Communications in Computer and Information Science 1548

More information about this series at http://www.springer.com/series/7899

Panos Liatsis · Abir Hussain ·
Salama A. Mostafa · Dhiya Al-Jumeily (Eds.)

Emerging Technology Trends in Internet of Things and Computing

First International Conference, TIOTC 2021
Erbil, Iraq, June 6–8, 2021
Revised Selected Papers

Springer

Editors
Panos Liatsis
Khalifa University
Abu Dhabi, United Arab Emirates

Abir Hussain
Liverpool John Moores University
Liverpool, UK

Salama A. Mostafa
Tun Hussein Onn University of Malaysia
Batu Pahat, Malaysia

Dhiya Al-Jumeily
Liverpool John Moores University
Liverpool, UK

ISSN 1865-0929 ISSN 1865-0937 (electronic)
Communications in Computer and Information Science
ISBN 978-3-030-97254-7 ISBN 978-3-030-97255-4 (eBook)
https://doi.org/10.1007/978-3-030-97255-4

This Springer imprint is published by the registered company Springer Nature Switzerland AG
The registered company address is: Gewerbestrasse 11, 6330 Cham, Switzerland

Preface

The First International Conference on Emerging Technology Trends in Internet of Things and Computing (TIOTC 2021) was organized by Al-Maarif University College, Al-Iraqia University, Salahaddin University, and Tishk International University, taking place (virtually) in the city of Erbil, Iraq, during June 6–8, 2021. TIOTC is an international conference focused on the latest topics related to computer science, the Internet of Things (IOT), computer networks and security, data science, artificial intelligence (AI), and machine learning.

Emerging technology is going to give a new dimension to the way we perform our everyday activities, leading to rapid advances in key areas of computer and information technology, such as the Internet of Things, artificial intelligence (AI), and their practical and theoretical applications. There are, therefore, challenges due to the changing nature of communications and computing in the Fourth Industrial Revolution. There is a huge amount of technology currently available, but the content is sometimes not specified or is significantly unemployed. Meaningfully deploying the content of these techniques relies on a comprehensive understanding of the vast number of technologies that are available today.

The Internet of Things (IoT) plays an important role in the current and future generation of information, networks, communication, and applications. Smart IoT is an exciting emerging research field that has great potential to transform both our understanding of fundamental computer science principles and our standard of living. IoT systems include heterogeneous, interacting, intelligent things, and distributed. In order to tackle challenges related to IoT, it is very important to have a better understanding of IoT applications in terms of reliable communication in constantly changing networks; heterogeneity and scalability; secure information handling and privacy preservation; and integrating and mediating things within intelligent systems.

The main aim of this conference was to gather state-of-the-art solutions that support robust systems with the ability to operate in dynamic and changing environments, including methods for industry and real-world problems. The theme of this conference was "Emerging Technology on Internet of Things (IoT)". Papers focusing on this theme were solicited, addressing applications in science and technology.

TIOTC 2021 received 182 submissions from authors in 19 countries around the world. All of the submitted manuscripts addressed either a theoretical or practical perspective that related to an aspect of the conference or presented relevant applications. All manuscripts underwent through a rigorous peer-review process and each paper received a minimum of three peer reviews. Based on the review reports, the Program Committee decided to accept only 27 papers for presentation at the conference, resulting in a strong program with an acceptance rate of less than 21%. The selected papers were distributed into main four tracks: Internet of Things (IoT): Services and Applications; IoT in Healthcare Industry; IoT in Communications and Distributed Computing; and Real World Application Fields in Information Science and

Technology. All of the selected papers are included in this volume of proceedings published in Springer's Communications in Computer and Information Science (CCIS) series.

We would like to thank the Program Committee, locally and internationally, and the reviewers for their collective time and effort in reviewing and soliciting the papers. Special thanks go to the team at Springer for their continuous support in publishing the proceedings. Finally, we also owe a great debt to all the researchers who submitted high-quality papers to our conference: TIOTC 2021.

December 2021

Panos Liatsis
Abir Hussain
Salama A. Mostafa
Dhiya Aljumaily
Li Zhang
Qaysar S. Mahdi
Essam Khaleel Abdullah

Organization

General Chair

Hoshang Kolivand	Liverpool John Moores University, UK

Technical Program Committee Chair

Dhiya Aljumaily	Liverpool John Moores University, UK

Technical Program Committee Co-chairs

Panos Liatsis	Khalifa University, Abu Dhabi, UAE
Abir Hussain	Liverpool John Moores University, UK
Salama A. Mostafa Alabdullah	Universiti Tun Hussein Onn, Malaysia
Li Zhang	Northumbria University, UK
Qaysar S. Mahdi	Tishk International University, Iraq
Essam Khaleel Abdullah	Salahaddin University, Iraq

Publication Chair

Jade Hind	Liverpool John Moores University, UK

International Scientific Committee

Mourad Oussalah	University of Oulu, Finland
Mathias Fonkam	American University of Nigeria, Nigeria
Farid Meziane	University of Derby, UK
Ajita Rattani	Wichita State University, USA
Alexei Lisitsa	University of Liverpool, UK
Miloudi Mohamed Tahar	UNESCO, France
Farhan Mohamed	Universiti Teknologi Malaysia, Malaysia
William Hurst	Wageningen University and Research, The Netherlands
Mohammed Zidan	Zewail City of Science and Technology, Egypt
Saad Bani-Mohammad	Al al-Bayt University, Jordan
Jabir Alshehabi Al-Ani	Lancaster University, UK
Ghani Hashim	Henri Poincaré University, France
Hanan Abdaulrahman Alharbi	Umm Al-Qura University, Saudi Arabia
Ali Al-Sabbagh	Florida Institute of Technology, USA
Mohammad Sarfraz	Aligarh Muslim University, India
Alaa Fareed Abdulateef	Universiti Utara Malaysia, Malaysia

Asma Alkalbani	Sultan Qaboos University, Oman
Hamid A. Jalab	University of Malaya, Malaysia
John Henry	Manchester Metropolitan University, UK
Adel Al-Jumaily	University of Technology Sydney, Australia
Omar Salim Abdullah	Universiti Kebangsaan Malaysia, Malaysia
Thar Baker	University of Sharjah, UAE
Rozlan Bin Alias	Universiti Tun Hussein Onn Malaysia, Malaysia
Qais Saif Qassim	Ibri College of Technology, Oman
Vijay Anant Athavale	Panipat Institute of Engineering and Technology, India
Suparawadee Trongtortam	Naresuan University, Thailand
Amando P. Singun Jr.	Higher College of Technology, Muscat, Oman
Wafaa M. Salih Abedi	City University College of Ajman, UAE
Omar Alani	University of Salford, UK
Muhsen Hammoud	Federal University of ABC, Brazil
Hossein Ahmadi	University of Birmingham, UK
Ataolalah Zarei	University of Windsor, Canada
Amjad Khan Rahman	Prince Sultan University, Saudi Arabia
Faris Amin M. Abuhashish	University of Petra, Jordan
Abdolvahab Ehsani Rad	Azad University, Iran
Tansila Saba	Prince Sultan University, Saudi Arabia
Hasan Chizari	University of Gloucestershire, UK
Parvane Esmaeili	Girne American University, Cyprus
Zahara Reaei	Azad University, Iran
Gabor Kecskemeti	Liverpool John Moores University, UK
Saba Jodaki	Azad University, Iran
Alireza Norouzi	Azad University, Iran
Majid Harouni	CMPLab, Iran
Fares Yousefi	Liverpool John Moores University, UK
Hamid Rastgari	Azad University, Iran
Rawaa Aljumeily	Belvedere British School, UAE
Shiva Asadianfam	Azad University, Iran
Malik Ghazi Qasaimeh	Princess Sumaya University for Technology, Jordan
Yousif Ahmed Hamad	Siberian Federal University, Russia
Pimsara Yaklai	Naresuan University, Thailand
Ala Al Kafri	Teesside University, UK
Rozaida Ghazali	Universiti Tun Hussein Onn Malaysia, Malaysia
Francis Li	University of Salford, UK
Ibrahim Idowu	Liverpool John Moores University, UK
Philip Duncan	University of Salford, UK
Chitinout Wattana	Naresuan University, Thailand
Saleh Mustafa Abu-Soud	Princess Sumaya University for Technology, Jordan
Joshua Meggitt	University of Salford, UK
Phillip Kendrick	Liverpool John Moores University, UK
Moamin A. Mohmoud	Universiti Tenaga Nasional, Malaysia
Ali Al Atababy	University of Liverpool, UK
Syed Zahurul Islam	Universiti Tun Hussein Onn Malaysia, Malaysia

Ammar Al Mhdawi	Newcastle University, UK
Wachira Punpairoj	Naresuan University, Thailand
Omar Alobaidi	Sussex University, UK
Attakrai Punpukdee	Naresuan University, Thailand
Mohammed Adbulhakim Alsaadi	University of Nizwa, Oman
Mohamed Alloghani	Abu Dhabi Health Service Company (SEHA), UAE
Udomlak Srichuachom	Naresuan University, Thailand
Shamaila Iram	University of Huddersfield, UK
Omar Aldhaibani	Liverpool John Moores University, UK
Rahmita Wirza O. K. Rahmat	Universiti Putra Malaysia, Malaysia
Jamila Mustafina	Kazan Federal University, Russia
Casimiro Aday Curbelo Montañez	OWIT, Spain
Pimsara Yaklai	Naresuan University, Thailand
Farhan Mohamed	Universiti Teknologi Malaysia, Malaysia
James Hahn	George Washington University, USA
David Al-Dabass	UK Simulation Society, UK
Kevin Kam Fung Yuen	Hong Kong Polytechnic University, Hong Kong
Maneerut Chatrangsan	Naresuan University, Thailand
Jade Janet Kayley Hind	Liverpool John Moores University, UK
Hasan Chizari	Imperial College London, UK
Parvaneh Esmaeili	Near East University, Turkey
Mutinta Mwansa	Liverpool John Moores University, UK
Ghani Hashim	Cihan University, Iraq
Anurut Asawasakulsorn	Naresuan University, Thailand
Fanny Klett	ADL Partnership Lab, Germany
Aine Mac Dermott	Liverpool John Moores University, UK
Robert S. Laramee	University of Nottingham, UK
Mohammed Al-Khafajiy	University of Reading, UK
David Tully	Scenegraph Studios, UK

National Scientific Committee

Moayad Yousif Potrus	Salahaddin University, Iraq
Mohammed W. Al-Neama	University of Mosul, Iraq
Salah Awad Salman	University of Anbar, Iraq
Israa Shaker Tawfic	Ministry of Science and Technology, Iraq
Mohammed Shweesh Ahmed	Tikrit University, Iraq
Itimad Raheem Ali	University of Information Technology and Communications, Iraq
Anwar Yahya Ibrahim	Babylon University, Iraq
Alaa Yaseen Taqa	University of Mosul, Iraq
Belal Al-Khateeb	University of Anbar, Iraq

Abid Salih Kumait	University of Kirkuk, Iraq
Ibrahim Ismail Hamarash	Salahaddin University Erbil, Iraq
Khattab M. Ali Alheeti	University of Anbar, Iraq
Qusay Fadhel Al-Doori	University of Technology, Iraq
Ahmad Saeed Mohammad	Mustansiriyah University, Iraq
Muntaser A. Salman	University of Anbar, Iraq
Imad Hussain Al Hussaini	University of Technology, Iraq
Hiba Basim Alwan Hussain Al-Dulaimi	Ministry of Finance, Iraq
Jabir Salman Aziz	Al-Nahrain University, Iraq
Huthaifa Q. Qadori	Al-Maarif University College, Iraq
Kayhan Zrar Ghafoor	Salahaddin University, Iraq
Idress Mohammed Husien	Kirkuk University, Iraq
Fawzi Al-naima	Al-Mamoon University College, Iraq
Mohammed Basil Alani	Al-Maarif University College
Abbas Mohamad Ali	Salahaddin University, Iraq
Athraa Juhi Jani	Mustansiriyah University, Iraq
Ahmed Sabah Abd-Alameer	University of Technology, Iraq
Husham Jawas Al Qayssy	Cihan University, Iraq
Jwan K. Alwan	University of Information Technology and Communications, Iraq
Tahseen Ahmed Tahseen	University of Tikrit, Iraq
Hasan Jaleel Hasan	University of Technology, Iraq
Hassan A. Jeiad	University of Technology, Iraq
Mohammed A. Abdulhameed	Imam Azam College, Iraq
Ahmed Sabaawi	Ninevah University, Iraq
Ruslan Saad Abdulrahman Al-Nuaimi	Al-Nahrain University, Iraq
Omed Salim Khalind	Salahaddin University, Iraq
Duraid Yahya Mohammed	Al Iraqia University, Iraq
Ahmed Jamal Ahmed	Al-Maarif University College, Iraq
Hassan A. Jeiad	University of Technology, Iraq
Haydar M. Al-Tamimi	University of Technology, Iraq
Abdul Monem S. Rahma	University of Technology, Iraq
Khudhair Thamir Abed	Al-Maarif University College, Iraq
Oras Ahmed Al-Ani	Electrical Engineering Technical College, Iraq
Hassan Muhialdeen	Al Iraqia University, Iraq
Ahmed Jamel	Al-Maarif University College, Iraq
Polla Abdul Hamid Fattah	Salahaddin University, Iraq
Yossra Hussain Ali Jawad	University of Technology, Iraq
Sarmad M. Hadi	Al-Nahrain University, Iraq
Gullanar Mohammed Hadi	Salahaddin University, Iraq
Omar Hussein Salman	Al Iraqia University, Iraq
Dler Salih Hasan	Salahaddin University, Iraq
Akeel A. Thulnoon	University of Anbar, Iraq

Essa Ibrahim Al-Juborie	University of Kirkuk, Iraq
Mohammed Khalid AlOmar	Al-Maarif University College, Iraq
Omer Abdulrahman Dawood	University of Anbar, Iraq
Ali Mahmood	University of Tikrit, Iraq
Murtadha Al-Hetee	University of Anbar, Iraq
Siddeeq Yousif Ameen	Duhok Polytechnic University, Iraq
Savriddin Khalilov	Tishk International University-Erbil, Iraq
Mohammed Hammed Yasen	University of Kirkuk, Iraq
Mohammed Ahmed Jaddoa	Al-Maarif University College, Iraq
Mohammed R. Hashim	Al-Maarif University College, Iraq
Taha Basheer Taha	Tishk International University-Erbil, Iraq
Ganesh Babu Loganathan	Tishk International University-Erbil, Iraq
Mohammad Abdulrahman Al-Mashhadani	Al-Maarif University College, Iraq
Emad Ahmed Mohammed	Northern Technical University, Iraq
Haider Abdula Haddad	Salahaddin University, Iraq
Baraa Albaker	Al-Iraqia University, Iraq
Taban Fouad Majeed	Salahaddin University, Iraq
Ahmed Hussain Ali	Ministry of Higher Education and Scientific Research, Iraq
Taban Fouad Majeed	Salahaddin University, Iraq
Shumoos Taha Al-Fahdawi	Al-Maarif University College, Iraq
Shaimaa Awadh Alayoubi	Salahaddin University, Iraq
Abeer Dawood Salman	Al-Maarif University College, Iraq
Ibraheem Nadher Ibraheem	Al-Mustansiriya University, Iraq
Ahmed Jasim Mohammed	University of Anbar, Iraq
Maytham M. Hammood	University of Tikrit, Iraq
Ahmed Hashim Mohammed	Al-Mustansiriyah University, Iraq
Qahtan Majeed Yas	University of Diyala, Iraq
Noor Haitham Saleem Al-Ani	Sulaimani Polytechnic University, Iraq
Mohammed Basil Alani	Almaarif University College, Iraq
Yusra Faisal	University of Mosul, Iraq
Taban Fouad Majeed	Salahaddin University, Iraq
Faten Azeez Alani	University of Mosul, Iraq
Hassan Hasson	Tishk International University-Erbil, Iraq
Omar Abdulmunem Aldabbagh	University of Mosul, Iraq
Mohammed I. Khalaf	Al-Maarif University College, Iraq
Hanaa Fathi Mahmood	University of Mosul, Iraq
Moceheb Lazam Shuwandy	Tikrit University, Iraq
Osamah Al-Mashhadani	Al-Ma'moon University College
Mafaz Alanezi	University of Mosul, Iraq

Ahmed Abduljabbar Hamad Alsabhany	Al-Maarif University College, Iraq
Harith Kamel Banieh	Anbar University, Iraq
Mohanad Abdulsattar Hammed	Al-Maarif University College, Iraq
Esra Adnan Abdul Jalil	Anbar University, Iraq
Mohammed Alzaidi	Al-Maarif University College, Iraq
Najwa Shehab Ahmed	University of Nahrain, Iraq
Azmi Shawkat Abdel Baqi	University of Anbar, Iraq
Noor Qusay Abdulmohsen	Al-Nahrain University, Iraq
Hussam Jasim	University of Anbar, Iraq
Alaa Al-Waisy	Imam Ja'afar Al-Sadiq University, Iraq
Huda Kadhim Tayyeh	University of Information Technology and Communications, Iraq
Ali Al-Nooh	University of Mosul, Iraq
Zohair Al-Ameen	University of Mosul, Iraq
Anwar Yahya Ibrahim	Babylon University, Iraq
Shaimaa Abbas Fahdel Al-Abaidy	University of Baghdad, Iraq

Official Sponsors

Al-Maarif University College, Al-Iraqia Univerity, Salahaddin University, and Tishk International University were the main sponsors for the conference and supported TIOTC 2021 financially. We would like to thank all sponsors for all the effort that made TIOTC 2021 successful.

Technical Sponsor

Applied Computing Research (ACR) Lab was the main technical sponsor of TIOTC 2021.

Contents

Internet of Things (IOT): Services and Applications

An Intelligent Flood Alert System Using LoRa on Basis of Internet of Things 3
Al Mohi Nur, Azana Hafizah Mohd Aman, Rosilah Hassan, Taj-Aldeen Naser Abdali, Zainab S. Attarbashi, and Aisha Hassan Abdalla Hashim

AGRIBOT: Energetic Agricultural Field Monitoring Robot Based on IoT Enabled Artificial Intelligence Logic 16
Ganesh Babu Loganathan, Qaysar Salih Mahdi, Idris Hadi Saleh, and Mohammad Mustafa Othman

Proof of Good Service Based on DAGs-To-Blockchain for IoT Applications 31
Istabraq M. Al-Joboury and Emad H. Al-Hemiary

A Lightweight Algorithm to Protect the Web of Things in IOT 46
Muthana S. Mahdi and Zaydon L. Ali

IoT Intrusion Detection Using Modified Random Forest Based on Double Feature Selection Methods 61
Adil Yousef Hussein, Paolo Falcarin, and Ahmed T. Sadiq

Network-Based Method for Dynamic Burden-Sharing in the Internet of Things (IoT) 79
Basim Mahmood and Yasir Mahmood

Internet of Things (IOT) in Healthcare Industry

Toward on Develop a Framework for Diagnosing Novel-COVID-19 Symptoms Using Decision Support Methods 93
Qahtan M. Yas and Ghazwan K. Ouda

Brain Tumours Classification Using Support Vector Machines Based on Feature Selection by Binary Cat Swarm Optimization 108
Wid Ali Hassan, Yossra Hussain Ali, and Nuha Jameel Ibrahim

Early Depression Detection Using Electroencephalogram Signal 122
Hasnisha Ladeheng and Khairul Azami Sidek

Automated Diagnosis of the Top Spread Infectious Diseases in Iraq Using SVM Technique 135
Hayder Hussein Thary, Duraid Y. Mohammed, and Khamis A. Zidan

Cardiac Arrhythmia Diagnosis via Multichannel Independent Component Analysis: An Approach Towards a Better Health Care System 150
Mohammad Sarfraz, Mudassir Hasan Khan, Duraid Yahya Mohammed, Mays Dheya Hussain, and Khamis A. Zidan

The Efficiency of Classification Techniques in Predicting Anemia Among Children: A Comparative Study 167
Qusay Saihood and Emrullah Sonuç

Automated Brain Tumor Segmentation and Classification Through MRI Images. 182
Sahar Gull, Shahzad Akbar, Syed Ale Hassan, Amjad Rehman, and Tariq Sadad

Eye Gaze Based Model for Anxiety Detection of Engineering Students 195
Khafidurrohman Agustianto, Hendra Yufit Riskiawan, Dwi Putro Sarwo Setyohadi, I. Gede Wiryawan, Andi Besse Firdausiah Mansur, and Ahmad Hoirul Basori

IOT in Networks, Communications and Distributed Computing

Integration Femtocells Based on Hybrid Beamforming with Existing LTE Macro-cell for Improving Throughput Towards 5G Networks 209
Mohammed K. Hussein and Nasser N. Khamiss

Performance Evaluation of CoAP and MQTT_SN Protocols 223
Rahaf A. Al-Qassab and Mohammed I. Aal-Nouman

Microsleep Detection of Automobile Drivers Using Electrocardiogram Signal 237
N. S. Nor Shahrudin, K. A. Sidek, M. R. Jalaludin, and N. A. N. Nazmi Asna

An Improved Video Coding Model for Future IMT Requirements. 253
Sarmad K. Ibrahim and Nasser N. Khamiss

Named Data Networking Mobility: A Survey 266
Wan Muhd Hazwan Azamuddin, Azana Hafizah Mohd Aman, Rosilah Hassan, and Taj-Aldeen Naser Abdali

A Spectrum Sensing Profile Based SDR for Cognitive Radio System: An Experimental Work 282
Muntasser S. Falih and Hikmat N. Abdullah

Real World Application Fields in Information Science and Technology

Novel Approximation Booths Multipliers for Error Recovery of Data-Driven Using Machine Learning 299
Sudhakar Sengan, Osamah Ibrahim Khalaf, Punarselvam Ettiyagounder, Dilip Kumar Sharma, and Rajakumari Karrupusamy

Applying an Efficient AI Approach for the Prediction of Bearing Capacity of Shallow Foundations 310
Faidhalrahman Khaleel, Mohammed Majeed Hameed, Deiaaldeen Khaleel, and Mohamed Khalid AlOmar

Training Adaptive Neuro Fuzzy Inference System Using Genetic Algorithms for Predicting Labor Productivity 324
Nehal Elshaboury

Approaches for Forgery Detection of Documents in Digital Forensics: A Review 335
Alaa Amjed, Basim Mahmood, and Khalid A. K. Almukhtar

A New Secret Sharing Scheme Based on Hermite Interpolation and Folded Magic Cube Rules. 352
Rafid Abdulaziz, Ali Sagheer, and Omar Dawood

Investigation on the Impact of Video Games on People Who Use New Technology. 365
Hoshang Kolivand, Shiva Asadianfam, and Daniel Wrotkowski

Author Index 381

Internet of Things (IOT): Services and Applications

An Intelligent Flood Alert System Using LoRa on Basis of Internet of Things

Al Mohi Nur[1], Azana Hafizah Mohd Aman[1](✉), Rosilah Hassan[1], Taj-Aldeen Naser Abdali[1], Zainab S. Attarbashi[2], and Aisha Hassan Abdalla Hashim[3]

[1] Centre for Cyber Security, Faculty of Information Science and Technology (FTSM), Universiti Kebangsaan Malaysia (UKM), 43600 Bangi, Selangor, Malaysia
{gp06116,P94546}@siswa.ukm.edu.my, {azana,rosilah}@ukm.edu.my

[2] Kulliyyah of Information and Communication Technology, International Islamic University Malaysia, Gombak, Malaysia
zainab_senan@iium.edu.my

[3] Kulliyyah of Engineering, International Islamic University Malaysia, Gombak, Malaysia
aisha@iium.edu.my

Abstract. The Internet of Things (IoT) is a network of devices, mechanical and digital machines, objects, or persons with unique identifiers to transfer data over a network. The internet helps people live and work more smartly. Technology contributes to helping from environmental threatening such as flooding, and tornadoes which cost people's lives. In this matter, IoT technology comes up with a lot of solutions. One of major well-known technology is the Long Range (LoRa). IoT technology which provides a low-power wide-area network protocol that uses radio frequency bands to transmit data. In this study, we proposed an Intelligent Flood Alert System (IFAS) to predict the early flooding by dropping the LoRa devices in certain places to take the required actions in the threatening of flooding and save people's lives. IFAS was tested in a real environment in different scenarios such as the water level, time duration, and maximum successful transmission coverage. In addition, the system provided three colors of alerts and a buzzer with different alerts to show the threatening level. The IFAS system proofed the ability to cover an area of 700 m.

Keywords: Internet of Things · LoRa · Wireless sensor network · Performance metrics

1 Introduction

The internet of things (IoT) is the upcoming leading technology for smart communication technology. IoT is a meaning of some physical objects network where some of the communication technologies are allowed to communicate and interact with each other and provide data. These objects could be mobile phones, radio frequency identification (RFID) tags, actuators, and sensors. In this current world, IoT has a big impact that affects human nature as well. IoT can affect the domestic and working field of a private

P. Liatsis et al. (Eds.): TIOTC 2021, CCIS 1548, pp. 3–15, 2022.
https://doi.org/10.1007/978-3-030-97255-4_1

user [1]. IoT is now related to logistics, automation, industrial manufacturing, business, transport, and so on. Statistics show that in the year 2020 there will be 50.1 billion devices connected to IoT [2].

So, the development of IoT is moving forward according to future expectations. The advantages of IoT in the current world and the future are huge but the technology Also adopting the deriving threats. To ensure the security of this big number of data and devices it is confirmed that related risks should be minimized [3, 4]. Infected IoT and the risk issues should be analyzed before it widely accepted.

Long Range (LoRa) is a wireless technology with a long coverage range. LoRa has spread spectrum modulation techniques derived from chirp spread spectrum technology. LoRa offers different features for IoT applications. It uses low power consumption and high secure data transmission at a low cost [5]. LoRaWAN is a protocol-based network that uses Low Power Wide Area Network (LPWAN) protocol. LPWAN is used to deliver the data in this technology. The structure of this LoRaWAN follows star network topology. The network consists of an end node, gateway, and sever. The data from the end node sends to the gateway and from the gateway, the data is forwarded to a server to visualize. This technology can utilize in public, private, and hybrid networks. LoRa uses 169 MHz, 433 MHz, 868 MHz, and 915 MHz radio frequency bands [6]. LoRa can transmit data up to 10 km in rural areas.

In this paper, we proposed a system termed Intelligent Flood Alert System (IFAS) using a LoRa-based wireless network to improve an intelligent flood alert system to measure different water levels, particularly in possible flood-affected areas. The testing environment is also used to evaluate the maximum distance of data transmission by this network and the performance during different indoor and outdoor environments. We experimented with this wireless network by taking the Packet Delivery ratio (PDR), Packet loss ratio (PLR), End-to-end delay (E2E), and Throughput.

2 Related Works

The previous studies have been focusing on applications of LoRa technology. In [7], a wireless sensor-based smart application system has built by the researchers to cultivate mushrooms based on wireless and mobile computing technology. To build the smart system, researchers have used temperature, humidity, and CO2 sensors to evaluate the data of the greenhouse environment. This type of greenhouse environment of mushroom cultivation changes the environmental factors frequently, so this automated sensor network can full fill the requirements. It needs an A/D converter, sensor, memory, microcontroller, wireless transceiver, and power module to build the wireless sensor node. Temperature and humidity requirements for mushroom incubation area and growth area are 75–85% humidity, 18–25 °C at day, and 15–18 °C at night, or 85–95% humidity, 22–25 °C at day, and 12–15 °C at night. The experiment results of this research show that the temperature and humidity in growth are 17 °C and 42% humidity and in incubation is 24 °C and 90% humidity. So, this wireless smart network can provide information about the environment and increase their income.

In [8], monitor the packet delivery ratio during rain attenuation, researchers have proposed a mesh network system based on LoRa technology. The effects of atmospheric attenuation in the signal transmission process at different line-of-sight and non-line-of-sight have been monitored by deploying the network in several situations. Also, the experiments have been conducted by collecting the maximum successful data transmission range of this network. To set up this network, the end node, master node, and gateway were deployed. The end node was made up with a LoRa RFM shield, Arduino UNO microcontroller, and DHT 11 temperature sensor. The master node and gateway were set up with a LoRa RFM shield and Arduino UNO microcontroller. In this network, the end node collects the temperature value by the DHT 11 sensor and sends it to the master node and the master node collects the data and sends it to the gateway. In the gateway, all the data sent from the end node can visualize in the serial monitor. The amount of data sends from the end to and the amount of data received by the gateway is collected to measure the PDR (Packet Delivery Ratio). The experiment result shows that during different volumes of rain, the PDR decreases significantly from 100% to 89.5%. Another experiment result shows that this mesh network can successfully transmit data up to 1.7 km in line-of-sight and up to 1.3 km in a non-line-of-sight environment with 100% PDR.

In [9], the best performance of spreading factor in different distance variations has been tested and analyzed by the researchers by using the 925 MHz ISM frequency band of QoS performance analysis on various reading factors. Different types of throughput are required like for maximum throughput value SF7, for the balanced high throughput and long-range capabilities SF8 is required, and for maximum range and optimal range SF11 is required. The variation of distance starts from 500 m to 1100 m. This network measures the Packet Loss, Throughput, End-to-End Delay, and RSSI value. The network was designed with the Arduino UNO and LoRa shield for client node and LG-01 as the gateway. This network used 925 MHz, ISM frequency band, transmitting power of 13 dbm, a bandwidth of 125 kHz and the code rate was 4/5. Experiment results show that the SF12 provides the maximum number of packet loss in every range of distance variation. SF8 provides a similar number of packet losses to SF12. For the experiments of throughput, the result shows that the SF7 provides the best throughput value up to 1927.3 bit/s for a short distance and SF8 provides the best throughput value of 1204.6 bit/s in the longer distance. Based on all the experiment results, they show that the SF7 has the best performance for maximum throughput value, SF8 has the high throughput value with long-distance, and SF11 has the best performance with maximum range and optimal range.

In research work [10], researchers have proposed a network setup in suburban and rural areas. By this network, they have collected the performance of this network in different line-of-sight and non-line-of-sight environments. As a result, they found that there is a huge role of the environment in the signal transmission process. [10] has proposed a LoRa based network to develop a flood alert system to study the issues and characteristics of IoT flood alert systems and IoT wireless communication technology.

Research in [11], A LoRaWAN network has been proposed by the researchers to increase the message delivery success rate. The network has been proposed as two approaches to a network that can solve this problem. The network was equipped with a 3.54 dBi antenna with an RN2483 LoRa module and the gateway was equipped with an IC880A LoRa concentrator and 8 dBi antenna. 8 different sensor boxes were deployed on the rooftop using the RN2483 module. The experiment results of this research show that the message delivery rate can highly increase in this network approach. But in some cases, this network provides the message delivery rate from 100% to 25.51%, and also the multi-helper reacts differently.

3 Intelligent Flood Alert System

This section shows the proposed network model IFAS, and the description of the physical components and software used in this study. A LoRa compatible water-level sensor is attached to the end node for measuring the level of water. Nodes are deployed at different locations, taking the readings at different conditions like indoor and outdoor and also at different distances. The readings of water level are sent from the end node to the gateway. The network is built with LoRa RFM 915 MHz shield, Arduino UNO board, 915 MHz SMA antenna, LED light sensor, buzzer sensor, and 5 V power supply are required to power this network. The complete design diagram of this proposed network is shown in Fig. 1. In addition, IFAS consist of two main categories:

i. **Hardware:** To build the network, for end node, shield LoRa RFM 915 MHz, Arduino UNO board, 915 MHz SMA antenna, 5 V power supply is required. A LoRa compatible water level brick sensor will be connected. For the gateway, LoRa RFM 915 MHz, Arduino UNO board, 915 MHz SMA antenna and 5 V power supply are used with a LoRa compatible buzzer module. A PC is required which is able to connect with the gateway and run the required application.
ii. **Software:** Instruments that will be used in this network will be Arduino compatible. Each of the devices like end node and gateway will be programmed as the end node can function as it measure the water level by the water level sensor and send to the gateway. The gateway will be programmed as it can receive data from the end node and send to the application server to visualize. Another function will be programmed to the gateway that is if the water level crosses the limit from the required level it will start functioning the buzzer module according to the increase of risk.

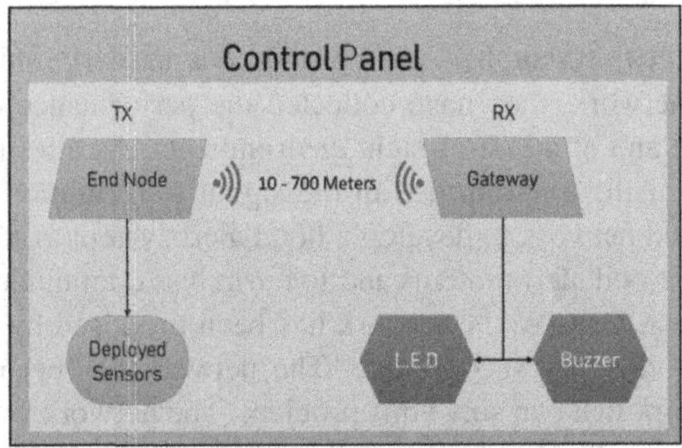

Fig. 1. Complete design diagram of IFAS system.

In this study, the LoRa shield is used to transmit data for a long-range. The Arduino UNO is used as the microcontroller board. In the second part of this network, a gateway collects data from the end node and activated the LED sensor and buzzer sensor according to the value of water-level. Gateway is connected to the application server through the USB port of Arduino UNO so that the data can be visualized. In Table 1 the network architecture is shown.

To notify the people living near the possible flood-affected areas, the LED light sensor and buzzer sensor respond according to the value of the end node. On the end node side, 0 mm to 100 mm of water-level is considered as low level of risk, from 101 mm to 200 mm is considered as a medium level of risk, and from 201 mm and above is considered as a high level of risk. On the gateway side when the water-level is between 0 mm–100 mm the green LED turns on and the buzzer beep every ten seconds. If the water-level is between 101 mm–200 mm the yellow LED turns on and the buzzer beeps every 5 s. For 201 mm and above the red LED turns on and the buzzer beeps every second. Table 2 shows different types of alerts for different levels of water by IFAS system.

Table 1. The proposed Intelligent Flood Alert System (IFAS) architecture

End node	Gateway
LoRa RFM 915 MHz	LoRa RFM 915 MHz
Arduino UNO	Arduino UNO
915 MHz SMA antenna	915 MHz SMA antenna
5 V power supply	5 V power supply
Water-level sensor	Traffic LED light module
	Buzzer sensor

Table 2. The types of alert for different water-level by IFAS system

Water level	LED color	Alert type/time
0–100 mm	Green	10 s
101–200 mm	Yellow	5 s
201-above mm	Red	1 s

4 Evaluation Measures

In this study, we adopted the evaluation measures based on the standard metrics that have been used in several studies for IFAS system performance. The evaluation metrics are as follows: Packet Delivery Ratio (PDR), Packet Loss Ratio (PLR), End-to-End delay (E2E), and Throughput [12–15].

4.1 Packet Delivery Ratio

The amount of the division maximum value of the data packet in the total number of data packets that all nodes send which is descried in the formula 1:

$$(PDR) = \frac{\text{Total packets received}}{\text{Total packets sent}} * 100 \tag{1}$$

4.2 Packet Lose Ratio

During simulation, the loss of packets is the total number of packages dropped. The lower value of the packet loss means that the specific routing protocol can perform better. The PLR calculation present in formula 2:

$$\text{PLR} = \frac{(Number\ of\ packet\ send - Number\ of\ packet\ received)}{Number\ of\ packet\ send} * 100 \tag{2}$$

4.3 End-To-End Delay

The data packet is averaged time based. On the basis of the first data packet forwarded to the destination, the time of transmission of the packet from the source was taken. The calculation of E2E delay using the formula 3:

$$\text{E2E Delay} = \frac{(Packet\ received\ time - Packet\ send\ time)}{Number\ of\ packets\ received} \tag{3}$$

4.4 Throughput

The throughput is defined as the amount at which messages are returned and is usually handled in bit/seconds. It is the percentage of the channel capacities used for data transmission in the telecommunications environment. The achievement for throughput can be present in formula 4:

$$\text{Throughput} = \frac{Received\ packet\ size}{(stop\ time - start\ time)} \tag{4}$$

Different indoor and outdoor environments and different locations to deploy the network and carried out the experiments were chosen. Data received by the gateway is calculated to obtain the value of PDR, PLR, E2E, and throughput by using the expression in (Sects. 4.1, 4.2, 4.3, and 4.4). All data are visualized in the serial monitor of the gateway. The results show the performance, stability, and consistency of the network. Figure 2 shows an example of device installation at different places for the experiments. The figure shows the distribution of node and gateway.

Fig. 2. The installation of IFAS system

5 Environment Setup

In this study, five types of experiments were conducted at different times of the day and in different locations the details were introduced in this section.

5.1 Water-Level Alert

For the low water-level experiment, the water-level sensor is drowned for a height of low water-level which means 0 mm–100 mm. As a result, the gateway side shows that the GREEN LED light is turned on and the buzzer starts the beep every 10 s. At the same time, in the serial monitor of the Arduino IDE application, it can be seen that the gateway receives data where the value of the water-level is between 15 mm–32 mm.

During the medium water-level experiment, the result shows that, on the gateway side, the YELLOW LED light is turned on and the buzzer is beeping every 5 s. In the serial monitor, it is visualized that the height of the water-level was from 107 mm–127 mm. For the experiment of a high water-level, results show that the LED light of the gateway side turns RED LED and the buzzer is beeping every second.

In the serial monitor, the value of the water-level is viewed between 243 mm–290 mm. In Fig. 3, the experiment results of the low water-level with green light are presented in Fig. 3a, medium water-level with yellow colour in Fig. 3b, and high water-level with red colour in Fig. 3c, with the value of the water-level sensor and the functions of LED lights are shown.

5.2 Surrounding Effects

To check the stability of this proposed network, the network is deployed in different environments so the performance of this network can be verified. Experiments were conducted in indoor and outdoor environments. The time duration of each experiment was one hour. During the experiment, the water-level sensor was drowned in 100 mm–200 mm of water to produce the communication between the devices.

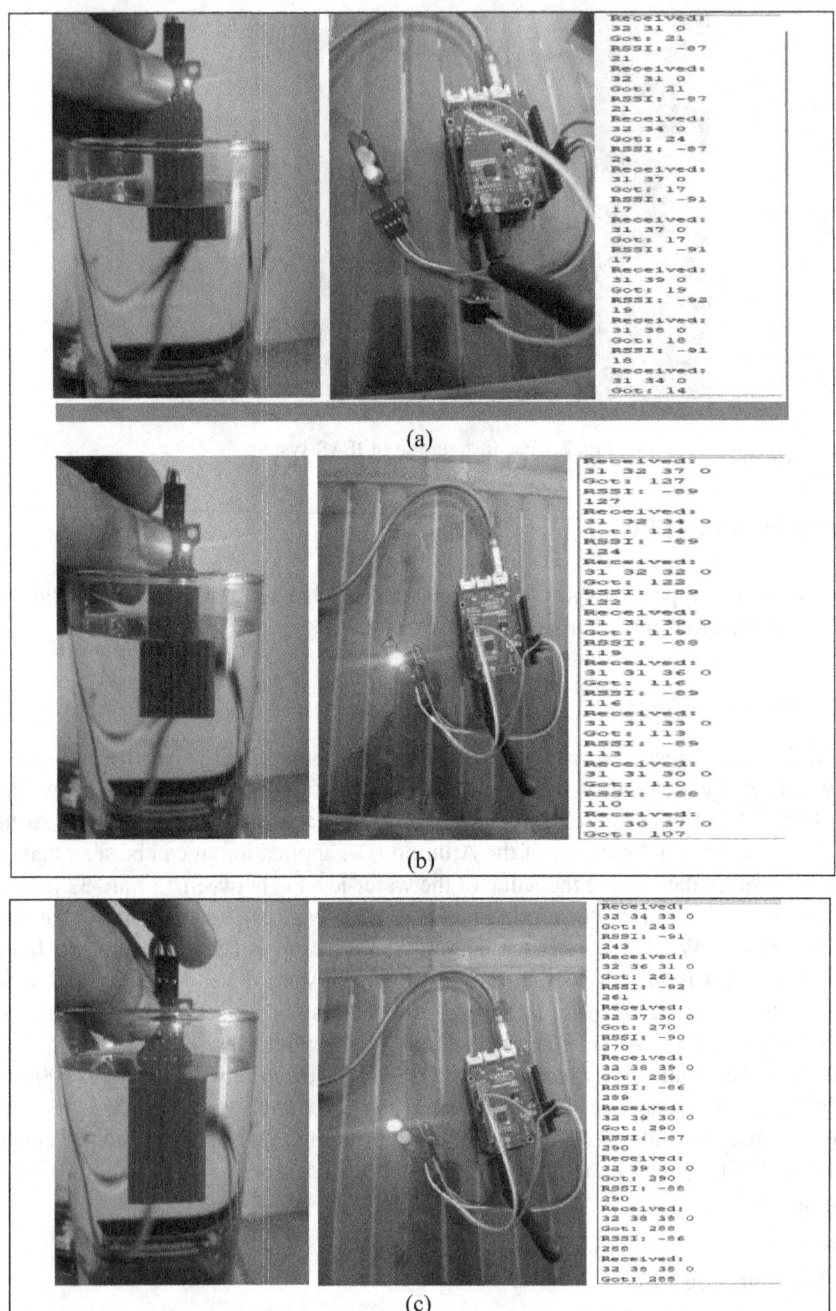

Fig. 3. Experiment in (a) low, (b) medium and (c) high water-level. (Color figure online)

Five experiments were conducted indoor and other five were conducted outdoor. For the indoor experiments, devices were installed 10 m away from each other. Experiments are done in five different days so that it can be easy to check if this network can provide the same performance every day or not. The results of all these indoor experiments show that, for each time, this network can actively perform.

Outdoor experiments were conducted in an area of 10 m distance on five different days. The results show that in this environment this network can also perform actively. Figure 4 shows the results of indoor and outdoor experiments on different dates.

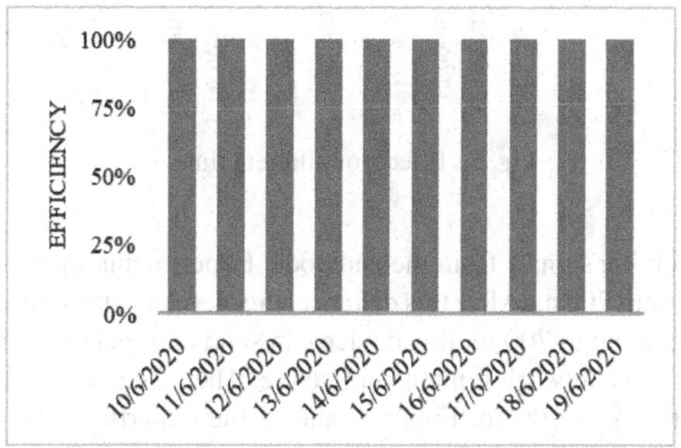

Fig. 4. Surrounding effects on different days.

5.3 Time Duration

Experiments to check the consistency of this proposed network are conducted in an indoor environment by sending and receiving data for a long duration. Distance between the end node and gateway was 10 m away from each other and there were some obstacles in between. Experiments were performed and the date was collected once every hour starting from 10.00 am till 10.00 pm, on the same day. For the experiment, the water-level sensor was drowned in 101 mm–200 mm water to continue the communication between the devices. As a result, it shows that the network provides the same performance in every situation of the time. It also shows that the device can perform activities for a long duration. In Fig. 5, the effects of time duration are shown.

5.4 Time Duration

In this proposed network, the end node sends data to the gateway, where the gateway performs like a notifier. To get the maximum distance of successful data transmission by this network, the network has deployed at different distances. Experiments were started from a 100 m distance by sending data of medium water-level, within five minutes of time duration.

The gateway was installed at 0 m and the end node was installed 100 m away from the gateway. Distance between the end node and the gateway increased gradually until the

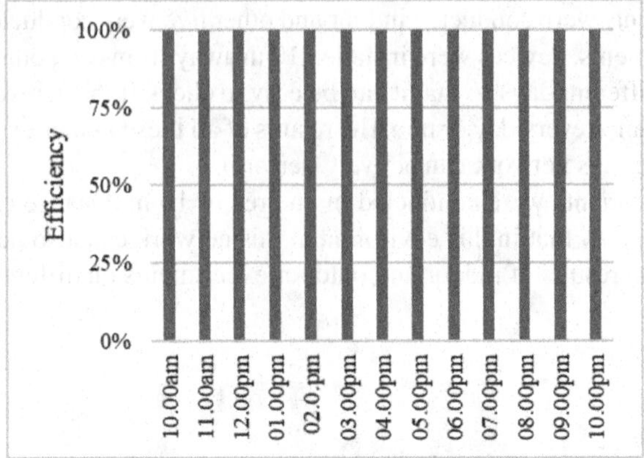

Fig. 5. Effects of different time.

gateway stops receiving signals from the end node. Experiments show that this network can communicate until 700 m. After this distance, this network stops the communication. The results show that up to 700 m, this device can send and receive data actively but in 800 m and 900 m, this network remains not active. Therefore, the maximum coverage range for this network is 700 m. Figure 6 shows the experiment results in different distances.

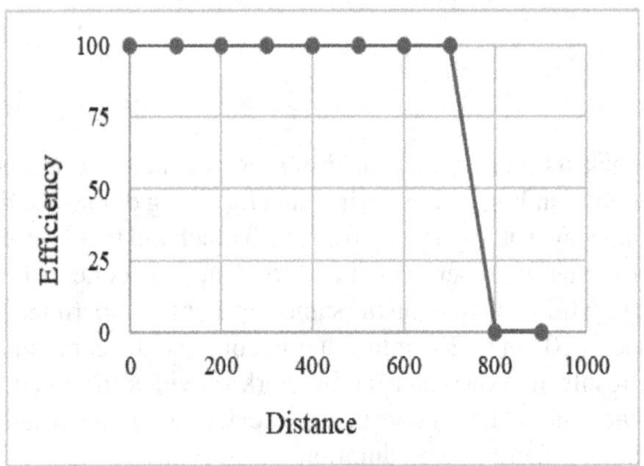

Fig. 6. Results in different distance.

6 Results and Discussion

To check the performance metrics of this proposed setup, the Packet Delivery Ratio, Packet Loss Ratio, End-to-End Delay, and the throughput are measured by calculating different amounts of data. For doing this experiment, data packets are sent from the end

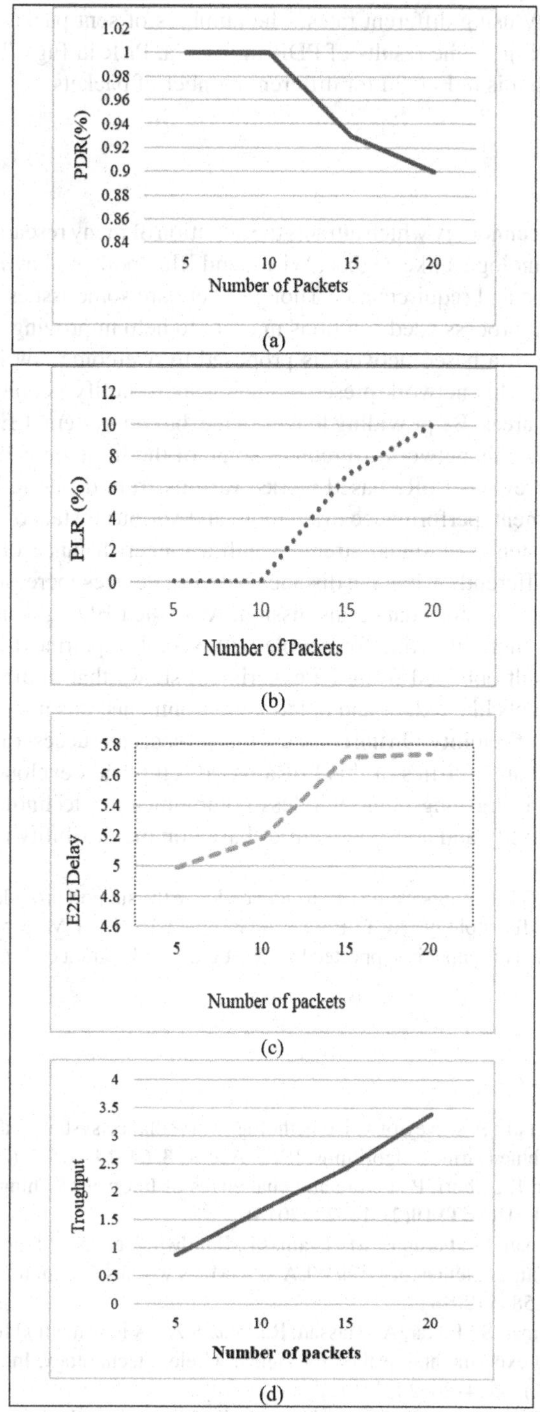

Fig. 7. Result of packet delivery ratio (a), packet loss ratio (b), end to end delay (c), and throughput (d).

node to the gateway using different rates. The numbers of sent packets are: 5, 10, 15, and 20 packets. In Fig. 7, the results of PDR in Fig. 7a, PLR in Fig. 7b, Fig. 7c shows E2E, and Throughput is in Fig. 7d for different number of packets.

7 Conclusion

LoRa is a wireless technology which attracts the attention of many researchers nowadays. Other wireless technologies like Zigbee, Wi-Fi, and Bluetooth are having less coverage range with high cost and requirements. Though, there are some issues regarding LoRa and its transmission process need solutions in order to help improving daily activity. In this paper, a new LoRa based network is proposed to overcome few issues regarding flood alert systems. This network presents a new way to notify people who are living near flood-affected areas. By providing longer range, buzzer system, LED light, and low power consumption, this network overcomes some of the limitations of other wireless technologies and previous LoRa based works. Results from different locations, times and dates, environment, performance evaluation, and various distances show the strong stability and consistency of signal strength with a longer distance of coverage. This network behaves differently when the distance between devices increases gradually, but from 800 m and above it stops data transmission. Also, the LED light and buzzer sensor make this network more effective for people with visual impairment and impervious. One significant result obtained from the experiment shows that in different times and different environments like indoor and outdoor environments, this network can perform with the same level of stability. On the contrary, this project can successfully show the best performance and characteristics of this LoRa based setup and developed an intelligent flood alert system using long-range wireless communication technology. Lastly, this IFAS model can modify and add new features based on the flexibility needed.

Acknowledgments. The authors would like to acknowledge the support provided by the Network and Communication Technology (NCT) Research Groups, FTSM, UKM in providing facilities throughout this paper. This paper is supported by UKM grant under grant code GGPM-2019–030.

References

1. Al-Dhief, F.T., et al.: A survey of voice pathology surveillance systems based on Internet of Things and machine learning algorithms. IEEE Access **8**, 64514–64533 (2020)
2. Jindal, F., Jamar, R., Churi, P.: Future and challenges of Internet of Things. Int. J. Comput. Sci. Inf. Technol. (IJCSIT) **10**(2), 13–25 (2018)
3. Hasan, M., Rahman, M., Faruque, M., Islam, M.: Bandwidth enhanced metamaterial embedded inverse L-slotted antenna for WiFi/WLAN/WiMAX wireless communication. Mater. Res. Express **6**(8), 085805 (2019)
4. Dahnil, D., Selamat, S., Bakar, A., Hassan, R., Ismail, A.: A new method for battery lifetime estimation using experimental testbed for zigbee wireless technology. Int. J. Adv. Sci. Eng. Inf. Technol. **8**(6), 2654–2662 (2018)
5. Husein, N., Hadi, A., Putri, D.: Evaluation of LoRa-based air pollution monitoring system. Int. J. Adv. Comput. Sci. Appl. **10**(7), 391–396 (2019)

6. Rahman, A., Suryanegara, M.: The development of IoT LoRa: a performance evaluation on LoS and Non-LoS environment at 915 MHz ISM frequency. In: 2017 International Conference on Signals and Systems (ICSigSys), pp. 163–167, 03 July 2017 (2017)
7. Kassim, M.R.M., Harun, A.N., Yusoff, I.M., Mat, I., Kuen, C.P.: Applications of wireless sensor networks in Shiitake Mushroom cultivation (2017). https://ieeexplore.ieee.org/document/8304516
8. Hossin, D.: Enhancement of packet delivery ratio during rain attenuation for long range technology. Int. J. Adv. Comput. Sci. Appl. **10**(10) (2019)
9. Widianto, E.D., Pakpahan, M.S.M., Faizal, A.A., Septiana, R.: LoRa QoS Performance Analysis on VarioISpreading Factor in Indonesia (2018). https://ieeexplore.ieee.org/document/8605471. 2018 International Symposium on Electronics and Smart Devices (ISESD)
10. Ahmed, A.K., Segaran, J.D., Hashim, F.R., Jusoh, M.T.: LoRa propagetion at 433 MHZ in tropical climate environment, 10 September 2017 (2018)
11. Wang, S.Y., Chen, T.Y.: Increasing LoRaWAN application -layer message delivery success rates. In: 2018 IEEE Symposium on Computers and Communications, PoD, pp. 1530–1346, 19 November 2018 (2018)
12. Abdali, T.A.N., Hassan, R., Muniyandi, R.C., Mohd Aman, A.H., Nguyen, Q.N., Al-Khaleefa, A.S.: Optimized particle swarm optimization algorithm for the realization of an enhanced energy-aware location-aided routing protocol in MANET. Information **11**(11), 529 (2020)
13. Abdali, A.T.A.N., Muniyandi, R.C.: Optimized model for energy aware location aided routing protocol in MANET. Int. J. Appl. Eng. Res. **12**(14), 4631–4637 (2017)
14. Al-Dhief, F.T., Sabri, N., Fouad, S., Latiff, N.A., Albader, M.A.A.: A review of forest fire surveillance technologies: mobile ad-hoc network routing protocols perspective. J. King Saud Univ.-Comput. Inf. Sci. **31**(2), 135–146 (2019)
15. AL-Dhief, F.T., Sabri, N., Salim, M.S., Fouad, S., Aljunid, S.A.: MANET routing protocols evaluation: AODV, DSR and DSDV perspective. In: MATEC Web of Conferences, vol. 150, p. 06024. EDP Sciences (2018)

AGRIBOT: Energetic Agricultural Field Monitoring Robot Based on IoT Enabled Artificial Intelligence Logic

Ganesh Babu Loganathan[1(✉)], Qaysar Salih Mahdi[2], Idris Hadi Saleh[3], and Mohammad Mustafa Othman[4]

[1] Mechatronics Engineering, Tishk International University, Erbil, Kurdistan, Iraq
ganesh.babu@tiu.edu.iq

[2] IT Services Department/Rectorate, Tishk International University, Erbil, Kurdistan, Iraq
qaysar.mahdy@tiu.edu.iq

[3] Tishk International University, Erbil, Kurdistan, Iraq
idrishadi@tiu.edu.iq

[4] Department of Physics/College of Education, University of Salahaddin-Hawler, Erbil, Iraq
muhamad.othman@su.edu.krd

Abstract. In these modern days agriculture is one of the major concern to take out from the loss and need to be improvised in next level of production ratio. The latest technologies such as Internet of Things and Artificial Intelligence are associated with many applications to improve the standards as well as provide a drastic support to customers to achieve their communication needs. In this paper, a new agricultural robot is designed called as agriBOT, in which it is used to monitor the entire agricultural field and the associated crops in an intelligent manner by using Artificial Intelligence logic. The agriBOT has a provision to act like a drone to survey all fields in an intelligent manner. This provision allows the robot to move in all fields even the crops are in so dense, in which the agriBOT is integrated with many smart sensors to monitor the crop details well such as Soil Moisture Level Identifier, Crop Leaf Image Accumulator, Rain Identification Sensor and Surrounding Temperature level Identification Sensor. These sensors are associated with the proposed agriBOT to make the robot as powerful and robust in association with Artificial Intelligence and Internet of Things (IoT) strategies. The Internet of Things is used to carry the local sensor data from the agriBOT to the remote server for processing as well as the data available into the remote server can easily be monitored by the respective farmer from anywhere in the world at any time. The alert is utilized over the proposed agriBOT to pass the emergency condition alerts to the respective farmers instantly as well as the Global Positioning System (GPS) is utilized to retrieve the location details of the crop and report that to the server immediately by using IoT. This paper introduced a new machine learning strategy to analyze the server data, in which it is called as Modified Convolutional Neural Scheme (MCNS). This approach of MCNS provides the facility to predict the climate conditions and the associated crop details instantly based on the data which is collected already and stored into the server. With the association of these two strategies made the proposed approach of agricultural field monitoring system too robust and efficient to analyze the crop related details as well as the plant lea disease is also identified by using this approach based on the images captured by

P. Liatsis et al. (Eds.): TIOTC 2021, CCIS 1548, pp. 16–30, 2022.
https://doi.org/10.1007/978-3-030-97255-4_2

the agriBOT in an intellectual manner. All these details are experimentally tested and the resulting section provides the proper proof for the mentioned things.

Keywords: Smart sensors · agriBOT · Modified convolutional neural scheme · MCNS · IoT

1 Introduction

In this modern era, each and every individual has an attention to do agriculture oriented business, but the major complexity is the locality of the people. Because the person need to do agriculture needs to stay near to the Agri-Land and monitor the field every day. This creates a complexity to every individual because of the civilization problems as well as the other major complexity is the crop diseases affect the agricultural business in drastic manner, so that it needs to be identified and resolve it in a proper way [3, 4]. These constraints are the major case of the agricultural field down and reduce the interest level of the person to do such business and many youngsters are not yet interested to do this agriculture. This paper is intended to develop a new agricultural architecture to support farmers and improve their life and lifestyle in next level as well as through this many youngsters gets attracted in this field and do the agricultural job as their profession. In many countries agriculture is the major financial source to improve the nation's economy level. In India 80% of the economy growth fully belongs to the agricultural fields as well as the associated things. Now-a-days, agricultural field is also gets lots of change with the adaption of new technologies such as Internet of Things and Artificial Intelligence. This tends to move the field of agriculture from loss to attain some profitability [1, 2].

Agriculture Field Monitoring is the most important and complex task to deal with some intelligent techniques, in which the ideologies such as AI, IoT and the machine learning features helps the farmers to improve their position in society as well as attaining the production ratio much better. The technologies such as Solar PV based power associations and the smart motor pump handling logics reduces the electricity consumption charges well with less power usages [5, 6]. These kinds of innovative solar technologies eliminate the struggle of the farmers by reducing the electricity charges in great manner. With the help of such smart devices and the associated things the manpower is highly reduced to do such agri based business as well as this logic provides a high level yield in outcome [7]. This paper is intended to design a new agricultural field monitoring system with powerful AI logics as well as the association of Internet of Things with proposed robotic design helps to monitor the crops and the field in clear manner. In this paper a novel machine learning strategy called Modified Convolutional Neural Scheme (MCNS) is implemented to provide clear classification logics of two strategic things such as plant leaf disease predictions as well as the environmental details prediction. These all are possible only with the help of integrating new robust machinery called agriBOT, in which it associates several sensor units and the digital camera to monitor the crop details and forward that to the remote server by using Internet of Things web services.

1.1 agriBOT: A Summary

This paper utilizes several latest technologies to propose a new algorithm to monitor the agricultural field in several constraints. A new robust machinery tool called agriBOT is designed with different sensors to acquire the details from the agricultural field and provide that details to the server with the help of Internet of Things associations. The smart sensors connected with the agriBOT are as follows: Soil.

Moisture Level Identifier, Crop Leaf Image Accumulator, Rain Identification Sensor and Surrounding Temperature level Identification Sensor. Along with this the agriBOT contains the Global System for Mobile Communications (GSM) and Global Positioning System (GPS) unit to identify the location details of the respective crop with exact latitude and longitude as well as the alert mechanisms are handled with the help of GSM. A small digital camera with high intensity coverage is placed into the agriBOT for capturing the crop images and pass it to the server unit for identifying the plant leaf diseases in an intelligent manner by using the proposed machine learning based classification logic called MCNS. The agriBOT design is fixed as like the flying drone, in which it can fly around the agricultural field for 30 to 45 min continuously with the power ratios handled by means of solar assisted battery units. The 12v DC power enabled Nano Solar PV Panels are placed into the agriBOT to capture the power source from the sunlight and stores that energy to the battery to provide the continuous flying ability to the agriBOT. The estimated flying distance of the proposed robot called agriBOT is around 2 to 5 feets above from the crop level, in which the level of flying is automatically controlled by the controller as well as the captured image analysis is also handled in a proper way [8]. The working of all sensors are illustrated one by one as follows.

Soil Moisture Level Identifier: The soil moisture sensor associated with the agriBOT is used to monitor the soil wet level and the crop growth belongs to that. The soil wet level is low means the water pump handling system immediately switch-on the pump and provides the sufficient level of water to the crops and switch it off when the soil wet level reaches the threshold ratio. This sensor is placed into the agri-land and the associated transmission unit passes the soil moisture level values to the agriBOT once it is nearer to the sensor, so that the agriBOT collects those values and pass it to the server for processing. The following figure, Fig. 1 shows the soil moisture sensor with the connectivity unit associated to the sensor for converting the digital values to analog.

Fig. 1. Soil moisture sensor

Crop Leaf Image Accumulator: The digital camera associated with the agriBOT is helpful to capture the plant leaf images from the agricultural land and pass that to the remote server unit for further processing. In which the crop leaf image accumulator acquires the plant leaf image from the agricultural field and identify the leaf diseases to prevent to surf further for other crops into the field. The classification process associated with the plant leaf disease model is used to identify the diseases affected in the respective plant as well as the alert will be passed to the farmers with respect to the location and the disease name as well. The following figure, Fig. 2 illustrates the perception of digital camera associated with the agriBOT.

Fig. 2. Digital agriBOT camera

Rain Identification Sensor: The rain detection sensor is used to identify the status of rainfall, in which the sensor produces the digital values such as either true or false. This sensor is associated with the agriBOT to detect the rainfall condition and provide the respective triggers to the controller to manage the status into the server unit for further training as well as the level indicates the rainfall means, the motor pump need to be cross-checked for off state. The soil moisture level indicates the level is low means the water pump position will be turned ON by the controller automatically. At the same time the rainfall is coming the pump will immediately be switched OFF by the trigger generated by using this rain identification sensor. The following figure, Fig. 3, illustrates the perception of rainfall identification sensor associated with the agriBOT.

Fig. 3. Rain identification sensor

Surrounding Temperature Level Identification Sensor: The climate conditions are the major concern of the agriculture field, in which the climate condition monitoring is the most essential task in such field. So, that a temperature identification sensor is associated with the agriBOT to identify the temperature level of the circumstance and report that properly to the server unit by means of Internet of Things enabling. These sensor readings are analog, in which these values are stored into the server for dual purpose such as training the data for future climate predictions as well as monitoring the details from the remote end. The following figure, Fig. 4, illustrates the perception of temperature level identification sensor associated with the agriBOT.

Fig. 4. Temperature sensor

1.2 Internet of Things with Machine Learning Process

The purpose of enabling the internet services to smart devices are to transfer the local device data to the remote server as well as the acquisition of triggers from the remote server end to the local devices. The recent technology called Internet of Things (IoT) provides such ability to the agriBOT to carry the sensor data from the agricultural field and pass that vales to the server end without any delay. Once the agricultural data reached into the server end the machine learning process begins and analyze the incoming data with proper thershold levels and produce the alert oriented tasks accordingly as well as the periodical data will be uploaded into the server without any interference. The machine learning process associated with the proposed approach called Modified Convolutional Neural Scheme provides a clear predictive analysis of the agricultural data and report it to the respective farmers accordingly. So, that the farmers can take an appropriate precautions to handle the affections in good way. The general process of training the agriBOT values and created the model based on that as well as the testing live input with that trained model will provide high end efficiency in outcome as well as the processing time complexity is highly redced with the help of this proposed metrics. The following figure, Fig. 5 illustrates the data with respect to the modern as well as latest technology assisted agricultral field management and monitoring lifecycle.

The rest of this paper describe regarding Related Study over Sect. 2, further section of Sect. 3 illustrates the proposed system methodologies in detail with proper algorithm flow and the Sect. 4 illustrates the Result and Discussion portion of the paper and the final section, Sect. 5 illustrates the concept of Conclusion and Future Scope of the proposed paper. These all will be explained in detail over the further section summaries.

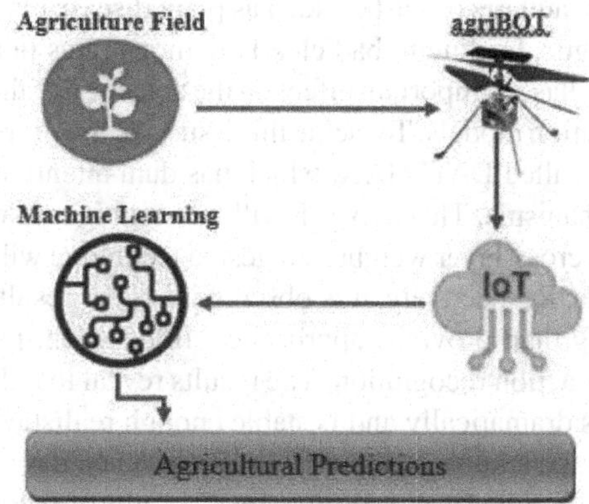

Fig. 5. Agri-field management and monitoring lifecycle

2 Related Study

In the year of 2020, the authors "Wei Zhao' et al. [10]" proposed a paper related to agricultural field development and the adaption of latest technologies such as Internet of Things with agricultural field. In this paper [10], the authors described such as: independent agriculture schemes are a potential option for bridging the gap between the labor shortage of agricultural tasks and the ongoing need to increase agricultural productivity. Automated mapping and navigation will be a cornerstone of the most independent farming system. Therefore, in this paper [10] authors introduce a ground-level mapping and navigation system based on machine viewing technology to produce a 3D farm map at the border as well as the cloud (Mesh SLAM) or Internet of Things. The technology in this framework includes three layers as sub-systems, i.e. (a) the ground level robot vehicle layer for frame selection with a single camera only, (b) the edge node layer for the data and communication edge image and (c) the general management and deep computation cloud layer. By enabling the robot vehicles to directly stream continuous frames into their respective edge node, they allow high efficiency and speed mapping level. Each edge node, which organizes a certain range of robots, introduces a new frame-by-frame Mesh-SLAM whose core constructs the map with a mesh based system with scalable units in order to reduce the data size of the function through a filtering algorithm. In addition, cloud computing enables vast arrangement and extremely deep computing. The system can be scaled to larger fields and complex environments by distributing the calculation power dynamically to the borders. The evaluation shows that: (a) the Mesh-SLAM algorithm exceeds the mapping and localization accuracy and yield prediction error (in cm resolution) and (b) the IoT architecture's scalability and versatility allow new consists of several modules or IoT sensors to be modularized and easily removed. We conclude that the tradeoff among price and efficiency greatly increases the feasibility and practicability of this system in real farms.

In the year of 2020, the authors "Qiang Dai' et al. [11]" proposed a paper related to plant leaf disease estimations with respect to dual attention laws based on fusion logics.

In this paper [11] the authors described such as plant disease classification of images obtained are usually vague, leading to bad clearly demonstrates in real critical applications. The image quality has an important effect on the accuracy of the recognition of pre-trained feature classification models. To tackle this issue, we are proposing a generational confrontational service called DATFGAN, which has dual attention and computational complexity fusion mechanisms. This network will turn ambiguous objects into elevated objects. In addition, our cross-layer weights suggested technique will substantially lower the quantity of variables. Respectively, it is observed that the results of DATFGAN are visually more appealing than province approaches. In addition, processed images are analyzed on the basis of action recognition. The results reveal that the improved method succeeds other methods dramatically and is stable enough realistic usage [11].

In the year of 2020, the authors "Ferhat Gölbol et al. [12]" proposed a paper related to systematic motion-controlled robot design for agriculture management system. In this paper [12] the authors described such as both domestic and international research, the benefits of autonomous farming over conventional agriculture have been stated. Motioning and trajectory preparation are one of the main problems to be overcome by an agricultural robot. In the literature, numerous configuration warning trends were created. A graphical motion planning framework available on Google maps is built in this work and A+ model is introduced. The vehicle location obtained via GPS is displayed in real time on the interface.

In the year of 2020, the authors "Omer Gulec' et al. [13]" proposed a paper related to design a new smart agricultural framework with Solar PV panel implementations for energy efficiency improvements with respect to wireless sensor network associations. In this paper [13] the authors described such as Current computer software technical advances impact various areas of production processes. One of the many areas influenced by these changes is the efficiency of an agricultural operation. The amount of production is increased with not only new models of farm production, but also with the use of technological developments in the manufacturing process. Also wireless sensor innovations are often used to capture distinctive effects to optimize output parameters and maintain the product at certain levels of quality. However, nodes that play an important role in such systems are susceptible to battery failure. Recently, the integration of foundry modules into the process is considered to ease this power issue. However, it is not enough to have certain nodes to boost the existence of the system. The paper proposes a new distributed linked dominant set method on wireless sensor network applications for precision farming with solar tracking nodes. In smart agricultural applications, the latest distributed dominant solar energy construction application, called CDSSEHA, is contrasted with the conventional flood methods and an efficient energy CDS method. According to the findings, in comparison with conventional flood approaches and the CDS based approach; the suggested methodology improved the resilience of the WSNs up to about six times and 1.4 times. In addition, the CDS building process represents just roughly 15% of the lifespan.

In the year of 2020, the authors "Lukáš Vacho et al. [14]" proposed a paper related to agricultural plant monitoring robot design with proper navigation features. In this paper [14] the authors described such as the method of navigation for mobile robot is applicable in the agriculture plant lines. The proposed clustering algorithm method uses data from the laser sensor Hokuyo. The created solution helps the plant to be identified in a row if the local navigation concept is used by a mobile robot. Crops in a row are common ways to build the polygon vertices. The moment of inertia is determined from this polygon, which defines the starting lineup including its plant lines. The moment of inertia is determined from this polygon, which defines the center line of the plant lines. This location is used for the algorithm of mobile robot control. The processed data by sensors do provide details on paths but also on barriers in the crop lines.

3 Proposed System Methodologies

This paper introduced a new novel methodology called Modified Convolutional Neural Scheme (MCNS), in which it provides a proper machine learning abilities to the agricultural field maintenance scheme as well as the agriBOT is initiated over this system

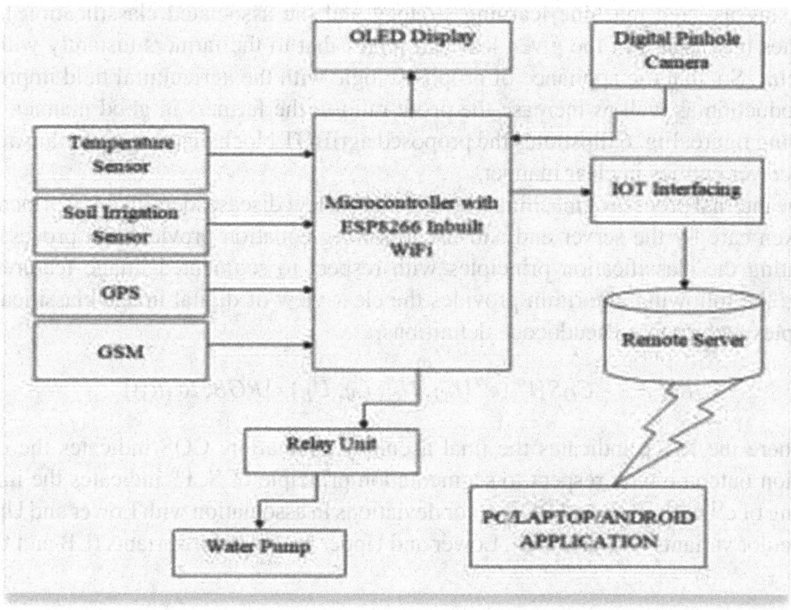

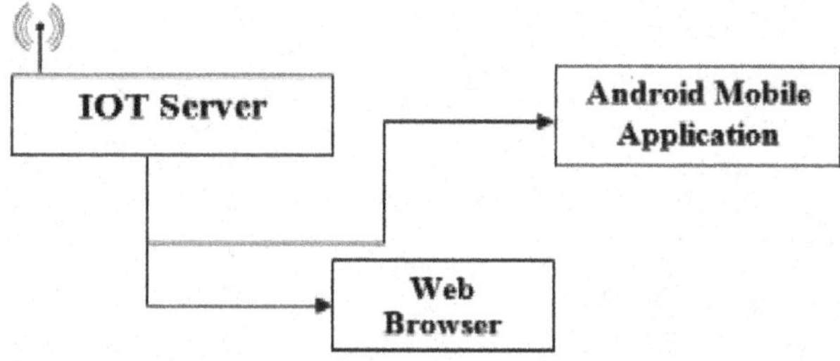

Fig. 6. Transmitter block of agriBOT and receiver block of agriBOT

to acquire the agri field data and pass it to the remote server with the help of Internet of Things (IoT) features. The proposed approach highly belongs to two things such as agriBOT and the Artificial Intelligence logic. The agriBOT is a robot, in which it has an ability to fly around the agricultural field and capture the data from the fields and pass it to the remote server entity to maintenance as well as manipulations. The manipulated results will be in a boolean format such as either true or false, in which the returned value from the prediction is true, the data is considered to be the most significant data as well as the alert mechanism is triggered to raise an alert to the respective farmer. And the prediction result is returned as false, the data is considered to be the regular periodical data and it is going to be stored into the remote server for monitoring purposes. The Artificial Intelligence logic is applied to the proposed approach to identify the incoming data is normal or abnormal, such kind of classifications are done in the server end for manipulating the incoming data from the agricultural field as well as the leaf images are cross-validated with respect to the disease detection principles.

The leaf disease detection principles are handled with the help of digital image processing assisted machine learning strategy and the associated classification logic identifies the disease of the given leaf and report that to the farmers instantly without any delay. So, that the appliance of proposed logic with the agricultural field improves the production as well as increase the profit ratio to the farmers in good manner. The following figure, Fig. 6 illustrates the proposed agriBOT block diagram with transmitter and receiver entities in clear manner.

The internal process of machine learning and the leaf disease identification principles are taken care by the server end and the following equation provides the process for estimating the classification principles with respect to segmented image features as well as the following algorithm provides the clear view of digital image classification principles with proper Pseudocode definitions.

$$R_{ACC} \leftarrow C_O S\{I^m(c^{vt}\{L_G, U_G, L_B, U_B\} \cdot [RGB, BGR])\} \tag{1}$$

Where the RAcc indicates the final accuracy estimation, COS indicates the classification outcome with respect to segmentation principle of S, I^m indicates the image masking of c^{vt} with RGB and BGR color deviations in association with Lower and Upper green color variants (LG and UG), Lower and Upper brown color variants (LB and UB).

Algorithm: Plant Leaf Image Classification

Input: *Extract the image features from the agriBOT memory unit/server storage.*

Output: *Disease Classification Result with Prediction Accuracy ratio.*

Step-1: *Initialize the function for image segmentation called "img_segment" with the input parameters of RGB and Hue-Saturation Value color variants.*

Step-2: *Define the lower and upper green value combinations for the plant leaf image gathered from agriBOT, in which it is acquired for feature extraction process.*

Step-3: *Specify the role for a healthy masking range for HSV image parameters, lower and upper green color variations.*

Step-4: *Initiate the lower brown values from the array variable generated by the extraction process.*

Step-5: *Identify the safe masking range feature to follow the image HSV, the lower and the upper color differences in parameters.*

Step-6: *Define the disease masking range with regard to the color matching scheme, both for green and brown variations.*

Step-7: *Concatenate the final masking results and store them in the finale mask variable.*

Step-8: *Return to the classification principles the final masking result.*

Pseudocode:

```
define img_segment (rgb_img,hsv_img):
Lower_Green+ Lower_Brown←array([25,0,20]);
Upper_Green+ Upper_Brown← array([100,255,255]);
h_mask←cvt.Range(hsv_img, Lower_Green, Upper_Green, , Lower_
Brown, Upper_Brown);
r1←cvt.bitwise_and(rgb_img,mask ➨h_mask);
result←cvt2.bitwise_and(r1, mask=final_mask);
return result;
```

Step-9: *Return the final results accuracy and subsequent prediction values.*

```
Acc(Result) ←array{result};
return Acc(Result);
```

4 Result and Discussions

In this paper a novel Modified Convolutional Neural Scheme (MCNS) is introduced, in which it appends the machine learning strategies to provide the high accuracy result estimations in association with Internet of Things enabled agriBOT principles. The agriBOT design is completed based upon the structural view of block diagram in figure, Fig. 6. The resulting section process the inputs accumulated from the agricultural field based on the data as well as the plant leaf. The details such as soil irrigation level and temperature conditions are estimated with respect to the prediction logics and the leaf estimations are processed with respect to the digital image processing principles, in which the classification and segmentation schemes are applied to extract the affected content from the leaf area and identify the disease to do a proper protections against that. The following figure, Fig. 7 illustrates the sample leaf images acquired from the agriBOT in various dimensions. The figure portrays the leaf with disease as well as the leaf without disease specifications. These leaves are not only belonging to the unique plants, instead these leaves are accumulated from different farm lands and agricultural fields for processing.

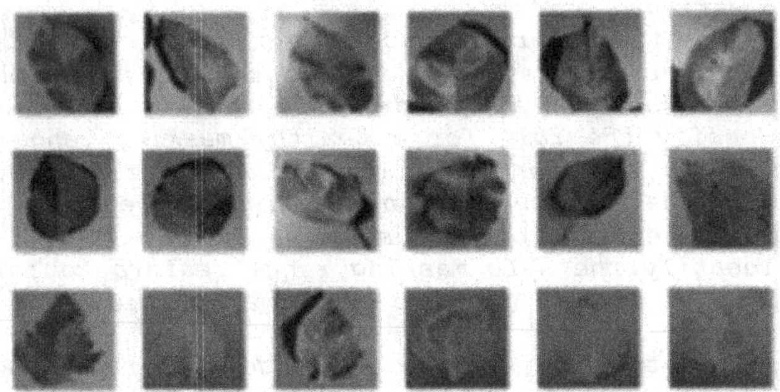

Fig. 7. Plant leaf images gathered from agriBOT

The following figure, Fig. 8 illustrates the plant leaf image RGB feature details extraction process resulting perception of the proposed approach MCNS, in which it shows the masking portion of green color ratio segmentation and masking portion of brown color ratio segmentation from input images and the outcome proof, is displayed further. The general segmentation process splits the affected portion alone from the leaf image, but in this proposed MCNS process based image segmentation scheme split out the green masking portion and the brown masking portions separately and concatenate the final resulting masked images for classification procedures, in which it also leads a way to attain high accuracy results in outcome.

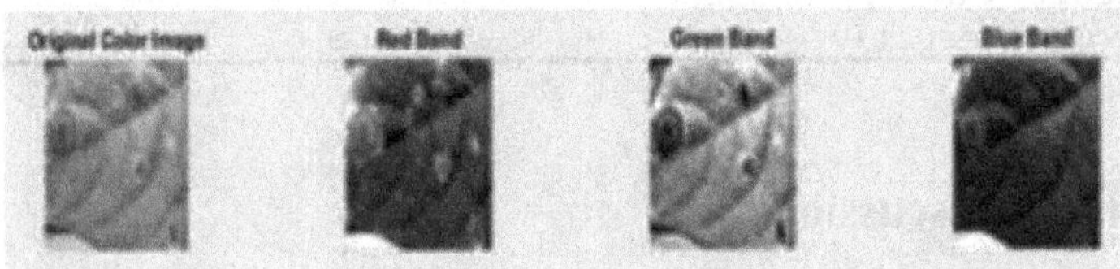

Fig. 8. Features extraction based on RGB color bands

The following figure, Fig. 9 (a) illustrates the histogram view of extracted features based on the plant leaf image RGB color variations as well as the basic image color perceptions acquired from the agriBOT. These histogram values are used to estimate the color variation ranges in pixel values as well as this is useful for easy understanding of the color ratios of the plant leaf image. Similarly the figure, Fig. 9 (b) illustrates the mask viws of the color bands in grayscale format.

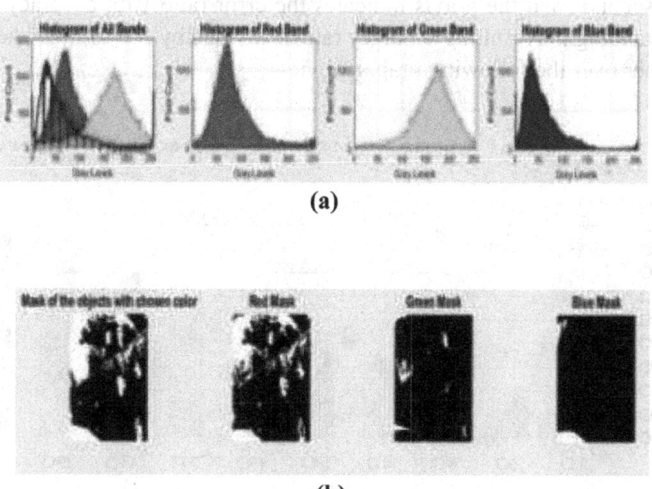

(a)

(b)

Fig. 9. (a) Histogram view of RGB color bands and (b) color masking view of the plant leaf images

The following figure, Fig. 10 shows the image classification portion of the input image, in which the plant leaf image acquired from agriBOT is analyzed with the help of proposed MCNS classification logic to attain the following outcome with better value predictions. The diseased portion boundaries are identified and marked clearly with red line specifications.

The following figure, Fig. 11 illustrates the agricultural data collection accuracy levels of the proposed approach of MCNS. The agriBOT collects the field data with the help of associated sensor units presented into the device. Those data will be passed to the server unit for manipulations with respect to the Internet of Things strategies. The

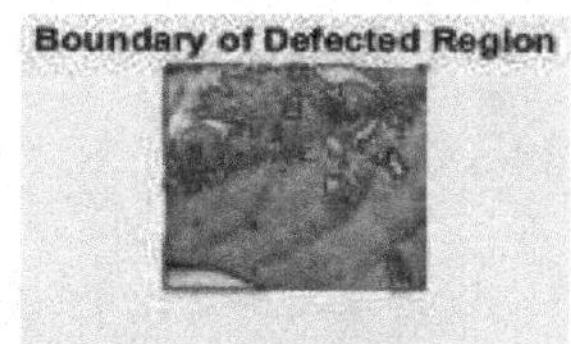

Fig. 10. Disease portion extraction from the leaf image

following figure, Fig. 11 portrays the view of data collection levels with respect to the data sent from agriBOT for a particular time period intervals.

The following figure, Fig. 12 illustrates the error ratio analysis of the proposed approach, in which the data collected from the agricultural field is processed with respect to the principles of Modified Convolutional Neural Scheme (MCNS). This figure portrays the processing time accuracy estimation range in association with the respective bit error ratio occurred while processing the agricultural data. In which the x-axis indicates the time in milliseconds and the y-axis indicates the error ratio with accuracy levels. For better understanding the resulting accuracy ratio is divided by 100 to show the error ratio in clear manner over the following graphical view.

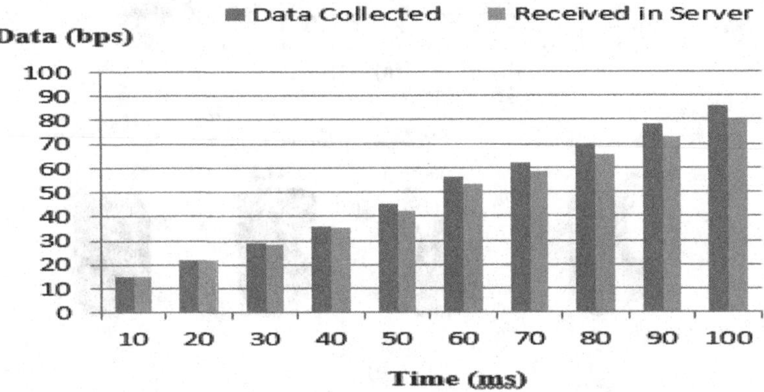

Fig. 11. Data collection vs. data received accuracy ratio

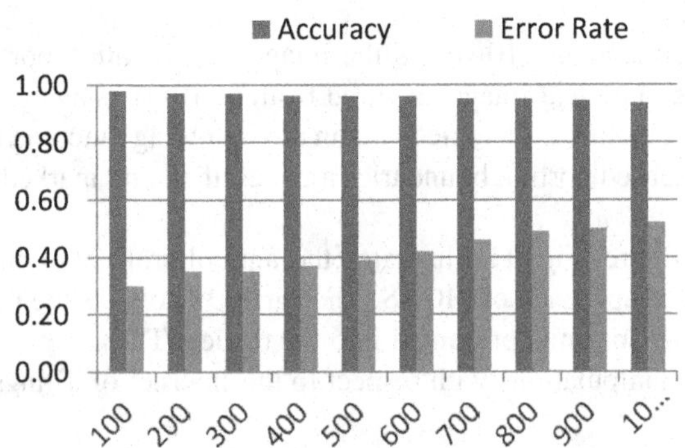

Fig. 12. Accuracy ratio vs. error rate estimation

The following figure, Fig. 13 (a) and (b) illustrates the temperature level and the rainfall ratio of the agriculture field with respect to the surveillance of 30 days continuously by using the designed agriBOT as well as the resulting efficiency are proved with the help of the following graphical results.

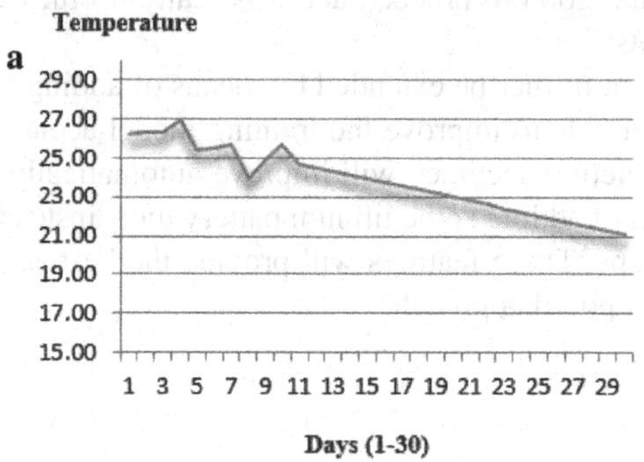

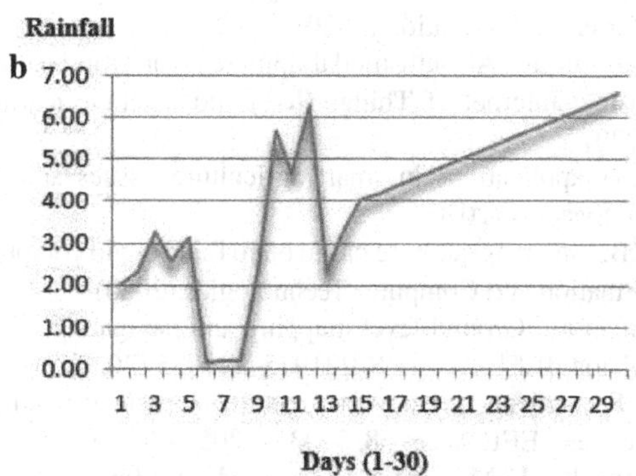

Fig. 13. (a) Temperature level estimation (b) rainfall level estimation

5 Conclusion and Future Scope

In this paper a new robotic structure is designed to provide support to the agricultural field and the farmers, in which it is designed with the association of smart sensors and the associated gadgets. The robot called agriBOT is operated with the nature of Artificial Intelligence and accumulates the temperature ranges and soil moisture levels in correct proposition as well as the resulting details are transferred to the remote server with the help of Internet of Things provisions. The outcome accuracy of the mentioned things are presented on the resulting section figures, Fig. 11 and Fig. 12. The proposed agriBOT acquire the agricultural information and pass it to the server end to manipulation, in which the server end receives the data and process it based on a novel machine learning procedure called Modified Convolutional Neural Scheme. This scheme identifies the climate changes and the associated water supplies to the crops are managed properly with the help of such approach in clear manner. The resulting section figure, Fig. 13 (a) and (b) illustrates the agricultural field temperature level and rainfall level indications in clear manner for the data of 30 days surveillance. The resulting section proves the proposed approach efficiency in terms of both image processing outcome wise as well as the machine learning processed basis also, so that the proposed approach presented into the paper is well and good to proceed and it is really useful for agricultural field monitoring environments.

In future the work can further be extended by means of adding some deep learning procedures on the server side to improve the training model accuracy ratio from 96% to 98%, so that the prediction accuracy will improve automatically. The agriBOT can be improvised by means of adding some lithium battery units instead of using the other expensive battery backups. These features will provide the best accuracy pattern with cost efficiency on the proposed approach.

References

1. Parvez, B., Haidri, R.A., Verma, J.K.: IoT in agriculture. In: International Conference on Computational Performance Evaluation (2020)
2. Shafi, U., Mumtaz, R., et al.: A multi-modal approach for crop health mapping using low altitude remote sensing, Internet of Things (IoT) and machine learning. IEEE Access **8**, 112708–112724 (2020)
3. Kassim, M.R.M.: IoT applications in smart agriculture: issues and challenges. In: IEEE Conference on Open Systems (2020)
4. Namani, S., Gonen, B.: Smart agriculture based on IoT and cloud computing. In: International Conference on Information and Computer Technologies (2020)
5. Zhao, W., Wang, X., et al.: Ground-level mapping and navigating for agriculture based on IoT and computer vision. IEEE Access **8**, 221975–221985 (2020)
6. Ferrag, M.A., et al.: Security and privacy for green IoT-based agriculture: review, blockchain solutions, and challenges. IEEE Access **8**, 32031–32053 (2020)
7. Castellanos, G., Deruyck, M., Martens, L., Joseph, W.: System assessment of WUSN using NB-IoT UAV-aided networks in potato crops. IEEE Access **8**, 56823–56836 (2020)
8. Kour, V.P., Arora, S.: Recent developments of the Internet of Things in agriculture: a survey. IEEE Access **8**, 129924–129957 (2020)
9. Subahi, A.F., Bouazza, K.E.: An intelligent IoT-based system design for controlling and monitoring greenhouse temperature. IEEE Access **8**, 125488–125500 (2020)
10. Zhao, W., Wang, X., Qia, B., Runge, T.: Ground-level mapping and navigating for agriculture based on IoT and computer vision. IEEE Access **8**, 221975–221985 (2020)
11. Dai, Q., Cheng, X., Qiao, Y., Zhang, Y.: Crop leaf disease image super-resolution and identification with dual attention and topology fusion generative adversarial network. IEEE Access **8**, 55724–55735 (2020)
12. Gölbol, F., Ölmez, H., Hacınecipoğlu, A., Ankaralı, M.M.: Developing a motion controller for autonomous agricultural robot. In: Signal Processing and Communications Applications Conference (2020)
13. Gulec, O., Haytaoglu, E., Tokat, S.: A novel distributed CDS algorithm for extending lifetime of WSNs with solar energy harvester nodes for smart agriculture applications. IEEE Access **8**, 58859–58873 (2020)
14. Vacho, L., HrubÝ, D., TÓth, L., PalkovÁ, Z.: identification of agricultural plant row using the clustering algorithm in the navigation of mobile robot. In: International Conference on Energy Efficiency and Agricultural Engineering (2020)

Proof of Good Service Based on DAGs-To-Blockchain for IoT Applications

Istabraq M. Al-Joboury(✉) and Emad H. Al-Hemiary

College of Information and Communication Engineering, Al-Nahrain University, Baghdad, Iraq
{estabriq_94,emad}@coie-nahrain.edu.iq

Abstract. Distributed ledgers based on decentralization are promising technologies to reliably and securely distribute data. Nodes in Blockchain can create a block that contains several transactions through consensus algorithms and is linked to the previous block using hash computation. It is expected to be integrated with smart technologies, such as the Internet of Things (IoT) to store and process data from sensors. However, IoT devices are resource-constrained embedded microcontrollers, which cannot handle the current Blockchain ledgers of high huge storage need, as well as the extensive tasks of consensus algorithms (e.g., Proof of Work). To remove centralization and to improve the linear structure, this paper proposes a new low latency distributed algorithm titled Proof of Good Service based on Directed Acyclic Graphs (DAGs)-to-Blockchain structure (PoGSDB). It is organized in 5 horizontal layers in permissioned mode with different features, namely: Common, Committee, Fog, Queen, and Cloud. A limited number of common, committee, and fog nodes are grouped. Each group has its DAG (named Cobweb ledger) based on uniform distribution. Common nodes send authenticated data with the public key to Committee. The latter receives and broadcasts it to its neighbors, then each node chooses a random number as a counter and autodecrement it. The winner node is the fastest committee node that reaches zero. The committee nodes rate the winner based on its speed and availability (rate scores from 1 to 5). Every stipulated time, the Cobweb ledger is selected from each group by fog node to send it with authentication to Cloud through the Internet. The cloud leader adds each Cobweb ledger to blocks after check the authentication and authorization. The rest nodes will rate the leader as in committee. Finally, the Queen node is used for monitoring the network and behavior of nodes. The proposed algorithm is emulated and evaluated in a healthcare scenario to mitigate overhead costs, verification time, and to increase throughput as compared to the traditional protocols.

Keywords: Internet of Things · Blockchain · Direct acyclic graphs · Distributed ledgers · Consensus algorithms

1 Introduction

With the prevalence of the Internet of Things (IoT), a large number of Things with lightweight resources, heterogeneous and ubiquitous features collaboratively produce a

P. Liatsis et al. (Eds.): TIOTC 2021, CCIS 1548, pp. 31–45, 2022.
https://doi.org/10.1007/978-3-030-97255-4_3

massive amount of data via the Internet [1]. It can be deployed and geographically scattered in any field with/without human intervention. This incurs several issues such as performance bottleneck, security, privacy, and verifying integrity. The traditional solutions depend on a trusted centralized entity such as Fog or Cloud computing technologies to mitigate the overhead and control the network [2]. However, those systems will suffer from a single point of failure in a real-world scenario, which may lead to loss of information. It is crucial because the system could hold sensitive data, so it is not efficient and suitable for sensitive applications [3]. Recently, authors proposed Distributed Ledger Technologies (DLTs) based decentralized architecture without depending on a third party to remove the challenges of centralization, and to provide high levels of data sharing and tractability. Integrating DLTs and IoT are projected to be an essential part of daily applications in the near future, such as in healthcare, education, and federal systems [4]. With DLTs based on a decentralized characteristic, IoT can achieve reliable and zero-failure architectures. Unfortunately, Bitcoin [5] and Ethereum [6] as examples of DLTs are not particularly designed for IoT applications, as the primary use was for cryptocurrency [7]. With traditional Blockchain (the fundamental concept of Bitcoin and Ethereum), IoT has a great potential to experience low throughput, long queue because of linear structure, and resource-intensive due to consensus algorithms. Thus, the current DLTs are inefficient for low-latency IoT systems that generate high volumes of data [8]. Looking forward, the size of Blockchain will expeditiously grow due to IoT-generated data. Consequently, full nodes will require large capabilities storage, memory, and processing to handle Blockchain. Additionally, it will cause high confirmation time to accept data, then new data will end up waiting to be confirmed [9]. To sum up, IoT-based the current DLTs have scalability issues. Hence, several authors propose solutions and consider one direction of scalability. It is still suffering either low through, high waiting time, or waste resources. It is a significant challenge to balance between these in one platform.

The main contributions of this paper are described as follows:

- Integrate DLTs with IoT to circumvent problems caused by vulnerabilities of centralized networks by ignoring the intermediary,
- Propose lightweight, feeless, and decentralized fashion consensus algorithm based on DAGs-to-Blockchain to efficiently and stability disseminate data and provide the tamper-proof feature with the increases of amount of data in real-time,
- Enhance the algorithm to meet single-board computing of Things requirements by designing a layered architecture to achieve fairness in terms of capabilities.
- Improve confirmation time and throughput by introducing no-chain and block-less in low-latency layers.
- Present a use case for the proposed algorithm that depends on the availability and accuracy of data.

The paper is outlined as follows: Sect. 2 describes the proposed consensus algorithm based on DAGs-to-Blockchain. Section 3, presents the experimental setup. Section 4, shows the results of performance evolution. Section 5, covers a use case. Finally, Sect. 6 concludes this paper.

2 System Design

This section introduces the overview and the model of our proposed consensus algorithm relying on DAGs-to-Blockchain structure.

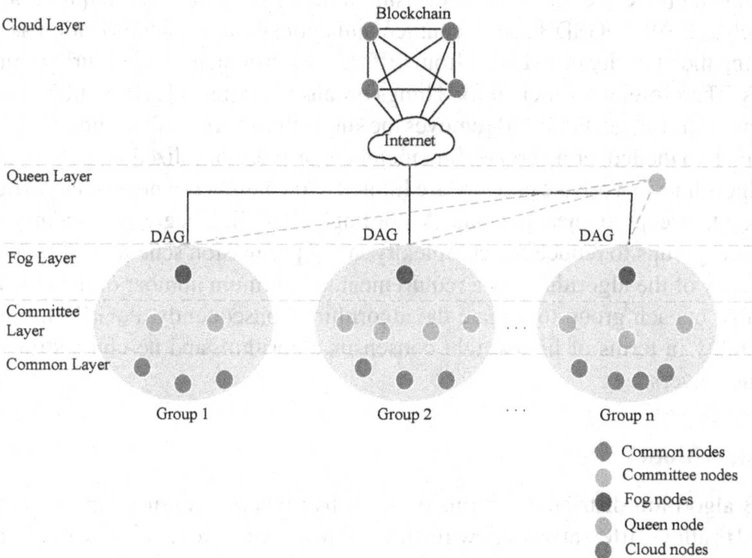

Fig. 1. The PoGSDB consensus algorithm.

2.1 System Overview

A novel consensus algorithm named Proof of Good Services based on DAGs-to-Blockchain structure (PoGSDB) is designed for lightweight, feeless, and resource-limited IoT devices, such as limited storage and computation processing, and to mitigate the scalability issue of the existing DLTs, and to provide low-latency distributed data securely. The main contributions of this algorithm are that the traditional Blockchain is worked in a horizontal model, which causes the unfair election of the leader. However, PoGSDB is proposed in hierarchical architecture with five layers as illustrated in Fig. 1, namely: Common, Committee, Fog, Queen, and Cloud, which leads to distribute the roles and responsibilities fairly between nodes in a hierarchical architecture. Nodes are playing different roles and different responsibilities in each layer, hence it reduces the misbehavior of nodes and increases the performance and trust in the network. Participants are identified in a permission mode to ensure that everyone will follow the regulation and to keep the network private and more secure. Each node in this protocol rates the other peers regarding their activities and their speed to process the data to motivate them to be always available and fast in response. A node may be punished for its bad behavior afterward. It depends on the DAGs-to-Blockchain data structure, in which the three layers (Common, Committee, and Fog) store data in DAGs (called Cobweb), and the Cloud layer preserves the received Cobweb ledger inside blocks in a sequence (called Blockchain). This is because DAG improves the low-latency layers that need fast response time; on the other hand, Blockchain increases security on the Cloud layer via the Internet that requires security over speed. Eventually, it will provide both features in this same architecture. (5) Instead of using a heavy-duty task that required a lot of work, such as PoW, PoGSDB uses a counter, authentication, and authorization as a way of verifying the integrity of IoT data from different environments and securing sensitive messages. Therefore, it is efficient for Things because it requires less computing power, processing, and storage. PoGSDB removes the single third party in the validation process to add data into the ledger by connecting members on a decentralized model. Most consensus algorithms in a private network are limited to the number of nodes that participate in deciding to accept to reject the data. Accordingly, PoGSDB segregates members into autonomous groups to reduce the complexity in the permission scheme and to increase the efficiency of the algorithm. As a requirement, a minimum number of devices would be available in each group to initiate the algorithm. Consequently, PoGSDB improves the scalability in terms of lightweight consensus algorithm, and no-chain structure in low-latency layers.

2.2 System Model

PoGSDB algorithm distributes its functions on five layers to ensure fairness between peers, and to allow different devices with different resources to join the network. Consider a limited number of participants are connected to establish a group. It assumes that there are `k` groups and a set of `p` nodes in each group. The layers of PoGSDB are described as follows:

Common layer: it contains common nodes, which represent sensors, actuators, and Things of IoT devices with lightweight resources as depicted in Fig. 2. It requires that at minimum one node in each group; otherwise, the group will be with no data. Each common node has private/public pair keys (`PrKi, PuKi`). `PrK` is privately saved in the network, while `PuK` is shared with all the peers. Initially, each node sends a specific message within a specific topic to identify itself and to declare that it will start sending messages containing sensor values. Common nodes are responsible for collecting, measuring IoT data from Things inside each group. Generating a JavaScript Object Notation (JSON) data format every `n` seconds that contains four information: `timestamp` represents the current time in seconds, `SensorValue` is the value from a sensor that can measure from the environment, and `DataID` is a unique hexadecimal identification for each data to facilitate the retrieval of data. `SensorData= {timestamp, SensorValue, DataID}`. Authenticating the source of data by signing it with its private key as a digital signature. Signing the data with a timestamp as well, which will be impossible to be forged. Forwarding the signed data to other members inside the group in a Peer-to-Peer mechanism. To clarify, this algorithm does not hash data because it is considered an energy-intensive scheme for IoT devices with limited resources.

Committee layer: it contains committee nodes, which have processing capabilities to process the received data from common nodes that connect to it. PoGSDB requires at minimum two committee members in each group to maintain the records. As in the

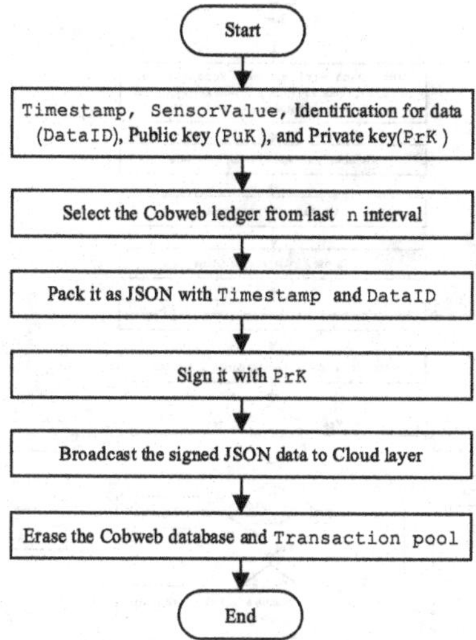

Fig. 2. The common layer's responsibilities

Common layer, each committee node has (PrKi, PuKi) set. The system assigns 4 score rates by default for each node to start processing the data. At the beginning of the process, the algorithm creates the genesis record with "dummy" values as the first data in the ledger inside each group. Each group has its genesis record and maintains an independent Cobweb ledger for fast and scalable processing data. At each n time, one leader from the committee nodes inside each group will be selected based on counting down a random number called counter range between x and y. In other words, each committee nodes chooses a number randomly and auto-decrements it during n seconds. Eventually, one of the nodes reaches zero faster than the others, which this node is considered the leader in a group.

The leader has the following roles during a short interval as shown in Fig. 3: publish a message for the rest of the nodes to declare that it becomes a leader and to wait for another phase. Receive the specific messages from each common node and are attached directly to thegenesis record. Collect the signed messages from common nodes. Disseminate every received message to the node's neighbors. Check if the received message has existed already in the Transaction pool. using the DataID. If it does not exist, then it will be added to the pool. To point out, the Transaction pool is used to store all the received messages without redundancy. After fetching the messages, committee nodes will verify the message if it is valid to ensure reputation: (i) by checking the message if it contains a signature, (ii) by validating the digital signature using the PuK of the source of that message, (ii) by checking the timestamp after the successful signature verification. Otherwise, the message will be rejected.

The valid data can be appended into the distributed Cobweb ledger system based on DAG: (i) select two random existing data in Cobweb ledger from the last n seconds. (ii) Check if these data will cause cyclic in the Cobweb ledger. Otherwise, select another

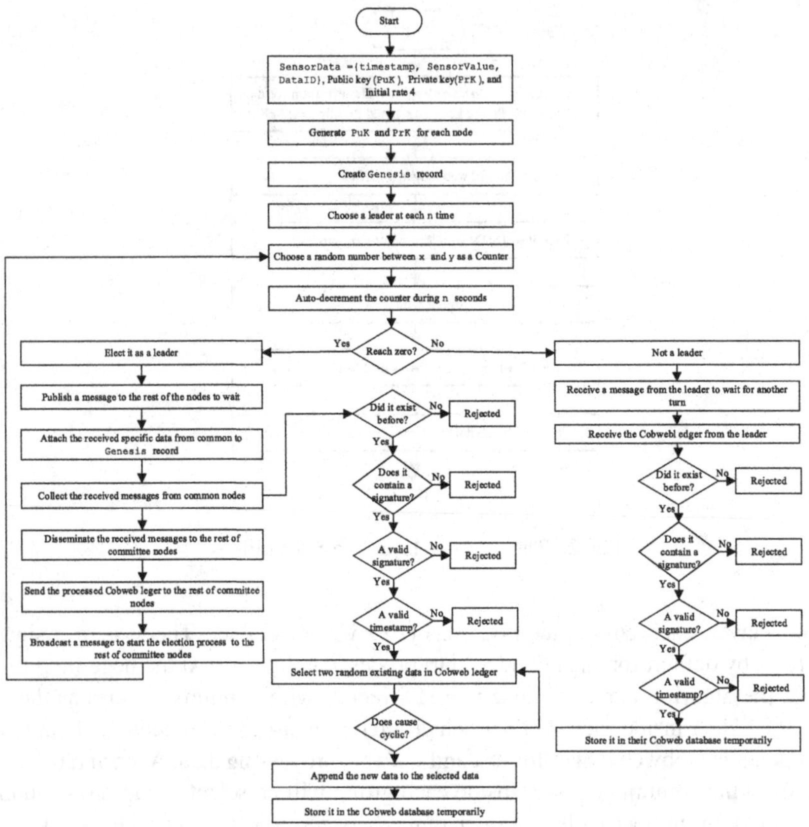

Fig. 3. Roles of the leader and normal nodes in the committee layer.

random existing data. (iii) Link the new data to the selected data (Edge between them). (iv) Store it temporarily and locally in the Cobweb database.

A new leader will be elected after n seconds, but the leader has to send the processed data in the Cobweb ledger to the rest of the committee nodes. Then, it will send a message to them to start the election process again. The other nodes will receive the Cobweb ledger from the leader. They have to follow the same step (number 4) of verifications so that can accept it and add it to their local Cobweb ledger temporarily.

Participants rate the leader based on its activity, which rate scores are from 1 to 5. The rate levels are decided based on the following: (i) node will rate 1, if it witnesses the messages have been changed or modified. (ii) A node will rate the leader by 2, if the leader becomes unavailable and did not process the data. (iii) If a node receives a successful message during a time frame, it will rate 3, 4, or 5 based on how fast it processes the data. Each node rates the leader, then the average will be calculated to find the final rate score. Therefore, the committee node needs to have a 3 or greater rate score to participate in the committee layer in the next round. Otherwise, it can join as a common node or will be disconnected from the network. As a result, PoGSDB motivates nodes to process data within record time and be available by giving them a good rate level. This also allows common nodes to connect to the trust committee members.

Fog layer: it contains a single node in each group referred to as a fog node, which is selected randomly from the committee layer. It has several responsibilities as shown in Fig. 4: Select the Cobweb ledger from the lastn interval. Pick it as a JSON with `Timestamp`, and `DataID`. Authentic the selected ledger with `PrK` of the fog node. Send it to the Cloud layer for further processing.

After sending the Cobweb ledger, each committee node includes the fog node will erase the Cobweb database and `Transaction pool` to reduce storage consumption, and to make IoT devices sufficiently lightweight.

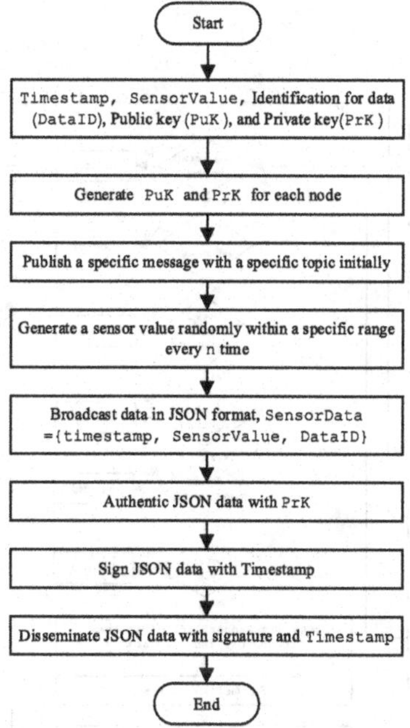

Fig. 4. The fog node's responsibilities every n interval.

Queen layer: this layer is used to perceive and maintain participants in the network through two steps: Monitor the groups, which represent Common, Committee, and Fog layers. Distribute the roles and responsibilities on the members in different layers mentioned above without influencing their decisions on accepting or rejecting the data.

Cloud layer: it contains high capacity storage node named cloud nodes similar to the full nodes in traditional Blockchain in Peer-to-Peer network. They contribute to the algorithm in terms of connectivity, permanent storage, and repudiation. It relies on Blockchain (not DAG). All cloud nodes have a unique `(PrKi, PuKi)` set. The system creates the initial record (`genesis`) with "no meaning" values in the Blockchain structure, which is the same in all cloud nodes. Choosing the leader is the same in the

Committee layer by counting down the counter that is specified between a determined range. The first cloud node's counter becomes zero, then it is the leader. Then, the leader will notify other nodes that it becomes a leader. The leader as illustrated in Fig. 5 is responsible for receiving the signed Cobweb ledger every n interval from the Fog layer. Broadcast the received messages to neighbors in Peer-to-Peer. Check the id of the received Cobweb should not have existed before. The leader must verify the message before appended it: (i) each message has to be packed with a signature. (ii) Check the authority of cloud and fog nodes through the username and password. (iii) Verify the authenticity of the message using a digital signature. (iii) Compare the timestamp of Cobweb from the origin timestamp. After successful verification, the leader inspects any cyclic in it, if it does then it will be rejected.

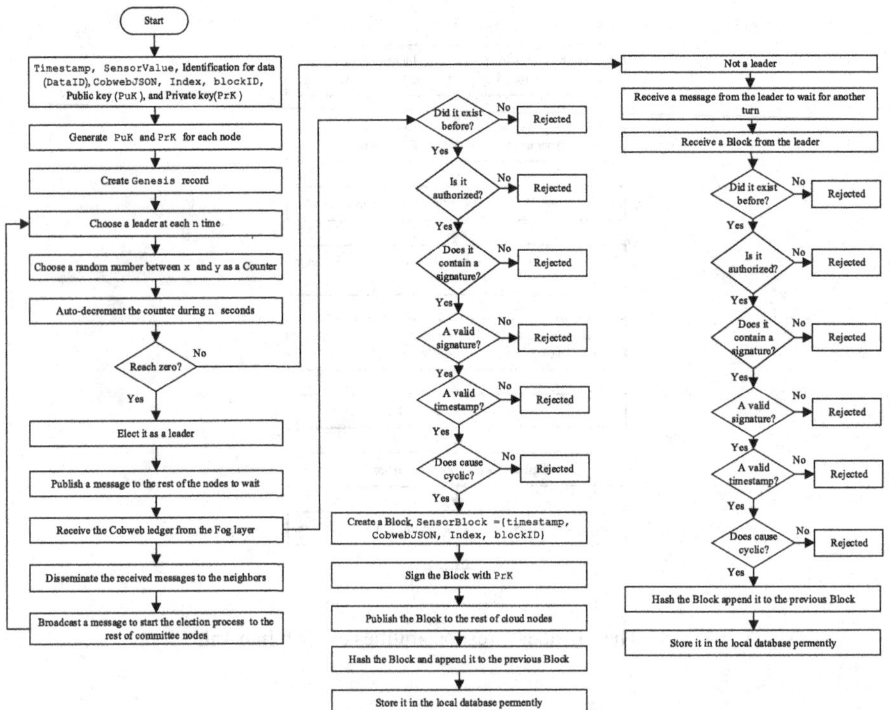

Fig. 5. The cloud node's responsibilities after receiving data from fog node.

The leader will create a block that contains the valid message (represents the Cobwed ledger), the current timestamp, unique id, and serial number. The serial number is auto-generated and increased to each block one-by-one. `SensorBlock= {timestamp, CobwebJSON, Index, blockID}`. The leader will sign the block to prevent the algorithm from fabricating the block and publish it to the rest of the cloud node. The other nodes will receive the block and check its validity according to the same process of the leader. If it is a valid block, then they will accept it. Every cloud node hashes the block and appends it to the end of the chain. In other words, the new block will point to the previous block through the hash function to ensure tamper-proof. Finally, it will be stored in their local Blockchain database permanently. After finishing the process, the cloud devices will rate the leader regarding its work as the same rate score in the Committee layer.

2.3 System Data Structure

DAGs-to-Blockchain data structure is proposed as illustrated in Fig. 6 to address the scalability issue of the line structure of the traditional Blockchain, which causes long confirmation time of transactions and low throughput. On the other hand, the traditional DAG such as in IoTA [10] usually leaves new transactions unattached to the ledger because it depends on the Coordinator node, which selects transactions and sends them to the nodes to confirm. However, this data structure solves these problems by allowing several groups creates stimulatingly independent DAGs that contain individual data (no-blocks) to make fast processing with low confirmation time (low-latency). Additionally, these DAGs will be inside the block for further processing to provide security and immutability of data. The traditional DLTs contain designated miners to mine the data, but this proposed algorithm can use different lightweight IoT devices to join the network and mine the data.

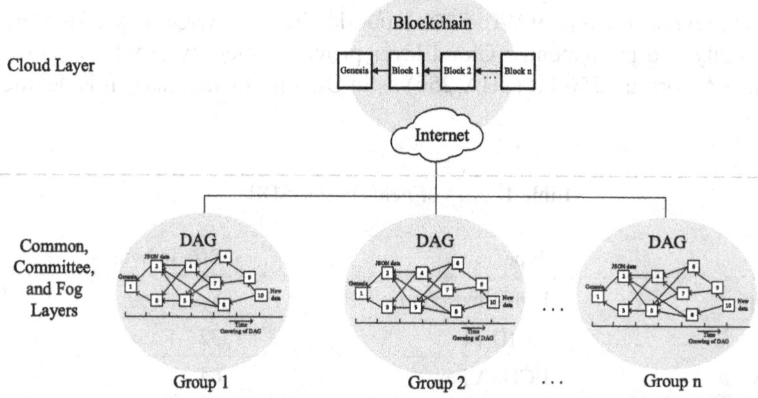

Fig. 6. DAGs-to-Blockchain data structure.

3 Experimental Setup

PoGSDB is set up on small Linux servers with proper capabilities to represent lightweight devices. The properties include 20 GByte of Dynamic Random-Access Memory (DRAM), 1 TByte of permanent storage, and it runs on Ubuntu server version 18.0.4 Long Term Standard (LTS) Operating system (OS). Node.js is used to prove the idea of the algorithm. PoGSDB is deployed in a real-time emulation scenario to provide accurate results. It is implemented on virtual machines that act as groups inside the physical server using VMware Workstation Pro version 15.5.2, which is used for virtualization. All peers inside a single group are identified by one IP address to represent the whole group. Access Point (AP) is enabled to connect the network through the same subnet mask. In this experimental setup, two virtual machines of 1000 nodes each are created. Nodes are connected in a Peer-to-Peer network through wireline communication across Common, Committee, and Fog layers. However, cloud nodes are connected via the Internet. Common nodes generate JSON data every 1 s with 124 bytes in size. Each data is identified uniquely using Universally Unique Identifier (UUID) version 4. This proposed algorithm uses asymmetric cryptography for digital signature, which is Standards for Efficient Cryptography 256-bits (secp256k1) of Elliptic Curve Cryptography (ECC) with the public key (65bytes) and the private key (32 bytes). In other words, it is a signature of data's content signed with common nodes' or fog node's private key. Additionally, the public key is used for signature validation and it is shared in advance. Regarding Elliptic Curve Discrete Logarithm Problem (ECDLP), a malicious user cannot extract the private key from the known public key. It requires O(k) operations in big O notation with brute force attack. The verification process is considered a lightweight method in IoT devices because it takes a negligible time to confirm. MQ Telemetry Transport (MQTT) application layer protocol is used to propagated data in publish/subscribe architecture. In the Cobweb ledger, data refers to two random previous data that were already verified during the last 5 min. It stores this information in the database, which means the edge of new data (the `DataID` of new data) is linked to the edges of the previous data (their `DataIDs`). For databases, MySQL is used to preserve data temporally and permanently. Cloud layer provides integrity proof on data using Secure Hash Algorithm 256-bit (SHA-256) as in Bitcoin. In summary, it is detailed in Table 1.

Table 1. Size of fields in PoGSDB.

Fields	Type	Size in byte
Timestamp	Unix timestamp	8
DataID	UUID v4	32
Public key	ECDSA key	64
Private key	ECDSA key	32
Authentication	ECDSA signature	72
Hash function	SHA-256	32

4 Results and Discussion

This section presents the performance evaluation of PoGSDB in an emulation environment in terms of confirmation time, throughput, central processing unit (CPU) utilization, and memory usage. The results ensure that if the proposed algorithm is suitable for limited-resources IoT devices. The algorithm is designed to work under private/permissioned mode. In the meantime of writing this paper, the results are mainly measured on the three layers (Things, Edge, and Fog). Further, the PoGSDB depends on the bandwidth and computational resources available to cloud nodes.

Listing 1: Cobweb Ledger in JSON

```
{
  "CobwebData":
        {
          "CobwebId": "8622018a....",
          "Timestamp": "1613053894",
          "SensorData": [
              "DataID": " 68295caa-4fe8-467e-89b0-d27c5357d149 ",
              "Timestamp": "1613050294",
              "SensorValue": "75"
                          ]
        },
  "Signature": "0x8f8c7........"

}
```

In this scenario, two virtual machines are employed to emulate two groups in the algorithm. Committee nodes collect data generated from common nodes and verify it using the public key of the source. Next, they will add it to the Cobweb ledger in their local storage. Fog node will select the Cobweb ledger, sign it with private key and `Timestamp`, and forwarded it to cloud nodes as described in listing 1. Once the received data is verified by the Committee layer, then it cannot be invalided because there is no concept of double-spending as data is not a currency, but is a sensor value. The output screenshot of the leader in the Committee layer is shown in Fig. 7.

It is excepted that the number of Things devices increases to billions, as result the number of records will grow exponentially. Consequently, the committee node cannot store the full copy of the Cobweb ledger due to its limited storage capacity. Therefore, the fog node selects the Cobweb ledger during the last 5 min and sends it periodically to cloud nodes as detailed in listing 2, then it clears it to reduce the storage overhead. This will not affect the DAG because the scheme does not depend on the history of a long period, but it requires a short interval to link the recent data with previous ones.

```
Start the process of choosing a leader:
The committee node chooses the number 5  randomly as a counter
Auto-Decrement the counter
    5
    4
    3
    2
    1
    0
This node became the leader
Send a message to other nodes for waiting for it
Process data for 1 minute
A new record is added to transaction pool
This new record is linked rondmly to two previous records that have been saved during the last minutein Cobweb ledger
A new record is added to transaction pool
This new record is linked rondmly to two previous records that have been saved during the last minutein Cobweb ledger
A new record is added to transaction pool
This new record is linked rondmly to two previous records that have been saved during the last minutein Cobweb ledger
Stop process data
Send a message to the rest of the committee nodes to start the process of chossing another leader
```

Fig. 7. Output screenshot of the leader in the committee layer.

LISTING 2: BLOCK IN JSON

```
{
  "Block":
        {
          "Index": "5",
          "Timestamp": "1612058994",
          "BlockID": " 16d7d4a7-5679-4288-92f8-84418bd62db8",
          "CobwebData": {} /* as the same as in lisiting 1
        },
  "Signature": "0x8f8c7.........",
  "Hash": " c671c846.........",
  "LashHash": "000066b3........."
}
```

Throughput: it is defined as the number of transactions per second (TPS) that the committee can handle. From the load test results as shown in Fig. 8, PoGSDB provides a good transaction rate of a varying number of nodes. The TPS increases regarding an increase in the number of nodes. This is because the work of processing data will distribute across the nodes. Every recent transaction is processed immediately because it does not need to wait in a queue to be confirmed immediately as there is no-chain in committee nodes. Additionally, Fig. 9 shows that average throughput remains stable even the size of Cobweb leger increases against time, which indicates that PoGSDB is a stable algorithm in the network when the number of nodes is 1000.

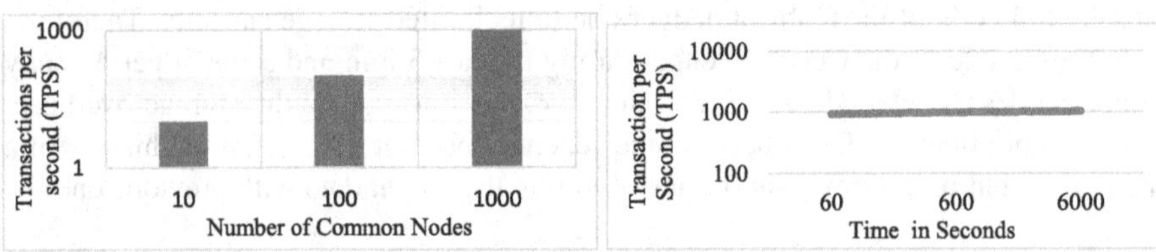

Fig. 8. Average TPS over several nodes. **Fig. 9.** Average TPS over time.

Confirmation time: it is referred to the time taken by data to be received, verified, and linked to the Cobweb ledger in each committee node. Figure 10 shows the average result of confirmation time over a different number of committee nodes with the same size of data.

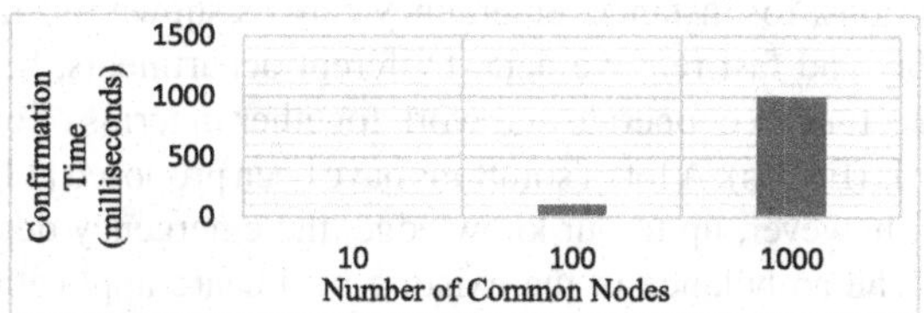

Fig. 10. Average confirmation time over a varying number of nodes.

The confirmation time increases as the number of common nodes increases. However, the delay is less than in the traditional DLTs because the data is processed simultaneously in a DAG-based ledger. For clarity, the results are measured in virtual machine scenarios and the network latencies need to be considered in the next work.

CPU utilization and memory usage: the average CPU utilization and average memory usage are measured in committee nodes during the interval (around 30 min) on virtual machines with a varying number of committee nodes. It is observed that CPU usage remains constant approximately 25 in percentage even the number of nodes increases. This is because the PoGSDB does not use heavy-duty tasks, instead, it uses a digital signature, `timestamp`, counter, and rate to verify data. Hence, it reduces CPU consumption. Moreover, memory usage remains constant as well, because committee nodes erase the old history of the Cobweb ledger every specific period.

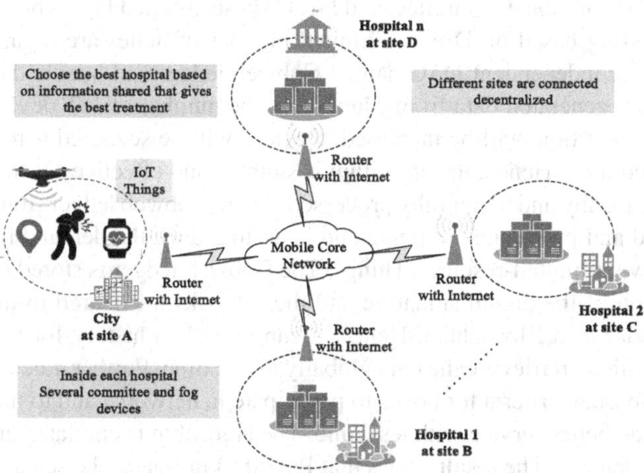

Fig. 11. Healthcare scenario for PoGSDB.

5 Use Case

PoGSDB can be implemented in any private application, but this paper concentrates on low-latency applications, for instance, emergency care as shown in Fig. 11. It requires low end-to-end delay and fast retrieve data. Different departments, hospitals, and any healthcare-related sector can cooperate and work together in terms of exchanging Electronic Health Records (EMRs). A lot of solutions have been proposed [11–14] for deploying DLTs with IoT; however, up to our knowledge, the emergency department has not to be covered yet. The ambulance in the existing healthcare applications chooses the nearest hospital regardless capabilities of a hospital to treat the patients. This threatens the patient life and reduces the quality of life. This paper aids the critical situations that need an immediate decision. Each department inside the hospital represents a group with permissioned nodes, which share data based on DAG. Additionally, interconnected hospitals will communicate together via exchanging Blockchain that contains DAGs to observe the history of patients. This helps the ambulance to choose the best hospital based on the previous records.

6 Conclusions and Future Work

In this paper, a novel consensus algorithm based on DAGs-to-Blockchain named PoGSDB is proposed in a permissioned and hierarchical architecture to address the scalability problem of integrating traditional DLTs with lightweight devices of IoT. Unlike the previous solutions, PoGSDB does not rely on solving intensive-task, no-chain, and no-block. However, it depends on layers to distribute roles and responsibilities on nodes. Additionally, the sensitive systems that need a fast response time, can take data from the grouped layers (Common, Committee, and Fog). These grouped layers provide efficient and fast processing based on DAG. A limited number of nodes are organized so that they will have an independent DAG named Cobweb ledger and handle data regarding the continuously generated data from Things. As the number of IoT devices increases rapidly, the waiting time will be increased. Devices will be scattered across groups as many as it is required. Hence, the algorithm is suitable and effective for IoT infrastructure. DAGs are locally and temporally processed. Then, Cobweb ledger from each group can be selected and propagated to the Cloud layer to reduce the demand for storage to be convenient with limited-resource Things. The Cobweb ledger is stored inside blocks after verification of the digital signature and these blocks are shared to the neighbors from cloud nodes as a Blockchain. Hence, it can provide a history for these Cobweb ledgers and facilitate retrieving the data globally at any time. Further, rate levels are one of the most important criteria for nodes to participate in networks and to motivate these nodes to provide better service with less time. The algorithm is emulated and evaluated in a real-time scenario. The result shows that PoGSDB mitigates the scalability issue in private networks and greatly increases the throughput by approximately 1K TPS with less waiting time around 1 s.

The future work will test the algorithm based on various parameters, such as different sizes of data and a different number of users. It will be implemented on real testbed devices, for example, Raspberry Pi to give realistic results. Comparison between

PoGSDB and other DLTs platforms will be evaluated. It can be integrated with Software Defined Network (SDN) to automate the whole network and reduce the complexity of programming.

References

1. de Matos, E., et al.: Context information sharing for the Internet of Things: a survey. Comput. Netw. **166**, 106988 (2020)
2. Ferrag, M., Derdour, M., Mukherjee, M., Derhab, A., Maglaras, L., Janicke, H.: Blockchain technologies for the Internet of Things: research issues and challenges. IEEE Internet Things J. **6**(2), 2188–2204 (2019)
3. Sengupta, J., Ruj, S., Das Bit, S.: A comprehensive survey on attacks, security issues and blockchain solutions for IoT and IIoT. J. Netw. Comput. Appl. **149**, 102481 (2020)
4. Nguyen, D.-L., Leyva-Mayorga, I., Popovski, P.: Witness-based approach for scaling distributed ledgers to massive IoT scenarios. In: 2020 IEEE 6th World Forum on Internet of Things (WF-IoT) (2020)
5. Wright, C. S .: Bitcoin: a peer-to-peer electronic cash system. SSRN Electron. J. (2008)
6. Ethereum/go-ethereum. https://github.com/ethereum/go-ethereum. Accessed 31 Mar 2021
7. Kim, H., Jang, J., Park, S., Lee, H.N.: Ethereum ECCPoW. arXiv preprint arXiv:2101.10729 (2021)
8. Tseng, L., Wong, L., Otoum, S., Aloqaily, M., Othman, J.: Blockchain for managing heterogeneous Internet of Things: a perspective architecture. IEEE Netw. **34**(1), 16–23 (2020)
9. Sori, A.A., Golsorkhtabaramiri, M., Rahmani, A.M.: Cryptocurrency grade of green; IOTA energy consumption modeling and measurement. In: 2020 IEEE Green Technologies Conference(GreenTech) (2020)
10. Miraz, M.: Blockchain of Things (BCoT): the fusion of blockchain and IoT technologies. SSRN Electron. J. 141–159 (2019)
11. Azaria, A., Ekblaw, A., Vieira, T., Lippman, A.: MedRec: using blockchain for medical data access and permission management. In: 2016 2nd International Conference on Open and Big Data (OBD) (2016)
12. Liang, X., Zhao, J., Shetty, S., Liu, J., Li, D.: Integrating blockchain for data sharing and collaboration in mobile healthcare applications. In: 2017 IEEE 28th Annual International Symposium on Personal, Indoor, and Mobile Radio Communications (PIMRC) (2017)
13. Khatoon, A.: A blockchain-based smart contract system for healthcare management. Electronics **9**(1), 94 (2020)
14. Al-Joboury, I.M., Al-Hemiary, E.H.: Automated decentralized IoT based blockchain using ethereum smart contract for healthcare. In: Marques, G., Kumar Bhoi, A., de la Torre Díez, I., Garcia-Zapirain, B. (eds.) Enhanced Telemedicine and e-Health. SFSC, vol. 410, pp. 179–198. Springer, Cham (2021). https://doi.org/10.1007/978-3-030-70111-6_9

A Lightweight Algorithm to Protect the Web of Things in IOT

Muthana S. Mahdi[1(✉)] and Zaydon L. Ali[2]

[1] Department of Computer Science, College of Science, Mustansiriyah University, Baghdad, Iraq
muthanasalih007@gmail.com
[2] College of Political Science, Mustansiriyah University, Baghdad, Iraq
zaydonlatif@uomustansiriyah.edu.iq

Abstract. The web of things is one of the most important innovations of modern technology. It aims to connect billions of devices, resulting in a vast number of contacts between devices and a huge volume of data. On the other hand, there are many security challenges to protect this information from risk exposure. It's crucial to note that these devices are compact and use very little power. As a consequence, using several rounds of data encryption would be exceedingly difficult and costly. Moreover, when fewer complex computations are used, integrity may be compromised. So, in this paper, a lightweight encryption algorithm called (L.W.A.E.S) is proposed. The proposed algorithm aims to achieve the highest speed in Cryptography (Encryption/Decryption) and reducing computational complexity. The MixColumns stage of the A.E.S algorithm is the most computationally challenging. So, it takes up the bulk of the time spent encrypting and decrypting data. The stage of MixColumns has been replaced by simple SHIFT processes in the proposed algorithm. It took just 1–8 s from the starting of the sensors' reading to the moment they were collected for the customer. The experimental results show that the modified algorithm (L.W.A.E.S) provides suitable security, the encryption techniques speed, low computational complexity, and light-weight in the manner of storage.

Keywords: Lightweight algorithm · Communications security · Web of things · Information security · Internet of Things · Cryptography

1 Introduction

Recently, the web of things (W.O.T) has shifted outward to becoming an emerging modern within spaces of exploration and implementation. The Internet of Things (I.O.T) may be a clear example of standard substances with the ability to detect and interact with comparable web-connected computers [1]. Currently, the broad band web has become widely used and open to anyone, which has led to an increase in information correspondence over the Internet and more sensors join it. Such a situation gives the right environment for the development of I.O.T [2]. Today, many research works focus on the complexities of the Internet of Things that want to be close to any entity in any place in

P. Liatsis et al. (Eds.): TIOTC 2021, CCIS 1548, pp. 46–60, 2022.
https://doi.org/10.1007/978-3-030-97255-4_4

the world. Electronic chips and sensors are embedded within the physical items around us, all of which transmit useful data [3].

The method of exchanging this vast pool of data begins with the computers themselves, which must be securely connected to an IoT platform that integrates information about multiple devices and implements demonstration calculations to exchange the most sensitive data for the applications. Since everything will be connected to the internet, the Internet of Things will carry the regular internet and the network of multi-use sensors to a whole different dimension [4]. Concerns that should be kept without thinking are ensuring issues with data visibility, ambiguity, and realism that will arise at the expense of security [5]. The Internet of Things is the starting point for connecting things, the operator, sensors, and any other intelligent techniques. I.O.T enables people to communicate in different places around the world (object to object) [6].

With the advent of the industrial internet, our world is now in the early stages of the digital period of change and enhancement (Web of Things) [7]. It takes up space by converging the overall industrial framework while constraining the advanced computing, sensing, analytics, and network development that the web provides. The Internet of Things (IoT) can be defined as a network of physical objects, product lines, homes, cars, buildings, and other things equipped with software, hardware, sensors, and a network connection that allows those devices to collect and transfer data [8]. Today the Internet has become ubiquitous and is known as the Internet of Things as an interactive relationship between the digital and physical worlds where the physical world interacts with the digital world using a large number of actuators and sensors. Moreover, the fast development in the field of communications and semiconductors has led to growing the development of the IoT so fast [9].

1.1 Lightweight Cryptography

The biggest risk related to IoT security concerning traditional IoT frameworks is that the device using the collects data from the real world could become a target for CyberAttacks. The aim of introducing IoT in the factory, in this case, is to increase performance and practicality by gathering data from a large number of sensors mounted in the generation equipment, evaluating it, and implementing an open, real-time control process [10].

If sensor data is cheated between that large preparation, the false scan will nearly start and off-base control will happen because such a situation could result in major injury. Also, since control orders and estimation data are exchanged insider facts about the organization and knowledge of the era, anticipating spills is critical from a competitiveness standpoint. Indeed, if there is no problem with the display, it is important to understand the long-term threats ((sizes of ROM, RAM, and circuits) and processing speed of power consumption (throughput, delay)) [11].

The estimation is the most important factor in determining a device's execution capability. Radio-frequency identification (R.F.ID) and energy collection systems need control, but battery-powered devices need the most control [12]. A tall Productivity is important for large information transmission devices such as vibration sensor or camera; although a low delay is important for real-time monitoring management with systems of orchestral rockets, etc. Since the control is dependent on the gear like the processor is in use or the degree of the circuit, the scale should be the primary point for the accuracy of the encryption methodology as well as the control [13].

Communicate IoT devices utilization a variety of protocols to operations of communication. Various wireless standards such as Bluetooth Low Energy (BLE), WiFi, ZWave, Zig-Bee, etc. The throughput is virtually based on the ability of parallel preparation. For security, due encrypting is the primary point of providing a sufficient degree of security for the existing cryptography [14]. When the length of the block is determined to shorter than standard encryption through prioritizing easiness of implementation, it's very still required to implement a properly proven methodology [15].

The rest of this paper is organized as follows. In Sect. 2 the related works are analyzed. Section 3 provides the details of the Proposed Algorithm. Section 4 discusses tests, experiments, and results. In Sect. 5 conclusions are given.

2 Related Works

This section will show a brief of some recent scientific papers on the use of security in the IoT, which relates to the security of the IoT and the various verification plans to properly manage the communications between the different objects in the web of things and achieve the best possible security. Yao, et al., in 2015 proposed "A lightweight scheme of attribute-dependent encryption for a WoT". These researchers suggested a lightweight non-coupling ABE method based on cryptography of elliptic bend. This method is based on a set of E.C.D.D.H rather than a set of bilinear Diffie-Hellman, which can reduce the management of information with communication and overhead. The A.B.E procedure ranks reasonably for applications of a single authority and is not important for a ubiquitous internet of things Apps [16]. Hagie-Chung et al. in 2016, proposed "A Key Assertion Plot among Lightweight Devices in the Internet of Things". The researcher recommended an agreement for low-power devices and low-speciation types to communicate with the customer's smart devices by certification and entry experts. This approach provides security from the center and reuses attacks, but it requires relatively large computational complexity [17]. Jan M. et al. in 2017 designed a lightweight validation strategy in the real world of the Internet of things. It might be encryption of load-based, as the system using a four-way hand-shake technicality to verify which characters are contained by the objects. Use the Advanced Encryption Standard (A.E.S), with a 128bit key, for a session of secure asset control. Although this scheme provides a defense against some attacks such as asset depletion, denial of services, replay, and physical alteration, the researcher did not perform the algorithms of random test mechanisms [18]. Esfahan A. et al. in 2017, proposed a lightweight validation method, based on hashes and XOR operation for machine to machine (M2M) within a mechanical environment of IoT. This proposal featured low-cost computation, session key understanding, and generic capacity. However, the researcher did not perform NIST tests [19].

3 The Proposed Algorithm

Increasing the speed of encryption/decryption algorithms while retaining a degree of protection is very critical for many apps that need a high level of security with minimal resources.

The problem with traditional algorithms is that the coding process is slow and there is a waste of time. The Advanced Encryption Standard (A.E.S) algorithm suffers from unnecessary time consumption to obtain the computational complexity required to achieve the necessary degree of security. Here in this paper, a new modification will be made to the A.E.S algorithm by replacing the stage of MixColumns with a randomly generated stage in each encryption session while reducing the number of rounds, which will lead to the algorithm speeding up. Consequently, this will increase the A.E.S algorithm speed without reducing the security level while reducing coding time. Moreover, the security level of the Light Weight A.E.S (L.W.A.E.S) algorithm can be improved utilization of the permutation phase, since it was a round of the operation. The proposed methodology for the L.W.A.E.S algorithm would ensure:

1- Accelerate the encryption/decryption operations by replacing the phase of MixColumns with simple SHIFT column processes.
2- Accelerate the encryption and decryption operations through decrease the number of the round (A.E.S).
3- Reducing the complexity of decryption by modifying the key through the following steps:
a- The use of a generator of random numbers with the removal of the subword stage.
b- RCON stage deletion and replace simple SHIFT processes.

Figure 1 shows the general diagram of the L.W.A.E.S algorithm compared to the A.E.S algorithm.

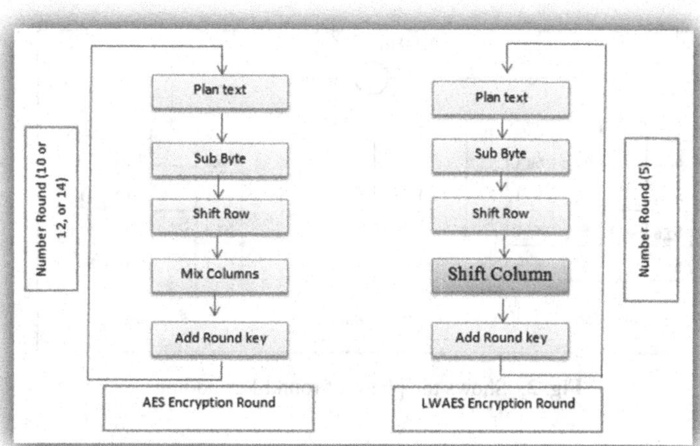

Fig. 1. Shows the L.W.A.E.S structure compared to the A.E.S structure.

The L.W.A.E.S scheme's first aim is to improve the speed of the algorithm. The most computationally intensive phase is MixColumns.

Since it is the most time-consuming phase in the A.E.S architecture, it occupies the majority of the time required for encryption/decryption. The MixColumns phase is replaced by SHIFT processes in the L.W.A.E.S architecture, and Algorithm 1 illustrates the steps of the phase-in detail.

Algorithm 1: Data encryption utilization the L.W.A.E.S

Inputs: State of the byte string [4][4].
Outputs: theState.
Begin
Step.1: Reading the number or text
Step.2: Convert the number or text to byte format.
Step.3: Round key = key expansion (input key, keyLength).
Step.4: State1=add the round-key(state, round key1)
Step.5: State2=sub-byte (state1)
Step.6: State3=shift-Row(state2)
Step.7: State4= Shift Column (state3)
Step.8: State final = add the round-key(state4, round key2)
End

There are four layers to the round roles.

A- Round key adding

The round main data is XORing with the data in the Box of State.
The entire algorithm is depicted in Fig. 2 below.

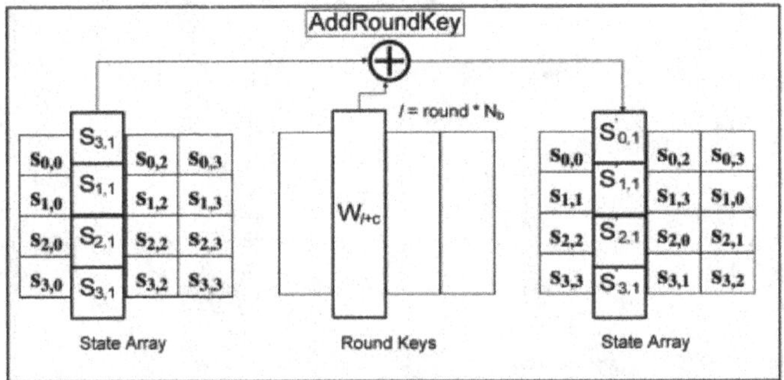

Fig. 2. Shows the phase of round-key adding.

B- Transformation of substitution

The data array byte is replaced with a new byte using S-box in this process. Figure 3 illustrates the relationship between the key and the cipher text.

C- Transformation of shiftraw

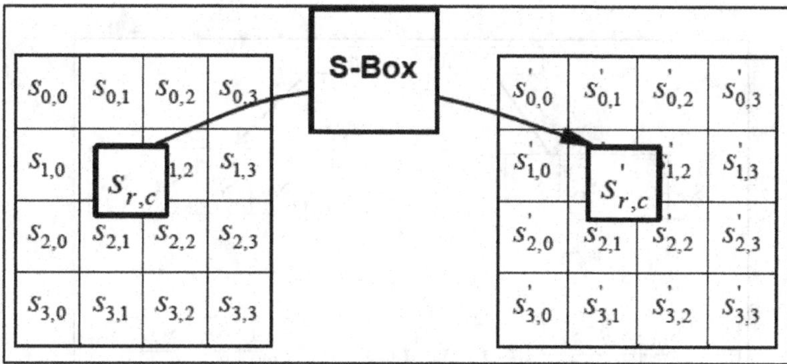

Fig. 3. Show the phase of substitution transformation.

The first row of the mechanism is left alone in this process. Within the 2nd push, each byte is shifted from one place to the cleared. Bytes within the third and fourth columns are moved by offsets of two and three respectively, as shown in Fig. 4.

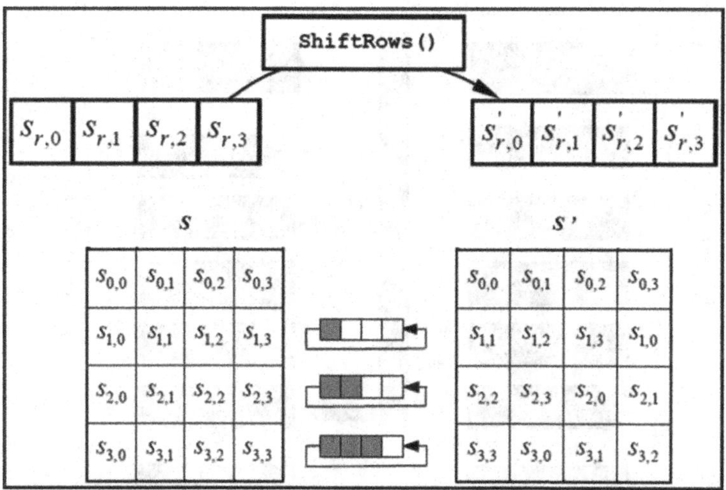

Fig. 4. Shows the stage of shiftraw transformation.

D- **Transformation of shift column**

Every byte in the 1st Column is shifted one location to the top, and each byte in the 2nd Column is shifted two positions to the top in this stage. Bytes in the 3rd and 4th columns were shifted by two and three offsets, respectively, as shown in Fig. 5 below.

Decryption is the opposite of encryption. It entails the conversion of encryption material to plain text. Figure 6 depicted the encryption and decryption scheme.

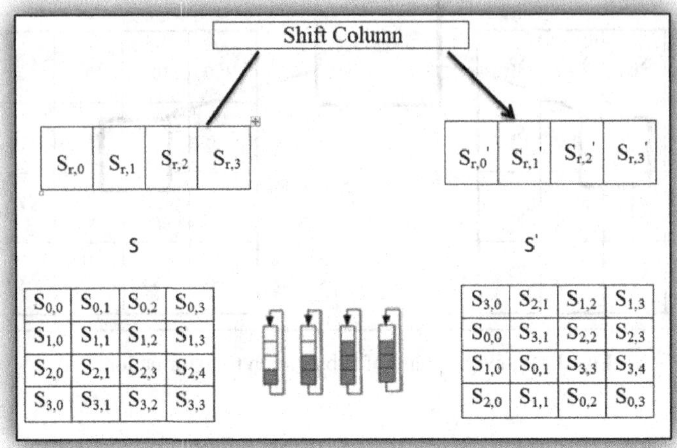

Fig. 5. Shows the stage of shift column transformation

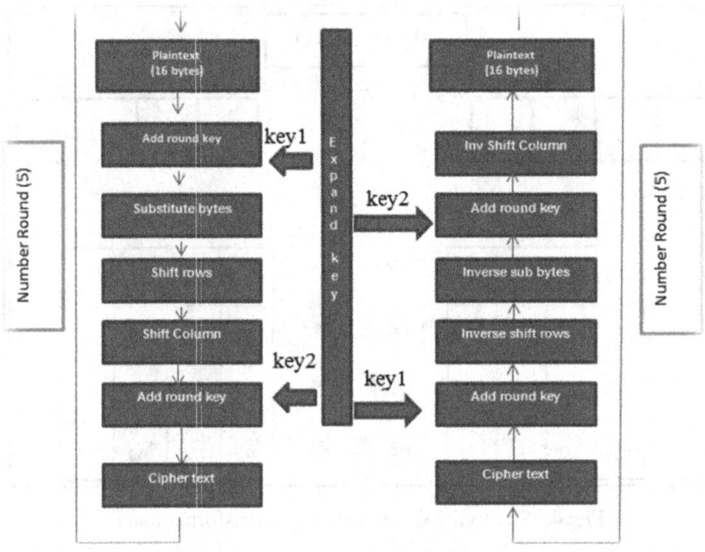

Fig. 6. Shows the stage of encryption and decryption L.W.A.E.S.

The L.W.A.E.S second aim is to ensure that the key operation is accelerated by altering the key steps to improve the speed of the encryption/decryption operations. To determine the 1st word of the key, the 1st and last columns are determined and then XOR will be done for them. After that, a Rot-word is worked in the second stage and will obtain w1, as depicted in Fig. 7 and Algorithm 2 respectively.

Algorithm 2: Light-WeightKey

Inputs: ByteString State [4] [4].
Outputs: TheState.
Begin
Step 1: XOR the first column with the last column.
Step 2: Rotate and shift one to get the desired result.
Step 3: w1 is obtained when output is added in the 1st column
Step 4: w2 is obtained by XORing between w1 and 2nd column in a state.
Step 5: w3 is obtained by XORing between w2 and 3rd column in a state.
Step 6: w4 is obtained by XORing between w3 and 4th column in a state.
End

Fig. 7.Shows the proposed light-weight key.

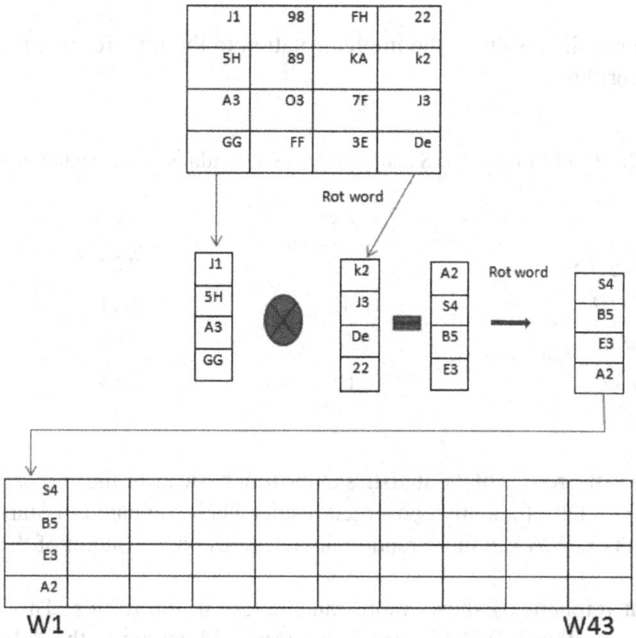

Fig. 7. Shows the proposed light-weight key.

4 Testing, Experiments, and Results

In this section, all the tests, experiments that were performed and the results obtained will be discussed.

4.1 The Algorithm of Random Test Strategies

Random Test Mechanisms Algorithms standard is used for the evaluation. The active archive's random quality check, as shown in Table 1 below, it includes (Frequency, Run, Pokers, and Serial).

Table 1. Random component test

Frequency test	Checks for random consistency of the Frequency test using dynamic text
Poker test	Checks for random consistency of the Poker test using dynamic text
Run test	Checks for random consistency of the Run test using text and LongRun
Serial Test	Checks the random consistency of the Serial-Test using dynamic text

Table 2 shows the results of the implementation to the fore Tests of the A.E.S and L.W.A.E.S algorithms.

Table 2. Results of the A.E.S and L.W.A.E.S algorithms implementation tests.

Tests\Algorithm	A.E.S	L.W.A.E.S
Frequency test ≤ 3.84	3.06	0.83
Poker test ≤ 14.07	12.41	11.84
Run test ≤ 9.48	9.26	3.68
Serial test ≤ 5.99	2.65	2.84

According to the results of the statistics of the four basic tests, the proposed algorithm is shown in Fig. 8 has efficiently converged results when compared to Standard A.E.S. The show results L.W.A.E.S more randomness degrees on the output of the was A.E.S algorithm.

The output (ciphertext) shows more randomness in the results. This proves that the proposed algorithm L.W.A.E.S provides more randomness to the A.E.S Standard algorithm and the reliability of the complexity characteristics.

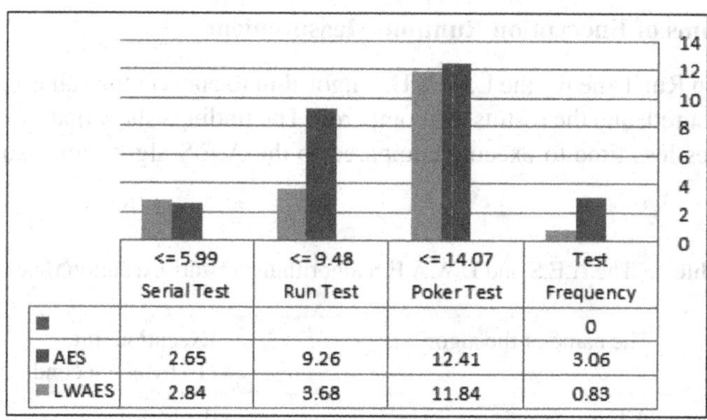

Fig. 8. Shows test results on the algorithms.

4.2 National Institute of Standards and Technology (NIST) Test Suite Algorithms

The NIST test is a set of statistical tests consisting of 16 tests developed to test the randomness of binary text. Encryption algorithms can be tested using NIST tests in a ready-made program to calculate the tests as shown in Table 3 for algorithm comparison.

Table 3. Shows the results of the **NIST** tests (**T = TRUE**)

Test	A.E.S	L.W.A.E.S
Frequency	T	T
Block frequency	T	T
Cumulative sums	T	T
Runs	T	T
Longest run	T	T
Rank	T	T
Discrete Fourier transform	T	T
Non-periodic templates	T	T
Overlapping	T	T
Universal	T	T
Approximate entropy	T	T
Random excursions	T	T
Random excursions varian	T	T
Serial	T	T
Lempel-Ziv compression	T	T
Linear complexity	T	T

4.3 Algorithms of Encryption Runtime Measurement

The encryption RunTime for the L.W.A.E.S algorithm to encrypt the same 128Bit block of data is measured, and the results are compared. The findings show that the L.W.A.E.S algorithm takes less time to execute compared to the A.E.S algorithm. Table 4 shows the results.

Table 4. The A.E.S and L.W.A.E.S algorithms' results execution times

No.	The name of the algorithm	Execution time (16 bytes)\Second
1	A.E.S	0.12
2	L.W.A.E.S	0.004

4.4 Experiment Results

To see how well the altered A.E.S algorithm performs. The efficiency of the altered A.E.S algorithm is evaluated by comparing the speed encryption method of the A.E.S, L.W.A.E.S, and Tiny Encryption Algorithm (T.E.A) algorithms using three text files of varying size. Table 5 shows the comparison operations.

Table 5. The results of the comparison between the A.E.S, L.W.A.E.S, and T.E.A algorithms

Size of file	A.E.S	T.E.A	L.W.A.E.S
1 kb	00: 00: 00: 112	00:00:00:75	00: 00: 00: 65
2 kb	00: 00: 00: 200	00:00:00:130	00: 00: 00: 100
3 kb	00: 00: 00: 323	00:00:00:190	00: 00: 00: 145

4.5 IOT System Security

In this section, all data transmitted among the server and clients in the system of smart Hotel is protected, and a thorough description of the system's protection will be given.

A. **Sensor Data Security**

Every two seconds, the server sends the sensor data readings. In accordance with the client choice of the administrator, the data is encrypted using one of the two encryption standards. When a client receives an encrypted text, he will attempt to decrypt it utilization the administrator's keys, thus completing an essential security component known as data security.

A.1- A.E.S Algorithm Based on Secure Sensor Temperatures

The data is encrypted by the A.E.S algorithm, so if the admin chooses the A.E.S data encryption type in the client size, the server encrypts the same data from the sensor and sends it to the client. Figure 9 shows an example of A.E.S encrypted sensor information.

```
Insecure WoT server started on port 8787

Current value for Temperature Sensor is { t: 3, timestamp: '2019-07-19T11:38:06.149Z' }

Temperature Sensor encryption using AES = 8029c7a084e0c6e49e9dfedb533399fc

Temperature Sensor decrypted = 3
```

Fig. 9. Shows the sample of A.E.S-encrypted sensor temperature.

A.2- L.W.A.E.S Algorithm Based on Secure Sensor Temperatures

If the A.E.S data encryption form is specified by the admin, the server is encrypting the same data of the sensor and sends it to the client using the L.W.A.E.S algorithm. Figure 10 shows an example of encrypted sensor data using L.W.A.E.S.

```
Insecure WoT server started on port 8787

Current value for Temperature Sensor is { t: 3, timestamp: '2019-07-19T11:38:06.149Z' }

Temperature Sensor encryption using LWAES = c312e9c354ca6fc15190600bdc04520a

Temperature Sensor decrypted = 3
```

Fig. 10. Shows the sample of L.W.A.E.S-encrypted sensor temperature.

4.6 The Case Study Evaluation of the IoT System

The scheme was implemented in this chapter using a variety of encryption methods. Sensor read data and control commands to adjust system status are encrypted. Two encryption methods are used in the system are A.E.S and L.W.A.E.S.

The server software component of the device is built utilizing the Node.J.S (v8.11) programming language, while the hardware is built utilizing a low-cost, lightweight, and powerful device (Raspberry Pi3/B+) with a 2.30 GHz 64bit 3-core processor and 4 GB-RAM running LinuxOS (Debian forked distribution named Raspbian).

The (A.E.S and L.W.A.E.S) algorithms use 128-bit key lengths in their implementation. The time it takes to encrypt/decrypt data read from sensors, as well as each control command to adjust a device's state, has been measured. Utilizing the machine encrypting shows how lightweight the proposed algorithm is, and the lower the number, the lower the overhead.

The A.E.S algorithm was used for comparison because it is similar in structure to the proposed algorithm and because of the strength of the A.E.S algorithm. The system was assessed in many ways, as detailed below.

A. Time of Encryption and Decryption

For the evaluations of any algorithm used in the I.O.T environments, the execution time was critical. This algorithm must take up the least amount of time and provide a high level of protection.

The algorithms are implemented in the proposed framework and measure the total time it takes to encrypt/decrypt the read data from the sensors as well as control commands to update the device's status. The system's encryption/decryption time when it's applied will be discussed, as well as a comparison of encryption/decryption algorithms.

Table 6 shows the time of encryption when utilizing Key (128bits). The time it takes the server to encrypt a fixed size of a message is directly influenced by the connected users' number, as discovered when increased the number of connected users.

Table 6. Time of data encryption with changing the user's number

Users number	Time of average encryption (A.E.S)	Time of average encryption (L.W.A.E.S)
One user	4 ms	1 ms
Two users	5 ms	2 ms
Four users	6 ms	3 ms
Six users	8 ms	4 ms
Eight users	10 ms	5 ms
Ten users	12 ms	6 ms
Twenty users	18 ms	7 ms

B. The use of memory

In the constrained resources of IoT computers, memory use was the main concern. Encryption techniques must not consume too much memory while in operation; otherwise, they would be unsuitable used in the IoT.

As a consequence, the memory usage of the algorithms used in the proposed method is assessed. The lower the memory consumption, the lower the overhead, and the smaller the memory sharing size, the better for sharing in an IoT environment.

Table 7 indicates that the A.E.S had the longest processing time (6.44 ms) and used the most memory (14 bytes), while the L.W.A.E.S had the shortest processing time (3.22 ms) and used the least memory (9 bytes).

Table 7. Memory use in the A.E.S and L.W.A.E.S algorithms results

Algorithm	Time of process (seconds)	Memory consumption (bytes)
A.E.S	6.44 ms	14 bytes
L.W.A.E.S	3.22 ms	9 bytes

5 Conclusions

In the not-too-distant future, the I.O.T will be an integral part of our everyday lives. Sensors and Many energy-restricted devices will be constantly interacting with one another, and their protection must not be put at risk. For this reason, in this paper, a lightweight protection algorithm (L.W.A.E.S) is proposed. The test appears to be effective in terms of making the computations a reasonable nominee for inclusion in I.O.T apps. The required time for the L.W.A.E.S algorithm implementation has been calculated and compared to the time required for the A.E.S algorithm implementation, showing that the L.W.A.E.S reduces the time in half. Following that, the proposed algorithm passes security checks to guarantee the safety of the encrypted data and cryptography method. The system provides speed in sending and receiving remote device control, memory use, and time of process are relevant parameters to test the algorithms that were used, and the results show that L.W.A.E.S is superior. Since the proposed methodology is less complicated, the randomized tests (Test of Frequency, Test of Run, Test of Poker, Test of Serial) of the proposed methodology approaches the results of standard algorithms, making it useful for data encryption.

References

1. Zikria, Y.B., Yu, H., Afzal, M.K., Rehmani, M.H., Hahm, O.: Internet of things (IoT): operating system, applications and protocols design, and validation techniques. Elsevier (2018)
2. Sreekantha, D.K., Koujalagi, A., Girish, T.M., Sairam, K.V.S.S.S.S.: Internet of Things (IoT) enabling technologies and applications—a study. In: Chiplunkar, N.N., Fukao, T. (eds.) Advances in Artificial Intelligence and Data Engineering. AISC, vol. 1133, pp. 1425–1442. Springer, Singapore (2021). https://doi.org/10.1007/978-981-15-3514-7_107
3. Want, R., Dustdar, S.: Activating the Internet of Things [Guest editors' introduction]. Computer **48**(9), 16–20 (2015)
4. Jain, A., Crespo, R.G., Khari, M. (eds.): Smart Innovation of Web of Things. CRC Press, Boca Raton (2020)
5. Reddy, J.R., Amrin, S., Reddy, C.R.: A brief review of Internet of Things and its applications (2020)

6. Romero-Mariona, J., Hallman, R., Kline, M., San Miguel, J., Major, M., Kerr, L.: Security in the industrial internet of things-the C-SEC approach. In: International Conference on Internet of Things and Big Data, vol. 2, pp. 421–428 (2016)
7. Khalaf, R., Mohammed, A., Essa, E., Ali, H.: controlling smart home activities using IoT. In: ICCISTA 2019 - IEEE International Conference on Computing and Information Science and Technology and their Applications (2019)
8. Harbi, Y., Aliouat, Z., Harous, S., Bentaleb, A., Refoufi, A.: A review of security in Internet of Things. Wirel. Pers. Commun. **108**(1), 325–344 (2019). https://doi.org/10.1007/s11277-019-06405-y
9. Kshetri, N.: Can blockchain strengthen the Internet of Things. IT Prof. **19**(4), 68–72 (2017)
10. Aljumeily, R.H.K., Mohammed, A.H.: Confidentiality, integrity and access control security services for actuator commands based IoT application. J. Adv. Res. Dyn. Control Syst. (2018)
11. Sadkhan, S.B., Salman, A.O.: Fuzzy logic for performance analysis of AES and lightweight AES. In: 2018 International Conference on Advanced Science and Engineering (ICOASE), pp. 318–323. IEEE (2018)
12. Perera, M.S., Halgamuge, M.N., Samarakody, R., Mohammad, A.: Internet of Things in healthcare: a survey of telemedicine systems used for elderly people. In: Marques, G., Bhoi, A.K., Albuquerque, V.H.C. (eds.) IoT in Healthcare and Ambient Assisted Living. SCI, vol. 933, pp. 69–88. Springer, Singapore (2021). https://doi.org/10.1007/978-981-15-9897-5_4
13. Sadkhan, S.B., Salman, A.O.: A survey on lightweight-cryptography status and future challenges. In: 2018 International Conference on Advance of Sustainable Engineering and its Application (ICASEA), pp. 105–108. IEEE (2018)
14. Iglesias-Urkia, M., Gómez, A., Casado-Mansilla, D., Urbieta, A.: Automatic generation of web of things servients using thing descriptions. Pers. Ubiquit. Comput.1–17 (2020). https://doi.org/10.1007/s00779-020-01413-3
15. Sardar, R., Anees, T.: Web of things: security challenges and mechanisms. IEEE Access **9**, 31695–31711 (2021)
16. Yao, X., Chen, Z., Tian, Y.: A lightweight attribute-based encryption scheme for the Internet of Things. Future Gener. Comput. Syst. **49**, 104–112 (2015)
17. Choi, K.C., Jun, M.S.: A design of key agreement scheme between lightweight devices in IoT environment. In: Park, J., Pan, Y., Yi, G., Loia, V. (eds.) Advances in Computer Science and Ubiquitous Computing, vol. 421, pp. 224–229. Springer, Singapore (2016). https://doi.org/10.1007/978-981-10-3023-9_37
18. Jan, M.A., Khan, F., Alam, M., Usman, M.: A payload-based mutual authentication scheme for Internet of Things. Future Gener. Comput. Syst. **92**, 1028–1039 (2019)
19. Esfahani, A., et al.: A lightweight authentication mechanism for M2M communications in industrial IoT environment. IEEE Internet Things J. **6**, 288–296 (2017)

IoT Intrusion Detection Using Modified Random Forest Based on Double Feature Selection Methods

Adil Yousef Hussein[1](✉), Paolo Falcarin[2], and Ahmed T. Sadiq[1]

[1] Computer Science Department, University of Technology, Baghdad, Iraq
[2] Software Systems Engineering (SSE) Research, University of East London, London, UK
paolo.falcarin@polito.it

Abstract. One of the fast-expanding technology today is the Internet of Things (IoT). It is very necessary, to protect these machines from adversaries and unwanted entry and alteration. Intrusion Detection Systems (IDS) are techniques that can be used in information systems to monitor identified threats or anomalies. The challenge that arises is that the IDS should detect attacks on time in high-speed network traffic data. This paper proposed a modified IDS in IoT environments based on hybrid feature selection techniques for the random forest that can be used to detect intrusions with high speed and good accuracy. IoTID20 dataset is used which has three target classes which are the binary class as normal or abnormal and the classes of categories and sub-categories for the binary class. The highest-ranked attributes in the dataset are selected and the others are reduced, to minimize execution time and improve accuracy, the number of trees in the random forest classifier is reduced to 20, 25, and 20 for binary, category, and sub-category respectively. The trained classifier is then tested and achieved accuracy approaches 100% for the binary target prediction, 98.7% for category and accuracy ranges from 78.1% to 95.2% for the sub-category target prediction. The proposed system is evaluated and compared with previous ones and showed its performance.

Keywords: IoT · IDS · IoTID20 dataset · Random forest · Hybrid feature selection

1 Introduction

Today, in the world of the Internet, trends seem to be starting to shift as a consequence of the emergence of connected devices that, like individuals, can create and transfer information over the Web. The Internet of Things (IoT) is a collection of cutting-edge inventions and software that have the potential to revolutionize our lifestyle. The IoT is pervasive and pervasive in about every aspect of life. IoT is used by governments around the world to collect data from various sectors and to offer better programs for health, governance, security, and development [1].

As the IoT gets more pervasive every day, threats against it rise. At present, there are billions of Internet-connected appliances. By 2020, the estimate will increase to 20

P. Liatsis et al. (Eds.): TIOTC 2021, CCIS 1548, pp. 61–78, 2022.
https://doi.org/10.1007/978-3-030-97255-4_5

billion [14]. An IoT will be a goal for attackers to conduct malicious behaviors and, through exponential expansion, raise the attack surface of IoT networks. As a result of many organizations suffering the loss of facilities, the results of cyber-attacks became more damaging, to recognize malicious activity in the smart infrastructure, IoT devices require a sophisticated instrument [2, 3].

Intrusion Detection Systems (IDS) are tools that can be used in information systems to track known threats or anomalies. IDS may be network-based or networks that are host-based. They may be used to protect a computer from the network or end-user. The network can be an IoT network, and an IoT system such as sensing equipment can be an end-user device. IDS may also be hardware and software in a single package of software [4]. There're 2 types of detection techniques: signature-based and anomaly-based detection. Through analyzing data traffic or records in-memory storage for particular patterns, signature-based approaches are effective in detecting defined threats. Anomaly-based detection is used to identify unknown threats by monitoring the actions of the entire system, objects, or traffic and comparing it with predefined behavior assumed to be normal. A potential intrusion is described as every deviation from standard operations [5]. An anomaly-based technique is well-tailored to the new climate due to the extreme complexity used mostly by crackers and the increase in zero-day attacks [3]. Anomaly-based IDS depend on Artificial Intelligence (AI) and Machine Learning (ML) to recognize anomalies. The theory behind AI and ML is to make a machine capable of learning on its own and to differentiate between the system activity that is normal or abnormal [6].

The enormous amount of traffic data on high-speed networks poses a major challenge to the performance of IDS in real-time [15]. As conventional IDSs normally concentrate on improving the performance of detection and lack adequate attention to timeliness, it is difficult for them to monitor traffic data in a short period. For attackers, this leaves an opening. It is also imperative to gain access to IDS solutions for real-time traffic data processing [16].

It is necessary to find a sophisticated scientific method or approach through which to reduce the number of features required for the study to determine whether there are anomalies or not and to discover interventions, as we are convinced there are many features that have been studied and analyzed do not effect on the decision to detect an intervention or identify anomalies, But it costs time and effort. Accordingly, classification was used to sort these features.

This paper suggests an IDS on hybrid feature selection techniques for the random forest that can detect intrusions and achieve high speed and good accuracy. We use the IoTID20 dataset [3] which utilizes three target classes, the binary class being normal or abnormal, and category and sub-category classes for the binary class.

The remainder of this paper is organized as follows. In the second section, the related work to the proposed method is discussed. The random forest algorithm is clarified in the third section. In the fourth part, The IoTID20 dataset description is done and the proposed architecture is addressed for anomaly identification in IoT systems. Section 5 discusses the outcomes and evaluations of the proposal. Finally, we wrap up the paper with suggestions for future research in the final section.

2 Related Work

Ullah and Mahmoud in 2020 [3] did the correlation of features, the ranking of features, and different machine-learning algorithms for classification, for analyzing and evaluating the IoTID20 dataset. To stabilize and interpret the IoTID20 dataset, they employed a machine learning models and column normalization strategies. The identification capabilities of a machine learning algorithm are harmed by associated characteristics. Twelve correlated attributes have been excluded from the dataset for IoTID20. The Shapira-Wilk algorithm was used to rate the features in the IoTID20 dataset, which tests the regularity of the feature-related distributions of appearances. Using a value greater than 0.50, more than 70% of the feature ranked, which indicates that they have a high rank. They evaluated the binary, category, and sub-category label datasets. Machine learning models are built using Random Forest, ensemble, GaussianNB, Support-Vector Machines (SVM), Logistic Regression, LDA, and Decision Tree classification methods. To evaluate the effect of the various classification models, they employed 3, 5, and 10 fold cross-validation measures. The maximum accuracy of the model was achieved by Decision Tree, Random Forest, and Ensemble classifiers, while the lowest accuracies were achieved by SVM and Logistic Regression.

Sherasiya and Upadhyay in 2016 [7] proposed a lightweight IDS using methods in ML. The purpose of the model is to detect nodes that have several identities within the IoT environment. The model works in wireless networks because it uses the strength of its wireless signal to distinguish between real and fake nodes, as well as the secret key and Identification to identify nodes with different identities when trying to bind to an IPv6 boundary router.

Fu et al. in 2011 [8] proposed a framework that had two steps. First, to detect anomalies in perception layer data, using the anomaly mining algorithm. Second, using a hierarchical intrusion scheme, i.e. using a central intrusion prevention system is not one of them, to distinguish between irregularities and unauthorized activity at the level of the network segment, but not as a whole. Fu et al. are now going to discriminate between three kinds of activities; polluting data, loss of service, and the Denial of Service (DoS).

Liu and Wu in 2014 [9] proposed an IoT lightweight anomaly-mining algorithm to look for data irregularities. They used the Jaccard coefficient with Euclidean distance, which are mathematical operations for determining how close two data sets are. They presume that each sensor generates several records of data. It can be determined how close the records are to each other by comparing the difference between two records from the same sensor. Consider placing a threshold dependent on the Jaccard coefficient, understanding the normal state of the record. If the similarity between the two data records is less than 0.8, so there is an abnormality. If a similarity of more than 0.8 has been detected, then the data is normal.

Hodo et al. in 2016 [10] provides an IoT threat analysis and uses an Artificial Neural Network (ANN) to counter these threats. A multi-level perceptron is equipped to be able to thwart Distributed Denial-of-Service/Denial-of-Service (DDoS/DoS) attacks using internet packet traces. The ANN procedure against a virtual IoT network is validated. The experimental results show 99.4% accuracy and can detect different DDoS/DoS attacks successfully. These accuracy results are high as the study classifies only DDoS/DoS attacks making their system not dependable.

Pajouh et al. in 2016 [11] presented a two-layer dimension reduction and two-tier classification module intrusion detection model designed to detect malicious behaviors such as User to Root (U2R) and Remote to Local (R2L) attacks. Their proposed model used the dimension reduction module, component analysis, and linear discrimination analysis to distribute the high-dimensional dataset to a lower one with fewer features. They then add a two-tier classification module to classify suspect actions using the K-Nearest Neighbor variant of Naïve Bayes and Certainty Factor. The findings of the experiment using the NSL-KDD dataset [19] shows 84.82% accuracy.

Assi and Sadiq in 2017 [18] proposed five key classification approaches that have been applied to identify network attacks using the NSL-KDD dataset [19] with three feature selection techniques. (J48 decision tree, SVM, Decision Table, Bayesian Network and Neural Network Back Propagation) are these approaches. (Correlation-based feature selection (CFS), Information Gain (IG), and Decision Table) are feature selection techniques. Several studies have been carried out to produce successful results using NSL-KDD preparation and research within the general attack (Normal and Anomaly). These were conducted using four forms of attack: DOS, User to Root attack (U2R), Root to Local attacks (R2L), and the Probing attack (Probe). The best results (80.3%) using the testing dataset and (93.9%) as an accuracy training dataset are provided by the J48 classification system with training data.

Assi and Sadiq in 2018 [20] proposed a feature selection technique based on the Modified Artificial Immune System. To maximize the efficiency and randomization of features, the proposed algorithm uses the benefits of the Artificial Immune System. Experimental findings based on the NSL-KDD dataset [19] have shown increased efficiency relative to other algorithms for feature selection (best first search, correlation, and information gain).

3 Feature Selection

Feature selection is the process of reducing the number of input variables when developing a predictive model.

It is desirable to reduce the number of input variables to both reduce the computational cost of modeling and, in some cases, to improve the performance of the model.

There are two main types of feature selection techniques: supervised and unsupervised, and supervised methods may be divided into wrapper, filter and embedded.

The information gain can also be used by assessing the gain of each variable in the context of the target variable. Information gain is the reduction of entropy by the transformation of a dataset. Information gain is measured by comparing the entropy of the dataset before and after the transition. A greater gain of information indicates a lower entropy or groups of samples of entropy. In a binary classification problem (two classes), for example, we can measure the data sample entropy as follows:

$$\boldsymbol{Entropy} = -\sum_{i-1}^{n} \boldsymbol{p}(\boldsymbol{m}_i) \log_2(\boldsymbol{p}(\boldsymbol{m}_i)) \tag{1}$$

Information gain provides a means of using entropy to measure how the purity of the dataset, e.g. class distribution, is influenced by a modification to the dataset. More purity or less surprise means lower entropy. For example, by dividing a dataset S by a random variable with several values, we may wish to determine the effect on purity. You should measure this as follows:

$$IG(S, a) = H(S) - H(S|a) \tag{2}$$

Where IG(S, a) is the dataset information S for variable a for a random variable, H(S) is the dataset entropy before some shift and H($S|a$) is the conditional dataset entropy for variable [12].

Gini Decrease calculates the importance of each feature as the sum of the number of splits that include the feature, proportionally to the number of samples that it divides. The improvement in the split-criterion is the significance measure attributed to the splitting variable at each split in each tree and is accumulated for each variable separately over all the trees in the forest [12].

A chi-square test X^2 is used in mathematics to test the independence of two cases. Provided the data of two variables, we can get observed count O and predicted count E. Chi-Square tests how the predicted number E and the observed number O deviate from each other [17]. The chi-square formula is shown in Eq. 3.

$$X^2 = \sum \frac{(O_i - E_i)^2}{E_i} \tag{3}$$

4 Random Forest

Random forests are an ensemble learning system that is used for classification, regression, and other tasks that function by constructing a multitude of decision trees at training time and generating the class that is the mode of the individual trees' classes (classification) or mean/average predictor (regression). Random decision forests are correct for the habit of decision trees. Random forests are a way to average many deep decision trees, trained with the intention of reducing the variance on various sections of the same training set. This comes at the cost of a slight rise in bias and some lack of interpretability, but usually improves the efficiency in the final model substantially. Forests are like pulling decision tree algorithm attempts together. In this way, teamwork of multiple trees increases the productivity of a single random tree [13] (Fig. 1).

Sadiq and Mohsen in 2018 [22] proposed a hybrid feature selection for Random Forest depends on the two measures, Information Gain, and Gini Index in different weight-based percentages. The key plan is to measure information gain for all random selection features and then look for the best split point in the node that offers the best value for a Gini Index hybrid equation.

Mohsen and Sadiq in 2019 [21] proposed a random forest algorithm using an accuracy-based ranking that relies on the accuracy of a single tree from the previous Random Forest assessment. The proposed model consists of two primary stages, the first being the training process responsible for the development of the tree and the evaluation phase containing two test tiers (evaluation test, and accuracy test).

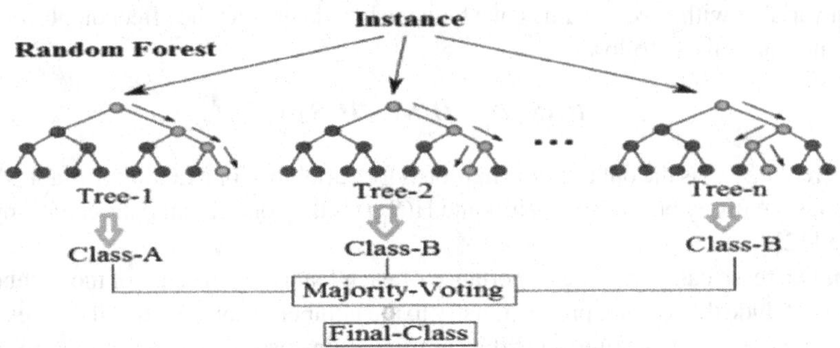

Fig. 1. Random forest classifier

5 Modified Random Forest

Random forest algorithm is considered one of the best classification methods, and their characteristic lie in the randomness they adopt in selecting the features for building trees. Consequently, a forest of trees may be dependent on the number of features available in the dataset. Sometimes, decisions or inaccurate classifications depend on weak features that do not affect the classification: this may cause a weakening of the accuracy of the general decision of the system and an increase in time that is not important in forecasting,

Therefore, one must take care of reducing the number of features by excluding weak features to achieve an increase in accuracy and a decrease in time. Many studies use feature selection methods or fixed a hybrid filter for more than one arrangement, but we have adopted the method of weighted hybridization. The overall ranking is done through Eq. 4,

$$\textbf{Hybrid Feature Selection Rank} = \mathbf{w} * \textbf{feature selection}_1 + (\mathbf{1} - \mathbf{w}) * \textbf{feature selection}_2 \quad (4)$$

This equation will ensure that the double feature selection is identified with different weights to ensure that the optimal characteristics (influence properties) are chosen to obtain the best results before the intrusion occurs, as we previously mentioned that (IoT) depends on many sensors whose output can be classified to (fixed data and dynamic data).

Certainly, static data will be ignored for not benefiting from its existence, in addition to deleting part of the dynamic data that does not have a direct or indirect impact on intrusion classification, and here random forests will act on the effective properties and thus this algorithm will build a forest of trees for affective features only, which will lead To predict with high accuracy, indeed through our experiments, we found that this equation, with a weight of 0.5, was effective and provided better results in the accuracy of prediction than it was recorded as shown at the table below:

In this paper, the modification that applied to the random forest by adding a hybrid feature selection equation depending on two filters, which are Gini and information gain, these filters, which can specify important features that affect the decision of detection the intrusion depending on the type of target, the first step in the modified random forest is import dataset to a feature's filters that ranking is based on the relevance for classification. Used Gini and information gain to decreasing features. Ranking differs based on the target class, which in our system may be binary, or sub-category, that will specify the highest features rank that equal, the numbers of trees, and choose the random feature and used as a root for the tree. The second step is splitting the dataset depending on the chosen root and then repeats these steps until complete building a random forest tree.

5.1 Dataset

IoTID20 dataset appeared in 2020 which contains 83 network features and three target classes. Binary, category, and sub-category are the label characteristics. Table 1 displays IoTID20 dataset's classes, Table 2 displays the network features. The IoTID20 dataset's main notable aspect is that it simulates a current IoT network connectivity pattern and is one of the only available to the public IoT datasets for intrusion detection [3].

IoTID20 features are ranked and reduced and then the datasets are split into two parts: 75% training and 25% testing and distribution of this dataset after this split is shown in Table 1.

Table 1. IoTID20 dataset split into training and testing datasets.

		Binary		Category		Sub_Category					
Dataset IoTID20	625783	Anomaly	585710	Anomaly-Scan	75,265	Hot Port	22,192	For Training 75%	16,644	For Test 25%	5,548
						Port OS	53,073	For Training 75%	39,805	For Test 25%	13,268
				Anomaly-Mirai	415,676	ACK Flooding	55,124	For Training 75%	41,343	For Test 25%	13,781
						Host BruteForceg	121,181	For Training 75%	90,886	For Test 25%	30,295
						HTTP Flooding	55,818	For Training 75%	41,864	For Test 25%	13,955
						UDP Flooding	183,553	For Training 75%	137,665	For Test 25%	45,888
				Anomaly-MITM ARP	35,377	MITM ARP Spoofing	35,377	For Training 75%	26,533	For Test 25%	8,844
				Anomaly-DOS	59,392	Synflooding	59,391	For Training 75%	44,544	For Test 25%	14,848
		Normaly	40073	Normal	40,073	Normal	40,073	For Training 75%	30,055	For Test 25%	10,018
								Tota Sample for Training	469,337	Tota Sample for Training	156,446

Based on the ranking from the previous step; the features are reduced and the reduced set is the input to the next steps. We performed several experiments that would be explained later; these experiments differ in the number of input features in the dataset after the reduction process based on the highest-ranked features. The reduced dataset is then split into 75% training dataset, and 25% testing dataset. The training dataset is used for training the random forest classifier for binary and sub-category targets. The number of trees in the random forest classifier is limited to decrease execution time and increase accuracy. The trained classifier is tested for the same target classes using the testing dataset.

Table 2. Displays the network features with dataset IoTID20

Feature name	Description
Flow_Duration	Flow duration
Tot_Fwd_Pkts, Tot_Bwd_Pkts	Total packets in the forward direction and backward direction
TotLen_Fwd_Pkts	Total size of packet in forward direction
Fwd_Pkt_Len_Max, Min	Maximum and Minimum size of packet in forward direction
Fwd_Pkt_Len_Mean	Average size of packet in forward direction
Bwd_Pkt_Len_Mean Fwd_Pkt_Len_Std	Mean and Standard deviation size of packet in forward direction
Bwd_Pkt_Len_Max, Min	Maximum, Minimum size of packet in backward direction
Bwd_Pkt_Len_Std	Standard deviation size of packet in backward direction
Flow_Byts s, Flow_Pkts s	flow byte and flow packets rate that is number of packets transferred per second
Flow_IAT_Mean, Flow_IAT_Std	Average and Standard deviation time between two flows
Flow_IAT_Max, Flow_IAT_Min	Maximum, Minimum time between two flows
Fwd_IAT_Tot, Bwd_IAT_Tot	Total time between two packets sent in the forward direction and backward direction
Fwd_IAT_Mean, Flow_IAT_Std	Mean and Standard deviation time between two packets sent in the forward direction
Fwd_IAT_Max, Fwd_IAT_Min	Maximum, Minimum time between two packets sent in the forward direction
Bwd_IAT_Mean, Bwd_IAT_Std	Mean and Standard deviation time between two packets sent in the backward direction
Bwd_IAT_Max, Bwd_IAT_Min	Maximum and Minimum time between two packets sent in the backward direction
Fwd_PSH_Flags, Bwd_PSH_Flags	Number of times the PSH flag was set in packets travelling in the forward direction and backward direction (0 for UDP)
Fwd_URG_Flags, Bwd_URG_Flags	Number of times the URG flag was set in packets travelling in the forward direction and backward direction (0 for UDP)
Fwd_Header_Len, Bwd_Header_Len	Total bytes used for headers in the forward direction and backward direction
Fwd_Pkts s	Number of forward packets per second

(*continued*)

Table 2. (*continued*)

Feature name	Description
Bwd_Pkts s	Number of backward packets per second
Pkt_Len_Max, Pkt_Len_Min	Maximum and Minimum length of a flow
Pkt_Len_Mean, Pkt_Len_Std	Mean and Standard deviation length of a flow
Pkt_Len_Var	Minimum inter-arrival time of packet
FIN_Flag_Cnt, SYN_Flag_Cnt, RST_Flag_Cnt, PSH_Flag_Cnt	Number of packets with FIN, SYN, RST and PUSH,
ACK_Flag_Cnt, URG_Flag_Cnt, CWE_Flag_Cont, ECE_Flag_Cnt	Number of packets with ACK,URG, CWE and ECE
Down Up_Ratio	Download and upload ratio
Pkt_Size_Avg	Average size of packet
Fwd_Seg_Size_Avg, Bwd_Seg_Size_Avg	Average size observed in the forward direction and backward direction
Fwd_Byts b_Avg, Fwd_Pkts b_Avg	Average number of bytes and packets bulk rate in the forward direction
Fwd_Blk_Rate_Avg, Bwd_Blk_Rate_Avg	Average number of bulk rate in the forward direction and backward direction
Bwd_Byts b_Avg, Bwd_Pkts b_Avg	Average number of bytes and packets bulk rate in the backward direction
Subflow_Fwd_Pkts, Subflow_Fwd_Byts	The average number of packets and bytes in a sub flow in the forward direction
Subflow_Bwd_Pkts, Subflow_Bwd_Byts	The average number of packets, bytes in a sub flow in the backward direction
Init_Fwd_Win_Byts	Number of bytes sent in initial window in the forward direction and backward direction
Fwd_Act_Data_Pkts	Number of packets with at least 1 byte of TCP data payload in the forward direction
Fwd_Seg_Size_Min	Minimum segment size observed in the forward direction
Active_Mean, Active_Std	Mean and Standard deviation time a flow was active before becoming idle
Active_Max, Active_Min	Maximum and Minimum time a flow was active before becoming idle
Idle_Mean, Idle_Std	Mean and Standard deviation time a flow was idle before becoming active
Idle_Max, Idle_Min	Maximum and Minimum time a flow was idle before becoming active

5.2 Experimental Results

Several experiments are made to test the trained random forest classifier. These experiments differ in the number of attributes used in the dataset after ranking and reducing them by using by combining more than scoring methods to do The Hybrid Feature Selection Rank, and according to a certain weight (w), the one that achieved the best results is w = 0.5, and the number of trees in the random forest tree. Tables 5, 6, 7 and Tables 8, 9, 10 show the experiments done for the dataset classes and the accuracy achieved in each experiment. The highest achieved accuracy is 99.9%, 98.7%, and 78.1% using 20, 25, and 20 trees for binary, category, and sub-category respectively when relying on all features for the binary class, and the highest-ranked 40 features for the rest of the classes.

The accuracy of predicting the binary target approaches 100% where the number of used trees is the random forest algorithm is 20 and regardless of the number of used features. Table 3 shows a comparison between the proposed system for predicting the binary target (normal/ anomaly), and the other machine learning algorithms in terms of accuracy and time. The accuracy is specified by the total number of correct predictions divided by the total number of predictions. The accuracy of the proposed system and neural networks are the highest and the time of the neural network is very high, while the test time for Decision Tree and Naïve Bayes is the lowest while their accuracy is not

Table 3. The comparison between the proposed system and other algorithms predicting the binary target (normal/anomaly) in terms of accuracy and time.

Algorithm	Testing accuracy	Training time [s]
Modification system	***99.9%***	***19.6***
Neural network	99.8%	769.52
Decision tree	98.6%	7.6
Logistic regression	96.6%	14.76
Naïve Bayes	94.7%	5.7
SVM	65.5%	123.47

Table 4. The comparison between the proposed system and other algorithms predicting the category target (Normal/Scan, Mirai, MITM ARP, DOS) in terms of accuracy & time.

Algorithm	Testing accuracy	Training time [s]
Modification system	***98.7%***	***13.41***
Neural network	95.7%	704.33
Decision tree	98.7%	12.64
Logistic regression	74.2%	30.64
Naïve Bayes	75.1%	2.43
SVM	42.9%	281.8

high compared to others. The overall evaluation shows the superiority of our proposed algorithm.

Table 4 shows a comparison between the proposed system for predicting the category target (normal/Scan, Mirai, MITM ARP, DOS), and other machine learning algorithms in terms of accuracy and time. The accuracy of the proposed system and Decision Trees are the highest and their time is not high, while the test time for Naïve Bayes is the lowest while the accuracy is very low. The overall evaluation shows the superiority of the Decision Tree and our proposed algorithm.

All: is used the classical Random Forest

The 40 Feature that we selected for category and sub_category target: (Bwd_Pkt_Len_Max, Bwd_Seg_Size_Avg, Bwd_Pkt_Len_Mean, Pkt_Len_Max, Bwd_Header_Len, Init_Bwd_Win_Byts, Pkt_Len_Mean, Subflow_Bwd_Byts, TotLen_Bwd_Pkts, Fwd_Seg_Size_Avg, Fwd_Pkt_Len_Mean, Pkt_Size_Avg, Fwd_Pkt_Len_Max, Src_Port, Bwd_Pkt_Len_Min, Fwd_Pkt_Len_Min, Bwd_IAT_Tot, Protocol, Flow_Pkts/s, Flow_Duration, Bwd_IAT_Max, Flow_IAT_Min, Flow_IAT_Max, Bwd_IAT_Mean.1, Subflow_Fwd_Byts, TotLen_Fwd_Pkts, Dst_Port, ACK_Flag_Cnt, Bwd_IAT_Min, Idle_Min, Idle_Max, Idle_Mean, Flow_IAT_Mean, Pkt_Len_Min, Bwd_Pkts/s, Fwd_Pkts/s, Fwd_Act_Data_Pkts, Flow_Byts/s, SYN_Flag_Cnt, Fwd_Header_Len)

All: is used the classical Random Forest

The 40 Feature that we selected for category target: (SYN_Flag_Cnt, Bwd_IAT_Min, Bwd_IAT_Mean.1, Bwd_IAT_Max, Bwd_IAT_Tot, Init_Bwd_Win_Byts, Fwd_Act_Data_Pkts, Bwd_Header_Len, Fwd_Pkts/s, Subflow_Fwd_Byts, TotLen_Fwd_Pkts, Fwd_Seg_Size_Avg, Fwd_Pkt_Len_Mean, Flow_Pkts/s, Flow_Duration, Fwd_Pkt_Len_Min, Fwd_Pkt_Len_Max, Flow_IAT_Mean, Subflow_Fwd_Pkts, Tot_Fwd_Pkts, Flow_IAT_Min, Src_Port, Bwd_Pkts/s, Flow_IAT_Max, ACK_Flag_Cnt, Bwd_IAT_Mean, Idle_Mean, Idle_Min, Idle_Max, Idle_Std, Pkt_Len_Max, Bwd_Pkt_Len_Min, Flow_IAT_Std, Bwd_Pkt_Len_Max, Bwd_Seg_Size_Avg, Bwd_Pkt_Len_Mean, Pkt_Len_Min, Pkt_Len_Mean, Bwd_Pkt_Len_Std, Subflow_Bwd_By

The 50 Feature that we selected for sub_category target: (SYN_Flag_Cnt, Bwd_IAT_Min, Bwd_IAT_Mean.1, Bwd_IAT_Max, Bwd_IAT_Tot, Init_Bwd_Win_Byts, Fwd_Act_Data_Pkts, Bwd_Header_Len, Fwd_Pkts/s, Subflow_Fwd_Byts, TotLen_Fwd_Pkts, Fwd_Seg_Size_Avg, Fwd_Pkt_Len_Mean, Flow_Pkts/s, Flow_Duration, Fwd_Pkt_Len_Min, Fwd_Pkt_Len_Max, Flow_IAT_Mean, Subflow_Fwd_Pkts, Tot_Fwd_Pkts, Flow_IAT_Min, Src_Port, Bwd_Pkts/s, Flow_IAT_Max, ACK_Flag_Cnt, Bwd_IAT_Mean, Idle_Mean, Idle_Min, Idle_Max, Idle_Std, Pkt_Len_Max, Bwd_Pkt_Len_Min, Flow_IAT_Std, Bwd_Pkt_Len_Max, Bwd_Seg_Size_Avg, Bwd_Pkt_Len_Mean, Pkt_Len_Min, Pkt_Len_Mean, Bwd_Pkt_Len_Std, Subflow_Bwd_Byts, TotLen_Bwd_Pkts, Pkt_Size_Avg, Dst_Port, Flow_Byts/s, Fwd_Pkt_Len_Std, Pkt_Len_Var, Pkt_Len_Std, Subflow_Bwd_Pkts, Tot_Bwd_Pkts, Fwd_IAT_Tot)

Table 11 shows the accuracy of algorithms proposed by Ullah and Mahmoud [3] for predicting sub-category (Normal/Host Port/Port OS/ACK Flooding/Host Brute-Force/HTTP Flooding/UDP Flooding/MITM ARP Spoofing/Synflooding) on the IoTID20 dataset, they achieved high accuracy using their decision tree, random forest, and ensemble algorithms, but their proposed system uses all the data in the training step which makes the algorithms suffer from overfitting and make it not dependable.

Table 5. Experiments using a different number of trees and features educed using Gini Decrease and Information Gain (where w1 = 0.6, w2 = 0.4)

Target	15 Trees					20 Trees					25 Trees					30 Trees				
	No. Feature					No. Feature					No. Feature					No. Feature				
	35	40	45	50	All	35	40	45	50	All	35	40	45	50	All	35	40	45	50	All
Label	99.0	99.0	99.1	99.2	99.0	99.3	99.3	99.3	99.3	99.4	99.3	99.3	99.4	99.5	99.2	99.3	99.3	99.4	99.5	99.4
Category	98.5	98.2	98.2	98.2	98.1	98.5	98.1	98.1	98.2	98.0	98.1	98.5	98.4	98.4	98.3	98.3	98.4	98.5	98.5	98.2
Sub-Category	73.3	77.1	77.0	77.7	77.3	74.1	76.7	77.2	77.4	77.4	74.2	77.1	77.9	77.9	77.0	74.0	77.0	76.9	77.2	77.1

Table 6. Experiments using a different number of trees and features educed using Gini Decrease and Information Gain (where w1 = 0.4, w2 = 0.6)

Target	15 Trees					20 Trees					25 Trees					30 Trees				
	No. Feature					No. Feature					No. Feature					No. Feature				
	35	40	45	50	All	35	40	45	50	All	35	40	45	50	All	35	40	45	50	All
Label	99.2	99.2	99.2	99.2	99.3	99.3	99.3	99.4	99.4	99.4	99.3	99.3	99.4	99.4	99.4	99.3	99.4	99.5	99.5	99.4
Category	98.6	98.5	98.4	98.5	98.1	98.7	98.3	98.5	98.3	98.2	98.3	98.6	98.4	98.4	98.2	98.5	98.4	98.4	98.5	98.3
Sub-Category	74.0	77.6	77.9	78.0	77.3	74.2	77.0	77.5	77.7	77.3	74.2	77.9	77.9	77.9	77.6	74.2	77.8	77.6	77.6	77.5

Table 7. Experiments using a different number of trees and features educed using Gini Decrease and Information Gain (where w1 = w2 = 0.5)

Target	15 Trees					20 Trees					25 Trees					30 Trees				
	No. Feature					No. Feature					No. Feature					No. Feature				
	35	40	45	50	All	35	40	45	50	All	35	40	45	50	All	35	40	45	50	All
Label	99.9	99.9	99.9	99.9	99.9	99.9	99.9	99.9	99.9	99.9	99.9	99.9	99.9	99.9	99.9	99.9	99.9	99.9	99.9	99.9
Category	98.7	98.5	98.5	98.5	98.2	98.7	98.5	98.5	98.5	98.2	98.3	98.7	98.5	98.5	98.3	98.7	98.6	98.6	98.6	98.3
Sub-Category	74.4	78.1	78.0	78.1	77.5	74.3	78.1	77.9	78.0	77.6	74.3	78.1	77.9	77.9	77.6	74.3	78.0	77.9	78.0	77.6

Table 8. Experiments using a different number of trees and features educed using Chi-Square and Information Gain (where w1 = 0.6, w2 = 0.4)

Target	15 Trees					20 Trees					25 Trees					30 Trees				
	No. Feature					No. Feature					No. Feature					No. Feature				
	35	40	45	50	All	35	40	45	50	All	35	40	45	50	All	35	40	45	50	All
Label	99.9	99.9	99.9	99.9	99.9	99.9	99.9	99.9	99.9	99.9	99.9	99.9	99.9	99.9	99.9	99.9	99.9	99.9	99.9	99.9
Category	98.5	98.5	98.4	98.2	98.2	98.4	98.5	98.5	98.5	98.2	98.0	98.4	98.6	98.6	98.2	98.5	98.3	98.5	98.6	98.3
Sub-Category	71.1	71.5	75.8	77.4	76.4	71.5	71.5	75.6	75.5	75.5	71.4	71.4	76.9	77.0	77.5	71.5	71.5	76.9	77.0	77.1

Table 9. Experiments using a different number of trees and features educed using Chi-Square and Information Gain (where w1 = 0.4, w2 = 0.6)

Target	15 Trees					20 Trees					25 Trees					30 Trees				
	No. Feature					No. Feature					No. Feature					No. Feature				
	35	40	45	50	All	35	40	45	50	All	35	40	45	50	All	35	40	45	50	All
Label	99.9	99.9	99.9	99.9	99.9	99.9	99.9	99.9	99.9	99.9	99.9	99.9	99.9	99.9	99.9	99.9	99.9	99.9	99.9	99.9
Category	98.5	98.5	98.4	98.2	98.2	98.4	98.5	98.5	98.5	98.2	98.0	98.4	98.6	98.6	98.2	98.5	98.3	98.5	98.6	98.3
Sub-Category	71.1	71.6	76.0	77.5	76.7	71.7	71.7	77.8	76.9	76.5	71.5	71.5	77.3	78.0	77.6	71.5	71.5	77.5	77.8	77.4

Table 10. Experiments using a different number of trees and features educed using Chi-Square and Information Gain (where w1 = w2 = 0.5)

Target	15 Trees					20 Trees					25 Trees					30 Trees				
	No. Feature					No. Feature					No. Feature					No. Feature				
	35	40	45	50	All	35	40	45	50	All	35	40	45	50	All	35	40	45	50	All
Label	99.9	99.9	99.9	99.9	99.9	99.9	99.9	99.9	99.9	99.9	99.9	99.9	99.9	99.9	99.9	99.9	99.9	99.9	99.9	99.9
Category	98.7	98.6	98.4	98.4	98.2	98.8	98.6	98.5	98.5	98.2	98.2	98.6	98.6	98.6	98.2	98.7	98.7	98.6	98.6	98.3
Sub-Category	71.8	71.7	77.9	78.0	77.7	71.8	71.7	77.9	77.9	77.5	71.7	71.6	77.9	78.0	77.7	71.7	71.6	77.9	78.0	77.6

Table 11. The accuracy of different algorithms in [3] for predicting sub-category

Algorithm	Accuracy
SVM	40%
Gaussian NB	73%
LDA	70%
Logistic regression	40%
Decision tree	**88%**
Random forest	**84%**
Ensemble	**87%**

Table 12 shows a comparison between the proposed system and other algorithms predicting the sub-category (Normal/Host Port/Port OS/ACK Flooding/Host Brute-Force/MITM ARP Spoofing/UDP Flooding/HTTP Flooding/Synflooding) with regards to time and accuracy. The accuracy of the proposed system and Decision Trees are the highest, while the time for Naïve Bayes and the proposed system is the lowest. The accuracy of Naïve Bayes is not dependable.

Table 12. The comparison between the proposed system and other algorithms predicting the sub-category (Normal/Host Port/Port OS/ACK Flooding/Host BruteForce/MITM ARP Spoofing/UDP Flooding/ HTTP Flooding/Synflooding) with regards to time and accuracy.

Algorithm	Testing accuracy	Training time [s]
Modification system	**78.1%**	**21.82**
Neural network	73.6%	648.85
Decision tree	**79.4%**	63.67
Logistic regression	50.7%	38.73
Naïve Bayes	52.5%	**3.66**
SVM	15.8%	45143.91

5.3 Discussion

Trying to enhance the accuracy of predicting the sub-category target, most false predictions are in predicting Ack Flooding and HTTP Flooding classes as we can see that in confusion matrix in Fig. 2 and Fig. 3 the Rcc analysis for this classes with different algorithms predicting. Removing these two classes and using the proposed system to predict the rest of the seven sub-categories (Normal/ Host Port/ Port OS/ Host BruteForce/ UDP Flooding/ MITM ARP Spoofing/ Synflooding) classes, the results are achieved in Table 13 and show the superiority of the proposed system in both accuracy and time.

Confusion Matrix

Confusion matrix for Random Forest (showing number of instances)

Actual \ Predicted	DoS-Synflooding	MITM ARP Spoofing	Mirai-Ackflooding	Mirai-HTTP Flooding	Mirai-Hostbruteforceg	Mirai-UDP Flooding	Normal	Scan Hostport	Scan Port OS	∑
DoS-Synflooding	14832	4	0	0	10	0	1	0	0	14847
MITM ARP Spoofing	1	8095	7	10	633	3	9	24	62	8844
Mirai-Ackflooding	0	0	3174	7583	545	2477	0	0	2	13781
Mirai-HTTP Flooding	0	2	7248	3676	575	2451	0	0	2	13954
Mirai-Hostbruteforceg	1	646	204	194	28908	128	8	48	158	30295
Mirai-UDP Flooding	0	2	3690	3796	480	37920	0	0	0	45888
Normal	1	39	10	8	65	7	9835	42	11	10018
Scan Hostport	0	77	3	4	110	1	5	3316	2032	5548
Scan Port OS	1	128	3	3	276	1	5	635	12216	13268
∑	14836	8993	14339	15274	31602	42988	9863	4065	14483	156443

Fig. 2. The confusion matrix for the sub-category target.

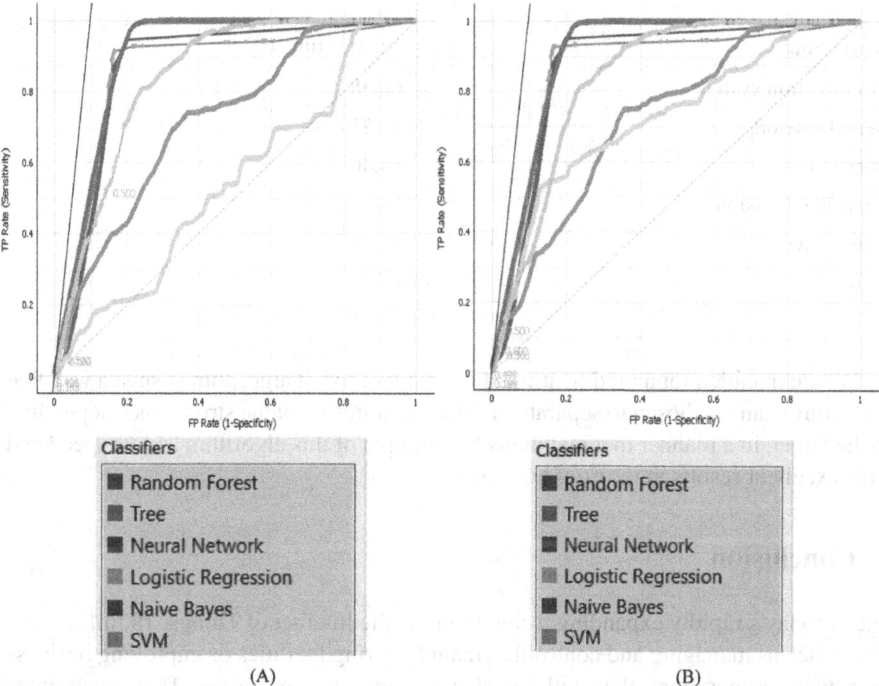

Fig. 3. ROC Analysis for (A) Ack Flooding, and (B) HTTP Flooding classes in sub-category target.

Table 13. The comparison between the proposed system and other algorithms predicting the sub-category (Normal/Host Port/Port OS/Host BruteForce/UDP Flooding/MITM ARP Spoofing/Synflooding) target in terms of accuracy and time.

Algorithm	Testing accuracy	Training time [s]
Modification system	**95.2%**	**14.41**
Neural network	89.3%	855.72
Decision tree	96.2%	20.33
Logistic regression	60.5%	28.55
Naïve Bayes	65.2%	2.5
SVM	21.9%	337.9

When employing the proposed system in a hierarchical architecture by predicting the binary target then predicting the category and sub-category targets. Comparing the cumulative time for the proposed system with the other machine learning algorithms shows the superiority of the proposed system as shown in Table 14.

Table 14. Comparison between the overall proposed system and other algorithms predicting the binary, category, and sub-category targets in terms of the cumulative time.

Algorithm	Cumulative time [s]
Modification system	**60.38**
Neural network	2129.22
Decision tree	84.40
Logistic regression	84.95
Naïve Bayes	14.13
SVM	45683.06

We are intended for a modification of the random forest algorithm in such a way that the features can be chosen to separate the weak features from the strong ones depending on the target, in a manner that maintains the strength of this algorithm and its speed and gives excellent results in terms of accuracy.

6 Conclusion

One of today's rapidly expanding technologies is the Internet of Things. To fulfill many goals, such as managing and controlling manufacturing facilities or improving business procedures or operations, they will then share it with approved parties. There are billions of the Internet-connected devices at present. The number will climb to 20 billion by 2020 as indicated by Gartner Research; so the number of attack targets is growing. It is very important to protect these devices against adversaries and unwanted entry and alteration. This study suggested an IDS in IoT environments on hybrid feature selection techniques for the random forests that can detect intrusions and achieve high speed and accuracy. The IoTID20 dataset uses three target classes, the binary class being normal or abnormal, and category and sub-category classes for the binary class. IoTID20 has 83 network features, using information gain and Gini decrease, these features are ranked. It selects the highest-ranked attributes. The lower-ranked features are excluded, as they do not affect the classification in determining the anomaly, and by experimenting with that and by adopting different ratios for both information gain and Gini decrease, the results mentioned in this paper were obtained. Then the reduced dataset is split into 75% training and 25% testing. For binary, category, and sub-category target classes, the training set is used to train the random forest classifier. To decrease execution time and improve accuracy, the number of trees in the random forest classifier is reduced to 20 for binary, 25 for the category, and 20 for the sub-category. Then the trained classifier is tested and 100% accuracy approaches are obtained for the binary target prediction, 98.7% for the category, and 78.1% to 95.2% for the sub-category of target prediction. The system proposed is checked and compared to previous systems and showed higher performance. Future directions include trying to enhance the accuracy of predicting sub-categories using deep learning techniques.

References

1. Alghuried, A.: A model for anomalies detection in internet of things (IoT) using inverse weight clustering and decision tree (2017)
2. Press, G.: Internet Of Things By The Numbers: What New Surveys Found (forbes.com) (2018). Accessed 1 Dec 2020
3. Ullah, I., Mahmoud, Q.H.: A scheme for generating a dataset for anomalous activity detection in IoT networks. In: Goutte, C., Zhu, X. (eds.) Advances in Artificial Intelligence. LNCS (LNAI), vol. 12109, pp. 508–520. Springer, Cham (2020). https://doi.org/10.1007/978-3-030-47358-7_52
4. Gordon, A. (ed.): Official (ISC) 2 Guide to the CISSP CBK. CRC Press, Boca Raton (2015)
5. Prabha, K., Sree, S.S.: A survey on IPS methods and techniques. Int. J. Comput. Sci. Issues (IJCSI) **13**(2), 38 (2016)
6. Buczak, A.L., Guven, E.: A survey of data mining and machine learning methods for cyber security intrusion detection. IEEE Commun. Surv. Tutor. **18**(2), 1153–1176 (2015)
7. Sherasiya, T., Upadhyay, H.: Intrusion detection system for Internet of Things. Int. J. Adv. Res. Innov. Ideas Educ.(IJARIIE) **2**(3) (2016)
8. Fu, R., Zheng, K., Zhang, D., Yang, Y.: An intrusion detection scheme based on anomaly mining in Internet of Things (2011)
9. Liu, Y., Wu, Q.: A lightweight anomaly mining algorithm in the Internet of Things. In: IEEE 5th International Conference on Software Engineering and Service Science, pp. 1142–1145. IEEE (2014)
10. Hodo, E., et al.: Threat analysis of IoT networks using artificial neural network intrusion detection system. In: International Symposium on Networks, Computers and Communications (ISNCC), pp. 1–6. IEEE (2016)
11. Pajouh, H.H., Javidan, R., Khayami, R., Ali, D., Choo, K.K.R.: A two-layer dimension reduction and two-tier classification model for anomaly-based intrusion detection in IoT backbone networks. IEEE Trans. Emerg. Top. Comput. **7**, 314–323 (2016)

12. Duda, R.O., Hart, P.E.: Pattern Classification. Wiley, Hoboken (2006)
13. Friedman, J., Hastie, T., Tibshirani, R.: The Elements of Statistical Learning, vol. 1, no. 10. Springer, New York (2011). https://doi.org/10.1007/978-0-387-21606-5
14. Middleton, P., Kjeldsen, P., Tully, J.: Forecast: the Internet of Things, worldwide, Gartner Research (2013)
15. Jamshed, M.A., et al.: Kargus: a highly-scalable software-based intrusion detection system. In: Proceedings of the 2012 ACM Conference on Computer and Communications Security, pp. 317–328 (2012)
16. Jin, D., Lu, Y., Qin, J., Cheng, Z., Mao, Z.: SwiftIDS: real-time intrusion detection system based on LightGBM and parallel intrusion detection mechanism. Comput. Secur. **97**, 101984 (2020)
17. Meesad, P., Boonrawd, P., Nuipian, V.: A chi-square-test for word importance differentiation in text classification. In: Proceedings of International Conference on Information and Electronics Engineering, pp. 110–114 (2011)
18. Assi, J.H., Sadiq, A.T.: NSL-KDD dataset classification using five classification methods and three feature selection strategies. J. Adv. Comput. Sci. Technol. Res. **7**(1), 15–28 (2017)
19. Tavallaee, M., Bagheri, E., Lu, W., Ghorbani, A.A.: A detailed analysis of the KDD CUP 99 data set. In: IEEE Symposium on Computational Intelligence for Security and Defense Applications, pp. 1–6. IEEE (2009)
20. Assi, J.H., Sadiq, A.T.: Modified artificial immune system as feature selection. Iraqi J. Sci. 733–738 (2018)
21. Mohsen, K.S., Sadiq, A.T.: Random forest algorithm using accuracy-based ranking. J. Comput. Theor. Nanosci. **16**(3), 1039–1045 (2019)
22. Sadiq, A.T., Musawi, K.S.: Modify random forest algorithm using hybrid feature selection method. Int. J. Percept. Cogn. Comput. **4**(2), 1–6 (2018)

Network-Based Method for Dynamic Burden-Sharing in the Internet of Things (IoT)

Basim Mahmood[1,2] and Yasir Mahmood[1,2](✉)

[1] Computer Science Department, College of Computer Science and Mathematics, University of Mosul, 41002 Mosul, Iraq
{bmahmood,yaser.ali}@uomosul.edu.iq
[2] BioComplex Laboratory, Exeter, UK
bmahmood@biocomplexlab.org

Abstract. The burden-sharing issue has become one of the most frequent challenges in the field of parallel computing under the Internet of Things (IoT). Distributing loads to processors is not an easy task to perform. In the IoT literature, many approaches have been suggested to come up with optimal burden-sharing. However, there still exists a limitation in providing simple, low-cost, and efficient approaches. Therefore, this paper proposes a network-based method for burden-sharing in IoT CPUs. The main idea behind the proposed method is to utilize concepts from network science in developing a method for efficiently distributing loads to the IoT CPUs. These processors belong to the IoT-connected devices, which can be located in local or remote networks. To this end, a weighted graph is generated whose nodes are the CPUs of the IoT devices and the edges formed if these devices are accessible to each other. The cost of accessing a node from another is assigned to the weight of the edge between the two nodes. The findings showed that the proposed method outperformed the benchmarking approaches in terms of missed deadline tasks. Moreover, the proposed method is easy to implement and does not need complex computations, which is of interest to the IoT developers.

Keywords: Parallel processing · Multiprocessing · Burden sharing · Load balancing · Complex networks

1 Introduction

In computing, the term *Burden Sharing* or *Load Balancing* refers to a kind of process that assigns a set of tasks to resources aiming at having efficient processing [1]. The main reason behind the advent of this term is to reduce the time consumed for executing a particular task as well as obtaining more efficient performance of the network [2]. Moreover, this field has attracted the research community to design and develop techniques and algorithms that enable performing fast computations. The current development in the fields of *IoT* and *Big Data* makes the concepts of burden-sharing and parallel computing more useful and a promising trend for IoT developers [2].

P. Liatsis et al. (Eds.): TIOTC 2021, CCIS 1548, pp. 79–90, 2022.
https://doi.org/10.1007/978-3-030-97255-4_6

The amount of data exchanged in our everyday activities (e.g., work and social activities) is noticeably increased. Therefore, it is needed to adopt techniques that can deal with and process a large amount of data optimally in terms of execution time and delay. In fact, distributing loads to processors is not an easy task since it is a dynamic process for most of our daily-used applications. It needs to take into consideration the availability, accessibility, and status (e.g., loads) of system processors [3–5]. In dynamic systems such as the IoT, the status of resources (e.g., processors) is changed at every single moment and it is difficult to have prior information or track their status within the system or network [6]. Therefore, designing burden-sharing algorithms for dynamic systems needs a lot of attention and many considerations during the developing phase.

One of the key factors that support designing dynamic burden-sharing algorithms is inspiring theories or concepts from the other fields of science. It is believed that sciences complement each other, and integrating disciplines can be a powerful tool to be inspired for addressing a variety of aspects such as burden-sharing issues. In this context, the field of complex networks can be considered the intersection between graph theory and statistical mechanics (multidisciplinary). Therefore, the characteristics of complex networks are applicable to the field of burden-sharing [7–9].

This work introduces a novel network-based method for burden-sharing. It should be mentioned that the difference between the proposed approach and the literature is that it uses simple calculations to achieve efficient burden sharing, which is the contribution of this work.

The rest of this paper is organized as follows; the next section presents the works that are related to the topic of this study. Section 3 illustrates our proposed approach and its details. In Sect. 4 we present the obtained results and discuss them in detail. Finally, we conclude this work in Sect. 5 along with future works.

2 Related Works

The field of parallel computing has become crucial in most of our life's applications [10]. This field of research has attracted many researchers and developers to contribute to designing algorithms that minimize the overall execution time of tasks as well as reduce the delay time [10, 11]. Moreover, the area of burden-sharing or load balancing is also considered a crucial area in the IoT literature. Liu et al. [3] proposed a strategy that reduced the delay time when migrating a request among the multi-server system. In their proposed strategy, each server within the system had information on the other accessible servers including the average response time. Then, they tried to minimize that average insofar as it made a server a good candidate to migrate a request. On the other hand, the area of dynamic burden-sharing in parallel computing systems brought the attention of the researchers in many aspects such as dealing with real-time tasks. Tang et al. [12] developed a dynamic load balancing strategy (DLBS). The algorithm has the ability to maximize the throughput of a network and dynamically balance the loads to network processors. Bokhari et al. [13] also used the DLBS algorithm and found that it minimized the execution time within the whole network. They also found that the DLBS algorithm fitted the multiprocessor interconnection networks.

Furthermore, the design of parallel processing and load balancing algorithms can be inspired from other sciences' theories. In this regard, Pilavare et al. [14] designed a bio-inspired approach based on the concepts of Genetic Algorithms (GA) for enhancing the performance of the network in terms of balancing the loads. Their approach focused on the issue of the processors being idle and the starvation issue. The Ant Colony Optimization (ACO) approaches were also used by the researchers in designing algorithms for load balancing such as the works of [15] and [16]. On the other hand, some works were inspired from sociological concepts such as the work of Abdullah and Alnooh [9]. They involved the preferential attachment concept in sociology in designing a load balancing algorithm. Their algorithm outperformed some of the well-known algorithms in the literature in distributing loads to network processors.

Besides, Adil in [18] proposed a protocol to solve the load balancing problem of the IoT networks in a congestion-free and priority-based communications infrastructure. The traffic management of his proposed protocol was based on priority-based information that balances power consumption with a balanced traffic environment. The results showed that, increasing the life of the IoT devices that were deployed in the network. Chen [19] proposed a method for IoT resource scheduling optimization. The method was based on the ACO algorithm. In the method, various costs and factors were taken into consideration in the IoT virtual machine. They considered a set of virtual machine states. Then, they dynamically calculated and adjusted each resource's scheduling. After that, the IoT scheduling was based on resource load log-data and current IoT upload status. In another study, Sahoo et al. [20] developed an efficient switch migration-based load balancing framework. It aimed to effectively assign switches to an underutilized controller. A Technique for Order Preference by Similarity to an Ideal Solution (TOPSIS) was used in the proposed framework. In the same context, Wang et al. [21] refined and optimized Spark's current load balancing strategy based on the computing performance of each node in the Spark cluster. Then, the authors proposed a node mapping algorithm to perform tasks based on the TENAA Genetic Algorithm. Finally, Xiao et al. [22] used the time-sharing (TS) mechanism instead the first-come-first-serve (FCFS) mechanism in fog computing nodes (FCNs). Then a collaborative load-balancing algorithm for the TS mechanism was proposed for FCNs. The algorithm was a variant of a work-stealing scheduling algorithm and based on the Nash bargaining solution (NBS) for a cooperative game between FCNs.

According to the literature, the majority of the proposed approaches and algorithms need complex computations, which is not desired. Hence, the contribution of this work is to fill the gap of the literature and achieve efficient burden sharing for the IoT devices using simple calculations.

3 The Proposed Approach

This section describes the environment that was designed to simulate the experiments of the proposed approach as well as the settings of the simulation environment. Also, it presents a detailed description of the proposed approach and its parameters.

3.1 Simulation Environment

In this work, a special-purpose model called *Parallel Computing Model* (*PCM*) was designed (see Fig. 1). It has the ability to crawl the IoT devices and simulated a real parallel computing environment since it deals with processors belonging to local and remote devices under the IoT framework. PCM model was designed using NetLogo Simulator, which is a multi-agent-programming-modeling environment [17]. PCM considers IoT environment with several networks $N_1, N_2, \ldots, N_n$ that include terminals (devices) $T_1, T_2, \ldots, T_m$. Each terminal has a processor(s) $P_1, P_2, \ldots, P_r$. In PCM, terminals are loaded with many tasks to be carried out. When a terminal has a heavy load of tasks and there exists some of them that need to be migrated for execution purposes, the proposed model (as will be discussed later) will target a specific processor within its local network, or task migration will be performed to a processor located in a remote network. Since the designed environment is dynamic, the migration strategy depends on the current status of networks' terminals in terms of availability, current load status, accessibility, the cost to reach, and other parameters. Moreover, each processor in PCM has the ability to track the status of all the environments' processors, which is useful when targeting a processor for task migration. The selection of tasks to be migrated is based on the *nearest deadline*. In this case, the proposed approach tries to meet tasks deadline as much as possible.

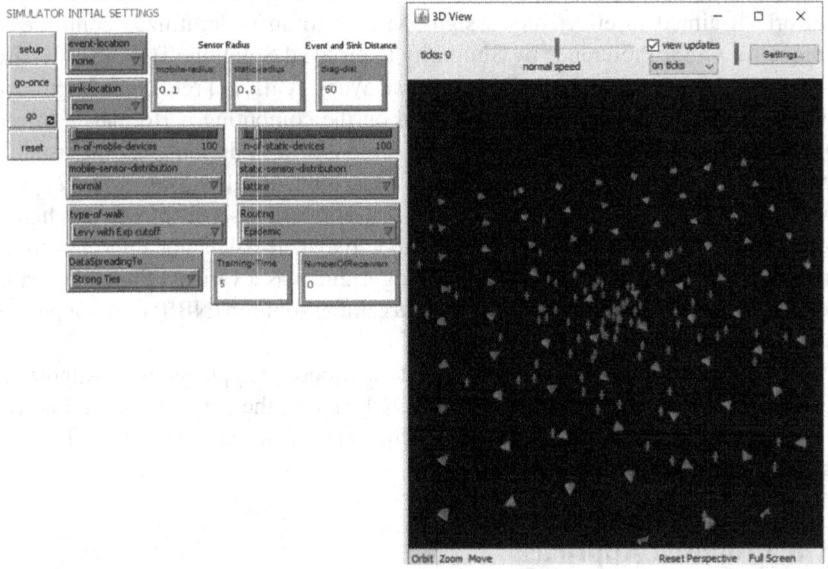

Fig. 1. Simulator interface showing how the configurations and how the devices are distributed within the simulation environment

3.2 The Proposed Method

Burden sharing algorithms aimed to minimize the turnaround time of tasks. Therefore, the goal of the proposed method is to carry out multiple tasks simultaneously and eventually reduce the execution and delay times. This work considers local and remote processors for executing tasks. For a processor, its local processors can be positioned in the same terminal or processors in its local network. While the remote processors of a processor are located in a remote terminal/network. The proposed model is considered a graph $G(V, E)$ in which each processor is represented as a vertex V (node) such that $V_1, V_2, \ldots, V_r$ for r processors in the environment and connected with edges E such that $E_1, E_2, \ldots, E_j$ for j edges in the graph. The edge between two vertices is created when both can access each other. The generated graph is weighted, the weight between two vertices is driven by their positions. Figure 2 shows how the graph is generated in the simulations. For all terminals (T_m), if the source and target processors are located in the same terminal (T_k), then the weight ($W_{source,target}$) is set to 0. Otherwise, the weight is set to the estimated Cost ($C_{source,target}$) needed for the source processor to access the target processor. Algorithm 1 shows how the weight between two processors is assigned.

Algorithm 1: Assigning weights among network processors.

```
BEGIN
  FOR ALL CPU pairs ∈ T_m DO
   IF CPU_source & CPU_target ∈ T_k THEN
        W_source,target = 0
   ELSE
        W_source,target = EC_source,target
   END IF
  END FOR
END
```

As mentioned in the previous section, the proposed model enables each processor to keep track of the other processors in the environment including the local and the remote ones. This means every processor within the environment has a Track Dynamic List (TDL) that contains information about the other processors within the environment. Here, the TDL list of a processor may contain tens or hundreds of entries. In the proposed approach, each processor is considered to have a TDL_i and is updated periodically according to a predetermined period value. The entries in the *TDL* of a processor at time t ($TDL_i(t)$) can be static or dynamic as follows:

- **Processor ID** (*static*): used to identify processors.
- **Position P** (*static*): it can be local or remote but the proposed method prefers the local processors because the cost of accessing them is significantly less than reaching remote processors.
- **Availability A** (*dynamic*): means, is this processor available at time t? Processors may not be available at particular times due to many reasons such as system failure issues or under heavy load.
- **Access Cost C** (*dynamic*): the estimated cost (time) consumed from the source processor to the targeted processor.
- **Current Load L** (*dynamic*): it reflects how much a processor is loaded with tasks.

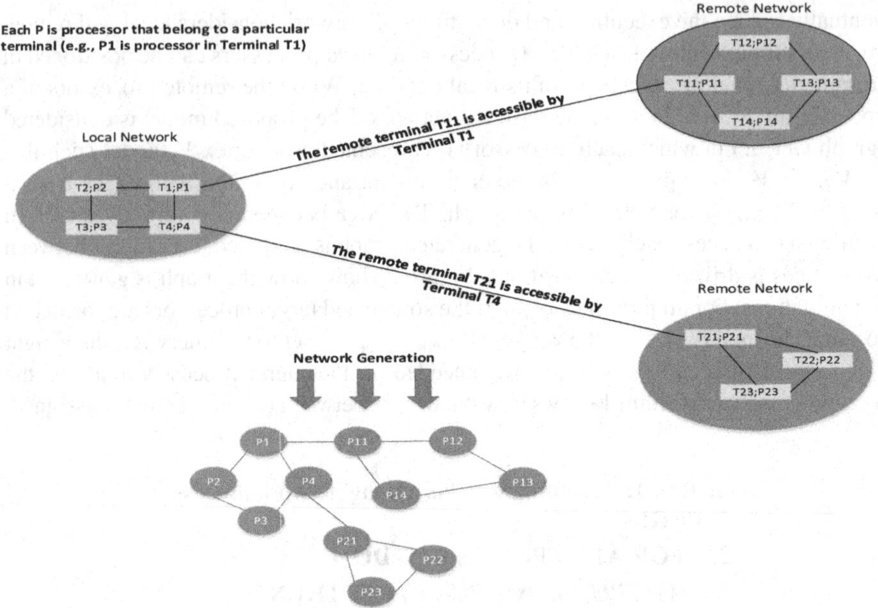

Fig. 2. Network generation strategy of the proposed approach.

In this work, the strategy that was followed when deciding on a processor to be the destination for the migrated tasks depended on the aforementioned entries in a way that guaranteed to minimize the turnaround time of tasks. In that case, each processor looks to its *TDL* list and targets one of the processors in the list. Based on the pre-experiments, a snapshot was taken of the system CPU loads at a time aiming to plot the histogram. It was found that the loads were normally distributed as shown in Fig. 3. According to the characteristics of the normal distribution, there is *95%* of the loads are positioned between two standard deviations (from both sides of the mean). This means the left-most *2.5%* of the loads are the actual least loaded CPUs in the system. This was useful for the proposed method in selecting the targeted processors since it was designed to be more restricted by the least loaded CPUs within the system. The proposed method has also utilized another factor, which was the other entries of the *TDL*. The proposed method tended to target the local CPUs rather than the remote ones. It also preferred to take into consideration the distance between the source and target machines since it plays a significant role in reducing the time consumed in executing the migrated tasks. In this strategy, a network measurement called *shortest path length* [23] was used to accurately reflect the access cost from one processor to another. Algorithm 2 shows the strategy proposed in selecting the target CPU within the system. Now, the strategy followed on which tasks should be migrated first was based on the nearest deadline tasks. It is important to immediately migrate the tasks the are approaching their deadlines. The proposed method can be summarized in four stages as shown in Fig. 4.

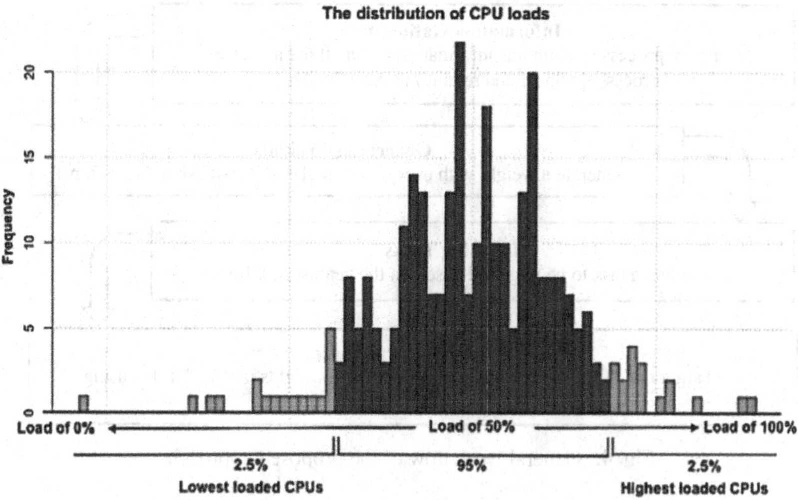

Fig. 3. Loads distribution followed a normal distribution.

Algorithm 2: The strategy followed by a machine in targeting a CPU (*P*) within the system (local/remote).

Given that M_i is a machine in a system and has a task to migrate.

```
BEGIN
  FOR ALL Pr ∈ System
    UPDATE TDLr
    SELECT the lowest 2.5% of the loads
    FOR EACH item DO
           SET weight (Mi, Pr) = 1
    END FOR
  END FOR
END
```

4 Results

As mentioned in the previous section, the NetLogo simulator was used to implement the experiments. The number of devices involved in the environment was 200 (100 mobile devices that can move in the environment and 100 static devices that are stationary). Each device was considered to have one processor and10,000 tasks were distributed to the devices. Deadlines were randomly assigned to each task for evaluation purposes. The proposed method was benchmarked with 3 approaches mentioned in the related works; namely, 1) Abdullah and Alnooh [9] that is called AA algorithm for short, 2) Tang et al. [12] (DLBS algorithm), and 3) Liu et al. [3] (Liu algorithm). These approaches are close to the design of the proposed in terms of their concept and parameters.

Furthermore, the simulations were running 50 times for each experiment aiming at having more accurate results. The average of the obtained results was calculated for

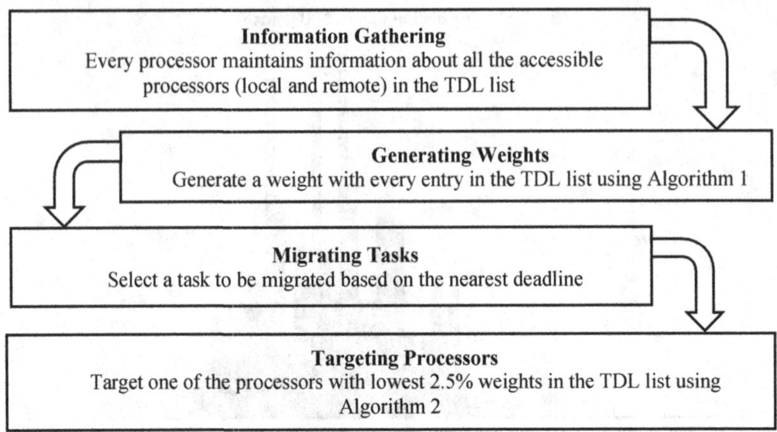

Fig. 4. General work flow of the proposed approach

each approach involved in this work. It should be mentioned that, in the simulator, the positions of the devices are changed from one experiment to another. In other words, the positions of the devices (static and dynamic) were changed in each experiment aiming to provide a different scenario and eventually different results. Therefore, the proposed approach assumes 50 different scenarios. The benchmarking indicator of the experiments was the number of missed deadlines tasks. This indicator expresses how efficient the proposed method compared to the other algorithms. The strategy used in evaluating the experiments was based on assessing the experiments 10 by 10 and observe the behavior of the proposed algorithm in a cumulative way.

All the simulations were started with a training time without executing tasks. The reason behind this step was to initialize the lists and the parameters of the algorithms (e.g., *TDL* and weights). According to the pre-experiments, the best training time was *500 ticks*, and each tick represents a second in the simulator. It should be mentioned that not all the tasks were involved in the environment at the same time; instead, every tick, 100 tasks were involved, which imitated a real IoT environment. The simulations stopped when all the tasks were assigned to processors (local or remote). After that, the number of tasks that missed their deadline was observed in each algorithm for every *10* experiments separately and cumulatively.

Figure 5 shows the performance of the proposed method compared to the benchmarking. As can be seen, the least number of missed deadline tasks were obtained from the proposed method. The figure also shows that the performance of the approaches was measured every 10 experiments and continued cumulatively until it reached *50* experiments. This enabled to accurately observe the behavior of the approaches. Moreover, the overall variations were observed in the *50* experiments for each algorithm. Therefore, a statistical boxplot was used to visualize the variations of the algorithms of this work. Figure 6 depicts that relatively stable behaviors were obtained in all the algorithms.

However, it was necessary to prove that the obtained results were statistically significant since close behaviors were gained from all the simulated algorithms. Therefore, the variations were analyzed using statistical techniques. A one-way Analysis of Variance ANOVA was used assuming two hypotheses:

Null Hypothesis: The means of all the approaches were equal as follows:

$$H0\colon \mu_{(proposed)} = \mu_{(AA)} = \mu_{(DLBS)} = \mu_{(Liu)}$$

Null Hypothesis: The means of all the approaches were NOT equal as follows:

$$H0\colon \mu_{(proposed)} \neq \mu_{(AA)} \neq \mu_{(DLBS)} \neq \mu_{(Liu)}$$

This test used a confidence level of 95% ($\alpha = 0.05$). The result showed that the significance level was greater than the *p-value*. Therefore, the Null Hypothesis of equal means is rejected, which confirmed that our results were statistically significant.

Finally, as shown, the proposed method outperformed the benchmarking algorithms not only because it gained fewer missed deadlines tasks, but also it is simple to implement and does not need complex computations. This point can be considered as the strong side of the proposed method.

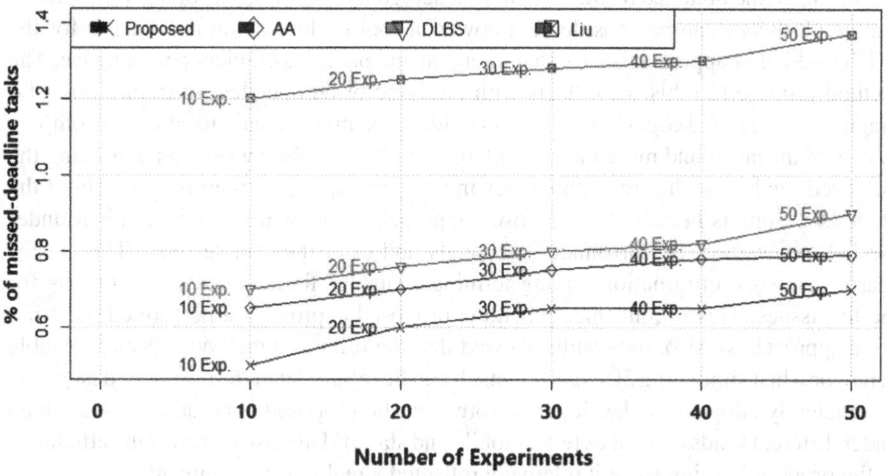

Fig. 5. Performance evaluation of the proposed method

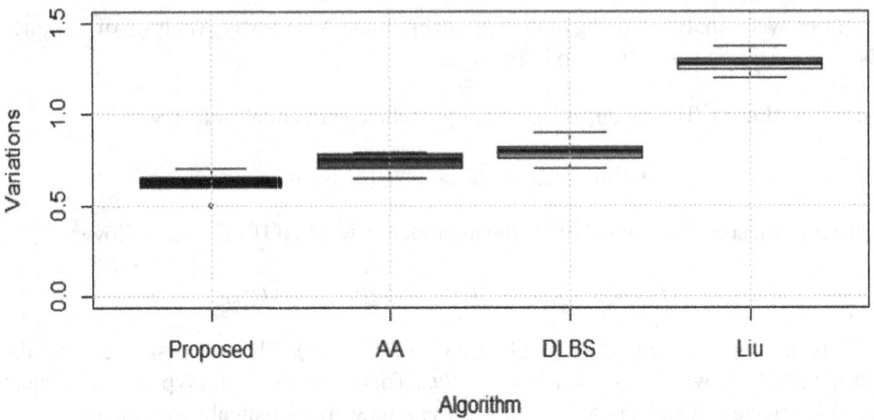

Fig. 6. Evaluation of the variations of the algorithms

5 Discussions

According to the obtained results, it can be observed that the concepts of network science and graph theory can be considered a powerful tool in developing approaches for the IoT. This kind of approach is easy to implement and provides efficient performance. The method proposed in this work deals with the issue of burden-sharing in the form of a graph with nodes and edges. In fact, this consideration makes it easy to convert a complex system to an easier and more understandable one. This is clear when benchmarking the proposed method with three approaches in the literature. The main reason behind the obtained results is because the proposed approach assumes that every terminal under the IoT is aware of its surrounded terminals and even the remote ones. This means sharing network information among terminals enables finding efficient solutions for the IoT issues. This is confirmed when the proposed approach outperformed the other three approaches. Also, the results showed that the proposed method reflected a stable behavior when simulating 50 experiments. It can be inferred that the proposed design can be efficiently adopted by developers. Moreover, the proposed approach was examined under different kinds of devices (e.g., mobile and static). This also confirms the efficiency of the proposed design since it relatively reflected a real IoT environment.

6 Conclusions and Future Works

In this work, a network-based method for CPU burden-sharing in the Internet of Things was proposed. It was based on concepts inspired from network science. Each terminal in the IoT was represented as a node and two nodes were considered to be connected if they can access each other. The weight of each edge represented the access cost between the two connected terminals. Moreover, each terminal has information on the status of the other terminals in terms of load level and the other dynamic parameters. In each terminal, the proposed method considered that the nearest deadline tasks should be immediately migrated to the least loaded terminal (local or remote). The proposed method was benchmarked with three other algorithms in the literature. The results reflected a stable behavior and efficient performance of the proposed method in terms of the number of missed deadline tasks. The proposed method is also considered simple to implement with minimum calculations. Besides, network science concepts can be considered a powerful tool in developing approaches for IoT issues.

It should be mentioned that the limitation of the proposed method was when having several tasks of the same deadlines. In this work, the proposed method selected randomly one of these tasks. To address this issue, it is needed to include the priority of tasks in addition to the deadline aiming at migrating the most appropriate task. However, this will add more parameters to the method and increase the level of complexity. In fact, this issue is considered in future work. Another limitation in this work is the privacy of the devices when sharing their information. This issue can be considered a big concern and needs to adopting some privacy policies and security protocols under the IoT framework.

Since this work is in progress, in the future, it is planned to involve more parameters (e.g., priority of tasks) taking into consideration the simplicity aspect of the design. It is also planned to implement a real IoT application and measure the performance in a real environment considering a large scale of data exchanged.

Acknowledgment. We are grateful to the Computer Science Department/University of Mosul for all the provided support during the work in this research.

References

1. Zhang, Y., et al.: Parallel processing systems for big data: a survey. Proc. IEEE **104**(11), 2114–2136 (2016)
2. Kaminisky, A.: Big CPU, Big Data: Solving the World's Toughest Computational PROBLEMS with Parallel Computing. CreateSpace Independent Publishing Platform (2016)
3. Liu, C., Li, K., Li, K.: A game approach to multi-servers load balancing with load-dependent server availability consideration. IEEE Trans. Cloud Comput. **9**, 1–13 (2018)
4. Czarnul, P.: Parallel Programming for Modern High Performance Computing Systems. CRC Press, Boca Raton (2018)
5. Iwata, A.: Parallel computing device, parallel computing system, and job control method. United States patent US 10,180,858, 15 January 2019
6. Wan, J., et al.: Toward dynamic resources management for IoT-based manufacturing. IEEE Commun. Mag. **56**(2), 52–59 (2018)
7. Zhang, Z., Zhang, X.: A load balancing mechanism based on ant colony and complex network theory in open cloud computing federation. In: 2010 the 2nd International Conference on Industrial Mechatronics and Automation, vol. 2, pp. 240–243. IEEE, 30 May 2010
8. Xiao, Y., Xue, Y., Nazarian, S., Bogdan, P.: A load balancing inspired optimization framework for exascale multicore systems: a complex networks approach. In: 2017 IEEE/ACM International Conference on Computer-Aided Design (ICCAD), pp. 217–224. IEEE, 13 November 2017
9. Alnooh, A.H., Abdullah, D.B.: On the impact of real time parameters into the design of cloud load balancers. J. Theor. Appl. Inf. Technol. **96**(15) (2018)
10. Tyagi, R., Gupta, S.K.: A survey on scheduling algorithms for parallel and distributed systems. In: Mishra, A., Basu, A., Tyagi, V. (eds.) Silicon Photonics & High Performance Computing. AISC, vol. 718, pp. 51–64. Springer, Singapore (2018). https://doi.org/10.1007/978-981-10-7656-5_7

11. Milani, A.S., Navimipour, N.J.: Load balancing mechanisms and techniques in the cloud environments: systematic literature review and future trends. J. Netw. Comput. Appl. **71**, 86–98 (2016)
12. Tang, F., Yang, L.T., Tang, C., Li, J., Guo, M.: A dynamical and load-balanced flow scheduling approach for big data centers in clouds. IEEE Trans. Cloud Comput. **6**(4), 915–928 (2016)
13. Bokhari, M.U., Alam, M., Hasan, F.: Performance analysis of dynamic load balancing algorithm for multiprocessor interconnection network. Perspect. Sci. **8**, 564–566 (2016)
14. Pilavare, M.S., Desai, A.: A novel approach towards improving performance of load balancing using genetic algorithm in cloud computing. In: 2015 International Conference on Innovations in Information, Embedded and Communication Systems (ICIIECS), pp. 1–4. IEEE, 19 March 2015
15. Ragmani, A., El Omri, A., Abghour, N., Moussaid, K., Rida, M.: A performed load balancing algorithm for public cloud computing using ant colony optimization. Recent Patents Comput. Sci. **11**(3), 179–195 (2018)
16. Dam, S., Mandal, G., Dasgupta, K., Dutta, P.: An ant-colony-based meta-heuristic approach for load balancing in cloud computing. In: Applied Computational Intelligence and Soft Computing in Engineering, pp. 204–232. IGI Global (2018)
17. Tisue, S., Wilensky, U.: NetLogo: design and implementation of a multi-agent modeling environment. In: Proceedings of Agent, vol. 2004, pp. 7–9, 4 October 2004
18. Adil, M.: Congestion free opportunistic multipath routing load balancing scheme for internet of things (IoT). Comput. Netw. **184**, 107707 (2021)
19. Chen, R.: effective scheduling simulation of internet of things load balanced sharing of resources. In: 2019 IEEE 5th International Conference on Computer and Communications (ICCC), pp. 2136–2140. IEEE, 6 December 2019
20. Sahoo, K.S., et al.: ESMLB: efficient switch migration-based load balancing for multicontroller SDN in IoT. IEEE Internet Things J. **7**(7), 5852–5860 (2019)
21. Wang, S., Zhang, L., Zhang, Y., Cao, N.: Spark load balancing strategy optimization based on internet of things. In: 2018 International Conference on Cyber-Enabled Distributed Computing and Knowledge Discovery (CyberC), pp. 76–763. IEEE, 18 October 2018
22. Xiao, H., Zhang, Z., Zhou, Z.: GWS—a collaborative load-balancing algorithm for internet-of-things. Sensors. **18**(8), 2479 (2018)
23. Mahmood, B., Menezes, R.: A social-based strategy for memory management in sensor networks. In: SENSORNETS, pp. 25–34, 19 February 2016

Internet of Things (IOT) in Healthcare Industry

Toward on Develop a Framework for Diagnosing Novel-COVID-19 Symptoms Using Decision Support Methods

Qahtan M. Yas[1(✉)] and Ghazwan K. Ouda[2]

[1] Department Computer of Science, College of Veterinary Medicine, University of Diyala, Baqubah 32001, Iraq
qahtan.myas@uodiyala.edu.iq

[2] Department Computer of Science, College of Education for Humanities, University of Diyala, Baqubah 32001, Iraq

Abstract. A novel coronavirus disease is considered the most dangerous epidemic spread in the world recently. The world health organization (WHO) has named this epidemic a novel COVID-19. According to the literature review, the most important symptoms that confirm the infection with this epidemic are high temperature, coughing, shortness of breath, and chest pain. In general, these symptoms have become the actual cause of most deaths for people who have the novel COVID-19 epidemic. These symptoms adopted in this study as essential criteria. The conflict between criteria formatted a challenge in this study. This paper aims to propose a framework for diagnosing the disease symptoms based on multiple criteria using an analytical hierarchy process (AHP) method. Therefore, decision support methods most suitable to solve various criteria problems. The results reported the most important criterion at the mean (0.407) and ±SD (0.166) for the fever. The least important criterion of the chest pain at the mean (0.116) and ±SD (0.070). While the cough criterion at the mean (0.254) and ±SD (0.099) and the shortness of breath criterion at the mean (0.223) and ±SD (0.127), respectively. This study presented an optimal framework for physicians to immediately diagnose coronavirus symptoms for the person with this disease.

Keywords: Novel-Covid-19 · Fever · Cough · Shortness of breath · Chest pain · Diagnosing symptoms · Multi-criteria · Analytical hierarchy process

1 Introduction

Briefly defined "Pandemic" is the outbreak of an epidemic in the wide geographical area that crossing the countries boundaries to be infecting a large number of humans as happens in the world nowadays. In late 2019, a new epidemic appeared that infects the human respiratory system in Wuhan city, China. In the earliest of 2020, the world health organization (WHO) has announced a new type of coronavirus called (Novel-COVID-19) [1, 2]. However, due to the outbreak declared a state of health emergency in all countries of the world to be taken preventive measures to preserve the safety and

P. Liatsis et al. (Eds.): TIOTC 2021, CCIS 1548, pp. 93–107, 2022.
https://doi.org/10.1007/978-3-030-97255-4_7

health of people [3]. The Investigations by many health care centers have proven the causes for the spread of this disease through human-to-human contact. Initial tests for people with this disease recorded several symptoms, which confirmed infected with the disease. The first symptom identified when the patient's temperature increases over 36 °C, which confirmed the infection with the disease. In addition, other symptoms were also diagnosed for the disease are coughing and shortness of breath and chest pain, as well as other symptoms [1, 2, 4, 5].

Several studies used different methods of diagnosing the disease, such as computerized tomography for the chest, which gives more details about lung diseases [6]. In some countries, diagnosed cases according to some visitors and travelers returning from endemic areas as well as from local residents [7]. On the other hand, some studies have used statistical methods to estimate the number of deaths and the rate infection by this disease after its spread in most countries of the world [8]. This study aims to provide an optimal framework for diagnosing the most critical symptoms of emerging coronavirus to help physicians present health services to the infected in this disease. Almost no study has addressed the diagnosis of COVID-19 symptoms yet. Therefore, this paper proposed a new framework to diagnose the novel COVID-19 based on multi-criteria decision-making techniques.

Decision support methods or MCDM techniques considered a significant part of operation research (OR) when persons take their difficult decision in real-time. MCDM techniques included several methods developed by researchers. These techniques relied on the behavior of the decision-making problem [9]. In some methods, the decision-maker calculates the weights according to the criteria selected [10–12]. One of the most important decision-making techniques is the analytical hierarchy process (AHP) that depends on the principle of the pairwise [13]. This method has been used in many scientific and industrial sectors and health and educational institutions [14–17]. This technique based on the doctors' preferences between the criteria selected in this study. According to the physicians' answers, the weights calculated of criteria based on the pairwise principle. This paper aims to present an optimal method for diagnosing the novel COVID-19 epidemic symptoms based on the analytical hierarchy process method. The organizing of the paper presented the background of the novel coronavirus in the introduction. Section 2 included the method implemented for diagnoses coronavirus symptoms. Section 3, discussion of the results. Section 4, a summary of the study.

1.1 Overview of COVID-19 Symptoms

This section presented a comprehensive review of all articles, including various symptoms of the novel COVId-19 epidemic. According to the literature review, the most acute symptoms identified to diagnose the emerging coronavirus disease. The indication of the patient's temperature rise above 36° is evidence of infection in the disease and the wave of coughing with shortness of breath that leads to a feeling of chest pain that formed more significant symptoms of the disease. Thus, the condition's symptoms represented essential criteria in our study (see Table 1).

Table 1 included several studies that adopted these criteria to identify symptoms of the novel COVID-19 epidemic. The highest percentage reported for fever at 97%, while

Table 1. Overview of COVID-19 symptoms

No.	Reference	Cough	Fever	Shortness of breath	Chest pain
1	[18]	√	√	×	×
2	[19]	√	√	×	×
3	[20]	√	√	√	×
4	[21]	√	√	√	√
5	[6]	√	√	×	×
6	[22]	√	√	×	×
7	[23]	×	√	×	×
8	[24]	×	√	×	×
9	[1]	√	√	√	√
10	[25]	√	√	×	×
11	[26]	√	√	×	×
12	[27]	√	√	×	×
13	[28]	√	√	×	×
14	[29]	√	√	×	×
15	[30]	√	√	×	×
16	[31]	√	√	×	×
17	[32]	√	√	×	×
18	[33]	√	√	×	×
19	[34]	√	√	×	×
20	[35]	×	√	×	×
21	[2]	√	√	√	√
22	[8]	√	√	√	×
23	[36]	√	√	√	×
24	[37]	√	√	×	×
25	[7]	√	√	√	×
26	[38]	√	√	×	×
27	[39]	√	√	×	√
28	[40]	√	×	×	×
29	[41]	√	√	×	×
30	[42]	√	√	×	×
		90%	**97%**	**23%**	**13%**

the lowest rate reported for chest pain at 13% and the coughing recorded at 90% and shortness of breath at 23%, respectively.

2 Methodology

The study's main objective is to present a methodology for the diagnosis of the most important symptoms of the emerging coronavirus disease using the analytical hierarchy process. A new framework proposed based on the analytical hierarchy process method to calculate the weights of the main criteria in this study. In addition, this framework provides a comprehensive instant for physicians to identify the priority of these symptoms when beginning the diagnosis of coronavirus disease for the people has infected.

2.1 Selection of Criteria

According to the literature review, the symptoms of the disease are identified in this study. Almost 40 articles have been thoroughly reviewed to identify signs of COVID-19. These articles provided a clear vision of the most important symptoms that confirm the infection in the novel coronavirus disease. Thus, the most important criteria identified based on the literature review in this study.

In this study, physicians play an important role as experts in the medical field. The experts were selected from the faculty of Medicine in Diyala University, such as Professor

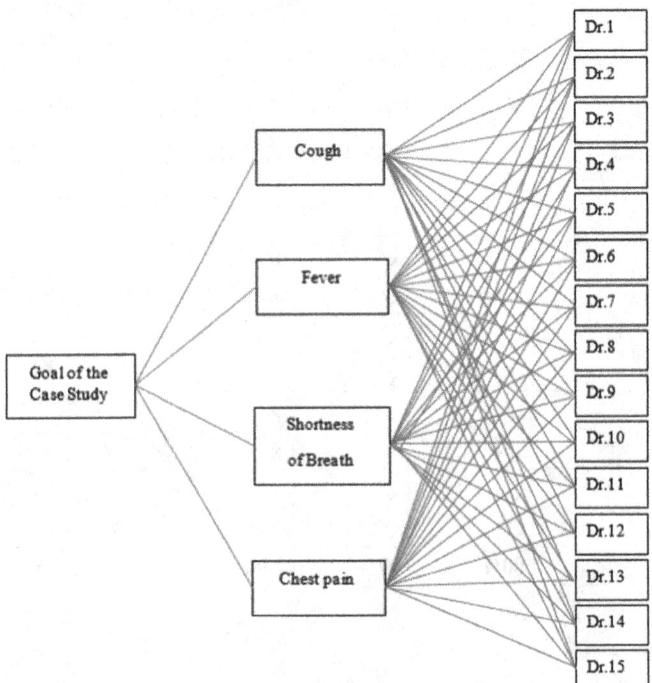

Fig. 1. Structure of the analytical hierarchy process

and Assistant Professor, as well as physicians working in Baqubah hospital. About 15 physicians' opinion was collected to identify a priority among symptoms of COVID-19, according to an approach invented by [13] (Fig. 1).

2.2 Calculation of Pairwise Comparisons

The AHP considered one of the most common decision-making methods based on multi-criteria is developed by [13, 43] to be conducting pairwise comparisons and calculate weights. This method usually included some inconsistencies in judgments due to the nature of humans are not typically consistent. The ratio metrics derived from the primary Eigenvector, and the consistency index is derived from the primary Eigenvalue. Consequently, the number of pairwise comparisons can be made according to the following formula:

$$\mathbf{n * (n - 1)/2} \tag{1}$$

where n represents the number of criteria, which selected during the evaluation process. The comparison process of criteria n represent pairs for the number of relative weights. Therefore, the criteria and weights represented ($C1$ .... Cn) and ($W1$.....Wn). In this matrix can be represented comparison process as follows:

$$C = \begin{array}{c|ccc} & C1 & C2 \;\ldots\ldots & Cn \\ \hline C1 & W1/W1 & W1/W2 \;\ldots\ldots & W1/Wn \\ C2 & W2/W1 & W2/W2 \;\ldots\ldots & W2/Wn \\ . & & & \\ . & & & \\ Cn & Wm/W2 & Wm/W2 \;\ldots\ldots & Wm/Wn \end{array} \tag{2}$$

where C represents the multiple vectors of weights $W = (W1, W2, \ldots Wn)$. The weight results in multiplication by $(W * n)$. The n represents the eigenvector, and the W represents the Eigenvalue for C, respectively. This matrix depends on the pairwise ratio calculated from the ratio of weights for each element to all other ratios. This method based on calculating the weights of the criteria according to their importance. The decision making relies on the importance of criteria due to conflicts between them. However, these criteria are consistent with the objectives chosen to investigate each activity [13]. Table 2 includes four elements of the decision matrix to determine the priority for each pair.

2.3 Configuration of Consistency Ratio

This stage considered important when collecting the various doctors' answers, then converting them into numerical values and insert them in the decision matrix. The decision matrix includes several measures that must be implemented, such as normalization and

Table 2. Pairwise comparison matrix

Criteria	A	B	C	D
A	1	A/B	A/C	A/D
B	B/A	1	B/C	B/D
C	C/A	C/B	1	C/D
D	D/A	D/B	D/C	1

aggregation, then calculating the weights and ranking them. The consistency ratio is the most important step to ensure the accuracy of results for the AHP method. Therefore, it is necessary to verify the consistency values for each criterion after calculating the weights for them. Often the researchers faced issues of inconsistency in the evaluators' answers collected from the questionnaire. Typically, inconsistency affects the results of the general test. Therefore, it is necessary to test the consistency values for all evaluators' answers to ensure the accuracy of the results [44].

The consistency ratio (CR) can be measured to identify the consistency of pairwise, which called a consistency index. Theoretically, the CR measure if larger than 0.10, then indicates inconsistency in the pairwise comparison, whereas a CR measures if equal or less to 0.10 that indicates the valid consistency measure for the comparison process [45]. The CR measure can be represented by following this formula:

$$CR = CI/RI \tag{3}$$

where CI represents the consistency index obtained from the formula:

$$CI = (\max - n)/(n - 1) \tag{4}$$

Then Random Index (RI) represent in Table 3. Random Index [43].

Table 3. Random index

N	1	2	3	4	5	6	7	8	9	10	11	12	13	14	15
RI	0.00	0.00	0.58	0.90	1.12	1.24	1.32	1.41	1.45	1.49	1.51	1.54	1.56	1.58	1.59

2.4 Calculation of Physicians' Preferences

In this section, we focus on the comparison process for Covid-19 parameters according to the pairwise principle. Basically, the items in the decision matrix are arranged based on the judgments of physicians or experts. Although, they have a concern about the importance of the elements related to all aspects of the goal regarding the diagnosis of COVID-19 symptoms. Table 4, illustrated the fundamental measure of criteria judgments in this method. This measure is valid not only with applications relied on experts but also the theoretical comparison for large-scale data. An important question when two criteria are compared for the following types. Therefore, comparing two criteria should be most important for the experts.

Table 4. Fundamental measure of criteria

Priority of measure	Description of measures
1	Equal favors
3	Slightly favors
5	Strong favors
7	Very strong favors
9	Extremely favors
2, 4, 6, 8	Intermediate values between the two adjacent judgments

On the other hand, this study adopted fifteen physicians and experts from the faculty of medicine at the University of Diyala and Baquhba Hospital in Iraq. These physicians and experts have a broad background on the epidemic and contagious diseases according to their curriculum vitae. These experts were asked, and their answers were calculated according to the pairwise comparison structure in Fig. 2. The experts' preferences discuss in detail in the next section.

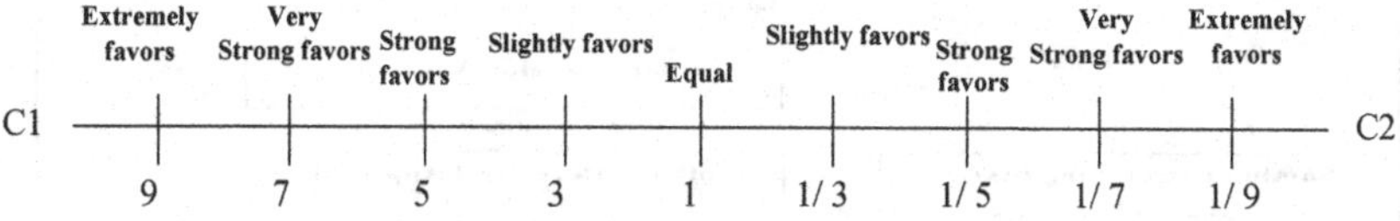

Fig. 2. Pairwise comparisons structure

2.5 Structure of Decision Matrix

This section shows the matrix constructing and distributing the criteria on it. AHP method implemented to calculate the weights according to the physicians' preferences. According to the pairwise principle, this method applies mathematical calculations to convert the physicians' judgments and generate required weights for each criterion. In contrast, calculation the consistency ratio for judgments that represent the internal consistency values entered. Thus, all answers of evaluators gathered based on pairwise comparisons to create a reciprocal matrix. The matrix includes each criterion values within any level and determines the priority of each feature compared with its parent. The criteria features obtained represent the importance of each feature is related to the goal. Table 5, illustrates calculation weights based on the analytical hierarchy process approach for physicians' preferences.

Table 5. Calculation weights based on the analytical hierarchy process approach

physicians' judgments	Criteria	Original Matrix				Normalization Matrix				Aggregation	weights
		Cough	Fever	Shortness of Breath	Chest Pain	Cough	Fever	Shortness of Breath	Chest Pain		
	Cough	C	C/F	C/SoB	C/C.P	C/sum1	(C/F) /sum2	(C/SoB) /sum3	(C/C.P) /sum4	Sum-C	W1= sum(C/n)
	Fever	F/C	F	F/SoB	F/C.P	(F/C) /sum1	F/sum2	(F/SoB) /sum3	(F/C.P) /sum4	sum-F	W2= sum(F/n)
	Shortness of Breath	SoB/C	SoB/F	SoB	SoB/C.P	(SoB) /sum1	(SoB/F) /sum2	(SoB) /Sum3	(SoB/ C.P) /sum4	sum-SoB	W3= sum(SoB/n)
	Chest Pain	C.P/C	C.P/F	C.P/SoB	C.P	(C.P) /sum1	(C.P/F) /sum2	(C.P/SoB) Sum3	(C.P) /sum4	Sum-C.P	W4= sum(C/n)
	SUM	**Sum1**	**Sum2**	**Sum3**	**Sum4**						1

2.6 Developing Diagnostic Framework for COVID-19 Symptoms

Recently, the decision matrix constructed based on the physicians' preferences using the principle of pairwise for comparison between criteria. However, a new diagnostic framework of COVID-19 symptoms developed based on MCDM techniques. The framework provided a clear landscape to evaluate of criteria that have been selected in this study. Essentially, the AHP method implemented in the proposed framework to calculate and rank the weights of criteria according to the physicians' preferences in this study. Figure 3 shows a new framework developed for the diagnostic of COVID-19 symptoms.

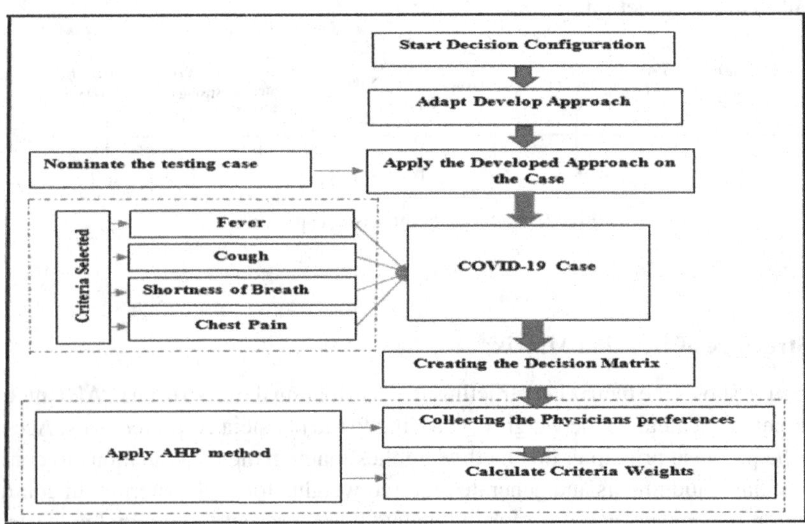

Fig. 3. Develop diagnostic framework for COVID-19 symptoms

3 Results and Discussion

In the final step, we discussed the results collected from the implementation of the decision matrix according to the AHP method. Table 4 included all physicians' preferences based on multi-criteria. The table illustrated each stage of collecting the original data, the normalization data, aggregation, and calculating weights. In addition, the testing stage of the consistency to ensure the accuracy of the results. According to the hierarchical analysis process, the results of fifteen experts verified and obtained the consistency ratios greater than 0.1; otherwise, it is ignored. See Table 6 shows the results of comparison matrices and local importance.

Table 7 shows the final results values of the criteria weights for each evaluator by physicians according to the AHP method rules. The table provided the weights for each criterion collected based on the physicians' preferences using the questionnaire. Thus, 15 expert answers collected in the medical field to determine the priority of each criterion to the other, based on the pairwise principle.

In this study, the mean and the standard deviation are calculated for their extreme importance in determining the importance of each criterion for decision making. Table 8 shows the statistical calculations of criteria in the decision matrix (DM). These measures calculated according to the comparison values between the criteria selected according to the preferences of the evaluators in the health care sector in Iraq. Results of the comparison showed that the values of the fever criterion reported the highest value at the mean (0.407) and ±SD (0.166), while the lowest value reported for the chest pain at the mean (0.116) and ±SD (0.070). The value of the cough criterion is at the mean (0.254) and ±SD (0.099) and the value of the shortness of breath at the mean (0.223) and ±SD (0.127), respectively. Figure 4 shows the status of the results according to the mean values and the standard deviation of the various criteria.

Table 6. Results of comparison matrices and local important

Dr.1	**Cough**	**S- of- B**	**Chest Pain**	**Fever**	**important Weights**	**Dr.2**	**Cough**	**S- of- B**	**Chest Pain**	**Fever**	**Important Weight**
Cough	**1.000**	5.000	9.000	0.111	0.220	**Cough**	**1.000**	3.000	7.000	0.200	
S- of- B	0.200	**1.000**	9.000	0.143	0.130	**S- of- B**	0.333	**1.000**	9.000	1.000	0.274
Chest Pain	0.111	0.111	**1.000**	0.111	0.034	**Chest Pain**	0.143	0.111	**1.000**	0.111	0.256
Fever	9.000	7.000	9.000	**1.000**	0.615	**Fever**	5.000	1.000	9.000	**1.000**	0.033
			CV	**CI**	**CR**				**CV**	**CI**	**CR**
			5.776	0.592	0.658				4.944	0.315	0.349

Dr.3	Cough	S- of- B	Chest Pain	Fever	important Weights	Dr.4	Cough	S- of- B	Chest Pain	Fever	important Weights
Cough	**1.000**	9.000	3.000	0.333	0.338	**Cough**	**1.000**	1.000	7.000	9.000	0.521
S- of- B	0.111	**1.000**	7.000	1.000	0.237	**S- of- B**	1.000	**1.000**	0.200	0.143	0.137
Chest Pain	0.333	0.143	**1.000**	0.200	0.057	**Chest Pain**	0.143	5.000	**1.000**	1.000	0.155
Fever	3.000	1.000	5.000	**1.000**	0.368	**Fever**	0.111	7.000	1.000	**1.000**	0.187
			CV	**CI**	**CR**				**CV**	**CI**	**CR**
			5.989	0.663	0.737				6.604	0.868	0.965

Dr.5	Cough	S- of- B	Chest Pain	Fever	important Weights	Dr.6	Cough	S- of- B	Chest Pain	Fever	important Weights
Cough	1.000	1.000	1.000	0.333	0.164	**Cough**	1.000	3.000	1.000	0.333	0.184
S- of- B	1.000	1.000	5.000	1.000	0.322	**S- of- B**	0.333	1.000	5.000	0.143	0.163
Chest Pain	1.000	0.200	1.000	7.000	0.280	**Chest Pain**	1.000	0.200	1.000	0.200	0.102
Fever	3.000	1.000	0.143	1.000	0.235	**Fever**	3.000	7.000	5.000	1.000	0.550
			CV	**CI**	**CR**				**CV**	**CI**	**CR**
			6.202	0.734	0.816				4.960	0.320	0.356

Dr.7	Cough	S- of- B	Chest Pain	Fever	important Weights	Dr.8	Cough	S- of- B	Chest Pain	Fever	important Weights
Cough	1.000	0.333	3.000	0.333	0.141	**Cough**	1.000	0.333	7.000	1.000	0.284
S- of- B	3.000	1.000	7.000	0.143	0.262	**S- of- B**	3.000	1.000	3.000	0.143	0.243
Chest Pain	0.333	0.143	1.000	0.200	0.061	**Chest Pain**	0.143	0.333	1.000	0.333	0.068
Fever	3.000	7.000	5.000	1.000	0.536	**Fever**	1.000	7.000	3.000	1.000	0.405
			CV	**CI**	**CR**				**CV**	**CI**	**CR**
			5.130	0.377	0.419				5.521	0.507	0.563

Dr.9	Cough	S- of- B	Chest Pain	Fever	important Weights	Dr.10	Cough	S- of- B	Chest Pain	Fever	important Weights
Cough	1.000	9.000	7.000	0.333	0.348	**Cough**	1.000	9.000	7.000	0.111	0.313
S- of- B	0.111	1.000	3.000	0.143	0.089	**S- of- B**	0.111	1.000	1.000	0.143	0.060
Chest Pain	0.143	0.333	1.000	0.200	0.059	**Chest Pain**	0.143	1.000	1.000	0.333	0.091
Fever	3.000	7.000	5.000	1.000	0.505	**Fever**	9.000	7.000	3.000	1.000	0.537
			CV	**CI**	**CR**				**CV**	**CI**	**CR**
			4.808	0.269	0.299				6.226	0.742	0.824

Dr.11	Cough	S- of- B	Chest Pain	Fever	important Weights	Dr.12	Cough	S- of- B	Chest Pain	Fever	important Weights
Cough	1.000	0.333	7.000	0.200	0.219	**Cough**	1.000	0.333	5.000	0.200	0.198
S- of- B	3.000	1.000	0.333	0.143	0.133	**S- of- B**	3.000	1.000	0.333	0.143	0.134
Chest Pain	0.143	3.000	1.000	0.333	0.142	**Chest Pain**	0.200	3.000	1.000	0.333	0.148
Fever	5.000	7.000	3.000	1.000	0.506	**Fever**	5.000	7.000	3.000	1.000	0.520
			CV	**CI**	**CR**				**CV**	**CI**	**CR**
			5.963	0.654	0.727				5.594	0.531	0.591

Dr.13	Cough	S- of- B	Chest Pain	Fever	important Weights	Dr.14	Cough	S- of- B	Chest Pain	Fever	important Weights
Cough	1.000	0.333	5.000	0.200	0.162	**Cough**	1.000	0.333	5.000	1.000	0.268
S- of- B	3.000	1.000	5.000	0.143	0.230	**S- of- B**	3.000	1.000	1.000	5.000	0.430
Chest Pain	0.200	0.200	1.000	1.000	0.139	**Chest Pain**	0.200	1.000	1.000	1.000	0.171
Fever	5.000	7.000	1.000	1.000	0.468	**Fever**	1.000	0.200	1.000	1.000	0.130
			CV	**CI**	**CR**				**CV**	**CI**	**CR**
			6.223	0.741	0.823				4.895	0.298	0.332

Dr.15	**Cough**	**S- of- B**	**Chest Pain**	Fever	**important Weights**
Cough	1.000	0.200	1.000	3.000	0.172
S- of- B	5.000	1.000	3.000	5.000	0.525
Chest Pain	1.000	1.000	1.000	1.000	0.205
Fever	0.333	0.200	1.000	1.000	0.099
			CV	**CI**	**CR**
			4.736	0.245	0.272

Table 7. Rustles of physicians' preferences

Experts	Cough	Shortness of breath	Chest pain	Fever	SUM
Dr-1	0.220	0.130	0.034	0.615	1.000
Dr-2	0.274	0.256	0.033	0.437	1.000
Dr-3	0.338	0.237	0.057	0.368	1.000
Dr-4	0.521	0.137	0.155	0.187	1.000
Dr-5	0.164	0.322	0.280	0.235	1.000
Dr-6	0.184	0.163	0.102	0.550	1.000
Dr-7	0.141	0.262	0.061	0.536	1.000
Dr-8	0.284	0.243	0.068	0.405	1.000
Dr-9	0.348	0.089	0.059	0.505	1.000
Dr-10	0.313	0.060	0.091	0.537	1.000
Dr-11	0.219	0.133	0.142	0.506	1.000
Dr-12	0.198	0.134	0.148	0.520	1.000
Dr-13	0.162	0.230	0.139	0.468	1.000
Dr-14	0.268	0.430	0.171	0.130	1.000
Dr-15	0.172	0.525	0.205	0.099	1.000

Table 8. Statistical calculations of criteria

Criteria	Mean	±SD
Fever	0.407	0.166
Cough	0.254	0.099
Shortness of breath	0.223	0.127
Chest pain	0.116	0.070

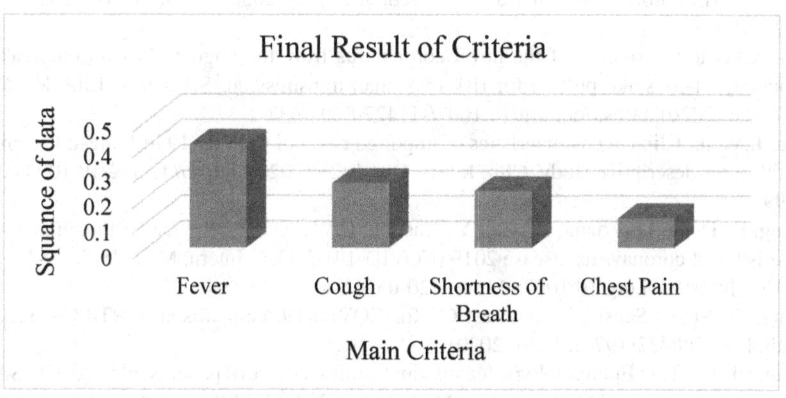

Fig. 4. Statistical results of criteria

4 Conclusion

Emerging coronavirus disease hit worldwide in late 2019. This pandemic is the most severe disease that diffuses around the world so far. The most important symptoms of this disease are severe fever, coughing, shortness of breath, and chest pain that has been identified between the infected by this disease. In this stage, a new framework developed to help physicians for diagnosing the symptoms of the disease directly. This framework relies on multi-criteria decision-making techniques. Given the conflict between these criteria, the best approach for solving this problem is the analytical hierarchy process applied in this study. This technique relied on the principle of pairwise and determining the priority of criteria. Consequently, the mean and standard deviation statistically calculated for the criteria selected. The results reported the most important criterion at the mean (0.407) and ±SD (0.166) for the fever, and the least important for the criterion of the chest pain at the mean (0.116) and ±SD (0.070). While the cough criterion at the mean (0.254) and ±SD (0.099) and the shortness of breath criterion at the mean (0.223) and ±SD (0.127), respectively. The limitations of the study due to the paucity of reliable data relevant to the objective of the study, as well as in regards to the government policy. Therefore, we adapted only four main symptoms reported in the previous studies. In recommendations, the framework considers a proper template to apply with another case study in future work.

Acknowledgment. The author would like to thank the University of Diyala\Scientific Research Committee (SRC) for supporting this major research project and also to some friends who gave me good advice while working on this research.

References

1. Wang, Y., Wang, Y., Chen, Y., Qin, Q.: Unique epidemiological and clinical features of the emerging 2019 novel coronavirus pneumonia (COVID-19) implicate special control measures. J. Med. Virol. **92**(6), 568–576 (2020). https://doi.org/10.1002/jmv.25748
2. Deng, S.-Q., Peng, H.-J.: Characteristics of and public health responses to the coronavirus disease 2019 outbreak in China. J. Clin. Med. **9**(2), 575 (2020). https://doi.org/10.3390/jcm9020575
3. Xu, X., et al.: Evolution of the novel coronavirus from the ongoing Wuhan outbreak and modeling of its spike protein for risk of human transmission. Sci. China Life Sci. **63**(3), 457–460 (2020). https://doi.org/10.1007/s11427-020-1637-5
4. Wu, J., et al.: Clinical characteristics of imported cases of COVID-19 in Jiangsu Province: a multicenter descriptive study. Clin. Infect. Dis. 1–23 (2020). https://doi.org/10.1093/cid/ciaa199
5. Jiang, F., Deng, L., Zhang, L., Cai, Y., Cheung, C.W., Xia, Z.: Review of the clinical characteristics of coronavirus disease 2019 (COVID-19). J. Gen. Intern. Med. **35**(5), 1545–1549 (2020). https://doi.org/10.1007/s11606-020-05762-w
6. Fang, W., et al.: Sensitivity of chest CT for COVID-19: comparison to RT-PCR Yicheng. Radiology **200432**(1976), 1–30 (2020)
7. Young, B.E., et al.: Epidemiologic features and clinical course of patients infected with SARS-CoV-2 in Singapore. JAMA - J. Am. Med. Assoc. **323**(15), 1488–1494 (2020). https://doi.org/10.1001/jama.2020.3204

8. Yang, S., et al.: Early estimation of the case fatality rate of COVID-19 in mainland China: a data-driven analysis. Ann. Transl. Med. **8**(4), 128 (2020). https://doi.org/10.21037/atm.2020.02.66
9. Yas, Q.M., Mahdi, A.F., AL-Shamary, A.K.J., Radam, N.S.: A multi criteria analysis in ranking composite material using gray relational analysis: a case study. In: 2020 International Conference on Electrical, Communication, and Computer Engineering (ICECCE), pp. 1–7 (2020)
10. Majumder, P., Biswas, P., Majumder, S.: Application of new TOPSIS approach to identify the most significant risk factor and continuous monitoring of death of COVID-19. Electron. J. Gen. Med. **17**(6), 1–12 (2020). https://doi.org/10.29333/ejgm/7904
11. Yas, Q.M., Zadain, A.A., Zaidan, B.B., Lakulu, M.B., Rahmatullah, B.: Towards on develop a framework for the evaluation and benchmarking of skin detectors based on artificial intelligent models using multi-criteria decision-making techniques. Int. J. Pattern Recognit. Artif. Intell. **31**(3) (2017). https://doi.org/10.1142/S0218001417590029
12. Yas, Q.M., Zaidan, A.A., Zaidan, B.B., Hashim, M., Lim, C.K.: A systematic review on smartphone skin cancer apps: coherent taxonomy, motivations, open challenges and recommendations, and new research direction. J. Circuits, Syst. Comput. **27**(5) (2018). https://doi.org/10.1142/S0218126618300039
13. Saaty, T.L.: How to make a decision: the anyaltic hierarchy process. Eur. J. Oper. Res. **48**(1), 9–26 (1990). https://doi.org/10.1007/978-1-4419-6281-2_31
14. Yas, Q.M.: A new methodology for evaluation and benchmarking of skin detector based on ai model using multi criteria analysis (2018)
15. Yas, Q.M., Zaidan, A.A., Zaidan, B.B., Rahmatullah, B., Karim, H.A.: Comprehensive insights into evaluation and benchmarking of real-time skin detectors: review, open issues & challenges, and recommended solutions. Measurement **114**, 243–260 (2018). https://doi.org/10.1016/j.measurement.2017.09.027
16. Jumaah, F.M., Zaidan, A.A., Zaidan, B.B., Bahbibi, R., Qahtan, M.Y., Sali, A.: Technique for order performance by similarity to ideal solution for solving complex situations in multi-criteria optimization of the tracking channels of GPS baseband telecommunication receivers. Telecommun. Syst. 1–19 (2017). https://doi.org/10.1007/s11235-017-0401-5
17. Zaidan, A.A., Zaidan, B.B., Alsalem, M.A., Albahri, O.S., Albahri, A.S., Qahtan, M.Y.: Multi-agent learning neural network and Bayesian model for real-time IoT skin detectors: a new evaluation and benchmarking methodology. Neural Comput. Appl. **32**(12), 8315–8366 (2020)
18. Rodriguez-Morales, A.J., et al.: Clinical, laboratory and imaging features of COVID-19: a systematic review and meta-analysis. Travel Med. Infect. Dis. 101623 (2020). https://doi.org/10.1016/j.tmaid.2020.101623
19. Li, Q., et al.: Early transmission dynamics in Wuhan, China, of novel coronavirus-infected pneumonia. N. Engl. J. Med. **382**(13), 1199–1207 (2020). https://doi.org/10.1056/NEJMoa2001316
20. Xu, Z., et al.: Pathological findings of COVID-19 associated with acute respiratory distress syndrome. Lancet Respir. Med. **8**(4), 420–422 (2020). https://doi.org/10.1016/S2213-2600(20)30076-X
21. Chen, H., et al.: Clinical characteristics and intrauterine vertical transmission potential of COVID-19 infection in nine pregnant women: a retrospective review of medical records. Lancet **395**(10226), 809–815 (2020). https://doi.org/10.1016/S0140-6736(20)30360-3
22. Wu, Z., McGoogan, J.M.: Characteristics of and important lessons from the coronavirus disease 2019 (COVID-19) outbreak in china: summary of a report of 72314 cases from the chinese center for disease control and prevention. JAMA - J. Am. Med. Assoc. **323**(13), 1239–1242 (2020). https://doi.org/10.1001/jama.2020.2648

23. Zhang, W., et al.: The use of anti-inflammatory drugs in the treatment of people with severe coronavirus disease 2019 (COVID-19): The experience of clinical immunologists from China. Clin. Immunol. 108393 (2020). https://doi.org/10.1016/j.clim.2020.108393
24. Hendin, A., La Rivière, C.G., Williscroft, D.M., O'Connor, E., Hughes, J., Fischer, L.M.: End-of-life care in the emergency department for the patient imminently dying of a highly transmissible acute respiratory infection (such as COVID-19). CJEM 1–5 (2020). https://doi.org/10.1017/cem.2020.352
25. Naicker, S., Yang, C.W., Hwang, S.J., Liu, B.C., Chen, J.H., Jha, V.: The novel coronavirus 2019 epidemic and kidneys. Kidney Int. **97**(5), 824–828 (2020). https://doi.org/10.1016/j.kint.2020.03.001
26. Hu, Z., et al.: Clinical characteristics of 24 asymptomatic infections with COVID-19 screened among close contacts in Nanjing, China. Sci. China Life Sci. **63**(5), 706–711 (2020). https://doi.org/10.1007/s11427-020-1661-4
27. Ahorsu, D.K., Lin, C.Y., Imani, V., Saffari, M., Griffiths, M. D., Pakpour, A.H.: The fear of COVID-19 scale: development and initial validation. Int. J. Ment. Health Addict. 1–9 (2020). https://doi.org/10.1007/s11469-020-00270-8
28. Soetikno, R., et al.: Considerations in performing endoscopy during the COVID-19 pandemic. Gastrointest. Endosc. 1–25 (2020). https://doi.org/10.1016/j.gie.2020.03.3758
29. Moghbelli, H., et al.: Comparative genomic analysis revealed specific mutation pattern between human coronavirus SARS-CoV-2 and Bat-SARSr-CoV RaTG13. Block Caving – Viable Altern. **21**(1), 1–9 (2020). https://doi.org/10.1016/j.solener.2019.02.027
30. Liu, W., Li, H.: COVID-19: attacks the 1-beta chain of hemoglobin and captures the porphyrin to inhibit human heme metabolism. ChemRxiv, no. 1, p. 31 (2020). https://doi.org/10.26434/chemrxiv.11938173.v6
31. Chen, Z., et al.: Efficacy of hydroxychloroquine in patients with COVID-19: results of a randomized clinical trial. medRxiv, vol. 7, pp. 1–11 (2020). https://doi.org/10.1101/2020.03.22.20040758
32. Li, X., Geng, M., Peng, Y., Meng, L., Lu, S.: Molecular immune pathogenesis and diagnosis of COVID-19. J. Pharm. Anal. **10**(2), 102–108 (2020). https://doi.org/10.1016/j.jpha.2020.03.001
33. Nikam, R.M., Kapadnis, K.H., Borse, R.Y.: A survey on epidemic growth of corona virus-Covid-19 in global world: issues, concern and possible remedial parameters. Int. J. Res. Appl. Sci. Eng. Technol. **8**(3), 938–941 (2020)
34. De Paepe, A.E., et al.: Family cluster of middle east respiratory syndrome coronavirus infections, Tunisia, 2013. J. Chem. Inf. Model. **53**(9), 1689–1699 (2014). https://doi.org/10.1017/CBO9781107415324.004
35. Kim, I., Lee, J., Lee, J., Shin, E., Chu, C., Lee, S.K.: KCDC risk assessments on the initial phase of the COViD-19 outbreak in Korea. Osong Public Heal. Res. Perspect. **11**(2), 67–73 (2020). https://doi.org/10.24171/j.phrp.2020.11.2.02
36. Rasmussen, S.A., Smulian, J.C., Lednicky, J.A., Wen, T.S., Jamieson, D.J.: Coronavirus disease 2019 (COVID-19) and pregnancy: what obstetricians need to know. Am. J. Obstet. Gynecol. **222**(5), 415–426 (2020). https://doi.org/10.1016/j.ajog.2020.02.017
37. Wang, D., et al.: Clinical characteristics of 138 hospitalized patients with 2019 novel coronavirus-infected pneumonia in Wuhan, China. JAMA - J. Am. Med. Assoc. **323**(11), 1061–1069 (2020). https://doi.org/10.1001/jama.2020.1585
38. Rothan, H.A., Byrareddy, S.N.: The epidemiology and pathogenesis of coronavirus disease (COVID-19) outbreak. J. Autoimmun. **109**(February), 102433 (2020). https://doi.org/10.1016/j.jaut.2020.102433
39. Yang, W., et al.: Clinical characteristics and imaging manifestations of the 2019 novel coronavirus disease (COVID-19): a multi-center study in Wenzhou city, Zhejiang, China. J. Infect. **80**(4), 388–393 (2020). https://doi.org/10.1016/j.jinf.2020.02.016

40. Heymann, D.L., Shindo, N.: COVID-19: what is next for public health? Lancet **395**(10224), 542–545 (2020). https://doi.org/10.1016/S0140-6736(20)30374-3
41. Zhou, F., et al.: Clinical course and risk factors for mortality of adult inpatients with COVID-19 in Wuhan, China: a retrospective cohort study. Lancet **395**(10229), 1054–1062 (2020). https://doi.org/10.1016/S0140-6736(20)30566-3
42. Pan, F., et al.: Time course of lung changes on chest CT during recovery from 2019 novel coronavirus (COVID-19) pneumonia. Radiology 200370 (2020). https://doi.org/10.1148/radiol.2020200370
43. Saaty, T.L., Ozdemir, M.S.: Why the magic number seven plus or minus two. Math. Comput. Model. **38**(3–4), 233–244 (2003). https://doi.org/10.1016/S0895-7177(03)90083-5
44. Saaty, T.L., Vargas, L.G.: Inconsistency and rank preservation. J. Math. Psychol. **28**(2), 205–214 (1984). https://doi.org/10.1016/0022-2496(84)90027-0
45. Al-Azab, F.G.M., Ayu, M.A.: Web based multi criteria decision making using AHP method. In: Proceeding of the 3rd International Conference on Information and Communication Technology for the Moslem World: ICT Connecting Cultures, ICT4M 2010, pp. 1–6 (2010). https://doi.org/10.1109/ICT4M.2010.5971886

Brain Tumours Classification Using Support Vector Machines Based on Feature Selection by Binary Cat Swarm Optimization

Wid Ali Hassan(✉), Yossra Hussain Ali, and Nuha Jameel Ibrahim

Department of Computer Science, University of Technology, Baghdad, Iraq
cs.19.74@grad.uotechnology.edu.iq, {110017, 110009}@uotechnology.edu.iq

Abstract. Magnetic resonance imaging (MRI) is one of main imaging modalities which has become extremely important in the diagnosis of brain tumors in real life also it has a major role in suggested computer systems for classification and segmentation of tumors due to the advancements in computer science and information technology. Researchers all over the world have worked hard to develop methods for diagnosing and classifying brain tumors. This paper presents an intelligent segmentation and classification approach worked on brain MR images to support doctors in diagnosis processes. However, the approach will consist of 4 phases. Pre-processing will be performed to enhance the MRI image, followed by Binary thresholding combined with Morphology operation to perform segmentation, followed by feature extraction fusion consisting of Local Binary Pattern (LBP), Gray Level Co-Occurrence Matrix Occurrence Matrix (GLCM), and Connected Regions. Modified Binary Cat Swarm Optimization (BCSO) combined with Support Vector Machine (SVM) is employed to perform feature selection and classification. The module provides the desired accuracy, which is better than SVM alone and artificial fish swarm. The achieved result shows the feasibility of employing a binary cat swarm to resolve the optimization problem of the extracted features.

Keywords: Brain tumor · Magnetic resonance imaging (MRI) · Binary cat swarm optimization (BCSO) · Segmentation · Medical image classification and Support vector machine (SVM)

1 Introduction

Gliomas are considered as the common type of brain tumor which can be partitioned into four grades based on the WHO system, where a benign tumor has a place with grade I and grade II and a malignant tumor has a place with grade III and grade IV [1].

Medical imaging systems have several types of modalities that are used to identify tumors. This paper is working on Magnetic Resonance Image (MRI) but there are many other modalities, such as Computed Tomography (CT) and Positron Emission Tomography (PET) [6].

P. Liatsis et al. (Eds.): TIOTC 2021, CCIS 1548, pp. 108–121, 2022.
https://doi.org/10.1007/978-3-030-97255-4_8

MRI is the most used in classifying and evaluating tumors because of its high resolution. There are various types of MRI scans, which are T1 contrast enhancement images, because of the contrast concentration in the vessels of the brain region, the edges of the tumor region look sharper. Active and necrotic tumor regions may be more readily identified in these images, meanwhile the edema area looks brighter in T2. To distinguish the edema region from the CSF, flair is used [1, 3].

Classification is a learning processes which can be worked with supervision or unsupervision based on one of machine learning algorithms. The input data will be used to train the classifier by extracting its features which are often coming with redundant or irrelevant features due to this absolute fact, we need to apply one of the metaheuristic search algorithms to get rid of the unnecessary features and select the necessary one. The process of selecting and finding the optimal subset of feature that are essential to a given task, decreasing computing time and enhance the classification accuracy.

Metaheuristic algorithms merge random search functions that are inspired by natural processes, such as particle swarm optimization (PSO), based on birds' behaviors simulation and genetic algorithms (GA), reflects the process of inherited from parents to children and gene mutation [2, 4].

In this study, we presented binary Cat swarm optimization (CSO) as a feature selection and optimization conjunction with linear SVM as a classifier. Binary Cat swarm optimization (CSO) is a new version of the original Cat swarm optimization which was initially invented by Chu et al. in 2006, inspired by the actions of cats, which has a new simulation methodology for discovery and exploitation phases. In this algorithm, the swarm of cats is divided into two groups, each group operating its selected mode either seeking or tracing wherein the seeking represents the cats' behavior at rest meanwhile the tracing mode emulates the tracking and capturing their targeted food [5]. Our main contribution in this paper is given below:

1- Initially, we employ preprocessing technique for tumor using one of Adaptive Histogram Equalization (AHE) techniques, which is responsible for increasing the contrast of MRI image that leads to the enhancement of the classification accuracy.
2- Employ a fast and non-complex processing method for segmentation, such as binary thresholding and morphologies operations, to define the region of interest based on studied medical knowledge, leading to shorter overall segmentation time when compared with conventional segmentation algorithms.
3- The typical feature selection algorithms have limitations; this research proposes a modification on binary Cat swarm optimization in conjunction with a support vector machine for feature selection and classification.

The paper's results in the experimental section of this have demonstrated that MBCSO-SVM is better than SVM and AFSO in classification accuracy.

The remaining sections are arranged as follows: Sect. 2 shows the related works and Sect. 3 show the proposed system description in detail. Section 4 describes the experimental results that are obtained when applying the proposed system on MRI slides images. Finally, in Sect. 5 we provide our conclusions and future work.

2 Related Works

Applying artificial intelligence for medical data whether it is clinical data or medical images has been an interesting area for many researchers, despite many researchers had suggested approaches for tumor classification and segmentation. This research field remains one of the top hot fields because of the lack of accuracy in diagnosis.

However, many researchers have employed classical machine learning algorithms for classification, such as Artificial Neural Network (ANN), Support Vector Machine (SVM). etc.

In 2019, J. Amin et al. [1] have proposed an entropy-based feature selection, followed by a brain tumor multi-classifier.

In 2019, B. Tahir et al. [7] have proposed a segmentation and classification framework for flair MRI sequence based on Otsu method thresholding of pixels.

In 2017, H. Dong et al. [8] have proposed an automatic segmentation and classification module using U-Net Based Fully Convolutional Network.

In 2006, C. J. Tu et al. [9] have proposed a hybrid method of PSO with SVM for feature selection.

In 2014, K.-C. Lin et al. [10] have proposed a modified Cat swarm optimization for feature selection followed by SVM as classifier.

3 The Propose System

The following subsections discuss the proposed system steps briefly as illustrated in Fig. 1.

3.1 Data Set

For experimental evaluation, we used the Brain Tumor Segmentation Challenge (BRATS) dataset; BRATS is freely accessible to researchers. BRATS is an MRI data coming in MHA format, containing 320 MRI greyscale images, each of 240×240 pixels and have four sequences with names T1, T1-contrast, T2 and FLAIR, consist of two classes (high-grade gliomas HGG and low-grade gliomas LGG) where 200 images are identified as LGG and 120 as HGG according to WHO [11], however, this experimental evaluation has been done by T2 sequence.

3.2 Preprocessing

Since the MRI images come with a special medical image format called MHA, which is commonly used in medicine graphic visualization applications, such as a toolkit. We needed to write a piece of code to transform them to image. Since MRI images usually have suffered from low contrast because of used equipment or the process of scans, in this paper Adaptive Histogram Equalization (AHE) had been applied as a preprocessing technique to enhance the contrast of images which will positively affect the quality of an image [6].

3.3 Segmentation

Thresholding is the simplest technique of image segmentation, where image is partitioned into regions dependent on intensity values of one or more thresholds. Based on the analysis of image intensity, we selected a specific threshold value *TH*, 1 is assigned when the pixels are above threshold and 0 is assigned to those which are shown below; it is given by the following equation [12]:

$$g(x, y) = \begin{cases} 1 \; if \; (x, y) \geq TH \\ 0 \; otherwise \end{cases} \tag{1}$$

In our case we applied binary thresholding as main process to segment the brain image followed by morphological operations to fine tune the segmentation processing and to remove unwanted small regions and points by generating a small matrix of binary pixels called a structural element, which will test all locations on the image by comparing the corresponding pixel with the neighborhood. This paper applied the Dilation and Erosion morphological operations.

Dilation is defined as a procedure of fixed steps that can be applied to both binary and grayscale images. Dilation produces artifacts by extending the limits that would make the tiny gaps much smaller in the regions that are starting to expand, M is dilated by N, written as M ⊕ N, as explained in the following equation:

$$M \oplus N = \{z|(N)z\cap \neq \varnothing\} \tag{2}$$

Erosion is like dilation, applying a procedure of fixed steps that can be applied to both binary and grayscale images working on the boundaries of structures where the size of the pixels is decreased by the effect of this process and the size of the holes continues to expand. M is eroded by N, written as M ⊖ N, defined in the following equation [13]:

$$M!N = \left\{z|(N)z \cap M^C \neq \varnothing\right\} \tag{3}$$

The segmentation steps described above have been represented in Fig. 2 using four samples from the data set, and Fig. 3 shows the final results of segmentation.

3.4 Feature Extraction

Feature extraction is an important step in any brain tumor classification scheme, this proposed system used texture, shape and intensity features when extracted feature vector. The texture features and intensity features are generated by GLCM and LBP and shape features are extracted using connected regions. Despite of being time consuming, the key benefit of using GLCMs is that it shows spatial information and occurrence details in another word, GLCM can track based on a given direction which can affect positively on feature vector because tumors may have textural characteristics in a particular direction. Meanwhile, different patterns of glioma may be recognized by the power of LBP, by extracting LBPs of neighbor pixels in order to describe local image texture spatial structure. Since the shape characteristics vary for different tumor types, extracted information of shape depending on connected regions in the image may provide powerful

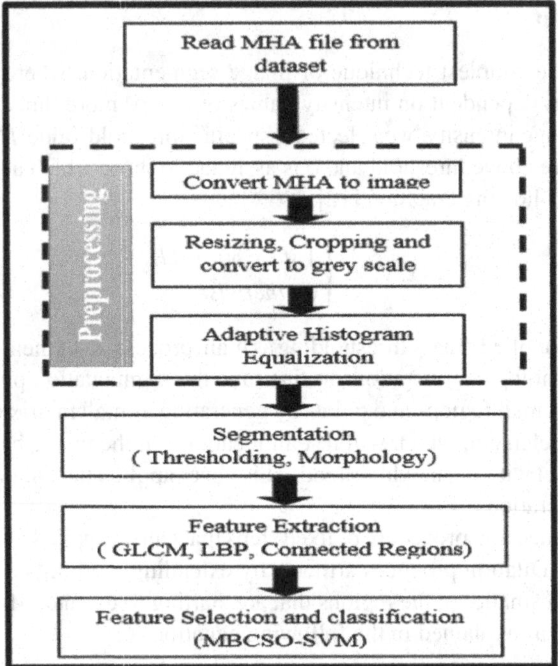

Fig. 1. Flow diagram explaining the proposed system.

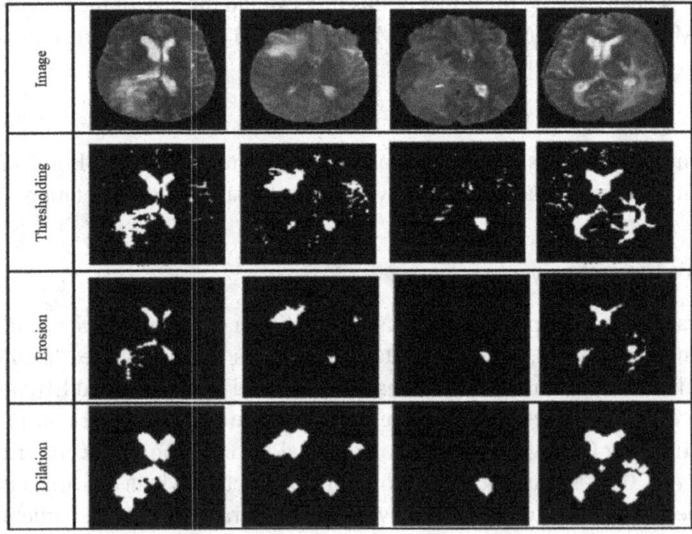

Fig. 2. Showing segmentation steps result for four image samples.

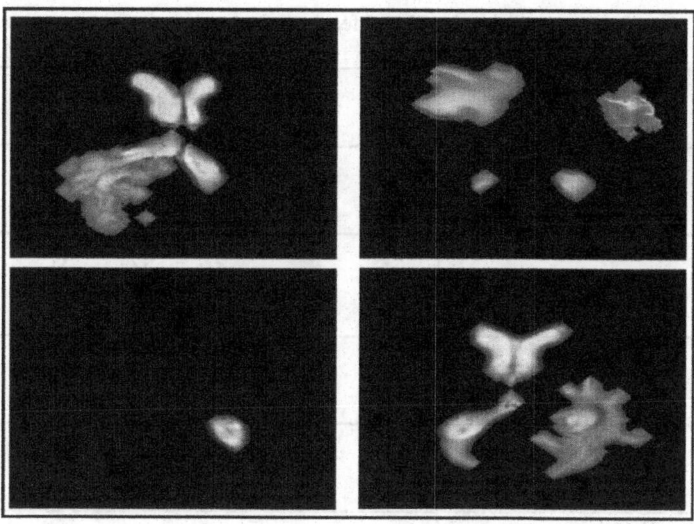

Fig. 3. Segmentation final result.

information for image classification. Based on these facts, the fusion of GLCMs, LBP, connected regions are applied to differentiate between tumors classes. The most popular 9 GLCM features are used in this work, as shown in the following table (Table 1):

We calculated Area, Perimeter and Circularity which are the main shape features by using the mythology of connected regions; the shape is defined as a binary representation of the object's scope in another word it refers to an object's geometrical features where these features are measured using the external boundary. The formulas used to calculate shape features are given in following table (Table 2):

As shown in Table 2, perimeter and area are calculated using boundary pixels, meanwhile, circularity is calculated based on area and perimeter, LBP have two parameters, the number of neighborhood pixel is assigned to parameters called P and a radius is assigned to parameters R. In this paper, the parameters are assigned as the following P = 8 and R = 1, as in the following equation:

$$LBP_{nR}^{riu2} = \begin{cases} \Sigma_{i=0}^{p-1} s(x_i - x_C) & \textit{if pattern is uniform} \\ p_{+}1 & \textit{if pattern is nonuniform} \end{cases} \tag{4}$$

After generating the LBP descriptor and from the histogram of the image, six features are extracted, the formulas used to calculate these features are given in the following table, (Table 3) [15]:

The final feature vector length that has been generated from this feature fusion is 19, as shown in Fig. 4.

Table 1. GLCM features' formula

Feature Name	Formula
Contrast	$\sum_{1;j=0}^{n-1} P_{i,j}(\mathrm{i}-j)^2$
Correlation	$\sum_{i,j=0}^{n-1} p_{i,j}\left[\frac{(\mathrm{i}-\mu_i)(j-\mu_j)}{\sqrt{(\sigma_i^2)(\sigma_i^2)}}\right]$
Dissimilarity	$\sum_{1;j=0}^{n-1} P_{i,j}\lvert i-j\rvert$
Energy	$\sum_{1;j=0}^{n-1} P_{i,j}^2$
Entropy	$\sum_{1;j=0}^{n-1} P_{i,j}(-\ln P_{i,j})$
Homogeneity	$\sum_{1;j=0} \frac{p_{i,j}}{1+(\mathrm{i}-j)^2}$
Mean	$\mu_i = \sum_{i,j=0} i\,(\rho_{i,j})\ , \mu_j = \sum_{i,j=0} j\,(\rho_{i,j})$
Variance	$\sigma i^2 = \sum_{1,j=0}^{n-1} \quad p_{i,j}(\mathrm{i}-\mu_i)^2,$ $\sigma j^2 = \sum_{i,j=0}^{n-1} \quad p_{i,j}(j-\mu_j)^2$
Standard Deviation	$\sigma_i = \sqrt{\sigma_i^2}\ , \sigma_j = \sqrt{\sigma_j^2}$

Table 2. Shape features' formula

Feature Name	Formula
Perimeter	$\sum_{i,j=0}^{MN} E_d(i,j)$
Area	$\sum_{i,j=0}^{m,n} b(i,j)$
Circularity	$\frac{4\pi A}{p^2}$

Table 3. LBP features' formula

Feature Name	Formula
Skewness	$s_s = \frac{1}{\sigma_b^3}\sum_{b=0}^{G-1}\left(b-\bar{b}\right)^3 P(b)$
Kurtosis	$s_k = \left[\frac{1}{\sigma_b^4}\sum_{b=0}^{G-1}\left(b-\bar{b}\right)^4 P(b)\right] - 3$
Energy	$s_N = \sum_{b=0}^{G-1}[P(b)]^2$
Entropy	$s_E = \sum_{b=0}^{G-1} P(b)\log_2\{P(b)\}$
Median	$Med(x) = \begin{cases} x\left[\frac{n}{2}\right] & \text{if } n \text{ is even} \\ \frac{\left(x\left[\frac{n-1}{2}\right]+x\left[\frac{n+1}{2}\right]\right)}{2} & \text{if } n \text{ is odd} \end{cases}$

Feature Name	Sample A	Sample B	Sample C	Sample D
lbp_energy	0.288024704	0.294499039	0.248874965	0.274275099
lbp_entropy	2.225701017	2.211394627	2.3591166	2.285768381
lbp_median	6	6	5	5
skewness x	-0.012469472	-0.05382709	0.007142933	-0.020208858
skewness y	0.02759486	0.029088306	-0.018967801	0.02088448
Kurtosis x	1.633251711	1.638935799	1.6604582	1.660222805
Kurtosis y	1.673052298	1.676416586	1.666088962	1.656573814
Contrast	246.7627101	210.2108894	243.082528	410.4259104
Correlation	0.967569951	0.96525995	0.965206073	0.949962914
Dissimilarity	6.402836134	6.078886555	6.696253501	9.480742297
Energy	0.407644105	0.415457182	0.340807009	0.381322398
Entropy	1.306075688	1.276948137	1.345325405	1.614254809
Homogeneity	0.505698816	0.51237407	0.455032167	0.458725569
Mean	1.52588E-05	1.52588E-05	1.52588E-05	1.52588E-05
Variance	2.53538E-06	2.63351E-06	1.77207E-06	2.2185E-06
STD	0.001592287	0.001622808	0.00133119	0.001489462
Perimeter	325.8528137	292.2609307	359.5807358	335.7817459
Area	33376	32946	37194	34883
Circularity	3.950037328	4.84697782	3.614846974	3.887850227

Fig. 4. Feature vector samples.

3.5 Feature Selection and Classification

3.5.1 Binary Cat Swarm Optimization (BCSO)

In 2013, Y. Sharaf et al. [5] had developed a binary Cat swarm optimization (BCSO) as a newly developed algorithm from continuous algorithm simulating the Cat behavior. The major differences in the new version are in position vector which consists of one and zero. This change causes some important variations between the CSO and the BCSO. In this algorithm, the swarm of cats is divided into two groups, each group operating its selected mode either seeking or tracing, wherein the seeking represents the cats' behavior at rest meanwhile, the tracing mode emulates the tracking and capturing of their targeted food. This algorithm is operated to solve optimization problems.

In BCSO, each cat in the population has a location which represents a possible solution set, velocity which is a distance difference in a specific dimensional space, the accuracy of generated solution set was treated as fitness value. BCSO randomly distributes cat's generation into two modes (seeking mode and tracing mode), optimal solution set is finally demonstrated by the location of the cat with the highest classification accuracy.

However, below a list of the essential factors playing a major role (as will be explained in each mode) in CSO algorithm:

- **SMP** determines the value of the seeking thread pool.
- **CDC** refers to the counts of dimensions considered to shift.
- **SPC** Self-position considering flag.
- **MR** is a mixture ratio.
- **C1** is a constant value defined by the user.
- **W** is the weight.
- **Vmax** is the maximum velocity that should be reached.
- **SRD** refers to the dimension is selected to mutate.
- **PMO** refers to mutation operation Probability.

A. **Seeking Mode**

This mode is a simulation of the action of the cat in the resting mode where all chosen cats make minor change in their current location. Like CSO, BCSO seeking Mode have four parameters except SRD which replaces by mutation operation (PMO), the 5 steps of seeking mode are as follows:

Step 1: If SPC is set to True, make SMP-1 copies the catK and keeping the original position as one of candidates, otherwise make SMP copies the catK.
Step 2: The major difference in the BCSO seeking mode from the original CSO is in this step, where for each of the SMP copies, pick as many CDC dimensions as possible and randomly change these CDC dimensions according to the PMO.
Step 3: By using the cost function, calculate the fitness values (FS) of all cats.
Step 4: If the fitness values of all cats are the same, give same probability value to all cats, otherwise calculate the probability of cat according to the following equation:

$$P_i = \frac{FS_i - FS_b}{FS\ max - FS\ min} \tag{5}$$

Step 5: Use roulette wheel to replace the current position with the selected cat.

B. **Tracing Mode**

The biggest difference between the original CSO and the developed version (BCSO) is the velocity concept. Velocity in CSO means the difference between the existing and the past location, but in BCSO it means the probability of mutations in each cat direction. Algorithm:

1- Create swarm of cats.
2- Initialize the cat positions randomly with values 1 or 0.
3- Initialize the necessary parameters for each cat.
4- Evaluate each cat by the fitness function.
5- keep the needed information of the cat that has the best fitness in global best cat (Gbest).
6- Separate the swarm to perform one of their modes based on the MR flag value.
7- check the termination condition; if satisfied, terminate the program, and otherwise repeat since step (4).

3.5.2 Support Vector Machine (SVM)

SVM was introduced in 1995 by Vapnik [16]; SVM is a supervised learning method that have been widely used for solving regression and classification problems. The principles behind SVM working are Vapnik-Chervonenkis (VC) dimension and structural risk minimization theory [16, 20]. The fundamental concept of SVM method is the establishment of an ideal hyperplane for the isolation of data from various classes. Although there may be a number of hyperplanes, only one can optimize the distance between classes.

Every classification method has its benefits and drawbacks, so what is making SVM suitable for this task?

- SVM is a classical method that is well-suitable for binary classification tasks.
- SVMs is very useful in information evaluation in case of non-regularity in the data or the data have an unknown distribution.
- according to the large number of dimensions in the features vector, SVM would be the better choice since the main goal of SVM is to find the optimal hyperplane for an N-dimensional feature space, which assists in the accurate separation of associated data into various classes.
- Ease of use and even with minimal training sets, the classification accuracy is high.

This research uses the linear SVM [17] with linear kernel. The SVM takes data (feature vector) as input and builds a classifier based on it.

3.5.3 The proposed MBCSO-SVM

In this paper, we developed a modified binary Cat swarm optimization method (MBCSO) to improve searching ability of BCSO; however, we kept each of seeking and tracing mode with no change but we examined a new way to evaluate fitness by employing SVM with linear kernel to evaluate the set of selected features by each cat. The steps of the proposed MBCSO-SVM are presented as follows:

1- Select N number of cats and set the necessary parameters.
2- By using SVM, calculate the fitness of every cat.
3- Based on MR value, assign each cat to one mode.
4- Perform the operations of assigned mode.
5- Find the best cat.
6- Stop and produce the best cat if the terminal conditions are met, otherwise, return to (3).

4 Experimental Result

In this paper, BRATS 2015 dataset was employed to measure the efficiency of the proposed classification method. However, the experiment was done by Python programming language with a personal laptop, which is considered as low level of specifications and that may increase the processing time. To find the optimal configuration, we have retried the experiment many times with different parameters. Table 4 lists the optimal parameter (the definition of all parameters is described previously in BCSO) values that we defined in our swarm.

Table 4. MBCSO parameters.

SMP	CDC	SPC	MR	c1	w	Vmax	SRD	PMO
5	8	True	2	2	0.9	100	2	0.8

The condition of the termination was determined as "achieving the same value of the accuracy of the classification despite the continuous adjustment of the solution set used in the classification for the specific number of iterations."

We tried 4-fold cross-validation to ensure the reliability of the experiment. The verification of all values was repeated four times, also we used 80% of samples within each class for training to avoid over fitting during training process, where in each iteration, the dataset was separated into 4 segments (one for test and the others were used as training). Table 5 and Table 6 show the accuracy archived by different experiments on BRATS 2015 and BRATS 2013, where the experiment was repeated five times with changing the number of cats in the swarm from two to six each time, i.e., use two cats in the swarm in the first experiment, three cats are used in second experiment… etc.

Tables 5 and 6 shows the number of cats set in each experiment (as input), number of selected features (Nf) that result from this experiment which led to this classification accuracy (Ac) (as output).

The results of experimental assessment revealed that there is an inverse relationship between the number of cats in the swarm and the number of features selected, where the number of selected features declines as the number of cats increases.

Table 5. Accuracy achieved using different numbers of cats on BRATS 2015.

Number of cats in swarm (Nc)	2	***3***	4	5	***6***
Number of selected features (Nf)	13	***11***	11	8	***7***
Classification accuracy (Ac)	96.3	***98.1***	98.1	96.3	***98.1***

Table 6. Accuracy achieved using different numbers of cats on BRATS 2013.

Number of cats in swarm (Nc)	2	***3***	4	5	***6***
Number of selected features (Nf)	11	***9***	9	8	***6***
Classification accuracy (Ac)	92.3	***94***	94.1	91.7	***94***

In BRATS 2015, the best accuracy achieved with MBCSO-SVM is 98.1% when Nc = 3 with features vector's length of 11, meanwhile we achieved same accuracy of 98.1% by using double number of cats Nc = 6, where the length of features vector is 7. We found the same scenario when we test the proposed method with BRATS 2013.

Table 7 shows the results obtained when we applied Fish swarm optimization (FSA) in conjunction with linear SVM to compare the efficiency with the proposed MBCSO-SVM. Table 8 shows the parameter values that were used in FSA.

The proposed method satisfies the desired accuracy from the classification process and taking into account fewer selected features in comparison with FSA-SVM.

Table 7. Accuracy achieved using different method comparing with the proposed method.

Data Set	No of Classes	No of Generated Features	Group 1 No Feature Selection - SVM		Group 2 Feature Selection (FSA) - SVM		Group 3 Proposed Method	
			No of Features	Accuracy	No of Features	Accuracy	No of Features	Accuracy
Barts 2013	2	20	20	81%	10	80%	*6*	***94%***
Brats 2015	2	20	20	89%	8	89%	*7*	***98%***

Table 8. FSA parameters.

Try times	Visual	step	crowd
3	0.2	0.3	5

Table 9 shows the comparison between the existing systems and proposed method, where in 2017, R. Mathew A and Dr. B. Anto P [18] had proposed an SVM classifier on BRATS 2015 and has achieved 86% accuracy and in 2018, A. Selvapandian and K. Manivannan [19] proposed a classification method that achieved 86% accuracy on BRATS. Meanwhile in 2019, J. Amin et al. [1] achieved a 93% accuracy.

Table 9. Comparison between proposed and previous techniques.

Ref	Year	Feature extraction method	Classifiers	Accuracy
[19]	2017	Discrete wavelet transforms	SVM	86%
[20]	2018	GLCM	ANFIS classification	86%
[1]	2019	HOG, LBP and SFTA	Multiple classification method	93%
Proposed	**2021**	**LBP, GLCM and Connected Regions**	**SVM**	***98%***

5 Conclusion

This paper presented a new hybrid method for brain tumor segmentation and classification by using MRI modalities to identify Glioma tumors according to their grade (HGG and LGG). By employing Adaptive Histogram Equalization (AHE) for image contrast enhancement, a unified approach for MRI image contrast enhancement was provided. Additionally, a completely automated segmentation approach based on thresholding and morphological operations has been developed, which offers both fast and accurate segmentation for the whole tumor region when compared to the manually determined ground truth. Then, a novel fully automatic method for brain tumor classification has been developed by using the discrete binary cat swarm algorithm in combination with a support vector machine. We used a binary-coded algorithm to manage the encoding of the selection of features. Experiments were conducted on the Brats-2015 dataset reveal that MBCSO-SVM is one of the best approaches in solving optimization problems in terms of iterations and accuracy. Also, it is superior to AFSA in the number of selected features and classification accuracy. For future work, a private dataset should be used to validate the proposed framework also BCSO has a wide space for development; for example, random tracing technique and finding a way to dynamically set all of the parameters and applying the CSO method to the continuum optimization problem.

References

1. Amin, J., Saba, T., Sharif, M.: Brain tumor classification: feature fusion. In: 2019 International Conference on Computer and Information Sciences. Published online, pp. 1–6 (2019)
2. Lin, K.-C., Chen, S.-Y., Hung, J.C.: Feature selection for support vector machines base on modified artificial fish swarm algorithm. In: Park, J.J.H., Pan, Y., Chao, H.-C., Yi, G. (eds.) Ubiquitous Computing Application and Wireless Sensor. LNEE, vol. 331, pp. 297–304. Springer, Dordrecht (2015). https://doi.org/10.1007/978-94-017-9618-7_28
3. Gupta, N., Bhatele, P., Khanna, P.: Glioma detection on brain MRIs using texture and morphological features with ensemble learning. Biomed Signal Process Control. **47**, 115–125 (2019). https://doi.org/10.1016/j.bspc.2018.06.003
4. Lin, K.C., Huang, Y.H., Hung, J.C., Lin, Y.T.: Feature selection and parameter optimization of support vector machines based on modified cat swarm optimization. Int. J. Distrib. Sens. Netw. **11**, 365869 (2015). https://doi.org/10.1155/2015/365869
5. Sharafi, Y., Khanesar, M.A., Teshnehlab, M.: Discrete binary cat swarm optimization algorithm. In: 2013 3rd IEEE International conference on computer, control and communication IC4 2013, 2013, May 2014. https://doi.org/10.1109/IC4.2013.6653754

6. Sameer, M.A.: Automatic Brain Tumor Segmentation and Classification Based on Convolutional Neural Networks (2020). https://ieeexplore.ieee.org/xpl/conhome/9253044/proceeding
7. Tahir, B., et al.: Feature enhancement framework for brain tumor segmentation and classification. Microsc. Res. Tech. **82**(6), 803–811 (2019). https://doi.org/10.1002/jemt.23224
8. Dong, H., Yang, G., Liu, F., Mo, Y., Guo, Y.: Automatic brain tumor detection and segmentation using U-Net based fully convolutional networks. In: Valdés Hernández, M., González-Castro, V. (eds.) MIUA 2017. CCIS, vol. 723, pp. 506–517. Springer, Cham (2017). https://doi.org/10.1007/978-3-319-60964-5_44
9. Tu, C.J., Chuang, L.-Y., Chang, J.-Y., Yang, C.-H.: Feature selection using PSO-SVM. In: Proceedings of the International Multiconference of Engineers and Computer Scientists (IMECS 2006), pp. 138–143 (2006)
10. Lin, K.-C., Huang, Y.-H., Hung, J.C., Lin, Y.-T.: Modified cat swarm optimization algorithm for feature selection of support vector machines. In: Park, J.J.(H., Zomaya, A., Jeong, H.-Y., Obaidat, M. (eds.) Frontier and Innovation in Future Computing and Communications. LNEE, vol. 301, pp. 329–336. Springer, Dordrecht (2014). https://doi.org/10.1007/978-94-017-8798-7_40
11. Menze, B.H., Jakab, A., Bauer, S., et al.: The Multimodal Brain Tumor Image Segmentation Benchmark (BRATS). IEEE Trans. Med. Imaging. **34**(10), 1993–2024 (2015). https://doi.org/10.1109/TMI.2014.2377694
12. Zhaowen, Y.: Brain Tumor Segmentation: A Comparative Analysis. Published online (2015)
13. Ilhan, U., Ilhan, A.: Brain tumor segmentation based on a new threshold approach. Procedia Comput Sci. **120**, 580–587 (2017). https://doi.org/10.1016/j.procs.2017.11.282
14. Shijin Kumar, P.S, Dharun V.S.: Extraction of texture features using GLCM and shape features using connected regions. Int. J. Eng. Technol. **8**(6), 2926–2930 (2016). https://doi.org/10.21817/ijet/2016/v8i6/160806254
15. Bhagat, P.K., Choudhary, P., Singh, K.M.: A comparative study for brain tumor detection in MRI images using texture features. Elsevier Inc. (2019). https://doi.org/10.1016/b978-0-12-819361-7.00013-0
16. Vapnik, V.N.: The Nature of Statistical LearningTheory. Springer, New York, NY, USA (1995)
17. Murty, M.N., Raghava, R.: Linear support vector machines. SpringerBriefs Computer Science, pp. 41–56. Springer, New York (2016). https://doi.org/10.1007/978-3-319-41063-0_4
18. Mathew, A.R., Anto, P.B.: Tumor detection and classification of MRI brain image using wavelet transform and SVM. In: Proceedings of IEEE International Conference on Signal Processing and Communication ICSPC 2017, 2018-January(July), pp. 75–78 (2018). https://doi.org/10.1109/CSPC.2017.8305810
19. Selvapandian, A., Manivannan, K.: Fusion based Glioma brain tumor detection and segmentation using ANFIS classification. Comput. Methods Programs Biomed. **166**, 33–38 (2018)
20. Cortes, C., Vapnik, V.: Support-vector networks. Mach. Learn. **20**(3), 273–297 (1995)

Early Depression Detection Using Electroencephalogram Signal

Hasnisha Ladeheng and Khairul Azami Sidek(✉)

Department of Electrical and Computer Engineering, Kulliyyah of Engineering, International Islamic University Malaysia, P.O. Box 10, 50728 Kuala Lumpur, Malaysia
azami@iium.edu.my

Abstract. Nowadays, depression has become such a widespread illness. It has been affecting people's health which can lead to suicide. Some studies relate depression with nervous system and some of them relate stress with the reduced brain activity within the left frontal lobe. Hence, an early depression detection system is an initiative to detect early depression. In this research, the detection of early depression was done using the EEG signal because the EEG signal is taken from our brain which has the cognitive ability. The cognitive skill is the best to explain and influence our emotions which results to certain actions and reactions. EEG is also widely used because it is non- invasive method as it does not require the skull to be punctured or anything to be inserted into the brain. To achieve the desired results, few steps were done which are data acquisition, pre-processing, feature extraction and classification. The results obtained show that there is a decrease in alpha waves and increase in beta waves of depressed patients. The accuracy rates for alpha and beta waves are comparable with the previous literatures.

Keywords: Depression · EEG · Alpha · Beta · Mindlink

1 Introduction

Depression is one of the most common medical illnesses that remain a burgeoning issue which affect humankind worldwide regardless of their age, gender, background, socioeconomic statuses and educational backgrounds. According to Oxford dictionary, depression is described as a mental disorder characterized by feelings of extreme despondency and dejection, usually with feelings of inadequacy and guilt, typically accompanied by loss of energy and appetite and difficulty to sleep [1]. Many previous researches have been performed to study and investigate depression using different techniques, methods and mechanisms. One of the previous studies found depression to be a disorder affecting a person as a whole and contributing to changes in feelings, perceptions, attitudes, brain and body. Depression has many potential causes. For example, it may be a reaction to an unusual or traumatic event that has a distressing effect on a person for a long time, such as traumas like witnessing criminal victimization, child abuse, intimate partner violence or repeated bullying [2].

P. Liatsis et al. (Eds.): TIOTC 2021, CCIS 1548, pp. 122–134, 2022.
https://doi.org/10.1007/978-3-030-97255-4_9

More than 300 million people worldwide suffer from depression, which is an increase of more than eighteen percent between 2005 and 2015. According to the World Health Organization (WHO) report, in 2020, depression will become the second-largest cause of illness that threatens human life [3]. In United States, diagnoses of depression rose by 33% between 2013 and 2016. Although women are statistically more than twice as likely as men to be diagnosed with depression, over the three-year period, both men and women experienced the same 33% increase [4]. Women experience more depression compared to man in the 3 years study. Depression is more prevalent in women because women tend to express more sensitivity compared to men.

Depression plays a role in more than one half of all suicide attempts. When depression goes deeper and control the body and mind, the pain of depression becomes unbearable. The chemical imbalance and extreme desperation will drive the brain to find ways to end the pain. That is when suicidal thought starts. Depressive disorders can affect thought in such a way that a person cannot think clearly or rationally. The disorder may cause hopelessness and helplessness thoughts which can lead to suicidal ideation. According to the 2017 National Health and Morbidity Study of Malaysia, there was a growing suicide trend among young people between the ages of 13 and 17, and about 10% had suicidal thoughts compared to 7.9% in 2012 [5]. Dealing with depression can be very isolating and it is very hard to handle it alone. Thus, an early depression detection system is proposed because there is a need to assist people with mental health problem to detect and recognize whether they have depression symptoms. Early detection can help a person to seek treatment and make changes to their life routines to help them manage their mental health.

Currently, the clinical detection of depression is mainly based on questionnaire and interview. However, the result from this method cannot be considered as accurate as people can give dishonest responses to the questionnaire and interview and lie about their mental condition. To provide solution to this problem, previous researchers developed depression detection methods using the brainwave signals to analyse the mental state of the person as the signal from our brain is something that cannot be forged. Human beings cannot control their biological and physiological signals as well as they control their mind. Hence, they cannot fake their mental condition.

There are many researchers that have been studying the detection of depression through several of methods such as using speech and text-based detection. However, researches have shown that detection of depression based on physiological signal is more accurate than other methods. This is because the approach is non-invasive, and it is easy to analyse the signal. There are three types of non-invasive methods using biomedical signal such as photoplethysmogram (PPG), electrocardiogram (ECG) and electroencephalogram (EEG). Thus, this research will concentrate on early depression detection using EEG signal because the EEG signal is taken from our brain which has the cognitive ability. The cognitive skill is the best to explain and influence our emotions which results to certain actions and reactions. Besides that, EEG also has a very high temporal resolution, on the order of milliseconds rather than seconds.

This paper is organized in 4 sections. In Sect. 2, the methodology of the research is discussed. Section 3 analyzes the experimental results. In Sect. 4, the work is concluded and future works are discussed.

2 Methodology

2.1 Data Acquisition

This study collects data from 10 participants aged between 21 to 60 years old (8 females and 2 males). The consent forms are given to each of them before the experiment was conducted. Initially, the participants were required to self- evaluate their mental conditions using the self-administered screening tool – PHQ-9. PHQ-9 is a case-finding instrument used in primary care clinic for depression screening. Based on the total scores obtained from the screening tool, the participants were categorized into four different group which are minimal, mild, moderate and moderately severe as shown in Table 1.

Table 1. Depression level classification for ten participants.

Level of depression	Participant
Minimal	3 and 5
Mild	2, 6, 8 and 9
Moderate	1, 4 and 10
Moderately severe	7

The experiment started with the participant asked to seat comfortably. Then, they were asked to open and close their eyes to ensure that the signals are captured at all electrode positions. All the participants were required to watch a short two minutes video while their EEG data being recorded by using the EEG acquisition device. The MindLink EEG collector device will be placed on the frontal scalp at Fp1, Fp2 and Fpz as shown in Fig. 1 because these positions are closely connected to emotions and are uncovered by hair, making the data collection much easier. This device applies Bluetooth to transmit the EEG data in range up to 10 m. This MindLink EEG collector device can be paired with Android, Windows, iOS and MAC OS devices.

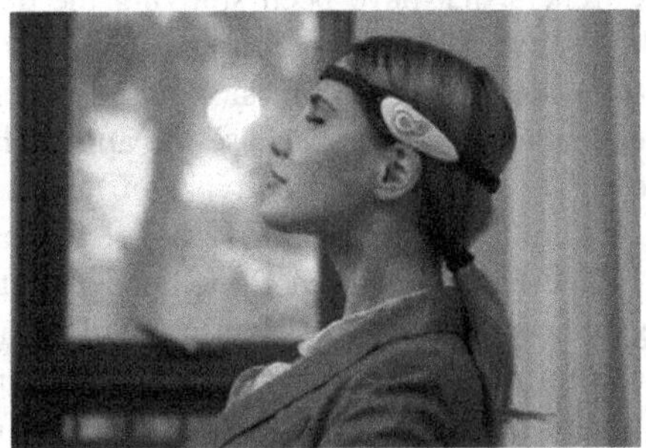

Fig. 1. The MindLink EEG collector device placement on the forehead [6].

EEG Recorder application as shown in Fig. 1 works with the MindLink EEG collector device. It captures all available signal values and stores them as comma delimited text

The data is recorded at one second intervals. This application can only be downloaded on iOS and MAC OS. Data obtained from the EEG Recorder application will be transferred to Microsoft Excel. The data will be processed in Matlab in the pre-processing stage.

2.2 Pre-processing

Pre-processing plays a vital role in the analysis of signals. Since EEG signals are the electrical signals that cerebral neurons emit during brain activity, the signals are very weak. In fact, because the electrode placements are close to the eyes, the electrical signals originating in the eye called electrooculographic signals are often interfering with the signals. In addition, skeletal muscle electrical activities and external electromagnetic radiation may also contaminate the resulting data. Hence, the rawdata must first be de-noised. In this pre-processing, Matlab software was used to filter the raw signals. The EEG signals were filtered using Butterworth filter with sampling frequency set to 256 Hz. The high pass Butterworth filter use cut off frequency of 0.3 Hz while the low pass Butterworth filter use cut off frequency of 56 Hz.

A high pass filtration design is intended to filter the DC component in the RC circuit. In the RC circuit, the more RC component, the stronger the high pass filtration low frequency. To minimize the impact of the voltage from the galvanic skin response across the head, the EEG use a high pass filter to attenuate frequencies below 5 Hz. A low pass filter is needed to reject noise at higher frequencies than the EEG signals.

2.3 Feature Extraction

Feature extraction from the data can help to enhance the accuracies of training and testing of the classifier. In this stage, feature selection was done to choose which brainwaves is the most appropriate to be used to detect early depression in the participants. Alpha and Beta waves were chosen since both waves are associated with mental activities.

Alpha waves, as shown in Fig. 2. are associated with a state of relaxation represent the brain shifting into an idling gear, waiting to respond when needed. If we close our eyes and begin picturing something peaceful, there is an increase in alpha brainwaves. However, when our alpha waves take a backseat, we will start to experience anxiety, insomnia, and depression. This shows that Alpha waves is a reliable feature that can be used to detect early depression. This statement can be supported since according to Hosseinifard et al., Alpha power has the highest accuracy in classifying depressed with healthy groups [7]. Besides that, Mantri et al. stated that Alpha band is reportedly responsible for identifying healthy people from patients with depression [8].

As for Beta waves, as shown in Fig. 3, they will be generated when the brain is aroused and actively involved in mental activities. In conscious thought and critical thinking, they are involved and appear to have a stimulating effect. Having the proper amount of Beta waves helps one to concentrate. Anxiety, high arousal, an inability to relax and stress are triggered by the prominence of this wave, while its suppression can contribute to daydreaming, depression and poor cognition. This proves that Beta waves is suitable to be used in detecting early depression in an individual. This can be supported since according to Cai et al., the absolute power of the Beta wave is a reliable feature that can be used to detect depression [9].

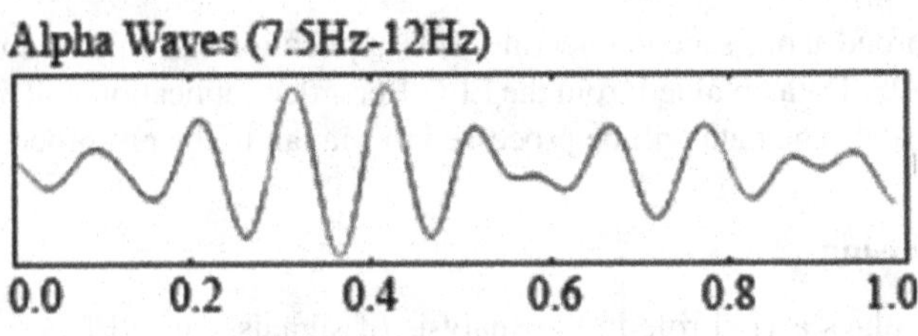

Fig. 2. Alpha waves pattern.

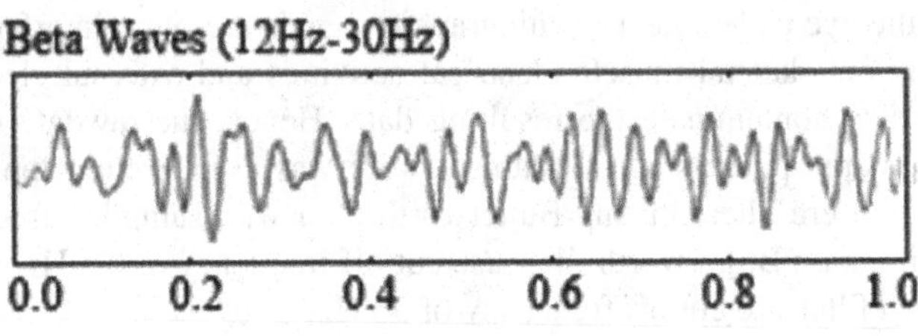

Fig. 3. Beta waves pattern.

2.4 Classification

Classification which is also called as decision making is the act of classifying something into a systematic arrangement in groups or categories, based explicitly on defined criteria. There are two ways of classifying data which are statistical and non- statistical approaches. This research will use statistical analysis in Time Domain and T- test method to classify the EEG signals.

2.4.1 Time Domain Analysis

Two parameters, which are mean amplitude and standard deviation were analysed in this stage. Mean amplitude was studied to determine how significant the difference in the mean amplitude of the alpha and beta waves measured to classify them into few categories. Standard Deviation is a measure of how spread out the data set is and commonly represent by the symbol 'σ'. A higher standard deviation indicates that the data is more dispersed. As shown in Eq. 1, it is mathematically defined as the square root of the variance.

$$\sigma = \sqrt{\frac{\sum |x - \mu|^2}{N}} \quad (1)$$

σ – standard deviation
Σ – summation
μ – mean of data set
N – number of data points in population.

2.4.2 T-Test Method

T-test was used to evaluate the significant differences in alpha and beta waves amplitude between the minimal and moderately severe categories of depression. The level of significant values for alpha and beta waves was set according to the accuracy rate achieved for that brainwave signals. The formula for T-test is shown in Eq. 2.

$$t = \frac{(\overline{x_1} - \overline{x})}{\sqrt{\frac{s_1{}^2}{n_1} - \frac{s_2{}^2}{n_2}}} \tag{2}$$

$\overline{x}1$ – observed mean of first sample
$\overline{x}2$ – observed mean of second sample
S1 – standard deviation of first sample
S2 – standard deviation of second sample
n1 – size of first sample
n2 – size of second sample.

3 Results and Analysis

3.1 Raw and Filtered EEG Signals for Ten Participants

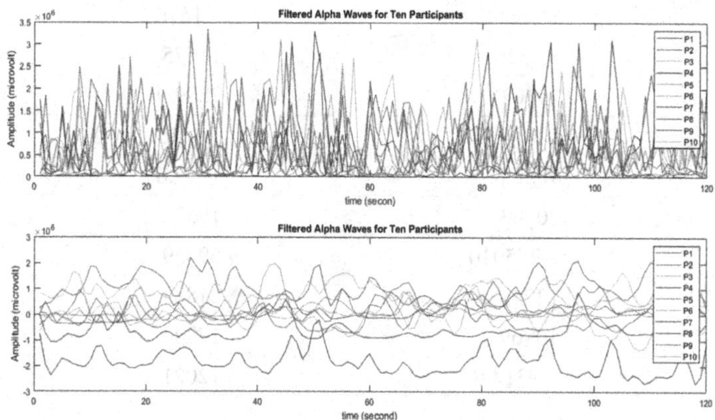

Fig. 4. Raw and filtered alpha waves for ten participants.

Figures 4 and 5 shows the raw and filtered alpha waves and beta waves for all ten participants obtained during the pre-processing stage. The EEG signals were filtered using Butterworth filter with sampling frequency set to 256 Hz. The high pass Butterworth filter use cut off frequency of 0.3 Hz while the low pass Butterworth filter use cut off frequency of 56 Hz.

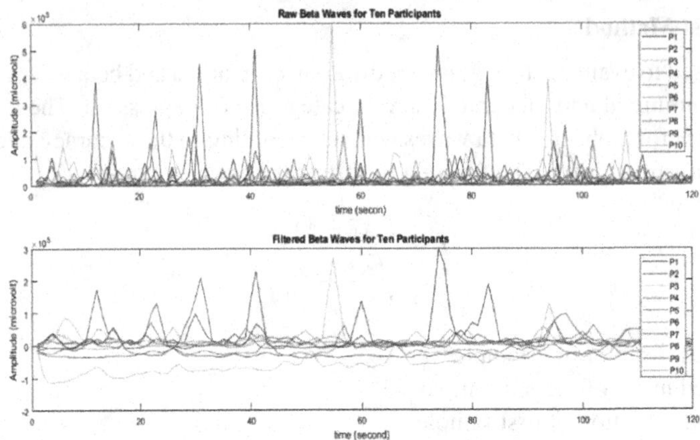

Fig. 5. Raw and filtered beta waves for ten participants.

3.2 Alpha and Beta Waves Pattern of Ten Participants

(See Table 2).

Table 2. Mean alpha and beta waves for ten participants.

Participant	Mean alpha waves	Mean beta waves
1	−8085.5	−1576
2	44.5201	11675
3	29102	7889.9
4	−7042.3	−1065.8
5	9866.8	1997.6
6	20103	19326
7	−255010	69459
8	12741	21889
9	10969	17240
10	−9312.6	12021

Based on Fig. 6, it can be seen that Participant 7 has the lowest amplitude of alpha waves compared to other participants and Participant 3 has the highest amplitude. As for beta waves, as shown in Fig. 7, it is clear that Participant 7 has the highest amplitude of beta waves compared to other participants while Participant 1 and Participant 4 both have the lowest amplitude. Since Participant 7 is in the moderately severe level of depression, an assumption can be made where the higher the level of depression the participant suffer, the lower the amplitude of alpha waves and the higher the amplitude of beta waves.

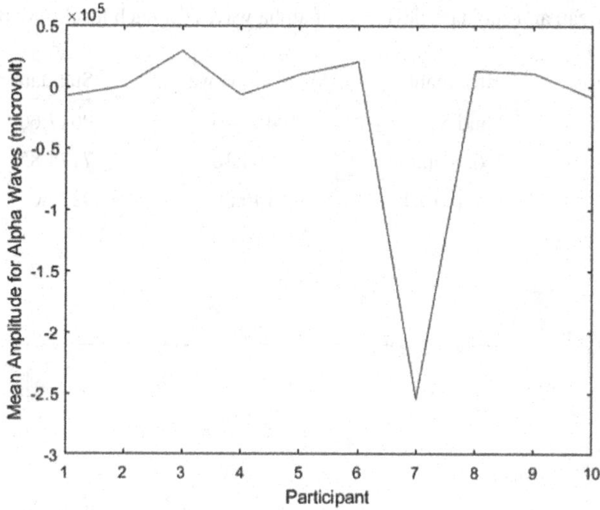

Fig. 6. Alpha waves pattern of ten participants.

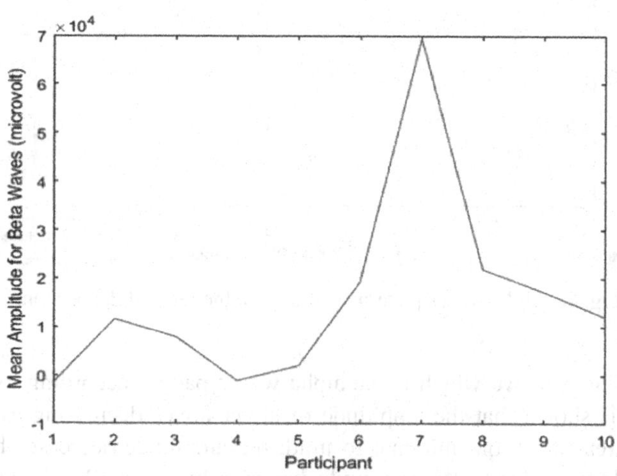

Fig. 7. Beta waves pattern of ten participants.

3.3 Alpha and Beta Waves Pattern According to the Level of Depression

3.3.1 Alpha Waves

(See Table 3).

Table 3. Mean and standard deviation of alpha waves for each level of depression.

Level of depression	Participant	Mean alpha waves	Standard deviation
Minimal	3 and 5	19484.40	9617.60
Mild	2, 6, 8 and 9	10964.38	7174.85
Moderate	1, 4 and 10	−8146.80	927.86
Moderately severe	7	−255010.00	–

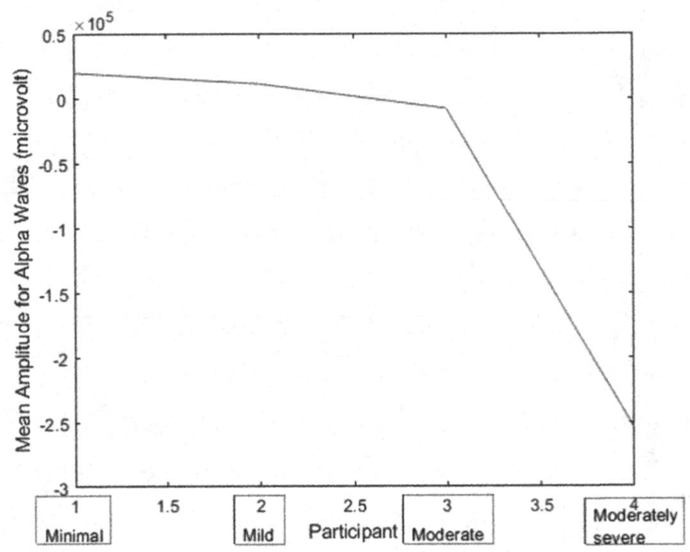

Fig. 8. Alpha waves pattern according to the level of depression.

Based on Fig. 8 above which is the alpha waves pattern according to the level of depression, it is shown that the amplitude of alpha waves decreasing as the level of depression increasing. From minimal to mild, the amplitude decreases by −43.73% while from mild to moderate, the amplitude decreases by −174.30%. In the moderately severe level of depression, the amplitude of alpha waves decreases drastically by –3030.19% from the moderate level of depression. All the calculations are shown below.

Percentage difference by group of alpha waves

- Minimal –> mild

$$\frac{10964.38 - 19484.4}{19484.4} \times 100\% = -43.73\%$$

- Mild –> moderate

$$\frac{-8146.8 - 10964.38}{10964.38} \times 100\% = -174.30\%$$

- Moderate – > severely moderate

$$\frac{-255010-(-8146.8)}{8146.8} \times 100\% = -3030.19\%$$

3.3.2 Beta Waves

(See Table 4).

Table 4. Mean and standard deviation of beta waves for each level of depression.

Level of depression	Participant	Mean beta waves	Standard deviation
Minimal	3 and 5	4943.75	2946.15
Mild	2, 6, 8 and 9	17532.5	3761.37
Moderate	1, 4 and 10	3126.4	6292.88
Moderately severe	7	69459	–

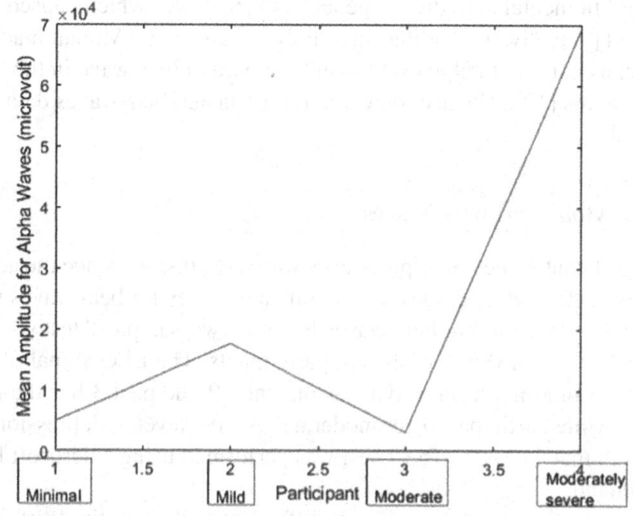

Fig. 9. Beta waves pattern according to the level of depression.

Based on Fig. 9 above, it can be stated that the amplitude of beta waves increasing as the level of depression increasing except from mild to moderate. From minimal to mild, the amplitude decreases by 254.64%. However, from mild to moderate, the amplitude decreases by −82.17%. This may be because there was participant in that level of depression self-evaluate his mental conditions incorrectly by ticking the score in the PHQ-9 form not according to what he felt. In the moderately severe level of depression, the amplitude of alpha waves increases drastically by 2126.69% from the moderate level of depression. All the calculations are shown below.

Percentage difference by group of beta waves

- Minimal –> mild

$$\frac{17532.5 - 4943.75}{4943.75} \times 100\% = 254.64\%$$

- Mild –> moderate

$$\frac{3126.4 - 17532.5}{17532.5} \times 100\% = -82.17\%$$

- Moderate –> severely moderate

$$\frac{69459 - 3126.4}{3126.4} \times 100\% = 2126.69\%$$

Hence, it can be said that the assumption made in the previous subchapter is true since the amplitude of alpha waves decreases as the level of depression increases, and the amplitude of beta waves increases as the level of depression increases. This statement can be supported since according to Kan and Lee, depressed patients had lower alpha waves than normal patients [10]. Besides that, Jain said that when the brain is aroused and actively engaged in mental activities, it generates beta waves which caused an increase in beta waves [11]. Finally, the findings in a study conducted by Mohammadzadeh et al. confirm the mean decrease in alpha waves and increase in beta wave in the brain waves of depressed patients [12]. The accuracy rate for alpha and beta waves data is 80% and 70%, respectively.

3.4 T-Test for Alpha and Beta Waves

The level of significant values for alpha waves was set at $p < 0.2$ since the accuracy rate for alpha waves is 80% while the level of significant values for beta waves was set at $p < 0.3$ since the accuracy rate for beta waves is 70%. Two-sample T-test was performed against the alpha and beta waves of the ten participants. The EEG signal of Participant 3 was used for the minimal level of depression since Participant 3 has the lowest total score of PHQ-9 while Participant 7 for moderately severe level of depression since only Participant 7 is in that category. The T-test was performed using Microsoft Excel using the 'ttest' command.

For alpha waves, there was a significant difference in the amplitude of minimal and moderately severe level of depression since the p-value obtained is 0.025423 ($p < 0.2$). As for beta waves, there was also a significant difference in the amplitude of minimal and moderately severe level of depression since the p-value obtained is 0.083151 ($p < 0.3$).

From the p-value obtained for alpha and beta waves in the T-test, it can be concluded that minimal and moderately severe level of depression have a significant difference in term of amplitude for both alpha and beta waves. This finding can be supported using the hypothesis made from the previous subchapter where the amplitude of alpha waves decreases as the level of depression increases, and the amplitude of beta waves increases as the level of depression increases.

4 Conclusion and Future Works

In conclusion, all objectives of this research have been achieved. Early depression detection system was managed to be investigated. There are several ways to detect early depression using the physiological and psychological signals. Other techniques required different equipment and applications which will produce varying results. In this study, early depression was detected based on psychological signals which is the EEG signals.

Next, an early depression detection using EEG signal of the subject has been developed by using the Matlab software. Based on the results obtained, it is proven that there is a mean decrease in alpha waves and increase in beta wave in the brain waves of depressed patients. The accuracy rate obtained for alpha waves data is 80% while beta waves is 70%. These accuracy rates are comparable with the previous literatures. The possible reason for the less accuracy of the results could be due to the small sample size. This study only used ten participants which gave a large impact to the accuracy rate even if only a small error present in the data.

In this project, four stages which are data acquisition, pre-processing, feature extraction and classification have been performed to get the results. Alpha and beta waves were analyzed to study the mental condition of the ten participants. In the future, in order to provide a more accurate results of detecting early depression using EEG signals, a few factors can be considered which are a larger sample size should be used and exploring other form of classification methods.

The accuracy rate of the results in this research can be improved by using a larger sample size. A larger sample size would have a smaller margin of error and give a more reliable mean value. Since there are more data, the estimation is more accurate. The confidence in the estimation increases as the sample size increases, the uncertainty decreases and will produce a greater accuracy.

Other forms of classification Methods that uses deep learning with high accuracy such as Deep belief Network (DBN) and Long Short Term Memory (LSTM) also can be explored to achieve a high level of accuracy. Deep learning are currently multiple times superior compared to the approaches used by classical machine learning. By using deep learning classifier, the accuracy level increases while the number of errors decreases.

References

1. Depression: Definition of Depression by Oxford Dictionary on Lexico.com also meaning of Depression. https://www.lexico.com/definition/depression. Accessed 02 Mar 2020
2. Depression, Suicide and Healing by Psychological Services, Harper College. http://dept.harpercollege.edu/psych-services/outreach/modules/depression/depression_print.html. Accessed 02 Mar 2020
3. Shen, J., Zhao, S., Yao, Y., Wang, Y., Feng, L.: A novel depression detection method based on pervasive EEG and EEG splitting criterion. In: 2017 IEEE International Conference on Bioinformatics and Biomedicine (BIBM), Kansas City, MO, pp. 1879–1886 (2017). https://doi.org/10.1109/BIBM.2017.8217946
4. Goldhill, O.: Depression diagnosis is up 33% in the US, and that's a good thing, 12 May 2018. https://qz.com/1276314/depression-diagnosis-is-up-33-in-the-us-and-thats-a-good-thing/. Accessed 03 Mar 2020

5. Institute for Public Health, National Institutes of Health, Ministry of Health Malaysia. NATIONAL HEALTH AND MORBIDITY SURVEY (NHMS) 2017: Key Findings from the Adolescent Health and Nutrition Surveys, p. 14, Rep. Perpustakaan Negara Malaysia (2018). http://iku.moh.gov.my/images/IKU/Document/REPORT/NHMS2017/NHMS2017Infographic.pdf. Accessed 05 Mar 2020
6. BrainLink Lite V2.0 by Macrotellect (n.d.). https://www.mindtecstore.com/Macrotellect-BrainLink-Lite-EEG-Headset-V20_1. Accessed 17 June 2020
7. Hosseinifard, B., Moradi, M.H., Rostami, R.: Classifying depression patients and normal subjects using machine learning techniques. In: 2011 19th Iranian Conference on Electrical Engineering, Tehran, pp. 1–4 (2011)
8. Mantri, S., Patil, D., Agrawal, P., Wadhai, V.: Non invasive EEG signal processing framework for real time depression analysis. In: 2015 SAI Intelligent Systems Conference (IntelliSys), London, pp. 518–521 (2015). https://doi.org/10.1109/IntelliSys.2015.7361188
9. Cai, H., Sha, X., Han, X., Wei, S., Hu, B.: Pervasive EEG diagnosis of depression using deep belief network with three-electrodes EEG collector. In: 2016 IEEE International Conference on Bioinformatics and Biomedicine (BIBM), Shenzhen, pp. 1239–1246 (2016). https://doi.org/10.1109/BIBM.2016.7822696
10. Kan, D.P.X., Lee, P.F.: Decrease alpha waves in depression: an electroencephalogram(EEG) study. In: 2015 International Conference on BioSignal Analysis, Processing and Systems (ICBAPS), Kuala Lumpur, pp. 156–161 (2015). https://doi.org/10.1109/ICBAPS.2015.7292237
11. Jain, A.: Introduction to brain waves & its types (part 1/13), 17 November 2020. https://www.engineersgarage.com/tech-articles/introduction-to-brain-waves-its-types-part-1-13/. Accessed 30 Jan 2021
12. Mohammadzadeh, B., Sattari, K., Lotfizadeh, M.: Determining the relationship between depression and brain waves in depressed subjects using Pearson correlation and regression. Int. J. Epidemiol. Res. **3**(4), 376–385 (2016)

Automated Diagnosis of the Top Spread Infectious Diseases in Iraq Using SVM Technique

Hayder Hussein Thary(✉), Duraid Y. Mohammed, and Khamis A. Zidan

Computer Engineering Department, College of Engineering, Al-Iraqia University, Baghdad, Iraq
{hayder_thary,khamis_zidan}@aliraqia.edu.iq

Abstract. Flu and Typhoid Fever Infectious diseases are developed an ongoing concern for many health systems around the world due to the pressure of large visits to health centers by patients. This presents pressing needs for developing an adequate, quick, and accurate recognition technique to reduce overloads on health centers and doctors to diagnose the suspected patients using advanced computing technologies. This study firstly showed that Typhoid and flu are at the top of the common list of infectious diseases attacking the Iraqi community by utilizing a tailor-made questionnaire. Most of the previous studies have neglected infectious disease gravity that increased due to the lack and scarcity of data. In this study, the dataset was collected and processed as shown later, which was then employed as features in the diagnosis process. The obtained data are classified into three named classes: healthy people, patients with flu, and patients with Typhoid. A machine learning model is used for solving this diagnose problem by using the Support Vector Machine (SVM) technique. The proposed method used 16 features of each sample to classify the samples in a three-class named before. Hence, the feature selection algorithms were not included in this study due to the small size of the dimensionality of the features and to minimize the computed cost. The suggested method illustrates promising and excellent diagnosis performance with 94.1% of classification accuracy. Consequently, the technique proposed has shown precisely discriminates between Flu and Typhoid diseases.

Keywords: Infectious disease diagnosis · SVM · Flu diagnosis · Typhoid diagnosis

1 Introduction

Ever-increasing volumes of affected cases nowadays have raised a pressing issue of how to diagnose these diseases and extract information from them. Automated diagnosis of diseases has become a tangible solution to the problem of this particular detection challenge. Indeed, infectious diseases are the trouble typically caused by the organisms, and they are communicable from one to another depends on the nature of the infection [1]. Recently, infectious diseases represent one of the major causes of mortality. To be clearer, according to the data available, infectious diseases causing 3.0 million deaths

P. Liatsis et al. (Eds.): TIOTC 2021, CCIS 1548, pp. 135–149, 2022.
https://doi.org/10.1007/978-3-030-97255-4_10

worldwide in 2016 [2]. In addition, it is endorsed that influenza viruses, which are one of the infectious diseases, often change so that the composition of influenza vaccines needs to be changed every year so that they are effective for the circulating virus. A new virus subtype spreads for some years, infecting a considerable majority of the population and potentially killing million [3]. A seasonal influenza epidemic, with less distinct seasonality in the tropics, with annual attack rates of 5–10% in adults and 20–30% in children can occur due to influenza viruses [4]. Flu is very infectious and easily spread to other people [5]. Similarly, Typhoid disease worries doctors, researchers, and the teams who work with it. Typhoid is common in many countries around the world especially these countries with low hygiene levels. It is endemic for those and might lead to a big health concern. Statistics show that there are 21000000 Cases per year and 200,000 deaths around the world [6]. Furthermore, it was estimated that roughly 11–20 million TF status and 128000-161000 were associated with the annual loss of their lives [7]. TF is a systemic infection caused by Salmonella Typhi, typically by the ingestion of infected food or water. Typhoid infections continue to be the main disease of general health in countries around the world, particularly in the twenty-first decade [8, 9]. In Iraq country, the residents changing place in quick movements lead to varied in character and volume of population behaviour, consequently rise to grow people risk of infectious diseases, particularly Tuberculosis patients, Typhoid patients, hepatitis patients, allergic conjunctivitis, and German measles patients [10, 11].

Biotechnology has a big evolved recently. Consequently, Biologists are joining the big data. Therefore, scientists are beginning with grappling with the massive datasets. With the advent of high-throughput resulting incessantly in a simple data production consequently ushering the science of applied biology into the area of big data, with that way all labs need to manipulate data to gain research answers [12, 13]. To make it clearer, data that are gathered and checked are used in biotechnology instruments, which are found in new and modern hospitals to produce the capability for collecting and sharing data in big information systems. Machine Learning techniques are considered offensive for the analysis of the gathered medical data for that great work is done related to diagnostic troubles. Hospitals need to minimize the cost of clinical tests and this result can be achieved by employing appropriate computer-based information and/or decision support systems using artificial intelligence [14]. Furthermore, machine learning techniques have been deployed in several fields, one of the most important fields is healthcare [15]. The default medical diagnostic process is named a disease classification method. In which a clinician before diagnosis a disease should analyze a set of symptoms that makes the clinician's job hard [16]. Thus, the disease diagnosis is considered the main challenge that needs to be tackled prior to treatment [17].

A good system of medical diagnosis represents a set of steps to be followed carefully, thus ensuring accurate results. Considering that, it's all about human life so it's a highly essential thing. Improving the health status of patients is done by making an accurate diagnosis which often aids a therapy administration [18]. Indeed, biomedical datasets can employ by a set of different types of methods and algorithms used in data mining tools to extract information. Some of which examples of the utilizing algorithms are Decision Trees (DT), Fuzzy Logic, Neural networks (NNs), Naive Bayes, logistic regression, K-nearest neighbour (KNN), and the support vector machine (SVM), etc.

[19–21]. In this study, patients are diagnosed whether they are affected with typhoid, influenza, or healthy, based on the symptoms affecting the patients, such as sex, age, fever, headache, runny nose, sneezing, cough, tiredness, diarrhea, sweating, abdominal pain, fatigue, ESR, white blood cell and widal Test. In the current study data collected using questionnaires method from different laboratories, consequently to determine the highest rate of 15 infectious diseases in the Iraqi community during 2019 then another questionnaire followed to identify symptoms with normal ranges used for diagnosing both diseases. Symptoms of each disease are considered as features ones. All features are taken as input for the machine learning model for predicting results. by using one of the machine learning techniques (SVM) to perform an automatic design process to diagnose diseases for a given patient efficiently concerning accuracy and area under the curve (AUC) of the receiver operating characteristic (ROC).

The outline of this paper is organized as follows: in Sect. 2, related work followed by Sect. 3 which illustrates the materials and techniques including questionnaire design and dataset description finally model proposed elaborate in details. In Sect. 4, experimental results are explained. Finally, this work discussed the conclusion in Sect. 5.

2 Related Work

In the biotechnology field, Computer technology plays a significant role in the diagnosis of infectious diseases, when it has been an ongoing process in the Information Technology domain there were several studies accomplished on some of the existing systems. These systems were used to the diagnosis process of infectious diseases including Typhoid and flu. Some of these earlier systems are presented in the following:

In [22] in 2015, Arturo López Pineda and the rest of the authors demonstrated that influenza could be detected using a various approach of machine learning techniques and made a comparison between them by used a Topaz, which is a natural language processing (NLP) tool, used for extracting influenza-related findings and to encode them into one of three values:- Missing, acute, and nonacute. By illustrating the use of machine learning (ML) and natural language processing (NLP) via the treatment of the missing value information which had a big effort for the diagnosis of infectious disease.

In [23] in 2014, Oguntimilehin A illustrates a Clinical Decision Support System (DSS) which makes a simulation of expert human reasoning or help as an assistant of a clinician in the medical domain is increasingly important. Two of the datasets that have been used on Typhoid samples were gathering at different periods one used for training data and another used for testing data. By employing an algorithm that was a decision tree for the diagnosis generated using the C4.5 algorithm.

In [18] in 2013, O.W. Samuel A Web-Based Decision Support System is employed through a Fuzzy Logic (FL) to diagnose Typhoid disease which is a main causing of illness and deaths in most developing regions. With the ability to operate on the internet networks, however, the system can run by any clinical specialist and trained health care personal.

In [24] in 2013 Adetunmbi A.O, the authors employed one of a machine learning algorithms to perform medical diagnosis of Typhoid. Indeed, 100 samples had been used for the training set, while another 50 samples had been used for module testing. The rough set is one of machine learning technique has been used for training the system including an (18) rules were generated through the training stage. The proposed system detection rate has been measured later.

In [25] in 2004 Alfred Young Itah explained that Typhoid has been diagnosed by employing a correlation study on Widal agglutination Reaction and Diagnosis. a number total of eighty (80) patients who considered suspected of getting a Typhoid infection were screened for the presence of salmonella kind using blood, urine, and stool samples along with Widal agglutination tests. The result of statistical investigation discovered an important variance between the Widal agglutination reaction and clinical samples of cultural prediction. Therefore, it is powerfully proposed that a single serological investigation could not be a good choice and a reliable diagnosis of Typhoid disease.

3 Materials and Techniques

There is no adequate dataset for flu and Typhoid diseases that fitting with the main objective of this research which is to develop an automated technique for diagnosing

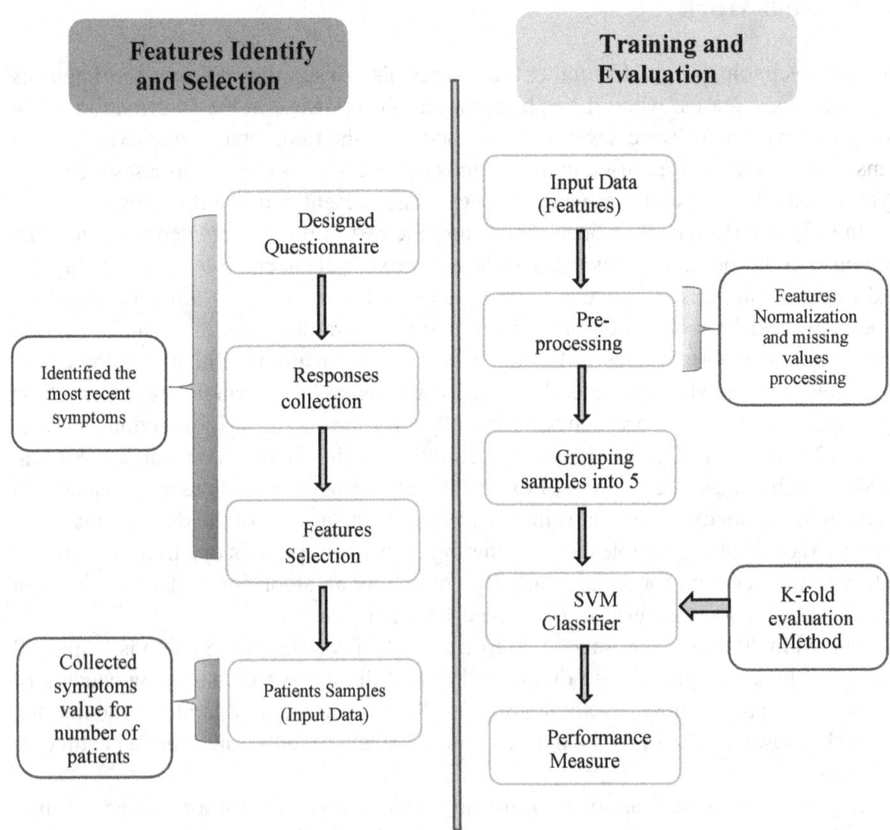

Fig. 1. The proposed framework

and classifying patient symptoms into either Flu or Typhoid. Consequently, this research is started by data samples gathering through a designed questionnaire for this purpose. Then features ranges for both diseases have been identified based on response analysis as illustrated later on in this paper.

The proposed framework is illustrated in Fig. 1. Firstly, two questionnaires have been designed and used for data collection. Both of these two questionnaires had been established based on the Iraqi community. The next step consists of training the dataset and evaluate. In order, to classify patients to any of the three classes obtaining a collected dataset for pre-processing level. The SVM classifier is applied for classifying samples once the dataset is prepared well. Then followed by performance measures to the model that has been built.

3.1 Questionnaire Design

3.1.1 Most Common Diseases Questionnaire

The most prevalent infectious diseases in Iraq have not been extensively investigated, according to a review of the literature. A clear understanding of the top spread diseases is very essential and motivated the current research. Consequently, this has been done through a specially designed questionnaire to collect data from different laboratories and clinicians, to assess the specific index rank of each of the 15 infectious diseases named (Influenza Flu, Typhoid, Hepatitis, Allergic conjunctivitis, German measles, Tuberculosis, Cholera, Meningitis, Scabies, Malaria, Rabies, Chickenpox, Elephantiasis, and SARS) in Iraqi community during 2019.

In order, to identify the rank of 15 infectious diseases, the 15 diseases were ranked using indices with values ranging from (1–5). The list of diseases was then ranked by laboratory specialists and clinicians based on their occurrence in the Iraqi population. The highest spread disease needs to be ranked with 5 by the person who fills out the designed questionnaire, while the lowest one needs to be ranked with 1. Then, a specific disease rank was determined via finding the average overall responses. For example, the weight of Typhoid disease has been calculated by the summation of all response values divided by the number of collected samples (115). Consequently, the weight of each disease as defined by [26] can be computed by:

$$\boldsymbol{Disease_{wight}} = \frac{\sum \boldsymbol{samples_{responce}}}{N} \tag{1}$$

where N represents the total number of responses.

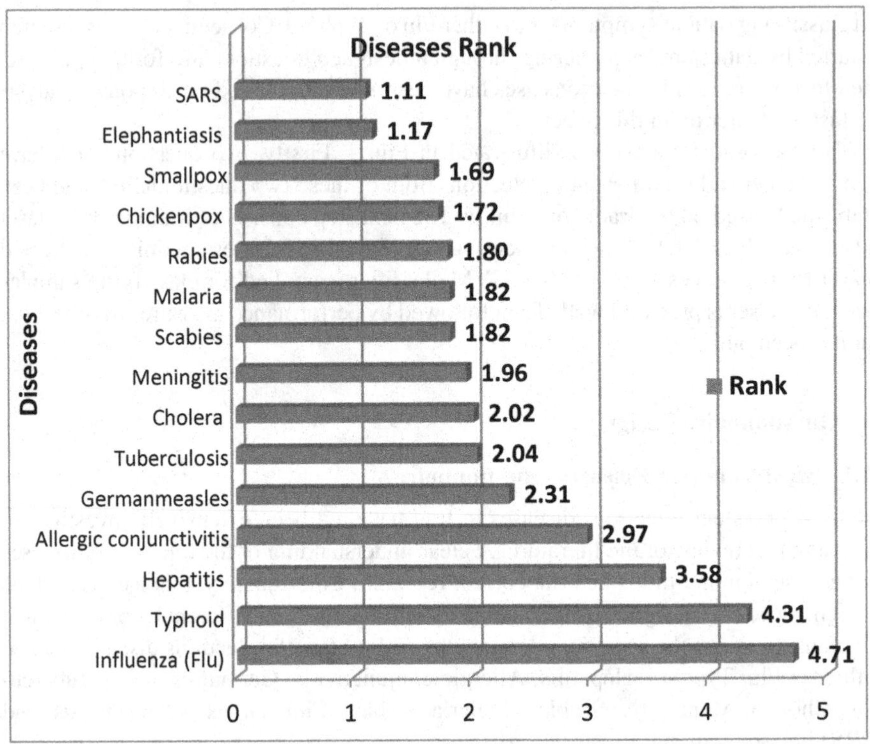

Fig. 2. Diseases rank

Figure 2 demonstrates the weight of each included disease that is computed based on responses average that computed using Eq. (1).

As shown in Fig. 2 which indicate that the widespread infectious diseases in the Iraqi community were influenza (Flu) with 4.71 weight followed by Typhoid disease with 4.31.

3.1.2 Symptoms Questionnaire

Furthermore, it can be seen that the limited works relating to infectious diseases in Iraq and that there are no previous studies especially focusing on flu and Typhoid. Therefore, conducted out another questionnaire to identify the most associated symptoms for the highest two indicate diseases (Flu and Typhoid) besides supported blood test factors which are required in some cases. In addition to highlighting its normal ranges which are collected by the same questionnaire and validated with other studies.

Typically, the identification tools rely on clinical checks, microbiological, and radiological tests as necessary. The designed questionnaire for symptoms of data collection producing the data had been collected to identifying blood test factors and their normal ranges. As illustrated in Table 1 that described disease symptoms for each disease also, demonstrated blood test factors of diagnosis diseases. Table 1 shows that there are seven and eight symptoms that are used to diagnose Flu and Typhoid respectively. The first four listed symptoms are considered as common between the two named diseases.

Table 1. Disease symptom and blood test factors

Symptoms	Flu	Typhoid
	Fever	Fever
	Headache	Headache
	Cough	Cough
	Fatigue	Fatigue
	Runny nose	Diarrhea
	Tiredness	Sweating
	Sneezing	Abdominal pain
		Vomiting
Blood test	ESR	Widal test
	WBC	

Besides, showing the blood test factor which is considered as a feature of the disease and is used for diagnosis of each disease. ESR means the Erythrocyte Sedimentation Rates a blood test that detects and monitors inflammation in the body. It tests how rapidly erythrocytes (red blood cells) stabilize at the bottom of a blood sample test tube if the range is more than 15 ml/1 h this indicates that there is an inflammation. On the other hand, WBC means White Blood Cell which is mainly normal ranges between (4000–11000). While the Widal test is a presumptive serological test for enteric fever whereby bacteria causing Typhoid are mixed with a serum containing specific antibodies obtained from infected persons. It's can be positive or negative.

3.2 Dataset Preparation and Analysis

Datasets for both flu and Typhoid have been collected using a tailored designed questionnaire concerning determinants of each symptom. The data set consists of 101 responses (samples) with 16 symptoms and blood test factors that are set as features as will be described later in this paper. The main objective of this dataset is to highlight Table 1 disease symptoms that can be employed for diagnoses of the flu and Typhoid patients. Data analysis involves major steps, done in roughly this order: data preparation and describe the data (statistics on data).

3.2.1 Data Preparation

Collected data has been checked for performing accuracy, i.e., checked the normal ranges of features. So far, the collected data has been entered and saved to the computer for analyzing, transforming the data to a (CSV extension) so it can be analyzed using Excel.

However, the collected Dataset as aforementioned before consists of 101 samples. Each one of these samples corresponding to the patient. Table 2 demonstrates single sample features (symptoms) and their data types. Besides, the values of some features that data type is numeric was normalized. Moreover, the normalize method will be described in the preprocess section.

Table 2. Samples values (features)

#	Features	Data type	Value
1	Sex	Flag value	0
2	Age	Numeric	0.525423729
3	Fever	Numeric	0.4
4	Headache	Flag value	1
5	Runny nose	Flag value	0
6	Sneezing	Flag value	1
7	Cough	Flag value	0
8	Tiredness	Flag value	0
9	Diarrhea	Flag value	1
10	Vomiting	Flag value	1
11	Sweating	Flag value	0
12	Abdominal pain	Flag value	1
13	Fatigue	Flag value	1
14	ESR	Numeric	0.785714286
15	White blood cell	Numeric	0.97398568
16	Widal test	Flag value	1
17	Class	Numeric	1

3.2.2 Descriptive Statistics

All features of the dataset have been described in a statistics way. Thus, providing a simple summary of it. However, statistics presented quantities description of features in a manageable scheme. As shown in Table 2 demonstrates an example of one sample (patient) input data that diagnosed to have Typhoid disease based on the symptoms provided.

On the other hand, the dataset consists of 59 females, 42 males. The patients' ages have ranged from 6 to 65 years. So far, as shown in Fig. 3 present that 27 persons were tested to have Typhoid disease while 46 persons tested to have flu disease and the remnant samples (28) tested with no infected diseases.

It has been found that the flu disease usually diagnosis with seven symptoms while Typhoid has eight symptoms. In Iraqi society, these symptoms are usually common, and

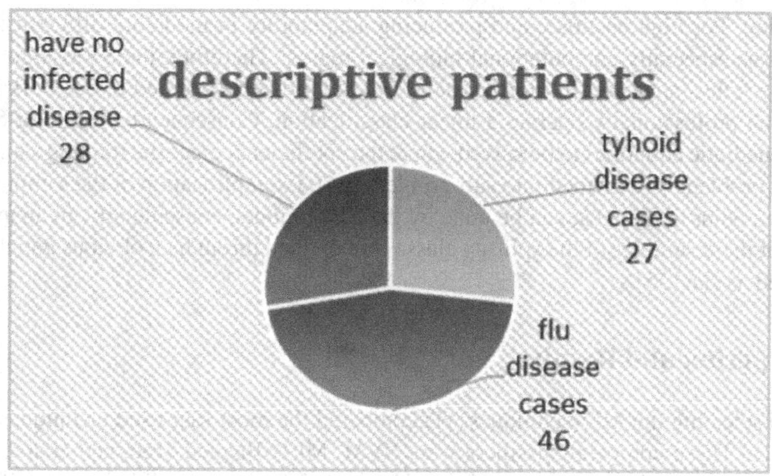

Fig. 3. Collected data taxonomy

this can be confirmed by the WHO [7, 27], NHS [5, 28], CDC [29, 30], and ECDC [31, 32]. However, symptoms of most infectious diseases are usually present in an overlapping fashion as shown in Table 1, since these disease diagnosis schemes are typical symptoms based and may lead to misdiagnosis.

3.3 Pre-processing Phase

Data pre-processing for the machine learning step is essential. Thus, there is an essential step for transforming the features into homogenous values that produce numerical stability. This is represented by the data normalization stage. Normalization helps the classifier to operate efficiently. Indeed, normalization is a pre-processing step in which all values are converted to values ranged between 0 and 1. However, there are different kinds to apply the normalization to the features. Min-Max is the common normalization method. Which has been selected and implemented in this study. Min-max normalization performed by substituting the min and max of features ranges in the formula below:

$$B_{normalized} = \frac{(\mathrm{B} - \mathrm{MIN(B)})}{(\mathrm{MAX(B)} - \mathrm{MIN(B)})} \tag{2}$$

where B represents feature value, MIN represents the minimum input value and MAX represents the maximum input value.

3.4 Supervised Learning-SVM

SVM is a supervised learning method that provides robust statistical approaches to classification. The SVM trained model assigns unseen samples to one of two classes and can be also assigned for multi classes, making it a non-probabilistic linear classifier. in addition to linear classification, SVMs can efficiently perform a non-linear classification utilizing a kernel trick. SVM is used widely in medical diagnosis for classification and regression. For high accuracy and producing adaptability in modeling different types of datasets especially computational biological region. Therefore, the SVM algorithm guarantees this. an aspect of bioinformatic was additionally specified in the work [33]. SVM can professionally operate a linear classification. Consequently, Training SVM needs quadratic equations to be solved where the coefficient equals the training samples. Indeed, problems are divided into sub-problem [34]. Exemplification of the samples, as there is a point in the area, can be done by the SVM model, consequently, by mapping it so that these samples of the split-up classes are divided through an obvious gap that is as varied as can [35].

4 Experimental Results

Toward selecting the ML techniques, via compared the most four used techniques performance. These compare classifiers were SVM, MLP, Bagged Tree, and coarse tree. randomly selected the training samples and basis on 5-fold cross-validation to verify the effectiveness of the proposed algorithm besides omitting the over-fitting phenomenon. An important finding that comes from this paper is that SVM is the best algorithm selected based on Table 3 which shows SVM efficiency over the other three algorithms. SVM has the highest performance established for the classification method that classifies patients to have flu, Typhoid, or unaffected. Table 3 also demonstrated the model's accuracy, training time, and total misclassification cost. As shown in Fig. 4 the comparative analysis of different algorithms accuracy, illustrate that the SVM algorithm has the best performance with 94.1% compared to MLP and other algorithms.

Table 3. Model characteristics

Model	Accuracy	Training time (sec)	Misclassification samples
SVM	94.1%	1.8544	6
Multi-layer perceptron (MLP)	88.1188	0.8146	12
Tree (coarse tree)	87.1%	0.83428	13
Bagged trees	83.2%	5.8376	17

This work was implemented using the MATLAB R2020a platform. The diagnosis performance of the implemented model is evaluated by applying K-fold cross-validation to gain the strength of the SVM classifier 5-fold cross-validation used in the training dataset. to mitigate overfitting which is mean when a classifier doesn't generalize well from the training data to unseen data. The collected dataset is first grouped into 5 equalized subsets. Each of these was implemented as a test dataset while the learning model is trained on all remained samples and an equivalent number of samples randomly selected from the lasting four datasets.

As shown in Fig. 6, describes the performance of this classifier. Consequently, the effectiveness of the classifier model is accurately measured performance via the calculation of the numbers of true and false samples that have been classified. There is a

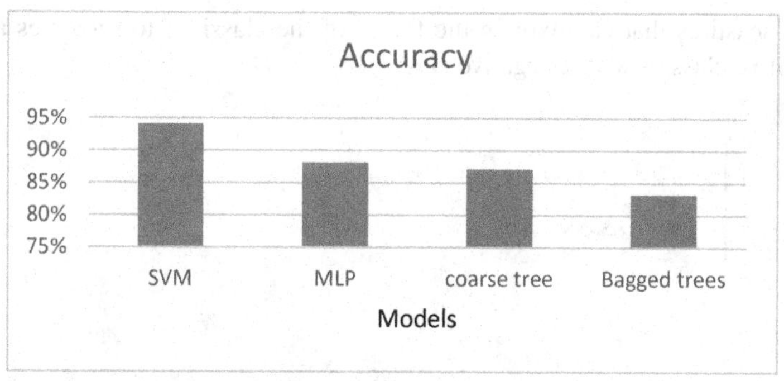

Fig 4. Graphical representation of comparative analysis of algorithms performance

25-sample predicted true with no infected disease of flu or TF, while 26 samples are classified as Typhoid patients and 44 classified as flu patients. A total of 6 misclassification errors has occurred. To obtain an accuracy of the SVM classifier as defined by [36] by using the following formula:

$$SVM\_accuracy = \frac{TP + TN}{TP + TN + FP + FN} \tag{3}$$

where TP present true positive which mean predicted yes (they have the disease), and they truly have the disease.

TN presents true negative which means predicted no, and the patients have not been affected.

FP present false positive which mean predicted yes, but they don't have the disease.

FN presents a false negative which means predicted no, but they do have the disease.

As shown in Fig. 5 ROC of the classifier Receiver Operating Characteristic (ROC) curve which is a graphical plot that represents by two axes the horizontal axes (X-axes) represent a false positive rate while vertical axes (Y-axes) represent the true positive rate. Consequently, it has been plotting in a form of the function to differentiate cut-off points. For every point on the ROC, curve plotting produces a sensitivity pair equivalent to a specific decision threshold. However, the ROC curve is showing the performance of a classifier over a series via the trade-offs between sensitivity and specificity for each cut-off. While the area under the curve (AUC) curves were produced depend upon the predicted result. The True Positive Rate and False Positive rate as defined by [36], can be calculated as the following formulas:

$$TruePositive\_rate = \frac{TP}{\mathrm{TP + FN}} \tag{4}$$

$$TrueNegative_{rate} = \frac{TN}{FN + TN} \tag{5}$$

$$Precision_{rate} = \frac{TP}{TP + FP} \tag{6}$$

These two factors are important for analyzing the classifier. These two factors also have known Sensitivity (TP rate) and Specificity is known (TN rate). They represent statistical measures that can explain the fitting of the classifier to separates a sample with a positive class or with a negative class.

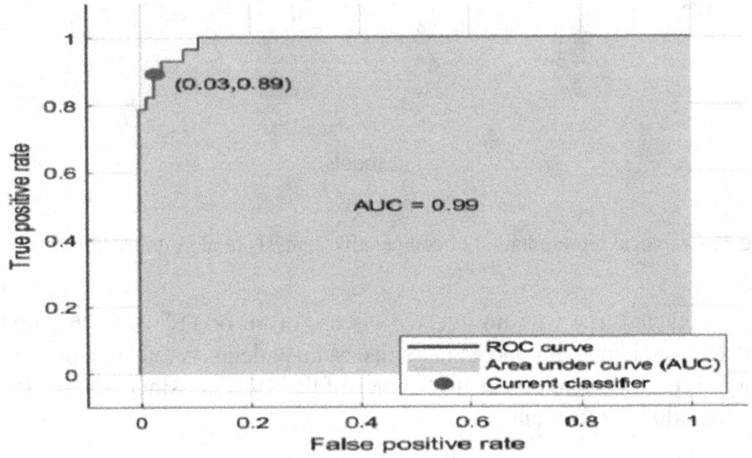

Fig. 5. ROC of classifier

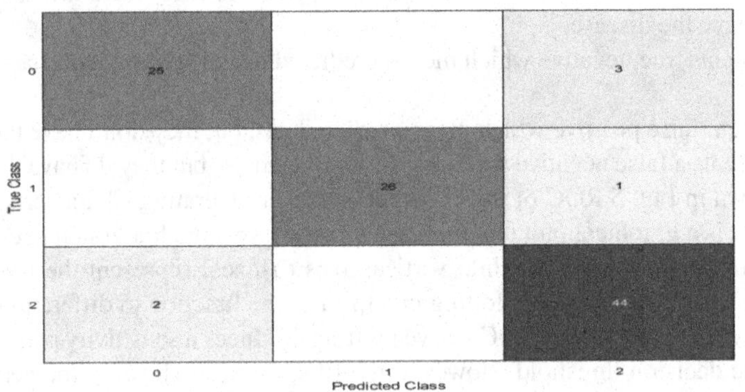

Fig. 6. Confusion matrix

Sensitivity could be defined as the detection of disease rate which identified those with the disease. Therefore, it needs to be maximized while the True negative rate which also known as specificity is the detection of those without disease and should be minimized for an accurate diagnosis. Precision is the rate of correctly predicted positive samples to the total predicted positive samples as shown in Table 4.

Table 4. Classifier performance

Sensitivity	Specificity	Precision
0.9793	0.8928	0.9693

5 Conclusion

It takes a relatively simple approach to the problem. The suggested design is shaped by acquiring important information through tailor-made questionnaires. Conducted evaluation of some classification techniques shows that Flu and Typhoid disease can be precisely detected using relatively simple algorithms. The experimental results demonstrated that the statistical symptoms besides blood test features that were acquired from patients are sufficient to discriminate the Flu disease from Typhoid patients employing SVM. This is a satisfactory result because most of the provided symptoms of a patient highly separable. It is also noted that the suggested method provides significantly outperforms with a simple and low computational load. Another gain of the current method is that designed to minimize the number of health centers and physician visits. The proposed method achieves the highest accuracy of 94.1% for two infectious diseases by comparing it to another similar existing system that used only one disease for diagnosing and less performance. Moreover, the proposed method is better than especially in dealing with overlapping features between both diseases. The diagnosis process can be done online systems by submitting patient symptoms. In contrast to earlier findings, however, blood test factors are considered expensive and not easy to acquire compared with other normal symptoms. Hence, Further improvement and investigation are needed to supplement accuracy and solving the disease symptoms overlapping challenge. It will also be interesting to extend the proposed automatic diagnostic technique to include more infectious diseases to advance automated diagnostic techniques.

Acknowledgments. The authors would like to acknowledge the appreciation to medicine college, Al-Iraqi University for their involvement in the conducted work through the efficient validation of the collected data and results.

References

1. Signore, A.: About inflammation and infection. EJNMMI Res. **3**, 1–2 (2013). https://doi.org/10.1186/2191-219X-3-8
2. World Health Organization: The top 10 causes of death. https://www.who.int/en/news-room/fact-sheets/detail/the-top-10-causes-of-death. Accessed 05 Apr 2020
3. Green Facts: Global Public Health Threats. https://www.greenfacts.org/en/global-public-health-threats/l-2/5-influenza-pandemic.htm. Accessed 19 July 2020
4. WHO: Weekly epidemiological record Relevé épidémiologique hebdomadaire. Geneva (2012)
5. National Health Service: FLU. https://www.nhs.uk/conditions/flu/. Accessed 02 Aug 2020

6. Kasuku, W., Bouland, C., Epumba, B., Biey, E.: Typhoid fever a public health problem in hospitals: case study at a work station in Kinshasa, DR Congo. Juniper Online J. Public Health **2**, 1–4 (2017). https://doi.org/10.19080/JOJPH.2017.02.555586
7. World Health Organization: Typhoid. https://www.who.int/news-room/fact-sheets/detail/typhoid. Accessed 06 Mar 2020
8. World Health Organization: Typhoid: Immunization, Vaccines and Biologicals. https://www.who.int/immunization/diseases/typhoid/en/. Accessed 02 June 2020
9. Bhan, M.K., Bah, R., Bhatnagar, S.: Typhoid and paratyphoid fever (2005). www.thelancet.com
10. Lischer, S.K: Security and displacement in Iraq: responding to the forced migration crisis (2008). http://www.mitpressjournals.org/doi/pdf/10.1162/isec.2008.33.2.95
11. Eiset, A.H., Wejse, C.: Review of infectious diseases in refugees and asylum seekers—current status and going forward. Public Health Rev. **38**, 1–16 (2017). https://doi.org/10.1186/s40985-017-0065-4
12. Marx, V.: The big challenges of big data (2013). https://doi.org/10.1038/498255a
13. Mattmann, C.A.: Computing: a vision for data science (2013). https://doi.org/10.1038/493473a
14. Pradhan, M.: Data mining & health care: techniques of application. Int. J. Innov. Res. Comput. Commun. Eng. **02**, 7445–7455 (2014). https://doi.org/10.15680/ijircce.2014.0212029
15. Salkuti, S.R.: A survey of big data and machine learning (2020). https://doi.org/10.11591/ijece.v10i1.pp575-580
16. Mitchell, T.M.: Machine Learning. McGraw-Hill Science/Engineering/Math; (March 1, 1997) (1997). https://doi.org/10.1007/978-3-642-21004-4_10
17. Selwal, A., Raoof, I.: A multi-layer perceptron based intelligent thyroid disease prediction system (2019). https://doi.org/10.11591/ijeecs.v17.i1.pp524-532
18. Samuel, O.W., Omisore, M.O., Ojokoh, B.A.: A web based decision support system driven by fuzzy logic for the diagnosis of typhoid fever. Expert Syst. with Appl. J. **40**, 4164–4171 (2013)
19. Corinna, C., Vladimir, V.: Support-Vector Networks. Kluwer Academic Publishers, Holmdel (1995). https://doi.org/10.1007/s40031-014-0099-7
20. Sarojini, B., Ramaraj, N., Nickolas, S.: Enhancing the performance of LibSVM classifier by kernel f-score feature selection. In: Ranka, S., et al. (eds.) IC3 2009. CCIS, vol. 40, pp. 533–543. Springer, Heidelberg (2009). https://doi.org/10.1007/978-3-642-03547-0_51
21. Herron, P.: Machine learning for medical decision support: evaluating diagnostic performance of machine learning classification algorithms (2004)
22. Pineda, A.L., Ye, Y., Visweswaran, S., Cooper, G.F., Wagner, M.M., Tsui, F. (Rich): comparison of machine learning classifiers for influenza detection from emergency department free text report. J. Biomed. Inform. J. **58**, 60–69 (2015). http://dx.doi.org/10.1016/j.jbi.2015.08.019
23. Oguntimilehin, A., Adetunmbi, A.O., Olatunji, K.A.: A machine learning based clinical decision support system for diagnosis and treatment of typhoid fever. Int. J. Adv. Res. Comput. Sci. Softw. Eng. **4**, 961–969 (2014)
24. Oguntimilehin, A., Adetunmbi, A.O.: ABiola OB: a machine learning approach to clinical diagnosis of typhoid fever. Int. J. Comput. Inf. Technol. **02**, 671–676 (2013)
25. Itah, A.Y., Akpan, C.J.: Correlation studies on Widal agglutination reaction and diagnosis of typhoid fever. Southeast Asian J. Trop. Med. Public Health **35**, 88–91 (2004)
26. Deisenroth, M.P., Faisal, A.A., Ong, C.S.: Mathematics for Machine Learning. Cambridge University Press (2020). https://doi.org/10.1017/9781108679930
27. World Health Organization: Influenza (Seasonal). https://www.who.int/news-room/fact-sheets/detail/influenza-(seasonal). Accessed 09 Dec 2019

28. National Health Service: Typhoid Fever. https://www.nhs.uk/conditions/typhoid-fever/symptoms/. Accessed 05 June 2020
29. Centers for Disease Control and Prevention(CDC): Influenza (Flu). https://www.cdc.gov/flu/symptoms/index.html. Accessed 01 Aug 2020
30. Centers for Disease Control and Prevention (CDC): Typhoid Fever and Paratyphoid Fever. https://www.cdc.gov/typhoid-fever/symptoms.html. Accessed 08 June 2020
31. European Centre for Disease Prevention and Control, (ECDC): Factsheet about seasonal influenza. https://www.ecdc.europa.eu/en/seasonal-influenza/facts/factsheet. Accessed 03 June 2020
32. European Centre for Disease Prevention and Control, (ECDC): Facts about typhoid and paratyphoid fever. https://www.ecdc.europa.eu/en/typhoid-and-paratyphoid-fever/facts. Accessed 08 July 2020
33. Dash, S., Patra, B., Tripathy, B.K.: A hybrid data mining technique for improving the classification accuracy of microarray data set. Int. J. Inf. Eng. Electron. Bus. **4**, 43–50 (2012). https://doi.org/10.5815/ijieeb.2012.02.07
34. Sain, S.R., Vapnik, V.N.: The Nature of Statistical Learning Theory. Springer, Holmdel (1996). https://doi.org/10.1007/978-1-4757-2440-0
35. Burges, C.J.C.: A Tutorial on Support Vector Machines for Pattern Recognition. Kluwer Academic Publishers (1998)
36. Awad, M., Khanna, R.: Efficient Learning Machine. Apress, Berkeley (2015). https://doi.org/10.1007/978-1-4302-5990-9

Cardiac Arrhythmia Diagnosis via Multichannel Independent Component Analysis: An Approach Towards a Better Health Care System

Mohammad Sarfraz[1](✉), Mudassir Hasan Khan[1], Duraid Yahya Mohammed[2], Mays Dheya Hussain[2], and Khamis A. Zidan[2]

[1] Department of Electrical Engineering, Centre for Interdisciplinary Biomedical and Human Factors Engineering, Aligarh Muslim University, Aligarh 202002, India
msarfraz@zhcet.ac.in

[2] College of Engineering/Computer Engineering Department, AL-Iraqia University, Adhamyh, Baghdad, Iraq

Abstract. With the evolving lifestyle, many cardiac ailments are becoming more frequent, and it has become necessary to provide detailed surveillance of the heart's functioning to ensure healthy living. ECG signals provide details regarding the various forms of arrhythmias. However, owing to the complexities and non-linearity of ECG signals, it is impossible to examine these signals manually. Conventional approaches for specialist inspection of ECGs on paper or television are inadequate for ambulatory, long-term monitoring, and sports ECGs. Automated applications that use signal processing and pattern recognition would be extremely beneficial. Identification of arrhythmias from ECGs is an essential branch of biomedical signal processing and pattern recognition. Motion-induced artifacts are well-known to be a major source of misrecognition and misdiagnosis.

On the other hand, the feature extraction method has a significant effect on the reliability and performance of ECG pattern recognition. This paper proposes new approaches and algorithms for pre-processing multi-channel ECG signals and neural networks for arrhythmia classification using independent component analysis (ICA) with two distinct goals: (1) to eliminate motion-induced or associated artifacts, and (2) to better select the features and allow more effective pattern recognition. When processing noisy ECG data with the MIT dataset, cross-validation reveals a major improvement. For noisy signals, classification sensitivity of 97.9% and positive predictivity of 98.1% was achieved in this work. A tenfold neural validation rule was used to achieve 99.3% accuracy in arrhythmia classification. The lower the signal-to-noise level, the more significant is the improvement. This proposed algorithm would be a valuable method for physicians in justifying their diagnosis. With its quick reaction time, the proposed algorithm can be easily integrated into an automated healthcare management system.

Keywords: Health care · Independent component analysis · Machine learning · Arrhythmia computer-aided diagnosis · Feature extraction · Neural network

P. Liatsis et al. (Eds.): TIOTC 2021, CCIS 1548, pp. 150–166, 2022.
https://doi.org/10.1007/978-3-030-97255-4_11

1 Introduction

Cardiovascular disorders (CVDs) are the leading cause of death worldwide. Early diagnosis and treatment of patients with pre-existing risk factors such as cardiovascular abnormalities and diabetes hypertension will save lives. According to the WHO, 31% of people in this world are losing their life due to cardiovascular ailments [1–3]. These include various types of heart arrhythmias, coronary artery disease, heart failure, congenital heart disease, tachycardia, bradycardia, etc. It is now necessary to systematically study these diseases, and routine diagnosis of the heart's condition is essential. The electric impulses of ECGs provide a database of the heart's health over time, allowing doctors to recognize different common and irregular cardiovascular disorders. Basically, ECG is the electrical signature of heart behavior.

Furthermore, it needs to be analyzed to explain the signal patterns and identify pathological conditions. An expert can accomplish the feature extraction and pattern recognition task with a visual ECG signal waveform on screen or paper [4]. However, the complexity and the duration of ECG signals make manual analysis very time-consuming. Manual ECG analyses are also prone to errors. On the other hand, ECG monitoring warrants long-term monitoring and close to real-time recognition, which human specialists can hardly handle. For these reasons, automated signal processing and pattern recognition methods have become prevalent and effective ECG application tools. A typical computer-based ECG analysis system can do the pre-processing of signals, detect beats, feature extraction, and classification algorithms [5]. This process will considerably help in the automatic detection of various problematic conditions and identify various arrhythmias. The above procedure represents an important and essential of present-day biomedical application of signal processing and pattern recognition.

The Independent Component Analysis (ICA) and Blind Source Separation (BSS), when applied to ECG and other biomedical signals, are considered new applications of the above techniques but have a high expansion area of research. Many efforts have been made to discover feeble characteristics from signals, like extraction of extra information of heart and body through the potential of blind signal separation [6–8]. Hidden factors of biomedical signals were successfully revealed using independent component analysis [9, 10]. The method of using the ICA and BSS to separate motion-induced noise was proposed by the authors [11–13]. This paper presents detail about ICA's use to improve diagnostic accuracy and computational efficiency by (1) signal cleaning and (2) better-improved feature selection.

2 ECG Signal Processing

The electrical potential produced due to heart muscles' action, i.e., heartbeats, gives the details of the heart's condition and is known as Electrocardiogram (ECG). This ECG is measured with the help of specially designed electrodes that are placed on the surface of the body. In technical terms, the ECG can be regarded as the electrical impression of the heart's performance. For obtaining the ECG, several electrodes are placed on the human body's surface at some designated positions, and the voltages for different configurations of these electrodes are measured. These voltages are amplified with differential voltage amplifiers and recorded with some processing with a recorder's help. The commonly used method is the Three-lead ECG recording method based on the principle of the Einthoven triangle, where the measurement is done with the help of three electrodes [14]. How the lead voltages are defined in the Einthoven triangle method is shown below.

$$\begin{aligned} Lead\ I &: V_I = \Phi_L - \Phi_R \\ Lead\ II &: V_{II} = \Phi_F - \Phi_R \\ Lead\ III &: V_{III} = \Phi_F - \Phi_L \end{aligned} \tag{1}$$

Here, 'Φ' is the value of potential measured by the electrodes placed at specific locations. The relationship between the lead voltages when Kirchhoff's law is applied is shown below.

$$V_I + V_{III} + V_{II} \tag{2}$$

Thus, out of these three independent leads are only two. We derived the data taken for this study from the MIT-BIH dataset [15] as the data of Lead II.

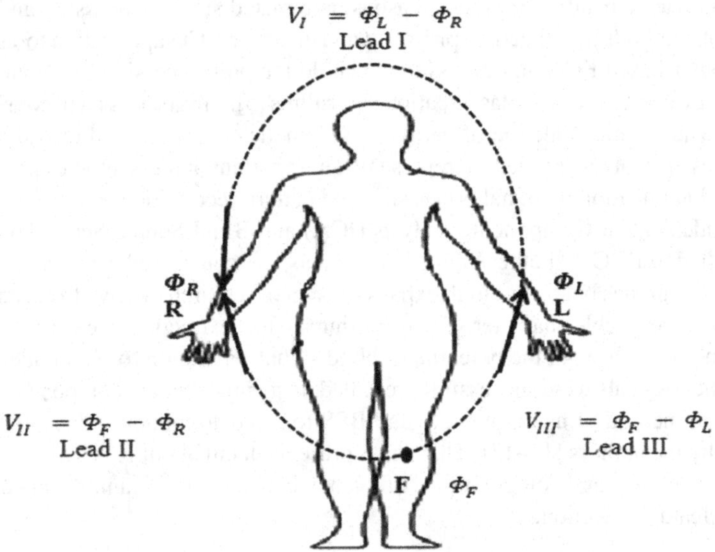

Fig. 1. Einthoven triangle and leads the definition

There are lots of noise and artifact signals present in the ECG signal due to other bioelectric signals generated by the movement of various body organs. These artifacts are often called 'em,' and their ectopic nature makes it complicated to get removed with the help of conventional filtering techniques. Now, this problem is rectified by inserting an extra electrode. This method will transform the problem of artifact removal into an independent component analysis. Two different linear combinations of pure ECG signal combined with lumped noise signal N, i.e., first in the case of Lead II, and another is the combined signal measured as of extra electrode, respectively [16]. ICA technique can separate the pure ECG and the lumped noise N from these two signals if they are statistically independent.

The classification of ECG signals will assist us in recognizing different health problems and illnesses associated with the cardiovascular system. Algorithms are proposed for classifying multiple pulse disturbances and cardiovascular disorders. The success of pattern recognition is heavily reliant on the extracted features and their selection in suitable spaces. This paper aims to investigate the useful features of ICA in order to achieve important characteristics or features of different types of arrhythmias and to develop a pattern recognition technique with a high degree of accuracy and computational efficiency.

3 Noise Reduction Using ICA (Proposed Method)

The noise and artifacts are the unwanted signals which are needed to be filtered or removed first during the processing of ECG signals. Work is done by [12], which utilized ICA filtering to separate artifacts caused by the breathing process from the ECG signals and showed good results. Another research work that was carried out by [12] has used an MIT-BIT noise stress database in their study. The linearly mixed signals were separated with the help of the BSS separation technique.

$$x1(t) = a_{11}s1(t) + a_{12}s2(t) \tag{3}$$

$$x2(t) = a_{21}s1(t) + a_{22}s2(t) \tag{4}$$

Equation 3 and 4 are the simple demonstration of ICA with $x1$ and $x2$ are the sound signals received by the microphones where the parameter a depend on the distance of the microphone from the speaker. Simultaneously, the parameter s denotes the actual speaker's voice. The architecture used for this purpose comprised a high pass filter, an ICA-based two-layer network, and a self-adaptive step size. The output means the behavior of the signals was used to derive the desired step size. It was found that when compared to a range of different algorithms, this two-layered algorithm that employed the ICA algorithm and whitening technique together proved to have high convergence. To measures independence for ICA, some common contrast functions are commonly used. Moments provide a great deal of information in the numerical form about the distribution—the first-moment measure central tendency.

$$E[x] = \int_{x=-\infty}^{+\infty} p_x(x)x dx \tag{5}$$

Second Moment

$$E\left[x^2\right] = \int_{x=-\infty}^{+\infty} p_x(x)x^2 dx \tag{6}$$

Third Moment

$$E\left[x^3\right] = \int_{x=-\infty}^{+\infty} p_x(x)x^3 dx \tag{7}$$

$$E\left[(x-\bar{x})^3\right] = \int_{x=-\infty}^{+\infty} p_x(x)(x-)^3 dx \tag{8}$$

The *fourth moment* $E\left[x^4\right]$ if the probability density function is

$$E\left[x^4\right] = \int_{x=-\infty}^{+\infty} p_x(x)x^4 dx \tag{9}$$

Kurtosis is the classical method of measuring Non-Gaussianity in ICA estimation

$$kurt(s) = E\left\{s^4\right\} - 3\left(E\left\{s^4\right\}\right)^2 \tag{10}$$

Entropy which is a measure of the uniformity of the distribution of a bounded set of values, Entropy H of discrete-valued signal S is defined as

$$H(S) = -\sum P(S = a^i) log P(S = a^i) \tag{11}$$

In order to remove the unwanted noise and artifact signals, many ICA algorithms were studied and analyzed by [17] more comprehensively and comparatively. Some ectopic types of motion artifacts are difficult to detect and get removed by usual methods. Hence, algorithms that were derived from the PCA-ICA technique were used by [11] to remove these motion artifacts. They used the FastICA algorithm for the estimation of Negentropy.

$$J(x) = H_G(x) - H(x) \tag{12}$$

$H(x)$ is the entropy and $H_G(x)$ is the entropy of a Gaussian random vector whose covariance matrix is equal to that of (x). Consequently, this idea was further enhanced by [16]. They proposed the extraction of features of ECG signals incorporating a two-lead design and feature extraction to remove motion artifacts successfully.

In the proposed work, we placed an extra electrode at the point where negligible ECG is achieved. A fraction of noise signal, N' (a linear attenuated version of the motion artifacts and noise N) is contained in the signal of Lead II. Similarly, a portion of noise signal N" is contained in the signal of extra lead which is placed on the point of negligible ECG. Different body motions lead to the formation of various types of motion artifacts and noise signals present in both the leads homogeneously with a range of mixing ratios. ICA is one of the most useful techniques by which these two, i.e., pure ECG and noise signal, can be easily separated from each other.

The ambulatory noise signal is separated from the pure and clean ECG signal using a blind source separation technique that finds its roots from ICA. They are highly uncorrelated, which gives good separation results [18, 19]. Separating the pure ECG and the noise signal through the blind source separation technique requires that there should have zero dependencies on each other. The data is recorded with the help of a multi-lead ECG. An investigation of the reliability of this method is done with the help of only two signals. The need here is to separate the ECG signal from the motion artifact of the electrode. ECG data from the MIT-BIH dataset is used as the signal for the modified

Lead II whereas the noise signal from electrode motion is taken from the MIT noise stress test database.

$$\begin{aligned} \textit{Modified Lead II} &= S1 + N' \\ \textit{Limb Electrode} &= S2 + N'' \end{aligned} \tag{13}$$

Here, the ECG signal and some fraction of electrode motion artifact are present in the modified lead II. In contrast, the limb electrode also consists of ECG data with some electrode-generated motion artifacts, but the ECG content in this limb electrode is minimal. The maximum portion constitutes the 'em' noise signal. Some other parts, such as the lumbar curve, etc., also receive the minimum amount of ECG and can be used to record motion artifacts in place of limb electrodes.

The noise signals and motion artifacts are removed from the pure ECG signal with the help of the FastICA algorithm, which is selected based on a quantified study done by [17]. Various ICA algorithms were compared taking different parameters into account. Figure 1 shows the proposed setup, which is used to complete our work. After the separation procedure is completed, we are left with two independent signals, one is the ECG, and the other is the noise and artifact component. It is too difficult to identify these signals with normal reading or analysis. They are unique in their properties and nature compared to the original signals in the frequency and time domain. It is important to recognize this waveform with the help of statistical properties automatically by using kurtosis. The kurtosis can be defined as the fourth-order cumulant used to obtain meaning observations, zero for Gaussian densities, as explained in our case. The kurtosis has a much lower value for a signal of continuous noise than the usual ECG. In our study, we have taken 30 as the threshold value. The noise component can be considered continuous if the kurtosis's modulus is below 30, which is the threshold value. In the absence of any component with the modulus of kurtosis for a designated threshold, the component which has the maximum value is chosen. The extremely simple behaviour of kurtosis makes it a desirable feature for selection. Kurtosis can be calculated by the computational use of the fourth moment of the data sample. Moreover, the correlation coefficient taken as 0.2 in our case distinguishes between the pure ECG signal and the noise signals. The clean ECG signals will have a value lower than 0.2, whereas the noise signal will have a greater value than 0.2 (Fig. 2).

The effect of overlapped noise and artifact signals on the pure ECG signal is shown by mixing noise signals in pure ECG data of two lead ECGs artificially, as shown in Fig. 3. We lost most parts of the factual information, and it was challenging to gather information from these signals by conventional or manual means. This problem is then resolved by applying the FastICA algorithm to two lead ECG data to separate the noise signal from pure ECG data, as shown in Fig. 4. This ICA technique can easily separate noise from the actual signal, which is proved by comparing the signal extracted from this method with that of the original signal, as shown in Fig. 5.

The evaluation of the proposed algorithm to reduce the noise and motion artifact signals [20] is done by generating a database in which pure ECG signals are combined with noise with different amounts of concentration to make a variety. The selection of 100 sets of 10 s is made for individual arrhythmias from the above dataset. Now, for each of the six combinations having a range of 24 dB to -12 dB of a variety of SNR is

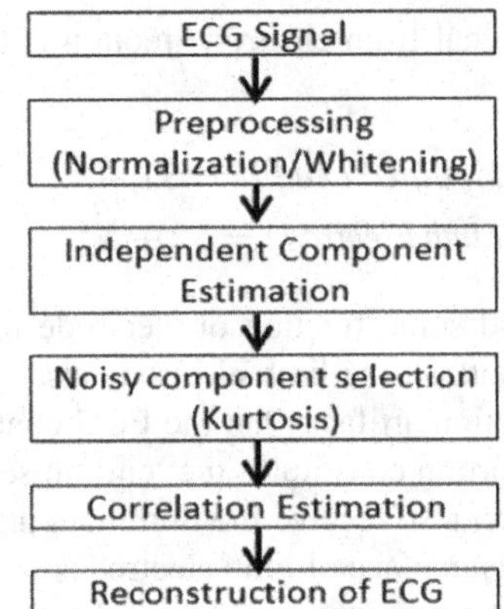

Fig. 2. Flowchart showing removal of noise and motion artefact

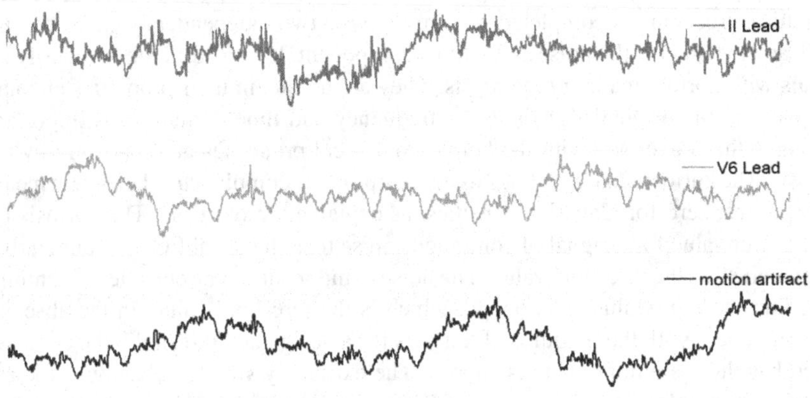

Fig. 3. Motion artifacts/noise signals contained in Ambulatory ECG signals

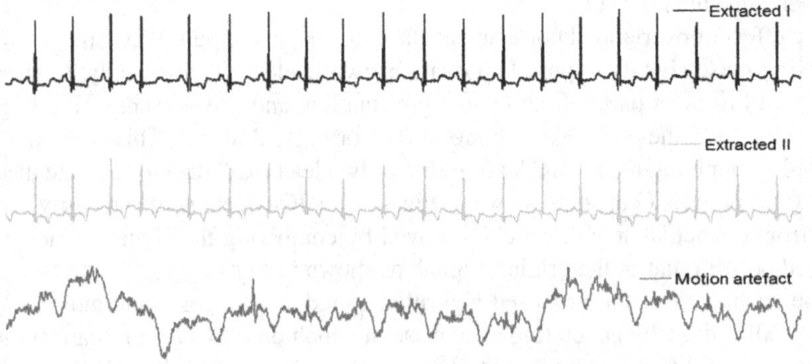

Fig. 4. ECG signals of the two leads after extraction

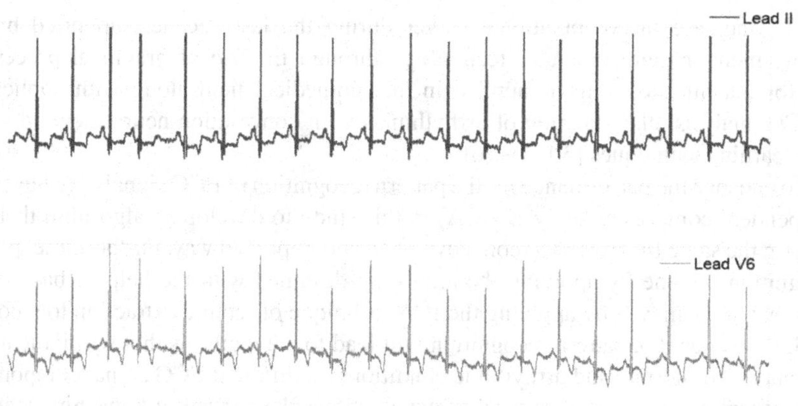

Fig. 5. Actual acquired data from ECG leads

acquired, resulting in the formation of 4800 sets having a diverse range of SNR present in them, taking their sampling frequency to be 360 Hz. After that, the pure ECG signals are intermixed with the required SNR containing motion artifact and noise signals by multiplying the desired gain factor with the 'em' signal and then adding this whole achieved signal to the pure ECG signal. SNR's value is taken in steps of six in the range of 24 dB to −12dB. Finally, a comparison between the reference 'em' signal and the obtained output signal is made. Any improvement in the signal's quality is detected with the help of a beat detection algorithm and classification performance of pure ECG signal and the ECG signal containing noise.

4 Feature Selection by ICA (Proposed Method)

For mutually independent component signals from a set of signals, it is essential to use a statistical signal processing technique. Hence, a type of blind separation scheme called independent component analysis is used [19, 21–23].

Researchers had done a lot of work on feature extraction and found ICA to be useful in a variety of research works [2, 3, 16, 17]. Although its domain is recent in research, when we talk about the feature extraction used to classify ECG signals by classifiers [24], this technique finds a high perspective. Moreover, the categorization of the features which are extracted by the above method is done according to the process, such as time-domain methods used by [25] as well as [26] and transformation methods used by [27] as well [28]. Arrhythmia detection using the tachycardia ECG segment intervals with the convolution neural network by [29–31]; similarly, [32] and [33] proposed an algorithm for selecting important features where along with the input features, they also incorporated the information of the output class. This extra information about the class helped enhance the system performance for feature extraction, to classify ECG signals. Although the results obtained were appreciable after applying the feed-forward neural network, its application was limited to the bio-signal datasets only and not applied to other signals of some type or a multiclass signal combination.

The increase in computational power during the last decade, supported by the advancement in semiconductor technology through the use of graphical processing unit for machine learning, is applied in the biomedical field along with application in ECG analysis, classification of arrhythmias with convolution neural networks, and deep learning techniques [30, 34–36].

To enhance the performance for the pattern recognition of ECG signals, we have used independent component analysis (ICA) in this study to develop an algorithm that will perform the same function in a more developed and improved way. Furthermore, pattern recognition is done by applying the algorithm designed with the help of basic functions that are achieved by applying the ICA technique of feature extraction to a normal ECG. Consequently, pattern recognition will lead to a hypothesis that will indicate the dependency of normal and arrhythmic conditions on different ECG signal components. An artificial neural network is used as the classifier. We can call it a machine learning classifier with input as a combination of ICA obtained features and R-R interval and QRS segment power. The accuracy of pattern recognition was significantly improved during the training process and validated using the MIT-BIH Arrhythmia Database. The number of inputs to the classifier is reduced to simplify the process and enhance its performance in real-time applications. In this study, we discuss the principle algorithm, and then the results are validated in this work.

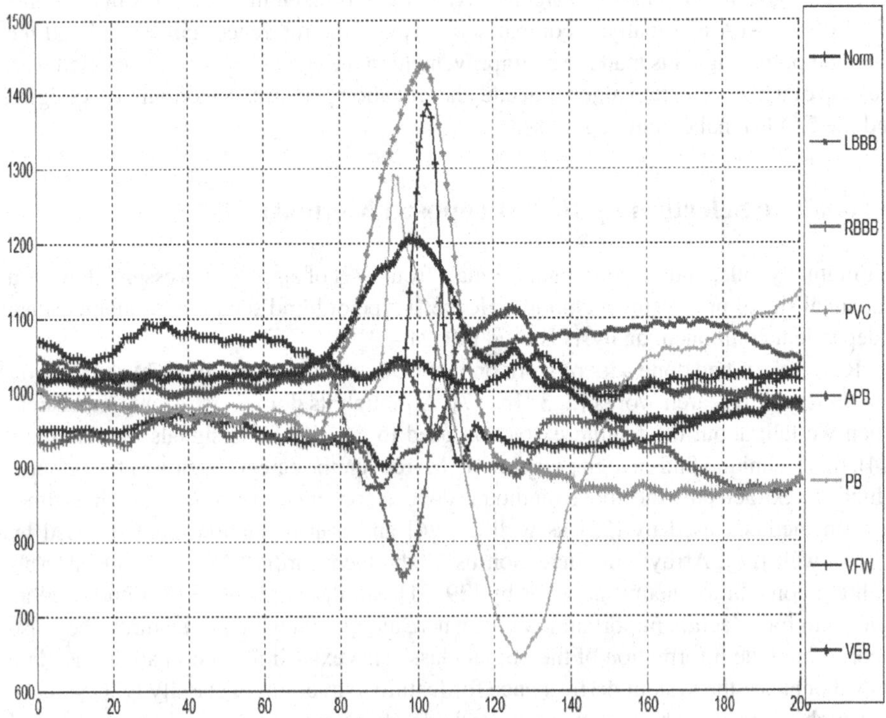

Fig. 6. ECG heartbeats of eight types

The MIT-BIH database of arrhythmia is used to complete the study work to get promising results. As we all know, the maximum information about the diagnostic condition is of heat beats lying near the R peak of the QRS segment, which has a period of 0.06 to 0.10 s. Hence, this portion of the required range around R-peak is selected for our study. The selection of different data points is made, 200 in number, coming out to be about 0.0556 s duration of the ECG signal with the sampling frequency of 360 Hz. These 200 samples consisting of the P wave and T wave also have all the required information of our need in a single pulse, including normal and noisy signals. Generalized structural and morphological characteristics of various types of arrhythmias are shown in Fig. 6. In our previous work, the same size and specifications of the signals were used [16, 17, 37].

5 Results

This work focused on using the BPNN classifier in the training stage as we have already discussed that we have taken eight types of ECG like NORM, LBBB, RBBB, or PVC. Hence, there will be eight inputs, which are feature vectors, whereas the eight output values are selected, starting from 1 up to 8, one for each type of ECG signal. We need to achieve superior classification by adjusting the different essential parameters in this stage. The number of ICs also affects the accuracy and other performance to a large extent. So, in this stage, they are varied starting from the lowest, i.e., five and going up to 40, and the accuracy achieved for each number is analyzed. The selection of ICs was based on a 10-fold approach. It was found that with an initial increase of IC numbers, the accuracy increased rapidly. After the number reaches 15, the accuracy became stable and formed a plateau, and any more increment in the IC count will not increase the classifier accuracy significantly. The average accuracy of the classifier hanged about more or less around 99.4%. Furthermore, after the training process, the neural network classifier was used on other sample types of the ECG signals. Its performance was again analyzed by doing sensitivity and specificity calculations.

The neural network classifier consisted of an input layer with 18 neurons, a hidden layer with 20 neurons, and an output layer with eight neurons. The number of neurons in the output layer is equal to the number of samples of different ECG signals to perform these signals' classification functions.

A hyperbolic tangent is being done for the input and hidden layer, whereas, for the output layer, the choice of identity function is made. BPNN bias values and weights are adjusted and updated with the help of the Levenberg-Marquardt optimization method [38]. The learning rate was set to be 0.1. During the training period, many iterations are reduced to a low count by establishing a criterion having a value of 0.01 in mean-square error. On an average of 10 times, the required time during the classifier's training period was found to be 1.6 s, which was done using MATLAB in its computing environment.

Accuracy was significantly improved when the pure ECG separation from the noise signal was incorporated with ICA, even when the signal is of low quality with a considerable amount of noise. We noted from the above results that the classification accuracy increased when ICA does noise removal in all noise cases. Still, the sensitivity and positive predictivity were improved up to 40% when a significant amount of noise is present in the ECG signal, as shown in Fig. 7 and Fig. 8. We also achieved enhanced classification accuracy (Tables 1 and 2).

Table 1. Classification sensitivity compared before and after source separation

Noise (dB) sensitivity (%)	−12	−6	0	6	12	18	24
ICA Filtering	93.3	94	95.1	97.1	97.6	98	97.9
Basic Filtering	55.6	61.1	80.6	83.2	92.9	96.5	96.5

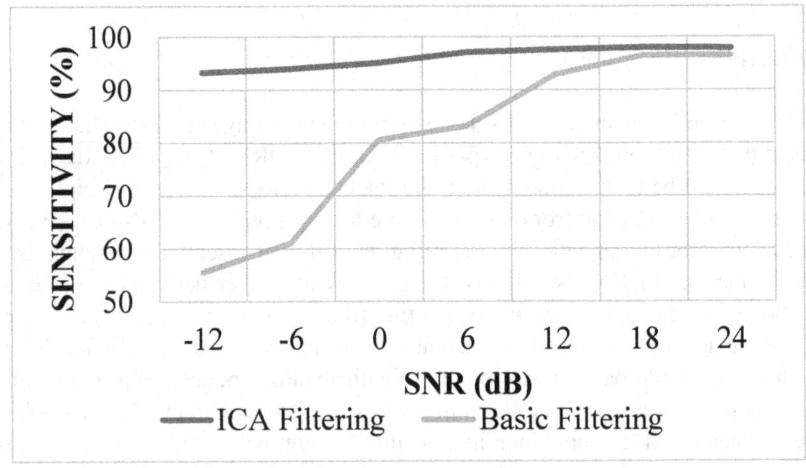

Fig. 7. Sensitivity before and after ICA filtering

Table 2. Classification of positive predictive value compared before and after source separation.

Noise (dB) predictivity (%)	−12	−6	0	6	12	18	24
ICA filtering	94.1	93.8	94.7	97.4	97.8	98.1	98.1
Basic filtering	55.9	59.9	81.6	82.5	93.6	96.4	96.1

The confusion matrix is indicated in Fig. 9, where the sensitivity, specificity, and overall accuracy of all the eight classes of ECG are shown. The last column and last row indicate the positive predictive value of each arrhythmia individually and the individual sensitivity of each arrhythmia type, respectively, with an accuracy of 99.8%, which is the highest value shown by the confusion matrix in its bottom-right cell (Tables 3, 4 and 5).

Figure 10 indicates a range of accuracy with different folds when the current set is used. We found that the highest record was 99.6% among the recorder accuracy, with the average coming out to be 99.3%. We also achieved the highest accuracy with ANN,

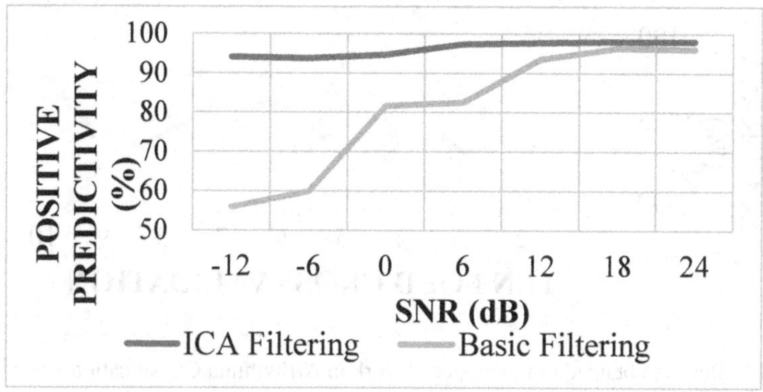

Fig. 8. Positive predictivity before and after ICA filtering

Confusion Matrix

Output Class \ Target Class	1	2	3	4	5	6	7	8	
1	200 13.8%	0 0.0%	0 0.0%	0 0.0%	0 0.0%	0 0.0%	0 0.0%	0 0.0%	100% 0.0%
2	0 0.0%	199 13.7%	0 0.0%	0 0.0%	0 0.0%	0 0.0%	0 0.0%	0 0.0%	100% 0.0%
3	0 0.0%	0 0.0%	200 13.8%	0 0.0%	0 0.0%	0 0.0%	0 0.0%	0 0.0%	100% 0.0%
4	0 0.0%	1 0.1%	0 0.0%	198 13.7%	0 0.0%	0 0.0%	0 0.0%	0 0.0%	99.5% 0.5%
5	0 0.0%	0 0.0%	0 0.0%	0 0.0%	200 13.8%	0 0.0%	0 0.0%	0 0.0%	100% 0.0%
6	0 0.0%	0 0.0%	0 0.0%	0 0.0%	0 0.0%	200 13.8%	0 0.0%	0 0.0%	100% 0.0%
7	0 0.0%	0 0.0%	0 0.0%	2 0.1%	0 0.0%	0 0.0%	200 13.8%	0 0.0%	99.0% 1.0%
8	0 0.0%	0 0.0%	0 0.0%	0 0.0%	0 0.0%	0 0.0%	0 0.0%	50 3.4%	100% 0.0%
	100% 0.0%	99.5% 0.5%	100% 0.0%	99.0% 1.0%	100% 0.0%	100% 0.0%	100% 0.0%	100% 0.0%	**99.8% 0.2%**

Fig. 9. Eight classes' classification with the proposed method

Table 3. Details of accuracy for different arrhythmias with above work

Fold	1	2	3	4	5	6	7	8	9	10
Accuracy	99.6	99.4	99.3	99.6	99.3	99.6	99.6	99.4	99.3	99.8

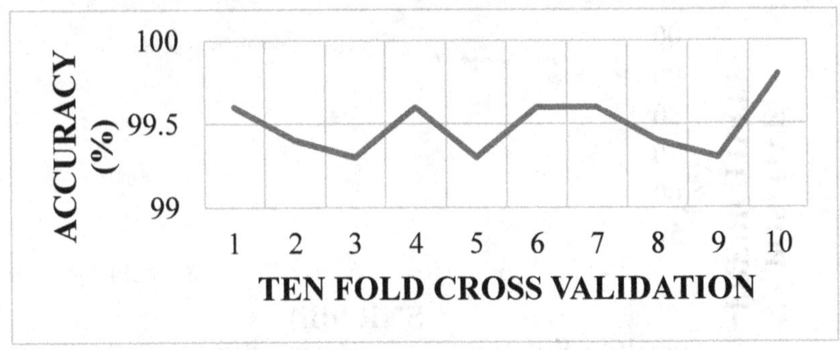

Fig. 10. Results obtained in the proposed work in Arrhythmia Classification Accuracy

Table 4. Details of positive predictive value in case of different arrhythmias using the above work

FOLD	1	2	3	4	5	6	7	8	9	10
NORM	100.0	100.0	100.0	100.0	100.0	100.0	100.0	100.0	99.5	100.0
LBBB	100.0	100.0	100.0	100.0	99.5	100.0	100.0	100.0	100.0	100.0
RBBB	100.0	99.5	98.5	99.5	99.5	100.0	99.0	100.0	99.0	100.0
PVC	99.5	100.0	99.5	99.0	99.5	100.0	100.0	98.5	99.5	99.5
APB	99.5	97.6	99.0	99.5	100.0	98.5	99.0	100.0	99.0	100.0
PB	99.0	99.5	100.0	99.5	100.0	99.5	99.0	100.0	100.0	100.0
VEB	98.5	100.0	98.5	99.0	96.6	99.0	99.5	98.5	99.0	99.0
VFW	100.0	96.2	94.3	100.0	96.2	100.0	100.0	100.0	92.6	100.0

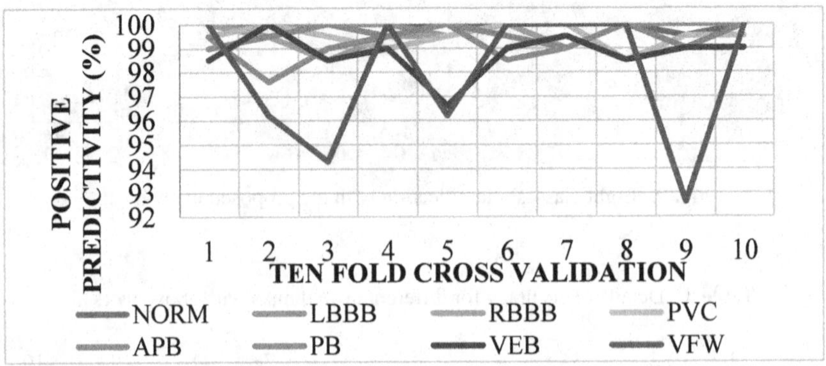

Fig. 11. Positive predictive value results using the above work

Table 5. Details of sensitivity for in case of different arrhythmias with the above method

FOLD	1	2	3	4	5	6	7	8	9	10
NORM	100	100	100	100	100	100	100	100	100	100
LBBB	99	99	99	99	99	99	99	99	98.5	99.5
RBBB	100	100	100	99.5	100	99.5	99.5	100	99.5	100
PVC	99	99	99	99	99	99	99	99	99	99
APB	100	100	100	100	100	100	100	100	100	100
PB	100	98.5	96.5	100	96.5	100	100	100	99.5	100
VEB	98.5	99	99.5	99	99.5	99.5	99	99.5	97.5	100
VFW	100	100	100	100	100	100	100	98	100	100

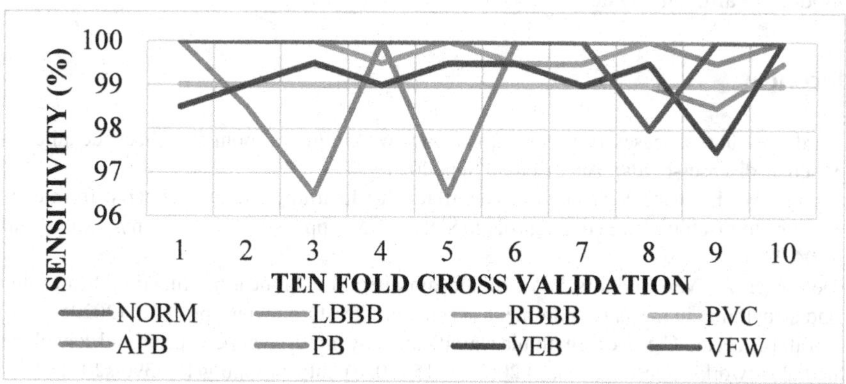

Fig. 12. Sensitivity results using the above work

and the least was acquired by using SVM. Figures 11 and 12 indicate the specificity and sensitivity performance level affected by different ICA features extracted with the help of various ANN classifier folds. We achieved the highest level of specificity of about 100% with Normal beats. In contrast, the proposed algorithm reduced specificity to 98.6% and 96.4% in VEB and VFW due to their reduced data set size.

6 Conclusions

During the Holter device and telemedicine applications, there are some uncommon noises present in the ECG data. The Fast ICA algorithm is connected with the kurtosis and a correlation function to detect and reduce noise in the ECG signal. PCA and ICA performance are investigated for carrying out denoising in the recorded ECG signals in ambulatory conditions.

The proposed method is automatic, and the component selection is done based on the correlation coefficient and kurtosis. When filtering is done using the above method and a comparison between filtered and non-filtered signals is done in high noise signals, it was found that the sensitivity during beat detection was 100%. The FastICA algorithm proposed in our study requires less time with high computational simplicity, which makes it superior to any other ICA technique for medical applications.

Classification sensitivity of 97.9% and positive Predictivity of 98.1% were achieved for noisy signals. Accuracy as high as 99.3% was achieved when the classification was done using the neural network classifiers, even when the ICs count was less. Not only accuracy but also other performance parameters like sensitivity, specificity, etc., were also better when features were extracted using ICA techniques as compared to any other technique, and computer simulations proved this. It was also demonstrated that the recognition performance improvement is also affected by selecting significant features, making the feature set selected more vigorous to classify various types of ECG arrhythmias. We can conclude that the proposed method/work proved to be very efficient and valuable in detecting various ECG arrhythmias types for real-time applications in the modern health care system.

References

1. Cardiovascular diseases (CVDs). https://www.who.int/news-room/fact-sheets/detail/cardiovascular-diseases-(cvds). Accessed 30 Sept 2020
2. Ravuri, M., Kannan, A., Tso, G.J., Amatriain, X.: Learning from the experts: from expert systems to machine-learned diagnosis models, no. Ml, pp. 1–16 (2018). http://arxiv.org/abs/1804.08033
3. Demolder, A., Von Kodolitsch, Y., Muiño-mosquera, L.: Myocardial function, heart failure and arrhythmia in marfan syndrome: a systematic literature review, pp. 1–20 (2020)
4. Savalia, S., et al.: Cardiac arrhythmia classification by multi-layer perceptron and convolution neural networks. Sensors (Switz.) **20**(7), 1–15 (2020). https://doi.org/10.3390/s20113069
5. Jacobsen, M., et al.: Reliable detection of atrial fibrillation with a medical wearable during inpatient conditions. Sensors (Switz.) **20**(19), 1–15 (2020). https://doi.org/10.3390/s20195517
6. Belgacem, N., Chikh, M.A., Reguig, F.B.: Supervised classification of ECG using neural networks (2003). http://dspace.univ-tlemcen.dz/handle/112/837
7. ECG arrhythmias recognition system based on independent component analysis feature extraction (2006). https://doi.org/10.1109/tencon.2006.343781
8. Yu, S.N., Chou, K.T.: Integration of independent component analysis and neural networks for ECG beat classification. Expert Syst. Appl. **34**(4), 2841–2846 (2008). https://doi.org/10.1016/j.eswa.2007.05.006
9. James, C.J., Hesse, C.W.: Independent component analysis for biomedical signals. Physiol. Meas. **26**(1), R15 (2004)
10. Wang, J.-S., Chiang, W.-C., Yang, Y.-T.C., Hsu, Y.-L.: An effective ECG arrhythmia classification algorithm. In: Huang, D.-S., Gan, Y., Premaratne, P., Han, Kyungsook (eds.) ICIC 2011. LNCS, vol. 6840, pp. 545–550. Springer, Heidelberg (2012). https://doi.org/10.1007/978-3-642-24553-4_72
11. Romero, I.: PCA and ICA applied to noise reduction in multi-lead ECG. Comput. Cardiol. **2010**(38), 613–616 (2011)
12. Wisbeck, J.O., Barros, A.K., Yy, A.K.B., Ojeda, R.G.: Application of ICA in the separation of breathing artifacts in ECG signals (1998). http://citeseerx.ist.psu.edu/viewdoc/summary?doi=10.1.1.40.3057

13. Raj, S., Ray, K.C.: Sparse representation of ECG signals for automated recognition of cardiac arrhythmias. Expert Syst. Appl. **105**, 49–64 (2018)
14. Malmivuo, J., Plonsey, R.: Bioelectromagnetism: Principles and Applications of Bioelectric and Biomagnetic Fields. Oxford University Press, Oxford (1995)
15. Moody, G.B., Mark, R.G., Goldberger, A.L.: PhysioNet: a web-based resource for the study of physiologic signals. IEEE Eng. Med. Biol. Mag. **20**(3), 70–75 (2001). https://doi.org/10.1109/51.932728
16. Sarfraz, M., Li, F.: Independent component analysis for motion artifacts removal from electrocardiogram. Glob. Perspect. Artif. Intell. **1**(4), 49–55 (2013)
17. Sarfraz, M., Li, F., Javed, M.: A comparative study of ICA algorithms for ECG signal processing. In: Proceedings of the International Conference on Advances in Computing and Artificial Intelligence, pp. 135–138 (2011)
18. Castells, F., Rieta, J.J., Millet, J., Zarzoso, V.: Spatiotemporal blind source separation approach to atrial activity estimation in atrial tachyarrhythmias. IEEE Trans. Biomed. Eng. **52**(2), 258–267 (2005). https://doi.org/10.1109/tbme.2004.840473
19. Hyvärinen, A., Oja, E.: Independent component analysis: algorithms and applications. Neural Netw. **13**(4–5), 411–430 (2000). https://doi.org/10.1016/s0893-6080(00)00026-5
20. Sarfraz, M.: Role of independent component analysis in intelligent ECG signal Processing. University of Salford (2014)
21. Karhunen, J., Oja, E., Hyvärinen, A.: Independent Component Analysis. Wiley, Hoboken (2001)
22. Naik, G.R., Kumar, D.K.: An overview of independent component analysis and its applications. Inform. An Int. J. Comput. Inform. **35**(1), 63–81 (2011)
23. Owis, M.I., Abou-Zied, A.H., Youssef, A.B.M., Kadah, Y.M.: Study of features based on nonlinear dynamical modeling in ECG arrhythmia detection and classification. IEEE Trans. Biomed. Eng. **49**(7), 733–736 (2002). https://doi.org/10.1109/TBME.2002.1010858
24. Li, H., Yuan, D., Wang, Y., Cui, D., Cao, L.: Arrhythmia classification based on multi-domain feature extraction for an ECG recognition system. Sensors **16**(10), 1744 (2016)
25. Afonso, V.X., Tompkins, W.J., Nguyen, T.Q., Luo, S.: ECG beat detection using filter banks. IEEE Trans. Biomed. Eng. **46**(2), 192–202 (1999). https://doi.org/10.1109/10.740882
26. De Chazal, P., O'Dwyer, M., Reilly, R.B.: Automatic classification of heartbeats using ECG morphology and heartbeat interval features. IEEE Trans. Biomed. Eng. **51**(7), 1196–1206 (2004). https://doi.org/10.1109/tbme.2004.827359
27. Acharya, R.U., et al.: Classification of cardiac abnormalities using heart rate signals. Med. Biol. Eng. Comput. **42**(3), 288–293 (2004). https://doi.org/10.1007/BF02344702
28. Al-Fahoum, A.S., Howitt, I.: Combined wavelet transformation and radial basis neural networks for classifying life-threatening cardiac arrhythmias. Med. Biol. Eng. Comput. **37**(5), 566–573 (1999). https://doi.org/10.1007/bf02513350
29. Kim, B.H., Pyun, J.Y.: ECG identification for personal authentication using LSTM-based deep recurrent neural networks. Sensors (Switz.) **20**(11), 1–17 (2020). https://doi.org/10.3390/s20113069
30. Acharya, U.R., Fujita, H., Lih, O.S., Hagiwara, Y., Tan, J.H., Adam, M.: Automated detection of arrhythmias using different intervals of tachycardia ECG segments with convolutional neural network. Inf. Sci. (Ny) **405**, 81–90 (2017). https://doi.org/10.1016/j.ins.2017.04.012
31. Yildirim, O., Talo, M., Ciaccio, E.J., San Tan, R., Acharya, U.R.: Accurate deep neural network model to detect cardiac arrhythmia on more than 10,000 individual subject ECG records. Comput. Methods Programs Biomed. **197**, 105740 (2020)
32. Kwak, N., Choi, C.H.: Feature extraction based on ICA for binary classification problems. IEEE Trans. Knowl. Data Eng. **15**(6), 1374–1388 (2003). https://doi.org/10.1109/TKDE.2003.1245279

33. Kwak, N., Choi, C.-H., Choi, J.Y.: Feature extraction using ICA. In: Dorffner, G., Bischof, H., Hornik, K. (eds.) ICANN 2001. LNCS (LNAI and LNB), vol. 2130, pp. 568–573. Springer, Heidelberg (2001). https://doi.org/10.1007/3-540-44668-0_80
34. Zheng, Z., Chen, Z., Hu, F., Zhu, J., Tang, Q., Liang, Y.: An automatic diagnosis of arrhythmias using a combination of CNN and LSTM technology. Electron. **9**(1), 1–15 (2020). https://doi.org/10.3390/electronics9010121
35. Oh, S.L., Ng, E.Y.K., Tan, R.S., Acharya, U.R.: Automated diagnosis of arrhythmia using combination of CNN and LSTM techniques with variable length heart beats. Comput. Biol. Med. **102**(June), 278–287 (2018). https://doi.org/10.1016/j.compbiomed.2018.06.002
36. Hannun, A.Y., et al.: Cardiologist-level arrhythmia detection and classification in ambulatory electrocardiograms using a deep neural network. Physiol. Behav. **176**(1), 139–148 (2018). https://doi.org/10.1016/j.physbeh.2017.03.040
37. Sarfraz, M., Li, F., Javed, M.: A blind source separation method to eliminate noise artifacts in ECG signals, vol. I, pp. 112–119 (2013)
38. Jang, J.S.R., Sun, C.T., Mizutani, E.: Neuro-fuzzy and soft computing-a computational approach to learning and machine intelligence [book review]. IEEE Trans. Automat. Contr. **42**(10), 1482–1484 (1997). https://doi.org/10.1109/tac.1997.633847

The Efficiency of Classification Techniques in Predicting Anemia Among Children: A Comparative Study

Qusay Saihood(✉) and Emrullah Sonuç

Faculty of Engineering, Department of Computer Engineering, Karabuk University, 78050 Karabuk, Turkey
esonuc@karabuk.edu.tr

Abstract. Anemia is the most common disease among children under school age, especially in developing countries, due to a lack of understanding about its causes and preventive measures. In most cases, anemia refers to malnutrition and is closely related to demographic and social factors. Previously, statistical methods were used to predict anemia among children and identify associated factors. It was concluded that this is not a good way. Following the success of machine learning (ML) techniques in exploring knowledge from clinical data in healthcare, it was a good chance to explore the knowledge of social factors associated with childhood anemia. In this study, we compared the performance of eight different ML techniques for predicting anemia in children using social factors to find the most appropriate method. ML techniques achieved promising results in predicting and identifying factors associated with childhood anemia. Multilayer perceptron (MLP) has the best accuracy of 81.67% with all features, while Decision Tree (DT) has the best accuracy of 82.50% when we applied feature selection methods. The explored knowledge of the social factors associated with anemia can guide nutritional practices and factors essential to child health. Additionally, identified factors can help prevent anemia outbreaks for appropriate intervention by governments and healthcare organizations.

Keywords: Machine learning · Classification · Anemia in children · Iron deficiency · Social factors

1 Introduction

Anemia is one of the most common blood diseases worldwide [1]. Anemia is defined as a disordering which the red blood cell count or hemoglobin concentration is lower than the normal range for a person [2]. The basic function of hemoglobin is to transport oxygen, and if there is not enough hemoglobin, the blood's ability to transport oxygen to body tissues will be reduced [3]. Anemia affects people in both developed and developing countries, but it is more widespread in developing countries where it is estimated that anemia affects 3.5 billion people in these countries [4]. In particular, children under school age are more likely to have anemia, as it is estimated that 42% of children in this

P. Liatsis et al. (Eds.): TIOTC 2021, CCIS 1548, pp. 167–181, 2022.
https://doi.org/10.1007/978-3-030-97255-4_12

age suffer from anemia [5]. There are several types of anemia, but iron deficiency anemia is one of the most common types of anemia, especially among children under five [6]. Several studies indicate the close association between anemia due to iron deficiency and children's social and demographic factors [7]. Children with iron deficiency anemia may suffer from many health problems in the short and long term. Some of these problems are low growth index, decreased perception and concentration, as well as mental disorders, and mental retardation [8]. Also, countries with widespread anemia suffer significant economic losses [9].

Due to the insidious nature of the disease, people cannot know the condition due to its widespread symptoms, but the disease itself is rampant, and it is a serious and worrying issue [10]. People's ignorance about child nutrition and the importance of social factors in child health are among the main reasons for the high rates of children with anemia at the national and international levels [10]. Therefore, it is crucial to transfer the required knowledge of the causes of anemia to reduce its prevalence [11]. Previously, researchers built many prediction systems by building algorithms based on expert advice. Also, many statistical methods (Chi-square, Logistic regression) have been used to measure the prevalence of anemia [12]. Although such studies may be useful in diagnosing the disease, they do not extend to deep data processing, which may detect different relationships and patterns that may be useful in determining the etiology of anemia [13].

Machine learning technologies have predictive power and discover functional patterns from complex data [14]. It could be a helpful method to explore the social factors associated with anemia in children [13]. Disease prediction is one of the practical applications of machine learning in healthcare. Also, the use of machine learning techniques is not limited to predicting disease only but also includes determining the causal inference from the predictive power of each variable [15]. This study aims to predict anemia in children and identify the factors associated with it using classification techniques, such as Decision Tree (DT), Support Vector Machine (SVM), Random Forest (RF), Naïve Bayes (NB), Logistic Regression (LR), Linear Discriminant Analysis (LDN), K-Nearest Neighbor (KNN) and Multilayer perceptron (MLP). The data used in this study was collected in Iraq for a set of children (600 samples).

The rest of the paper is organized as follows. Section 2 contains a discussion of related works, especially works dealing with anemia classification using artificial intelligence methods over the last five years. Section 3 explains the Materials and Methods, which is also divided into several parts: data collection, pre-processing phases, machine learning techniques, and performance measurement metrics. Section 4 deals with the results achieved. Section 5 contains a discussion of the results. Section 6 contains the conclusion and future work.

2 Related Work

Artificial intelligence (AI) techniques have recently achieved great success in exploring knowledge from health data within the healthcare sector. Mainly data mining techniques have been used extensively in diagnosing and predicting diseases. Anemia is a widespread and dangerous disease, especially in children. The incidence of anemia is closely related to socio-demographic factors [13]. In this section, a literature review (for the last five years) deals with predicting and diagnosing anemia using AI techniques.

Boubaker Sue et al. [15] focused on exploring social factors that are considered critical factors in children's health by using machine learning techniques (ANN, SVM, NB, RF and KNN) to predict anemia and malaria in children. The dataset used in the study was obtained from Demographic and Health Surveys (DHS) conducted from 2015 to 2016 in Senegal. ANN achieved the highest accuracy of 84.17% in predicting anemia and 94.74% in predicting malaria.

Jahidur Rahman Khan et al. [11] proposed new methods using data mining techniques to replace traditional data analysis methods. They proposed a model to predict states of anemia (Not anemia, Mild, Moderate, Severe) in children under the age of five by using data mining techniques includes association rule mining and DT. According to the results, the proposed model is not competitive in predicting anemia in respect of their experiments.

Priyanka Anand et al. [16] have used five ML techniques (LDA, KNN, RF, DT, and LR) to predict anemia in children under the age of 36 months from the risk factors associated with the occurrence of the disease. The study was conducted on a dataset that was collected from the outpatient clinics of a hospital in India. RT achieved the highest accuracy of 67.18% among other methods. Jahidur Rahman Khan et al. [17] also used SVM and the same methods as in [16]. ML techniques tested on the dataset taken by Bangladesh Demographic and Health Survey. RF achieved the highest accuracy of 68.53% among other techniques.

Dithy, M. D. and V. KrishnaPriya [18] proposed using a Gausnominal classification algorithm with a sequential selection process ADD-Left Remove-Right (ALRR) to predict anemia (not anemia, mild, severe or moderate) in young children and pregnant women. They focused on understanding the relationship between iron deficiency and demographic factors. The results showed that the proposed system performed better accuracy with 76.24% as compared to ANN, which has 65.0% accuracy.

Yıldız et al. [19] designed a decision support system to classify 12 types of anemia using NB, ANN, SVM and Boosted and Bagged Trees. The system was tested on a dataset obtained from a university hospital in Turkey with 25 features. In addition, different feature selection methods were used to create eight different datasets. This system achieved acceptable results for each of the algorithms used in the classification, and the best accuracy of 85.6% was obtained by using Bagged Decision Trees.

NB, Bayesian Network (BN), MLP and LR were used in [20] with and without feature selection techniques. Using all the features, LR achieved the highest accuracy with 87.3%, followed by MLP, BN, and NB to achieve accuracy of 87.1%, 85.1% and 83.6%, respectively. Using features selection, MLP and LR achieved the highest accuracy of 86.1%, followed by BN with an accuracy of 85.3% and NB with an accuracy of 84.6%.

A new type of random prediction (RP) with an improvised method for selecting median-based features is developed for predicting anemia in pregnant women [21]. The proposed method compared with ANN, Gausnominal [18] and VectNeighbour [22] and is very competitive among those methods.

3 Materials and Methods

The proposed system, which is shown in Fig. 1, consists of three phases.

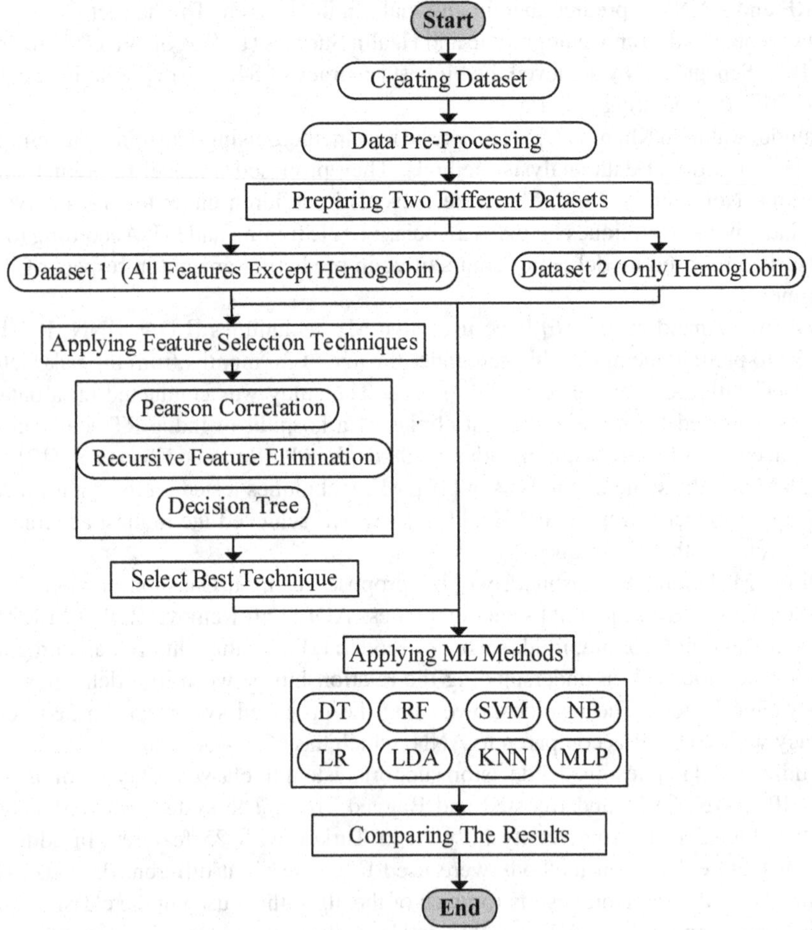

Fig. 1. Flowchart of the method.

In the first phase, the dataset was used in this study is described. The second phase consists of several steps. First, the data is prepared by pre-processing. Second, the dataset is divided into two subsets. Dataset 1 consists of all the features (socio-demographic factors, pediatric medical information, child nutrition practice and mother's nutritional knowledge) without the hemoglobin level feature. Dataset 2 consists of only one feature which is the hemoglobin level. Third, feature selection is used on Dataset 1. Important features are selected, and features that are not associated with anemia or strongly correlated with another variable are removed. In the third phase, we present classification algorithms to predict anemia and compare the performance of different classifiers by calculating the accuracy of each classifier.

Ethical Authorization: The dataset used in this study was collected by performing a cross-sectional study. It was conducted at Haditha General Hospital and out clinics in Haditha City, Al Anbar Governorate, Iraq, and was overseen by a specialist doctor. This study lasted for three months, from (2020/10/01) to (2021/01/01). The covered population in this study are children from the age of 6 months to under the age of 6 years. The data was collected through a questionnaire that contains a set of social factors (socio-demographic factors, pediatric medical information, child nutrition practice and mother's nutritional knowledge) that are associated with the occurrence of anemia in children. Written consent was obtained from the child's guardian, the hospital and the out clinics doctors to conduct this study.

3.1 Data Collection

The dataset used in this study has 600 samples collected from Haditha General Hospital and the out clinics in Haditha City in the Iraqi Al Anbar Governorate with a license from the hospital ethics committee. The features that impact anemia in children were selected according to previous medical studies and the recommendation of an experienced medical professional. All features used in the dataset are explained in Table 1.

Table 1. Description of dataset features.

Attribute name	Type	Description
1-Id	Numeric	The primary key consists of 600 rows
2- Child's age	Numeric	From 6 months to under 6 years
3-Gender	Numeric	0 = Female, 1 = Male
4-Mother's age	Numeric	0 = Age < 30, 1 = Age ≥ 30
5-Mother's education level	Numeric	0 = Illiteracy,1 = Primary, 2 = Secondary, 3 = University and above
6-Mother's occupational level	Numeric	0 = Un Employee, 1 = Employee
7-Father's education level	Numeric	0 = Illiteracy,1 = Primary, 2 = Secondary, 3 = University and above
8-Father's occupational level	Numeric	0 = Un Employee, 1 = Employee

(*continued*)

Table 1. (*continued*)

Attribute name	Type	Description
9-Residence	Numeric	0 = rural, 1 = urban
10-socio-economic status	Numeric	0 = Poor, 1 = Moderate, 2 = Good
11-Hemoglobin level	Numeric	
12-Short stature for age	Numeric	0 = Abnormal, 1 = Normal
13-Fever in the last 15 days	Numeric	0 = No, 1 = Yes
14-Previous history of anemia	Numeric	0 = No, 1 = Yes
15-Diarrhea in the last 15 days	Numeric	0 = No, 1 = Yes
16-Type of breastfeeding	Numeric	0 = Abnormal, 1 = Normal, 3 = Max
17-Consume milk powder	Numeric	0 = No, 1 = Yes
18-Consume sugary drink	Numeric	0 = No, 1 = Yes
19-Consume yogurt	Numeric	0 = No, 1 = Yes
20-Consume solid/ semisolid food	Numeric	0 = No, 1 = Yes
21-Duration of breastfeeding	Numeric	0 = Abnormal, 1 = Normal,
22-Consumption of meat	Numeric	0 = No, 1 = Yes
23- Consumption of dark-green leafy vegetables	Numeric	0 = No, 1 = Yes
24-Consumption of foods that are sources of iron	Numeric	0 = No, 1 = Yes
25-Consumption of liver	Numeric	0 = No, 1 = Yes
26-Know the optimal time of complementary feeding	Numeric	0 = Unknow, 1 = Know, 2 = Not Sure
27-Know the first complementary food	Numeric	0 = Unknow, 1 = Know, 2 = Not Sure
28-know the optimum food of supplemental iron	Numeric	0 = Unknow, 1 = Know, 2 = Not Sure
29-Know nutrients related to anemia	Numeric	0 = Unknow, 1 = Know, 2 = Not Sure
30-Know the optimal time of breastfeeding	Numeric	0 = Unknow, 1 = Know, 2 = Not Sure
31-Anemia state	Numeric	0 = Not Anemic (171 samples), 1 = Anemic (429 samples)

The target (anemic, not anemic) was determined by relying on the normal level of hemoglobin (HGB) according to the WHO criteria shown in Table 2.

Table 2. Hemoglobin levels for ages [14].

Age of child	Not-Anemia	Anemia
6 months	HGB ≥ 11.1	HGB < 11.1
6 months to 2 years	HGB ≥ 10.5	HGB < 10.5
2 years to 6 years	HGB ≥ 11.5	HGB < 11.5

3.2 Data Pre-processing

Data pre-processing is an important stage for both data mining and machine learning techniques. This is because real-world data tends to be inconsistent, noisy, and may contain missing data, redundant data, and irrelevant data. It negatively affects the performance of the algorithms and may result in inaccurate knowledge and incorrectly learned. Pre-processing is used to clean data, scaling data, and transform data into a format that matches the algorithms used. In addition, feature selection to select the best features [18].

Data Cleaning. In this stage of the pre-processing steps, the missing data and the duplicate data are checked. The missing values can be handled in several ways, such as replacing the value with the median or mean or mode of that attribute [15]. In this study, the missing value of a feature is replaced with the mean value of that feature column. There were seven values of residence and ten values of short stature are missed, which was compensated by using the mean value of the feature column. In addition, it was ensured that there were no duplicate values.

Data Transforming. In this stage of the pre-processing steps, all categorical features in the dataset are converted to a unified numeric representation. Due to there are categorical and numeric features in the dataset.

Data Normalization. Normalization is the process of converting the values of numeric columns in a dataset to a common scale without distorting the ranges of values. In this study, data normalization was used with the MLP algorithm only using the Min-Max normalization method.

The final dataset after the pre-processing process consists of 600 rows and 31 columns and does not contain any null or duplicate values and is represented in numeric form.

Feature Selection. The aim of using feature selection techniques in machine learning is to find the best set of features that can be used to construct useful models. It involves evaluating the relationship between each input variable and the target variable according to specific evaluation criteria and selecting the input variables with the strongest relationship to the target variable. Feature selection is used to improve decision accuracy, minimize the dimensions of the dataset and minimize the time in implementing the ML training process. There are four main methods of feature selection techniques: filter approach, wrapper approach, embedded approach, and hybrid methods [23].

More than one feature selection technique has been experimented with to choose the best method suiting the work of ML techniques that are used in this study.

Pearson Correlation. Pearson correlation is one of the filter methods to feature selection that uses a statistical method to determine the association between two variables X and Y. It calculates the intensity of the correlation between each function of the input dataset and the category (target). This test's result ranges from 1 to −1, suggesting a weak correlation is indicated by a value near 0. A value indicates a strong positive correlation near 1, and a value indicates a strong negative correlation near −1 [24].

Recursive Feature Elimination. Recursive Feature Elimination (RFE) is a feature selection wrapper method to define features by looking at smaller collections of features regularly. The estimator is trained on the initial set of features. The coef_attribute or feature value is used to determine the significance of each feature. The less important features are then trimmed from the original dataset. This process is repeated until the highest accuracy is reached and each function is rated [25].

Decision Tree. One of the essential advantages of the decision tree algorithm is the feature importance characteristic that defines each of the input variables according to their importance in determining the class(target). This characteristic is used to identify important features and be used to select features [26]. Table 3 shows the features chosen by all of the feature selection techniques used.

3.3 Classification Methods

ML is concerned with designing algorithms that allow computers to learn on their own without the need to program each rule to make a decision or extract a specific pattern by training it on many datasets that help it understand and build its concept. There are two types of learning: supervised and unsupervised learning. In supervised learning, algorithms train a model using inputs (features) and outputs (targets), intending to generate reasonable predictions for new data inputs. In unsupervised learning, algorithms train a model using inputs only without specifying the outputs. Through the training process, algorithms build relationships and patterns used to make predictions on new data [27].

Table 3. Features selected by feature selection techniques.

Feature selection techniques	Number of features selected	Features selected
Pearson correlation	8	{mother's age, mother's education level, father's occupational level, fever, previous history of anemia, type of breastfeeding, consume sugary drink, consumption of liver}
Recursive Feature Elimination	14	{child's age, gender, mother's age, mother's education level, father's education level, father's occupational level, fever, previous history of anemia, type of breastfeeding, consumption of foods that are sources of iron, know the optimal time of complementary feeding, know the first complementary food, know the optimum food of supplemental iron, know the optimal time of breastfeeding}
Decision Tree	12	{child's age, gender, mother's education level, father's education level, residence, fever, type of breastfeeding, duration of breastfeeding, know the optimal time of complementary feeding, know the optimum food of supplemental iron, know nutrients related to anemia, know the optimal time of breastfeeding}

One of the most important and widely used supervised ML techniques is classification. There are two types of classification, binary and multiple classification that depend on the number of outputs [28]. Since we predict an anemia state in children (anemic or not-anemic), binary classification was used in this study.

Decision Tree (DT). DT is a supervised machine learning algorithm and is used for both classification and regression problems. The DT looks like a tree-like flowchart where the data is divided continuously depending on a specific parameter. DT does not require many data cleaning processes in the pre-processing stage. Also, it is not limited to a specific type of data [29].

Support Vector Machine (SVM). SVM is widely used for classification but also can be used for and regression. The classification is done by linearly or non-linearly dividing the dataset's input space. This process is performed by determining the hyperplane in an n-dimensional vector space between two classes of elements. It can be than one hyperplane separating two classes. In this case, since large margins improve test sample prediction, the hyperplane with the largest margin distance is chosen [19].

Random Forest (RF). Usage of RF in medical diagnostics has grown in popularity. RF contains a number of decision trees. Each decision tree displays a vote that reflects the item's classification decision [30].

Naïve Bayes (NB). The Bayes' theorem is used to create NB classifiers, a set of classification algorithms of supervised machine learning algorithms. The predictors are assumed to be independent in this classification technique. The NB classifier, in general, assumes that the existence of one feature in a class has no bearing on the existence of any other feature [27].

Logistic Regression (LR). LR is a supervised classification method that uses a statistical model to predict the likelihood of an event by fitting data to a logistic curve. A dichotomous variable is used to assess the outcome. Several expected variables, which can be numerical or categorical, are used in logistic regression. LR is commonly used in health care and the social sciences. It is also used extensively in marketing to explore consumers' propensity to buy a product or not [31].

Linear Discriminant Analysis (LDA). LDA is a popular algorithm in both supervised and unsupervised machine learning that is used to identify patterns and solve dimensional problems in data pre-processing steps while building the model. It is proposed by R. Fischer. It locates the hyper-projection plane that reduces class variance while increasing the distance between predicted class means. LDA uses Bayes' theorem to get the predictions. LDA differs from NB in that it assumes that the contrast is the same for all classes, while NB assumes that the variables are independent [32].

K-Nearest Neighbor (KNN). KNN is an easy-to-use method for classification and regression problems. KNN stores all available cases and classifies new classes based on the plurality of its neighbors' votes. Most of the time, a majority vote is used between data elements in a neighborhood to determine an X rating, with or without regard to a weighting based on distance. However, it needs to choose an appropriate value for k on which classification success will highly depend [33].

Multilayer Perceptron (MLP). MLP is a type of classifier that connects to a neural network. Unlike other classification algorithms like SVM and NB, MLP performs the classification task depending on the underlying neural network. The multilayer sensory structure of MLP consists of three layers of nodes: the first layer is an input layer, the second layer is a hidden layer, and the third layer is an output layer. The training data is entered into the first layer, where it is multiplied by randomly initialized weights. After that, some biases are added, and an activation function is applied to the whole result. The output is passed to the next layer, which repeats the process, with each layer's input data coming from the previous layer except the first [34].

3.4 Performance Measurement

The performance of classification techniques was evaluated using three quality measures that are accuracy, sensitivity and specificity. Anemic samples were considered positive "1", and not-anemic samples were considered negative "0".

- **True Positives (TP):** Anemic children who are predicted as anemic.
- **True Negatives (TN):** Not-anemic children who are predicted as not-anemic.
- **False Positives (FP):** Not-anemic children who are predicted as anemic.
- **False Negatives (FN):** Anemic children who are predicted as not-anemic.

$$\text{Accuracy} = (TN + TP)/(TN + TP + FN + FP) \tag{1}$$

$$\text{Sensitivity} = TP/(TP + FN) \tag{2}$$

$$\text{Specificity} = (TN/(TN/FP) \tag{3}$$

4 Experiments and Results

The eight ML techniques are built using a scikit-learn library that is a powerful library used to implement ML models and pre-processing and model validation phases. The dataset consists of 600 samples with 429 positive samples of anemic children and 171 negative samples of not-anemic children. 80% of the data was used as a training set and 20% used as a test set.

4.1 Experimental Results on Dataset 1

Anemia in children was predicted using Dataset 1, which contains all the features (socio-demographic factors, pediatric medical information, child nutrition practice and mother's nutritional knowledge) except the hemoglobin level.

Table 4 shows the results of the algorithms. MLP achieved the best accuracy of 81.67%. DT ranks second with an accuracy of 80.00%.

Table 4. Performance comparison of ML algorithms on Dataset 1.

Algorithms	Accuracy	Sensitivity	Specificity
DT	80.00%	87.95%	62.16%
SVM	75.00%	91.56%	37.83%
RF	79.17%	95.18%	43.24%
NB	60.00%	73.49%	29.72%
LR	70.00%	97.59%	8.10%
LDA	70.83%	97.59%	10.81%
KNN	76.67	73.49%	83.78%
MLP	81.67%	91.56%	59.45%

4.2 Experimental Results on Dataset 2

In this section, anemia in children was predicted by using hemoglobin levels only. SVM, NB, LR, LDA and MLP algorithms achieved the highest accuracy of 92.50%. Results are shown in Table 5.

Table 5. Performance comparison of ML algorithms on Dataset 2.

Algorithms	Accuracy	Sensitivity	Specificity
DT	91.67%	95.18%	83.78%
SVM	92.50%	100.0%	75.67%
RF	91.67%	97.59%	78.37%
NB	92.50%	100.0%	75.67%
LR	92.50%	100.0%	75.67%
LDA	92.50%	100.0%	75.67%
KNN	91.67%	97.59%	78.37%
MLP	92.50%	100.0%	75.67%

4.3 Experimental Results on Dataset 1 Using Feature Selection Techniques

Three different feature selection techniques (Pearson correlation, Recursive Feature Elimination and Decision Tree) were used on Dataset 1 to determine the most appropriate method to get better accuracy on ML techniques.

As shown in Table 6, remarkable improvement was observed for DT, SVM, RF, NB LR, and LDN. DT achieved the best result using feature selection techniques with an accuracy of 82.50%, while MLP and KNN cannot improve their results.

Table 6. Comparison of ML algorithms using feature selection techniques on Dataset 1.

Algorithms	Feature selection techniques	Accuracy	Sensitivity	Specificity
DT	Decision Tree	82.50%	85.54%	75.67%
SVM	Recursive Feature Elimination	79.16%	89.15%	56.75%
RF	Recursive Feature Elimination	80.00%	96.38%	43.24%
NB	Recursive Feature Elimination	68.33%	86.74%	27.02%
LR	Pearson correlation	70.83%	100.0%	5.40%
LDA	Recursive Feature Elimination	71.67%	98.79%	10.81%
KNN	Recursive Feature Elimination	69.17%	68.67%	70.27%
MLP	Recursive Feature Elimination	79.17%	89.15%	56.75%

5 Discussion

The ML techniques have achieved promising results in diagnosing anemia and exploring the knowledge of social factors associated with it. This study proved that socio-demographic factors could be considered good predictors of anemia in children. It can be concluded that a clear correlation between the educational level of the father and mother, place of residence and the appearance of anemia, in addition to the importance of the mother's nutritional knowledge and her ability to identify complementary feeding. Also, it can be said that both the type of breastfeeding and the period of normal breastfeeding affects the risk of anemia.

According to the accuracy, the performance of the eight classification techniques was compared, and MLP is the best method without using feature selection techniques. When feature selection techniques are used on Dataset 1, DT is the best method, RF and MLP are very competitive techniques. When we analyze the results of the other studies [15–17] in the literature among the classification techniques used in the study, SVM has the best accuracy in [15], RF has the best accuracy in [16, 17]. Furthermore, the deep learning model in [15] has the best accuracy.

6 Conclusion and Future Works

This study compares eight different ML techniques (DT, SVM, RF, NB, LR, LDA, KNN, MLP) to predict anemia in children using social factors as features. These techniques successfully diagnose anemia thorough analysis and deep understanding of data and achieved good results in predicting anemia. We tested the proposed methods in three stages. In the first stage, we use Dataset 1, which contains social factors, and the results indicate that MLP algorithm achieved the highest accuracy of 81.67%. The second stage uses only the hemoglobin level as a feature, and the results show that SVM, NB, LR, LDA and MLP algorithms achieved the highest accuracy of 92.50%. In the last stage, we try to make classification using feature selection methods and the results indicate that DT outperforms the rest of the algorithms with an accuracy of 82.50%. The results confirm the importance of using social factors to predict anemia in children, which are considered factors associated with disease occurrence. In addition, it is important to choose the appropriate feature selecting technique for features used by the model. As future work, we recommend improving the performance of ML techniques and the use of deep learning techniques to predict anemia in children. Also, different types of classes can be used (Not-anemic, Mild, Moderate, Severe) to predict the anemia in more detail.

References

1. Kawo, K.N., Asfaw, Z.G., Yohannes, N.: Multilevel analysis of determinants of anemia prevalence among children aged 6–59 months in Ethiopia: classical and Bayesian approaches. Anemia 2018 (2018)
2. Gautam, S., et al.: Determining factors for the prevalence of anemia in women of reproductive age in Nepal: evidence from recent national survey data. PloS One **14**(6), e0218288 (2019)
3. Berhe, B., et al.: Prevalence of anemia and associated factors among pregnant women in Adigrat General Hospital, Tigrai, northern Ethiopia, 2018. BMC Res. Notes **12**(1), 1–6 (2019)
4. Ewusie, J.E., et al.: Prevalence of anemia among under-5 children in the Ghanaian population: estimates from the Ghana demographic and health survey. BMC Public Health **14**(1), 1–9 (2014)
5. Al-Alimi, A.A., Bashanfer, S., Morish, M.A.: Prevalence of iron deficiency anemia among university students in Hodeida Province, Yemen. Anemia 2018 (2018)
6. Adem, O.S., Tadsse, K., Gebremedhin, A.: Iron deficiency aneamia is moderate public health problem among school going adolescent girls in Berahle district, afar Northeast Ethiopia. J. Food Nutr. Sci. **3**, 10–16 (2015)
7. Gebreweld, A., et al.: Prevalence of anemia and its associated factors among children under five years of age attending at Guguftu health center, South Wollo, Northeast Ethiopia. PloS One **14**(7), e0218961 (2019)
8. Huang, Z., et al.: Prevalence and risk factors of anemia among children aged 6–23 months in Huaihua, Hunan Province. BMC Public Health **18**(1), 1–11 (2018). https://doi.org/10.1186/s12889-018-6207-x
9. Tezera, R., et al.: Prevalence of anemia among school-age children in Ethiopia: a systematic review and meta-analysis. System. Rev. **7**(1), 1–7 (2018). https://doi.org/10.1186/s13643-018-0741-6
10. Mattiello, V., Schmugge, M., Hengartner, H., von der Weid, N., Renella, R.: Diagnosis and management of iron deficiency in children with or without anemia: consensus recommendations of the SPOG pediatric hematology working group. Eur. J. Pediatr. **179**(4), 527–545 (2020). https://doi.org/10.1007/s00431-020-03597-5
11. Meena, K., et al.: Using classification techniques for statistical analysis of anemia. Artif. Intell. Med. **94**, 138–152 (2019)
12. Dey, S., Raheem, E.: Multilevel multinomial logistic regression model for identifying factors associated with anemia in children 6–59 months in northeastern states of India. Cogent Math. Stat. **3**(1), 1159798 (2016)
13. Dukhi, N., et al.: Artificial intelligence approach for analyzing anaemia prevalence in children and adolescents in BRICS countries: a review. Curr. Res. Nutr. Food Sci. J. **9**(1), 1–10 (2021)
14. Aswad, S.A., Sonuç, E.: Classification of VPN network traffic flow using time related features on apache spark. In: 2020 4th International Symposium on Multidisciplinary Studies and Innovative Technologies (ISMSIT). IEEE (2020)
15. Sow, B., et al.: Assessing the relative importance of social determinants of health in malaria and anemia classification based on machine learning techniques. Inform. Health Soc. Care **45**(3), 229–241 (2020)

16. Anand, P., Gupta, R., Sharma, A.: Prediction of anaemia among children using machine learning algorithms
17. Khan, J.R., et al.: Machine learning algorithms to predict the childhood anemia in Bangladesh. J. Data Sci. **17**(1), 195–218 (2019)
18. Dithy, M.D., Priya, V.K.: Predicting anemia in pregnant women by using gausnominal classification algorithm. Int. J. Pure Appl. Math. **118**(20) 3343-9 (2018)
19. Yıldız, T.K., Yurtay, N., Öneç, B.: Classifying anemia types using artificial learning methods. Eng. Sci. Technol. Int. J. **24**(1), 50–70 (2021)
20. Mohammed, M.S., Ahmad, A.A., Murat, S.A.R.I.: Analysis of anemia using data mining techniques with risk factors specification. In: 2020 International Conference for Emerging Technology (INCET). IEEE (2020)
21. Dithy, M.D., KrishnaPriya V.: Anemia screening in pregnant women by using random prediction (RP) classification algorithm. Int. J. Rec. Technol. Eng. (IJRTE), 8(02) (2019)
22. Dithy, M.D., KrishnaPriya V.: Anemia screening in pregnant women by using vect neighbour classification algorithm. J. Adv. Res. Dyn. Control Syst. **11**(04) (2019)
23. Das, A.K., Sengupta, S., Bhattacharyya, S.: A group incremental feature selection for classification using rough set theory based genetic algorithm. Appl. Soft Comput. **65**, 400–411 (2018)
24. Saidi, R., Bouaguel, W., Essoussi, N.: Hybrid feature selection method based on the genetic algorithm and pearson correlation coefficient. In: Hassanien, A.E. (ed.) Machine Learning Paradigms: Theory and Application. SCI, vol. 801, pp. 3–24. Springer, Cham (2019). https://doi.org/10.1007/978-3-030-02357-7_1
25. Isabelle, G., Jason, W., Stephen, B., Vladimir, V.: Gene selection for cancer classification using support vector machines. Mach Learn. **46**(1–3), 389–422 (2002). https://doi.org/10.1023/A:1012487302797
26. Sugumaran, V., Muralidharan, V., Ramachandran, K.I.: Feature selection using decision tree and classification through proximal support vector machine for fault diagnostics of roller bearing. Mech. Syst. Signal Process. **21**(2), 930–942 (2007)
27. Panda, D., Dash, S.: Predictive system: Comparison of classification techniques for effective prediction of heart disease. In: Satapathy, S.C., Bhateja, V., Mohanty, J.R., Udgata, S.K. (eds.) Smart Intelligent Computing and Applications. SIST, vol. 159, pp. 203–213. Springer, Singapore (2020). https://doi.org/10.1007/978-981-13-9282-5_19
28. Mohan, S., Thirumalai, C., Srivastava, G.: Effective heart disease prediction using hybrid machine learning techniques. IEEE Access **7**, 81542–81554 (2019)
29. Ghiasi, M., Zendehboudi, S., Mohsenipour, A.: Decision tree-based diagnosis of coronary artery disease: CART model. Comput. Methods Programs Biomed. **192**, 105400 (2020)
30. Ayon, S.I., Islam, M.M., Hossain, M.R.: Coronary artery heart disease prediction: a comparative study of computational intelligence techniques. IETE J. Res. 1–20 (2020)
31. Chao, C.-M., et al.: Construction the model on the breast cancer survival analysis use support vector machine, logistic regression and decision tree. J. Med. Syst. **38**(10), 1–7 (2014). https://doi.org/10.1007/s10916-014-0106-1
32. Ricciardi, C., et al.: Linear discriminant analysis and principal component analysis to predict coronary artery disease. Health Inform. J. **26**(3), 2181–2192 (2020)
33. Cai, Z., et al.: An intelligent Parkinson's disease diagnostic system based on a chaotic bacterial foraging optimization enhanced fuzzy KNN approach. Comput. Math. Methods Med. **2018** (2018)
34. Sharifzadeh, F., Akbarizadeh, G., Kavian, Y.: Ship classification in SAR images using a new hybrid CNN–MLP classifier. J. Indian Soc. Remote Sens. **47**(4), 551–562 (2018). https://doi.org/10.1007/s12524-018-0891-y

Automated Brain Tumor Segmentation and Classification Through MRI Images

Sahar Gull[1], Shahzad Akbar[1], Syed Ale Hassan[1], Amjad Rehman[2(✉)], and Tariq Sadad[3]

[1] Department of Computing, Riphah International University, Faisalabad Campus, Faisalabad, Pakistan

[2] Artificial Intelligence and Data Analytics LAB (AIDA), Prince Sultan University, Riyadh, Saudi Arabia

rkamjad@gmail.com

[3] Department of Computer Science and Software Engineering, International Islamic University, Islamabad, Pakistan

Abstract. The brain tumor is considered a hazardous infection and may cause death. Therefore, early detection of brain tumors can improve the survival rate. This paper presents convolutional neural network method for segmentation and classification of brain tumors using magnetic resonance images. The proposed method has achieved an accuracy of 98.97%, specificity of 97.35%, sensitivity of 97%, precision of 97.90%, and F1-score of 96% for brain tumor segmentation. While on brain tumor classification, the proposed method shows accuracy 98.25%, sensitivity 98%, specificity 98.5%, precision 97.21% and F1-score 97%. The BRATS 2020 dataset has been utilized for training and testing the proposed method for brain tumor segmentation and classification.

Keywords: Brain tumor segmentation · Magnetic resonance images · BRATS 2020 dataset · Brain tumor classification · Convolution neural network

1 Introduction

In the last few decades, human intellectual disorders have been assumed to be resolved. However, due to uncertain human nature, the tumor is yet considered a danger to humanity. The brain tumor is assumed to be one of the fatal diseases ever experienced [1]. The brain is the highly diverse and central organ of the human body, including nerve cells and muscles that regulate the body's primary functions, including breathing, muscle activity, and senses. The functionality of each cell requires energy and varies that it may be growing; energy is being wasted, reactive, and aberrant [2]. The tissue as a tumor is created by this mass collection of abnormal cells. Tumors in the brain have formed brain cells unnatural [3]. In 2015 [4], Nearly 23,000 tumor cases in the United States (USA) have been reported. In 2017 [5], One of the significant causes of cancer Infirmity and morbidity worldwide is a brain tumor. Also, the abnormal development of the brain tumor does not propagate to other parts of the body except the brain. A slowly growing benign brain tumor has multiple limits and never spreads out. Whereas cells in

P. Liatsis et al. (Eds.): TIOTC 2021, CCIS 1548, pp. 182–194, 2022.
https://doi.org/10.1007/978-3-030-97255-4_13

a vital region are not malignant, benign tumors may cause life threats. This tumor often expands quickly and poses unusual borders and occurrence in other areas of the brain. Secondary (metastatic) brain tumors start elsewhere in the body like cancer. The World Health Organization (WHO) has been developed a ranking system for standardizing connectivity and forecasting brain tumor outcomes. The increasing rate of brain tumor types of Glioma (45%), meningioma, and pituitary (15%), among all other brain tumors [6], and are dangerous for brain activity.

Medical imaging approaches like Magnetic Resonance Imaging (MRI) provide considerable detail about the shape, size, and area of the brain tumor [7]. MRI is used to take 2D and 3D images of human body organs. It is the most reliable technique that provides high-quality images of brain tumors that can be identified at their early stages [8]. The MRI was invented in 1969 by Raymond V. Damadian, the first person to use MRI for analyzing the human body. MRI technique can be used for the treatment of brain tumors, using high-resolution images [9]. MRI is commonly used for different human body parts for 2D images and may vary from system-to-system specification. The intensity of the 3D brain is represented in the MRI processing [7].

Four typical types of MRI brain tumors include T1, T2, T1CE, and Flair. The T1 MRI images recognize the tissues, T2 MRI images recognize the edema zone with positive signals. T1CE images detect the tumor edge in the tumor's complex cell area without remarkable signal of the distinguishing specialist (gadolinium particles) [10]. As the necrotic cells cannot identify the administrator, the exceptional hypo portion of the tumor patient indicates that it can be segmented into a comparable strategy from the complex cell region for T1CE images to recognize the tumor edge. In Flair images, the molecular water signals are diluted to allow the perception of the CSF [11].

Besides, machine learning (ML) and deep learning (DL) models are sub-domains of artificial intelligence (AI) such as CNN have been utilized for segmentation and classification. In radiology, these techniques offer a great deal of knowledge to understand diagnosis, treatment, and perception with a chance of effectiveness [12, 13]. ML and DL image processing have a significant role in diagnosing acute diseases [14–19]. The radiologist deployed a CNN-based computer-aided diagnosis (CAD) [20, 21] method to detect various diseases.

In brain tumor detection, there are different stages. The primary stage is preprocessing that converts inaccurate real-world data into feasible data for evaluation to attain better performance [22]. This stage has been used to minimize the noise, rebuild an image, and detect the tumor in the image by texture [23]. The segmentation is referred to as the separation and analysis of a single pixel within the image. This step eliminates the pixel values from the texture features. Segmentation is the way of visual image that is divided into parts through identical features. Every pixel in the image has a label that shares identical characteristics with pixels with a single label. The DL provides the nature of the qualitative and quantitative arrangement of the brain tumor [24]. After 2012, the DL methodologies depends on a CNN that has increased a significant result within the ImageNet pc vision competition, and DL became popular within the field of pc vision [25]. Deep learning allows object segmentation processes [26], the retrieval of characteristics from segmented objects, and the probability that features to be evaluated [27]. The most common types of structural MRI images [28] are shown in Fig. 1.

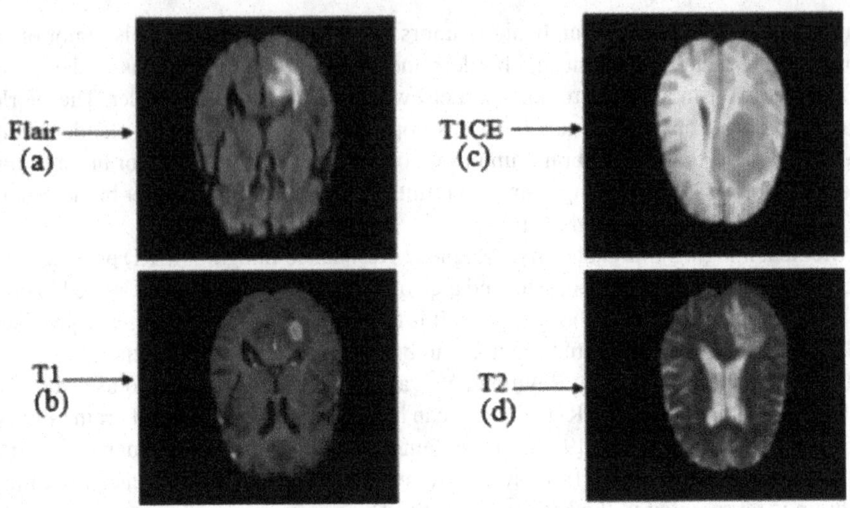

Fig. 1. Basic types of MRI images

Figure 1 shows typical types of MRI. In the images of (a), the molecular water signals are diluted to allow the perception of the CSF. In the complex cell area, the tumor edges can be identified without the remarkable signal of the identifying expert, (b) MRI images recognize the tissues, (d) MRI images the edema zone with positive signals in the image, and the (c) images recognize the tumor edge.

In summary, the significant contributions of this research are listed as follows.

- Developed a new DL model for automated brain tumor detection, providing more accurate and reliable results.
- In comparison to the state-of-the-art methods, the proposed method showed the highest segmentation and classification accuracy.
- Our CNN-based model provides quick detection of tumors, less error rate, and a computational time of 3.43%.
- The proposed method enhances the efficiency through a more extensive, and more diverse dataset.

The strength of this study is automated brain tumor detection which leads to a more extensive, and more diverse dataset, and it takes less time in the detection of a tumor that enhanced the performance of the proposed methodology.

This paper consists of six sections. In Sect. 1, a brief introduction of brain tumors has been described. Section 2 elaborates the related work such as existing models, techniques of deep learning, working, and results. In Sect. 3, the methodology has been proposed that explains the pre-processing phase, segmentation, classification of brain tumors. In Sect. 4, experiments and results of the proposed methodology have been discussed. Section 5 consists of the discussion in which discuss critical analysis, and Sect. 6 has been illuminated the conclusion and future direction of this domain.

2 Related Work

The DL techniques help classify the tumor segments, grading, successively mapping brain tumor shape, texture, and estimating patients' survival based on MRI image datasets [13, 25].

Sajid et al. [29] developed an approach based on the patch-based technique for detecting brain tumors. This method contracts the over-fitting method that has been used for unbalancing data issues and batch normalization. The N4ITK technique has been used for the bias field correction. The outcomes indicate that the dice score was 0.86, specificity of which was 0.91, and the sensitivity was 0.86 on the BRATS 2013 dataset.

Yogananda et al. [30] developed an automated DL-based model for brain tumor segmentation for solving multi-class segmented into binary segmentation on the 3D-Dense-UNet. The outcomes of the proposed model were Dice score for WT 0.92, ET 0.80, and CT 0.84 on the dataset of 20 test cases. Dice scores for WT 0.90, TC 0.80, and ET 0.78 on the BRATS 2017 dataset and WT 0.90, TC 0.82, ET 0.80 on BRATS 2018 dataset, respectively.

Akil et al. [31] built an automated CNN-based model for the segmentation of glioblastoma. The developed CNN model used a selective focus technique in three versions of the CNNs to enhance the unique features from high and low-level MRI images. The proposed method outcomes were depicted the WT 0.90, TC 0.83, and ET 0.83, and a median Dice score increased 74% to 85% on the BRATS 2018 dataset.

Naser et al. [32] developed a CNN-based U-Net and DL models model focused on pre-trained Vgg-16 CNN architecture to improve brain tumor segmentation. The automated segmentation, diagnosis, and grading were utilized from MRI images. The developed U-Net method results were depicted DSC 0.84 mean value, and an accuracy of 0.92 was attained. In the classification, the accuracy of 0.89, sensitivity 0.87, specificity 0.92, at MRI image level and sensitivity of the level of 0.97, the accuracy of 0.95, and specificity of 0.98 at patient-level with Flair MRI.

Thaha et al. [33] developed an enhanced CNN method through BAT algorithm to automate brain tumors. The tiny kernels were utilized in CNN to allocate a lower weight for the system with a good influence upon overfitting. The skull removal and pre-processing phase were used for enhanced imaging algorithms. The outcomes of the proposed model indicate that the performance was improved over existing methods. The Accuracy of E-CNN is 92%, precision 87%, and Recall 90% on BRATS 2015 dataset.

Laukamp et al. [34] developed a DL approach with multi-parametric for automated segmentation of meningiomas. Meningiomas were detected using MRI data sets for the treatment of meningiomas. The deep learning models (DLM) for glioma cases were used as an independent dataset, and the BRATS benchmark dataset was applied to segment the image of the brain tumor. The outcomes indicate that the Dice average coefficients for the overall tumor volume were 0.81 ± 0.10 and 0.46–0.93, and the T1CE range was 0.78 ± 0.19 and 0.27–0.95.

Sajjad et al. [35] built a method that was based on CNN for brain tumor detection. A DL technique was used to separate the tumor portion of the MRI. The segmented data was further extended by utilizing the criteria to maximize the number of data samples. At the same time, VGG-19 CNN architecture was used for multi-grade classification. In the comprehensive choice of classification, the radiologist deployed a CNN-based computer-aided diagnosis (CAD) method. The results indicate an accuracy of 94.58%, the sensitivity of 88.41%, and specificity of 96.12% on the publicly available dataset.

Amin et al. [36] built a model based on four MRI classifications for brain tumor detection. In the fusion phase, discrete wavelet transform (DWT) with wavelet kernel offered details about the tumor area to reduce noise that was applied on the dataset. The threshold method was based on the CNN model for the tumor and non-tumor areas in particular. For the suggested approach, the five publicly accessible datasets were used and achieved the best results. The proposed method results indicate that on fused images, the accuracy was 0.97 on BRATS 2018 datasets.

Sharif et al. [37] developed a DL feature selection method for brain tumor segmentation and detection in two phases. In the first one, the SbDL strategy was to increase the functionality of the DL through the particle swarm optimization (PSO) algorithm in segmented and confirmed brain tumors. Moreover, the classification of brain tumors used a SoftMax classifier, that optimized functions were validated. The change of comparison helped to coordinate better segmentation of the image and CNN functions. The findings revealed that the Dice score for CT was 83.73%, WT 93.7%, and ET 79.94% on a BRATS 2017 dataset, while the Dice score for CT was 88.34%, WT 91.2%, and ET 81.84% on the BRATS 2018 dataset. The overall accuracy for all BRATS datasets was over 92% in the brain tumor rating.

Zhou et al. [38] developed an automated method built on the CNN for the segmentation of brain tumors. The first issue was missing spatial information, and secondly, the multi-scale procedure was not sufficient. The 3D Atrous convolution was used to minimize the first issue. In the pyramid of a multi-scale history structure, the second issue of 3D Atrous convolution was addressed. The outcomes depict that the WT, TC, ET was 0.83, 0.68, 0.60 for AFPNet and 3D CRF on the BRATS 2013 dataset and WT, TC, ET was 0.82, 0.68, and 0.60 on the BRATS 2015 dataset, and the performance of AFPNet and 3D CRF for the Lesion structure on the BRATS 2018 dataset the WT was 0.8658, TC 0.7688, and ET 0.74434 respectively.

Agarwal et al. [39] developed a model that was built on transfer learning. The main goal of this study was to propose a DL model that enhanced the performance of brain tumor classification. In this research, the developed CNN-based VGG-16 model classified the MRI images into two classes. The outcomes showed that the proposed model attained accuracy 96.5% in training and 90% accuracy in testing with low complexity on the public dataset.

The comprehensive study of previous related works considered tiny and local datasets in state-of-art methodologies and offers low performance. It took more time for the segmentation of the tumor. The existing techniques (AFPNet, 3D CRF, DWT) provided high complexity and the VGG-16 model was performed better results than others. Our proposed method removes the noise during the pre-processing phase and enhances the background object on the MRI image. The pre-processing step improves the background of the MRI image and obtained the most useful information from the MRI image to supply the CNN. The three layers of convolution have been used to extract the features which provided efficient and reliable performance, and the VGG-19 model has been used for classification.

3 Proposed Methodology

3.1 BRATS Dataset

In this work, the BRATS 2020 [28] dataset has been utilized to trained and tested the proposed model. The model has been trained on 80% of the data, and 20% of the dataset has been used to test brain tumor detection. High-grade glioma (HGG) and low-grade glioma (LGG) images have been included in BRATS 2020 [40] dataset considering for binary classification. Four different modalities have been scanned in the dataset: T1, T1CE, T2, and FLAIR for each subject. These approaches are rigidly computed with the four MRI modalities and anisotropic resolutions, resampled to the isotropic. In the proposed methodology, the BRATS 2020 dataset comprises a total of 2345 MRI images, of which 1870 MRI images for the training phase (374 segmentation, 374 Flairs, 374 T1, 374 T1-CE, and 374 MRI images for T2) and 476 MRI images for the testing phase (119 flair, 119 T1, 119 T1-CE and 119 MRI images for T2). Numerous parameters have been applied for testing error rate, accuracy, sensitivity, specificity, and computational time. Some BRATS dataset names, sizes, and brain tumor types have been listed in Table 1.

Table 1. BRATS dataset with brain tumor types

Serial no.	Dataset name	Dataset size	Brain tumor types
1	BRATS 2015	274 MRI images	220 HGG, 54 LGG
2	BRATS 2016	465 MRI images	220 HGG, 54 LGG, 191 unknown Grades
3	BRATS 2017	285 MRI images	210 HGG, 75 LGG
4	BRATS 2018	1425 MRI images	1050 HGG, 375 LGG
5	BRATS 2019	1675 MRI images	1295 HGG, 380 LGG
6	BRATS 2020	2345 MRI images	1435 HGG, 620 LGG, 290 unknown Grades

3.2 Proposed Model for CNN Based Brain Tumor Segmentation

An automated method has been developed for the detection of brain tumors. The different layers have been used in the proposed model. Pre-processing has been conducted to enhance image quality, remove noise, and better visualize tumor pixels by implementing the Gabor filter [41]. The Skull stripping has been used for the removal of the skull. In the convolution layer, the one patch of dimension is $32 \times 32 \times 3$, and kernel/filter has been deployed to extracts the features from the MRI image. The convolution layer has been applied three times in the proposed methodology. The Batch normalization layer has been used to improve the learning speed, avoid overfitting, and provide regularization, then used the ReLu as an activation layer. The two Max-pooling layers have been added to diminish feature dimensionality in the proposed method. The Max-Pooling layer strategy has been supplied for down-sampling in CNN layers and reduced the feature at each level. After that convolution layer has been used to extract features and then batch normalization, the ReLu (activation) layer has been applied to normalize the pixel values. Subsequently, again convolution layer, activation layer, and Max-pooling layer have been applied for improving the performance of the proposed method. The transpose layer has been used for the up-sampling and contains many learning parameters to help create a resultant image. The fully connected layer takes the previous layer's output and flattens them to convert the three-dimensional matrix into the one-dimensional matrix that has an input of the next stage. Later, the SoftMax layer transforms the input values into 0 and 1. The pixel classification layer has been used for analysis through spectral information, cross-entropy losses, and ignore the undefined pixel labels. Finally, the post-processing removed the small positives around the corners of the MRI images. In post-processing, the global threshold technique has been used for each portion. Moreover, for brain tumor classification, the CNN pre- trained architecture VGG-19 [42] has been used to classify MRI images. The proposed methodology for brain tumor detection has been shown in Fig. 2 and Fig. 3.

3.3 Training Details

In the training phase, the 32 × 32 × 3 patches have been taken as input. The pre-processing and skull stripping layer have been employed. The first convolution layer by the size of filter 64 × 3 × 3, padding [0 0 0 0], and stride [1 1] have been utilized. Later, the batch normalization layer has been applied, and then the activation function has performed. The max-pooling layer (2 × 2) has been selected with padding [0 0 0 0] and stride [1 1]. Then the second convolution layer has been selected with padding [1 1 1 1], and stride [1 1], and then the batch normalization and activation function have been re-applied. The third convolution layer has been selected with padding [0 0 0 0], and stride [1 1], and the batch normalization, the activation function has been employed. In last convolution layer with the padding [0 0 0 0], and stride [1 1] with activation layer have been utilized. In second phase Max-Pooling layer, padding [0 0 0 0], stride [1 1] has been utilized. The trained model has been guarded as just a new process and developed for the analysis.

4 Experiments and Results

4.1 Performance Matrices

Various metrics have been obtained from the confusion matrix to demonstrate classifier performance, particularly to each tumor class. Significant matrices (accuracy, recall or sensitivity, specificity, precision, and F1-Score) has been measured using the following formulas

$$\text{Accuracy} = \frac{\text{TP} + \text{TN}}{(\text{TP} + \text{FN} + \text{TN} + \text{FP})} \times 100 \tag{1}$$

$$\text{Sensitivity or Recall} = \frac{\text{TP}}{\text{TP} + \text{FN}} \tag{2}$$

$$\text{Specificity} = \frac{\text{TN}}{\text{TN} + \text{FP}} \tag{3}$$

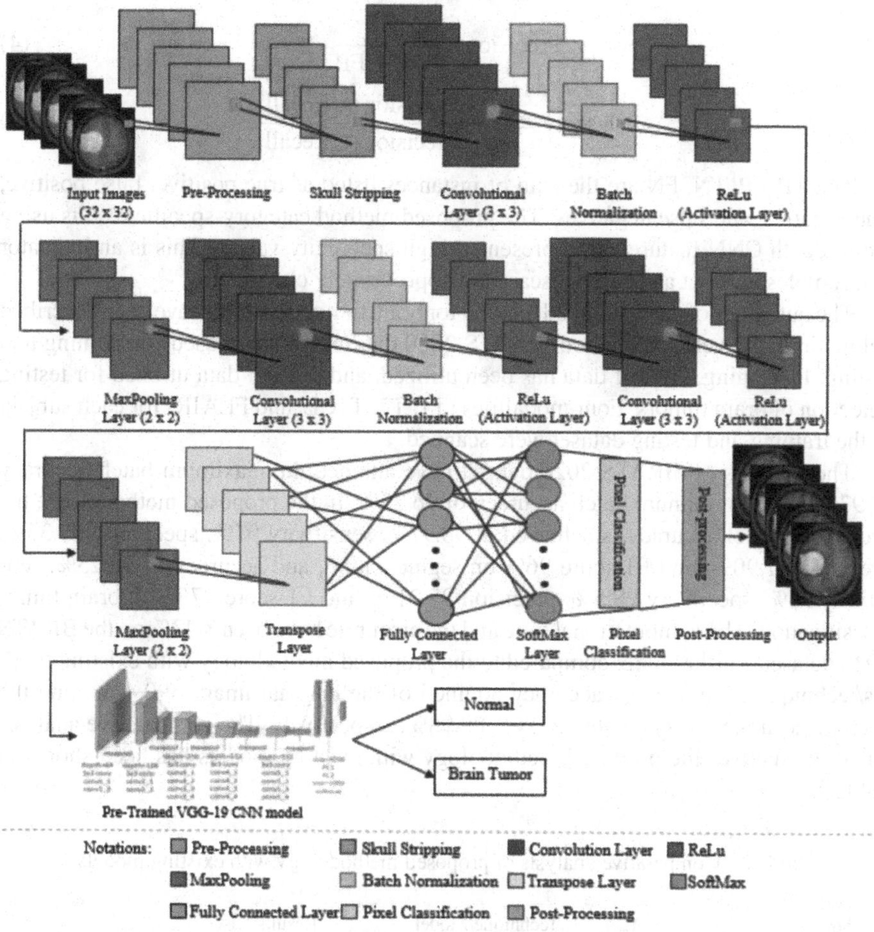

Fig. 2. Proposed methodology for brain tumor segmentation and classification

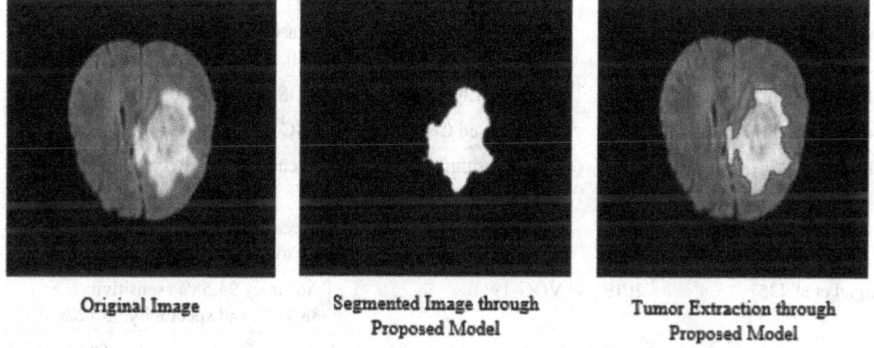

Fig. 3. Brain tumor segmentation results through proposed method

$$\text{Precision} = \frac{\text{TP}}{\text{TP} + \text{FP}} \tag{4}$$

$$\text{F1-score} = 2 \times \frac{\text{Precision} \times \text{Recall}}{\text{Precision} + \text{Recall}} \tag{5}$$

The TP, FP, TN, FN are the sum of instances listed as true positive, false positive, true negative, and false negatives. The proposed method category-specific results using the in-depth CNN features have presented high specificity values. This is an indicator that samples without a specific disease are appropriately classified.

The outcomes of the developed method for brain tumor detection have been described below. In the developed method, BRATS 2020 dataset has been used for training and testing. In training, 80% of data has been utilized, and 20% of data utilized for testing detection of brain tumors. Four modalities (T1, T2, T1CE, and FLAIR) for each subject in the training and testing dataset were scanned.

The findings on BRATS 2020 dataset have attained the maximum batch accuracy of 97.45% and minimum batch accuracy of 96.25%. In the proposed methodology, the proposed model accuracy is achieved at 98.97%, sensitivity 97%, specificity 97.35%, precision 97.90%, and F1-score 96% on segmentation, and accuracy of 98.25%, sensitivity 98%, specificity 98.5%, precision 97.21%, and F1-score 97%, on brain tumor classification. The computational time and the error rate have been 3.43% on the BRATS 2020 dataset. Furthermore, compared to the proposed methodology with existing models/techniques, the average accuracy attained of the original images 90.42%, and the average accuracy of segmented images 89.98%, respectively. The comparative analysis has been made of the proposed methodology with existing models has been shown in Table 2.

Table 2. Comparative analysis of proposed methodology with existing models

Author	Year	Technique/Model	Results
Sajid et al. [29]	2019	N4ITK	Dice score 0.86, sensitivity 0.86, specificity 0.91
Yogananda et al. [30]	2020	3D-Dense-UNets, 3 fold cross-validation	Dice score for WT, TC, ET was 0.90, 0.82, 0.80 on the BRATS 2018 dataset and WT, ET, CT was 0.92, 0.80, 0.84 on 20 test cases dataset
Akil et al. [31]	2020	Based on CNN	MDS for WT 0.90, CT 0.83, ET 0.83
Naser et al. [32]	2020	U-Net-based CNN, Vgg16	DSC 0.84, Accuracy 0.92
Thaha et al. [33]	2019	BAT algorithm, CNN	Accuracy 92%, Recall 90%, precision 87%
Laukamp et al. [34]	2019	DLM	Dice coefficients for CT 0.78 ± 0.19, for total tumor 0.81 ± 0.10
Sajjad et al. [35]	2019	VGG-19	Accuracy 94.58%, sensitivity 88.41%, and specificity 96.12%

(*continued*)

Table 2. (*continued*)

Author	Year	Technique/Model	Results
Amin et al. [36]	2020	DWT	Accuracy 0.97
Sharif et al. [37]	2020	SbDL, PSO Approach	Dice score for CT 88.34%, WT 91.2%, ET 81.84%
Zhou et al. [38]	2020	AFPNet, 3D CRF	ET 0.74434, WT 0.8658, TC 0.7688
Agarwal et al. [39]	2021	VGG-16 model	Accuracy 96.5%
Proposed Methodology	**2021**	**Based on CNN**	**Accuracy 98.97%, sensitivity 97%, specificity 97.35%, precision 97.90%, and F1-score 96% on segmented images, and accuracy 98.25%, sensitivity 98%, specificity 98.5%, precision 97.21%, and F1-score 97%,on classification images**

5 Discussion

A framework of the developed methodology has been illustrated as the developed approach that contains two main steps: the first step is segmentation, and the second step is a classification of brain tumors. The developed model consists of binary classification. The proposed method has been segmented tumor through MRI images for segmentation, and in classification, CNN architecture VGG-19 has been utilized to classify the MRI images. It could be noticed from the analysis that the proposed segmentation model works substantially on regions of low contrast tumors. The various strategies of brain tumor detection from MRI have been discussed in the related work section.

Comparing results with existing work in literature provides evidence of the novelty and efficiency of the developed methodology. The outcomes indicate that our proposed model is improved than existing models for the detection of brain tumors.

6 Conclusion

In this study, the automated CNN-based model has been developed for the detection of brain tumors. The brain tumor has been segmented through MRI images in the proposed model. Whereas for the brain tumor classification CNN architecture VGG-19 has been used to classify the MRI images. Before classification, a pre-processing layer improved the MRI images of low-contrast and filtered noisy elements that enhanced performance. The proposed model has been composed of binary classification, and the BRATS 2020 dataset has been utilized for training and testing. The 80% data of MRI images have been utilized in training, and 20% data of MRI images have been utilized in testing. The proposed model results presented a maximum batch accuracy of 97.45% and a minimum batch accuracy of 96.25%. The proposed model achieved accuracy 98.97%, sensitivity 97%, specificity 97.35%, precision 97.90%, and F1-score 96% on segmented images. Whereas the accuracy of 98.25%, sensitivity 98%, specificity 98.5%, precision

97.21%, and F1-score 97% on classification images although the computational time and error rate is 3.43%. The results conclude that the low error rate has offered the highest accuracy. Moreover, the proposed methodology efficiently segmented and classified the brain tumor through MRI images. The proposed method improved the performance, detected tumors quickly, and enhanced results than the existing models. In this study, we detected brain tumors efficiently, and cost-effectively through the proposed method.

In the future, implementing a deep reinforcement model may be performed to enhance robustness and accuracy for brain tumor classification.

Acknowledgment. This research is supported by the Riphah Artificial Intelligence Research Lab (RAIR), Riphah International University, Faisalabad Campus, Pakistan. The authors are thankful for the support.

Declaration of Competing Interest. The authors claim that this study does not include conflicts of interest.

References

1. Havaei, M., et al.: Brain tumor segmentation with deep neural networks. Med. Image Anal. **35**, 18–31 (2017)
2. Nema, S., Dudhane, A., Murala, S., Naidu, S.: RescueNet: an unpaired GAN for brain tumor segmentation. Biomed. Signal Process. Control **55**, 101641 (2020)
3. Razzak, M.I., Imran, M., Xu, G.: Efficient brain tumor segmentation with multiscale two-pathway-group conventional neural networks. IEEE J. Biomed. Health Inform. **23**, 1911–1919 (2018)
4. Siegel, R.M., Jemal, K.: Cancer statistics, 2015. CA Cancer J. Clin. **65**, 5–29 (2015)
5. Siegel, R.M., Jemal, K.: Cancer statistics, 2017. CA Cancer J. Clin. **67**, 7–30 (2017)
6. Swati, Z.N.K., et al.: Content-based brain tumor retrieval for MR images using transfer learning. IEEE Access **7**, 17809–17822 (2019). https://doi.org/10.1109/ACCESS.2019.2892455
7. Işın, A., Direkoğlu, C., Şah, M.: Review of MRI-based brain tumor image segmentation using deep learning methods. Procedia Comput. Sci. **102**, 317–324 (2016). https://doi.org/10.1016/j.procs.2016.09.407
8. Kumar, S., Dabas, C., Godara, S.: Classification of brain MRI tumor images: a hybrid approach. Procedia Comput. Sci. **122**, 510–517 (2017)
9. Damadian, R., Goldsmith, M., Minkoff, L.: NMR in cancer: XVI. FONAR image of the uve human body. Physiol. Chem. **9**, 97–100 (1977)
10. Wang, G., Li, W., Ourselin, S., Vercauteren, T.: Automatic brain tumor segmentation using cascaded anisotropic convolutional neural networks. In: Crimi, A., Bakas, S., Kuijf, H., Menze, B., Reyes, M. (eds.) BrainLes 2017. LNCS, vol. 10670, pp. 178–190. Springer, Cham (2018). https://doi.org/10.1007/978-3-319-75238-9_16
11. Dogra, J., Jain, S., Sharma, A., Kumar, R., Sood, M.: Brain tumor detection from MR images employing fuzzy graph cut technique. Recent Adv. Comput. Sci. Commun. **13**(3), 362–369 (2020). https://doi.org/10.2174/2213275912666181207152633
12. Ravishankar, P., Smith, D., Avril, S., Kikano, E., Ramaiya, N.: Uterine carcinosarcoma: a primer for radiologists. Abdom. Radiol. **44**(8), 2874–2885 (2019). https://doi.org/10.1007/s00261-019-02038-8

13. Hosh, M., Antar, S., Nazzal, A., Warda, M., Gibreel, A., Refky, B.: Uterine sarcoma: analysis of 13,089 cases based on surveillance, epidemiology, and results database. Int. J. Gynecol. Cancer **26** (2016)
14. Akbar, S., Akram, M., Sharif, M., Tariq, A., Ullah Yasin, U.: Arteriovenous ratio and papilledema based hybrid decision support system for detection and grading of hypertensive retinopathy. Comput. Methods Programs Biomed. **154**, 123–141 (2018). https://doi.org/10.1016/j.cmpb.2017.11.014
15. Akbar, S., Akram, M., Sharif, M., Tariq, A., Ullah Yasin, U.: Decision support system for detection of papilledema through fundus retinal images. J. Med. Syst. **41**, 66 (2017). https://doi.org/10.1007/s10916-017-0712-9
16. Akbar, S., Akram, M., Sharif, M., Tariq, A., Khan, S.: Decision support system for detection of hypertensive retinopathy using arteriovenous ratio. Artif. Intell. Med. **90**, 15–24 (2018). https://doi.org/10.1016/j.artmed.2018.06.004
17. Akbar, S., Sharif, M., Akram, M., Saba, T., Mahmood, T., Kolivand, M.: Automated techniques for blood vessels segmentation through fundus retinal images: a review. Microsc. Res. Tech. **82**(2), 153–170 (2019). https://doi.org/10.1002/jemt.23172
18. Akram, M., Akbar, S., Hassan, T., Khawaja, S., Yasin, U., Basit, I.: Data on fundus images for vessels segmentation, detection of hypertensive retinopathy, diabetic retinopathy and papilledema. Data Brief **29**, 105282 (2020). https://doi.org/10.1016/j.dib.2020.105282
19. Akbar, S., Hassan, T., Akram, M.U., Yasin, U.U., Basit, I.: AVRDB: annotated dataset for vessel segmentation and calculation of arteriovenous ratio. In: Proceedings of the International Conference on Image Processing, Computer Vision, and Pattern Recognition (IPCV), pp. 129–134 (2017)
20. Hassan, S.A.E., Akbar, S., Gull, S., Rehman, A., Alaska, H.: Deep learning-based automatic detection of central serous retinopathy using optical coherence tomographic images. In: 2021 1st International Conference on Artificial Intelligence and Data Analytics (CAIDA), pp. 206–211. IEEE (2021)
21. Hassan, S.A., Akbar, S., Rehman, A., Tariq, U., Abbasi, R.: Recent developments in detection of central serous retinopathy through imaging and artificial intelligence techniques a review. arXiv preprint arXiv: 10961 (2020)
22. Ayemi, B.A., Rai, S., Bora, D.J.: Machine learning based techniques for brain tumor analysis: a review. UGC Care Group I Listed J. **10** (2020)
23. Ramarao, N., Kavya, P., Deepa, M.S., Gowda, S., Vaishnovi, H.: Review of methods for automatic segmentation of brain tumor in MRI images. Int. J. Eng. Tech. Res. **9** (2020)
24. Zhao, F., Yang, X., Zhang, H., Ren, Y.: Ultrasonographic findings of uterine carcinosarcoma. Gynecol. Obstet. Invest. **84**(3), 277–282 (2019). https://doi.org/10.1159/000481885
25. Krizhevsky, A., Sutskever, I., Hinton, G.E.: ImageNet classification with deep convolutional neural networks. Commun. ACM **60**, 84–90 (2017)
26. Rehman, A., Khan, M., Saba, T., Mehmood, Z., Tariq, U., Ayesha, N.: Microscopic brain tumor detection and classification using 3D CNN and feature selection architecture. Microsc. Res. Tech. **84**(1), 133–149 (2021). https://doi.org/10.1002/jemt.23597
27. Suzuki, K.: Overview of deep learning in medical imaging. Radiol. Phys. Technol. **10**(3), 257–273 (2017). https://doi.org/10.1007/s12194-017-0406-5
28. Kaggle Brain Tumor Dataset. https://www.kaggle.com/awsaf49/brats2020-training-data
29. Sajid, S., Hussain, S., Sarwar, A.: Brain tumor detection and segmentation in MR images using deep learning. Arab. J. Sci. Eng. **44**(11), 9249–9261 (2019). https://doi.org/10.1007/s13369-019-03967-8
30. Yogananda, C.G.B., et al.: A fully automated deep learning network for brain tumor segmentation. Tomography **6**, 186 (2020)

31. Akil, M., Saouli, R., Kachouri, R.: Fully automatic brain tumor segmentation with deep learning-based selective attention using overlapping patches and multi-class weighted cross-entropy. Med. Image Anal. **63**, 101692 (2020)
32. Naser, M.A., Deen, M.J.: Brain tumor segmentation and grading of lower-grade glioma using deep learning in MRI images. Comput. Biol. Med. **121**, 103758 (2020)
33. Thaha, M.M., Kumar, K., Murugan, B.S., Dhanasekeran, S., Vijayakarthick, P., Selvi, A.S.: Brain tumor segmentation using convolutional neural networks in MRI images. J. Med. Syst. **43**, 1–10 (2019)
34. Laukamp, K.R., et al.: Fully automated detection and segmentation of meningiomas using deep learning on routine multiparametric MRI. Eur. Radiol. **29**(1), 124–132 (2019). https://doi.org/10.1007/s00330-018-5595-8
35. Sajjad, M., Khan, S., Muhammad, K., Wanqing, W., Ullah, A., Baik, S.: Multi-grade brain tumor classification using deep CNN with extensive data augmentation. J. Comput. Sci. **30**, 174–182 (2019). https://doi.org/10.1016/j.jocs.2018.12.003
36. Amin, J., Sharif, M., Gul, N., Yasmin, M., Shad, S.: Brain tumor classification based on DWT fusion of MRI sequences using convolutional neural network. Pattern Recogn. Lett. **129**, 115–122 (2020). https://doi.org/10.1016/j.patrec.2019.11.016
37. Sharif, M., Li, J., Khan, M., Saleem, M.: Active deep neural network features selection for segmentation and recognition of brain tumors using MRI images. Pattern Recogn. Lett. **129**, 181–189 (2020). https://doi.org/10.1016/j.patrec.2019.11.019
38. Zhou, Z., He, Z., Jia, Y.: AFPNet: a 3D fully convolutional neural network with atrous-convolution feature pyramid for brain tumor segmentation via MRI images. Neurocomputing **402**, 235–244 (2020)
39. Agerwal, A.K.: Brain Tumor Classification Using CNN. Mili-Link (2021)
40. Henry, T., et al.: Top 10 BraTS 2020 challenge solution: brain tumor segmentation with self-ensembled, deeply-supervised 3D-U Net like neural networks. arXiv preprint arXiv: 01045 (2020)
41. Tahir, B., et al.: Feature enhancement framework for brain tumor segmentation and classification. Microsc. Res. Tech. **82**(6), 803–811 (2019). https://doi.org/10.1002/jemt.23224
42. Rajinikanth, V., Raj, A.N.J., Thanaraj, K.P., Naik, G.R.: A customized VGG19 network with concatenation of deep and handcrafted features for brain tumor detection. Appl. Sci. **10**(10), 3429 (2020). https://doi.org/10.3390/app10103429

Eye Gaze Based Model for Anxiety Detection of Engineering Students

Khafidurrohman Agustianto[1(✉)], Hendra Yufit Riskiawan[1], Dwi Putro Sarwo Setyohadi[1], I. Gede Wiryawan[1], Andi Besse Firdausiah Mansur[2], and Ahmad Hoirul Basori[2(✉)]

[1] Information Technology Department, Politeknik Negeri Jember, PO BOX 164, Mastrip, Jember, Indonesia
{yufit,dwi.putro,wiryawan}@polije.ac.id

[2] Faculty of Computing and Information Technology in Rabigh, King Abdulaziz University, Rabigh 21911, Makkah, Saudi Arabia
{abmansur,abasori}@kau.edu.sa

Abstract. Education is a vital component for country development, particularly in the engineering or technology field. The engineering students must maintain their focus and attention due to the complexity of their study. The objective of this research is to observe student anxiety who is taking a course in engineering fields. Students with anxiety disorders show moderate interest in learning, have a weak performance on exams and assignments. Stress detected from the eye gaze. It has a pattern that represents the anxiety condition of engineering students. The main contribution of our paper is providing an observation result on how to deal with the anxiety experienced by engineering students using eye gaze by identifying eye movement patterns from students. The eye gaze pattern divided into 16 areas (A1, A2, A3, A4, B1, B2, B3, B4, C1, C2, C3, C4, D1, D2, D3, and D4). The research results show 85.5% accuracy. These results provide a guideline for how teachers can rapidly comprehend students' anxiety condition and perform a particular action to help students gain their optimum learning result.

Keywords: Student modeling · Engineering students · Eye gaze · Anxiety detection system

1 Introduction

The development of education is a critical issue for every country. It is also found in Indonesia goverment, thereby triggering a lot of research on developing an e-learning or education system to support students in getting their excellent education with an intelligent tutoring system one of them is research conducted by [1] which uses metacognitive approach.

The anxiety/Mood disorders factor is one essential element that engineering students mostly faced during their study [2]. Gaudioso et al. [3] proposed an Adaptive Educational System Known as AESs to help students analyse suitable course material for

P. Liatsis et al. (Eds.): TIOTC 2021, CCIS 1548, pp. 195–205, 2022.
https://doi.org/10.1007/978-3-030-97255-4_14

students. So the problem of anxiety becomes something that needs attention in higher education. Destarianto et al. [4] focused on modelling the student's motivational system by encouraging their study to obtain success and evade failure [5].

A mood disorder can be an obstacle during the learning process, and it also can strive for severe health and social life [6]. The e-learning reflects the study through an online platform, so it has altered the education system platform. Online learning uses the internet as its backbone communication to deliver educational content [7, 8]. This technology is beneficial to abandon the limitless of humans in terms of time, place, and suppleness.

This study aims to deal with the anxiety experienced by engineering students using eye gaze by identifying eye movement patterns from students. The eye gaze pattern is divided into 16 areas (A-1, A-2, A-3, A-4, B-1, B-2, B-3, B-4, C-1, C-2, C-3, C-4, D-1, D-2, D-3, and D-4). For every determined area, coordinates of the points are chosen then grouped into two central regions known as inside and outside. The inner part is A-1, B-1, C-1, and D-1, while the outside area is A-2, A-3, A-4, B-2, B-3, B-4, C-2, C-3, C-4, D-2, D-3, and D-4.

2 Related Works

Jirotka, M and Stahl, B.C. discuss that responsible technology practically is a technology designed to help humanity achieve happiness. The need for reliable technology such as Artificial Intelligence (AI) and big data against the COVID19 has shown the closed interaction between humans and technology [9]. Furthermore, online learning can also monitor students' dropout rates early by proactively tracking students who have a high risk of leaving the course. It also can help to recognize the issue that student-facing during the learning process [10]. They used Logit Leaf Model (LLM) to measure achievement and clarity. The enthusiasm of study at engineering faculty is a critical factor for every student because of the nature of courses in an engineering field that is quite hard. Student motivation monitoring is essential to maintain their performance. They use a coaching role model and a plan-based approach [11].

Maintaining student motivation for engineering faculty is a challenging task where the workload is quite heavy, such as an initial planetary mission plan [11]. The other study focuses on investigating the classroom layout that may affect student learning experience, refer to Fig. 1. Researchers study the correlation between student learning environment and their engagement toward academic performance [12]. The other researcher focused on improving the learning behavior by an improved e-book system affiliated with social media such as Facebook to boost students' motivation. They analyze the student's behavioral pattern, comments in the e-book system [13]. Their result concluded that their finding encourages low participation students. The assimilation of social media and learning platforms has shown an increment of alleged interactivity of students. They express their likeness by sharing, liking, or posting their opinion in the system [13]. The researcher agrees that digital information technology is responsible for helping students with their learning process to obtain more efficient results. Their finding argued that common skills have tremendous positive encouragement [14]. Based on the critical analysis of the previous work on the e-learning field and its correlation with human achievements. We can conclude that there is a strong correlation between the e-learning system, student behavior analysis as responsible technology to help students in particular, or humanity in general, refer to Table 1 for summarisation.

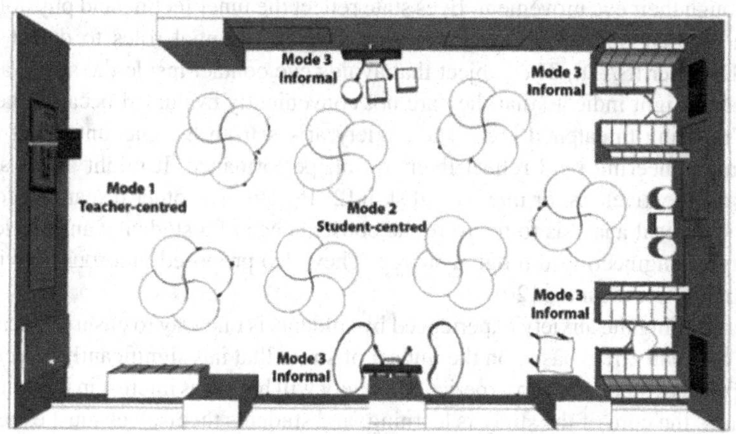

Fig. 1. Various typical classroom layout

Table 1. E-learning analysis as responsible technology

Authors	Finding	Correlation with responsible technology
[7, 8]	E-learning is a technology to overcome the limitlessness of humans in terms of time, place, and suppleness	E-learning has a significant factor in boosting student performance
[11]	Improve motivation of engineering student	E-learning analysis may help in detecting students that already bored and less focused
[13]	Utilize social media to attract student active engagement	Assimilation between social media and e-learning increase student participation
Proposed approach	Early anxiety detection through eye gaze model	Eye gaze technology and e-learning have a strong correlation as responsible technology to capture student attention during the learning process

Temper illnesses in adults rise significantly and become communal wellness crises, the older person the risk of losing their mood also higher. Hence, the issue of anxiety becomes something that needs attention in higher education. Significantly higher education techniques that have a higher anxiety potential, current research portray a strong relationship between advanced stress with student failure [6]. Focus for child learning is also being studied by considering their eyes gaze when they felt fear during the learning process [15].

Human emotion originated from their brain, and the expression of emotion is conveyed through their eye movement. Eyes state reflect the inner feeling and physiological condition of their body [16]. Gaze perceptions play essential roles to detect Social Anxiety Disorder (SAD). The subject that avoids eye contact inside the social anxiety environment might indicate that they are not conveniently evaluated because they feel like they're being threatened [17]. The anxiety arises from the encounter met by the student in engineering field reflect their overall performance. It might affect student enthusiasm, attentiveness, or intellectual skill [2, 18, 19]. The other researcher focused on using statistical analysis to measure the consequence of a student's anxiety level in the faculty of engineering through a survey. They also proposed vigorous activities to overwhelm the nervousness [20].

Understanding the anxiety experienced by students is one way to ensure education is achieved optimally. It is based on the impact of stress that has significantly affected the learning process; students who experience anxiety will have less interest in learning [21]. As we know, the core of the study is learning, and students themselves must experience learning. This research identifies anxiety by looking at eye gaze. Another investigation conducted by Grillon, H. using eye-tracking to assess phobias experienced by a person [22]. In contrast, the other study uses eye-tracking to analyze cognitive and psychological behavior with Computer Graphics& Animation (CG&A) [23].

They provide high-level tracking for eye gaze to ensure the behavior and psychology captured during the interaction. Moreover, stress levels among students were also investigated through eye gaze to monitor student's perception of learning [24]. Simultaneously, Wang's study utilizes eye gaze to detect anxiety readings bias from facial expressions [25]. The signal from the human body will distress the emotion and cognition of a person [26]. The other researcher provides a personalized learning model and analyses their behavior and failure through Role-Sphere Influence [27–29]. To assess the condition of anxiety/emotional processes of students using Tobi as a tool that reads the eye gaze of students. The eye gaze read then will be classified into 16 segments, where the evaluation of the student eye gaze's focus points will determine the level of anxiety experienced. This study divides anxiety classes into anxiety and not anxiety. We are passionate about making extreme classes, and this is with the aim of the system to quickly identify engineering students who experience anxiety.

3 Research Method

Since the literature review has been completed, the next phase is collecting data. The dataset in this study was obtained by identifying the patterns of eye movement from students. Then the eye gaze pattern was divided into 16 areas of the monitor screen (A-1, A-2, A-3, A-4, B-1, B-2, B-3, B-4, C-1, C-2, C-3, C-4, D-1, D-2, D-3, and D-4), in the form of X and Y values. The Resolution of the monitor was 1365x767. The boundary of the areas depicted is shown in Fig. 2 below.

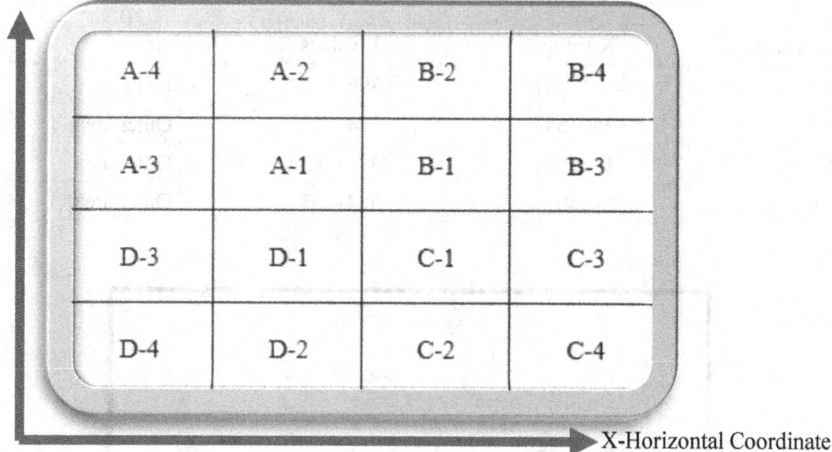

Fig. 2. Areas boundaries of the monitor screen

The designated area is classified into two main groups: inner and outer. The internal space is A-1, B-1, C-1, and D-1, while the outer region is A-2, A-3, A-4, B-2, B-3, B-4, C-2, C-3, C-4, D-2, D-3, and D-4.

Table 2 represents the X and Y values of each area. For example, area A1 where X value is between 351 and 687 while Y value is between 192 and 395 (Fig. 3).

Table 2. X and Y values of each area.

Area name	X values	Y values	Area
A-1	351–687	192–395	Inner area
A-2	351–687	1–191	Outer area
A-3	1–350	192–395	Outer area
A-4	1–350	1–191	Outer area
B-1	688–1030	192–395	Inner area
B-2	688–1030	1–191	Outer area
B-3	1031–1365	192–395	Outer area
B-4	1031–1365	1–191	Outer area
C-1	688–1030	396–583	Inner area
C-2	688–1030	584–767	Outer area
C-3	1031–1365	396–583	Outer area
C-4	1031–1365	584–767	Outer area

(*continued*)

Table 2. (*continued*)

Area name	X values	Y values	Area
D-1	351–687	396–583	Inner area
D-2	351–687	584–767	Outer area
D-3	1–350	396–583	Outer area
D-4	1–350	584–767	Outer area

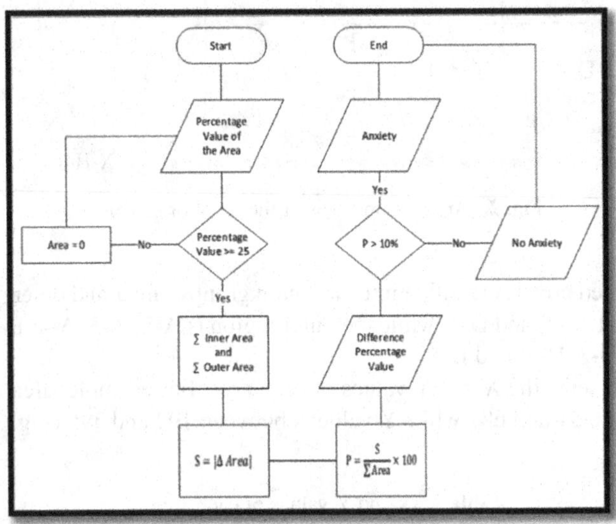

Fig. 3. Flowchart of the anxiety detection

4 Result and Discussion

We adopt the WebGazer [30] system to detect user's eye gaze through webcam during the experimental study, as shown in Fig. 4 and Fig. 5.

WebGazer uses a simple 3D game that is controlled through eye gaze focus. Figure 4 is the result of the tracking process when user miss their attention, while Fig. 5 demonstrates the user with a total concentration toward the 3D objects and their face surrounded by a green rectangle.

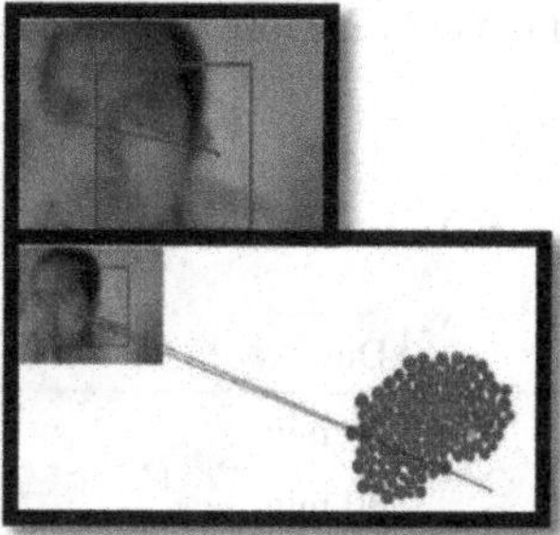

Fig. 4. User being tracked with red colour because lost the focus (Color figure online)

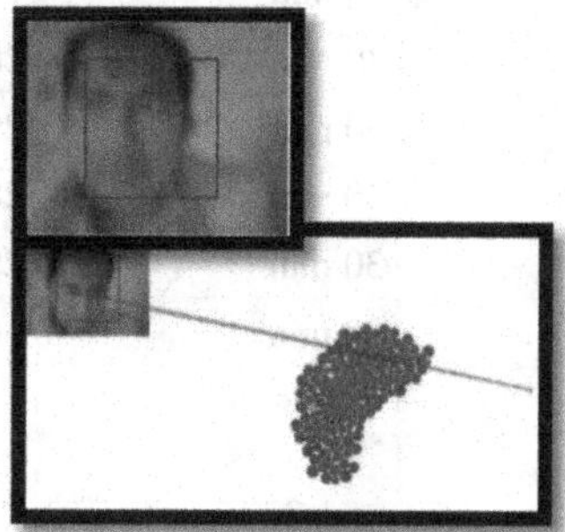

Fig. 5. User being tracked with red colour because lost the focus (Color figure online)

The anxiety detection process starts with a percentage value from each area. The system will give the area a zero value if the percentage value is less than twenty-five. It will then add up the value of the inner and the outer regions as well after the system finds an area with a percentage value above twenty-five. Using Eq. (1), the system will calculate the absolute value of the difference between the inner and the outer area. Where Δ is the difference between the inner and the outer area.

$$\mathrm{S} = |\Delta Area| \tag{1}$$

$$\mathrm{P} = \frac{S}{\sum Area} \times 100 \tag{2}$$

Afterward, the system will calculate the S value's ratio to the total cost of the inner and outer area. Following calculation using Eq. (2) as mentioned above. P is the ratio of S value to the full value of the inner and outer area, and S is the absolute value of the difference between the inner and the outer area. Finally, the last phase is to detect the anxiety of the respondents. The system would make some limited selections for the P-value. If the P-value were lesser than ten, it would recognize that the respondent was in an anxiety state. But if the p-value were above ten, then the system would detect no anxiety. Overall, the purpose of calculations is to count the domination of the eye gaze that pointed to every area. Table 3 depicts the total of data processed in this anxiety detection. The total numbers of data are 23.560. For each respondent that involved, the amounts of data around 280.

Table 3. The implementation of system and device.

Resp.	Dist.	Dur.	Numbers of data
1	100 cm	30 min	299
2	100 cm	30 min	293
3	100 cm	30 min	275
4	100 cm	30 min	273
5	100 cm	30 min	284
6	100 cm	30 min	284
7	100 cm	30 min	295
8	100 cm	30 min	285
9	100 cm	30 min	298
10	100 cm	30 min	300
.			.
.			.
.			.
81	100 cm	30 min	292
82	100 cm	30 min	290
83	100 cm	30 min	283
Total			23.560

The duration of data taken was 30 min, and approximately the distance between the monitor screen to the respondent's eye is 100 cm. Figure 6 below shows the variance of data in this study. The x-axis of the graph is the respondent to this study, while the y-axis represents the amount of data obtained.

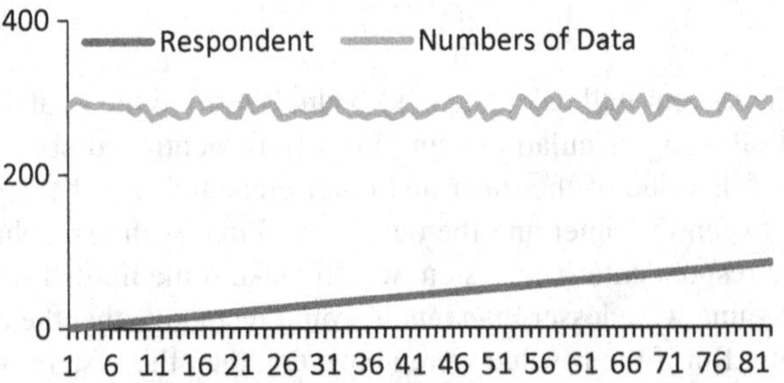

Fig. 6. The variance of data in anxiety detection

Table 4. The system evaluation by the psycologist

Resp.	System Res	Psycologist Res	Evaluation Res
1	Anxiety	Anxiety	Succeed
2	Anxiety	Anxiety	Succeed
3	Anxiety	Anxiety	Succeed
4	Anxiety	Anxiety	Succeed
5	No Anxiety	No Anxiety	Succeed
6	Anxiety	Anxiety	Succeed
7	Anxiety	Anxiety	Succeed
8	Anxiety	No Anxiety	Failed
9	No Anxiety	Anxiety	Failed
10	Anxiety	Anxiety	Succeed
.			.
.			.
.			.
81	No Anxiety	No Anxiety	Succeed
82	No Anxiety	No Anxiety	Succeed
83	Anxiety	No Anxiety	Failed

The evaluation of the anxiety detection system involved a psychologist. The discovery of anxiety by the psychologist was carried out on eighty-three students. From the system evaluation, around seventy-one of the eighty-three respondents had similar results to the psychologist's analysis result—the score around 85.5% accuracy. Table 4 shows the result of the system evaluation by the psychologist. The difference between the detection results by the system and the psychologist could be due to the difference between the factors used. The psychologist might not only use eye gaze as a consideration in determining the outcome of detecting anxiety but also several other factors that he knows can influence anxiety.

5 Conclusion

The study was initiated to detect the anxiety of engineering students during their research. Sensing student anxiety in the early phase of study might give the teacher time to help students. The instrument used in the detection process was an eye-tracking device and WebGazer application. This study's primary purpose is to help students aware of their anxiety and give them a suggestion to overcome their fear to achieve optimum performance. The detection process is conducted by looking at the results of the dominance of eye movements. When the respondent's eyes are more often facing the outside area, the person can be anxious, and if it is more often looked into the inner room, that person can be said to be focused or not worried. The result had been evaluated by comparing its products with the analysis from a psychologist expert. The results of this comparison obtained an accuracy value of 85.5%. Therefore, results provide a novel finding of how teachers can understand students' anxiety conditions early. Then offer a policy to help student gain their best performance. Future works might have physiological sensors such as sweat or heartbeat sensors to capture student physiological signals during their study.

Acknowledgements. This work was supported by the Deanship of Scientific Research (DSR), King Abdulaziz University, Jeddah Saudi Arabia and Information Technology Department, Politeknik Negeri Jember. The authors, therefore, gratefully acknowledge the DSR technical and financial support.

References

1. Agustianto, K., Permanasari, A.E., Kusumawardani, S.S., Hidayah, I.: Design adaptive learning system using metacognitive strategy path for learning in classroom and intelligent tutoring systems, vol. 1755, no. 1, p. 070012 (2016)
2. Vitasari, P., Wahab, M.N.A., Othman, A., Herawan, T., Sinnadurai, S.K.: The relationship between study anxiety and academic performance among engineering students. Procedia - Soc. Behav. Sci. **8**, 490–497 (2010)
3. Gaudioso, E., Montero, M., Hernandez-del-Olmo, F.: Supporting teachers in adaptive educational systems through predictive models: a proof of concept. Expert Syst. Appl. **39**(1), 621–625 (2012)
4. Destarianto, P., Etikasari, B., Agustianto, K.: Developing automatic student motivation modeling system. In: Journal of Physics: Conference Series, vol. 953, p. 012114 (2018)
5. Dewanto, W.K., Agustianto, K., Sari, B.E.: Developing thinking skill system for modelling creative thinking and critical thinking of vocational high school student. In: Journal of Physics: Conference Series, vol. 953, p. 012115 (2018)
6. Cybulski, M., Cybulski, L., Krajewska-Kulak, E., Orzechowska, M., Cwalina, U., Kowalewska, B.: Occurrence of mood disorders among educationally active older adults in Bialystok, Poland: a cross-sectional study. Ann. Gen. Psychiatry **19**, 35 (2020). (in English)
7. Allen, I., Seaman, J., Poulin, R., Straut, T.T.: Online Report Card - Tracking Online Education in the United States (2015). Accessed Sept 2020
8. Reinig, M.: The Theory and Practice of Online Learning. University of Washington Press (2010)
9. Jirotka, M., Stahl, B.C.: The need for responsible technology. J. Responsible Technol. **1**, 100002 (2020)
10. Coussement, K., Phan, M., De Caigny, A., Benoit, D.F., Raes, A.: Predicting student dropout in subscription-based online learning environments: the beneficial impact of the logit leaf model. Decis. Support Syst. **135**, 113325 (2020)
11. López-Fernández, D., Ezquerro, J.M., Rodríguez, J., Porter, J., Lapuerta, V.: Motivational impact of active learning methods in aerospace engineering students. Acta Astronautica **165**, 344–354 (2019)
12. Byers, T., Imms, W., Hartnell-Young, E.: Comparative analysis of the impact of traditional versus innovative learning environment on student attitudes and learning outcomes. Stud. Educ. Eval. **58**, 167–177 (2018)
13. Zarzour, H., Bendjaballah, S., Harirche, H.: Exploring the behavioral patterns of students learning with a Facebook-based e-book approach. Comput. Educ. **156**, 103957 (2020)

14. Hernández-Lara, A.B., Serradell-López, E., Fitó-Bertran, À.: Students' perception of the impact of competences on learning: an analysis with business simulations. Comput. Hum. Behav. **101**, 311–319 (2019)
15. Michalska, K.J., et al.: Anxiety symptoms and children's eye gaze during fear learning. J. Child Psychol. Psychiatry **58**(11), 1276–1286 (2017). (in English)
16. Ntonia, I., Ntonias, S.: Differential hemispheric activation in emotional responses: evidence by conjugate lateral eye movements. Ann. Gen. Psychiatry **5**(1), S303 (2006)
17. Schulze, L., Renneberg, B., Lobmaier, J.: Gaze perception in social anxiety and social anxiety disorder. Mini Rev. **7**(872) (2013). (in English)
18. Carberry, A.R., Lee, H.-S., Ohland, M.W.: Measuring engineering design self-efficacy. **99**(1), 71–79 (2010)
19. Vitasari, P., Wahab, M.N.A., Herawan, T., Othman, A., Sinnadurai, S.K.: A pilot study of pre-post anxiety treatment to improve academic performance for engineering students. Procedia - Soc. Behav. Sci. **15**, 3826–3830 (2011)
20. Nandhini, S., et al.: A statistical exploration on effects of anxiety faced by engineering students. Int. J. Adv. Sci. Technol. **28**(15), 892–898 (2019)
21. Holmes, A., Richards, A., Green, S.: Anxiety and sensitivity to eye gaze in emotional faces. Brain Cogn. **60**(3), 282–294 (2006). (in English)
22. Grillon, H., Riquier, F., Thalmann, D.: Eye-tracking as diagnosis and assessment tool for social phobia. In: 2007 Virtual Rehabilitation, pp. 138–145 (2007)
23. Subrahmaniam, S.: CG&A with eye tracking for cognitive behavior analysis and psychoanalysis. In: 2013 Sixth International Conference on Developments in eSystems Engineering, pp. 132–137 (2013)
24. Jyotsna, C., Amudha, J.: Eye gaze as an indicator for stress level analysis in students. In: 2018 International Conference on Advances in Computing, Communications and Informatics (ICACCI), pp. 1588–1593 (2018)
25. Wang, L., Xie, Y.: Attention bias during processing of facial expressions in trait anxiety: an eye-tracking study. In: Proceedings of 2011 International Conference on Electronics and Optoelectronics, vol. 1, pp. V1-347–V1-350 (2011)
26. Rehg, J.M., et al.: Decoding children's social behaviour. In: 2013 IEEE Conference on Computer Vision and Pattern Recognition, pp. 3414–3421 (2013)
27. Basori, A.H., Abdul Hamid, A.L.B., Firdausiah Mansur, A.B., Yusof, N.: iMars: intelligent municipality augmented reality service for efficient information dissemination based on deep learning algorithm in smart city of Jeddah. Procedia Comput. Sci. **163**, 93–108 (2019)
28. Firdausiah Mansur, A.B., Yusof, N., Basori, A.H.: Comprehensive analysis of student's academic failure classification through role-sphere influence and flow betwenness centrality. Procedia Comput. Sci. **116**, 509–515 (2017)
29. Firdausiah Mansur, A.B., Yusof, N., Basori, A.H.: Personalized learning model based on deep learning algorithm for student behaviour analytic. Procedia Comput. Sci. **163**, 125–133 (2019)
30. Papoutsaki, A., Sangkloy, P., Laskey, J., Daskalova, N., Huang, J., Hays, J.: Webgazer: scalable webcam eye tracking using user interactions. Presented at the Proceedings of the Twenty-Fifth International Joint Conference on Artificial Intelligence, New York, New York, USA (2016)

IOT in Networks, Communications and Distributed Computing

Integration Femtocells Based on Hybrid Beamforming with Existing LTE Macro-cell for Improving Throughput Towards 5G Networks

Mohammed K. Hussein(✉) and Nasser N. Khamiss

Information and Communication Engineering, College of Information Engineering, Al-Nahrain University, Baghdad, Iraq

Abstract. In recent years, the mobile data traffic levels have been expected to be 1000-fold per geographical area. Unfortunately, existing communication systems suffer from the Shannon limit. Integration of the key 5G technologies such as millimeter waves (mmWave), massive multiple-input multiple-output (Massive MIMO), and Small-Cells (SC) systems is to achieve the increase in the network throughput and capacity, as well as the enhancement of the spectral efficiency, and energy efficiency. Our objective develops a new hybrid beamforming algorithm for indoor environments working in the 5G networks to achieve the desired goals. The contribution of this study designs and simulates the hybrid beamforming (HBF) that included the analog precoding and combining based on MMSE criteria and the digital precoding based on the Kalman precoding with the mathematical model in detail compared with other algorithms in the literature. Also, it proposes the heterogeneous network that included femto-cells, based on a real channel model to analyze our algorithm and calculate the throughput in all aspects of the 5G network. The proposed HBF achieves spectral efficiency closer to fully digital precoding, meaning that our solution is in the best state under different conditions. The proposed 5G HetNets enhance the macro-cell throughput under different scenarios, such as 2301.6 times compared with the LTE macro-cell.

Keywords: Massive MIMO · Millimeter-Wave · Small-Cells · Heterogeneous Networks

1 Introduction

Recent years have seen an exponential increase in connected devices and data traffic for mobile wireless networks [1]. Some technologies such as smart cities, smart homes, and the Internet of Things (IoT) are becoming a reality. Simultaneously, the Cisco Visual Networking Index (VNI) has estimated the Traffic Forecast 2017–2022. The video traffic was 59% in 2017, and it will be 79% of the total traffic in 2022 [2]. The mobile data traffic levels are expected to be 1000-fold per geographical area [3]. Unfortunately, existing communication systems suffer from the Shannon limit. It means that a modulation and coding scheme, long with the limited bandwidth of the microwave spectrum, cannot

P. Liatsis et al. (Eds.): TIOTC 2021, CCIS 1548, pp. 209–222, 2022.
https://doi.org/10.1007/978-3-030-97255-4_15

meet these challenges [4, 5], and [6]. It is because that the research community turns attention into the fifth generation (5G) networks, which enable applications in various fields [6]. Recent studies have confirmed a need to fundamentally modify a mobile system architecture and radio technology for achieving 5G goals. Therefore, an integration of the key technologies such as millimeter waves (mmWave), Massive multiple-input multiple-output (Massive MIMO), and Small -Cells (SC) systems is to achieve the increase in the network throughput and capacity, as well as the enhancement of the spectral efficiency, and energy efficiency [7–11], and [12].

The wavelength of mmWave bands is very small, which causes a propagation loss compared to the microwave bands. However, The Massive MIMO makes mmWave bands suitable by deploying more antennas in a small physical area to achieve high-gain antennas. Furthermore, the Massive MIMO system plays a vital role exploited both the spatial freedom and array gain in enhancing beamforming gain and array gain (spectral efficiency and energy efficiency). Also, the beamforming technique adds up the signals in desired directions and nulls in different directions (constructive and destructive). Thus, the narrow and directional beams are a crucial factor to eliminate interference, and then it focuses antennas energy on the desired direction [13–16], and [17].

Beamforming architecture can be classified into three main categories: Digital Beamforming (DBF), Analog Beamforming (ABF), and Hybrid Beamforming (HBF). In more detail, the DBF requires a dedicated radio chain (RF) equips with a single antenna that leads to more cost and consumed energy. It is because that the DBF is unpractical. On the contrary, the ABF is an energy-efficient solution based on inexpensive phase shifters, facilitating beam steering. However, it is limited to one data stream, leading to severe performance limitations in a multi-user scenario. Thus, it is not easy to cancel interfering signals. As a result, the HBF is a promising approach that exploits the small matrix digital beamforming and the high matrix analog beamforming to meet these challenges [18–31], and [32].

The remainder of the paper is organized as follows: Sect. 2 surveys related research articles, Sect. 3 describes the system model and analyses problem formulation, and Sect. 4 discusses the simulation results. Finally, the conclusion is reported in Sect. 5.

Notations: This paper considers A and **a** as a matrix and a vector. On the other hand, A^H, A^{-1}, A^T, $|A|$, and $\|A\|_F$ represent $\mathbb{C}$ the Hermitian, inverse, transpose, determinant, and Frobenius norm of a matrix, respectively. $\mathbb{C}$ is the field of complex numbers. Finally, I and $[\cdot]$ denote the identity matrix and the expectation operator.

2 Related Works

Existing research efforts have been conducted to investigate the performance of ultra-dense small-cells integrated with The LTE macro-cells, known as a Heterogeneous Network (HetNet). In [33], the authors proposed integrating ultra-dense small-cells with the LTE macro-cells to maximize the throughput system. However, the authors did not indicate the details of the study, mainly used hybrid beamforming. The authors in [34] showed a significant compromise between the coverage and link rate in mm-wave HetNets, where there are small-cells within macro-cells as multiple tiers. In [7], the authors presented a survey that facilitates understanding research problems in ultra-dense small-cells with massive MIMO. The authors in [11] presented the survey that focuses on mm-wave HetNets and discussed the system architecture and key technologies extensively to meet the 5G goals. Also, the authors indicated the significant research challenges and open issues. In [35], the authors showed the benefits and challenges that resulted in the wireless backhaul architecture based on mm-wave massive MIMO. Another approach to evaluate the effect of the small cell user density on power consumption was demonstrated in [36]. The authors in [37] discussed and compared many wireless backhaul architectures, in which macro-cells and small-cells are considerable. The authors in [38] presented small-cell planning to enhance energy efficiency within the existing LTE macro-cell. According to the beamforming, there are some studies focused on beamforming as the Zero Forcing hybrid precoding as the digital part, and the codebook as analog part as in [39], the MMSE hybrid precoding as the digital part, and the codebook as analog part as in [40], and also the Kalman hybrid precoding as the digital part and the codebook as analog as in [41].

Our objective proposes a new hybrid beamforming algorithm working in the 5G networks to achieve the desired goals. The contribution of this study designs and simulates the hybrid beamforming that included the analog precoding and combining based on MMSE criteria and the digital precoding based on the Kalman precoding with the mathematical model in detail compared with other algorithms in the literature. Also, it proposes the heterogeneous network that included femto-cells, based on a real channel model to analyze our algorithm and calculate the throughput in all aspects of the 5G network.

3 System Model

The proposed heterogeneous network model is shown in Fig. 1. It is based on the existing LTE macro-cells that serve mobile macro stations (MSs) at the sub-6 GHz band. On the other hand, femto-cells with the mm-wave band help the MSs within the limited area. The LTE macro-cell works as a helper that provides all coverage areas when the femto-cells fail or do not exist.

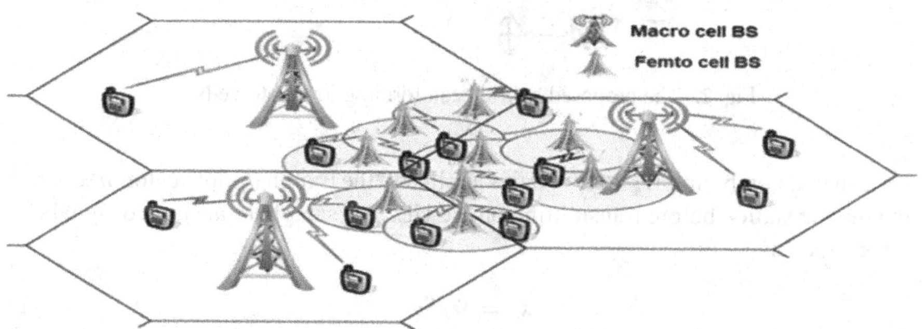

Fig. 1. The proposed HetNet.

LTE macro-cells works with femto-cells to split the large coverage areas into small ones supplied with high bandwidth of millimeter-wave. Femto-cells BS equips with a large number of antennas to maximize throughput underutilized the proposed hybrid beamforming.

The LTE macro uses the DBF and depends on the frequency-division duplex (FDD) system, in which each user estimates the channel state information (CSI) from the received downlink training sequences. After that, it feeds them back to the BS over the uplink control channel since the characteristics of the uplink (UL), and downlink (DL) channels are highly uncorrelated.

The femto-cells BS uses the time-division duplex (TDD) system based on the reciprocity of the UL and DL channels to overcome the problem of the resource-consuming feedback channel. The femto-cells BS exploits it to estimate the UL and DL channel due to the same frequency in forward and reverse links.

The femto-cells BS is given in Fig. 2, in which multi-users Massive MIMO systems incorporate with the hybrid precoding solution, and the mm-Wave channel is considered. The femto-cells BS equips with the number of antenna N_{BS} supplied from Nt_{RF} RF chains at the BS, known as fully-connected architecture. It maps Ns data streams on the N_{BS} and simultaneously serves K MSs. On the other hand, the MS equips with the number of antenna N_{MS} and single RF chains to receive the Ns at the receive side.

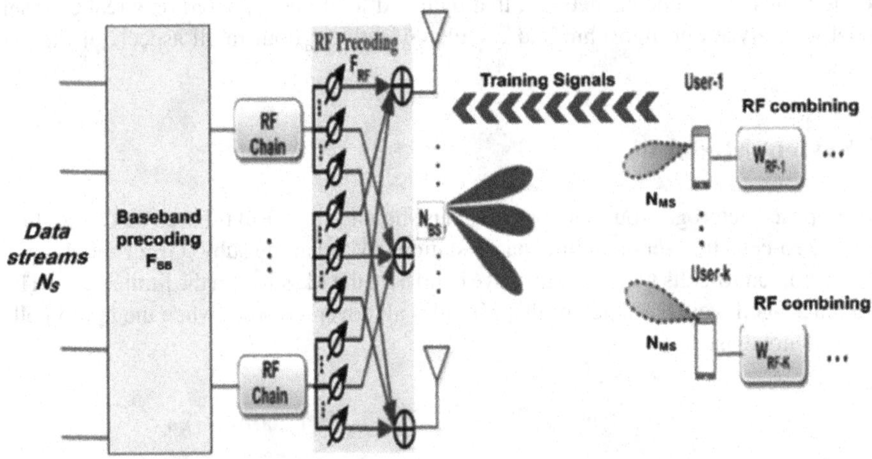

Fig. 2. The proposed hybrid beamforming for femto-cells.

An analog combining $W_k \in \mathbb{C}^{N_{MS}\, x\, k}$ is applied to the training/pilot vector $S_k \in \mathbb{C}^{k\, x\, l}$ at the mobile station before transmitting on the UL. The sampled transmitted signal can be expressed as:

$$x_k = W_k S_k \tag{1}$$

The femtocells BS consists of $F_{BB} \in \mathbb{C}^{N_{RF} x K}$ digital precoding and $F_{RF} \in \mathbb{C}^{N_{BS} x K}$ analog precoding applied to the received signal. Thus, the estimated signal after decoding processes can be expressed as:

$$s_{\hat{k}} = \underbrace{H_k^H F_{RF}^H F_{BBk}^H W_k S_k}_{Desired\ signal} + \underbrace{\sum_{j \neq k}^{K} H_k^H F_{RF}^H F_{BBj}^H W_K S_j}_{Interference\ signal} + \underbrace{F_{RF}^H F_{BBk}^H n_k}_{Noise} \tag{2}$$

Where $n_k \in \mathbb{C}^K$ is the Gaussian noise vector and H_k is the channel matrix between the BS and the *kth* user. The generated channel model is a realistic radio channel known as QUAsi Deterministic RadIo channel GenerAtor (QuaDRiGa). The Fraunhofer Heinrich Hertz Institute has developed the QuaDriGa for heterogeneous configurations and deployment conditions [42].

The sum achievable rate of the system related to *Kth* user is given as:

$$R_k = \sum_{k=1}^{K} \log_2 \left[1 + \frac{\left| H_k^H F_{RF}^H F_{BBk}^H W_k S_k \right|^2}{\left| \sum_{j \neq k}^{K} H_k^H F_{RF}^H F_{BBj}^H W_K S_j \right|^2 + \sigma_k^2} \right] \tag{3}$$

Where σ_k^2 and $|S_k|^2$ are the average noise power and the average total signal power.

3.1 Problem Statement and Proposed Hybrid Beamforming

The hybrid precoding and combining can be designed based on optimizing the sum rate of the proposed system. Also, it can be described through equations as following:

$$\begin{gathered} \underbrace{max}_{F_{RF}, F_{BB}, W} = \sum_{k=1}^{K} R_K \\ \textbf{s.t.} \\ \begin{cases} |(F_{RF})i, j| = \frac{1}{\sqrt{N_{BS}}} \\ |(W_K)i, j| = \frac{1}{\sqrt{N_{MS}}} \\ \|F_{BB}\|_F^2 = K \end{cases} \end{gathered} \tag{4}$$

The above Eq. (4) is not easy to solve since it is a non-convex optimization problem. Therefore, it is decomposed into two sub-problems as the analog and digital stage at the precoding/combining design. In the analog stage, the sub-problem can be reformulated based on maximizing the antenna array gain, which can be represented as the effective channel written as:

$$Heff = H_k^H F_{RF}^H W_k \tag{5}$$

As explained above, the data rate will be increased gradually if the antenna array gain is increased. Therefore, the effective channel can be reformulated as follow:

$$\underbrace{max}_{F_{RF},W} = \sum_{k=1}^{K} \left\| H_k^H F_{RF}^H W_k \right\|_F^2$$
$$\text{s.t.}$$
$$\begin{cases} |(F_{RF})i,j| = \frac{1}{\sqrt{N_{BS}}} \\ |(W_k)i,j| = \frac{1}{\sqrt{N_{MS}}} \end{cases} \tag{6}$$

The proposed solution attempts to apply the MMSE criterion on the uplink channels for obtaining the analog precoding and combining as shown in the following equations:

$$AP_{xx} = \left(H_k^H H_k + \frac{K\sigma^2}{P} I \right)^1 H_k^H \tag{7}$$

Here, the angle $\phi_{i,j}$ of the matrix AP_{xx} is considered the basis for determining the analog combining for the kth MS when the amplitudes are constant, as shown in Eq. (7). Therefore, the analog combining can be calculated as follow:

$$W_k = \frac{1}{\sqrt{N_{MS}}} e^{i(\text{angle } \phi\, \text{i,j})} \tag{8}$$

Next, the MMSE criterion is applied to the analog combining and the channel as written:

$$b_k = W_k H_k^H \tag{9}$$

$$AC_{XX} = \left(b_k^H b_k + \frac{K\sigma^2}{P} I \right)^1 b_k^H \tag{10}$$

Similarly, the analog precoder based on the angle $\Omega_{i,j}$ of the matrix AC_{xx} can be formulated as follow:

$$F_{RF} = \frac{1}{\sqrt{N_{BS}}} e^{i(\text{angle } \Omega\, \text{i,j})} \tag{11}$$

On the other hand, the digital part can manage the interferences among the MSs if the effective channel is available. In other words, the analog precoding and combining are determined in the analog part above, and then the effective channel is calculated. In this step, we select a Kalman filter as the digital part since it optimally estimates a current value depends on past measurements. The Kalman precoding uses a dynamic model of a system to estimate the desired values. The proposed precoding centralizes on update equations to compute F_{BB} and considers the error estimate as follows:

$$\text{Kalman Gain } G(k) = C(k|k-1) H_{eff}^H \left[H_{eff} C(k|k-1) H_{eff}^H + Lk \right]^{-1} \tag{12}$$

$$\text{Error Estimate } e(k) = \frac{I - H_{eff} F_{BB}(k|k-1)}{\left\| I - H_{eff} F_{BB}(k|k-1) \right\|_F^2} \tag{13}$$

$$\text{Update Estimate } F_{BB}(k|k) = F_{BB}(k|k-1) + e(k)G(k) \tag{14}$$

$$\text{Update Covariance Matrix } C(k|k) = \left[I - G(k)H_{eff} \right] C(k|k-1) \tag{15}$$

$$\text{Normalize } F_{BB} = \sqrt{p} \frac{F_{BB}}{\| F_{BB} F_{RF} \|_F} \tag{16}$$

Where *Lk* is the covariance matrix of the noise that sets (1/ SNR)*I, and p the transmitted power.

Figure 3 summarizes the processes followed in the Kalman algorithm.

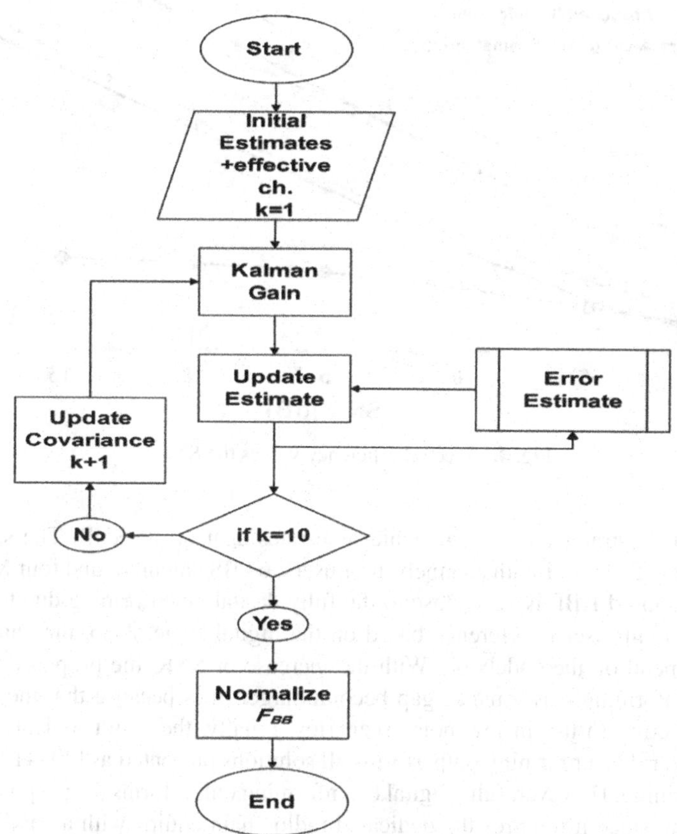

Fig. 3. The flowchart of the proposed digital part.

4 Simulation Results

In this section, the femto-cell is operated at 60 GHZ with 2 GHZ bandwidth. The average achievable rate is used to evaluate the performance. The simulation and comparison are presented between the proposed HBF and analog beamforming, fully digital beamforming, and single-user without interference along with [39, 40], and [41]. The results are more than 1000 random channel implementations on average. MATLAB 2019a software is a simulation tool and environment for the proposed method.

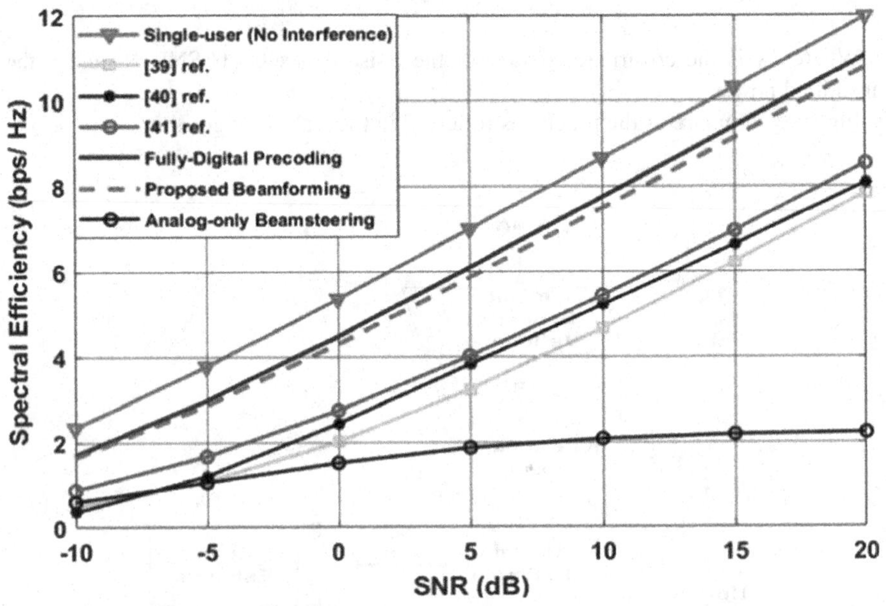

Fig. 4. Spectral efficiency versus the SNR.

Figure 4 illustrates the average achievable rates against the SNR. The simulation parameters are five multi-path channels, four users, 64 BS antennas, and four MS antennas. The proposed HBF is very close to the fully digital beamforming due to the cancellation of multi-user interference based on the digital stage. Also, the analog stage does not depend on the codebook. With the increase of SNR, the proposed HBF and analog beamforming performance gap become larger. It is because that the proposed HBF is preferred to use in low noise scenarios. Finally, the result indicates that the proposed hybrid beamforming outperforms all solutions presented as [39–41], and analog beamforming. However, fully digital beamforming outperforms the proposed hybrid beamforming since it requires the dedicated radio chain equips with a single antenna that leads to more cost and consumed energy.

Figure 5 considers the same settings described in the above figure but sets SNR 10 dB. The figure shows that the proposed HBF is decreased slightly by increasing the number of users than other solutions. Our solution uses the Kalman filter with limited iteration

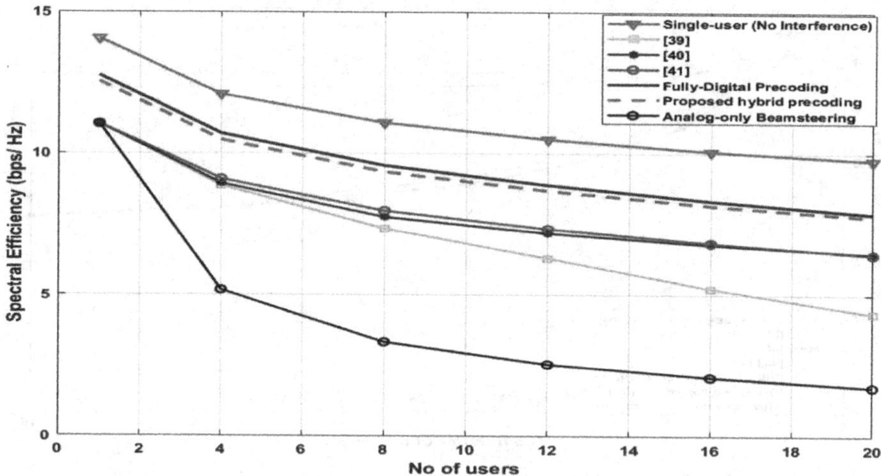

Fig. 5. Spectral efficiency versus the number of users.

to cancel interference between users and increase the array gain based on extracting the angles from MMSE criteria.

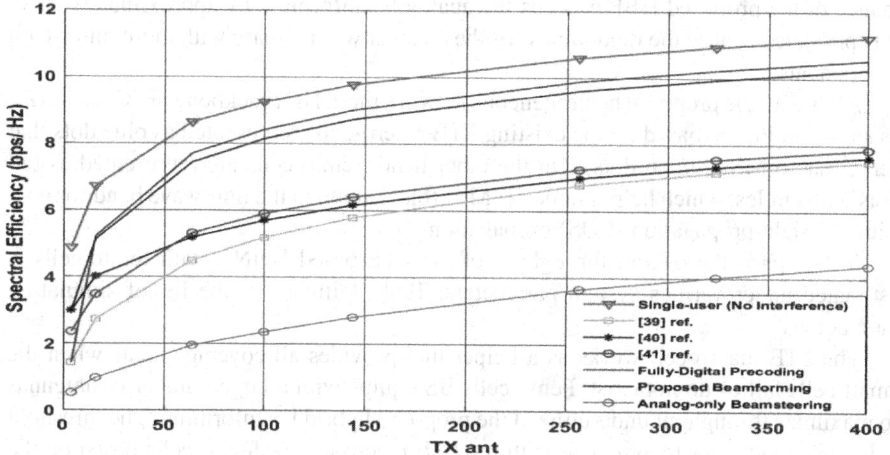

Fig. 6. Spectral efficiency against the BS antennas

Figure 6 considers the same configuration described above but sets the number of users four and confirms that the number of antennas benefits in growing the desired data rate. The BS antennas are increased to grow the desired data rate. The results indicate that the proposed HBF outperforms other solutions. The performance gap between fully digital beamforming and our method is approximately constant with the increasing number of antennas.

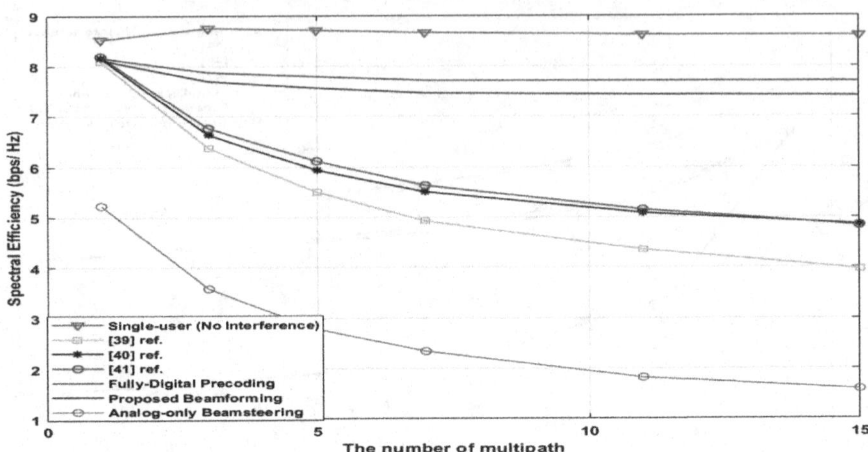

Fig. 7. Spectral efficiency against the number of multi-path.

Figure 7 considers the same configuration described above but sets 64 BS antennas. In the multi-path scenario, the proposed HBF illustrates the best performance than other solutions. Hence, the proposed solution is better in facing the multi-path since the digital stage of the proposed solution can eliminate interferences between signals. The performance of the proposed HBF exceeds the analog beamforming by approximately 21%. It is possible because the randomness of the channel will increase with more multi-path components.

After that, the proposed heterogeneous network model is a backbone of 5G networks, as shown in Fig. 8, based on the existing LTE macro-cells represented as blue dots that serve macro MSs (green dots). On the other hand, femto-cells are represented as red dots with circles, which help femtocells MSs (black dots) in the mm-wave band for near Line Of Sight propagation (LOS) propagation.

In this part, the overall throughput of the LTE-based HetNet with femto-cells is estimated under various system parameters. Table 1 illustrates the list of simulation parameters.

The LTE macro-cell works as a helper that provides all coverage areas when the small-cells fail or do not exist. Femtocells BS equips with a large number of antennas to maximize throughput underutilized the proposed hybrid beamforming. The threshold value is an indicator to associate with the LTE macro-cell or femto-cells based on the only SNR due to the variation in the interference level within one frame. In this work, the MSs with the (8 dB or more) SNR are associated with femtocells, while other users are associate with the LTE macro-cell.

Results illustrated in Table 2 shows that throughput of the macro-cell area is approximately enhanced up to 1162 times compared with the LTE macro-cell. Simulation results show that femtocells serve closed UEs with a package of advantages; as shown above, 88% of MSs are supplied from these femto-cells, resulting in this increase.

Results are presented in Table 3 that the throughput enhancement for the macro-cell area is up to 2301.6 times compared with the LTE macro-cell. The reasons are also the

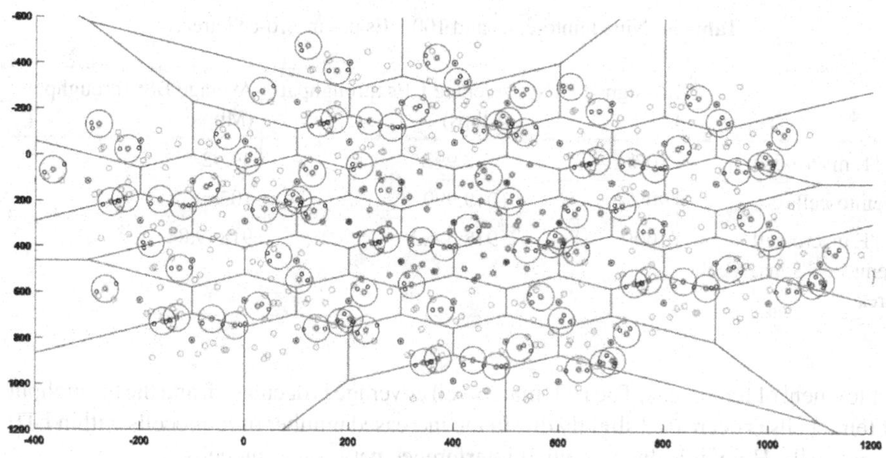

Fig. 8. The proposed HetNet layout.

Table 1. List of simulation parameter

Model parameter	Macro-cells	Femto-cells
Multiple access	OFDM, with normal cyclic prefix	OFDM, with normal cyclic prefix
System bandwidth	20 MHz FDD	2 GHz TDD
Carrier frequency	2.6 GHz	60 GHz
Number of cells	Seven heterogeneous hexagonal	3, 9 per macro-cell area
Number of users	50, 100 per macro-cell area	
Tx powers	47 dBm	20 dBm
Tx antenna elements	6	128 arrays
BS heights	25 m	10 m
UE heights	1.5 m	1.5 m
Propagation model	3GPP 38.901 UMa NLOS	3GPP 38.901 UMi LOS
Inter-site distance	200 m	

Table 2. Three femto-cells and 50 UEs per macro-cell area.

	Assigned UEs	Average UEs throughput (Mbps)	Average BSs throughput (Mbps)
LTE macro-cell	12%	6.7166	40.3
Femto-cells	88%	1063.641	15600
LTE macro-cell + femto-cells macrocell area	100%	936.81	46840

Table 3. Nine femto-cells and 100 UEs per macro-cell area.

	Assigned UEs	Average UEs throughput (Mbps)	Average BSs throughput (Mbps)
LTE macro-cell	10%	3.992	39.92
Femto-cells	90%	1019.999	10200
LTE macro-cell + femto-cells macrocell area	100%	918.3983	91879.84

deployment of femtocells. The LTE macro-cell coverage is decreased, and the throughput of femtocells is decreased slightly due to the increased number of femtocells within LTE macro-cells. Here, it is due to mutual interference between femtocells.

5 Conclusions

Overall, this work offers a successful approach towards 5G networks. The outcome of various experimentations concludes that femtocells serve closed UEs with a package of advantages. However, it is mandatory to solve issues related to the integration of 5G technologies. The design of hybrid beamforming is the main challenge. The proposed HBF passes all simulation scenarios with better spectral efficiency under different parameters than other solutions. It uses the Kalman filter with limited iteration to cancel interference between users and increase the array gain based on extracting MMSE angles. The proposed HBF achieves spectral efficiency closer to fully digital precoding, meaning that our solution is in the best state under different conditions. The proposed 5G HetNets enhance the macro-cell throughput under different scenarios, such as 2301.6 times compared with the LTE macro-cell. The realistic channel usage in this simulation undoubtedly fulfills the fact that the proposed method is a more practical solution.

References

1. Chen, W.C.: 5G mmWAVE technology design challenges and development trends. In: 2020 International Symposium on VLSI Design, Automation and Test (VLSI-DAT), pp. 2–5. VLSI-DAT 2020 (2020)
2. Paper, W.: Cisco Visual Networking Index: Forecast and Methodology Cisco Visual Networking Index: Cisco Visual Networking Index: Forecast and Methodology. Forecast Methodol. 2015–2020 (2015)
3. Lee, S.: Cooperative non-orthogonal multiple access for future wireless communications. EAI Endorsed Trans. Ind. Netw. Intell. Syst. **5**, 156078 (2018)
4. Hemadeh, I.A., Satyanarayana, K., El-Hajjar, M., Hanzo, L.: Millimeter-wave communications: physical channel models, design considerations, antenna constructions, and link-budget. IEEE Commun. Surv. Tutor. **20**, 870–913 (2018)
5. Uwaechia, A.N., Mahyuddin, N.M., Ain, M.F., Abdul Latiff, N.M., Za'bah, N.F.: On the spectral-efficiency of low-complexity and resolution hybrid precoding and combining transceivers for mmWave MIMO systems. IEEE Access **7**, 109259–109277 (2019)

6. Sherif, A.B., Kazi, M.S.H., Shahid, M., Linglong, D., Jonathan, R.: Millimeter-wave massive MIMO communication for future wireless systems: a survey. IEEE Commun. Surv. Tutor. **20**, 836–869 (2018)
7. Rajoria, S., Trivedi, A., Godfrey, W.W.: A comprehensive survey: small cell meets massive MIMO. Phys. Commun. **26**, 40–49 (2018)
8. Taheribakhsh, M.: 5G implementation: major issues and challenges. In: 2020 25th International Computer Conference, Computer Society of Iran (CSICC), pp. 1–5 (2020)
9. Umer, A., Hassan, S.A., Pervaiz, H., Ni, Q., Musavian, L.: Coverage and rate analysis for massive MIMO-enabled heterogeneous networks with millimeter wave small cells. In: 2017 IEEE 85th Vehicular Technology Conference (VTC Spring) (June 2017)
10. Manap, S., Dimyati, K., Hindia, M.N., Abu Talip, M.S., Tafazolli, R.: Survey of radio resource management in 5G heterogeneous networks. IEEE Access **8**, 131202–131223 (2020)
11. Kazi, B.U., Wainer, G.A.: Next generation wireless cellular networks: ultra-dense multi-tier and multi-cell cooperation perspective. Wirel. Netw. **25**(4), 2041–2064 (2018). https://doi.org/10.1007/s11276-018-1796-y
12. Zhang, T., Biswas, S., Ratnarajah, T.: Performance analysis of cache aided hybrid mmwave sub-6 GHz massive MIMO networks. In: 2020 IEEE 21st International Workshop on Signal Processing Advances in Wireless Communications (SPAWC) (May 2020)
13. Varshney, N., De, S.: Optimum downlink beamwidth estimation in mmWave communications. IEEE Trans. Commun. **69**, 544–557 (2021)
14. Erden, F., Ozdemir, O., Guvenc, I.: 28 GHz mmwave channel measurements and modeling in a library environment. In: 2020 IEEE Radio and Wireless Symposium (RWS), pp. 52–55 (January 2020)
15. Li, T., Zhao, F.: A spectral efficient hybrid precoding algorithm for mmwave MIMO systems. Procedia Comput. Sci. **174**, 584–590 (2020)
16. Ghosh, A., Ratasuk, R., Mondal, B., Mangalvedhe, N., Thomas, T.: LTE-advanced: next-generation wireless broadband technology. IEEE Wirel. Commun. **17**, 10–22 (2010)
17. Tatineni, M.: Hybrid precoding/combining for single-user and multi-users in mm-Wave MIMO systems. Int. J. Innov. Technol. Explor. Eng. **9**, 134–139 (2019)
18. Yassin, M.R.A., Abdallah, H.: Hybrid beamforming in multiple user massive multiple input multiple output 5G communications system. In: 2020 7th International Conference on Electrical and Electronics Engineering ICEEE 2020, pp. 215–220 (2020)
19. Molisch, A.F., et al.: Hybrid beamforming for massive MIMO: a survey. IEEE Commun. Mag. **55**, 134–141 (2017)
20. Zhou, Z., Ge, N., Wang, Z., Chen, S.: Hardware-efficient hybrid precoding for millimeter wave systems with multi-feed reflectarrays. IEEE Access **6**, 6795–6806 (2018)
21. Souto, N., Silva, J., Pavia, J., Ribeiro, M.: An alternating direction algorithm for hybrid precoding and combining in millimeter wave MIMO systems. Phys. Commun. **34**, 165–173 (2019)
22. Alluhaibi, O., Ahmed, Q.Z., Pan, C., Zhu, H.: Hybrid digital-to-analog beamforming approaches to maximise the capacity of mm-wave systems. In: 2017 IEEE 85th Vehicular Technology Conference (VTC Spring), 4 June 2017
23. Uwaechia, A.N., Mahyuddin, N.M.: A comprehensive survey on millimeter wave communications for fifth-generation wireless networks: feasibility and challenges. IEEE Access **8**, 62367–62414 (2020)
24. Ahmed, I., et al.: A survey on hybrid beamforming techniques in 5G: architecture and system model perspectives. IEEE Commun. Surv. Tutor. **20**, 3060–3097 (2018)
25. Xiao, M., et al.: Millimeter wave communications for future mobile networks. IEEE J. Sel. Areas Commun. **35**, 1909–1935 (2017)

26. Carrera, D.F., Member, S., Vargas-rosales, C., Member, S., Villalpando-hernandez, R.: Performance improvement for multi-user Millimeter-wave massive MIMO systems, pp. 1–15 (2020)
27. Lin, T., Cong, J., Zhu, Y., Zhang, J., Letaief, K.B.: Hybrid beamforming for millimeter wave systems using the MMSE criterion. IEEE Trans. Commun. **67**, 3693–3708 (2019)
28. Shaheenbanu, M., Suma, M.N.: Investigation on hybrid precoding for multi-user MIMO systems. In: 2019 IEEE International WIE Conference on Electrical and Computer Engineering (WIECON-ECE), pp. 1–4. WIECON-ECE 2019–Proceedings (2019)
29. Blandino, S., et al.: multi-user hybrid MIMO at 60 GHZ using 16-antenna transmitters. IEEE Trans. Circuits Syst. I Regul. Pap. **66**, 848–858 (2019)
30. Duan, K., Du, H., Wu, Z.: Hybrid alternating precoding and combining design for mmwave multi-user MIMO systems. In: 2018 IEEE/CIC International Conference Communication China, pp. 217–221. ICCC 2018 (2019)
31. Seo, B.: Hybrid combiner design for downlink massive MIMO systems. ETRI J. etrij. 2019–0123 (2020)
32. Said, S., Saad, W., Shokair, M.: MMSE algorithm based two stages hybrid precoding for millimeter wave massive MIMO systems. Analog Integr. Circuits Signal Process. **98**(3), 565–573 (2018). https://doi.org/10.1007/s10470-018-1354-7
33. Abdullah, Q., et al.: Maximising system throughput in wireless powered sub-6 GHz and millimetre-wave 5G heterogeneous networks. Telkomnika Telecommun. Comput. Electron. Control **18**, 1185–1194 (2020)
34. Liu, C.H.: Coverage-rate tradeoff analysis in mmwave heterogeneous cellular networks. IEEE Trans. Commun. **67**, 1720–1736 (2019)
35. Gao, Z., Dai, L., Mi, D., Wang, Z., Imran, M.A., Shakir, M.Z.: MmWave massive-MIMO-based wireless backhaul for the 5G ultra-dense network. IEEE Wirel. Commun. **22**, 13–21 (2015)
36. Aldırmaz Çolak, S.: Impact of small cell user density on performance of small cells sleeping technique for HetNet. Pamukkale Univ. J. Eng. Sci. **25**, 519–524 (2019)
37. Jaber, M., Imran, M.A., Tafazolli, R., Tukmanov, A.: 5G backhaul challenges and emerging research directions: a survey (2016)
38. Wang, Y.C., Lee, S.: Small-cell planning in LTE HetNet to improve energy efficiency. Int. J. Commun. Syst. **31**, 1–18 (2018)
39. Alkhateeb, A., Leus, G., Heath, R.W.: Limited feedback hybrid precoding for multi-user millimeter wave systems. IEEE Trans. Wirel. Commun. **14**, 6481–6494 (2015)
40. Nguyen, D.H.N., Le, L.B., Le-Ngoc, T.: Hybrid MMSE precoding for mmWave multiuser MIMO systems. In: 2016 IEEE International Conference on Communications (ICC), pp. 1–6. IEEE (2016)
41. Vizziello, A., Savazzi, P., Chowdhury, K.R.: A kalman based hybrid precoding for multi-user millimeter wave MIMO systems. IEEE Access **6**, 55712–55722 (2018)
42. Jaeckel, S., Raschkowsk, L., Borner, K., Thiele, L., Burkhardt, F.E.: Quasi deterministic radio channel generator user manual and documentation. Fraunhofer Heinrich Hertz Inst. Wirel. Commun. Netw. Einsteinufer **37**, 10587 (2017). Berlin Ger. (ed.), Tech. Rep. v2.0.0, Fraun-hofer Heinrich Hertz Institute, Einsteinufer 37, 10587 Berlin, Ger. 1–133

Performance Evaluation of CoAP and MQTT_SN Protocols

Rahaf A. Al-Qassab and Mohammed I. Aal-Nouman(✉)

Department of Information and Communication Engineering, College of Information Engineering, Al-Nahrain University, Baghdad, Iraq
{rahaf.ammar,m.aalnouman}@coie-nahrain.edu.iq

Abstract. Internet of Things (IoT) protocols are a set of rules or standards that are used to facilitate communication between connected devices over a wireless network. One of the most important requirements of a wireless sensor networks (WSN) is power efficiency because it depends on the life span of the batteries of sensor nodes. This paper resolves to evaluate the performance of application-layer IoT protocols such as CoAP (Constrained Application Protocol) and MQTT_SN (Message Queuing Telemetry Transport for Sensor Networks) in terms of power efficiency. Contiki-OS and Cooja Simulator were utilized to conduct the simulation of the protocols and to collect the data of the nodes which was used to calculate the power consumption. Simulation Results show that CoAP is relatively more power efficient than MQTT_SN. It was also evaluated that the highest power consumption is happening at different power states for each protocol.

Keywords: IoT · CoAP · MQTT_SN · Protocols · Contiki-OS · Cooja · Powertrace

1 Introduction

The protocols evaluated in this paper are application-layer protocols used for the Internet of Things, a system where internet-connected sensors collect environmental data for communication with other devices over a wireless network [1]. CoAP is a lightweight, low power IOT application protocol especially designed for constrained environments that do not support HTTP (The Hypertext Transfer Protocol) or TCP/IP (Transmission Control Protocol/Internet Protocol) [2]. MQTT_SN is an enhanced version of MQTT, designed for IoT sensor networks of efficient operation and low power. Both protocols were simulated using Contiki-OS' Cooja simulator with the power information of the nodes collected through the Powertrace application [3]. This data was used to calculate the power consumption of the client nodes. Power efficiency was chosen as the metric of evaluation in this paper because it is a very important requirement of IoT and WSN due to the dependency of sensor nodes on batteries. Most IoT applications require objects and sensors to operate for very long periods of time, therefore, power efficiency is crucial for IoT applications. Hypothetically, CoAP should be more power efficient than MQTT_SN due to its constrained nature.

P. Liatsis et al. (Eds.): TIOTC 2021, CCIS 1548, pp. 223–236, 2022.
https://doi.org/10.1007/978-3-030-97255-4_17

This paper is focused on evaluating the performance of CoAP and MQTT_SN with regard to power efficiency using Contiki-OS and Cooja Simulator. The contribution of this research is to evaluate the performance of the aforementioned protocols in different power states. This is an evaluation that has not been discussed previously in similar research. This finding will aid the developers to select a suitable protocol for their IoT applications and environment.

Similar Work: Many researchers have shown interest in this topic, [4] conducted two experiments to evaluate the performance of IoT communication protocols CoAP, MQTT and AMQP. The chosen metrics were throughput, message size and packet loss, of which CoAP showed the best results [5]. Evaluates the performance of CoAP and 6LoWPAN over the IEEE 802.15.4 radio link and demonstrates that CoAP is not particularly sensitive to the increase in the generation time of client request [6]. Performs a comparative study between CoAP and MQTT and comes to the conclusion that while CoAP performs better in terms of latency, MQTT has a higher performance when it comes to bandwidth. CoAP has also proven to be suitable in a medical application setting, [7] studies the performance of CoAP and MQTT for ECG with respect to elapsed time and comes to the conclusion that CoAP has a significantly better performance than MQTT in terms of large scalability IoT networks and with the constraint of elapsed time. However, [8] demonstrates that when it comes to not only medical applications but any IoT system that requires loss-less, low latency performance, MQTT is the most suitable due to its superior performance on data latency and reliability.

The rest of the paper will be organized as follows; Sect. 2 will be about the primary IoT architectures, Sect. 3 and 4 will discuss the CoAP protocol and the MQTT_SN protocol, respectively. Section 5 contains the simulation setup and Sect. 6 will discuss simulation results. Finally, the conclusion will be presented in Sect. 7.

2 IoT Architecture

There is no agreed on, standard architecture for IoT. Different researchers have proposed different architectures. However, the three-layer architecture is the most basic IoT architecture. This three-layer architecture consists of the perception layer, the network layer and the application layer. Figure 1(a) displays the three-layer IoT architecture.

The Perception layer represents the physical layer which includes sensor devices that collect environmental data. The Network layer is responsible for connecting the different components of a wireless sensor network. These components could be other sensors, smart objects and servers. As for the Application layer, it is the layer responsible for delivering application specific services to the user. It specifies different IoT applications such as smart home, smart city and smart healthcare [9].

Another popular architecture is the five-layer IoT architecture. This architecture is similar to the three-layer one but with the addition of two layers; The Access gateway layer and the Middleware layer. The access gateway layer is responsible for managing the communication in a particular IoT environment. The Middleware layer provides flexible association between hardware devices and applications [10]. The five-layer architecture is displayed in Fig. 1(b).

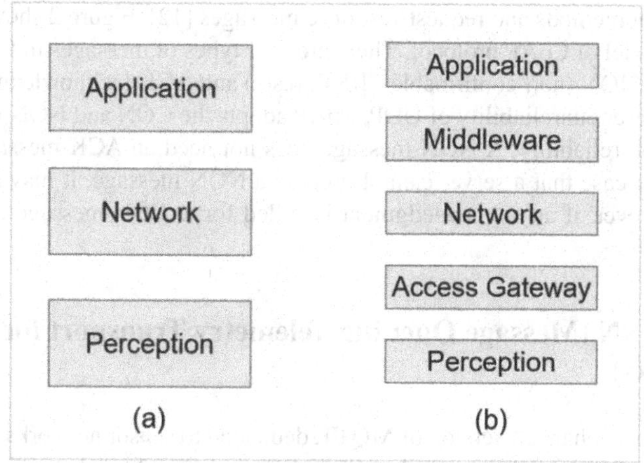

Fig. 1. (a) Three-layer IoT architecture [9]. (b) five-layer architecture [10].

This work is interested in evaluating the performance of application layer IoT protocols, in particular CoAP and MQTT_SN.

3 CoAP (Constrained Application Protocol)

CoAP is an IoT application layer protocol designed specifically for constrained (limited) hardware and applications. The insufficiency of HTTP in constrained IoT environments was the design motive of CoAP, but it was also the inspiration. Like HTTP, it follows a client-server model. CoAP is expected to perform a similar role as HTTP but for an IoT setting, rather than the traditional Internet, and has therefore been standardized as a web transfer protocol by IETF [11]. The main difference between HTTP and CoAP is in the transport layer. HTTP relies on TCP protocol, which is connection-oriented. Whereas CoAP relies on UDP, a connectionless protocol. CoAP employs a two-layer structure, the Message layer and the Request/Response layer. The former has been designed to deal with UDP and asynchronous switching, whereas the latter layer is concerned with

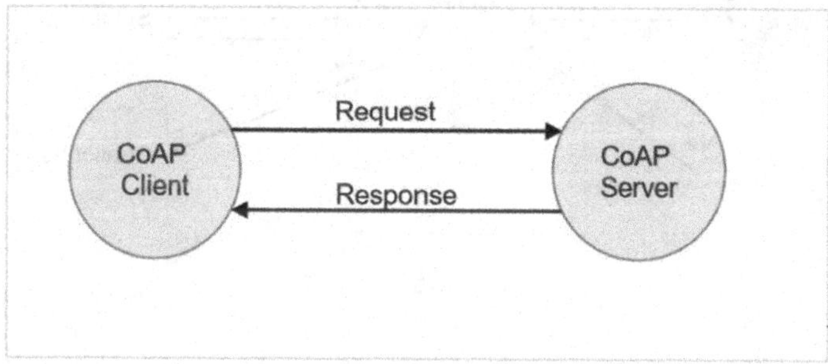

Fig. 2. CoAP protocol communication [14].

communication methods and request-response messages [12]. Figure 2 shows the communication model of CoAP protocol. There are four types of messages in CoAP –CON (confirmable), NON (non-confirmable), RST (reset) and ACK (acknowledgment) [13]. Due to the inherent unreliability of UDP, CoAP adopts the CON and NON messages to provide its own reliability. A NON message does not need an ACK message upon its delivery. In the case that a server cannot process a NON message, it may send a RST message. However, if an acknowledgment is called for, a CON message is employed [4].

4 MQTT_SN (Message Queuing Telemetry Transport for Sensor Networks)

MQTT_SN is an enhanced version of MQTT, dedicated to sensor networks. This protocol is designed for network sensors that are simple, lightweight and easy to apply [15]. Despite aiming to be as close as possible to MQTT, MQTT_SN has modifications that adhere to sensor network requirements such as restraints to the message length, unreliability, low bandwidth, etc. [12]. MQTT_SN is also optimized to be implemented on low-cost, battery-operated devices that have limited processing and storage capabilities [16]. MQTT_SN, like MQTT, uses a Publisher/Subscriber model to enable communication between constrained sensor nodes. In this model, a publisher will send messages on a specific topic to a broker, which then forwards the messages to a subscriber that has subscribed to this particular topic. MQTT clients can publish and subscribe messages synchronously to the broker for particular topics. MQTT devices can be connected to different resources such as sensors, backend servers or even graphical clients capable of communicating with MQTT [17]. MQTT_SN is designed to better cope with the

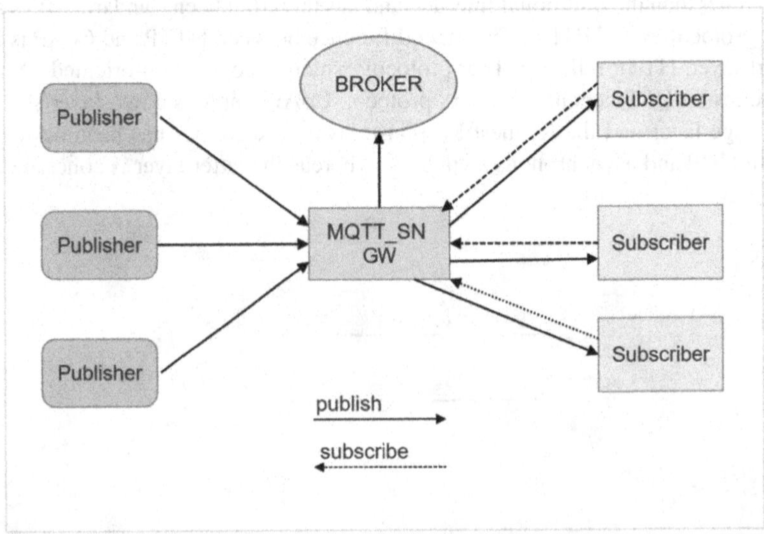

Fig. 3. MQTT_SN protocol communication model [16].

constraints of WSN [18]. The architecture of MQTT_SN is represented in Fig. 3, where every publisher is publishing a different topic and sending MQTT messages to the broker via a MQTT_SN GW (MQTT_SN gateway). The broker is then forwarding the messages to the subscribed devices, also through the MQTT_SN GW. The only difference between this architecture and the MQTT architecture is the addition of an MQTT_SN GW [16]. The MQTT_SN clients deploy the MQTT_SN GW to connect to a MQTT server.

5 Simulation Setup

For simulation purposes, Contiki OS and COOJA simulator were used. Contiki-OS is an operating system for the Internet of Things, made for networked, memory-constrained systems and focused on IoT devices of low power. Contiki OS is implemented in C programming language and deploys a make build environment for cross-compilation on most platforms [5]. It also comes with network stacks such as the uIP (micro IP) stack (with support for IEEE802.15.4 – TSCH, IPv6, 6LoWPAN, RPL and CoAP) and the Rime stack [19]. Contiki OS offers a wide variety of microcontrollers and device platform ports, called motes, in addition to examples and reusable applications and tools. Various simulators were researched for this work, including OMNET++, NS-2 and NETSIM. Contiki OS was found to be the most suitable for the purpose of this paper.

COOJA is a WSN simulator built in Contiki-OS specialized for sensor nodes. This simulator focuses on network connectivity and protocol performance [20]. It has been developed in JAVA programming language, but the sensors that are simulated can also be programmed in C programming language. Cooja has the ability to emulate the behavior of real motes which makes it the better choice out of similar simulators, for evaluating the performance of IoT protocols. Another advantage of COOJA simulator is its ability to simulate the application software concurrently in high level algorithm development and low level hard driver development.

It must be mentioned that an additional Contiki tool, called Powertrace, was used in this work. Powertrace is a Contiki OS application that collects power data of motes either from a testbed or from a Cooja simulation. It uses power state tracking to estimate the power consumption of the system [3]. In other words, it tracks the duration of activities of a node being in each power state by counting the number of ticks at every interval. There are 6 defined power states: CPU, LPM, TRANSMIT LISTEN, IDLE_TRANSMIT and IDLE_LISTEN. Only the first four states were used to calculate the average power consumption of each node. Powertrace was integrated into the simulations by adding it to the source code of the nodes that we want to calculate power consumption for. The Makefile was also adjusted so that Cooja could recognize the application.

In this work, the mote platform chosen for the nodes is the Tmote Sky platform, which is based on MSP430 micro-controller with 10 KB of RAM and IEEE 802.15.4 chip-con wireless transceiver.

5.1 CoAP Implementation

To simulate the CoAP protocol, Tmote Sky motes were used for all the nodes. The simulation contained one CoAP server, ten CoAP client nodes representing sensor devices and one border router. Table 1 depicts the simulation parameters, which were applied to both simulations.

Figure 4 shows the network diagram for the CoAP simulation. The circular nodes represent the CoAP client sensors, which can communicate with the CoAP server directly, or through a gateway represented by the border router. CoAP clients can also communicate with each other. The CoAP clients are periodically sending request messages to the server, which replies with a response message.

Table 1. Simulation parameters

Parameter	Value
Simulation time	600000 ms (10 min)
Mote type	Tmote sky
Radio environment	Unit Disk Graph Medium (UDGM)
Node count	10 nodes (client)
Mote startup delay	1 ms
Seed	Random
MAC/adaptation layer	ContikiMAC

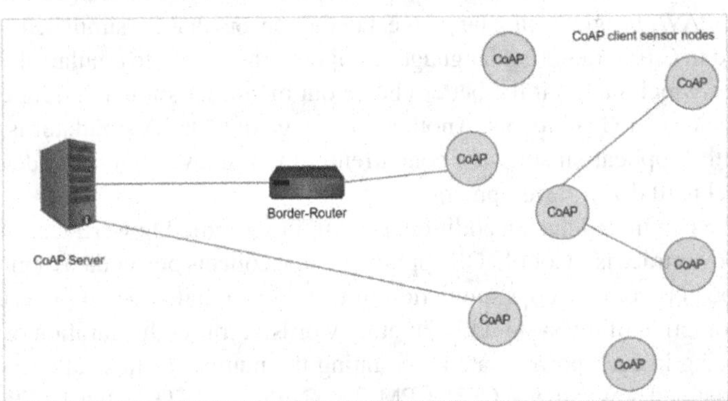

Fig. 4. CoAP simulation network diagram.

5.2 MQTT_SN Implementation

To achieve MQTT_SN implementation, a border router was used in addition to one publisher and multiple subscribers. In this topology, the border router is acting as the main server. The publisher is publishing a certain topic and there are multiple subscribers that have subscribed to that topic. Every time the publisher sends a message to the broker, the broker will filter that message and then forward it to the intended subscriber. For this simulation, the RSMB (Really Small Message Broker) broker was used for sending and receiving messages instead of the main MQTT broker, Mosquitto, as the Mosquitto codebase does not support MQTT_SN. Figure 5 displays the network diagram for the MQTT_SN simulation.

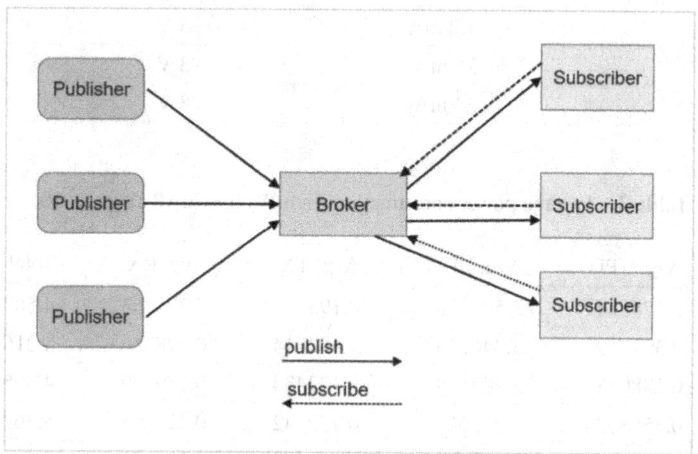

Fig. 5. MQTT_SN network diagram.

6 Simulation Results

In order to find the power information of each node, a Contiki OS application called Powertrace, was used. Powertrace records the power state data of each node during simulation, the information is then displayed in mote output. Every power state has a number of ticks for every time interval. To calculate the average power consumption of each node for both CoAP and MQTT_SN, the CPU, LPM, TRANSMIT LISTEN and IDLE_TRANSMIT power states were used.

The average power consumption of every node at every one of the four states was calculated. Summing the average power consumption at every state gave us the total power consumption of every node. The calculation of the power consumption (in mW) is formulized as [21],

$$Power\_Cons(mW) = \frac{Energest\_value \times Current \times Voltage}{RTIMER\_SECOND \times Runtime} \tag{1}$$

Where Energest_value is the difference between the number of clock ticks (in a particular state) between two time intervals, Current is the current of the mote, Voltage is the voltage of the mote, RTIMER_SECOND is the number of ticks per second for rtime and Runtime is the simulation runtime. Table 2 depicts the voltage and current values of Tmote Sky for every power state. The information was taken from the Tmote Sky datasheet.

Table 3 portrays the average power consumption at each of the four states for 10 client nodes for the CoAP simulation.

Where,

Table 2. Voltage and current values for the different power states [22].

Power state	Current	Voltage
CPU	2.3 mA	3 V
LPM	1.2 mA	3 V
TX	21 mA	3 V
RX	23 mA	3 V

Table 3. Average power consumption (in mW) for CoAP client nodes.

Node	Avg. CPU	Avg. LPM	Avg. TX	Avg. RX	Total
3	0.178524	3.509759	0.193617	0.705363	4.587264
4	0.307259	3.446235	0.684014	0.778946	5.216454
5	0.188013	3.505849	0.122434	0.789299	4.605596
6	0.350853	3.42366	0.772742	0.820007	5.367263
7	0.301138	3.449158	0.752078	0.776852	5.279225
8	0.276341	3.461396	0.749578	0.663982	5.151297
9	0.226019	3.485989	0.126077	0.914355	4.75244
10	0.282963	3.459092	0.757148	0.729349	5.228551
11	0.295175	3.45218	0.738463	0.687203	5.17302
12	0.316458	3.441622	0.728497	0.775772	5.262348

Avg. CPU = average time for which the mote was active.
Avg. LPM = average time for which the mote was in low power mode.
Avg. TX = average transmission time of mote.
Avg. RX = average listening time for mote.

Figure 6 displays a bar chart of the average power consumption of CoAP clients. We can see that the highest power consumption is that of node 6, with 5.36 mW. The other nodes have a similar power consumption.

From the collected data we noted that most of the power consumption of CoAP clients is happening during the Low Power Mode (LPM) power state. Figure 7 depicts the average power consumption of CoAP clients at every power state.

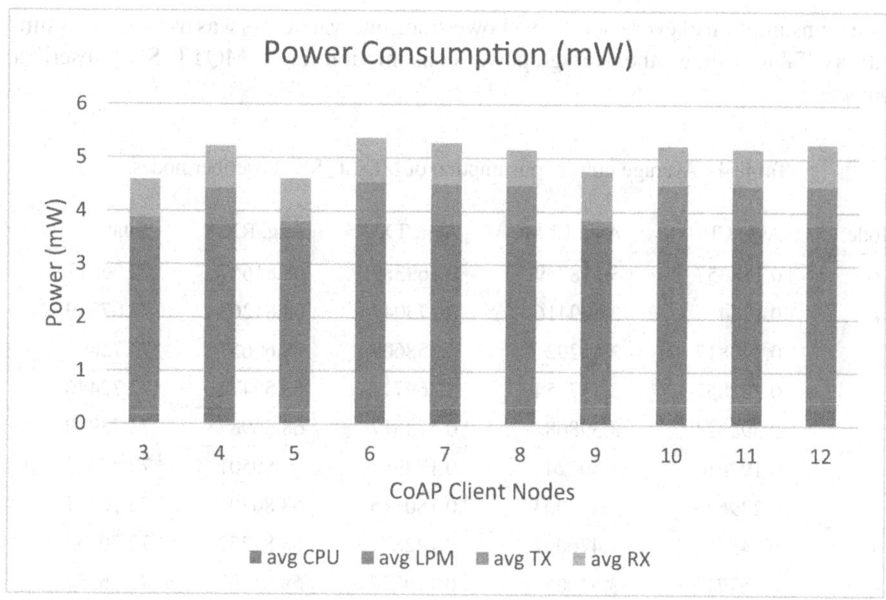

Fig. 6. Average power consumption of CoAP client nodes.

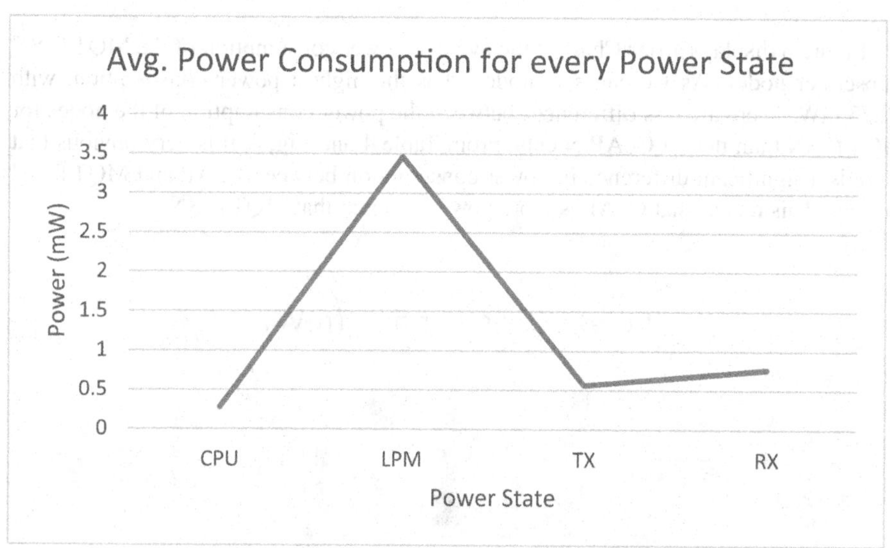

Fig. 7. Average power consumption of CoAP clients at every power state.

The same calculations were applied to MQTT_SN. The useful power state information was extracted from the Powertrace output and then used to calculate the average power consumption of every node. The Powertrace interval of 60 s was used for both simulations. Table 4 shows the average power consumption for 10 MQTT_SN Subscriber nodes.

Table 4. Average power consumption of MQTT_SN subscriber nodes.

Node	Avg. CPU	Avg. LPM	Avg. TX	Avg. RX	Total
3	0.158357	3.518759	0.169389	68.81667	72.66317
4	0.1784	3.509416	0.173042	68.81263	72.67349
5	0.330817	3.43292	0.358609	68.60657	72.72892
6	0.322857	3.437154	0.369714	68.59474	72.72446
7	0.398324	3.39868	0.572517	68.36987	72.73939
8	0.192613	3.502249	0.17996	68.80501	72.67983
9	0.239643	3.478003	0.180615	68.80401	72.70227
10	0.245154	3.476007	0.172871	68.81252	72.70655
11	0.157715	3.51906	0.170777	68.81502	72.66257
12	0.315397	3.440156	0.391973	68.56964	72.71716

Figure 8 displays a Bar Chart of the average power consumption of the MQTT_SN Subscriber nodes. As we can see, node 7 has the highest power consumption, with 72.73 mW. There are less differences between the power consumption of the nodes for MQTT_SN than that of CoAP clients. From Table 4 and Fig. 8, it is very obvious that there is a significant difference in power consumption between CoAP and MQTT_SN devices. This means that CoAP is more power efficient that MQTT_SN.

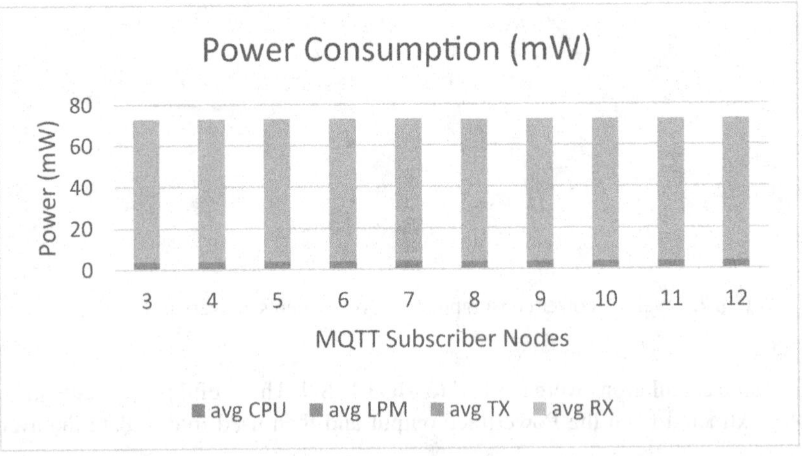

Fig. 8. Average power consumption bar chart for MQTT_SN subscriber nodes.

Most of the power consumption of MQTT_SN subscriber nodes is happening during the Radio Listen (RX) power state. This is displayed in Fig. 9, where the average power consumption of MQTT_SN subscriber nodes at every power state is shown.

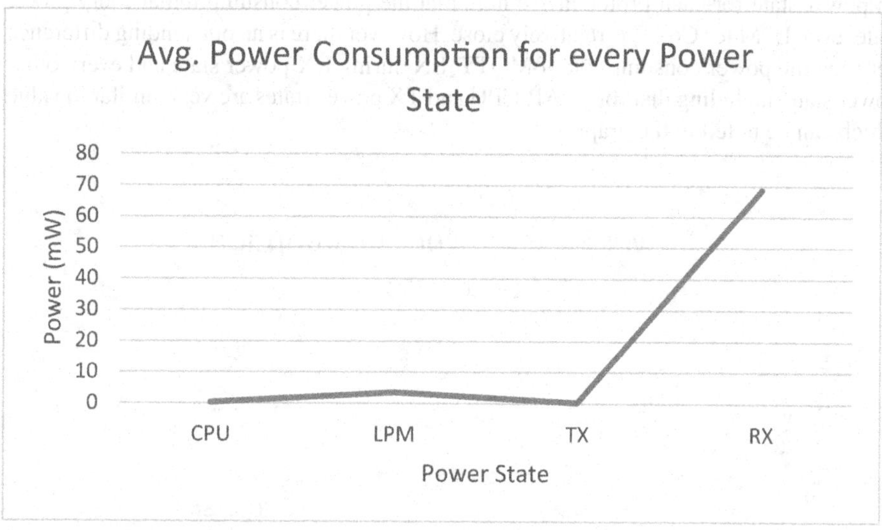

Fig. 9. Average power consumption of MQTT_SN subscriber nodes for every power state.

Figure 10 represents a line chart that compares between the total power consumption of CoAP and MQTT_SN at every one of the nodes. The line chart depicts the remarkable difference in power consumption of the protocols with MQTT_SN subscriber nodes consuming more power than CoAP client nodes.

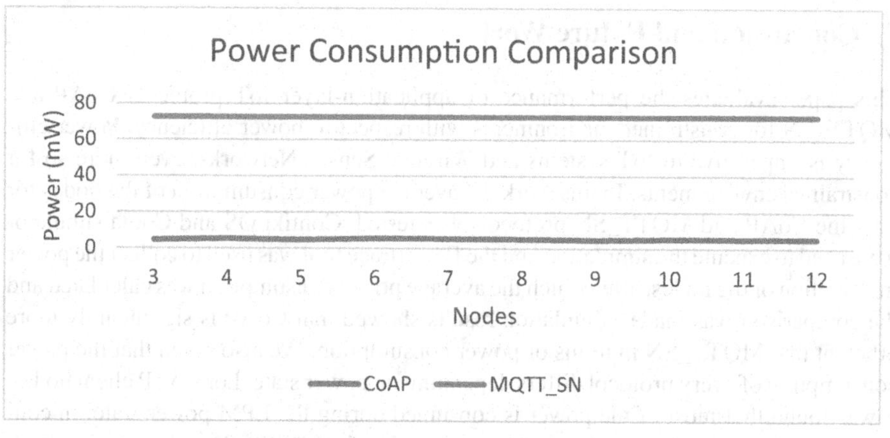

Fig. 10. Comparison between power consumption of CoAP and MQTT_SN.

Simulation results show that the power consumption of the nodes differ with every power state. The CoAP protocol consumes the most power during the Low Power Mode (LPM) power state, whereas MQTT_SN consumes the most power during the Radio Listen (RX) power state. Figure 11 depicts a comparison of power consumption based on power state for each protocol. We note that the power consumption at every power state, even LPM for CoAP, is relatively close. However there is an outstanding difference between the power consumption of MQTT_SN during RX power state and every other power state, including that for CoAP. CPU and TX power states are very similar in value which can be noted in the graph.

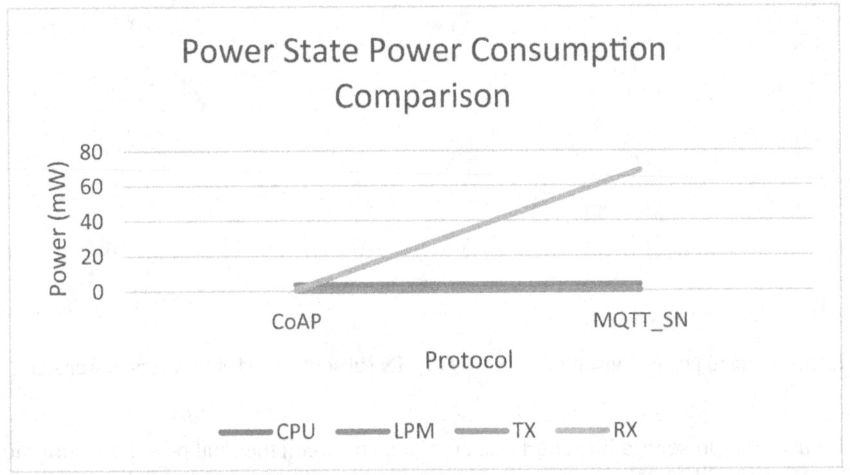

Fig. 11. Comparison of power consumption for different power states.

7 Conclusion and Future Work

This paper evaluates the performance of application-layer IoT protocols CoAP and MQTT_SN for constrained environments with respect to power efficiency. Power efficiency is imperative to IoT systems and Wireless Sensor Networks, even more so for constrained environments. In this work the average power consumption of the nodes for both the CoAP and MQTT_SN protocols was tested. Contiki OS and Cooja simulator were used to execute the simulation and the Powertrace tool was used to collect the power information of the nodes, after which the average power consumption was calculated and the comparison was made. Simulation results showed that CoAP is significantly more efficient that MQTT_SN in terms of power consumption. We also noted that the power consumption of every protocol differs depending on power state. For CoAP client nodes, it was found that most of the power is consumed during the LPM power state. In contrast, a significant amount of the power consumption for MQTT_SN subscriber nodes is happening during the RX power state. In the future, we hope to test these protocols for specific IoT scenarios to find out which one is more suitable for a particular application under different performance metrics, like throughput, end-to-end delay, latency, etc. in order to get a more accurate comparison.

References

1. Mahmoud, R., Yousuf, T., Aloul, F., Zualkernan, I.: Internet of things (IoT) security: current status, challenges and prospective measures. In: 2015 10th International Conference for Internet Technology and Secured Transactions (ICITST) (2015)
2. Dizdarević, J., Carpio, F., Jukan, A., Masip-Bruin, X.: A survey of communication protocols for internet of things and related challenges of fog and cloud computing integration. ACM Comput. Surv. (CSUR) **51**(6), 1–29 (2019)
3. Dunkels, A., Eriksson, J., Finne, N., Tsiftes, N.: Powertrace: network-level power profiling for low-power wireless networks. Swedish Institute of Computer Science (2011)
4. Moraes, T., Nogueira, B., Lira, V., Tavares, E.: Performance comparison of IoT communication protocols. In: 2019 IEEE International Conference on Systems, Man and Cybernetics (SMC) (2019)
5. Thombre, S., Islam, R.U., Andersson, K., Hossain, M.S.: Performance analysis of an IP based protocol stack for WSNs. In: 2016 IEEE Conference on Computer Communications Workshops (INFOCOM WKSHPS) (2016)
6. Hamdani, S., Sbeyti, H.: A comparative study of COAP and MQTT communication protocols. In: 2019 7th International Symposium on Digital Forensics and Security (ISDFS) (2019)
7. Kassem, I., Sleit, A.: Elapsed time of IoT application protocol for ECG: a comparative study between CoAP and MQTT. In: 2020 International Conference on Electrical, Communication, and Computer Engineering (ICECCE) (2020)
8. Yuang, C., Kunz, T.: Performance evaluation of IoT protocols under a constrained wireless access network. In: 2016 International Conference on Selected Topics in Mobile Wireless Networking (MoWNeT) (2016)
9. Sethi, P., Sarangi, S.R.: Internet of things: architectures, protocols, and applications. J. Electr. Comput. Eng. **2017**, 9324035 (2017)
10. Al-Qaseemi, S.A., Almulhim, H.A., Almulhim, M.F., Chaudhry, S.R.: IoT architecture challenges and issues: lack of standardization. In: 2016 Future Technologies Conference (FTC) (2016)
11. Rahman, W.U., Choi, Y.-S., Chung, K.: Performance evaluation of video streaming application over CoAP in IoT. IEEE Access **7**, 39852–39861 (2019)
12. Silva, E.F., Dembogurski, B.J., Vieira, A.B., Ferreira, F.H.C.: IEEE P21451-1-7: providing more efficient network services over MQTT-SN. In: 2019 IEEE Sensors Applications Symposium (SAS) (2019)
13. Hasan, H.M., Ahmed, A.I.: A comparative analysis for congestion mechanism in COAP and COCOA. Eng. Technol. J. (2018)
14. Ugrenovic, D., Gardasevic, G., Golic, D., Gazdic, V.: IoT wireless sensor networks for healthcare applications. In: 1st Conference of Medical and Biological Engineering in Bosnia and Herzegovina (CMBEBIH 2015) (2015)
15. Al Rasyid, M.U.H., Astika, F., Fikri, F.: Implementation MQTT-SN protocol on smart city application based wireless sensor network. In: 2019 5th International Conference on Science in Information Technology (ICSITech) (2019)
16. Standford-Clark, A., Truong, H.L.: MQTT for sensor networks (MQTT-SN) protocol specification. Int. Bus. Mach. (IBM) Corp. Version **1**(2), 1–28 (2013)
17. Jassim, E.K., Al-Hemiray, E.H.: Cognitive internet of things using MQTT protocol for smart diagnosis system. Iraqi J. Inf. Commun. Technol. **2**(3), 30–37 (2019)

18. Schütz, B., Bauer, J., Aschenbruck, N.: Improving energy efficiency of MQTT-SN in lossy environments using seed-based network coding. In: 2017 IEEE 42nd Conference on Local Computer Networks (LCN) (2017)
19. Kritsis, K., Papadopoulos, G.Z., Gallais, A., Chatzimisios, P., Theoleyre, F.: A tutorial on performance evaluation and validation methodology for low-power and lossy networks. IEEE Commun. Surv. Tutor. **20**(3), 1799–1825 (2018)
20. Sitanayah, L., Sreenan, C.J., Fedor, S.: A Cooja-based tool for coverage and lifetime evaluation in an in-building sensor network. J. Sens. Actuat. Netw. **5**(1), 4 (2016)
21. Han, S.: Contiki OS: using powertrace and energest power profile to estimate power consumption. Thingschat, 6 April 2015. http://thingschat.blogspot.com/2015/04/contiki-os-using-powertrace-and.html. Accessed 29 Apr 2021
22. TMOTESKY Tmote Sky User Manual Tmote-Sky-Datasheet. https://fccid.io/TOQTMOTESKY/User-Manual/Users-Manual-Revised-613136. Accessed 29 Apr 2021

Microsleep Detection of Automobile Drivers Using Electrocardiogram Signal

N. S. Nor Shahrudin(✉), K. A. Sidek(✉), M. R. Jalaludin, and N. A. N. Nazmi Asna

Department of Electrical and Computer Engineering, International Islamic University Malaysia, Jalan Gombak, P.O. Box 10, 50728 Kuala Lumpur, Malaysia
azami@iium.edu.my

Abstract. Microsleep can happen in any situations which could lead to accidents due to the driver's fatigue. One of the studies that have been done on observing the occurrence of microsleep is by analysing the electrocardiogram (ECG) signal. This study proposed to develop a steering wheel that extracts ECG signal from a driver in preventing microsleep through the data acquisition, pre-processing, feature extraction and classification stages. Firstly, the ECG signals were collected in normal and drowsy states. Then, the signals were filtered using the Savitzky Golay filter and Pan Tompkins's algorithm were selected to extract the R peak. The data was analysed using four classifications which are RR interval (RRI), standard deviation of normal to normal (SDNN), root mean square of successive differences (RMSSD) and p-value. Consequently, ECG in steering wheel managed to display a distinct difference for both states through all classifications, simultaneously capable in detecting the occurrence of microsleep.

Keywords: Electrocardiogram · Microsleep · Drowsiness · RR interval · SDNN · RMSSD

1 Introduction

Microsleep is a common term that every driver or motorcyclist is familiar with and aware about the possibility of fatal outcomes. It is a momentary and unintended, period of sleep which can last up to a full 10 s, and the person who experiences this situation will be drifted off the road without noticing it [1]. It also can occur at any time, to anybody and anywhere such as students in morning lectures, office workers during project meetings or truck drivers during midnight journeys.

In the United State of America, this issue is a serious concern as microsleep leads to thousands of vehicle crashes. According to the National Highway Traffic Safety Association (NHTSA) of the United State, there were 90,000 and more car accidents where 795 deaths were recorded in 2017 due to this issue. The NHTSA also mentioned that from 2013 until 2017, there were about 4,000 people dead due to this microsleep car accidents [2]. For local cases, the Road Safety Department of Malaysia have recorded that there were about 457 and more car accidents related to drowsy drivers from year 2016 until 2019 [3]. From these statistics, it shows that this issue can contribute a large

P. Liatsis et al. (Eds.): TIOTC 2021, CCIS 1548, pp. 237–252, 2022.
https://doi.org/10.1007/978-3-030-97255-4_18

number of road accidents in a country. More car accidents lead to higher funding from the government to cover the tragedy.

Events of microsleep do not occur surprisingly and without any explainable reasons. There are many possible causes which can lead to this issue and there are also early symptoms that can be detected before a person encounters this microsleep event. Sleep deprivation is commonly associated with microsleep accidents as many drivers still urge themselves to drive their automobile while in drowsy and fatigue conditions due to lack of sleep. This normally occurs during night-time as driving at this moment is more tiring and might pass the driver's bedtime. However, it does not mean that it will not occur during the daytime because a person may not have an adequate amount of good and quality sleep before beginning their journey. Lack of sleep occurs not just because of someone who needs to stay up late to complete their work, but it also occurs because of unintended sleep disorder such as obstructive sleep apnea, depression, narcolepsy, circadian disorder and other chronic diseases which force them away from a proper sleep [2]. Nevertheless, this issue has early symptoms such as yawning, missing an exit, inability to concentrate and inactiveness which is obvious for the driver or passengers to notice it.

Biological signals within our body portrays our actions and reactions based on the situation. Examples of biological signals include electroencephalogram (EEG), electrocardiogram (ECG) and electromyography (EMG) signals. These biosignals may be able to interpret a person's condition in a particular time for instance, whether a person is emotional, under stress, telling a lie, fatigue and even drowsy that leads to microsleep. ECG is a commonly used type of signal in hospitals and other medical institutions to assess a person's health condition for decades. Indicators obtained from the assessment of ECG waveforms paves the way for the next course of actions. Thus, this study will propose the design and development of a steering wheel which could detect microsleeps using the ECG signal.

2 Literature Review

2.1 Electrocardiography

Electrocardiography is a technique used to observe the activity of the heart through electricity produced by the body using electrical sensors. This method can give many information such as the segment of the heart that activates each heartbeat, the rhythm and rate of the heartbeat, and the nerve conduction passage of the heart [4]. Electrocardiogram is the result from electrocardiography which is a graph of voltage against time. It is typically a repetitive signal that has a pattern which can be divided into three phases and few main points. For the first phase, electrical impulse from the sinus node (SA) begins to spread through the atria from right to left which causes depolarization and produces a wave called the P wave. For the next phase, the electrical current spreads to the atrioventricular node (AV) where it will produce QRS complex waves where these waves indicate the depolarization of the ventricular part. Lastly, the T wave is produced during the recovery phase of the heart muscle and this process occurs due to the repolarization of the ventricle [5]. A typical ECG signal is shown as in Fig. 1.

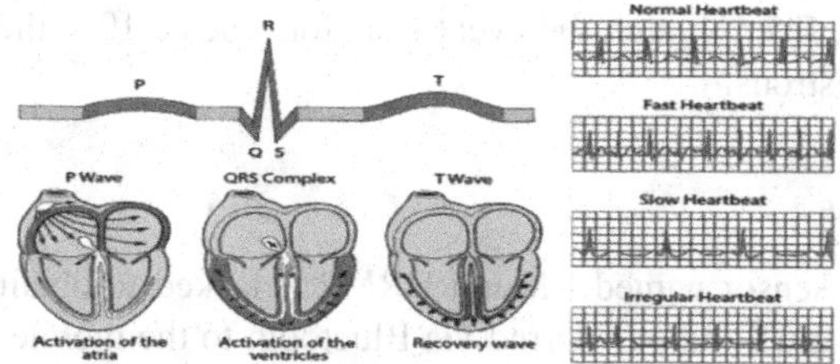

Fig. 1. ECG signal and the relation with heart nodes [4]

It is wise to note that ECG signals are one of the best and important biosignals as it can represent the cyclical contraction and relaxation of the heart muscles which can be used to discover any heart diseases and sleep disorders. The movement of the heart's muscle is dependent on the electrical pulse detected by placing electrodes at several places on a human's skin. Normally, a total of ten electrodes were used where six electrodes placed on the chest position and four electrodes placed on the limbs position. Then, the heart's electrical potential is measured from 12 angles or leads and is recorded continuously which typically lasts for ten seconds.

However, the number of electrodes used is dependent on the application, different electrode type and placing is used on human's skin. The most common electrode that is used in electrocardiography is the wet electrodes with gel which is the Silver - Silver chloride (Ag/AgCL) electrodes. Other than wet electrodes, dry electrodes are also used and it does not require any type of gel and skin preparation. However, this type of electrode leads to higher distortion compared to wet electrodes [6].

2.2 Microsleep

Microsleep is a short period of sleep which is uncontrollable and can occur without being noticed by the doers. This event frequently happens because a person might have lack of sleep and in fatigue where these lead to drowsy state. It is important to note that there are two main stages of sleep such as rapid eye movement sleep (REM) sleep and non-rapid eye movement (NREM) sleep. However, microsleep does not fall into these categories because none of the characteristics of the stages fit in the microsleep event as it is a temporary sleep and does not last for a long period [1].

According to a study from the Neuroimage Journal [7], 29 volunteers were picked and stayed awake for 22 h before being put in a dark fMRI machine to scan their brain. The investigation found that there was a reduction of activity in the thalamus region where this part is tasked to regulate the sleep activity. However, some other parts of the brain have increased their productivity because that particular region is responsible to keep the brain focused and stay awake. This can be concluded that some parts of the brain are in the waking state while some other parts have the urge to fall asleep during microsleep events. In addition, a study in 2011 from University of Wisconsin also stated that a brain can experience passive mode and enter the brief sleeping state while the rest part of the brain remains awake [7]. Thus, this shows that microsleep is different from a normal sleep stage. Experiencing microsleep for drivers may lead to fatality due to unwanted accidents. Even though the event lasts for at least 10 s, the impact could be devastating and disastrous.

2.3 Related Works

According to [8], a sensor named I-Mami HRM2 is tasked to obtain the ECG signal from the driver and it will be transferred via Bluetooth to the mobile phone for further measurement. In this system, decimation technique is used to minimise the complexity and size of the data by reducing the sampling rate to 50 Hz from the original frequency of 250 Hz using the low pass filter. This system also used the Hamming window function to analyse, manage and measure the data of the signal before proceeding to Fast Fourier Transform (FFT). FFT technique is used to get the spectrum of the signal by converting the heartbeat signal into the frequency domain. For the testing part, the power ratio of four males and four females is obtained during the awake stage and sleep stage where the power ratio is measured every 1 min in 120 min duration. A power ratio is the ratio of low frequency (LF) and high frequency (HF) of the spectral power for all NN intervals which 0.04 Hz to 0.15 Hz is the range for LF and 0.15 Hz to 0.4 Hz is the range for HF. The result shows that the mean value of power ratio for awake state and sleep state between the males and females does not have too much difference. The mean value for awake state is 0.240668 while 0.162554 is the mean value for sleep stage. The author believes that the drowsiness falls between these numbers. Thus, if the power ratio falls below 0.17 for 3 times, the alarm of the Android handheld device will be triggered. However, the limitation of this system is the system also depends on the I-Mami-MRM2 sensor where it needs to be placed on the user's or driver's chest which this method is found unsuitable and uncomfortable to be implemented.

In [9], the study proposed to develop an ECG-based Drivers' Status Monitoring (ECG-DSM) system that can detect the status of a driver which is normal, drowsy and drunk. The process of this study is divided into 4 stages which is ECG signal processing, feature extraction and building classifier, K-fold validation and safety analysis. In the first stage, the ECG signals obtained are filtered to remove the unwanted noises and separate it into multiple samples with one heartbeat duration using the bandpass filter and moving window integration. For the feature extraction stage, the cross-correlation coefficient of the ECG signals is obtained by using the kernel development to examine the similarity between the normal, drowsy and drunk situations. The final stage is the risk analysis where the Monte Carlo analysis method is implemented. The ECG-DSM system is divided into three time periods which is detection period, reaction period and execution period in order to alert the driver. Monte Carlo is used to help the analysis in these three periods become smoother and more predictable. The result of this study shows that the ECG-DSM can provide 91% accuracy for the detection time and 92.4% chances to avoid collision by using this system. However, there is still room for improvement as the misclassification rate is nearly 10% which still can be fatal for the drivers.

In study [10], a drowsiness detection was developed by combining intrusive and non-intrusive methods which are ECG signals detection and real-time video streaming of the driver's face. For the video streaming inputs, a camera was put in front of the driver to obtain the footage of the driver's face. After that, the footage was converted into frames so that the difference in pixels between the normal condition frame and the current condition frame can be calculated by using the frame difference algorithm. The threshold of the pixel value was 5. Thus, if the frame exceeds the threshold for a long time, then the driver will be considered as drowsy. For the ECG signals input, the data was obtained from the MIT-BIH database. A band pass filter and band rejection filter were used to eliminate the baseline wander with frequency of 0.5 Hz to 0.75 Hz and power line with frequency of 50 Hz respectively. Later on, the value of R peak obtained was used to calculate the heartbeat rate per minute (bpm) with a peak threshold of 85% of the maximum amplitude while the threshold of the bpm was set to between 60 to 100 bpm. However, the limitation of this study is frame comparison method is not convincing as the environment of a moving car is always changing which could disturb the calculation of the pixels and lead to inaccurate data.

In [11], the study aimed to design a drowsiness monitoring device embedded on the steering wheel which can obtain ECG signal from the drivers. A polyester based conductive fabric electrode was used as the sensor on the steering wheel and the data obtained will be transferred to a PC for further signal monitoring and processing. In order to remove the noises, an analogue signal conditioning circuit was implemented which consists of high pass filters, low pass filters and an amplifier to treat the signal before sending it to the PC. Two healthy male volunteers participated in the test and were required to drive for 2 h straight. The data obtained were analysed in the form of frequency and time domain for every normal, drowsy and fatigue state. The results of the study show that the mean value of LF/HF ratio increases while the mean value for RMSSD decreases from normal to fatigue and finally to drowsy states. Thus, the study has concluded that the embedded ECG sensor steering wheel system is capable of detecting the drowsiness level of a driver and can be useful to alarm the drivers from any further chaos. Yet, there is no system that uses the data for an alarm mechanism that can trigger the drivers when they are in drowsy state.

To summarize, ECG signals could be analysed for the purpose of detecting drowsiness but accurateness, long detection time and practical ways to acquire the data become a huge limitation for many of the past studies. Thus, this study will provide a better solution to utilize and obtain the ECG signals to prevent the microsleep accurately as possible. This will be further elaborate in the next section.

3 Research Methodology

In this section, the methodology used by this project will be elaborated. There will be four different parts which are data acquisition, pre-processing, feature extraction and classification Each of the parts will be briefly explained in the following subsections.

3.1 Data Acquisition

The process of computing electrical entities such as voltage and current by using the computer is called data acquisition (DAQ). There are three components in this system which are sensors, DAQ hardware and programmable software of the computer [12]. For this study, the electrical phenomena of a person's heart will be recorded by using the ECG module to form a signal. The hardware and software involved in this project will be explained much further in the next subsections.

3.1.1 Hardware Components

For this project, the hardware components used are copper foil, Arduino Uno and Ks0261 Keyestudio ECG module (AD8232). The components are connected to each other in order to obtain the desired signal from a person's heartbeat. Figure 2 shows the connection of the ECG module and the Arduino Uno.

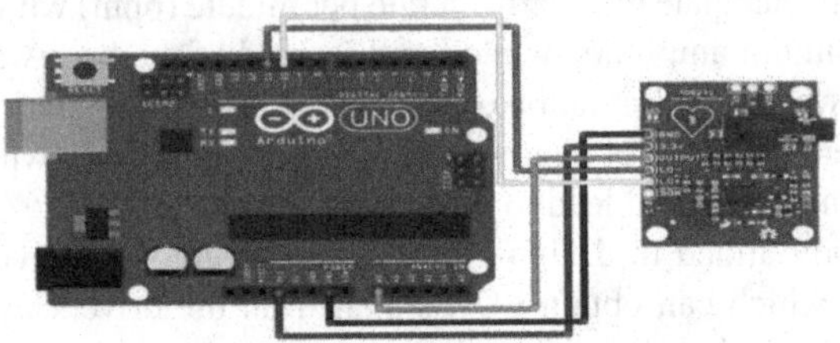

Fig. 2. Connection between Arduino UNO and ECG module [13]

a) **ECG Module (AD8232)**
   The AD8232 is an integrated signal conditioning block for ECG and other biopotential measurement applications. A raw ECG signal obtained from the human's skin may be very noisy. However, the AD8232 is designed to simply extract, amplify, and filter the signals for a better reading [14].
b) **Arduino Uno**
   Arduino Uno can be powered using external sources such as batteries or using the USB connection to a computer port. Arduino IDE is used to program the microcontroller to communicate with other devices [15].
c) **Sensor**
   Traditional ways to obtain the ECG signal are using three Silver/Silver Chloride (Ag/AgCl) electrodes by attaching it on the skin. For this project, a copper foil is used to replace the electrodes to act as the sensor to obtain the electrical activity of the heart. The main reason to use this material is due to its high conductivity properties which is the second highest among the metals [16]. Besides having a decent conductivity, this item also flexible to be embedded on a steering wheel.

3.1.2 Software Component

The software component used for the data acquisition part is the Arduino Software also known as Integrated Development Environment (IDE). This software is used to code and compile instructions for the physical Arduino to work. The written code will be uploaded to the hardware via USB connection. The coding used is a simplified version of both C++ and C programming language [15].

3.2 Pre-processing

During the acquisition process, the ECG signal might be disturbed by artifacts that leads to imperfect and hard to analyze signals. This condition occurs due to the movement of the body, electromagnetic fields interference, respiration, improper contact between the skin and electrode, and the electrical activity of the muscles [17]. Since noises could lead to misinterpretation of the desired ECG signal, the Savitzky-Golay filter is implemented to treat the contaminated signal with its ability to smoothen the signals while preserving the important features of the ECG waveform [18].

3.3 Feature Extraction

Feature extraction is commonly known as a process of reducing the original dataset by extracting the important components only to form a more simple and summarized information for further analysis [19]. Thus, in this study, the feature extraction process is aimed to extract fundamental components such as the amplitudes of the P-QRS-T wave and the interval between the peaks [20]. The Pan-Tompkins algorithm is the one that will be tasked to operate the extraction, where the algorithm will detect the amplitudes and the interval of the QRS complex. From the QRS complex, we can observe the R peak and the interval clearly for further calculations [21].

3.4 Classification

The classification involves the interval of RR peak as in Fig. 3, that used to calculate the standard deviation of the normal to normal (SDNN), root mean square of successive differences (RMSSD) and the average time between the two successive R waves intervals (RRI). Equation (1), (2) and (3) refers to the values of SDNN, RMSSD and the average time of the RRI respectively during the normal and drowsy state.

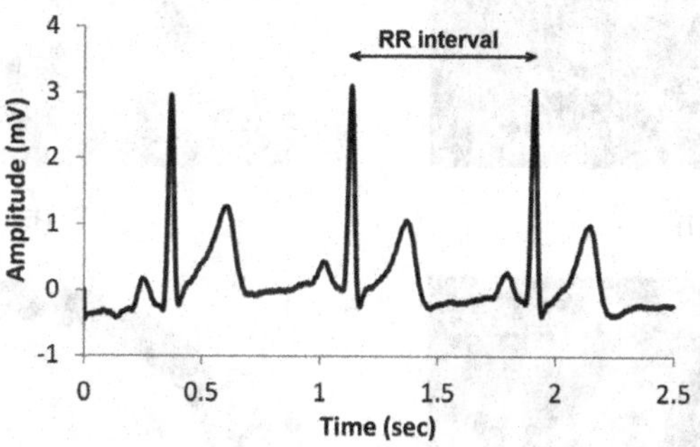

Fig. 3. RR interval [22]

$$SDNN = \sqrt{\frac{1}{\mathrm{N}-1}\sum_{i=1}^{N}\left(RR_i - \overline{RR}\right)^2} \tag{1}$$

$$RMSSD = \sqrt{\frac{1}{\mathrm{N}-1}\sum_{i=1}^{N}\left(RR_{i+1} - \overline{RR_i}\right)^2} \tag{2}$$

$$Average\ of\ RRI = \frac{1}{N}\sum_{i=1}^{N} RR_i \tag{3}$$

where, $N = Total\ number\ of\ RRI, RR_i = ith\ RR\ interval, \overline{RR} = mean\ of\ the\ RR\ interval$ and $\overline{RR_i} = average\ of\ the\ RR\ intervals\ up\ to\ the\ ith.$

P-value calculation is also used to analyse the difference of the ECG signals between normal and drowsy states. The null hypothesis (Ho) is tested to make sure there is no correlation between the ECG graph of normal and drowsy states. The p-value is false if the value is less than 0.05 which will indicate that there is correlation between the signals. In contrast, if the p-value is larger than 0.05, this will support the evidence of the null hypothesis which indicates that there is no correlation between the signals and have a significant difference between the data [23]. The p-value is calculated by t-statistic having $n-2$ degrees of freedom as shown in Eq. (4).

$$t = \frac{r\sqrt{n-2}}{\sqrt{1-r^2}} \tag{4}$$

Where $r = correlation\ coefficient$ and $n = number\ of\ observations.$

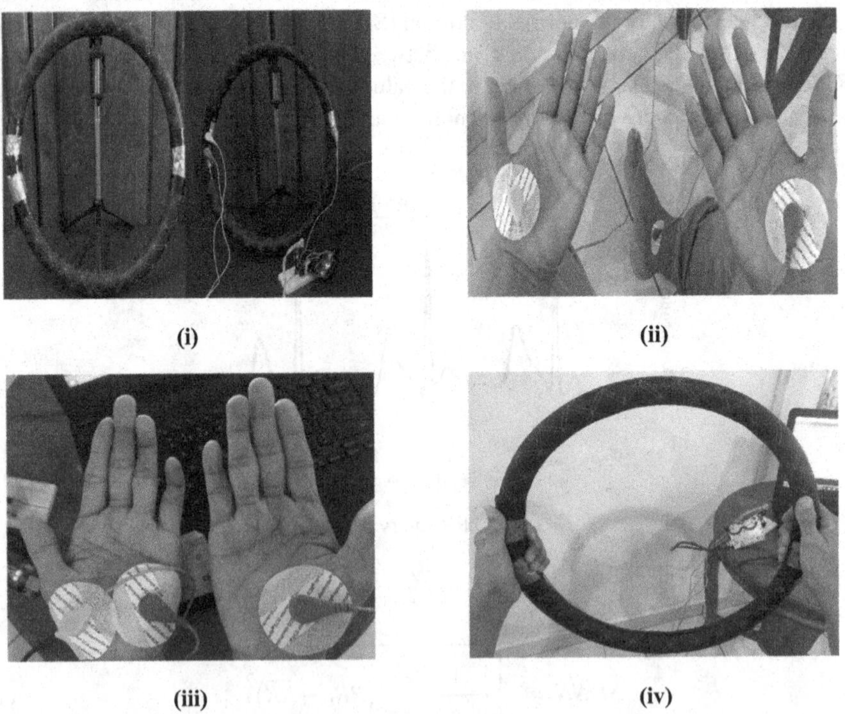

Fig. 4. **(i)** Steering wheel embedded with copper foil, **(ii)** Condition one, **(iii)** Condition two and **(iv)** Condition three

4 Experimentation Setup

The experimentation setup involved hardware components including the steering wheel embedded with copper coil, ECG pad, Arduino UNO, ECG module and a laptop. Figure 4(i) shows the placement of cooper foil on the steering wheel. For this experiment, the ECG signal is obtained in three different conditions. The first condition is where the ECG pads is placed on the subject's left palm, right palm and right leg as in Fig. 4(ii). The second condition is where two ECG pads is place on left palm and one ECG pad on the right palm as in Fig. 4(iii). While for the third condition, the subject is required to hold the steering wheel as in Fig. 4(iv).

5 Results and Analysis

Five subjects were involved in this project to obtain their data in all three conditions mentioned earlier in normal and drowsy states. The first state in this data acquisition

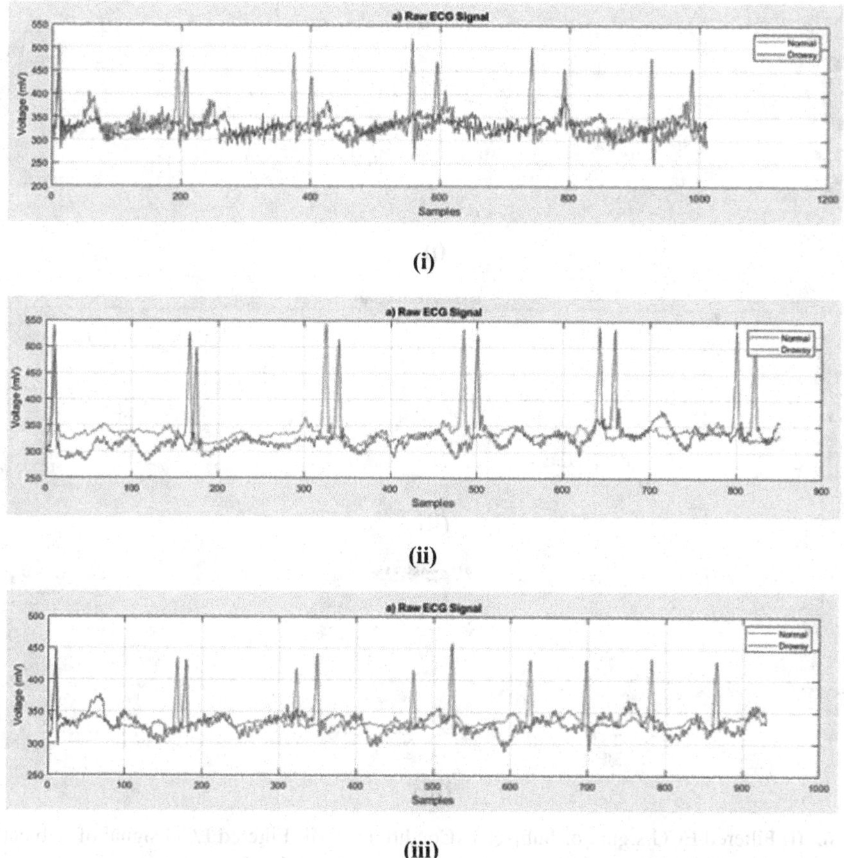

Fig. 5. **(i)** Raw ECG signal of Subject 1 (Condition 1), **(ii)** Raw ECG signal of Subject 1 (Condition 2) and **(iii)** Raw ECG signal of Subject 1 (Condition 3)

process is the normal state. During this state, the subjects need to be in a fully awake condition and free from drowsiness. The data was taken during the daytime around 11 am to 3 pm where the subjects were usually active doing their daily routines such as working or completing chores with a total duration of 5 min for each condition.

The drowsy state is taken when the subjects experience drowsiness condition. The experiment was done at night during the subject's bedtime around 11 pm to 2 am. Before the data was acquired, the subjects have taken a 30-min laying on the bed in the most relaxing position. Then, a duration of five minutes was allocated to take the data for each condition. Figures 5(i)–(iii) show the raw ECG obtained from three subjects in both normal and drowsy states for Subject 1.

From these figures, a huge difference can be detected especially on the interval between the R-peaks. The normal state signals have a shorter interval as compared to the drowsy state. However, these raw ECG signals needs to be filtered for further analysis. Thus, the Savitzky-Golay filter was used in this pre-processing stage to smoothen the signals. Figures 6(i)–(iii) show the results of the filtered ECG signals.

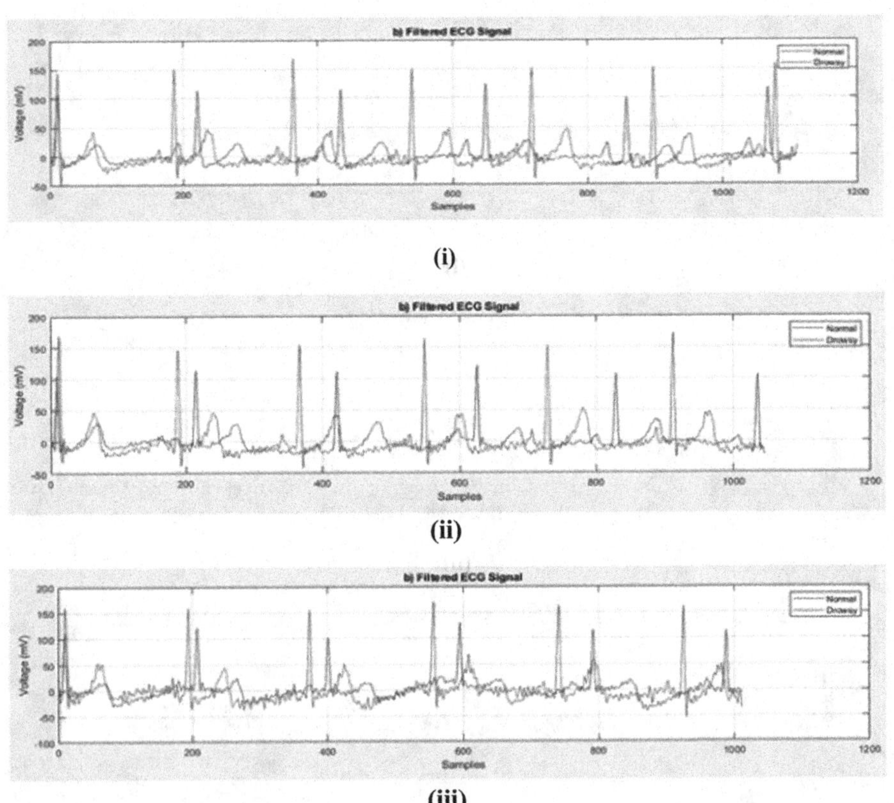

Fig. 6. **(i)** Filtered ECG signal of Subject 1 (Condition 1), **(ii)** Filtered ECG signal of Subject 1 (Condition 2) and **(iii)** Filtered ECG signal of Subject 1 (Condition 3)

The pre-processing stage filtered the ECG signal in removing the noises. The peaks were more visible and easier to detect the R peaks of the signals. In the third stage, R peaks of the filtered signals were extracted using the Pan Tompkins algorithm as in Figs. 7 (i) and (ii) for both normal and drowsy states of Subject 1.

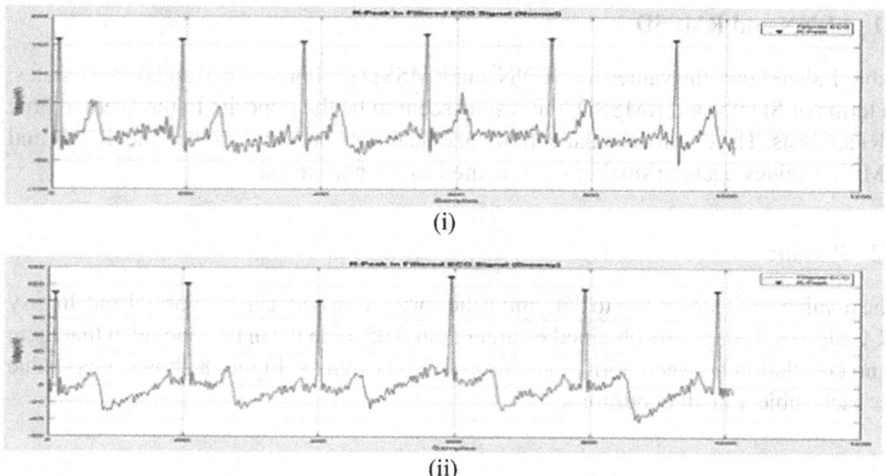

(i)

(ii)

Fig. 7. R peak detection of **(i)** normal and **(ii)** drowsy states of Subject 1 (Condition 3)

However, if the algorithm fails to detect the R peaks, the value will be affected the final results. There are four classification parameters used to analyse the difference between the normal and drowsy signals obtained from the subjects in all three conditions. These classification criteria include average time for RRI, SDNN, RMSSD and p-value as been tabulated in Table 1.

Table 1. RRI values for normal and drowsy state

Subjects	Conditions	RRI Normal (ms)	RRI Drowsy (ms)	SDNNN Normal (ms)	SDNN Drowsy (ms)	RMSSD Normal (ms)	RMSSD Drowsy (ms)
1	1	177.4	211.6	2.796	2.408	3.530	3.316
	2	179.8	205.4	2.775	1.817	3.884	2.474
	3	182.8	195.6	1.924	1.517	2.890	2.272
2	1	158.2	162.2	0.837	0.683	1.313	1.025
	2	154.2	171.6	2.588	2.302	3.583	3.123
	3	168.2	174.4	2.864	0.894	3.929	1.251
3	1	158.4	198.6	1.789	1.673	2.262	2.222
	2	168.2	185.0	2.582	2.345	3.641	3.535
	3	167.4	190.0	2.191	1.00	3.203	1.365
4	1	170.4	197.2	1.817	1.789	2.524	2.502
	2	170.0	189.0	2.739	2.345	4.004	3.215
	3	174.8	185.4	2.775	1.817	4.113	2.534
5	1	177.6	206.4	1.517	1.302	2.154	2.118
	2	181.6	202.8	1.517	1.049	2.835	2.156
	3	181.6	194.4	3.286	1.14	4.304	1.555

Based on the results, the RRI value for drowsy state is higher as compared to RRI of the normal state for every condition. This is due to the changes of cardiovascular activities during sleepy state that lowers the blood pressure as well as the heart rate which will cause the RRI to be longer as compared to the normal state [24].

5.1 SDNN and RMSSD

Table 1 also shows the values for SDNN and RMSSD for both normal and drowsy states. In terms of SDNN and RMSSD, the results seem to be the opposite to the average time RRI analysis. The cardiovascular activity and heart rate becomes slower, the SDNN and RMSSD values become smaller as compared to the normal state.

5.2 P-value

The p-value analysis is a test to determine the correlation between the normal and drowsy ECG signals. If the value obtained is larger than 0.05, then it can be concluded that there is no correlation between normal and drowsy ECG signals. Figure 8 shows the p-value for each subject in all conditions.

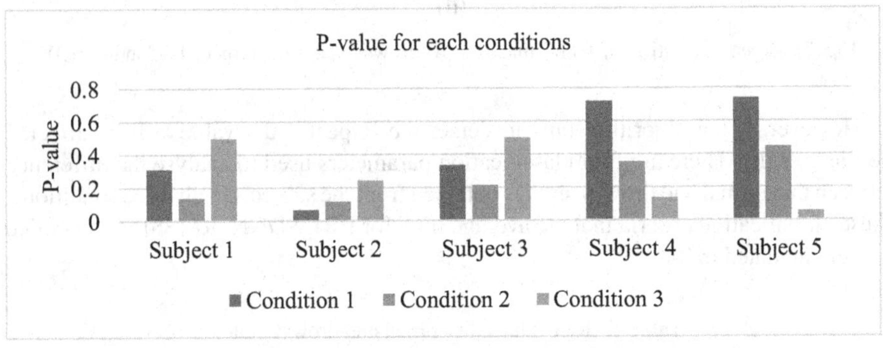

Fig. 8. P-value of normal and drowsy ECG signals

From the results obtained from the subjects, all the p-value calculated are larger than 0.05. This shows that there is no correlation between normal and drowsy ECG signals obtained from the experiment in all conditions. Condition Three will be the main focussed for the analysis of ECG acquisition on the steering wheel.

From the results discussed earlier, the data obtained from the subjects satisfy the idea that drowsy state have a longer interval for Condition One, Condition Two and Condition Three. The results of the calculation show that the value of SDNN and RMSSD of drowsy state is always smaller as compared to the normal state for every condition. From these early observations, it shows that Condition Three able to collect ECG signals as good as

Condition One and Condition Two while producing a desired result where the difference between normal and drowsy states are clearly shown.

For further analysis, the percentage difference of RRI, SDNN and RMSSD between normal and drowsy states are calculated to study the patterns and differences between the conditions. The results were tabulated in Table 2.

Table 2. Percentage difference of RRI, SDNN and RMSSD

Subjects	Conditions	Percentage difference of RRI (%)	Percentage difference of SDNN (%)	Percentage difference of RMSSD (%)
1	1	19.28	13.88	6.06
	2	14.24	34.53	36.3
	3	7.00	21.16	21.36
2	1	2.53	18.33	21.95
	2	11.28	11.06	12.83
	3	3.69	68.77	68.16
3	1	25.38	6.46	1.76
	2	9.99	9.17	2.90
	3	13.5	54.36	57.38
4	1	15.73	6.46	0.88
	2	11.18	14.37	19.7
	3	6.06	34.53	38.4
5	1	16.22	14.14	1.69
	2	11.67	30.81	23.95
	3	7.05	65.31	63.88

In terms of percentage difference in RRI, Condition Three for Subject 1, 3, 4 and 5 have a lower percentage as compared to Condition One. The percentage difference for Condition Three are 7%, 3.69%, 6.06% and 7.05% while for Condition One are 19.28%, 25.38%, 15.73% and 16.22% for Subject 1, 3, 4 and 5, respectively. Between condition Three and Condition Two, the same pattern appears for between Subject 1, 2, 4 and 5 where Condition Two have a bigger percentage difference as compared to Condition Three. The percentage difference for Condition Two are 14.24%, 11.28%, 11.18% and 11.67% against 7%, 3.69%, 6.06% and 7.05% of Condition Three for Subject 1, 2, 4 and 5, respectively. These differences occur due to the position and behaviour of the subjects during the test of Condition Three. An extra focus and muscle activities are required to hold the steering wheel could increase the heartbeat in the drowsy state causing the difference of the RRI between the conditions become smaller as compared to other conditions which are more relaxing.

For the SDNN and RMSSD, the percentage difference of each condition has a similar pattern between each other. The comparison between Condition Three and Condition One shows that the percentage difference of SDNN and RMSSD during drowsy state are always higher for every subject as compared to the normal state. However, the comparison is almost similar for Condition Three and Condition Two where the percentage difference of Condition Three is higher for most of the subjects except for Subject 1. Next, the value of RRI, SDNN, RMSSD and p-value for every subject have been averaged and the results were tabulated in Table 3. The average value obtained is consistent with the results discussed in previous sections.

Table 3. Average of RRI, SDNN, RMSSD and p-value for all subjects

	Average of RRI (ms)		Average of SDNN (ms)		Average of RMSSD (ms)		Average of p-value
Conditions	Normal	Drowsy	Normal	Drowsy	Normal	Drowsy	
1	168.4	195.2	1.751	1.571	2.357	2.237	0.433
2	170.76	190.76	2.44	1.972	3.589	2.9	0.252
3	174.96	187.96	2.608	1.274	3.688	1.795	0.286

The average of RRI for every condition shows that the drowsy state has a longer RRI as compared to the normal state. In addition, the RRI of drowsy state for Condition Three is the shortest among the other conditions with 187.96 ms. This supports the idea that an extra cardiovascular activity is presence while a subject is holding the steering wheel during the drowsy state. For the average of SDNN and RMSSD, the value obtained for drowsy state are smaller compared to the normal state with Condition Three having the smallest value of 1.274 ms and 1.795 ms for SDNN and RMSSD respectively in this state. Finally, the average p-value obtained for every condition also satisfy the point where there is no correlation between the ECG signals of normal and drowsy states with every condition have p-value more than 0.05.

The percentage difference of average RRI, SDNN and RMSSD have also been calculated and displayed in Table 4.

Table 4. Percentage difference of average RRI, SDNN and RMSSD

	Percentage Difference (%)		
Conditions	RRI	SDNN	RMSSD
1	15.91	10.27	5.09
2	11.71	19.20	19.19
3	7.43	51.16	51.31

The results show that Condition Three have the smallest percentage of 7.43% compared to Condition One and Condition Two. This conclude that the RRI of the test subjects does not have a big difference when conducting the steering wheel during drowsy state. While for SDNN and RMSSD, Condition Three have the highest percentage of 51.16% and 51.31% respectively.

6 Conclusion

The focus of this study would be the performance of the steering wheel which corresponding to Condition Three where the subjects are required to hold the steering wheel during the data acquisition. A comparison between conditions also have been made in this study. From this analysis, the RRI of Condition Three for drowsy state have the lowest percentage different while for SDNN and RMSSD, the percentage difference was the highest among the conditions. This was due to the change of cardiovascular activities that increased the heart rate during the drowsiness test as the subject required more strength and focus to hold the steering wheel as compared to other conditions where the subjects were in a more relaxing set up.

However, there are many improvements that can be done for future works such as having more test subjects for the analysis to produce an accurate and firm results. To add, any suitable material can be used to replace the copper foil to increase the lifespan of the product, better quality and more comfortable be used by any drivers.

Acknowledgments. This work was funded by the Fundamental Research Grant Scheme (FRGS) from the International Islamic University Malaysia (Project ID: FRGS19-056-0664).

References

1. Peters, B.: The causes, dangers, and prevention of microsleep. https://www.verywellhealth.com/description-of-microsleep. Accessed 12 Mar 2020
2. Insurance Information Institute: Facts and Statistics: Drowsy Driving. https://www.iii.org/fact-statistic/. Accessed 12 Mar 2020
3. Malaysia Road Safety Department: Statistic of Road Accidents and Injuries 2019. http://www.jkjr.gov.my. Accessed 12 Mar 2020
4. Shea, M.J.: Electrocardiography. https://www.msdmanuals.com/home/heart-and-blood-vessel-disorders/diagnosis-of-heart-and-blood-vessel-disorders/electrocardiography. Accessed 16 Apr 2020
5. Covington, T.: Drowsy driving statistic in 2020. https://www.thezebra.com/research/drowsy-driving-statistics/. Accessed 16 Apr 2020
6. Hurskyi, A., Matviykiv, O., Lobur, M.: Research of electrocardiography sensors for healthcare monitoring. In: 2017 13th International Conference on Perspective Technologies and Methods in MEMS Design (MEMSTECH) 2017, pp. 164–166 (2017)
7. Gregoire, C.: What's happening in your brain during 'microsleep'. https://www.huffpost.com/entry/microsleep-brain-sleep-deprivation_n_56d9ed81e4b0ffe6f8e958e6. Accessed 20 Apr 2020
8. Ke, K.W., et al.: Drowsiness detection system using heartbeat rate in android-based handheld devices. In: First International Conference on Multimedia and Image Processing (ICMIP), pp. 99–103 (2016)
9. Wan, W.H., et al.: A real-time drivers' status monitoring scheme with safety analysis. In: IECON 2018 - 44th Annual Conference of the IEEE Industrial Electronics Society, pp. 5137–5140 (2018)
10. Anilkumar, C.V., et al.: Design of drowsiness, heart beat detection system and alertness indicator for driver safety. In: 2016 IEEE International Conference on Recent Trends in Electronics, Information & Communication Technology (RTEICT), pp. 937–941 (2016)

11. Jung, S.J., Shin, H.S., Chung, W.Y.: Driver fatigue and drowsiness monitoring system with embedded electrocardiogram sensor on steering wheel. IET Intell. Transp. Syst. **8**(1), 43–50 (2014)
12. Engineer Ambitiously: Data Acquisition (DAQ). https://www.ni.com/en-my/shop/data-acquisition.html. Accessed 9 June 2020
13. Alam: ECG Graph Monitoring with AD8232 ECG Sensor and Arduino. https://how2electronics.com/ecg-monitoring-with-ad8232-ecg-sensor-arduino/. Accessed 9 June 2020
14. keyestudio: Ks0261 keyestudio AD8232 ECG measurement heart monitor sensor module. https://wiki.keyestudio.com/. Accessed 9 June 2020
15. Aqeel, A.: Introduction to Arduino Uno. https://www.theengineeringprojects.com/. Accessed 9 June 2020
16. TIBTECH: Conductive materials, metals and stainless steels properties table. https://www.tibtech.com/conductivite.php?lang=en_US. Accessed 9 June 2020
17. Maggio, A.C.V., et al.: Quantification of ventricular repolarization dispersion using digital processing of the surface ECG, pp. 182–206. InTech (2012)
18. Birle, A., et al.: Noise removal in ECG signal using Savitzky Golay filter. Int. J. Adv. Res. Electron. Commun. Eng. **4**(5), 1331–1333 (2015)
19. Ippolito, P.P.: Feature extraction techniques. https://towardsdatascience.com/feature-extraction-techniques. Accessed 12 June 2020
20. Karpagachelvi, S., et al.: ECG feature extraction techniques – a survey approach. Int. J. Comput. Sci. Inf. Secur. **8**(1), 76–80 (2010)
21. Pan, J., Tompkins, W.J.: A real-time QRS detection algorithm. IEEE Trans. Biomed. Eng. **BME-32**(3), 230–236 (1985)
22. Cornforth, D., Tarvainen, M., Jelinek, H.: How to calculate Renyi entropy from heart rate variability, and why it matters for detecting cardiac autonomic neuropathy. Front. Bioeng. Biotechnol. Comput. Physiol. Med. **2**, 34 (2014). https://doi.org/10.3389/fbioe.2014.00034
23. Glen, S.: P-value in statistical hypothesis tests: what is it? https://www.statisticshowto.com/probability-and-statistics/statistics-definitions/p-value/. Accessed 2 Jan 2021
24. Brandenberger, G., Viola, A.U.: Autonomic nervous system activity during sleep in humans. In: Cardinali, D.P., Pandi-Perumal, S.R. (eds.) Neuroendocrine Correlates of Sleep/Wakefulness, pp. 471–485. Springer, Boston (2006). https://doi.org/10.1007/0-387-23692-9_24

An Improved Video Coding Model for Future IMT Requirements

Sarmad K. Ibrahim[1(✉)] and Nasser N. Khamiss[2]

[1] College of Engineering, Mustansiriyah University, Baghdad, Iraq
eng_sarmadnet@uomustansiriyah.edu.iq
[2] College of Information Engineering, Al-Nahrain University, Baghdad, Iraq

Abstract. The annual need for digital wireless data continues to grow significantly, and the number of wireless devices is rapidly increasing, creating problems for current networks. Video data representing approximately 90% of the total data transmitted through networks constitute the most frequent data sent over these networks. To serve the greatest number of users, the volume of video data services needed by each user needs to be decreased. One of the goals of this paper is to improve existing mobile networks to help them meet the IMT-2022 specifications of high throughput and low latency. This paper is also devoted to developing a new video encoder model to provide the greatest number of users with video services by reducing the consumption of video data and cutting its volume. The proposed wireless scheme has the potential to support nearly 16% more consumers than LTE-ADV systems, while video encoding with the proposed wireless scheme can provide nearly 136% and 36% more users than LTE with H.265 and LTE-ADV with H.265, respectively.

Keywords: 4G · 5G · High-efficiency video coding · Ultra-high-definition · Filter bank multicarrier · International mobile telecommunications

1 Introduction

Wireless network connectivity has seen rapid technological advancement in the last 20 years. Using second-generation mobile technologies, a user could only make a phone call or deliver a short message service [1]. Furthermore, using fourth-generation technologies such as Long-Term Evolution (LTE), other practices such as high-speed Broadband connectivity, web gaming, video chatting, and video conferencing is now possible [2]. The Third-Generation Partnership Project consortium standardized LTE and its subsequent iterations [3].

Data traffic in mobile communications has risen significantly in recent years. Video providers account for a sizable portion of this data traffic [4]. In recent years, there has been an increased use of Internet-based applications, and more Internet-capable mobile terminals have been deployed throughout the world. The primary application driving the development of Long-Term Evolution Advanced (LTE-ADV) was to reach 1 Gbps peak data rates and to provide customers with a spectrum of telecommunications services [5].

P. Liatsis et al. (Eds.): TIOTC 2021, CCIS 1548, pp. 253–265, 2022.
https://doi.org/10.1007/978-3-030-97255-4_19

LTE-ADV uses multiple-component carrier aggregation [6–8] to boost the data rate to have a wide spectrum of bandwidth up to 100 MHz. The upcoming LTE update, called LTE-ADV -Rel.15, is still in its early stages, but it will allow DL data speeds of more than 3 Gbps and support emerging services like video calling, the Internet of Things, and smart cities. The LTE network roadmap must undergo several changes to satisfy International Mobile Telecommunications-2022 (IMT-2022) requirements, and the LTE specification will continue to incorporate new features [1].

The majority of data sent over these wireless networks is video data, indicating a pressing need to increase video transmission efficiency, as video data accounts for roughly 70%–90% of total data sent over networks. Advanced Video Coding (AVC/H.264) is the most common video coding format for wireless networks, and it's used to deliver a wide variety of application services to consumers. However, delivering high-definition content necessitates a wide bandwidth, which is impractical. By using sophisticated coding methods, high-efficiency video coding (HEVC/H.265) solves this challenge.

The Moving Picture Experts Group(MPEG) optimized it, and the bit rate is about half that of H.264 (at the same quality), making it a more realistic choice for providing HD, ultrahigh-definition (UHD), and 8K video services to consumers over wired and wireless networks. Currently, a network challenge exists due to the variety of video audiences and the speed of data speeds between devices, increasing in video file size to satisfy user requirements. Several researchers looked at various video coding output styles, based on two properties: subjective and objective consistency, as well as estimation approaches. When comparing AVC to HEVC, it was discovered that HEVC saved more bit rate while retaining the same efficiency.

In 2013, D. Grois and et al. [9] conducted a performance evaluation of H.265, H.264, and VP9 in terms of processing time. The results revealed that H.265 takes seven times longer to encode than VP9. The encoding times of VP9, on the other hand, are longer than those of AVC.

A. Jassal and al. [3] measured in 2016, using different buffer techniques, the value of each image frame given by video encoding and the approximate output under traffic conditions. The results showed a significant improvement over the baseline. In 2017, T. N. Huu and colleagues developed an efficient error concealment solution for real-world HEVC video transmissions that compensates for a missed entire frame and mitigates the error propagation issue [10]. The extension for H.265 was introduced by A. Ramanand and et al. in 2017 [11].

The findings revealed some of the most glaring unsolved issues in HEVC rate control. H. Azgin and et al. used FPGA to implement various angular prediction modes for HEVC in 2017 [12].

The proposed solution uses less energy than the standard solution. F. P. Pongsapan and et al. evaluated and examined HEVC over LTE in terms of PSNR with a set of videos in 2017 [13], using NS3 to test the performance. To determine the effect of a burst error, the authors used a variety of error rates. To reduce the bit rate, J. Huang and et al. combined two video coding standards, namely AVC and HEVC, into a single component in 2017 [14].

The results showed that using the high quantization value in H.265 and the low quantization value in H.264, the bit rate savings could be over 50%. To reduce complexity, In H.265 in 2019, Hai-Che Ting and colleagues suggested a modern convolutional neural network [15].

The results showed that the proposed method's complexity is reduced by up to 66% when compared to the H.265 standard, but bit rate increases and PSNR decreases. Jiang and colleagues reduced the complexity of H.265 for vehicular ad-hoc networks in 2019 [16].

The findings revealed that the proposed approach will minimize encoding time while rising delta bitrate as compared to H.265.

This paper aims to address the shortcomings of previous studies by proposing new video coding models and techniques that reduce complexity while maintaining quality. The rest of this paper is structured as follows. Section 2 introduces the proposed broadband system. Section 3 presents the proposed video coding. Section 4 illustrates the result of the proposed systems. Finally, the conclusion is presented in Sect. 5.

2 Proposed Broadband System

The existing cell phone cannot satisfy the demands of a broadband network, which involves high throughput, increased spectrum quality, and low latency.

As a consequence, 5G networks have been developed to address these needs; nevertheless, the expense of deploying and configuring 5G networks is greater than that of LTE-ADV networks, the challenge for communication engineers and operators working on 5G is to build 10 times the number of base stations required for LTE-ADV deployment.

Furthermore, 5G subscribers are projected to hit 1.9 billion by 2024, while LTE is expected to continue to be the leading broadband connectivity technology in terms of subscriptions for the far future, with approximately 5 billion subscriptions (From the Ericsson Versatility Report). As a result, improving mobile systems and increasing network capacity is a key topic for mobile system development and one of IMT-2020's goals.

The LTE interface protocol is based on a design similar to that of the 3.5G high-speed packet access protocol. The names of protocols and functions, on the other hand, are very similar; the differences are due to the multiple access techniques [17]. LTE is based on the packet data transmission method, which eliminates the need for old circuit switching systems. The user protocol stack is shown in Fig. 1.

The LTE system has bandwidth flexibility [19]. In the LTE system, The architecture achieves a higher data rate of approximately 1 Gbps. The proposed mobile framework is based on LTE-ADV, but with additional functionality. As shown in Fig. 2, the proposed system employs advanced technologies such as Modulation and Coding Scheme- proposed(MCS-Pro) and Filter Bank Multicarrier modulation- Offset Quadrature Amplitude Modulation (FBMC-OQAM).

Orthogonal frequency-division multiplexing (OFDM) is a multicarrier scheme that employs rectangular pulses during transmission and reception, resulting in a significant reduction in computational complexity due to the absence of the filter band and the use of a small number of FFT points. The CP also implies that the transmit pulse is

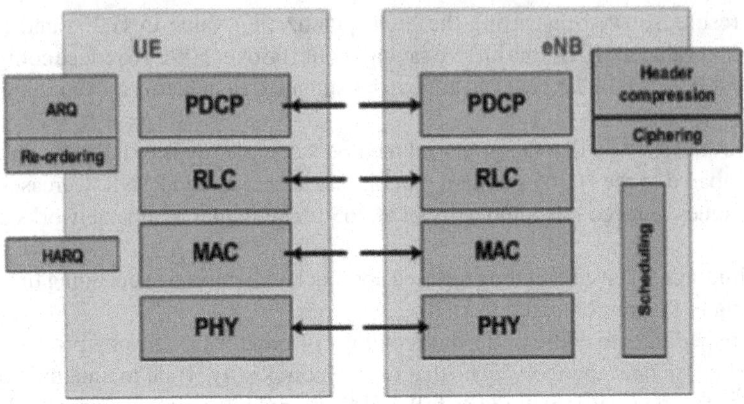

Fig. 1. Protocol stack on LTE [18].

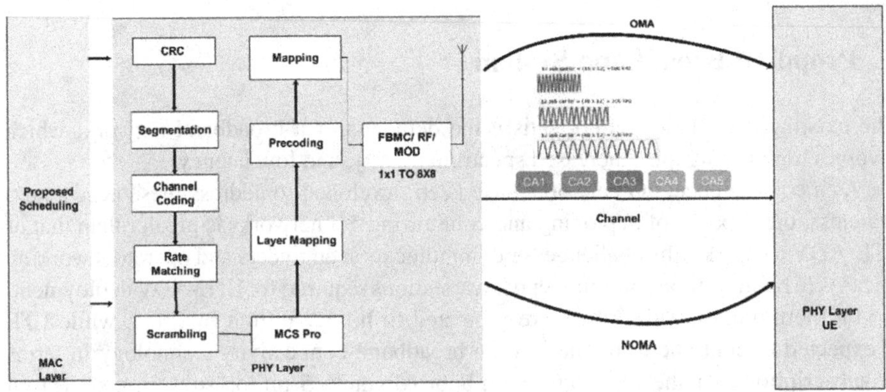

Fig. 2. Block diagram of the proposed system.

slightly longer than the received pulse; the duration of the rectangular pulse is equal to the duration of the real symbol plus the length of the CP. Furthermore, the rectangular pulse produces a lot of out-of-band (OOB) emissions and has low spectral efficiency. As shown in Fig. 3, FBMC is used to reduce OOB emissions in this study. Instead of the traditional MCS, which has a high coding efficiency, the proposed MCS is used. The proposed system is known as Pro-G, and its characteristics are listed in Table 1.

MCS recommended selecting the right modulation and coding quality to improve spectrum efficiency. MCS is selected as the best for each form of modulation, such as Quadrature Phase-Shift Keying (QPSK) and Quadrature Amplitude Modulation (16-QAM), where it determines three indices. However, the optimal pairs for 64-QAM and 256-QAM are three for 64-QAM and four for 256-QAM.

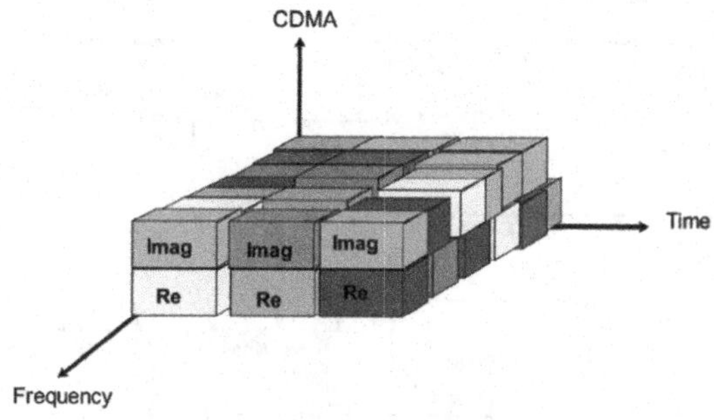

Fig. 3. Proposed FBMC

Table 1. Comparison of mobile system features

System	Proposed	LTE-ADV	LTE
Flexibility of bandwidth (MHZ)	1.25 to 60	1.25 to 20	1.25 to 20
Type of modulation	(MCS-Pro)	QPSK to 256QAM	QPSK to 64QAM
Waveform	FBMC	OFDM	OFDM
Size OF FFT (point)	128–3072	128–1024	128–1024
No. of carriers	72–3600	72–1200	72–1200
No. of RB	6–300	6–100	6–100
Carrier spacing frequency (KHZ)	15–60	15–30	15–30
No. of antenna	8 × 8	8 × 8	4 × 4

3 Proposed Video Coding for Future Mobile Systems

The standard video coding (H.265) is procedures in Fig. 4, which outline the configurations used to denote video coded data. H.265 sends blocks to the network abstraction layer [3].

Many changes have been introduced to H.265 including partition stability and further interpolation, a modern complicated and motion vector estimation, and support for several processes [3, 21, 22].

A block coding scheme is used in H.265 that involves coding tree units (CTU) and coding tree blocks, projection units, prediction blocks, transform units (TU), and transform blocks [23–26]. The proposed video coding for the proposed future video coding (PFVC) model is intended for use in today's and tomorrow's wireless mobile networks. The following are the key features of the proposed system: In a CTU, the Luma block can be up to 128 128 bytes in size. The number of directional intra modes in PFVC has been increased from 33 to 65, as in H.265. The raw video is first divided into CTUs. These units are subdivided into coding units (CUs) by a quadtree multitype layout, with a leaf coding unit describing an area that uses the same prediction mode.

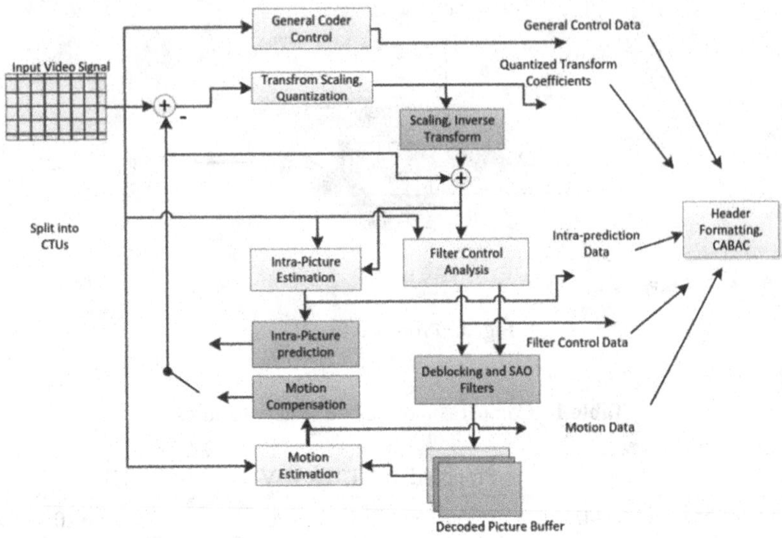

Fig. 4. The encoder of H.265 [20].

A quadtree is a nested multitype tree (MTT) with binary and ternary segmentation splits. In the coding tree structure, a CU can be square or rectangular. As a result, a quaternary tree (QT) structure is used to divide CTU into blocks. As shown in Fig. 5, the QT leaf nodes can then be further divided by a different type of construction (MTT structure). There are four types of splitting in an MTT system. The four forms of separating variance are horizontal binary, vertical binary, horizontal ternary, and vertical ternary.

A first flag (mtt split cu flag) is signaled in the MTT form to show if the node is partitioned further. As shown in Fig. 6, when a node is further partitioned, a second flag (mtt split cu vertical flag) indicates the splitting direction, and a third flag (mtt split cu binary flag) indicates whether the split is binary or ternary.

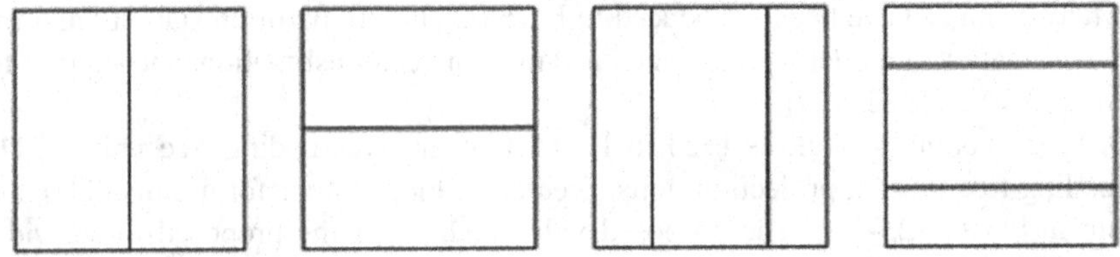

Fig. 5. Splitting types (vertical binary, horizontal binary, vertical ternary, and horizontal ternary) in the proposed model.

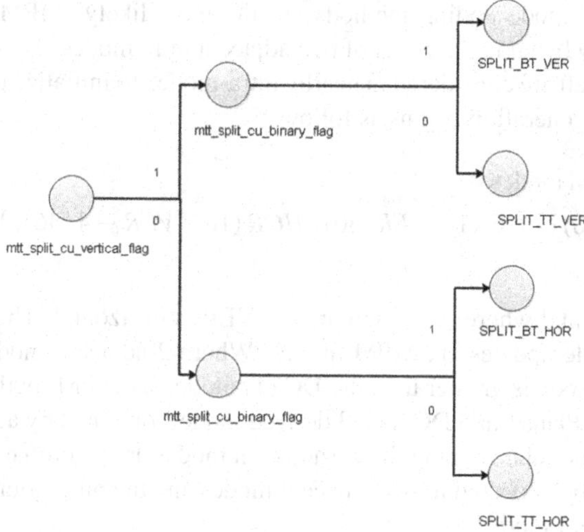

Fig. 6. Structure of proposed video coding model.

In PFVC, the number of directional intra modes was increased from 33 in H.265 to 65. As seen in Fig. 7, the current directional modes that are not present in H.265 are depicted by red dotted arrows, while the planar and DC modes stay unchanged in H.265. Furthermore, extra directional intra prediction modes are used in the chroma and luma blocks.

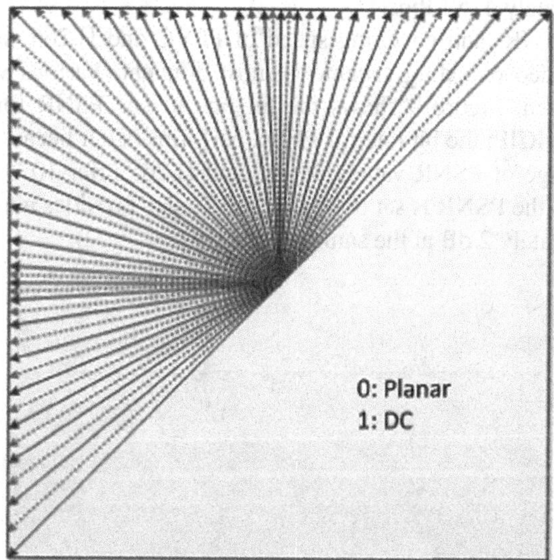

Fig. 7. Modes of Intra prediction in PFVC.

Six of the intramode coding methods are the most likely (MPM) mode used to minimize difficulty by taking account of two adjacent intra modes. Two adjacent blocks placed above and left are considered in nearby intra-mode. To initialize the default MPM list, six-MPM list generation begins as follows:

$$\text{Six Default MPM modes} = \{A,\ Planar\,(0)\ or\ DC\,(1),\ VER\,(50),\ HOR\,(18),\ VER - 4\,(46),\ VER + 4\,(54)\} \tag{1}$$

HOR is horizontal where A is angular, and VER is horizontal. The pruning of two adjacent intra mode updates six MPM modes. Where 2 adjacent modes are the same and the adjacent mode is greater than the DC (1) mode, six MPM modes can include 3 default modes (A, Planar, and DC) and 3 derived modes, obtained by added pre-defined offset values and modular running. If two adjacent modes are incompatible, the first two MPM modes will be allocated to two adjacent modes and the other four MPM modes to default and neighbor modes.

4 Simulation and Results

Two wireless mobile networks were introduced in the first device to transmit video through it. Figure 8 shows a contrast of throughput performance for two mobile systems, Pro-G and LTE-ADV, with varying antenna counts. Pro-G has a throughput of approximately 965 Mbps with 8 * 8 MIMO, which is higher than the 829 Mbps offered by LTE-ADV. Pro-G delivers approximately 483 Mbps with 4 * 4 MIMO, while LTE-ADV provides approximately 415 Mbps.

The bit rate, PSNR, and encoding speed of PFVC and H.265 were compared to ascertain which video encoding scheme is most efficient. Various video resolutions were used and tested. Figure 9 shows the bit rate versus PSNR for different video encoding modes at 4CIF; the bit rate for PFVC performs better because it is lower than H.265 across a range of PSNR values. PFVC and H.265 offer 1074 and 1412 Kbps, respectively. When the PSNR is set to 40 dB, PFVC also provides a higher PSNR than H.265 of approximately 2 dB at the same bit rate.

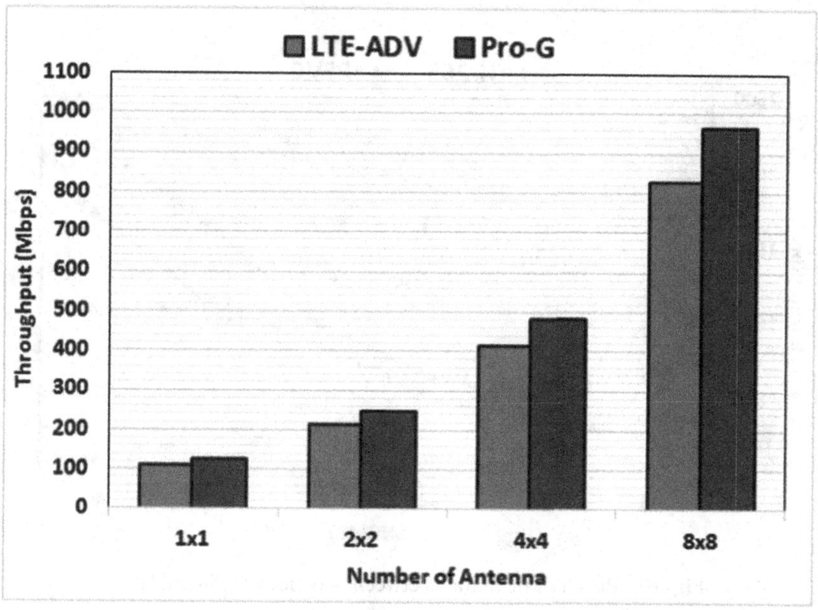

Fig. 8. Result of throughput for LTE-ADV and Pro-G systems

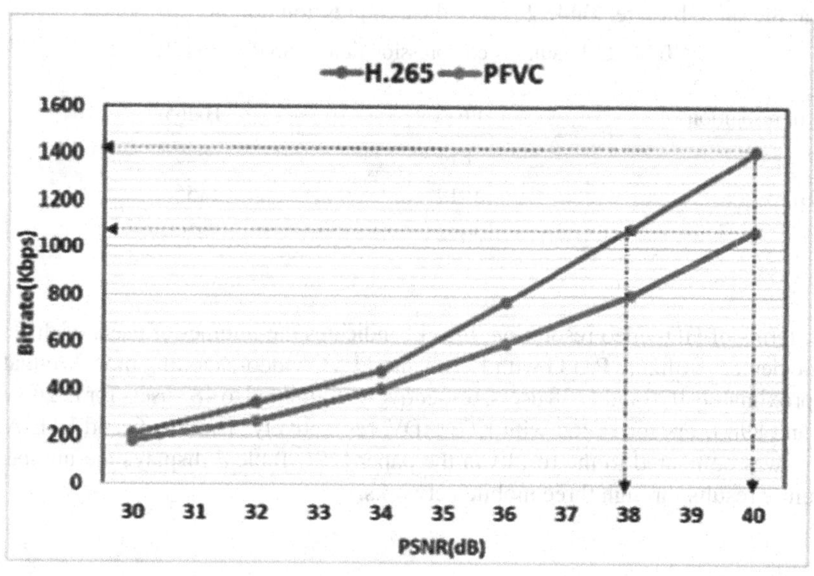

Fig. 9. Result of the bitrate between two video coding in 4CIF

Figure 10 represents the bit rate versus PSNR for various types of video encoding at 1080 HD, with PFVC outperforming H.265 because it has a lower bit rate over varying PSNR values. If the PSNR is set to 40 dB, PFVC and H.265 produce 1711 and 2181

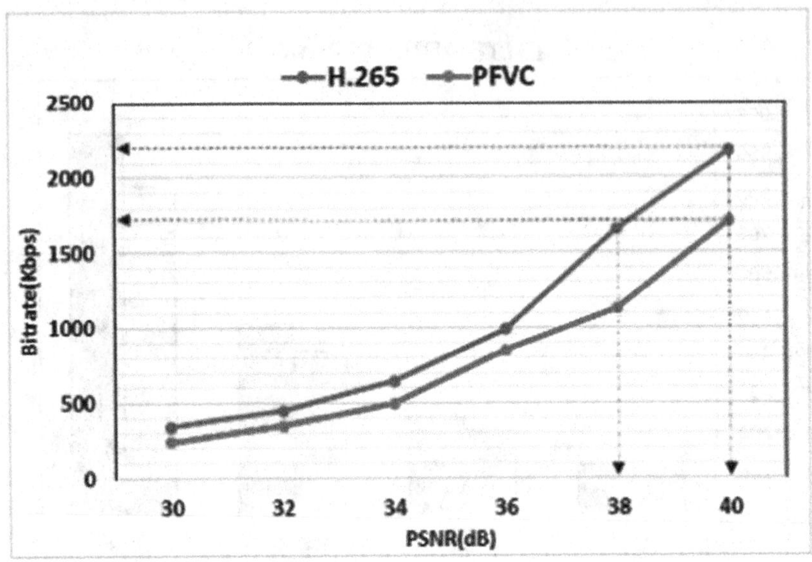

Fig. 10. Result of the bitrate between two video coding in HD

Kbps, respectively. PFVC also provides a higher PSNR than H.265 of approximately 2 dB at the same bit rate. Table 2 shows the compression output.

Table 2. Results of compression ratio (PSNR = 36 dB)

Type of resolution	PFVC	H.265
4CIF	814	628
720 HD	1919	1455
HD	3522	3020

In terms of HD video resolution, Fig. 11 indicates the number of users of different mobile devices utilizing Pro-G with H.265 and PFVC video-encoding models equating to approximately 976 and 1138 users, respectively, compared to 483 users for H.265 with LTE and 898 users for H.265 with LTE-ADV, respectively. The Pro-G and LTE-ADV system was compared to the results in the paper [27]. Table 3 displays the number of consumer results through three mobile networks.

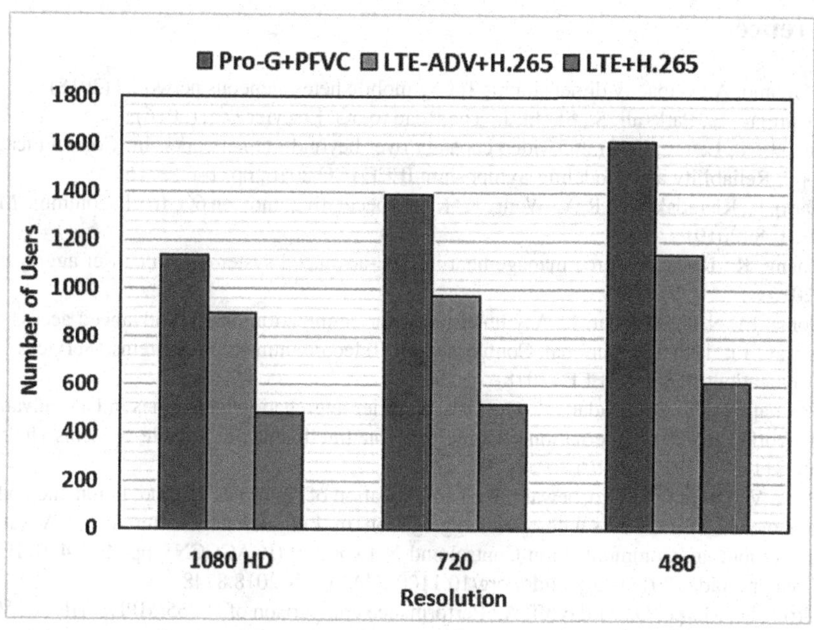

Fig. 11. Result of number of users for video coding time

Table 3. Number of video users for different video encoding

System	Resolution	PFVC	H.265
Pro-G	4CIF	1614	1246
	720	1395	1059
	1080	1138	976
LTE-ADV	4CIF	1486	1147
	720	1284	974
	1080	1048	898

5 Conclusion

In this article, two models were proposed. The first, the mobile wireless device channel technology, is proposed to increase spectral quality at low costs; the second, video coding, enables support to current and future video application requirements. The findings of the first model reveal that the suggested technique has a throughput of 16–16.5% greater than the LTE-ADV system. The findings of the video coding scheme reveal that PFVC has a lower bit rate than H.265 for various video resolutions. The results from the video coding scheme imply that PFVC has a lower bit rate than the H.265 for various video resolutions. The Pro-G with PFVC video encoding has approximately 136% more users than the LTE with H.265 and 36% more than the LTE-ADV with H.265.

References

1. Marcano, A.: Capacity dimensioning for 5g mobile heterogeneous networks (2018)
2. Dahlman, E., Parkvall, S., Skold, J.: The Road to 5G. Elsevier Ltd. (2016)
3. Jassal, A., Leung, C.: H.265 video capacity over beyond-4G networks. In: Communication QoS, Reliability and Modeling Symposium IEEE ICC 2016, pp. 1–6 (2016)
4. Tariq, F., Khandaker, M.R.A., Wong, K.-K.: A speculative study on 6G. IEEE Commun. Mag. **27**, 1–8 (2019)
5. Zhang, R.: Radio resource management in LTE-advanced systems with carrier aggregation (2016)
6. Somantri, N.T., Iskandar, I.: Asymmetric carrier aggregation on LTE-advanced access networks. In: 12th International Conference on Telecommunication Systems, Services, and Applications (TSSA). IEEE (2018)
7. Padmapriya, T., Saminadan, V.: QoE based carrier aggregation techniques in LTE-advanced networks. In: 2017 International Conference on Intelligent Sustainable Systems (ICISS), pp. 811–815. IEEE (2017)
8. Pana, V., Balyan, V., Groenewald, B.: Fair allocation of resources on modulation and coding scheme in LTE networks with carrier aggregation. In: International Conference on Advances in Computing, Communication Control and Networking (ICACCCN), pp. 467–470. IEEE, Greater Noida (2018). https://doi.org/10.1109/ICACCCN.2018.8748355
9. Grois, D., Marpe, D., Mulayoff, A.: Performance comparison of H.265/MPEG-HEVC, VP9, and H.264/MPEG-AVC encoders. In: Picture Coding Symposium (PCS), pp. 394–397. IEEE (2013)
10. Huu, T.N., Trieu, D.D., Jeon, B., Hoangvan, X.: Performance evaluation of frame-loss error-concealment solutions for the SHVC standard. IEIE Trans. Smart Process. Comput. **6**, 428–436 (2017)
11. Ramanand, A.A., Ahmad, I., Swaminathan, V.: A survey of rate control in HEVC and SHVC video encoding. In: IEEE International Conference on Multimedia & Expo Workshops (ICMEW), pp. 145–150 (2017)
12. Azgin, H., Mert, A.C., Kalali, E., Hamzaoglu, I.: An efficient FPGA implementation of HEVC intra prediction. In: 2018 IEEE International Conference on Consumer Electronics (ICCE), pp. 1–5 (2018). https://doi.org/10.1109/ICCE.2018.8326332
13. Pongsapan, F.P., Hendrawan: HEVC video compression performance evaluation on LTE network. In: 11th International Conference on Telecommunication Systems Services and Applications (TSSA), pp. 1–4. IEEE (2017)
14. Huang, J., Lin, M., Chang, P.: Transcoding or not? – a study of quantization configuration for H.264-to-HEVC transcoding. In: IEEE 6th Global Conference on Consumer Electronics (GCCE), pp. 2–3. Nagoya, Japan (2017)
15. Ting, H., Fang, H., Wang, J.: Complexity reduction on HEVC intra mode decision with modified LeNet-5. In: IEEE International Conference on Artificial Intelligence Circuits and Systems (AICAS), pp. 20–24. IEEE, Hsinchu (2019)
16. Jiang, X., Feng, J., Song, T., Katayama, T.: Low-complexity and hardware-friendly H.265/HEVC encoder for vehicular ad-hoc networks. Sensors. **19**, 1–15 (2019). https://doi.org/10.3390/s19081927
17. Bari, S.G., Jadhav, K.P., Jagtap, V.P.: High-speed packet access. Int. J. Eng. Trends Technol. (IJETT) **4**, 3422–3428 (2013)
18. Larmo, A., Lindström, M., Meyer, M., Pelletier, G., Torsner, J.: The LTE link-layer design. IEEE Commun. Mag. **47**, 52–59 (2009)
19. Kumar, A., Liu, Y., Sengupt, J.: LTE-advanced and mobile WiMAX: meeting the IMT-advanced specifications for 4G. IJCST **1**, 7–10 (2010)

20. Ibrahim, S.K., Khamiss, N.N.: Optimal usage of LTE advanced system to support multi-user in video streaming application. In: 2018 Third Scientific Conference of Electrical Engineering (SCEE), pp. 197–202. IEEE (2019)
21. Sullivan, G.J., Ohm, J.R., Han, W.J., Wiegand, T.: Overview of the high efficiency video coding (HEVC) standard. IEEE Trans. Circ. Syst. Video Technol. **22**, 1649–1668 (2012). https://doi.org/10.1109/TCSVT.2012.2221191
22. Winken, M., Helle, P., Marpe, D.: Transform coding in the HEVC test model. In: IEEE International Conference on Image Processing, pp. 3693–3696 (2011)
23. Sihag, K., Lamba, C.S.: Algorithm and architecture design of high efficiency video coding (HEVC) standard. Int. J. Comput. Sci. Mob. Comput. **5**, 171–178 (2016)
24. Ranjana, R., Mahesh, D.K.: Video compression using compact tool (HEVC). Int. J. Adv. Res. Computer . Sci. Softw. Eng. **6**, 140–143 (2016)
25. Uhrina, M., Frnda, J., Sevcik, L., Vaculik, M.: Impact of H.264/AVC and H.265/HEVC compression standards on the video quality for 4K resolution. Adv. Electr. Electron. Eng. J. **12**, 368–376 (2014). https://doi.org/10.15598/aeee.v12i4.1216
26. Ibrahim, S.K., Khamiss, N.N.: A new wireless generation technology for video streaming. J. Comput. Netw. Commun. Hindawi **2019**, 1–9 (2019)
27. Ibrahim, S., Khamiss, N.: Proposed of the wireless mobile system and video coding system in the heterogeneous network. Multimed. Tools Appl. **78**(23), 34193–34205 (2019). https://doi.org/10.1007/s11042-019-08230-8

Named Data Networking Mobility: A Survey

Wan Muhd Hazwan Azamuddin(✉), Azana Hafizah Mohd Aman, Rosilah Hassan, and Taj-Aldeen Naser Abdali(✉)

Center for Cyber Security, Faculty of Information Science and Technology (FTSM), Universiti Kebangsaan Malaysia (UKM), UKM, 43600 Bangi, Selangor, Malaysia
{p101964,p94546}@siswa.ukm.edu.my, {azana,rosilah}@ukm.edu.my

Abstract. Architecture technology Networking Data Named (NDN) is an alternative technology to the existing Internet Protocol (IP) network. These technologies can solve various problems such as safety and mobility. The basic concept of NDN uses content data for routing purposes rather than using location addresses such as IP addresses. However, NDN automatically supports consumer mobility, but mobility complainants are still challenging and require in-depth studies. Given the increase in Internet communication, network mobility support at NDN is essential. This paper comprehensively highlights the NDN background, the emergence of the Internet of Things (IoT) in NDN, and mobility in NDN.

Keywords: Information-centric networking · Named data networking · NDN mobility · Internet of Things

1 Introduction

Based on the evolution of the latest technology, the trend of data traffic consumption mobility increases throughout the year. According to statistical projections from the statista.com website, there is a variation of access from users using mobility Internet networks i.e. using online applications, virtual video playing, socially connected on virtual sites, making access like video streaming and executing online businesses. Data findings through this portal statista.com usage of traffic mobility beyond 55.64% of the total consumption of the network. Based on statista.com [1] shows the trend of traffic data mobilization rates that increase every year. It can be measured in 2018, of which 19.01 exabytes are used monthly. Expectations in 2022 of traffic data mobility usage will increase by 46% which reaches a value of 77.5 exabytes per month. Most digital marketing is more based on mobile-first concepts, causing lower personal computer usage due to cost and infrastructure constraints. Generally, the issue that can be highlighted in this research is when the use of high traffic data mobility will create traffic congestion and there will be no guarantee of the quality of mobility data to reach perfection. Figure 1 shows data access from 2017 to 2022.

Internet usage shows a significant improvement yearly. Following the advances in the use of the Internet, various latest technologies on the Internet network have been introduced to be an alternative for future networks. Nowadays, video streaming apps

P. Liatsis et al. (Eds.): TIOTC 2021, CCIS 1548, pp. 266–281, 2022.
https://doi.org/10.1007/978-3-030-97255-4_20

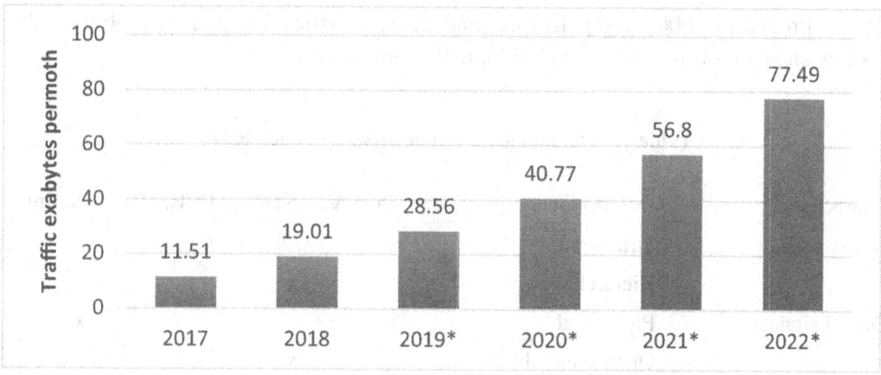

Fig. 1. Mobility data usage statistics from 2017 to 2022

are based on central content concepts that have been widely used in all communities. Among the apps that are getting widespread links are the use of social media apps such as Facebook, Twitter, YouTube, and Instagram. The use of this app allows users to share information with other users globally. The main issue in the latest internet network technology is the use of more unconducive strips as well as excessive latency content [2]. The frequent mobility issues on internet networks involve mobility and consumer mobility, complainants. Various ideas were introduced by researchers to listing several methods and in resolving problems that occurred. Among the methods introduced is a centralized content concept technology (Content-Centric). The ideology of this concept to solve mobility problems on the transmission of non-optimal content. Researcher Ted Nelson introduced an efficient method of adaptation in future Internet networks using Information-Centric Network (ICN) technology.

There have been four major architects of ICN started with the TRIAD project since the beginning of 2000. The project has become a reference center for architects who are actively developing nowadays. Among its architects the has developed are:

1. Data-oriented network architecture (DONA)
2. Content-Centric Network Architecture (CCN). This technology is better known as the Named Data Network (NDN).
3. Architecture Paradigm Routing Internet Subscription Producer (PSIRP). It has also been known as The Internet Technology Subscription of Producer (PURSUIT).
4. Network of Information (NetInf).

Network technology based on name-based objects (NDO) was introduced following improvements in the content on internet networks such as YouTube, Netflix, and so on. Typically, users should know the server IP address to enable access to the content but the introduction of ICN technology is an alternative method to access the Internet network. The main objective of the introduction to ICN technology is to ensure the efficient and effective transmission of content in communications systems such as peer-to-peer (P2P). To ensure that the objectives were achieved, the first study was introduced through the

TRIAD project in 2000 by [3]. To formulate characteristics for each technology, Table 1 below shows their respective technological characteristics.

Table 1. Technological characteristics of each ICN.

Characteristic	Description	DONA	NDN	PURSUIT	NetInf
Namespace	Structured	x		x	x
	Hierarchy		x		
Digital signature	PKI-based	x		x	x
	Open source-based		x		
Human readable	Yes		x		
	No	x		x	x
Granularity NDO	Packet		x		
	Object	x		x	x
Aggregate routing	Producer	x	x		x
	Explicit	x		x	
API	Synchronous	x	x		x
	Publish/subscribe			x	
Transport	IP	x	x	x	x
	Variety		x		x
Aggregation by NDO request	Resource handler	x			
	Named content		x		
	Name resolution system			x	x
	Hybrid				x

This article is divided into 6 sections starting with an introduction, methodology, the background of NDN, the emergence of IoT in NDN, Mobility in NDN, and a conclusion. For searching review articles, this article used several well-known databases such as IEEE Xplore [4], Science Direct [5], and google scholar [6]. Several keywords have been applied such as Information-Centric Networking, Named Data Networking, NDN mobility, Internet of Things.

2 Background of Named Data Networking

The architecture of NDN can be classified into three mains categories, namely architectural systems, service systems, and applications. Figure 2 elaborates the taxonomy of NDN. Next, details of each main category will be discussed in the next section.

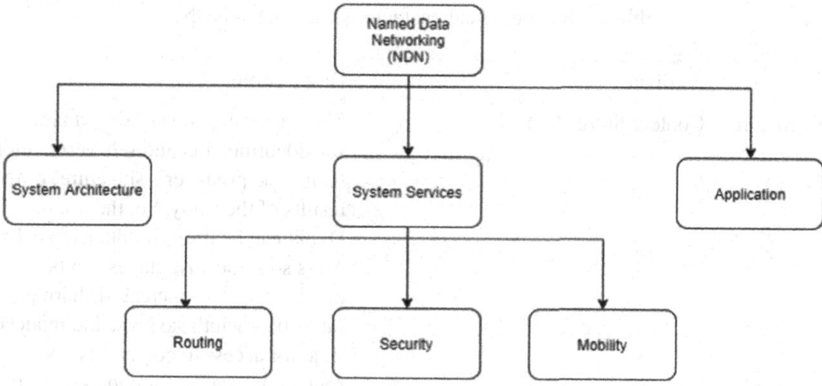

Fig. 2. NDN taxonomy

The NDN architecture operates by making content access by name like a process in internet access using names in DNS. Name access to content must be unique and no names overlap in the network. The Content Name (CN) on the NDN architecture is based on a hierarchical structure where the content access to be made must have a complete addressing such as CN/edu/svr/data-1/file-1. Figure 3 shows the structure architecture for NDN.

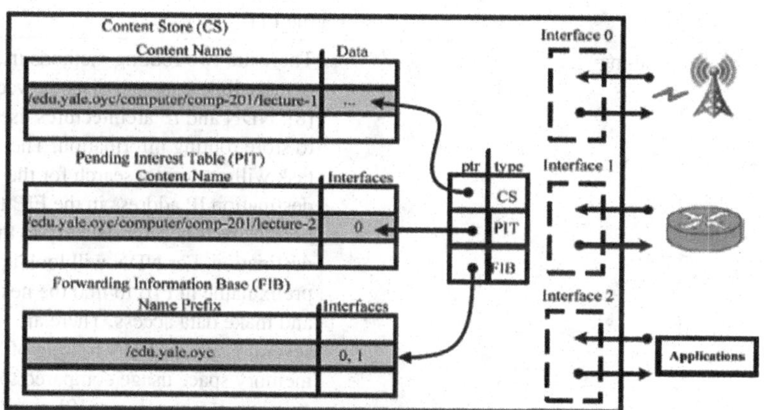

Fig. 3. Structure architecture NDN [7]

NDN communication uses the Interest packet (I_pkt) as the communication medium. When a user sends an I_pkt to a content producer, then the generation of a data packet (D_pkt) upon the reception response of I_pkt. CN is contained in both I_pkt and D_pkt. Table 2 shows a brief description for Named Data Networking:

Table 2. Technological characteristics of each NDN.

	Attribute	Description
Data structure	Content Store (CS)	The unique features of D_pkt are self-identification and self-verification (using the producer's signature) of the results of the study. So, the use of D_pkt can be used simultaneously by users so some advantages can be obtained such as increased sharing rates, bandwidth savings, and reduced time for access to content (NDN routers will cache for copies of D_pkt
	Pending Interest Table (PIT)	PIT provides an entrance for I_pkt while waiting for the presence of D_pkt. PIT is used to send D_pkt to the user. A name search for the content will be performed by the PIT search agent
	Forwarding Information Base (FIB)	The FIB's task is to ensure delivery to the next hop is successful based on the content of the name applied for. FIB is contained on the NDN router and uses the routing protocol to send I_pkt to the PIT
Services	Routing	There are two routing methods in NDN namely link-state and distance vector [8]. NDN and IP architectures use FIB to store routing information. The IP task will perform a search for the destination IP address in the FIB to find the next hop for delivery to the destination. For NDN will look up the prefix name in FIB to find the next hop and make data access. There are several issues in NDN routing of high memory space usage compared to existing IP technologies [9]

(continued)

Table 2. (*continued*)

	Attribute	Description
	Security	Content security is an important criterion in centralized data [10]. Key challenges in NDN architectural security are effective security operations, trust management, and privacy protection. The key requirements in the NDN element of security are data integrity, authentication of origin, and suitability of the data to be achieved. In the NDN architecture, it is a must to provide privacy to the content by creating an encryption process
	Mobility	In general, various methods are introduced to accommodate the mobility process in the ICN architecture, including using resolution handler methods, DNS-like servers, rendezvous, NRS, and routing-based naming. NDN mobility is divided into two aspects, namely from the point of view of mobile users and mobility producers
Application	ChronoChat	NDN ChronoChat is an instant messaging application that compatible with Android mobile devices. The main task in the ChronoChat chatroom is to make sure all clients can chat successfully. All users can use this application by making a connection to the NDN hub and also support ad-hoc communication and WiFi Direct [11]
	NDN Real-time Video Conferencing NDN-RTC	This application enables live video conferencing that using NDN libraries such as WebRTC, VP9 codec, and OpenFEC. NRN-RTC provides low latency and real-time video communication using the NDN platform [12]

(*continued*)

Table 2. (*continued*)

	Attribute	Description
	Geo-locating Nodes in Named Data Networking	NDN geo-location has provided better privacy performance compare to IP-based Internet. This technique supports ubiquitous caching communication [13]

3 Emergence of IoT in Named Data Networking

NDN communication model creates and supports various IoT technologies and applications. NDN can handle IoT device platform features and capabilities directly, including auto-configuration, service and peer exploration, bootstrapping, maintenance, stability, usability, robustness, and scalability. By using its application-specific hierarchical naming and forwarding approach, NDN makes system data extraction easy, reliable, and scalable [14]. Although NDN is based on named data rather than end-to-end communications, several applications have used the communication system provided in NDN to allow operations related to the discovery, control, and configuration of IoT devices. While for data aggregation, NDN's in-network caching makes data retrieval efficient and fail-safe, particularly if the devices are deployed in a hierarchical topology [15].Some of the technology such as implementation on smart cities, smart homes, smart healthcare, and smart grid system using IoT with NDN embedded on the system [16]. Each application will be discussed in the next section. Figure 4 shows the implementation of IoT by various sectors worldwide.

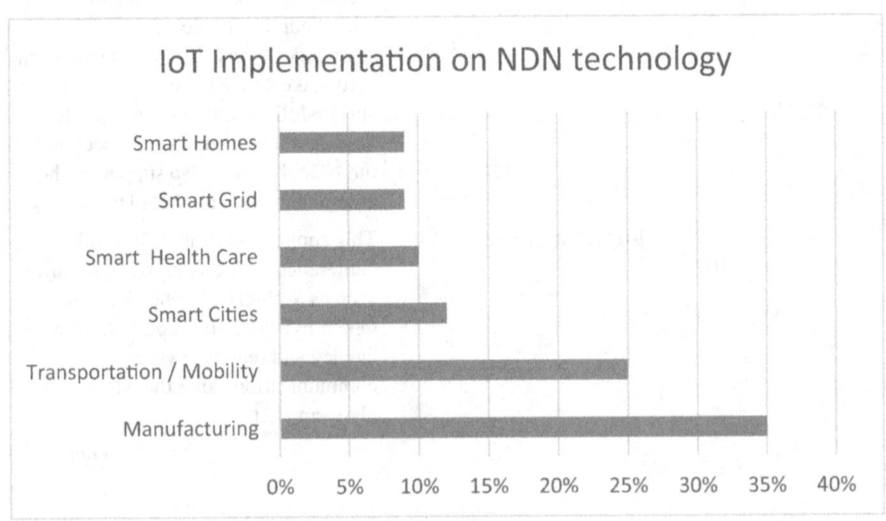

Fig. 4. IoT application on the year 2020 [17]

3.1 Smart Cities

A study from [18] stated that a large number of ubiquitous devices getting connected with providing multiservice. Implementation sensors on IoT networks give a lot of benefits such as improved quality of life, enhance power monitoring system, embedded parking, and security system. By using NDN technology provides a large namespace that supports multi ecosystem, devices, increase security and privacy, and can adapt many protocols to run in the application. There is the study by [19] used NDN-based IoT for developing smart cities to make sure all the netizen will be secured and safe. The advantages in these smart cities are consuming may find the content by discovering a provider. It's also provided a secure communication channel. However there some limitations in these smart city's system such as too long processing time caused by large overhead transmission content and not support in-network caching operation. In perspective of content-caching, study from [20] make some improvement on content-delivery by reducing latency and jitter. This can be done by distribute the content caching to make sure higher number of connected devices can be sustaining and improve the service quality.

3.2 Smart Homes

This technology has been embarking to update citizen lifestyle, to make life easy and simple. A various study has been done on applying NDN into smart homes technology. Focusing on security, a study from [21] has developed new architecture in NDN security to make controlled lightning by using Building Automation System (BAS). This system creates a command to control lighting by using names. The sensor will retrieve the command, make an execution, and return the data packet. Another study from [22] applies NDN technology to make an identification based on service to make sure communication satisfies and meets the service requirement.

3.3 Smart Healthcare

Smart healthcare can be defined as the implementation of IoT applications for the use of diagnostic, patient monitoring, treatment, and surgery [23]. All these applications using a variety of sensors, wireless network infrastructure, and personal computers. By applying NDN in this technology, it can be upgradable. Researcher [24] proposed NDN architecture for Ambient Assistant Living (AAL) applications that support various IoT models. They also claim that it is compatible with PSRIP communication. This communication is among the secure group.

3.4 Smart Grid

Smart grids purpose to control and distribute energy by using a smart system to increase efficiency on energy consumption. There are several challenges to smart grid deployment such as issues on scalability by implementing heterogeneous IoT devices, real-time data collection, and possible malicious attacks. A study from [25] stated that there is challenge need to face of such as designing and make reliable communication.

4 Mobility in Named Data Networking

When a mobile user moves from one location to another and communicates with a point of attachment (PoA) then the mobility user will send an uncertain request or a pending INTEREST packet to the mobility producer. The network-driven ICN infrastructure allows users to send unsatisfied packets when moving to a new location. This is because ICN contains an in-network caching process on providing content requested by mobility users without the need for access to mobility producers.

4.1 Producer Mobility

When the producer node moves, the Interest packet cannot be reached using FIB. If the FIB is contained on the router and has information that has been updated as a result of node movement, then the NDN operation can be carried out without any problems. There is a mobility solution that has been introduced such as studies by [26], and [27] to overcome issues of NDN mobility. Techniques for mobility producers such as rendezvous point, tunnel based-redirection, and indirection techniques will be discussed below: -

a) Rendezvous point

As a result of the discovery of this method, the rendezvous point uses a location management server called a rendezvous server to support mobility producers. The main key result of this study is to provide name resolution services to name content and locator for mobility producers [28]. The operation of this mobility producer is described in more detail in Fig. 5 below. The rendezvous server can store the user's location path, the latest prefix routing for data, node movement requests can be obtained by making requests on information that has been stored at the rendezvous point. However, the constraints of this solution are the increased latency rate on new name applications and the establishment of a Forward Information Base (FIB). This indicates a negative impact that is not in line with the goals of the introduction of ICN. Therefore, some methods and studies should be conducted to solve the problem that occurs.

b) Tunnel based-redirection technique

This method is similar to studies that have been conducted on previous indirection points but an improvement to internal router users. The main key to the development of this idea is to bring the message of Interest to the new location by using tunnels. The messages that will be sent through the tunnel are Prefix Update (PU) and Prefix Update Acknowledgment (PUA). The study of [30] stated that can reduce the rate of traffic consumption in mobility movement and avoid network disruption. Referring to Fig. 6 each information will be registered on the internal router. The method implemented is similar to Mobile IPv6 technology from the perspective of a combination of architecture and routing tables. However, the disadvantage of this method is that it can only be used for in-network cache to reduce overhead but cannot be used globally.

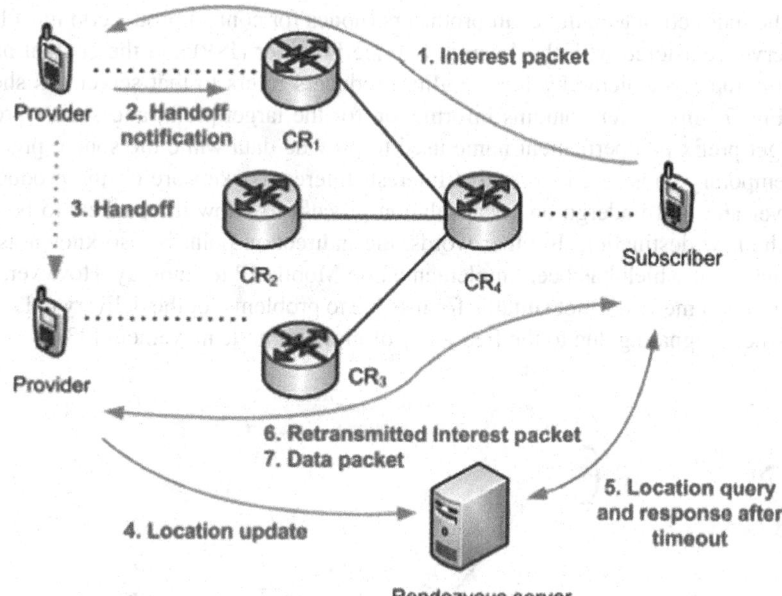

Fig. 5. NDN server rendezvous point technique [29]

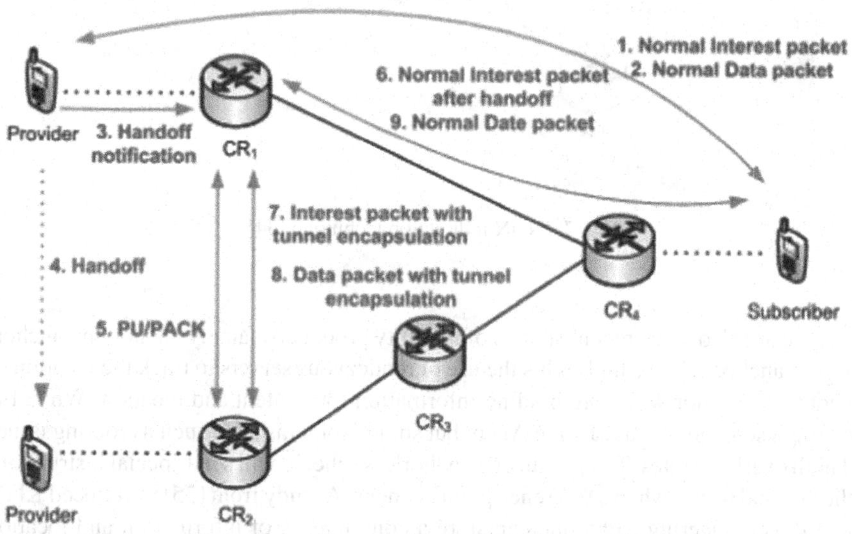

Fig. 6. NDN tunnel-based technique [31]

c) Indirection technique

This method is developed by adding a relay server element or known as an indirection server or indirection point. The advantage of the rendezvous point can reduce the handoff latency rate of the study results from [32]. To solve the problem in the indirection technique, all producers (nodes for content producers) must have a server registered with the Internet Service Provider (ISP) and the content name of the top layer hierarchy for mobility producers refers to that server. As shown in Fig. 7, this server contains information for the target prefix and source prefix, Target prefix is a permanent name used to provide data while the source prefix is a temporary name used to receive Interest. Interest packets are on the producer's server and will undergo an encapsulation process to allow the packets to be sent to the new destination. In other words, the indirection point is also known as the home agent which has been implemented on Mobile IP technology. However, this indirection method is not suitable for use due to problems for the delivery delay and overhead signaling due to the frequency of mobility node movement [33].

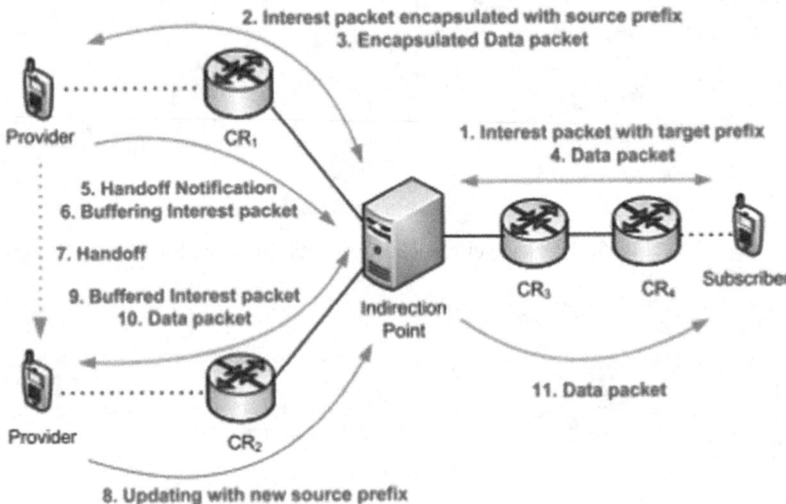

Fig. 7. NDN indirection technique [34]

There are also some recent studies of mobility producers namely anchor and anchorless. The anchor scheme highlights the use of rendezvous servers to track the location of the content. Anchor will store binding information for content and location. While the anchorless scheme will use Home Agent but some problems arise such as routing issues and high overhead rates. The producer's anchorless scheme will send special instructions to the original router when a reference point changes. A study from [35] introduced KITE where the engineering technique can store a combination of information and location on a rendezvous server. This method uses an anchor scheme. The issue that occurred was a problem with routing and overhead signaling. Subsequent studies use the anchorless method by [36] which works specifically in the management of micro-mobility in streaming applications. Studies from [37] show that mobility producers are used to updating Interest FIB data input on routers adjacent to mobility producers. Yet this study still has shortcomings as this technique has gone beyond the architectural principles of NDN. Further studies have made a revolution by introducing a hybrid scheme where the use of NeMo protocol is introduced in NDN. This study was introduced by [38] which is the only hybrid study for mobility producers. This technique introduces the use of BIT (Binding Information Table) to reduce the rate of use of FIB in NDN architecture. This technique is still in the process of development and has not undergone a metric performance validation process to test the performance of the hybrid technique. Table 3 shows a study of the latest technique of NDN mobility producers.

Table 3. A study of the latest techniques for NDN mobility producers

Author	Producer mobility technique	Advantages	Disadvantages
[39]	Rendezvous point	provide name resolution services (NRS) to name content and locators for mobility producers	Increased latency rates on new name applications and the establishment of a Forward Information Base (FIB)
[35]	Kite (anchor)	Stores a combination of information for content and location	Issues for routing and overhead signaling
[36]	Map-ME (Anchorless)	Micro mobility management for mobility producers specializing in streaming applications	No finding
[40]	Dual connection strategy (anchorless)	Ensure routing information is always updated as a result of the activities of mobility producers	Unable to cope when the movement of mobility producers is moving fast
[38]	NEMO (hybrid)	Use BIT tables to reduce the frequency of use of FIB tables	Implementing metric performance simulation. There were no findings of weakness in this study
[37]	T-Move	The mobility producer is used to update the FIB input and send the content to a router close to the producer	Exceeding the inner limits of NDN architectural principles

4.2 Mobility Performance Parametric

Based on previous research, a lot of technology has been proposed to overcome the issue of mobility on NDN. Each technique used various methods to prove their result such as by using mathematical modeling and simulation using a special simulator such as ns3. Table 4 below shows a comparison of performance metrics between previous studies.

Table 4. Comparison performance metric between producer mobility techniques

Author	Producer mobility technique	Parameter	Research technique	Simulation software/Mathematical equation
	MAP-Me (Anchorless)	Network size (m^2) – 400 × 400 Number of NDN router – 4 × 4 (16 nod) Number of producer mobility – 5 Mobility speed (m/s) – 1 – 15 ms Interest range (ms) – 300 Segment size (bytes) – 1024 Mobility model – RandomWayPointMobilityModel Comparison – Rocketfuel	Simulation	ndnSIM 2.0 ns-3
[35]	Kite	Network size (m^2) – 400 × 400 Number of NDN router – 11 range node – 100 m Number of mobility producer – 1 Mobility speed (m/s) – 2 Interest range (ms) – 100 Segment size (bytes) – 1024 Mobility model – RandomWalk2MobilityModel Comparison – Kite	Simulation	ndnSIM
[40]	Dual connection strategy (anchorless)	Distance router to AP – 150 m Distance between AP – 340 m Pro Mobility speed – 60 km/j Interest user transmission – 20 (1 Interest /50 ms) Hop count – 1 Delay – 10 ms	Simulation	ndnSIM

5 Conclusion

Based on the techniques that have been developed, a conclusion can be expressed by a deep study on producer mobility NDN has to find a variety of issues and methods to overcome it. Among them are the problems of high overhead rates as well as the frequency of packet loss during transmission between NDN routers issue must be solved by using a suitable technique on mobility NDN. For host-centric IoT technology, there are facing many challenges due to some IoT devices, security, and reliable communication. By embed NDN technology in IoT Technology, a content-centric paradigm has been introduced. In conclusion, further research needs to be done for finding more benefits in applying NDN as IoT communication.

Acknowledgments. This research is funded by research grant FRGS/1/2019/ICT03/UKM/02/1.

References

1. Statista: • Global mobile data traffic 2022 | Statista (2019). https://www.statista.com/statistics/271405/global-mobile-data-traffic-forecast/
2. Khan, S., Alvi, A.N., Javed, M.A., Roh, B.H., Ali, J.: An efficient superframe structure with optimal bandwidth utilization and reduced delay for internet of things based wireless sensor networks. Sensors (Switzerland) **20**(7), 1971 (2020). https://doi.org/10.3390/s20071971
3. Cheriton, D.R., Gritter, M.: TRIAD: a new next-generation Internet architecture, no. January 2000, pp. 1–20. Citeseer (2000). http://citeseerx.ist.psu.edu/viewdoc/summary?doi=10.1.1.33.5878%0Ahttp://citeseerx.ist.psu.edu/viewdoc/download;jsessionid=D6B317634A9F9D3BB6E72708328CC3DF?doi=10.1.1.33.5878&rep=rep1&type=pd
4. IEEE: IEEE Access: The Multidisciplinary Open Access Journal (2021). https://ieeeaccess.ieee.org/. Accessed 21 Mar 2021
5. Science Direct: ScienceDirect (2021). https://www.sciencedirect.com/. Accessed 21 Mar 2021
6. Google: Google Shcolar (2016). https://scholar.google.com/. Accessed 21 Mar 2021
7. Saxena, D., Raychoudhury, V., Suri, N., Becker, C., Cao, J.: named data networking: a survey. Comput. Sci. Rev. **19**, 15–55 (2016). https://doi.org/10.1016/j.cosrev.2016.01.001
8. Wang, L., Lehman, V., Mahmudul Hoque, A.K.M., Zhang, B., Yu, Y., Zhang, L.: A secure link state routing protocol for NDN. IEEE Access **6**, 10470–10482 (2018). https://doi.org/10.1109/ACCESS.2017.2789330
9. Walters, S.T., et al.: MAPIT: development of a web-based intervention targeting substance abuse treatment in the criminal justice system. J. Subst. Abuse Treat. **46**, 60–65 (2014). https://doi.org/10.1016/j.jsat.2013.07.003
10. Liu, T., Zhang, M., Zhu, J., Zheng, R., Liu, R., Wu, Q.: ACCP: adaptive congestion control protocol in named data networking based on deep learning. Neural Comput. Appl. **31**(9), 4675–4683 (2018). https://doi.org/10.1007/s00521-018-3408-2
11. Smith, T.V., Afanasyev, A., Zhang, L.: ChronoChat on Android, pp. 1–4 (2017)
12. Gusev, P., Burke, J.: NDN-RTC, pp. 117–126 (2015). https://doi.org/10.1145/2810156.2810176
13. Compagno, A., Conti, M., Gasti, P., Mancini, L.V., Tsudik, G.: Violating consumer anonymity: geo-locating nodes in named data networking. In: Malkin, T., Kolesnikov, V., Lewko, A.B., Polychronakis, M. (eds.) ACNS 2015. LNCS, vol. 9092, pp. 243–262. Springer, Cham (2015). https://doi.org/10.1007/978-3-319-28166-7_12
14. N. D. N. project team: Named Data Networking (NDN) - a future internet architecture, vol. 2018, no. Nov 28 (2010). http://named-data.net/%0Ahttps://named-data.net/publications/techreports/tr001ndn-proj/.%0Ahttps://named-data.net/
15. Aboodi, A., Wan, T.C., Sodhy, G.C.: Survey on the incorporation of NDN/CCN in IoT. IEEE Access **7**, 71827–71858 (2019). https://doi.org/10.1109/ACCESS.2019.2919534
16. Mohd Aman, A.H., Yadegaridehkordi, E., Attarbashi, Z.S., Hassan, R., Park, Y.J.: A survey on trend and classification of internet of things reviews. IEEE Access **8**, 111763–111782 (2020). https://doi.org/10.1109/ACCESS.2020.3002932
17. Scully, P.: Top 10 IoT applications in 2020 - which are the hottest areas right now? IoT Analytics (2020). https://iot-analytics.com/top-10-iot-applications-in-2020/
18. Zanella, A., Bui, N., Castellani, A., Vangelista, L., Zorzi, M.: Internet of things for smart cities. IEEE Internet Things J. **1**(1), 22–32 (2014). https://doi.org/10.1109/JIOT.2014.2306328
19. Piro, G., Cianci, I., Grieco, L.A., Boggia, G., Camarda, P.: Information centric services in smart cities. J. Syst. Softw. **88**(1), 169–188 (2014). https://doi.org/10.1016/j.jss.2013.10.029
20. Ahmed, S.H., Kim, D.: Named data networking-based smart home. ICT Express **2**(3), 130–134 (2016). https://doi.org/10.1016/j.icte.2016.08.007

21. Burke, J., Gasti, P., Nathan, N., Tsudik, G.: Securing instrumented environments over content-centric networking: the case of lighting control and NDN, pp. 394–398 (2014). https://doi.org/10.1109/infcomw.2013.6970725
22. Amadeo, M., Campolo, C., Molinaro, A.: Internet of things via named data networking: the support of push traffic (2014). https://doi.org/10.1109/NOF.2014.7119766
23. Saxena, D., Raychoudhury, V.: Design and verification of an NDN-based safety-critical application: a case study with smart healthcare. IEEE Trans. Syst. Man Cybern. Syst. **49**(5), 991–1005 (2019). https://doi.org/10.1109/TSMC.2017.2723843
24. Nour, B., et al.: A survey of internet of things communication using ICN: a use case perspective. Comput. Commun. **142–143**, 95–123 (2019). https://doi.org/10.1016/j.comcom.2019.05.010
25. Song, F., et al.: Smart collaborative caching for information-centric IoT in fog computing. Sensors (Switzerland) **17**(11), 1–15 (2017). https://doi.org/10.3390/s17112512
26. Hussaini, M., Nor, S.A., Ahmad, A.: Producer mobility support for information centric networking approaches: a review. Int. J. Appl. Eng. Res. **13**(6), 3272–3280 (2018). http://www.ripublication.com
27. Yan, Z., Zeadally, S., Zhang, S., Guo, R., Park, Y.J.: Distributed mobility management in named data networking. Wirel. Commun. Mob. Comput. (2016). https://doi.org/10.1002/wcm.2652
28. Kim, D., Ko, Y.-B.: On-demand Anchor-based mobility support method for named data networking. In: ICACT, pp. 19–23 (2017)
29. Kim, D., Ko, Y.B.: On-demand anchor-based mobility support method for named data networking (2017). https://doi.org/10.23919/ICACT.2017.7890049
30. Bi, Y., Han, G., Lin, C., Wang, X., Zhang, Q., Liu, Z.: Effective packet loss elimination in ip mobility support for vehicular networks. IEEE Netw. **34**(1), 152–158 (2020). https://doi.org/10.1109/MNET.2019.1900093
31. Zhang, S., et al.: Efficient producer mobility support in named data networking. IEICE Trans. Commun. **E100B**(10), 1856–1864 (2017). https://doi.org/10.1587/transcom.2016EBP3458
32. Alajlan, M., Belghith, A.: Supporting seamless mobility for real-time applications in named data networking. Proc. Comput. Sci. **110**, 62–69 (2017). https://doi.org/10.1016/j.procs.2017.06.117
33. Afanasyev, A., Burke, J., Refaei, T., Wang, L., Zhang, B., Zhang, L.: A brief introduction to named data networking. In: Proceedings - IEEE Military Communications Conference MILCOM, vol. 2019-Octob, pp. 605–611 (2019). https://doi.org/10.1109/MILCOM.2018.8599682
34. Zhang, Z., et al.: An overview of security support in named data networking. IEEE Commun. Mag. (2018). https://doi.org/10.1109/MCOM.2018.1701147
35. Zhang, Y., Xia, Z., Mastorakis, S., Zhang, L.: KITE: producer mobility support in named data networking. In: ICN 2018 – Proceedings of 5th ACM Conference on Information-Centric Networking, pp. 125–136 (2018). https://doi.org/10.1145/3267955.3267959
36. Augé, J., Carofiglio, G., Grassi, G., Muscariello, L., Pau, G., Zeng, X.: MAP-me: managing anchor-less producer mobility in content-centric networks. IEEE Trans. Netw. Serv. Manag. **15**(2), 596–610 (2018). https://doi.org/10.1109/TNSM.2018.2796720
37. Korla, S., Chilukuri, S.: T-move: a light-weight protocol for improved QoS in content-centric networks with producer mobility. Futur. Internet **11**(2), 1–17 (2019). https://doi.org/10.3390/fi11020028
38. Adhatarao, S., Arumaithurai, M., Kutscher, D., Fu, X.: NeMoI: network mobility in ICN. In: Biswas, S., et al. (eds.) COMSNETS 2018. LNCS, vol. 11227, pp. 220–244. Springer, Cham (2019). https://doi.org/10.1007/978-3-030-10659-1_10

39. Fotiou, N., Alzahrani, B.A.: Rendezvous-based access control for information-centric architectures. Int. J. Netw. Manag. **28**(1), e2007 (2018). https://doi.org/10.1002/nem.2007
40. Choi, J.H., Cha, J.H., Han, Y.H., Min, S.G.: A dual-connectivity mobility link service for producer mobility in the named data networking. Sensors (Switzerland) **20**(17), 1–16 (2020). https://doi.org/10.3390/s20174859

A Spectrum Sensing Profile Based SDR for Cognitive Radio System: An Experimental Work

Muntasser S. Falih[1(✉)] and Hikmat N. Abdullah[2]

[1] Department of System Engineering, Al-Nahrain University, Baghdad, Iraq
muntasser.saleem@coie-nahrain.edu.iq

[2] Department of Information and Communication Engineering, Al-Nahrain University, Baghdad, Iraq
hikmat.abdullah@coie-nahrain.edu.iq

Abstract. Cognitive Radio (CR) system is one of the key technologies that enables 5G and beyond. Spectrum Sensing (SS) is the basic step performed by CR operator to specify the spectrum opportunity, so it is must be reliable and efficiently implemented as much as possible while the later system actions depends on its decision. In this paper, a flexible SS profile based Software Defined Radio (SDR) is implemented for real time signal detection. Also, experimental scenario is achieved using commercial SDR platform. OFDM signal is transmitted using Hack Rf one with GUN radio software at transmitter side, while the sensing part is performed using RTL SDR and MATLAB for signal capturing and executing SS algorithms. The results show that the proposed profile is supported with many specification makes it is flexible to select different sensing algorithm with different received samples at the preferred detection accuracy.

Keywords: Cognitive radio · Spectrum sensing · SDR · RTL · GUN radio · Hack RF one

1 Introduction

Cognitive Radio (CR) is an intelligent radio system has ability to change its operation parameters according to the operation environment. The massive growth in the communicated wireless devices and the high data traffic generated by social media and high resolution multimedia application, this causes congestion in communication resources. By the way, Federal Communication Commission (FCC) reported that about 85% of allocated available spectrums are used in inefficient manner. Thus, there is a necessary need for a technology which makes up for utilizing the unused spectrum spaces. Finally, this can be achieved by using CR [1–3].

P. Liatsis et al. (Eds.): TIOTC 2021, CCIS 1548, pp. 282–295, 2022.
https://doi.org/10.1007/978-3-030-97255-4_21

CR system consists of many parts such as Spectrum Sensing (SS), spectrum sharing and spectrum mobility. SS is basic function in CR cycle by which the vacant spectrum band is identified. In CR system, the operating environment is structured in the form of wireless communication networks which are called Cognitive Radio Networks (CRNs). CRN is an association of computer network based on the stand negating between two sub-networks, these are; primary network includes the licensed users (PUs) and the secondary network that is the unlicensed users (SUs).From this point of view, SS role is very influence on all later CR activity. Wrong hole identification leads to harmful interfering with the licensed user and this is not recommended in CRNs standardization. Thus, SS approach must be selected under the required QoS levels by CRNs. In this context, there are many SS techniques like; Matched Filter, Cyclostatioary and Energy Detection (ED) [4, 5].

The SS algorithms implementation is the way to realize the system level designed algorithm and make it useful for standalone or hardware based real time SS applications. System implementation can be achieved using two approaches. The first approach is using programmable devices like FPGA or DSP processors, and the other is using commercial Software Define Radio (SDR) devices. The presented designs in the literature using both approaches are either do not include testing using real time spectrum data or suffer from the inflexibility specially when realizing Cooperative Spectrum Sensing (CSS) scenarios.

The reminder sections of this paper are structured as follow: In Sect. 2, we present the related works that associated to SS realization using SDR devices. Section 3 reviews the basic principles of spectrum sensing in CR system with brief desecration for the supported SS algorithm in the proposed profile. In Sect. 4 we illustrate the proposed framework, while Sect. 5 shows experimental scenario and its features. The experimental results presented in Sect. 6. The conclusions that extracted from this work presented in last section.

2 Related Works

There are many works associated with spectrum sensing realization using SDR platforms. For example: in [6] proposed an implementation scheme for SU to perform SS using USRP with GNU radio. The main drawback of this scheme is deepened of static block of GNU radio in ED implementation that causes an inflexibility to change, replace and modify the SS profile. In [7] proposed a framework for SU SS side uses USRP SDR with MATLAB. In this context, the author employed CED as SS. However, it did not take into account the use of efficient SS at low SNR and for MBSS and WBSS. As well as, the CSS topology did not take into account the real time applications which in nature suffer from fading effects. In [8] proposed an implementation scheme for modified ED SS algorithm using FPGA. The main drawback of this work is not considering the facilities of SDR devices that support the RF real time spectrum data for testing the proposed algorithm. In this paper an efficient and flexible SS profile is designed based MATLAB GUI interfaced with real-time spectrum capturing hardware. This is useful for different signal detection like Digital-TV signal which is based on OFDM. The main contributions of this paper can be defined as follows:

1. Design and implementation of a flexible SS profile supports different detection algorithms.
2. The designed profile supports the detection of wide frequency bands with tunable detection probability controlled by number of received samples and false alarm probability.
3. Real time interfacing RTL SDR hardware with MATLAB GUI for injects refreshed spectrum data.
4. Testing the proposed SS profile experimentally using real spectrum data.

3 Spectrum Sensing Principles

In CR system, the spectrum sensing is a necessary process and it is achieved in the beginning of CR life cycle. SS is used to detect the spectrum hole (white space) at specific frequency band. It based on binary hypothesis in which H0 represents spectrum hole and H1 represents the busy channel or PU presence. The following equation shows the detection hypothesis in noisy channel.

$$\mathrm{y(n)} = \begin{cases} w(\mathrm{n}); & \mathrm{H_0} \\ s(\mathrm{n}) + w(\mathrm{n}); & \mathrm{H_1} \end{cases} \tag{1}$$

Where y(n) is the received sample, w(n) is the Additive White Gaussian Noise AWGN samples collected from the transmission channel, s(n) is the PU signal sample, H0 and H1 are null and power hypothesis respectively. In this the work, energy detector is the used model and the test statistics of the received sample is defined as follows:

$$\mathrm{T} = \frac{1}{\mathrm{Ns}} \sum_{\mathrm{n=1}}^{\mathrm{Ns}} |\mathrm{y(n)}|^2 \tag{2}$$

Where Ns is the total number of received samples. The distribution of T is chi-squared with 2Ns degrees of freedom [9]. Energy detection can be achieved either in time or in frequency domain. Frequency domain energy computation is better than time domain because it gives efficient resolution over wider bandwidth. The traditional frequency domain energy computation called "preiodgram".

The performance of ED is measured by Receiver Operating Characteristics (ROC) that is represented by Probability of Detection (PD) and Probability of False Alarm (PFA) at certain SNR and Ns values. PD represents the correct detection when PU is present, PFA represents false detection alarm that indicates the presence of PU but actually, it is not there. From [10], PD and PFA in AWGN are calculated in case of unity noise variance as in Eqs. (3) and (4) respectively.

$$\mathrm{P_D} = \mathrm{P}\left[\mathrm{T} > \lambda\middle|_{\mathrm{H_1}}\right]\mathrm{Q}\left(\frac{\lambda - \mathrm{Ns}(1 + \mathrm{SNR})}{\sqrt{2\mathrm{Ns}(1 + \mathrm{SNR})}}\right) \tag{3}$$

$$\mathrm{P_{FA}} = \mathrm{P}\left[\mathrm{T} > \lambda\middle|_{\mathrm{H_0}}\right]\mathrm{Q}\left(\frac{\lambda - \mathrm{Ns}}{\sqrt{2\mathrm{Ns}}}\right) \tag{4}$$

Where λ is the threshold value, this value can be optioned form Eq. (4) as follow:

$$\lambda = \sqrt{2N_S}\,Q^{-1}(P_{FA}) + N_s \tag{5}$$

Where Q is complementary Q-function (Marcum function).

3.1 The Supported Spectrum Sensing Algorithms

The proposed sensing profile designed for noncooperative SS scenario. Thus a three sensing algorithms are injected in this profile. The first algorithm is the standard frequency domain Conventional Energy Detector (CED) which is same the classical energy detection but differs by taking Fourier Transform for the received samples. This sensing algorithm also called periodgram, the flowchart is presented in Fig. 1 [11].

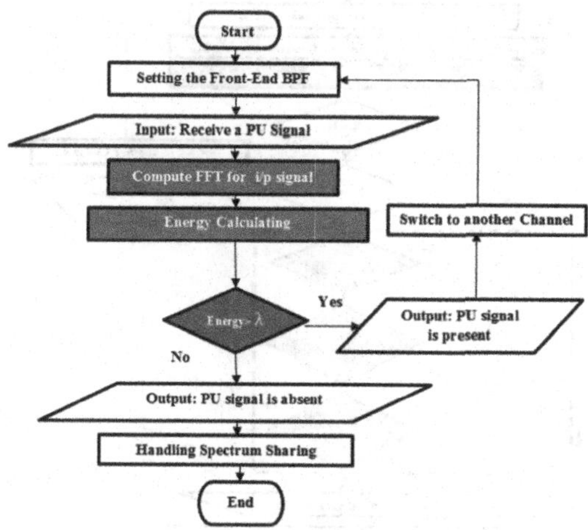

Fig. 1. CED algorithm flowchart

The other two spectrum sensing algorithms are developed by the same authors to increase the detection performance of CED. These algorithms are related to energy detection family but with some modification, the description of these algorithms are:

a. Knowledge Based Decision Procedure (KBDP algorithm): this algorithm is related to the double threshold energy detection family. In this algorithm PU detection mechanism is based on present energy level and the average number of previous energies. Moreover, the knowledge based decisions making approach is used to achieve soft decision in PU detection instead the classical decisions in which many detection opportunities are denied through precise matching verification. The justification of this scheme is to increase the detection accuracy by diminishing the unknown noise fluctuating, which in turn reduces the decision uncertainty. The detection mechanism in this algorithm is based on computing the values of present energy (resulting from current energy test over sensing time) and the average of M-previous energies (resulting from M previous tests). Then, Knowledge Based Decision Procedure

(KBDP) is applied on the computed values. A KBDP acts to make the decision based on inference intelligent knowledge instead of the certain threshold matching. The detailed operation of the proposed method can be explained as follows: first, the confusion region is divided into 3 equal sub-distances (SD). SDs are arranged from lower to higher by linguistic values LOW, NORMAL and HIGH, respectively. Figure 2 reveals detection mechanism of this algorithm. The full description of this algorithm is in [5].

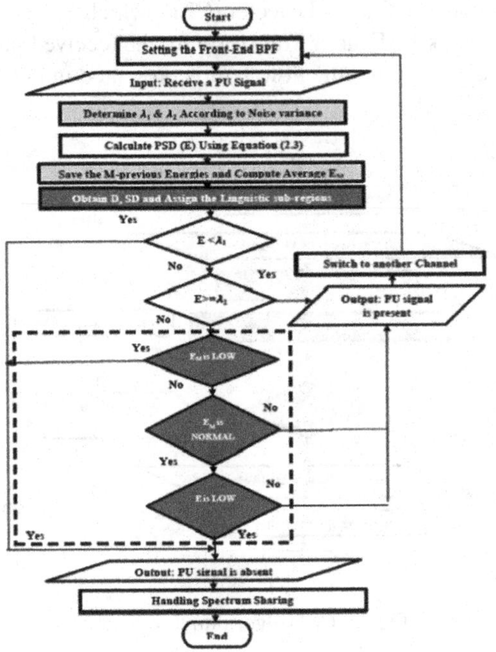

Fig. 2. KBDP algorithm flowchart

b. Average Ratio Discrete Cosine Transform (AR-DCT Algorithm): In this algorithm some advantages of using DCT transform in signal recognition has been utilized. This algorithm has two operation modes. The first mode performs spectrum sensing for every received samples using CED. The o/p of this checking gives H1 hypothesis when the received energy is greater or equal to the predefined threshold. Otherwise, the second mode is initiated where enhancing module based on DCT statistics is activated. The enhancement module will act to make further verification about the hypothesis decision produced by CED energy detector. The full explanation of this algorithm represented in [12], Fig. 3 shows its system level flowchart.

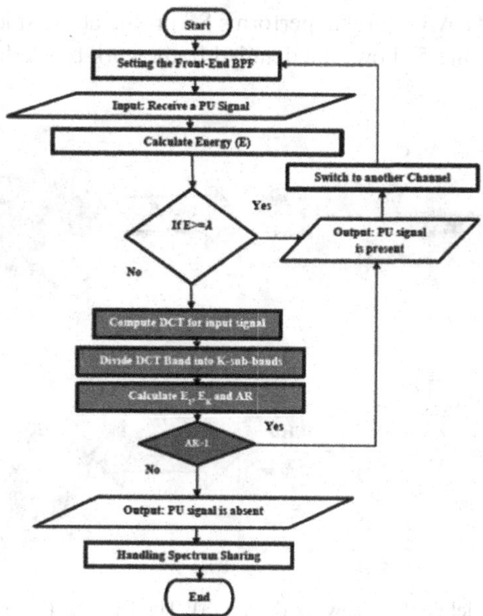

Fig. 3. AR-DCT algorithm flowchart

4 The Proposed Framework

This framework consists of; SDR transmitter as PU and SDR receiver supported with many SS algorithms as SU. This framework supports single user SS. Figure 4 reveals the general layout of this framework. The detailed structure of each side (PU and SU) can be explained as follows: the PU consists of Host Computer (H-PC), this contains the transmitting software program and SDR device. This PC is interfaced with suitable SDR using UHD driver to perform the PU functionality. In this work, the transmission program is GNU Radio Campion v.3 [13], which is block based signal flow graph software able to support most of the communication system tools for SDR devices in both of sink and source functions. Regarding the used SDR in PU side, HackRF One SDR is used for this function with coverage transmission and reception range from 70 kHz to 6 GHz [13]. Regarding to SU side, RTL SDR is used as spectrum data receiver [14]. This device is interfaced with H-PC using UHD driver, H-PC contains the SDR configuration command and the software of SS algorithm in turn the spectrum will be sensed. The last step is

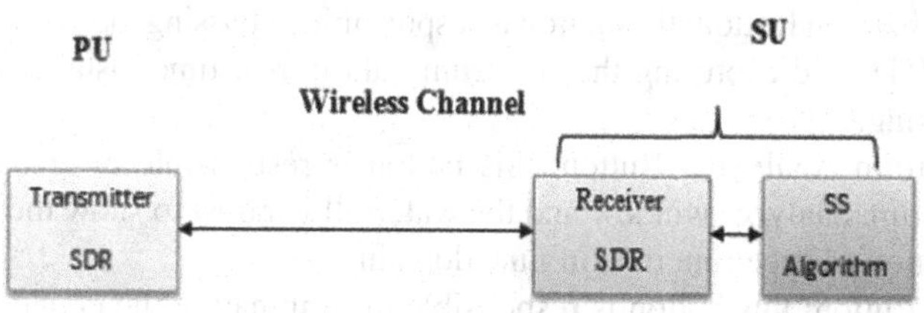

Fig. 4. Framework layout

carried out using MATLAB GUI that performs SS profile at SU side which is explained in the next section. Figure 5 shows the detailed framework block diagram.

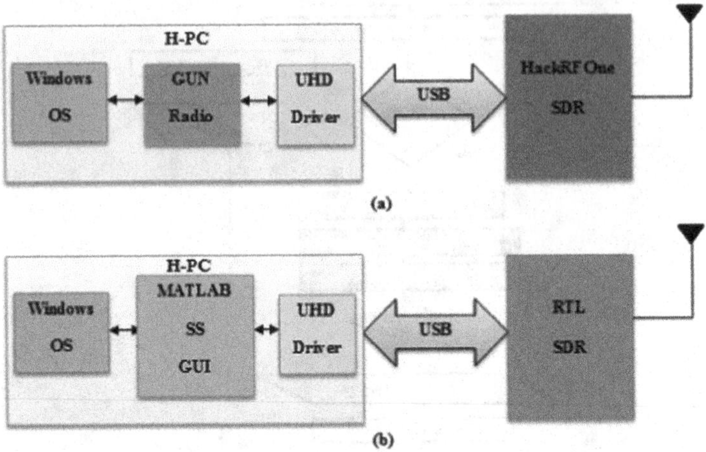

Fig. 5. The detailed framework design (a): The PU side (b): The SU side

4.1 The Proposed Spectrum Sensing Profile

This section presents the proposed SU profile that performs the SS process in real time fashion using SDR. This profile is designed using MATLAB GUN tools. This front-end supports two panels. The first panel is designed for managing RTL SDR initialization and configuration. In addition, this panel is supported with spectrum analysis tool to show the spectrum in forms of PSD and waterfall. The second panel gives the user the ability to manage SS processing. Hence, this panel contains a collection of SS algorithms which is selected based on user demand to perform the SS mechanism. Figure 6 depicts the designed GUI. From this figure, it can be seen, that each panel has settings which can be chosen according to the required function. The description of these settings can be defined as follows:

A. A.RTL Panel: this panel handles the initialization and the control of RTL SDR device. It captures the spectrum data and pass them to SS side. The accessories of this panel are:

   i. Initialization Button: this button is responsible of passing the setting parameters into RTL and capturing the spectrum data in real time fashion with periodic updating.
   ii. Spectrum Analyzing Button: this button is responsible of creating a digital spectrum analyzer window and the waterfall window to show the PSD and the variation of spectrum data in time domain.
   iii. Stop Button: this button is responsible of terminating the created RTL object and clear all the pushed parameters.

iv. Initialization Parameters Window: this window consists of many radio and text boxes to capture the user data that is related to the preferred Center Frequency (CF) and the required number of captured samples (Ns).

B. Spectrum Sensing Panel: this panel handles the SS process to find PU in the received spectrum that is supported from RTL side, the accessories of this panel are:

i. SS algorithms List box: this list contains the candidate SS algorithms that can be selected in SS testing. This profile supports four SS algorithms. Each algorithm is selected from each class of the proposed SS algorithm in the previous chapters.
ii. Enter PFA textbox: this box is designed to capture the target value of false alarm probability. This value is then used to compute the threshold value in SS process.
iii. SS Button: this button performs the SS process using the selected algorithm from the list box. This button is supported with all functions of these SS algorithms and switching among them based on user selection.

The aforementioned GUI is internally interconnected and synchronized. Thus, this enables passing of both control and spectrum data among their panels.

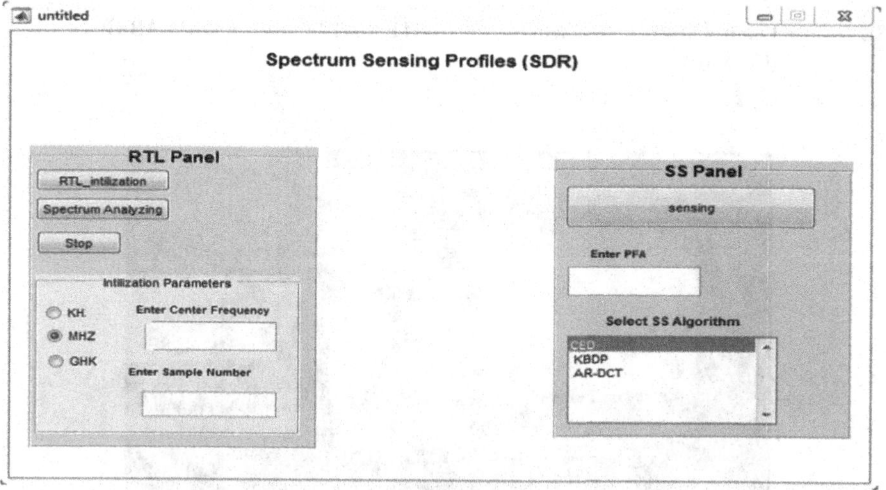

Fig. 6. GUI of the SS profile at SU side

5 The Experimental Scenarios

This scenario consists of PU who transmits OFDM signal and a single LOS SU who wish to perform the SS to detect PU status which is either present or absent. Table 1 reveals the suggested components of this scenario. This scenario is carried out in Collage of Information Engineering (COIE) building C at Electronic and Communication Lab (E & Comm. Lab). Figures 7 and 8 show the actual PU and SU sides, respectively. The distance between PU and SU is about 10 m. The PU OFDM signal is generated using the GNU radio blocks as shown in Fig. (9). These blocks are; data source of rate 1024 kbps, OFDM block which generates OFDM signal with the following specifications; length FFT samples is 2048, cyclic prefix length is 64 and mapper is 16-QAM. The remaining blocks are; constant multiplication block is used for providing constant gain, and osmocom sink block that represents the RF HackRFone transmitter configuration for adjusting the SDR transmitter parameters: Carrier Frequency (FC) = 100 MHz, RF gain = 300 dB, IF gain = 200 dB and baseband gain = 200 dB. This block injects the OFDM into SDR for air transmission. The other blocks are used for adjusting the frequency and magnitude gain sliders. Running this configuration is achieved by ticking the run icon in the tool bar of GNU radio. This acts to generate real OFDM transmission to be detected by SU at the receiver side.

Table 1. PU and SU components of experimental scenario.

	H-PC	OS	SDR Type	Software Tool
PU	Lenovo Z510 (Corei7)	Win10	HackRF One	GNU radio v3.7
SU	Lenovo Z510 (Corei5)	Win7	RTL 820T2	MATLAB GUI

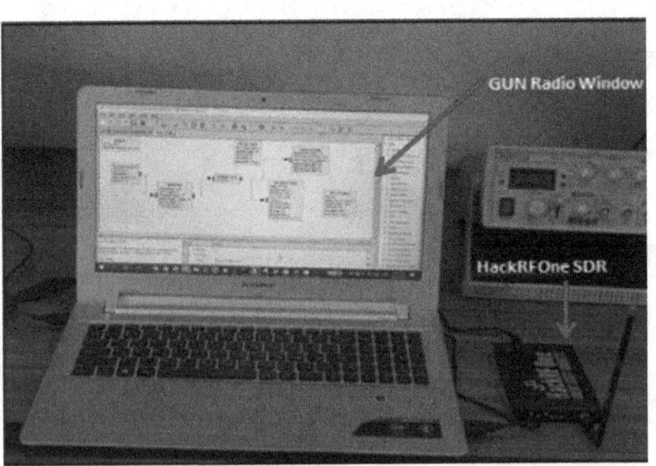

Fig. 7. PU transmitter side

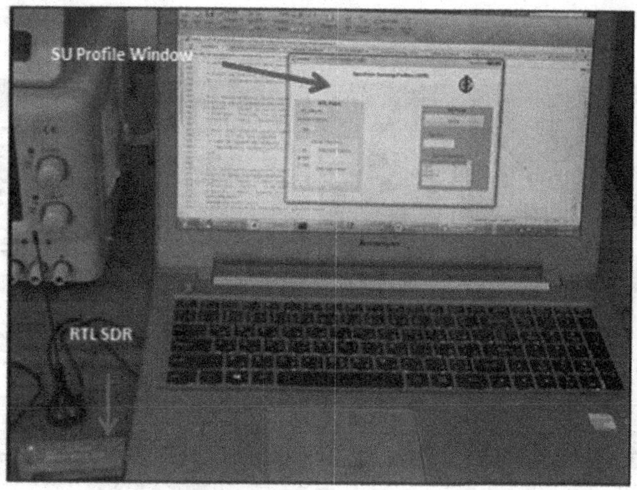

Fig. 8. SU reciever side.

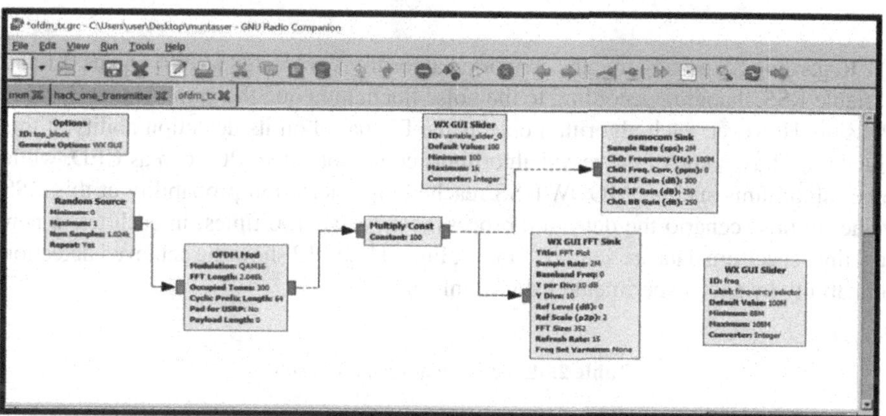

Fig. 9. GNU radio blocks for OFDM generation and transmission at PU side

6 The Experimental Results

To capture the transmitted signal, RTL at SU side is adjusted and initialized with FC = 100 MHz and Ns = 2048 using RTL initialization panel in SU profile. After that, ticking the spectrum analyzing button will show the FFT samples and spectrum waterfall as shown in Fig. 10.

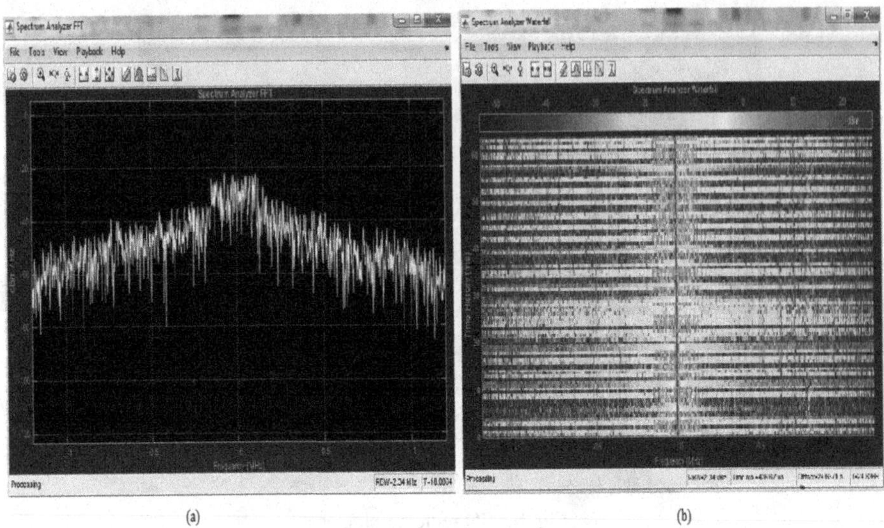

Fig. 10. Received signal vision (a): FFT spectrum (b): Waterfall

Regarding SS processing, the supported algorithms are tested at PFA equals 0.1 and variable RSS changing according to the noise fluctuation and the amplification level at PU side. However, each algorithm detects the PU based on its detection ability at this situation. Thus, some of the tested algorithms could not detect PU such as CED, while other algorithms such as MODWT SS reached high detection probability at this RSS value. In this scenario the detection process is repeated 100 times, in each test a new real time spectrum data are sensed. Table 2, Figs. 11 and 12 show the achieved detection probability by each experimented algorithm.

Table 2. Experimental scenario results

SS Algorithm	P_D/SNR(-30to-20)dB	P_D/SNR(-20to-10)dB
CED	0	0.44
KBDP	0.12	0.56
AR DCT SS	0.42	0.72

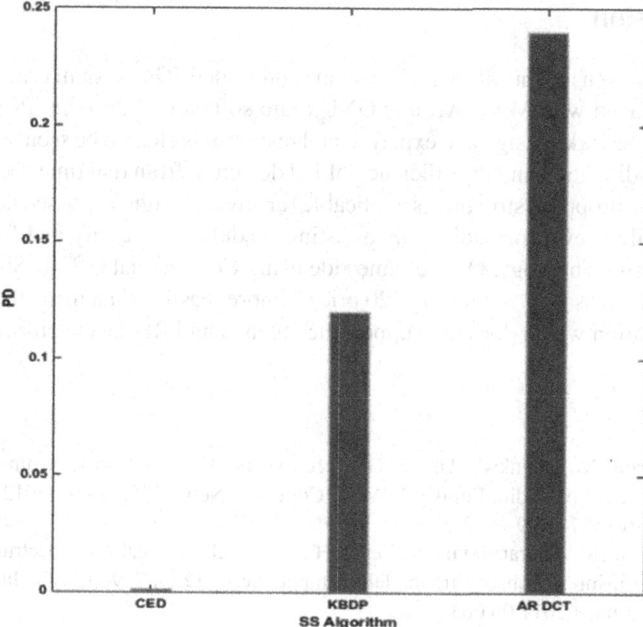

Fig. 11. Experimental results at SNR = (–30 to –20)

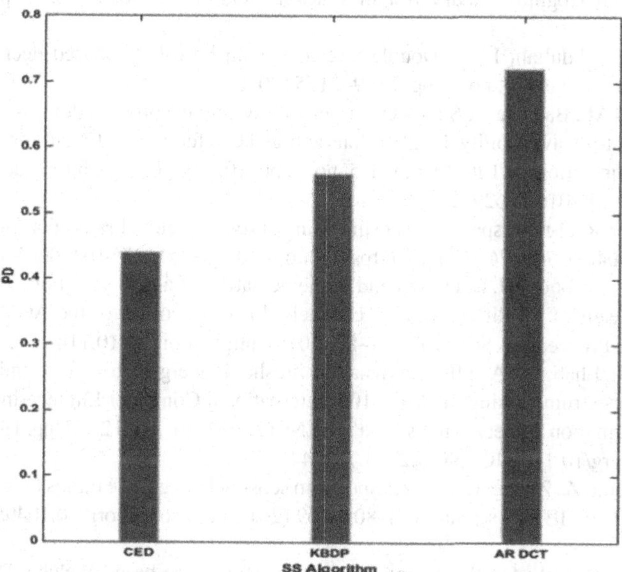

Fig. 12. Experimental results at SNR = (–20 to –10) dB

7 Conclusion

In this paper SS sensing profile for CR system is presented. This system is based on SDR devices interfaced with MALTAB and GNU radio software at different PCs. From the presented frameworks design and experimental results, it is clear to be seen the flexibility of profiles modification and the efficiency of PU detection from real time spectrum data. In addition, the proposed structure is applicable for any opportunistic based network with certain flexibility level for adding any assisting module for security and for advanced communication technology. On the same side using Commercial Off the Shelf (COTS) components such as RTL within sub $20 price is more feasible than using the float point system realization which does not support the antenna and RF data capturing.

References

1. Lu, L., Zhou, X., Onunkwo, U., Li, G.Y.: Ten years of research in spectrum sensing and sharing in cognitive radio. Eurasip J. Wirel. Commun. Netw. **2012**, 1–16 (2012). https://doi.org/10.1186/1687-1499-2012-28
2. Riahi Manesh, M., Subramaniam, S., Reyes, H., Kaabouch, N.: Real-time spectrum occupancy monitoring using a probabilistic model. Comput. Netw. **124**, 87–96 (2017). https://doi.org/10.1016/j.comnet.2017.06.003
3. Salahdine, F., El Ghazi, H., Kaabouch, N., Fihri, W.F.: Matched filter detection with dynamic threshold for cognitive radio networks. In: 2015 International Conference on Wireless Networks and Mobile Communications WINCOM 2015, no. October (2016). https://doi.org/10.1109/WINCOM.2015.7381345
4. Falih, M.S., Abdullah, H.N.: Evaluation of Different Energy Based Spectrum Sensing Approaches in Cognitive Radio System: Practical Perspective, vol. 6, no. 12, pp. 2015–2018 (2018)
5. Falih, M.S., Abdullah, H.N.: Double threshold with knowledge based decision spectrum sensing method, vol. 10, no. 1, pp. 2169–2175 (2018)
6. Llames, G.J.M., Banacia, A.S.: Spectrum sensing system in software-defined radio for determining spectrum availability. In: 2016 International Conference on Electronics, Information, and Communications ICEIC 2016, vol. 5, no. 2, pp. 100–106 (2016). https://doi.org/10.1109/ELINFOCOM.2016.7562961
7. Martian, A.: Real-time spectrum sensing using software defined radio platforms. Telecommun. Syst. **64**(4), 749–761 (2016). https://doi.org/10.1007/s11235-016-0205-z
8. Thabit, A.A., Ziboon, H.T.: Design and implementation of a new detection system based on statistical features for different noisy channels. In: Proceedings of the ACM International Conference Proceedings Series, pp. 81–88 (2019). https://doi.org/10.1145/3321289.3321294
9. Farag, H.M., Ehab, M.: An efficient dynamic thresholds energy detection technique for cognitive radio spectrum sensing. In: 2014 10th International Computer Engineering Conference: Today Information Society What's Next? ICENCO 2014, no. April 2015, pp. 139–144 (2015). https://doi.org/10.1109/ICENCO.2014.7050446
10. Song, J., Feng, Z., Zhang, P., Liu, Z.: Spectrum sensing in cognitive radios based on enhanced energy detector. IET Commun. **6**(8), 805–809 (2012). https://doi.org/10.1049/iet-com.2010.0536
11. Salman, E.H., et al.: On the energy detection performance based Welch's DCT algorithm in cognitive radio systems. In: 1st International Scientific Conference of Engineering Sciences 3rd Scientific Conference of Engineering Science ISCES 2018–Proceedings, vol. 2018-Janua, pp. 135–139 (2018). https://doi.org/10.1109/ISCES.2018.8340542

12. Toradmalle, D., Muthukuru, J., Sathyanarayana, B.: Certificateless and provably-secure digital signature scheme based on elliptic curve. Int. J. Electr. Comput. Eng. **9**(4), 3228–3231 (2019). https://doi.org/10.11591/ijece.v9i4.ppxx-xx
13. Del Barrio, A.A., et al.: HackRF + GNU Radio: a software-defined radio to teach communication theory. Int. J. Electr. Eng. Educ. (August) (2019). https://doi.org/10.1177/0020720919868144
14. Ugwuanyi, S.O., Ahaneku, M.A.: Radio frequency and channel investigation using software defined radio in MATLAB And simulink environment. Niger. J. Technol. **37**(4), 1049 (2018). https://doi.org/10.4314/njt.v37i4.26

Real World Application Fields in Information Science and Technology

Novel Approximation Booths Multipliers for Error Recovery of Data-Driven Using Machine Learning

Sudhakar Sengan[1](✉), Osamah Ibrahim Khalaf[2], Punarselvam Ettiyagounder[3], Dilip Kumar Sharma[4], and Rajakumari Karrupusamy[5]

[1] Department of Computer Science and Engineering, PSN College of Engineering and Technology, Tirunelveli 627152, Tamil Nadu, India
sudhasengan@gmail.com

[2] Al-Nariain University, Baghdad, Iraq

[3] Department of Information Technology, Muthayammal Engineering College, Rasipuram 637408, Tamil Nadu, India

[4] Department of Mathematics, Jaypee University of Engineering and Technology, Guna 473226, Madhya Pradesh, India

[5] Department of Computer Science and Engineering, School of Engineering Avinashlingam Institute for Home Science and Higher Education for Women, Coimbatore 641043, Tamil Nadu, India

Abstract. The multiplier is a primary function of the circuit that is frequently used in Digital Signal Processing. Estimated circuits were investigated for better efficiency/lower power consumption but are still troubled by errors. A modern DSP unit has an innovative approximate multiplier and a simple critical path. It uses a modern logic design less unique to neighbouring bases. Although many advanced energies save is maintained by Machine Learning approaches are erroneous, this proposed model is possible. A configurable error-correction device can deliver greater accuracy, depending on the circuit used. A configurable error-correction device can deliver greater accuracy, depending on the circuit used. When using these II-errors reducing methods, the outcomes are discussed as estimated multipliers AM1/AM2. Half of the least essential limited products for AM1/AM2 are reduced in a 16 × 16 configuration. In an 8 × 8 × AM1, error reduction takes precedence over pace, showing a 40.14% reduction in power dissipation.

Keywords: Approximate circuits · Digital signal processing · Error reduction · Machine learning

1 Introduction

The demand for energy-efficient communication devices may provide a feasible solution for estimated computations [1]. Digital media, identification, and data mining technologies are essentially error-tolerant and do not necessitate perfect computation precision. In Digital Signal Processing (DSP) systems [2], the effect is often left to human intuition

P. Liatsis et al. (Eds.): TIOTC 2021, CCIS 1548, pp. 299–309, 2022.
https://doi.org/10.1007/978-3-030-97255-4_22

to perceive. As a consequence of limited human interpretation, exact precision may not be expected, and an inexact result may suffice. Estimated circuits play a vital role in these applications as a viable method for minimizing area, power, and delay, resulting in improved energy efficiency [3]. Adders have been widely researched for estimated implementations as one of the primary devices of calculation circuits. The carry chain is generally smaller than the typical, and it is used to reduce significant bits. An error checking and regaining system has been suggested to encompass the system for a stable adder with mutable latency [4]. A carry that selects an addition-based variable-latency adder has been presented. As emerging technologies for modelling, analyzing, and evaluating estimated adders have been suggested, special techniques for modelling, analyzing, and evaluating them have been debated [5].

A multiplier typically has III-phases: limited invention-creation, Partial Product Accumulation (PPA), and finally, a Carry Propagation Adder (CPA) [6]. Estimated PPA is designed utilizing inaccurate 22 multiplier blocks in the Under-Designed Multiplier (UDM) [7, 8]. Simultaneously, appropriate adders are cast-off in an adder tree to aggregate the actual limited products; near 444, and 848-bit Wallace Tree (WT) multipliers are built using a carry-in prediction process. Then they're used in the development of AWTM. Using different estimated 4×4 and 8×8 multipliers, the AWTM can be designed into four different modes [9, 10]. For the final phase addition multiplier, estimated speculative adders have been addressed. The Error-Tolerant Multiplier split a multiplier into a simulation model for '1' and '0'.

A static grouping method is now being implemented by the Static Segment Multiplier (SSM). In *nxn* SSM, the *m* successive bits from the 2 input functions are multiplied by an *mxm* special multiplier (m-$^{n}/_{2}$). The choice of the input for the special multiplier is determined irrespective of whether the (n-m) MSBs of an input operand are all '0'. These estimated multipliers are intended for use with unsigned numbers. A Booth algorithm is widely used to implement signed multiplication [11, 12]. For fixed-width BMs, estimated models have been suggested. They have centred on Vedic Mathematics and discussion regarding Vedic multipliers. Due to its higher speed and reduced power usage, Vedic multipliers are currently being studied [13, 14]. They propose 8 and 16-bit multipliers that use fast adders to reduce the power delay product of multipliers for low-high applications. Compared with conventional multipliers, Vedic multipliers with quick adders attain massive interruption and power-delay output benefits.

Uniquely signed 16×16-bit approximate radix-8 Booth Multiplier (BM) designs are suggested. An approximately 2-bit adder collected from a 3-input XOR gate is first suggested [15, 16]. The estimated 2-bit adder's EDCC, reimbursement, and regeneration circuits are also discussed. The double-bit adder then becomes available in combination with approximately half of a typically utilized radix-8 block adder to generate a triplet without carrying over. A truncation technique used in the suggested signed approximate radix-8 BMs is referred to as ABM1/ABM2 to save even more power and time. The addition of partial items is then sped up using parallel processing by a WT. According to simulated results, the proposed approximate recoding adders (ARA8, ARA8-2C, and ARA8-2R) are more appropriate for a radix-8 BM than other approximate adders.

2 Problem Statement

A multiplier is made up of stages that involve PPA, aggregation, and final integration. WT, DADDA trees, and a CDA series are examples of PPA assemblies. An n-bit multiplier requires log_2(n) layers in a WT [17–19]. Each layer's adders run in parallel with no carry propagation, and the process repeats until only II-rows of limited products exist. As a result, the PPA stage's delay is $O(log_2(n))$. Also, the adders in a WT could be considered about 3:2 compressor, and they can be substituted with the other counters to reduce the delay even further [20]. The DADDA tree is related to the WT in form, but it requires as few adders as feasible. The carry and sum signals of the sum of the adders of one row are associated with the carrying of the mentioned row in a carry-adder array simultaneously. As a result, an n-bit multiplier's PPA delay is approximately $O(n)$, which is longer than the WT. The primary and symmetric arrangement of an array, on the other hand, necessitates a smaller space and thus reduce power dissipation. Approximation in generating PPA, PPA tree, adders' designs, and counters are used to estimate a multiplier. The current structures of estimated multipliers are briefly checked after this classification.

3 System Implementation

3.1 The Capacity to Create Sensor Data

The Under Designed Multiplier (UDM) employs a roughly 2-bit multiplier block attained by changing a single entry in its Karnaugh Map function. To save 1% bit, the accurate result "1001" and multiplying "11" and "11" is simplified to "111" in this approximation. The failure degree of the 22-bit multiplier block is (1 2) 4 = 116, considering that every $^i/_p$ bit's value is equally probable. The 22-bit multiplier could be used to create larger multipliers. While creating PPA, this multiplier creates an error, but the adder tree leftovers are correct.

3.2 Approximate Result in the PP-Tree

The Broken Array Multiplier (BAM), an inaccurate bio-inspired multiplier, is suggested. The BAM works by ignoring some CSA in an array multiplier in parallel and perpendicular orders. The MSBs have a multiplier section, and the LSBs have a non-multiplication section in the Error Tolerant Multiplier (ETM). Multiplication portion is allowed when the device of the MSBs is '0'; LSB segment prediction is used when the device of the MSBs is non-zero. A similar division scheme was also used to propose the Static Segment Multiplier (SSM). Compared to ETM, the SSM does not add any approximation to the LSBs.

Based on whether each operand's MSBs are all '0', the MSB/LSB within each operand is correctly multiplied. Since there is only a small change in accuracy and hardware cost than the ETM, this design is not included in the comparison report. The Approximate Wallace Tree Multiplier (AWTM) is built on a carry-in prediction system and a bit width-conscious approximate multiplication. An AWTM is divided into 4 sub-of-bit modules, about which the II- lowest is further sub-of-bit elements. 4 functionalities that accurately measure the AWTM prediction can be extracted from a WT, or the expected full adders can be referred to as a WT.

3.3 Using Approximate Counters

An estimated (4:2) counter is suggested for an inconsistent 4-bit WT multiplier in the Inaccurate Counter-based Multiplier. When all input signals are '1', the counter's carry and sum are computed as "10" (for "100"). Since the chance of having a PPA of '1' is 1 4, the approximate (4:2) counter's error rate is (1 4) 4 = 1 256. The inaccuracy of the 4-bit multiplier is used to create higher multipliers that provide Error Detection and Correction Circuits (EDCC). Accurate (3:2) and (4:2) compressors are enhanced in the compressor-based multiplier to accelerate the PPA point. Delay and sustainability of a compressor may increase using an improvement plug.

4 Proposed System

The suggested approximate multiplier structure is illustrated in the diagram below. The PPA is simplified in the proposed design (Fig. 1).

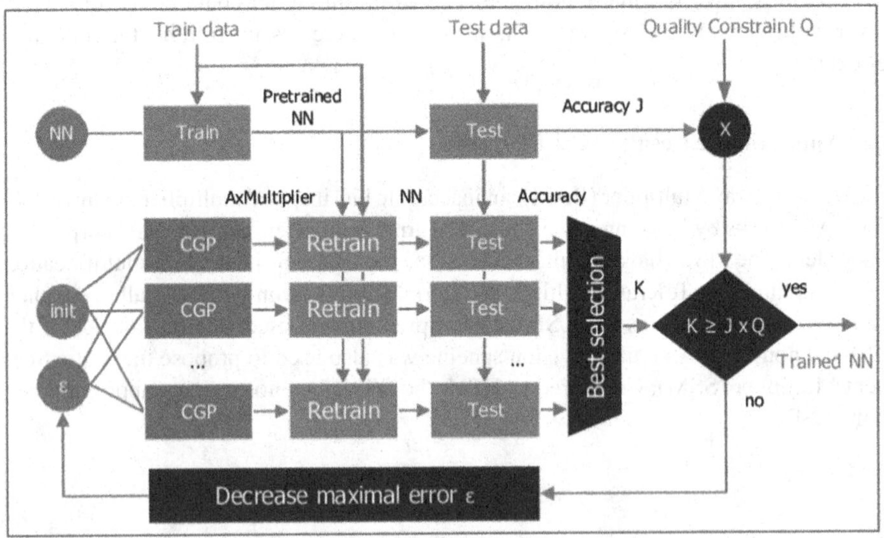

Fig. 1. Proposed system block diagram

4.1 Basic Simulation Flow

ModelSim can assist the design of this process (Fig. 2).

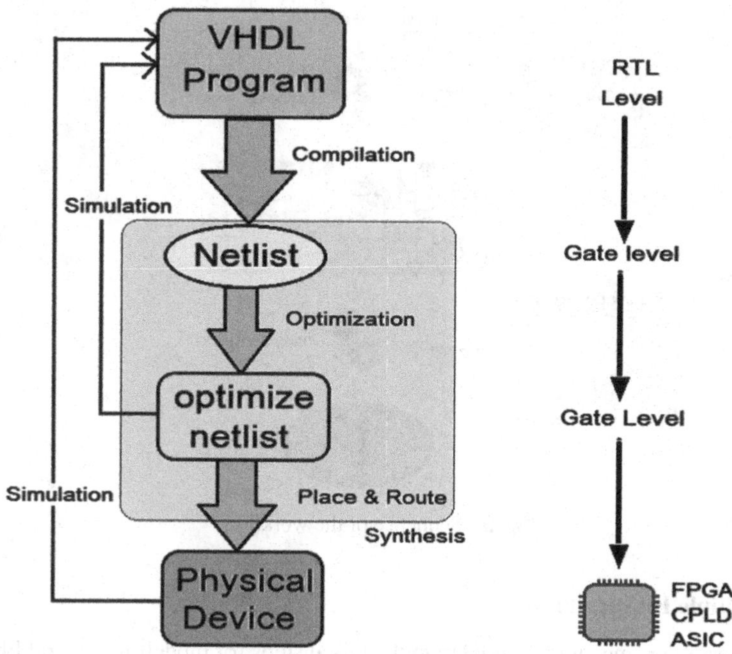

Fig. 2. Basic simulation flow

- The Working Library Formation. All models are collected in a library in ModelSim. Usually, you start a new ModelSim Simulation by creating the "work" library, which is the default language of a compiler library as a default design unit destination.
- The Compilation of Your Design. After developing the working model of your concept, you build the design units. All the ModelSim data formats are supported on all supporting platforms. Simulating your design on any platform doesn't require recompiling your design.

4.2 The Sequence of the Workflow

A paper serves as a study implementation and test environment for an HDL design even if you aren't expected to use ModelSim developments (Fig. 3).

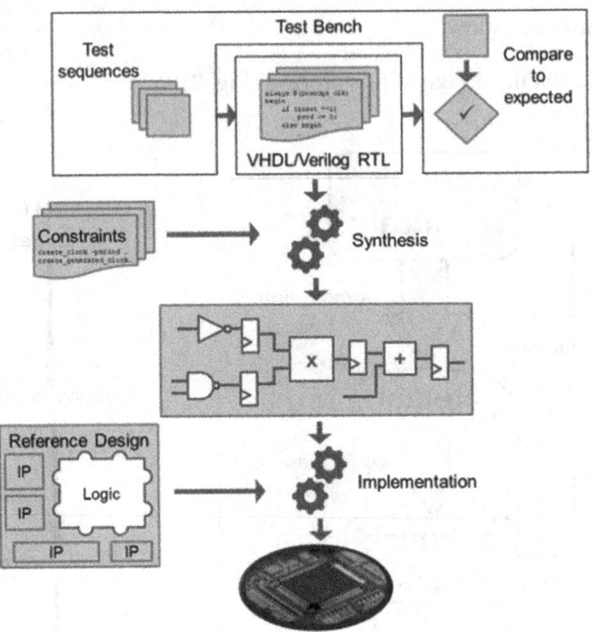

Fig. 3. Sequence of the workflow

4.3 Multiple Library Flow

This illustration is meant to demonstrate the initial steps for modelling several libraries. A design library typically serves as a static component supply for your resources. You can either build your resource libraries or receive them from a different development team or a third party. When the template is compiled, you have the appropriate resource libraries and determine which one to use in which order. For one particular example (Fig. 4), you might build your gate-level designs and test-level models in separate libraries. You may link the scheme to resource libraries within or outside the mission. To continue working on a scheme, you must follow these steps: build the plan and then attach the test bench.

4.4 Domain-Specific Platform

- The domain-specific framework is the next step of the targeted design platform hierarchy. Each domain-specific platform is published 3 to 6 months after the base platform and addresses one of the 3 major Xilinx FPGA user profiles (domains): embedded processing, DSP, or logic/connectivity. This is where the targeted design platform's true power and purpose begin to show. Domain-specific platforms add a predictable, dependable, and intelligently focused range of integrated technologies to the base platform, such as:
- Advanced concept strategies and technology
- FSD, or D-specific embedded, or IP-specific
- This hardware was designed solely for one or more particular tasks, standalone applications etc.

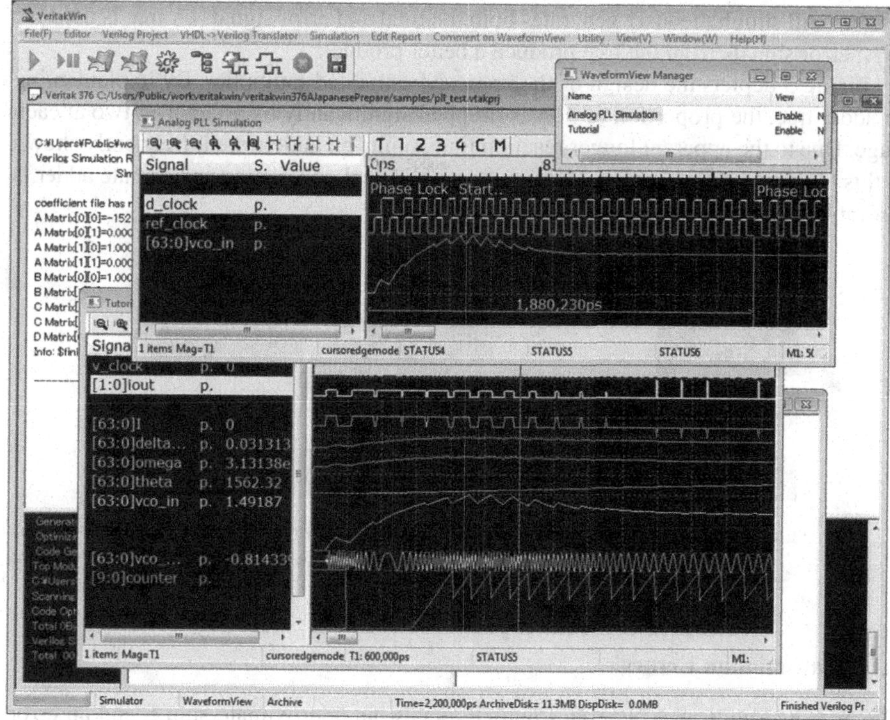

Fig. 4. Sequence of multiple library flow

- Performance designs Reference designs for embedded processing, connectivity, and DSP-performance models.
- Software and operating systems

A market-specific framework is a technology stack that allows software or hardware designers to rapidly design and deploy their applications or solutions. Market-specific systems combine both the base and domain-specific platforms and include higher-level features that can be utilized by customer-specific software/hardware designs, like Automobile, Product, Mil/Aero, Communications, and AVB ISM. The market-specific system will rely heavily on third-party focused IP instead of the base or domain-specific platforms.

5 Results and Discussions

An exciting aspect of the proposed approximate multiplier is that it is simple to use for approximate accumulation. It has been proved that significant errors can accumulate, and correcting them is difficult with currently estimated adders. It does away with this shortcoming by using the error signal but, at the same time, uses the recently developed approximation. The design approach has a communication channel with packet forwarding failures like conventional models. The estimated adder has a slightly higher error rate but still simultaneously generates both the total and error signals. A tree is used for PPA; error signals from the tree produce a better product.

Figure 5 depicts the design of the proposed estimated multiplier. By implementing an adder tree, the proportion of PPA is dropped significantly by a factor of two at each stage. Due to the apparent longer reaction time, multi-bit adders are infrequently shown in this logic tree type. Since it is easier than a classical adder, the approximate adder is desirable while implementing an adder tree.

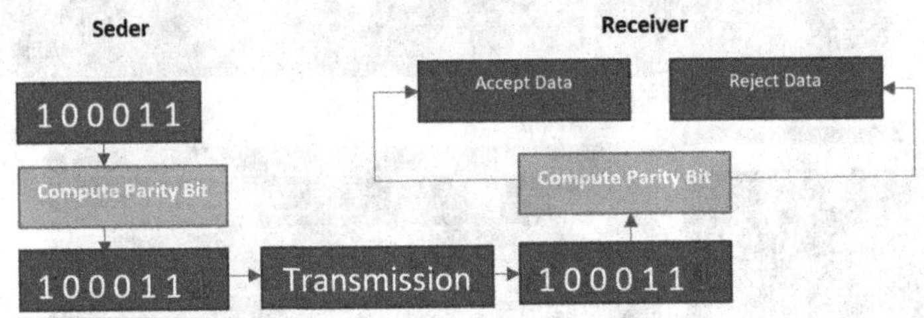

Fig. 5. An actual count with significant transmission errors

5.1 Transmission Errors

The expected multiplier generates output signals: an approximate sum S and an error E signal. Even though attempts were made to deal with the sum of each estimate's estimation methods, an error reduction circuit is used to set the maximum result rather than the adder's output. To reduce the errors, different components are selected: the first is called *"error iteration,"* and the second is termed *"error aggregation"*. Error

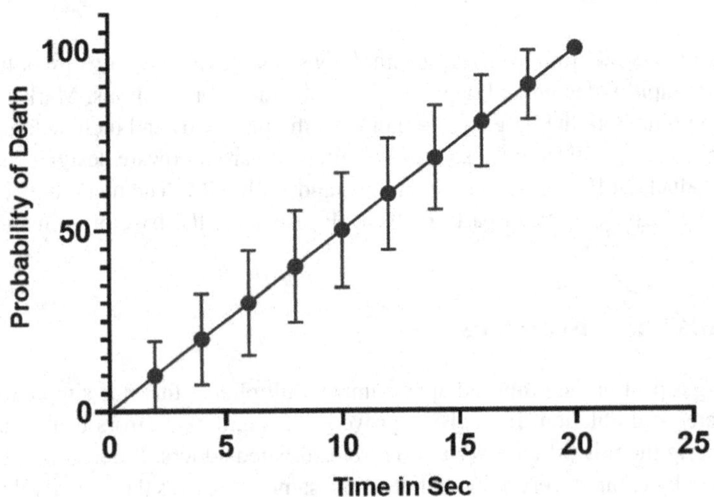

Fig. 6. Error accumulation tree for AM1

signals are managed to accumulate in the PPA tree's output port and then implemented to the total product tree. AM1 and AM2 are suggested as two approximate aggregation methods in Fig. 6 and Fig. 7; a complete and two NOR gate, quarter NOR cell, and an estimated NOR layer have been seen.

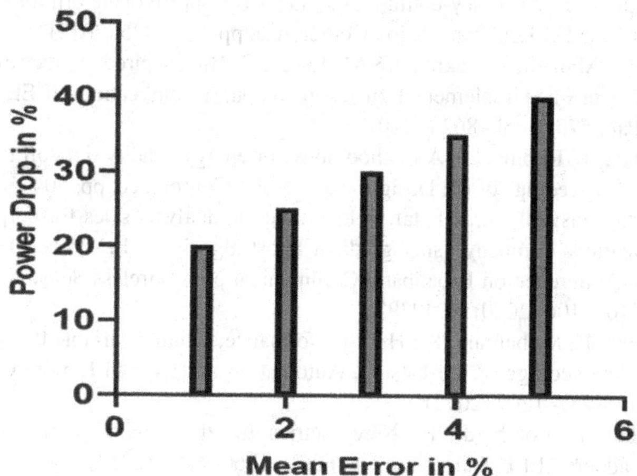

Fig. 7. Error accumulation tree for AM2

6 Conclusion and Future Work

Using a recently designed probabilistic, high-performance, and low-power PPA technique, this research achieved a high and low-power estimated product accumulation tree. As it is designed, the predicted adder creates both an approximate value and an error. 2 distinct 8-multiplier designs: AM1 and AM2, use approximate solutions. Besides, medications are focused on 16 × 16 products, significantly decreasing machine learning that works with TAM1 and TAM2 that visualize 16 × 16 PPA. The implemented approximate multipliers dissipated less power than frequency power. According to functional analysis, the suggested multipliers have relatively small error distances on a statistical basis and produce better precision. AM2 has greater precision than AM1 but a more significant delay and high-power consumption, according to simulations. With a slight degradation in NMED, Truncation-based designs significantly increase power and field. Subsequent approximate multipliers have outperformed the suggested ones, particularly concerning reliability. Delays and significant power reduction can be effectively achieved with high reliability; earlier models fail to mitigate both correctly. It has been proved that the suggested multipliers help to enhance and layer images.

Future work will focus on the synthesis of the overall network. Since the proposed accumulative and exponential precision models are not restricted to the presented application, future research will concentrate on incorporating these principles into other machine learning techniques. Further research on using packet forwarding decomposition methods to create incremental-precision models for other approximate computing models is also ongoing.

References

1. Verma, A.K., Brisk, P., Ienne, P.: Variable latency speculative addition: a new paradigm for arithmetic circuit design. In: Proceedings of the Design, Automation and Test in Europe Conference, pp. 1250–1255 (2008)
2. Kahng, A., Kang, S.: Accuracy-configurable adder for approximate arithmetic designs. In: Proceedings of the Design, Automation Conference, pp. 820–825 (2012)
3. Mahdiani, H.R., Ahmadi, A., Fakhraie, S.M., Lucas, C.: Bio-inspired imprecise computational blocks for efficient VLSI implementation of soft computing applications. IEEE Trans. Circuits Syst. I Reg. Pap. **57**(4), 850–862 (2010)
4. Huang, J., Lach, J., Robins, G.: A methodology for energy-quality tradeoff using imprecise hardware. In: Proceedings of the Design, Automation Conference, pp. 504–509 (2012)
5. Wiseas, O., Adriansyadh, A., Khalaf, O.I.: Prediction analysis sales for corporate services telecommunications company using gradient boost algorithm. In: Proceedings of the 2nd International Conference on Broadband Communications. Wireless Sensors and Powering. BCWSP, pp. 101–106 (2020). 9249397
6. Du, K., Varman, P., Mohanram, K.: High-performance, reliable variable latency carry select addition. In: Proceedings of the Design, Automation and Test in Europe Conference and Exhibition, pp. 1257–1262 (2012)
7. Liang, J., Han, J., Lombardi, F.: New metrics for the reliability of approximate and probabilistic adders. IEEE Trans. Comput. **62**(9), 1760–1771 (2012)
8. Miao, J., He, K., Gerstlauer, A., Orshansky, M.: Modeling and synthesis of quality-energy optimal approximate adders. In: Proceedings of the IEEE/ACM International Conference on Computer-Aided Design, pp. 728–735 (2012)
9. Sudhakar, Sengan., Chenthur Pandian, S.: Secure packet encryption and key exchange system in mobile ad hoc network. J. Comput. Sci. **8**(6), 908–912 (2012)
10. Sengan, S., Pandian, S.C.: Hybrid cluster-based geographical routing protocol to mitigate malicious nodes in mobile ad hoc network. Int. J. Ad Hoc Ubiquitous Comput. **21**(4), 224–236 (2016)
11. Keerthana, N., Vinod, V., Sudhakar, S.: A novel method for multi-dimensional cluster to identify the malicious users on online social networks. J. Eng. Sci. Technol. **15**(6), 4107–4122 (2020)
12. Hamad, A., AAl-Obeidi, A.S., Al-Taiy, E.H., Khalaf, O.I., Le, D.: Synchronization phenomena investigation of a new nonlinear dynamical system 4D by gardano's and lyapunov's methods. Comput. Mater. Contin. **66**(3), 3311–3327 (2021)
13. Ganesh Kumar, K., Sengan, S.: Improved network traffic by attacking denial of service to protect resource using Z-test based 4-tier geomark traceback (Z4TGT). Wirel. Pers. Commun. **114**(4), 3541–3575 (2020). https://doi.org/10.1007/s11277-020-07546-1
14. Alkhafaji, A.A.R., et al.: Payload capacity scheme for quran text watermarking based on vowels with Kashida. Comput. Mater. Contin. **67**(3), 3865–3885 (2021)
15. Al-Khanak, E.N., et al.: A heuristics-based cost model for scientific workflow scheduling in cloud. Comput. Mater. Contin. **67**(3), 3265–3282 (2021)
16. Tran, T.X., et al.: Effect of poly-alkylene-glycol quenchant on the distortion, hardness, and microstructure of 65Mn steel. Comput. Mater. Contin. **67**(3), 3249–3264 (2021)
17. Priyadarshini, A.U., Sudhakar, S.: Cluster-based certificate revocation by cluster head in mobile ad hoc network. Int. J. Appl. Eng. Res. **10**(20), 1604–16018 (2015)
18. Romero, C.A.T., Ortiz, J.H., Khalaf, O.I., Prado, A.R.: Web application commercial design for financial entities based on business intelligence. Comput. Mater. Contin. **67**(3), 3177–3188 (2021)

19. Javed Awan, M., Mohd Rahim, M.S., Nobanee, H., Yasin, A., Khalaf, O.I..: A big data approach to black Friday sales. Intell. Autom. Soft Comput. **27**(3), 785–797 (2021)
20. Zheng, X., Ping, F., Pu, Y., Montenegro-Marin, C.E., Khalaf, O.I.: Recognize and regulate the importance of workplace emotions based on organizational adaptive emotion control. Aggress. Violent Behav. **2021**, 101557 (2021)

Applying an Efficient AI Approach for the Prediction of Bearing Capacity of Shallow Foundations

Faidhalrahman Khaleel[1], Mohammed Majeed Hameed[1](✉), Deiaaldeen Khaleel[2], and Mohamed Khalid AlOmar[1]

[1] Department of Civil Engineering, Al-Maarif University College, Ramadi, Iraq
m.majeed@uoa.edu.iq

[2] Electrical Engineering Department, College of Engineering, University of Anbar, Ramadi, Iraq

Abstract. This study focused on presenting the potential of artificial intelligence (AI) modeling approach to predict the bearing capacity (Q_u) of shallow foundation. Accurate prediction of (Q_u) is very significant in geotechnical engineering and the experimental tests, costs, and efforts can be minimized if (Q_u) is accurately predicted. In this paper, extreme learning machine (ELM) and multiple linear regression (MLR) models are used along with cross-validation (CV) technique to predict the ultimate bearing capacity Q_u. The obtained results showed that CV-ELM is superior to the CV-MLR model in terms of producing high accurate estimations of Q_u. The CV-MLR produced more forecasted errors, giving a low correlation coefficient (CC) of 0.755 and a lower value of Index of Agreement (WI) of 0.819. Compared to the CV-ELM model, the prediction accuracy of the latter is higher with CC of 0.946, and WI of 0.945. The superiority of the CV-ELM model was measured in terms of MAE and RMSE during the testing phase. The obtained results showed a prediction improvement by 54.84% and 56.75%, for the MAE and RMSE, respectively, using the CV-ELM model over the standard CV-MLR model. Furthermore, uncertainty analysis was conducted and showed that the CV-MLR produced high uncertainty (about 90%). The proposed models in this study showed a robust and applicable computer aid technology for modeling the ultimate bearing capacity of the shallow foundation may contribute to the base knowledge of geotechnical engineering perspective.

Keywords: ELM · Cross-validation · Uncertainty analysis · Bearing capacity of shallow foundation

1 Introduction

A shallow foundation is a load-borne structure that directly transmits loads (from small to medium size structures) to the base soil. More specifically, A shallow foundation can be introduced as a type of foundation that has the ratio of its depth (D) to its width (B) equal to or less than four [1]. There are two basic criteria that must be fulfilled by a foundation, ultimate bearing capacity, and settlement. In general, ultimate bearing capacity can be

P. Liatsis et al. (Eds.): TIOTC 2021, CCIS 1548, pp. 310–323, 2022.
https://doi.org/10.1007/978-3-030-97255-4_23

defined as the maximum applied stress by the foundation to the soil leading to a settlement ratio (the ratio between footing settlement to the foot width) of 10% of footing width [2, 3]. Due to its importance in the design procedure of the shallow foundation, the estimation of ultimate bearing capacity has received a lot of attention from many researchers. For instance, Terzaghi (1943) [3] was the first researcher who proposed a universal theory of measuring the ultimate bearing capacity in shallow foundations. Following Terzaghi, many researchers like Hansen (1970) [4], Vesic (1973) [5], and Meyerhof (1963) [6] have proposed the so-called limit-equilibrium approach for estimating the ultimate bearing capacity. This approach offers the estimation of ultimate bearing capacity by using general soil foundation configuration and potential failure curve approximations [7]. However, the approximations underlay this approach limits the practical implementation due to the oversimplified assumptions and other restrictions which are hard to achieve. Particularly, due to the scale effect (the difference between the model of footing in the laboratory and real-life) which affects the stress distribution behavior, their findings show a large mismatch with the experimental measurements. Furthermore, taking large scaling footings is costly, timely and an experimentally challenging process [8]. Besides, the outcomes of classical numerical-based approaches in comparison to the experimental-based ones, do not always guarantee an acceptable level of accuracy [8]. Furthermore, taking into consideration the variety of soil properties and the underlying uncertainty in both laboratory and field experiments [7], the researchers were motivated to estimate the ultimate bearing capacity using different approaches. These approaches included plasticity hardening models and numerical approaches like finite difference method, finite element, soft computing, and artificial intelligence (AI) [9]. Using soft computing and AI to estimate the ultimate bearing capacity received growing attention in the last years by geotechnical engineers [10]. In what follows we will discuss some of the recent literature in the application of AI and soft computing for estimating the ultimate bearing capacity.

Khorrami et al. [7] used M5' Tree model to estimate the ultimate bearing capacity in the shallow foundation on granular soil and achieved desirable results. Nazir et al. [11] used Back Propagation feed-forward Artificial Network (ANN) to predict the ultimate bearing capacity of spread foundation in cohesionless soil. According to the literature, the artificial neural network (ANN) is considered one of the most efficient techniques in solving complex engineering issues [12]. Although the ANN approach which is trained using a backpropagation algorithm has achieved interesting successes in different sectors, it faces some limitations that hinder the prediction accuracy such as getting stuck in a local minimum, generalization issues as well as low convergence. Recently, an efficient algorithm appeared to train the ANN with a single hidden layer instead of a casual one called extreme learning machine (ELM) and showed better generalization, faster, and excellent performance compared to traditional ANN [13]. Against this background, we present novel AI modeling techniques called ELM to efficiently predict the ultimate bearing capacity of shallow foundations. The ELM approach along with cross-validation (CV) is used in this study to predict the ultimate bearing capacity of shallow foundations. Furthermore, we used CV technique to ensure obtaining the general performance of the ELM model by using all datasets in both training and testing phases. The proposed model is compared with CV-MLR (cross-validation and multiple linear regression) to examine its prediction accuracy. Both proposed models (CV-ELM, and CV-MLR) were performed on geometrical and physical datasets. To the best of the authors' knowledge, this is the first time in the literature to use ELM and CV-ELM models in geotechnical engineering. The structure of the paper is presented as following, section two discusses the methodology of the used approaches, data collection, and statistical measures; the results and discussion are placed in section three. lastly, section four of this paper is dedicated for conclusion and future studies.

2 Methodology

2.1 Data Collection and Statistical Description

There are several parameters used for evaluating the ultimate bearing capacity (Q_u) of the shallow foundations on granular soils, such as the foundation geometry, angle of shearing resistance, and unit weight. These parameters play an important role in the stress distribution and failure mechanism which, in turn, are used to address the problems of bearing capacity. The foundation length (L), width (B), depth (D) represent the foundation geometry in which D has the biggest effect on the ultimate bearing capacity [7]. The other important parameters that affect the ultimate bearing capacity are the specific gravity (γ) and, most importantly, the angle of internal friction (Ø). L, B, D, γ, and Ø are the core governing criteria according to Foye et al. [14]. In this study, 169 data readings from different researchers [15], Golder et al. [16], Subrahmanyam [17, 18], Muhs et al. [19], Muhs and Weiß [20], Briaud and Gibbens [21], Muhs and Weiß [22], Briaud and Gibbens [23], Cerato and Lutenegger [24], Akbas and Kulhawy [25], and Gandhi [26] are collected to be used for training and testing the performance of two machine learning models in order to estimate the bearing capacity. Table 1 shows the statistical description of each variable.

Table 1. Statistical description of all parameter used in this study

Dataset/Statistics	B (m)	L/B	D (m)	Ø (degree)	γ_{dry} (kN/m^3)	Q_u (kN/m^2)
U_{mean}	0.532	2.217	0.119	39.208	15.637	481.527
U_{min}	0.030	1.000	0.000	31.950	31.950	14.000
U_{max}	3.016	6.000	0.890	45.700	45.700	2847.000
U_{std}	0.564	1.919	0.208	3.439	3.439	472.378
U_{skew}	2.507	1.223	2.160	−0.338	−0.338	2.066
Correlation	0.477	−0.224	0.571	0.206	0.206	1.000

2.2 Multiple Linear Regression

Multiple regression analysis is a general system for analyzing the relationship between a set of independent variables to a single dependent variable or set of dependent variables.

The independent variables can be quantitative measures or categorical measures. The basic concept of multiple regression can be expanded to include other forms of dependent variables, such as categories or counts [27]. Among the various forms of regression analysis, the linear regression approach is commonly used by scientists to demonstrate the linear relationship between variables as shown in the following equation:

$$\acute{Y} = b_o + b_1x_1 + b_2x_2 + \ldots + b_ix_i + E \tag{1}$$

Where $\acute{Y}$ is the predicted value, b_o is the regression intercept, $b_1, b_2, \ldots, b_i$ are the regression weights (regression coefficients), $x_1, x_2, \ldots, x_i$ are the independent variables, and E is the error of the regression. The squared multiple correlation (R^2) is used to illustrate the fitness of the regression model.

2.3 Cross-Validation Technique

Cross-validation was originally used to test the authenticity of the predictive models and also used as an effective tool for estimating the hyperparameters for AI models [28]. Moreover, cross-validations are generally used to compare the vast number of fit models and to avoid overfitting. The two goals behind using cross-validation can be defined as follows [29]. First, to predict the efficiency of the trained model (using available data) by using an algorithm, i.e., to examine the algorithm's generalizability. Second, to evaluate the output of various algorithms on the data and find the best algorithm that fits the data. To achieve these two goals, there are various forms of cross-validation have been proposed, such as Leave one out cross-validation, Re-substitution validation, repeated K-fold cross-validation, Hold out validation, K fold cross-validation, etc. In Leave one out cross-validation, the number of K-folds is proportional to the number of available data instances, therefore it has high variance [29]. In Re-substitution validation, the training and testing phases in the model are carried out on all the available data therefore it suffers from over-fitting. Unlike the Re-substitution validation approach, in Hold out validation, the data is divided into two parts, training, and testing. K-fold cross-validation is a method of arbitrarily splitting the original samples into K subsamples. A single subsample is then assumed to be a validation data in order to test and train the model, where the remaining K − 1 subsamples are used as training data [30]. This process is replicated K times and each subsample is used as a validation data exactly once, then K outputs from folds can be averaged to provide a single estimate. It is important to remember that data is normally stratified (rearrangement of data to ensure that any fold is a fair representation of the whole data) before dividing it into the K segments.

2.4 Extreme Learning Machine

Extreme Learning Machine (ELM) is proposed by Huang et al. [31] and it has a simple structure of three layers known as the input layer, the output layer, and the hidden layer. The hidden layer is considered as the most important layer in the ELM system, with a variety of nonlinear hidden nodes. The ELM is considered as an improved variant of the conventional ANN due to its potential to solve regression problems taking into consideration the time consumption [32]. ELM is often presented as an effective and alternative tool for traditional modeling techniques such as ANN which has many drawbacks, such as overfitting, sluggish convergence, local minimum problems, poor generalization and longer learning time, and the necessity for iterative tuning its parameter [13].

The ELM model can be expressed mathematically as:

$$R_t = \sum_{r=1}^{i} B_r g_r(\alpha_r \cdot x_r + \beta_r),\quad r = 1, 2, \ldots, n, \tag{2}$$

Where R_t is the ELM target, i is the number of the hidden nodes, B_r is the weight value linking the rth hidden node with the output node, $g_r(\alpha_r \cdot x_r + \beta_r)$ is the function of hidden output, and (α_r, β_r) are the hidden node parameters that are initialized randomly.

The n equation above can be written in a compact form as

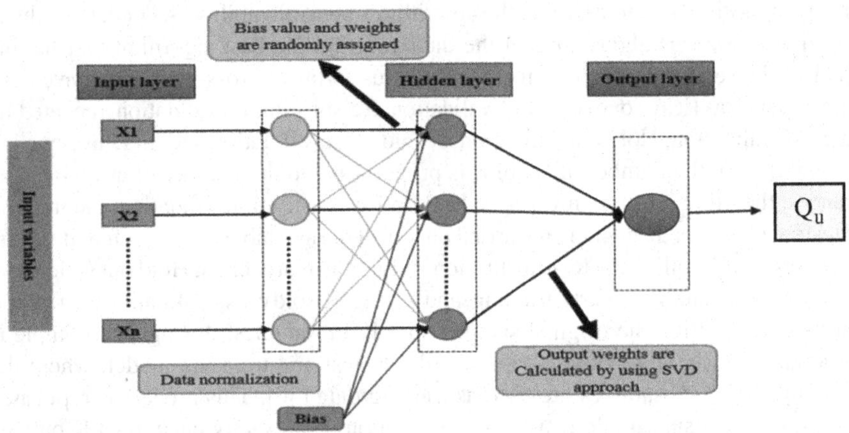

Fig. 1. Structure of ELM, including three layers (hidden layer, middle layer and output layer).

$$SB = T \tag{3}$$

Where **S** is defined as the neural network's hidden layer output matrix,

$$\mathbf{S}(\alpha_1, \ldots, \alpha_I,\ \beta_1, \ldots, \beta_I,\ x_1, \ldots, x_i) = \begin{bmatrix} g_r(\alpha_1 \cdot x_1 + \beta_1) \ldots g_i(\alpha_i \cdot x_1 + \beta_i) \\ \vdots \qquad\qquad \vdots \\ g_r(\alpha_i \cdot x_i + \beta_1) \ldots g_i(\alpha_i \cdot x_1 + \beta_i) \end{bmatrix}_{N \times i} \tag{4}$$

$$B = \begin{bmatrix} B_1^T \\ \vdots \\ B_i^T \end{bmatrix} \tag{5}$$

$$T = \begin{bmatrix} t_1^T \\ \vdots \\ t_i^T \end{bmatrix} \tag{6}$$

Where $(\cdot)^T$ is the transpose operator. Figure 1 shows the structure of ELM.

2.5 Model Development

In this study, two models have been developed to estimate the ultimate bearing capacity of shallow foundations. The cross-validation method was combined with the ELM and MLR techniques to establish new two models namely; CV-ELM, and CV-MLR. The main advantage of using the CV approach is to allow all the datasets to be used for training and testing the proposed models, that is, without splitting them. Thus, the general performance of each model is computed based on several statistical matrices to select the best model. In this study, K-fold cross-validation is used instead of the Leave one out one, because it is more efficient and requires less computational cost. As mentioned before, the collected data set includes 169 samples, therefore, the dataset was divided into 13 folds as shown in Fig. 2. Accordingly, each model (CV-ELM and CV-MLR) was trained and tested 13 times and then the general performance of each run was computed. Considering the ELM method, the hidden nodes in the hidden layer are computed using the trial-and-error method, where there is no explicit method to accurately calculate the hidden nodes' number [33]. Furthermore, during the development of the learning process of ELM, a strict method was used to enhance the efficiency of ELM performance depending on two loops. The internal loop was employed to eliminate the outliers of the performance of ELM throughout the training set via changing the weights and bias in the hidden layer. The external loop is applied to change the structure of the network in the case of huge variance between the training performance and the testing one. It is worth noting that if the performance of ELM was below the desirable level after carrying out both loops, the algorithm has the authority to use both loops (internal and external loops) simultaneously. Before training ELM, the dataset was normalized to follow the range from 0 to 1 as shown in Eq. 7. The normalization step is very important to speed up the learning process of ELM and to prevent impugnation as well as sweep effects of candidate variable ranges in the proposed model.

$$X_n = \frac{X_i - \alpha}{\beta - \alpha} \tag{7}$$

Where α, β are the minimum and maximum values in the trained dataset, and X_n is the normalized value of X at the ith iteration. Lastly, we used the log-sigmoid transfer function in the hidden layer of ELM while the output weight values are computed using the singular value decomposition approach.

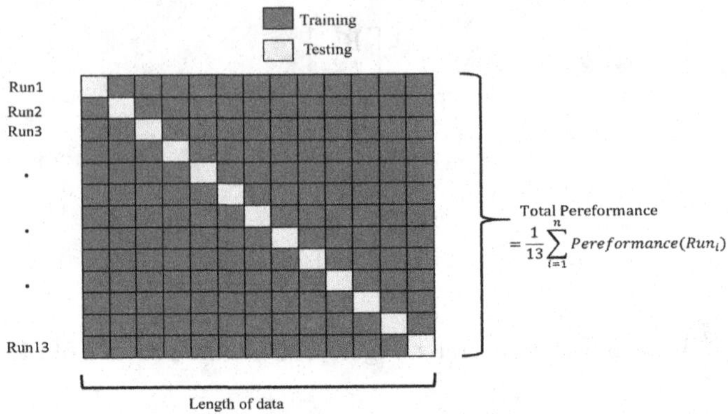

Fig. 2. K-fold cross-validation of 13 folds used as a powerful technique to examine the general performance for both ELM and MLR models.

2.6 Statistical Matrices

In order to examine the prediction performance of bearing capacity, the proposed models were tested with four statistical matrices. The statistical parameters are the correlation coefficient (r), root mean square error (RMSE), mean absolute error (MAE), and Index of Agreement or Willmott coefficient (WI). The mathematical expressions of these parameters are given as follows [13, 34–36]:

$$\mathrm{RMSE} = \sqrt{\frac{1}{N}\sum\nolimits_{i=1}^{N}\left(Q_{u_{obs_i}} - Q_{u_{pred_i}}\right)^2} \tag{8}$$

$$r = \frac{\sum_{t=1}^{n}\left[\left(Q_{u_{obs_i}} - \overline{Q_{u_{obs}}}\right)\left(Q_{u_{pred_i}} - \overline{Q_{u_{pred}}}\right)\right]}{\sqrt{\sum_{t=1}^{n}\left(CS_{obs_i} - \overline{Q_{u_{obs}}}\right)^2\sum_{i=1}^{n}\left(CS_{pred_i} - \overline{CS_{pred}}\right)^2}} \tag{9}$$

$$\mathrm{MAE} = \frac{1}{n}\sum\nolimits_{t=1}^{n}\left|Q_{u_{obs_i}} - Q_{u_{pred_i}}\right| \tag{10}$$

$$\mathrm{WI} = 1 - \frac{\sum_{i=1}^{n}\left(CS_{obs_i} - CS_{pred_i}\right)^2}{\sum_{i=1}^{n}\left(\left|Q_{u_{pred_i}} - \overline{Q_{u_{obs}}}\right| + \left|Q_{u_{obs_i}} - \overline{Q_{u_{obs}}}\right|\right)^2} \tag{11}$$

Where, $Q_{u_{obs_i}} - \overline{Q_{u_{obs}}}$ are the actual value of ultimate bearing capacity at i^{th} sample, and mean of observed ultimate bearing capacity, respectively. While $Q_{u_{pred_i}} - \overline{Q_{u_{pred}}}$ are referring to the predicted value of ultimate bearing capacity at i^{th} sample and mean of predicted ultimate bearing capacity, respectively.

3 Result and Discussion

This part of this current study presents the performance of CV-ELM and MLR-CV models in the prediction of ultimate bearing capacity (Q_u) of the shallow foundations. It is important to mention that the dataset includes 169 samples collected from open sources in the literature. Then, shuffling data-process are conducted to increase the quality of data which used for training and testing the models. Figure 3 shows the main process of conducting CV-ELM and MLR-CV models in this study.

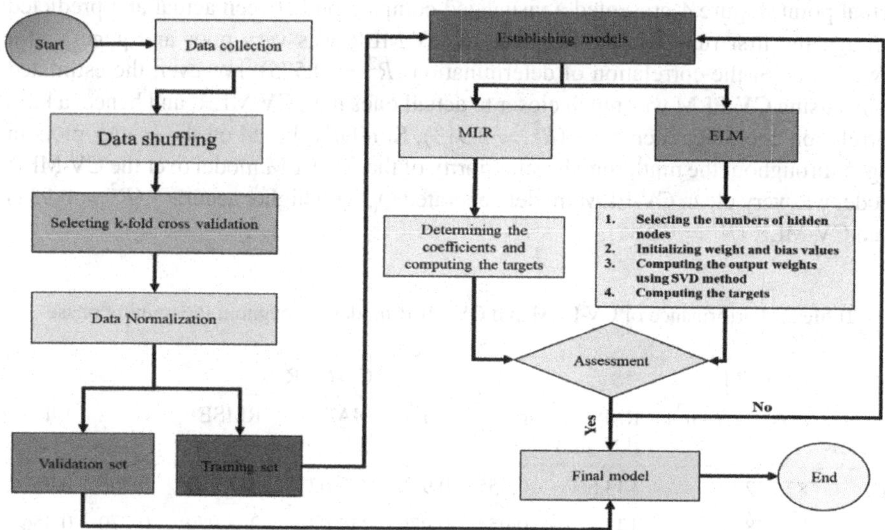

Fig. 3. Flowchart shows main processes of developing the proposed models.

The performance of CV-ELM and CV-MLR models in the training phase is illustrated in Table 2. The results showed that the CV-ELM model can predict the Q_u more precisely than CV-MLR in all cases with MAE of 72.192, RMSE of 130.852, r of 0.960, and WI of 0.979. However, the performance of CV-MLR is noticed to estimate Q_u with higher forecasting error (MAE = 219.402, RMSE = 302.535, r = 0.766, and WI = 0.852). Although CV-ELM was superior to the CV-MLR model, the training set does not reflect the reliability of the model without using the testing dataset. Besides, the calibration process of the models is carried out over the training set and, hence, the models may overfit the dataset. Therefore, the assessment of CV-ELM and CV-MLR through a testing set, where unseen data are introduced to both models, is crucial.

Table 3 summarizes the performances of each adopted model during the testing phase. The obtained results show that ELM approach still outperforms the MLR approach over all the 13 folds. Furthermore, the CV-ELM model predicts Q_u with higher accuracy than CV-MLR where there is high correlation obtained between actual and predicted values (r = 0.946, and WI = 0.945) and fewer forecasted error (MAE = 103.167, and RMSE = 160.552). The capacity of CV-MLR was however, noticed undesirable, generating higher estimated errors (MAE = 228.458 RMSE = 306.177, r = 0.755, and WI = 0.819). The superiority of the CV-ELM model is measured based on its ability to reduce the MAE and RMSE during the testing phase, where the obtained results show a prediction improvement by 54.84% and 56.75%, respectively, using the CV-ELM model over the standard CV-MLR model. Based on these results, it can be, interestingly, noted that there is a high consistency in the performance of CV-ELM during training and testing phases. For visualized assessment, two scatter plots were created for visually comparing the performance of each model during the first and ninth run. The choice of these runs due to the fact that, in these runs both models gives higher predictions. Scatter plots are very important in noticing how does each predicted point moves away from the actual point. Figure 4 presented a visualized comparison between actual and predicted through the first run. The performance of CV-MLR was very poor and generated a lower value of the correlation of determination ($R^2 = 0.585$). however, the estimated points using CV-ELM was much closer to actual ones than CV-MLR, and hence, a high correlation coefficient achieved ($R^2 = 0.913$). Similarly, based on the scatter plots in Fig. 5 throughout the ninth run, the superiority of the CV-ELM model over the CV-MLR model was very clear. CV-ELM model generated Q_u with higher accuracy ($R^2 = 0.932$) than CV-MLR ($R^2 = 0.585$).

Table 2. Performance of CV-ELM and CV-MLR models throughout the training phase

Run	CV-ELM				CV-MLR			
	MAE (kN/m^2)	RMSE (kN/m^2)	r	WI	MAE (kN/m^2)	RMSE (kN/m^2)	r	WI
1	87.332	143.660	0.955	0.976	227.021	311.785	0.765	0.852
2	82.858	141.128	0.954	0.976	214.096	298.989	0.770	0.856
3	56.369	121.140	0.968	0.984	227.005	310.818	0.766	0.852
4	61.675	119.878	0.961	0.980	202.577	278.864	0.764	0.850
5	96.475	160.472	0.940	0.968	218.532	302.376	0.767	0.853
6	93.748	148.161	0.947	0.972	217.563	303.656	0.753	0.842
7	80.804	138.749	0.957	0.978	220.445	304.715	0.771	0.857
8	51.473	97.238	0.979	0.989	221.914	302.447	0.771	0.856
9	65.349	127.215	0.964	0.982	227.364	310.121	0.764	0.851
10	81.653	139.386	0.953	0.976	213.825	298.361	0.762	0.849
11	43.021	106.019	0.975	0.987	219.259	302.341	0.769	0.854
12	69.522	130.218	0.961	0.980	219.574	300.611	0.772	0.857
13	68.218	127.813	0.963	0.981	223.056	307.867	0.764	0.851
Mean	**72.192**	**130.852**	**0.960**	**0.979**	**219.402**	**302.535**	**0.766**	**0.852**

It is important to validate the best model obtained from this study against several prediction models performed in the previous study. As it is clearly observed that the ninth run produced more accurate prediction of ultimate bearing capacity. Therefore, the CV-ELM is selected as a benchmark model and compared with efficient models conducted in previous studies. The models used in the comparison are support vector machine (SVM), Genetic Programming (GP), and M5 mode. Table 4 exhibits the performance accuracy of each model. It is clear that the proposed model of this study (CV-ELM) gives a less value of RMSE compared to predictions of the other models.

Table 3. Performance of CV-ELM and CV-MLR models throughout the testing phase

Run	CV- ELM				CV- MLR			
	MAE (kN/m^2)	RMSE (kN/m^2)	r	WI	MAE (kN/m^2)	RMSE (kN/m^2)	r	WI
1	56.362	66.368	0.965	0.982	150.918	172.626	0.756	0.865
2	115.702	164.163	0.955	0.966	290.600	361.815	0.719	0.833
3	75.974	101.489	0.948	0.954	154.692	193.717	0.659	0.772
4	137.939	217.571	0.976	0.975	334.929	534.201	0.777	0.759
5	115.031	174.718	0.980	0.950	237.206	317.166	0.766	0.796
6	165.048	225.751	0.954	0.965	212.353	307.077	0.949	0.868
7	80.371	119.643	0.957	0.975	260.562	292.947	0.639	0.773
8	143.152	289.299	0.749	0.775	200.124	314.812	0.688	0.705
9	38.499	53.356	0.985	0.988	171.491	207.999	0.739	0.831
10	101.854	153.594	0.993	0.985	264.281	362.397	0.780	0.869
11	136.954	281.482	0.923	0.821	225.958	317.194	0.710	0.798
12	93.412	135.967	0.952	0.975	255.182	347.495	0.809	0.873
13	80.874	103.774	0.962	0.980	211.653	250.851	0.820	0.897
Mean	**103.167**	**160.552**	**0.946**	**0.945**	**228.458**	**306.177**	**0.755**	**0.819**

3.1 Uncertainty Analysis

In order to examine the reliability of the CV-ELM and CV-MLR models in the prediction of Q_u, uncertainty analysis has been carried out. In a predictive model, the main sources of uncertainty lie in the uncertainty of model inputs are model structure, weights, and biases. The uncertainty in the model inputs is the most essential source for the model uncertainty. Since the data sets used in this study are collected from different sources, their data introduces a level of uncertainty in the model inputs. Consequently, the average uncertainty in the prediction can be determined by using the equation below:

$$A_U = \frac{1}{N}\sum\nolimits_{i=1}^{N}\left(\frac{|Q_{ua} - Q_{up}|}{Q_{ua}}\right) * 100 \tag{12}$$

Where A_U is the average uncertainty percentage, N is the number of data points, Q_{ua} is the observed data points, and Q_{up} is the predicted data points.

Average uncertainty was calculated through the first and ninth runs wherein these runs the performance of each suggested model gives higher prediction accuracy. Figure 6

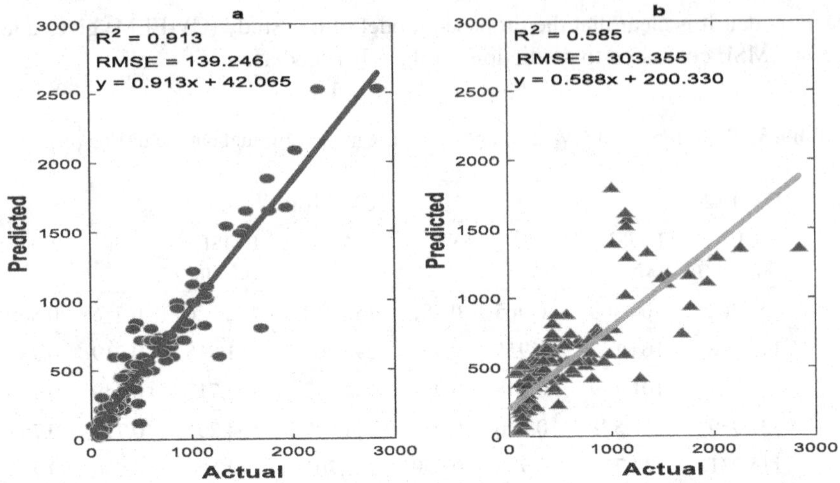

Fig. 4. A comparison between actual and predicted values of ultimate bearing capacity: first run. (a) ELM model, (b) MLR model.

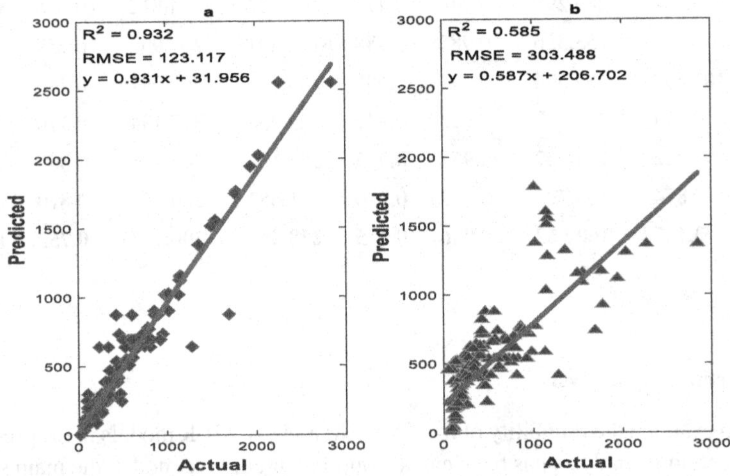

Fig. 5. A comparison between actual and predicted values of ultimate bearing capacity: ninth run. (a) ELM model, (b) MLR model.

Table 4. Validating the proposed model (CV-ELM) against several models conducted in the literature.

Source	Model	RMSE (kN/m^2)	MAE (kN/m^2)
Shahnazari et al. [37]	GP	114.8	76.5
Kordjazi et al. [38]	SVM	315.86	-
Khorrami et al. [7]	M5	130.14	86.08
Proposed	CV-ELM	53.356	38.499

presents the uncertainty analysis for both models during the two runs. Based on this figure, the uncertainty in the input variables has a significant effect on the outputs of the MLR model, and hence, large prediction errors produced ($A_U \approx 90\%$). However, the ELM is found to be less affected by the input uncertainties where the A_U is in the range of 20% to 28%. Thus, the ELM is more reliable than the MLR approach in estimating the ultimate bearing capacity of the shallow foundations.

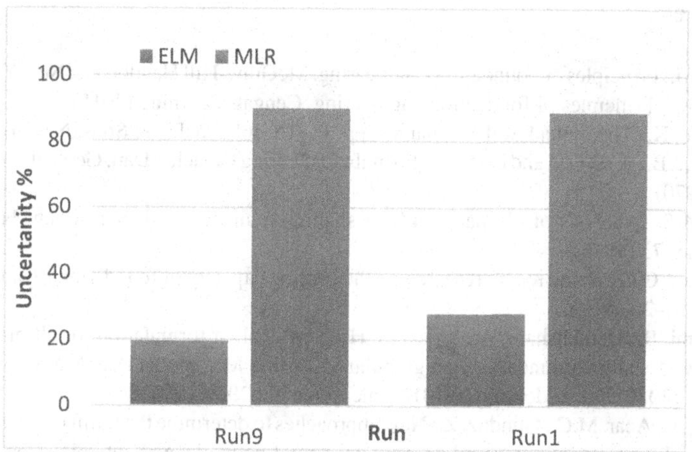

Fig. 6. Uncertainty analysis showing that the ELM model has less magnitude of uncertainty.

4 Conclusion and Future Work

Two different modeling approaches have been developed to predict the bearing capacity of shallow foundations called CV-ELM and CV-MLR. K-fold cross-validation is used with both MLR and ELM models to ensure all samples are used in the training and testing phases to obtain more reliable predictions. Furthermore, robust assessments were carried out to select the best predictive model. The obtained results revealed that the CV-ELM model has much better prediction accuracy compared to the CV-MLR model. In addition, the CV-MLR model could not capture the nonlinear relationship between the inputs and their correspondents. On the other hand, the CV-ELM model is equipped with a nonlinear activation function that enables it to capture the complex relation, and thus, enhances the accuracy of the obtained results. Since the datasets are collected from different sources and may contain different levels of uncertainty, the uncertainty analysis is carried out in this study to obtain more reliable assessments. Our findings clearly show that the CV-MLR has an inferior performance compared to the CV-ELM model, where the former produces a high level of uncertainty (about 90%). Accordingly, this study recommends the use of the ELM model as a promising machine learning-based approach to solve the geotechnical problems associated with the prediction of the bearing capacity. Finally, for future studies, the use of the feature selection tools to generate the training set for the ELM model looks a worth of investigating research direction, where the generated training set will have the most relevant and informative inputs only.

Acknowledgment. The authors would like to thank AL-Maarif University College for supporting this research.

References

1. Das, B.M.: Principles of Foundation Engineering. McGraw-Hill Handbooks, New York (2002)
2. Das, B.M.: Principles of foundation engineering. Cengage learning (2015)
3. Terzaghi, K.: Theoretical Soil Mechanics, pp. 11–15. John Wiley & Sons, New York (1943)
4. Hansen, J.B.: A revised and extended formula for bearing capacity. Dan. Geotech. Inst. Bullet. (28) (1970)
5. Vesić, A.S.: Analysis of ultimate loads of shallow foundations. J. Soil Mech. Found. Div. **99**(1), 45–73 (1973)
6. Meyerhof, G.G.: Some recent research on the bearing capacity of foundations. Can. Geotech. J. **1**(1), 16–26 (1963)
7. Khorrami, R., Derakhshani, A., Moayedi, H.: New explicit formulation for ultimate bearing capacity of shallow foundations on granular soil using M5' model tree. Meas. J. Int. Meas. Confed. (2020).https://doi.org/10.1016/j.measurement.2020.108032
8. Kalinli, A., Acar, M.C., Gündüz, Z.: New approaches to determine the ultimate bearing capacity of shallow foundations based on artificial neural networks and ant colony optimization. Eng. Geol. (2011).https://doi.org/10.1016/j.enggeo.2010.10.002
9. Derakhshani, A.: Estimating uplift capacity of suction caissons in soft clay: a hybrid computational approach based on model tree and GP. Ocean Eng. (2017). https://doi.org/10.1016/j.oceaneng.2017.09.025
10. Harandizadeh, H., Jahed Armaghani, D., Khari, M.: A new development of ANFIS–GMDH optimized by PSO to predict pile bearing capacity based on experimental datasets. Eng. Comput. **37**(1), 685–700 (2019). https://doi.org/10.1007/s00366-019-00849-3
11. Nazir, R., Momeni, E., Marsono, K., Maizir, H.: An artificial neural network approach for prediction of bearing capacity of spread foundations in sand. J. Teknol. **72**(3) (2015)
12. AlOmar, M.K., Hameed, M.M., AlSaadi, M.A.: Multi hours ahead prediction of surface ozone gas concentration: robust artificial intelligence approach. Atmos. Pollut. Res. (2020). https://doi.org/10.1016/j.apr.2020.06.024
13. AlOmar, M.K., Hameed, M.M., Al-Ansari, N., AlSaadi, M.A.: Data-driven model for the prediction of total dissolved gas: robust artificial intelligence approach. Adv. Civ. Eng. **2020** (2020)
14. Foye, K.C., Salgado, R., Scott, B.: Assessment of Variable Uncertainties for Reliability-Based Design of Foundations. J. Geotech. Geoenviron. Eng. (2006). https://doi.org/10.1061/(asce)1090-0241(2006)132:9(1197)
15. Eastwood, W.: A comparison of the bearing power of footings on dry and inundated sand. Struct. Eng. **29**(1), 1–11 (1951)
16. Golder, H.Q., Fellenius, W., Kogler, F., Meischeider, H., Krey, H., Prandtl, L.: The ultimate bearing pressure of rectangular footings. J. Inst. Civ. Eng. **17**(2), 161–174 (1941)
17. Subrahmanyam, G.: The effect of roughness of footings on bearing capacity (1967)
18. Weiß, K.: Der Einfluß der Fundamentform auf die Grenztragfähigkeit flachgegründeter Fundamente, Untersuchungen ausgef.... von Klaus Weiß: mit 14 Zahlentaf. Ernst (1970)

19. Muhs, H., Elmiger, R., Weiß, K.: Sohlreibung und Grenztragfähigkeit unter lotrecht und schräg belasteten Einzelfundamenten; mit 128 Bildern und 13 Zahlentafeln. Ernst (1969)
20. Muhs, H.: Ntersuchung von Grenztragfaehigkeit und Setzungsverhalten Flachgegruendeter Einzelfundamente in Ungleichfoermingen Nichtbindigen Boeden (1971)
21. Briaud, J.-L., Gibbens, R.: Behavior of five large spread footings in sand. J. Geotech. Geoenviron. Eng. **125**(9), 787–796 (1999)
22. Muhs, H.: Inclined load tests on shallow strip footings (1974)
23. Briaud, J.-L., Gibbens, R.: Large-scale load tests and data base of spread footings on sand. United States. Federal Highway Administration (1997)
24. Cerato, A.B., Lutenegger, A.J.: Scale effects of shallow foundation bearing capacity on granular material. J. Geotech. Geoenviron. Eng. **133**(10), 1192–1202 (2007)
25. Akbas, S.O., Kulhawy, F.H.: Axial compression of footings in cohesionless soils. II: Bearing capacity. J. Geotech. Geoenviron. Eng. **135**(11), 1575–1582 (2009)
26. Gandhi, G.N.: Study of bearing capacity factors developed from lab. Experiments on shallow footings on cohesionless soils. Ph. D. Thesis, Shri GS Institute of Tech and Science, Indore (MP) (2003)
27. Little, T.D.: The Oxford Handbook of Quantitative Methods, vol. 1. Oxford University Press, USA (2014)
28. Mosier, C.I.: I. problems and designs of cross-validation 1. Educ. Psychol. Meas. (1951). https://doi.org/10.1177/001316445101100101
29. Refaeilzadeh, P., Tang, L., Liu, H.: Cross-validation. Encycl. Database Syst. **5**, 532–538 (2009)
30. Hameed, M.M., AlOmar, M.K., Baniya, W.J., AlSaadi, M.A.: Incorporation of artificial neural network with principal component analysis and cross-validation technique to predict high-performance concrete compressive strength. Asian J. Civ. Eng. **22**(6), 1019–1031 (2021). https://doi.org/10.1007/s42107-021-00362-3
31. Huang, G.-B., Zhu, Q.-Y., Siew, C.-K.: Extreme learning machine: a new learning scheme of feedforward neural networks. In: 2004 IEEE international joint conference on neural networks (IEEE Cat. No. 04CH37541), vol. 2, pp. 985–990 (2004)
32. Deo, R.C., Downs, N., Parisi, A.V., Adamowski, J.F., Quilty, J.M.: Very short-term reactive forecasting of the solar ultraviolet index using an extreme learning machine integrated with the solar zenith angle. Environ. Res. **155**, 141–166 (2017)
33. Hameed, M.M., AlOmar, M.K., Baniya, W.J., AlSaadi, M.A.: Prediction of high-strength concrete: high-order response surface methodology modeling approach. Eng. Comput. 1–14 (2021).https://doi.org/10.1007/s00366-021-01284-z
34. Hameed, M.M., AlOmar, M.K.: Prediction of compressive strength of high-performance concrete: hybrid artificial intelligence technique. In: Khalaf, M., Al-Jumeily, D., Lisitsa, A. (eds.) Applied Computing to Support Industry: Innovation and Technology. ACRIT 2019. Communications in Computer and Information Science, vol. 1174, pp. 323–335. Springer, Cham (2020). https://doi.org/10.1007/978-3-030-38752-5_26
35. Tao, H., et al.: Global solar radiation prediction over North Dakota using air temperature: development of novel hybrid intelligence model. Energy Rep. **7**, 136–157 (2021). https://doi.org/10.1016/j.egyr.2020.11.033
36. Khalaf, J.A., et al.: Hybridized deep learning model for perfobond rib shear strength connector prediction. Complexity **2021**, 6611885 (2021). https://doi.org/10.1155/2021/6611885
37. Shahnazari, H., Tutunchian, M.A.: Prediction of ultimate bearing capacity of shallow foundations on cohesionless soils: an evolutionary approach. KSCE J. Civ. Eng. (2012).https://doi.org/10.1007/s12205-012-1651-0
38. Kordjazi, A., Nejad, F.P., Jaksa, M.B.: Prediction of ultimate axial load-carrying capacity of piles using a support vector machine based on CPT data. Comput. Geotech. **55**, 91–102 (2014)

Training Adaptive Neuro Fuzzy Inference System Using Genetic Algorithms for Predicting Labor Productivity

Nehal Elshaboury(✉)

Construction and Project Management Research Institute, Housing and Building National Research Center, Giza, Egypt
nehal.elshabory@hbrc.edu.eg

Abstract. The construction industry is labor-intensive and providing an accurate estimate for labor productivity is crucial for managing construction projects. In this regard, this research develops an adaptive neuro fuzzy inference system (ANFIS) model trained using genetic algorithms (GA) to enhance the prediction accuracy and reliability for construction labor productivity. The model is validated using data acquired from two high-rise buildings in Montreal, Canada. The performance of the optimized model is evaluated against that of the classic ANFIS model using correlation coefficient (R), mean bias error (MBE), and root mean square error (RMSE). The results of the evaluation metrics reveal that the ANFIS-GA model (R = 0.121, MBE = 0.331, and RMSE = 0.411) outperforms the classical ANFIS model (R = 0.040, MBE = 0.426, and RMSE = 0.537) for formwork labor productivity. It can be concluded that combining the ANFIS model with metaheuristic algorithms improves the forecasting accuracy of construction labor productivity.

Keywords: Labor productivity · Adaptive neuro fuzzy inference system · Machine learning · Metaheuristic algorithms

1 Introduction

The construction industry contributes to the gross domestic product growth and the economic development in both developed and developing countries [1, 2]. Furthermore, it has a remarkable contribution to employment growth [3, 4]. Therefore, improved construction productivity attracts more investment and generates work opportunities [5]. The labor cost accounts for 30–60% of the overall costs of a construction project, making the construction industry labor-intensive [6, 7]. Therefore, improving labor productivity would lead to enhancing the performance of construction projects [8]. However, the construction sector is subjected to several challenges, including declining productivity growth [9].

Productivity assesses the correlation between the resources consumed and the output produced [10]. In construction, productivity is commonly defined as a ratio of a quantity of output to a unit of resource input [4]. Generally speaking, productivity is related to

P. Liatsis et al. (Eds.): TIOTC 2021, CCIS 1548, pp. 324–334, 2022.
https://doi.org/10.1007/978-3-030-97255-4_24

the degree of utilization of resources to satisfy objectives. Besides, it is correlated to the degree of resource leveraging to fulfill objectives [11–13].

It is crucial to identify and quantify the relationships among influential factors to model construction labor productivity. The current conventional practice of estimating the productivity rates relies on a subjective judgment, historical or published productivity data. The accuracy and reliability of the first estimation method are influenced by personal prejudice and employee turnover. The published productivity data reflects the average productivity rates of the industry instead of measuring the performance of a contractor [14]. The most accurate estimate can be obtained from past project data [1]. This highlights the necessity to model construction labor productivity by considering influencing factors, leading to effective planning and scheduling of the construction projects [15].

The paper is organized as follows: Sect. 1 presents the background and motivation of this research. Section 2 comprehensively reviews the existing labor productivity estimation models. Section 3 provides a background on the materials and methods used in the model development. Section 4 proposes the framework for this research. Section 5 discusses a case study for labor productivity estimation using hybrid prediction models. Section 6 examines and analyzes the resulting models. Section 7 concludes this work and presents potential future research directions in this domain.

2 Literature Review

There are many techniques to study the relationship between influential factors and productivity rates [1]. One of the powerful techniques to model construction labor productivity is system dynamics simulation. For example, Nojedehi and Nasirzadeh [16] applied a fuzzy system dynamics simulation approach to improve construction labor productivity. The influential input and output factors were represented as fuzzy numbers based on the opinions of the experts involved in the project. Moreover, different scenarios were proposed to improve labor productivity and project performance. Khanzadi et al. [17] modeled the productivity of different contractors based on system dynamic simulation. The definitions and interrelationships among different parameters were determined based on the expert's judgment. The influence of input factors on contractor productivity was studied. In another study, Khanzadi et al. [18] combined the application of system dynamics and agent-based modeling to model labor productivity. The hybrid simulation approach considered the various influential factors and the interactions among project agents. The results affirmed the impact of the number and movement patterns of working groups on labor productivity. Durdyev et al. [4] determined the most important factors influencing construction labor productivity using a structural equation model. The model accounted for several factors, which were investigated using a questionnaire survey among the government authorities and construction players. The results confirmed the significance of the competency level of the management team and workforce in enhancing labor productivity.

Artificial intelligence has been a powerful tool in modeling construction labor productivity. It mostly refers to machine learning and metaheuristic algorithms. The machine learning algorithms refer to building a model based on input data, and training and testing/validating the trained model. Furthermore, metaheuristic algorithms do not consider the trend of data and instead, satisfy an objective function based on defined variables and constraints [19]. Artificial neural network (ANN) belongs to the machine learning class. It has been widely used in modeling labor productivity. For instance, Heravi and Eslamdoost [20] modeled labor productivity using a backpropagation neural network (BPNN) model. Bayesian regularization exhibited a better prediction performance when compared to the early stopping method. Furthermore, the influence of each input factor on the predictive performance of the models was measured using a sensitivity analysis. El-Gohary et al. [1] quantified the construction labor productivity using the ANN technique. Several activation and transfer functions were employed to measure construction labor productivity. The proposed model yielded more accurate results compared with the conventional methods. Golnaraghi et al. [10] evaluated the performance of BPNN, general regression neural network (GRNN), radial base function neural network (RBFNN), and adaptive neuro-fuzzy inference system (ANFIS) to estimate labor productivity. It was found that BPNN exhibited better performance for modeling construction labor productivity. Mlybari [21] applied GRNN, ANN, support vector machine (SVM), and multiple additive regression trees (MART) to estimate labor productivity. The results indicated that the GRNN model outperformed other intelligent-based methods for predicting labor productivity in concrete pouring and finishing and steel fixing.

In recent years, developing hybrid intelligent-based models has gained significant attention to improving model performance [22, 23]. Researchers utilized hybrid approaches to predict labor productivity. For instance, Cheng et al. [24] predicted the productivity loss caused by change orders in construction projects using an evolutionary fuzzy SVM inference model. Data cleaning, attributes reduction, and data transformation techniques were applied to improve data quality. Based on the results of assessment metrics, the proposed model yielded the most accurate results when compared to ANN, SVM, and evolutionary SVM inference models.

The ANFIS exhibited better performance in comparison with the ANN model in many applications [25, 26]. However, it encountered some problems in optimizing the parameters of the membership functions, negatively affecting the prediction accuracy. In an attempt to overcome this shortcoming, the ANFIS model could be optimized using metaheuristic algorithms [27, 28]. In this regard, this research aims at evaluating the performance of applying a hybrid intelligent model to forecast formwork labor productivity. The effectiveness of the proposed model is tested and verified using two high-rise buildings in Montreal, Canada. The model is implemented using an ANFIS model optimized using a genetic algorithm (GA). The metaheuristic algorithm is employed to get the optimum weight parameters of the membership function. Besides, the results of the optimized ANFIS model are compared against that of a standalone ANFIS model using three performance metrics. The proposed model can accurately predict labor productivity, providing more realistic estimates of construction projects' cost and time. Besides, accurate knowledge of labor productivity is necessary for controlling the progress of construction projects.

3 Materials and Methods

3.1 ANFIS Model Trained Using Genetic Algorithms

In this research, GA is applied to determine the parameters of the membership function in the ANFIS model, as shown in Fig. 1. After creating the fuzzy inference system using the input and target data, the membership functions are optimized using GA. The model output is computed and the error objective function is minimized using Eq. (1) [29]. The optimization process terminates when the best output is obtained.

$$\begin{aligned} \textit{Objective function} &= \min(\text{RMSE}) \\ &= \min\left(\sqrt{\text{mean}(e)^2}\right) = \min\left(\sqrt{\text{mean}(t-y)^2}\right) \end{aligned} \tag{1}$$

Where; t and y are the target and output data and e is the error objective function to be minimized.

3.2 Adaptive Neuro-Fuzzy Inference System

The ANFIS integrates the modeling capabilities of neural networks and fuzzy logic [30, 31]. Its structure comprises five layers. The first layer is responsible for fuzzifying the input parameters, while the firing strength of the rules is calculated in the second layer. The firing strength of the rules is normalized in the third layer. Finally, the fifth layer determines the system output based on the assigned rule outputs in the fourth layer. There exist three methods to generate the fuzzy inference system, namely grid partitioning, subtractive clustering, and fuzzy c-means clustering. The fuzzy c-means clustering method is used in this research because it yields the most reliable results among other methods [10].

3.3 Genetic Algorithms

GA was introduced by Holland [32] to mimic natural selection based on genetics. The population is shaped based on randomly generated chromosomes. The fitness functions of chromosomes determine whether or not these individuals will be selected as parents. The chosen individuals propagate their genes by reproducing offspring. Diversity in the generations is maintained using crossover and mutation. This process is repeated for a defined number of iterations, and the chromosomes in the final iteration are the solutions.

3.4 Performance Metrics

The prediction performance of the classical and hybrid machine learning models is evaluated using three performance evaluation metrics. These indicators give insights into the model accuracy and goodness of fit for the datasets. The mathematical formulas of the correlation coefficient (R), mean bias error (MBE), and root mean square error (RMSE) are shown in Eq. 2–4 [33, 34]. It could be noted that the closer the value of R to

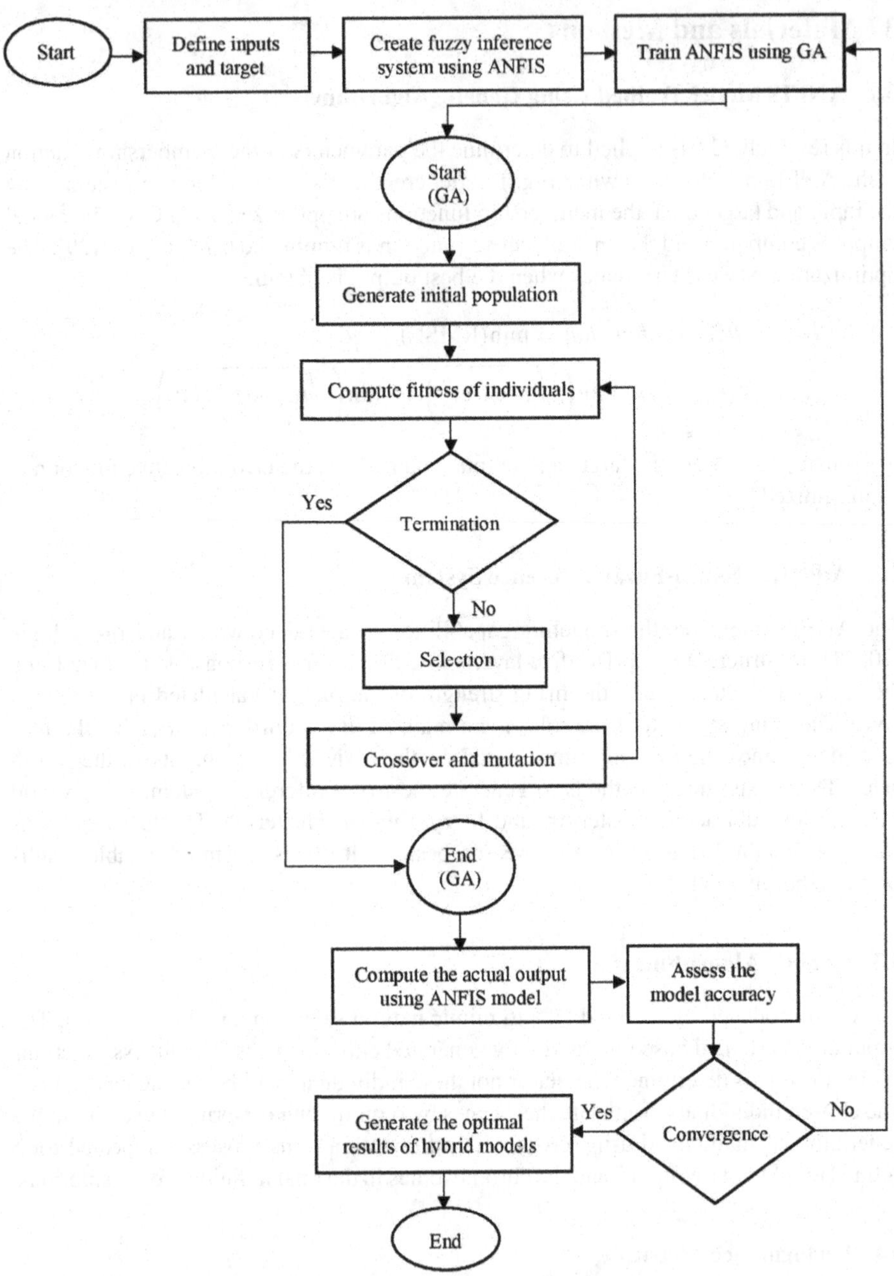

Fig. 1. Flowchart of the proposed hybrid machine learning model.

1, the better the model is performing. Besides, lower MBE and RMSE values indicate a better absolute fit of the model.

$$R = \frac{\sum_{i=1}^{n}((x_i - \overline{x})(y_i - \overline{y}))}{\sqrt{\sum_{i=1}^{n}(x_i - \overline{x})^2 \times \sum_{i=1}^{n}(y_i - \overline{y})^2}} \tag{2}$$

$$MBE = \frac{1}{n}\sum_{i=1}^{n}|x_i - y_i| \tag{3}$$

$$RMSE = \sqrt{\frac{1}{n}\sum_{i=1}^{n}(x_i - y_i)^2} \tag{4}$$

Where; n, x, y, $\overline{x}$, and $\overline{y}$ are the numbers of data samples, reported values, predicted values, mean reported values, and mean predicted values, respectively.

4 Model Development

Construction projects are dynamically changing with respect to time, cost, quality, and safety aspects. This complicated environment could be addressed by applying different machine learning models. Therefore, this research develops standalone and hybrid machine learning models for forecasting formwork labor productivity. As illustrated in Fig. 2, the framework comprises six steps: 1) identifying the input and output parameters from the available database, 2) dividing the data into training and testing datasets, 3) implementing the machine learning models, 4) reporting the predicted productivity, 5) validating the models using performance evaluation metrics, and 6) recommending the most suitable prediction model.

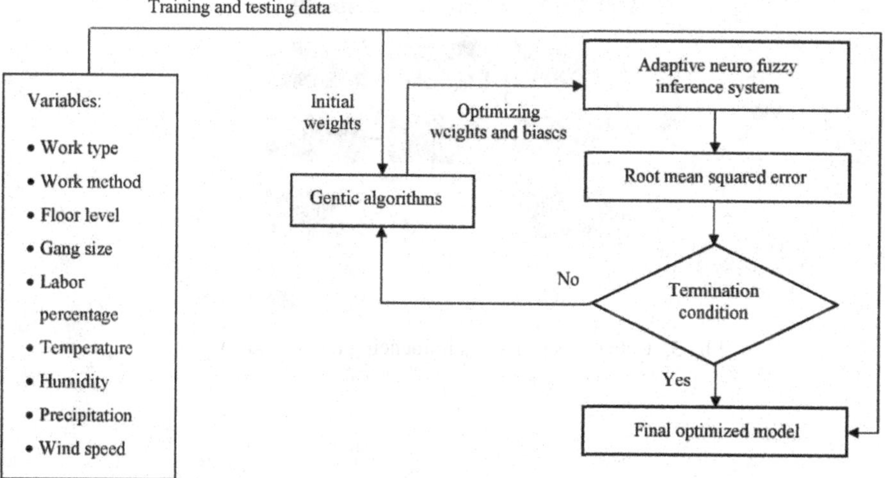

Fig. 2. Flowchart for modeling formwork labor productivity.

5 Case Study

The data utilized in this research is acquired from two high-rise buildings located in Montreal, Canada over eighteen months [35]. The structural system of the first building is a flat slab concrete system. This building is composed of 17 floors, covering a surface of 68,000 m^2, and it was constructed over three years. The structural system of the second building is similar to the first one. The gathered dataset comprises two hundred and twenty-one data points for formwork activity. As shown in Fig. 3, the labor productivity factors can be divided into project, crew, and weather categories. The work type, work method, and floor level factors belong to the project category. Meanwhile, the crew category covers data related to the gang size and labor percentage. Finally, the weather category comprises parameters related to temperature, humidity, precipitation, and wind speed.

The abovementioned categories and related-factors cause changes in labor productivity. Table 1 depicts more statistical parameters about the nine factors. It is worth noting that the work type refers to three distinct types of formwork; slabs (1), walls (2), and columns (3). Additionally, the work method comprises built-in place (1) and flying forms (2). The number of floors could be described in the floor level. Regarding the crew category, the gang size describes the number of persons in a crew, while the labor percentage is the ratio between the labor size to the gang size. For the weather category, the temperature, humidity, and wind speed are numerical variables, unlike precipitation which is a categorical variable. The first three variables are measured based on Celsius (°C), percentage (%), and km/h, respectively. Finally, precipitation can be classified into no precipitation (0), light rain (1), snow (2), and rain (3).

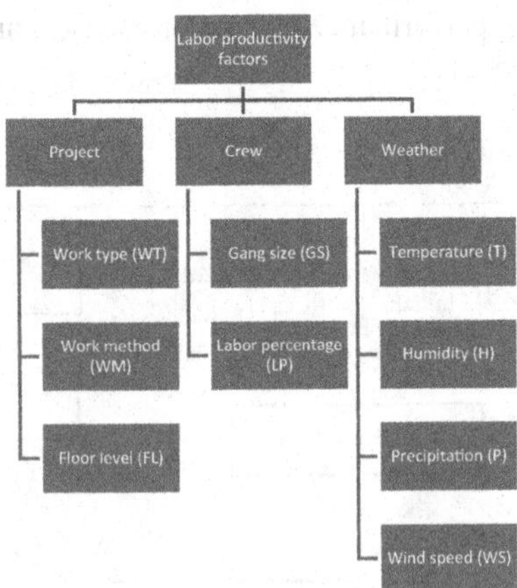

Fig. 3. Categories of factors influencing labor productivity.

Table 1. Statistical parameters of input and output variables for formwork labor productivity.

Variable	Minimum	Maximum	Median	Mean	Standard deviation
Work type	1.00	3.00	1.00	1.43	0.51
Work method	1.00	2.00	1.00	1.44	0.50
Floor level	1.00	17.00	12.00	11.38	3.75
Gang size	8.00	24.00	18.00	16.03	5.07
Labor percentage	29.00	47.00	36.00	35.49	3.79
Temperature	–26.00	25.00	3.00	4.08	12.03
Humidity	18.00	97.00	67.00	66.34	15.67
Precipitation	0.00	3.00	0.00	0.28	0.60
Wind speed	3.00	43.00	14.00	15.42	8.46
Productivity	0.82	2.53	1.51	1.57	0.35

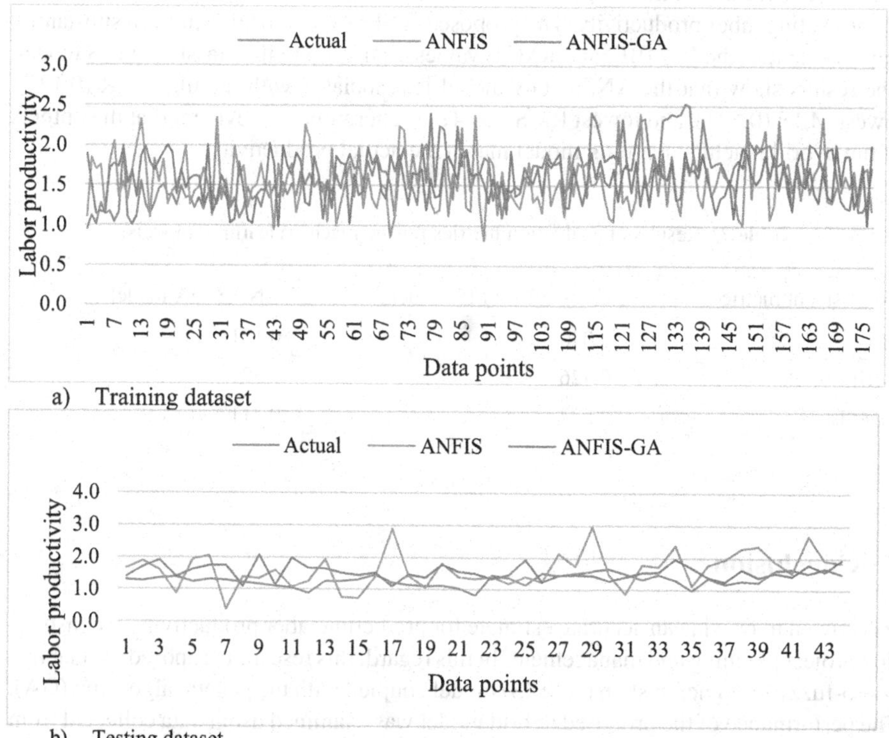

Fig. 4. Comparison of the actual and forecasted labor productivity using ANFIS and ANFIS-GA models; for a) training dataset and b) testing dataset.

6 Results and Discussion

This research conducts a comparative analysis between the performance of the ANFIS and ANFIS-GA models for forecasting formwork labor productivity in two high-rise buildings in Montreal, Canada. A comparison of the predicted and actual labor productivity values is plotted in Fig. 4. 80% and 20% of the dataset are selected for training and testing purposes, respectively. The function of training is adjusting the weights of membership functions, while the testing aims at assessing the performance of the trained models. For ANFIS, the number of clusters is set to 15, while the maximum number of epochs and iterations is 200. The initial step size, step size decrease rate, and step size increase rate values are adjusted as 0.01, 0.9, and 1.1, respectively. Concerning the parameters of GA, the population size, crossover rate, and mutation rate are 100, 0.7, and 0.5, respectively. The author coded the machine learning models using MATLAB R2015a.

As summarized in Table 2, the performance of the machine learning models is assessed using three measures (R, MBE, and RMSE). These metrics reflect whether or not the model outputs are matching with the actual productivity. It could be noted that the RMSE of the classic ANFIS model (i.e., 0.537) is relatively high (i.e., above 0.50). This implies that this model is incapable of mimicking the actual productivity. In order to address this limitation, ANFIS-GA is developed to provide an accurate estimate for predicting labor productivity. The proposed ANFIS-GA model exhibits a substantial improvement in the R, MBE, and RMSE values compared to the classic ANFIS model. The results show that the ANFIS-GA model is associated with the highest R (0.121), lowest MBE (0.331), and lowest RMSE (0.411). Therefore, it is evident that the outputs of the hybrid machine learning model match the actual productivity.

Table 2. Results of evaluation metrics for the machine learning models.

Assessment metric	Classical ANFIS model	ANFIS-GA model
R	0.040	0.121
MBE	0.426	0.331
RMSE	0.537	0.411

7 Conclusion

It is crucial to provide an accurate estimate for predicting labor productivity in construction project planning and management. In this regard, this research proposed an adaptive neuro-fuzzy inference system (ANFIS) model coupled with the genetic algorithm (GA). The performance of the proposed hybrid model was examined using data collected from two high-rise buildings in Montreal, Canada. The dataset was divided into 80% and 20% for training and testing purposes, respectively. The dataset comprised factors related to the project, crew, and weather conditions. The proposed model was compared with the classic ANFIS model using correlation coefficient (R), mean bias error (MBE), and root mean square error (RMSE) metrics. The results showed that the proposed ANFIS-GA model (R = 0.121, MBE = 0.331, and RMSE = 0.411) outperformed the classical ANFIS model (R = 0.040, MBE = 0.426, and RMSE = 0.537). Therefore, it is evident that coupling the ANFIS model with GA can be a useful tool for modeling formwork labor productivity. The findings of this study could be useful for providing the project managers and professionals with an accurate prediction for formwork labor productivity. This research could be extended in the future by comparing the proposed method against artificial intelligence-based methods for modeling productivity processes.

References

1. El-Gohary, K.M., Aziz, R.F., Abdel-Khalek, H.A.: Engineering approach using ANN to improve and predict construction labor productivity under different influences. J. Constr. Eng. Manag. **143**(8), 04017045 (2017)
2. Dixit, S., Mandal, S.N., Thanikal, J.V., Saurabh, K.: Evolution of studies in construction productivity: a systematic literature review (2006–2017). Ain Shams Eng. J. **10**(3), 555–564 (2019)
3. Dixit, S., Mandal, S.N., Sawhney, A., Singh, S.: Relationship between skill development and productivity in construction sector: a literature review. Int. J. Civ. Eng. Technol. **8**(8), 649–665 (2017)
4. Durdyev, S., Ismail, S., Kandymov, N.: Structural equation model of the factors affecting construction labor productivity. J. Constr. Eng. Manag. **144**(4), 04018007 (2018)
5. Duncan, J.R.: Innovation in the building sector: trends and new technologies. In: Technical Conference of the Institution of Professional Engineers of New Zealand. Building Research Association of New Zealand, Wellington (2002)
6. Gomar, J.E., Haas, C.T., Morton, D.P.: Assignment and allocation optimization of partially multi-skilled workforce. J. Constr. Eng. Manag. **128**(2), 103–109 (2002)
7. Hanna, A.S., Peterson, P., Lee, M.: Benchmarking productivity indicators for electrical/mechanical projects. J. Constr. Eng. Manag. **128**(4), 331–337 (2002)
8. Durdyev, S., Mbachu, J.: On-site labor productivity of New Zealand construction industry: key constraints and improvement measures. Australas. J. Constr. Econ. Build. **11**(3), 18–33 (2011)
9. Allen, S.G.: Why construction industry productivity is declining. Rev. Econ. Stat. **67**(4), 661–669 (1985)
10. Golnaraghi, S., Zangenehmadar, Z., Moselhi, O., Alkass, S.: Application of artificial neural network(s) in predicting formwork labor productivity. Adv. Civ. Eng. **2019**, 1–11 (2019)
11. Hanna, A.S.: Effectiveness of Innovative Crew Scheduling. Construction Industry Institute, Austin, United States (2003)
12. El-Batreek, A.H., Ezeldin, A.S., Elbarkouky, M.M.G.: A framework for construction labor productivity improvement in Egypt. In: 2013 Architectural Engineering Conference. ASCE, Reston (2013)
13. Abdel-Wahab, M., Vogl, B.: Trends of productivity growth in the construction industry across Europe US and Japan. Constr. Manag. Econ. **29**(6), 635–644 (2011)
14. Thomas, H.R.: Quantification of losses of labor efficiencies: innovations in and improvements to the measured mile. J. Legal Affairs Dispute Resolut. Eng. Constr. **2**(2), 106–112 (2010)
15. Song, L., AbouRizk, S.M.: Measuring and modeling labor productivity using historical data. J. Constr. Eng. Manag. **134**(10), 786–794 (2008)

16. Nojedehi, P., Nasirzadeh, F.: A hybrid simulation approach to model and improve construction labor productivity. KSCE J. Civ. Eng. **21**(5), 1516–1524 (2016)
17. Khanzadi, M., Kaveh, A., Alipour, M., Mohammadi, R.K.: Assessment of labour productivity in construction projects using system dynamic approach. Sci. Iran. **24**(6), 2684–2695 (2017)
18. Khanzadi, M., Nasirzadeh, F., Mir, M., Nojedehi, P.: Prediction and improvement of labor productivity using hybrid system dynamics and agent-based modeling approach. Constr. Innov. **18**(1), 2–19 (2018)
19. Golnaraghi, S., Moselhi, O., Alkass, S., Zangenehmadar, Z.: Predicting construction labor productivity using lower upper decomposition radial base function neural network. Eng. Rep. **2**(2), e12107 (2020)
20. Heravi, G., Eslamdoost, E.: Applying artificial neural networks for measuring and predicting construction labor productivity. J. Constr. Eng. Manag. **141**(10), 04015032 (2015)
21. Mlybari, E.A.: Application of soft computing techniques to predict construction labor productivity in Saudi Arabia. Int. J. Geomate **19**(71), 203–210 (2020)
22. Moazenzadeh, R., Mohammadi, B., Shamshirband, S., Chau, K.W.: Coupling a firefly algorithm with support vector regression to predict evaporation in Northern Iran. Eng. Appl. Comput. Fluid Mech. **12**(1), 584–597 (2018)
23. Aghelpour, P., Mohammadi, B., Biazar, S.M.: Long-term monthly average temperature forecasting in some climate types of Iran, using the models SARIMA, SVR, and SVR-FA. Theor. Appl. Climatol. **138**, 1471–1480 (2019)
24. Cheng, M., Wibowo, D.K., Prayogo, D., Roy, A.F.: Predicting productivity loss caused by change orders using the evolutionary fuzzy support vector machine inference model. J. Civ. Eng. Manag. **21**(7), 881–892 (2015)
25. Masoudi, S., Sima, M., Tolouei-Rad, M.: Comparative study of ANN and ANFIS models for predicting temperature in machining. JESTEC **13**(1), 211–225 (2018)
26. Gill, J., et al.: Adaptive neuro-fuzzy inference system (ANFIS) approach for the irreversibility analysis of a domestic refrigerator system using LPG/TiO2 Nanolubricant. Energy Rep. **6**, 1405–1417 (2020)
27. Varnamkhasti, M.J.: A hybrid of adaptive neuro-fuzzy inference system and genetic algorithm. J. Intell. Fuzzy Syst. **25**(3), 793–796 (2013)
28. Mohammadi, B., et al.: Adaptive neuro-fuzzy inference system coupled with shuffled frog leaping algorithm for predicting river streamflow time series. Hydrol. Sci. J. **65**(10), 1738–1751 (2020)
29. Termeh, S.V., et al.: Optimization of an adaptive neuro-fuzzy inference system for groundwater potential mapping. Hydrogeol. J. **27**(7), 2511–2534 (2019)
30. Aghdam, I.N., Varzandeh, M.H.M., Pradhan, B.: Landslide susceptibility mapping using an ensemble statistical index (Wi) and adaptive neuro-fuzzy inference system (ANFIS) model at Alborz mountains (Iran). Environ. Earth Sci. **75**, 553 (2016)
31. Jang, J.S.: ANFIS: adaptive-network-based Fuzzy inference system. IEEE Trans. Syst. Man Cybernet. **23**, 665–685 (1993)
32. Holland, J.: Adaptation in Natural and Artificial Systems. University of Michigan Press, Ann Arbor (1975)
33. Elshaboury, N., Marzouk, M.: Comparing machine learning models for predicting water pipelines condition. In: 2020 2nd Novel Intelligent and Leading Emerging Sciences Conference (NILES). IEEE, Giza (2020)
34. Sayegh, A.S., Munir, S., Habeebullah, T.M.: Comparing the performance of statistical models for predicting PM10 concentrations. Aerosol. Air Qual. Res. **14**(3), 653–665 (2014)
35. Khan, Z.U.: Modeling and Parameter Ranking of Construction Labor Productivity. Dissertation, Concordia University (2005)

Approaches for Forgery Detection of Documents in Digital Forensics: A Review

Alaa Amjed[1(✉)], Basim Mahmood[1,2], and Khalid A. K. Almukhtar[3]

[1] Computer Science Department, University of Mosul, Mosul 41002, Iraq
Alaa.csp52@student.uomosul.edu.iq, bmahmood@uomosul.edu.iq, bmahmood@biocomplexlab.org
[2] BioComplex Lab, Exeter, UK
[3] Ministry of Interior, Baghdad, Iraq

Abstract. The current technological era is witnessing a great revolution in the development of online applications. They are used for a variety of purposes when it comes to processing documents. A vast amount of online software applications is currently available for professionally editing documents. One of their most dangerous aspects is the manipulation/imitating of original documents. In this context, digital forensics science provides a lot of tools for examining documents from being forged or counterfeited. Moreover, most of the works in the literature focused on a particular aspect of digital forensics. However, this work provides a comprehensive review on the three main aspects of digital forensics; namely, image-processing-based, video-processing-based, and spectroscopy-based detection techniques. The review also provides the most recent updates in these aspects when detecting forged or counterfeited documents, which is of interest to the research community. Finally, this work can be considered a reliable guide for fresh digital forensics researchers.

Keywords: Forged documents · Forensics science · Forgery detection · Image forgery · Video forgery · Spectroscopy forgery

1 Introduction

Forensic science can be defined as the use of scientific theories and approaches in providing solutions for crimes and these solutions are suitable or can be used in a court of law [1, 2]. With the current revolution in technology, many software applications are developed and published to the public for many different kinds of purposes. People usually use these applications in their jobs, study, and other life activities. Managing and editing documents are the most frequent activities that are performed every day by people using their computers or smart devices [3]. However, these software applications can also be used in falsifying documents. This kind of tampering is considered illegal and prohibited by law. Official certificates, checks, currency bills, and transcripts are good examples of documents that can be forged [4]. Furthermore, everyday thousands of counterfeit document cases are reported around the world as a consequence of using

P. Liatsis et al. (Eds.): TIOTC 2021, CCIS 1548, pp. 335–351, 2022.
https://doi.org/10.1007/978-3-030-97255-4_25

these applications [5]. This case leads to what is currently known as "Digital Forensics", which means the use of technology tools and computer-based approaches for solving crime-related issues that can be legal evidence in courts [6].

Doubtful documents are usually called "*questioned documents*", which can be *forged* or *counterfeited* documents [4]. The main difference between both terms is that forgery reflects the intention of producing documents to defraud another one, while counterfeit is the intention of producing unauthorized imitation on a document [7, 8]. Most of the works in the literature focus on how to detect forged or counterfeit documents using similar approaches and techniques. For example, the methods that use image-processing or video processing techniques try to investigate the features of the questioned documents and deal with them as images or video frames. The investigation, in this case, can be performed on the features extracted from these images/frames. Furthermore, spectroscopy-based methods can also be used for investigating questioned documents [9]. Spectroscopy analysis is a way for investigating the interaction between matter and electronic radiation [10]. This interaction is represented as a function of the wavelength of the radiation and can be measured using special-purpose devices such as Laser-Induced Breakdown Spectroscopy (LIBS) [10, 11]. Spectroscopy approaches study the characteristics of matter's absorption when it is exposed to electromagnetic radiation [12]. Therefore, spectroscopy can be considered as a measurement of the radiation intensity of wavelength for a matter. The analysis of spectroscopy has been developed to become crucial in the development of forensic science [13].

The main problem for researchers when they work on forgery detection is the approach that is best involved [13]. The literature provides a large number of reviews and surveys but they are limited to a particular aspect (e.g., image processing, video processing, or spectroscopy analysis) [4]. However, it is needed to have reviews and surveys that take into consideration the main aspects of digital forensics. This is important especially for the fresh researchers in this field. Moreover, it is needed to have works that present most of the available approaches and let researchers choose the best ones that fit their background and qualifications. For instance, computer scientists prefer to use image processing techniques, but physicists prefer to use spectroscopy analysis. Besides, other researchers prefer to combine and integrate more than one approach in one efficient approach [4]. Therefore, this review presents the state-of-the-art in the field of forgery detection in digital forensic science. The studies are categories based on the technique used. This review considers three main areas, namely, image processing techniques, video processing techniques, and spectroscopy-based techniques. Recommendations are also provided to researchers when they perform forgery detection research. This work is important for fresh researchers because it provides the basic concepts of the forgery detection field in different directions.

This review is organized as follows: the next section introduces the techniques that are based on image processing. Section 3 presents the detection approaches used in video files. Section 4 describes the approaches that are based on spectroscopy. Finally, this work is concluded in Sect. 5.

2 Image-Processing-Based Forgery Detection Techniques

The Internet contains a vast amount of multimedia files such as images and videos. Some of these files might have been manipulated by scammers (see Fig. 1 (a), (b) and (c), (d)). Many approaches are already available in the literature that detects counterfeit documents using image processing techniques. Some of these approaches deal primarily with edge detection and feature extraction of the questioned document (e.g., in the form of an image) [15]. Moreover, edges information in an image is one of the most important data that can describe the target outline and its relative location within the target region. Edge detection is one of the most critical processes in image processing and can be considered a tool for detecting forgery/counterfeit. In this context, the detection schemes have continuously evolved through different techniques and algorithms that operate on machines and devices.

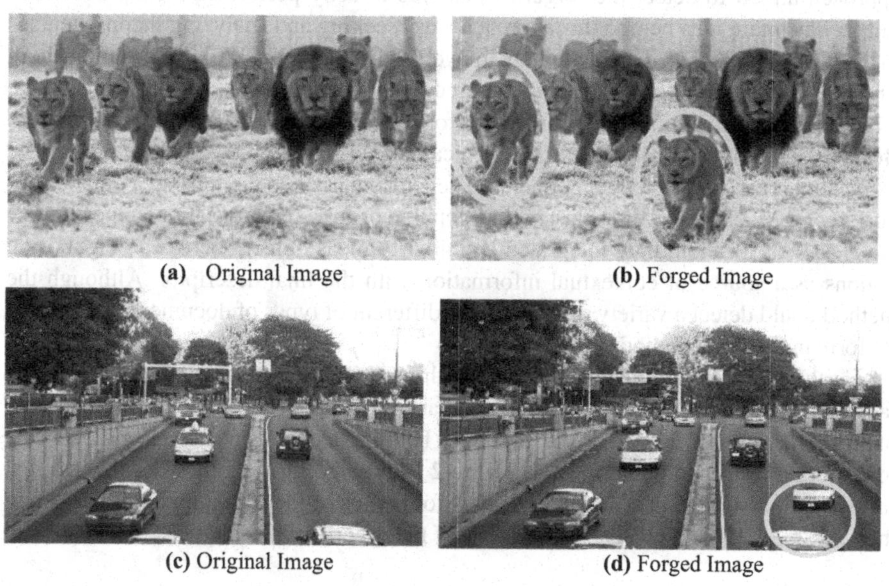

(a) Original Image (b) Forged Image

(c) Original Image (d) Forged Image

Fig. 1. Original vs Forged image [14].

According to the study of Barad and Goswami [16], image forgery detection approaches are divided into two types [16, 17]; active and passive approaches. The former can include digital watermarking and digital signature techniques. While the latter can be dependent such as copy-move or image splicing approaches, or independently such as image retouching or lighting condition approaches. Furthermore, the forgery process can be performed using printing papers, inks, currency, banknotes, etc. Gorai et al. [18] proposed an efficient method to detect fraud documents. Their method considered "Texture Features" such as local binary patterns and Gabor filters. Then, the method performed a process called "Histogram Matching" that aimed to analyze the document. RGB information and Texture features were extracted from the document's word. Then, a comparison was performed between the normalized histograms of two different images of the document in order to produce what was called a "Matching Score" for making a decision on that document. The main advantage of the approach, it consumed less time, fully unsupervised, and did not require any prior knowledge.

Other approaches in the literature have relied on the texture feature such as the study of Lamsal and Shakya [19]. They studied the identification and classification of counterfeit and genuine banknotes based on color and texture features. It presented a simple approach to the identification of counterfeit currency. A currency's color and texture features were mainly involved in the identification process. Entropy and correlation were used to analyze the texture features of the document. For the purpose of analyzing color features, it calculated skew and standard deviation. These two parameters were used in combination with the entropy and correlation as the parameters of the texture that, in turn, contributed to the classification of counterfeit currency image. Another study by Cruz et al. [20] proposed an approach using local binary patterns. The approach aimed to detect the forgeries that was directly performed on the document image. The main idea behind this approach was "seeking and analyzing inconsistencies in the intrinsic features of the document image", the authors said [20]. Information about fine-grained texture information was captured from the inconsistencies left in the image when a region is manipulated or forged, uniform local binary (LBP) patterns were used. Besides, the uniform LBP operators were calculated for the image patches that were extracted around connected components. Then, they classified them using a binary Support Vector Machines (SVM) classifier as genuine or forged regions. For supporting the the classifier decision, they integrated a similarity measurement between neighboring regions as a source of contextual information with the final descriptor. Although the method could detect a variety of forgeries in different of types of documents, the global performance of the method is low.

Furthermore, several techniques deal with particular objects in images such as the face. In recent years, face forgery detection has become popular due to the high number of forgery cases reported. In this regard, deep learning techniques play a significant role in detecting face manipulation [21]. Figure 2 shows several examples of fake and real facial manipulation [21]. The figure depicts four types of facial manipulation including their samples. Table 1 presents a summary of the described techniques.

Table 1. Summarizing the image-processing-based forgery detection techniques.

Authors	Doc. used	Methodology	Advantages	Limitations
Wang and Dant. [24] (2020)	Images	Deep learning (3DCNN)	Accu. = 90.2%	Complex
Marra et al. [23] (2019)	Images	Deep learning Features (CNN and Incremental Learning)	Accu. = 99.3%	Complex

(continued)

Table 1. *(continued)*

Authors	Doc. used	Methodology	Advantages	Limitations
Rossler et al. [22] (2019)	Images (video frames)	Deep Learning, Steganography, and Mesoscopic Features	Accu. = 94%	Complex
Yu et al. [21] (2018)	Images	Deep Learning Features (CNN)	Accu. = 99.5%	Complex
Cruz et al. [19] (2017)	Banknotes	Texture Features (Uniform Local Binary (LBP) and Binary Support Vector Machines (SVM)	Ability to detect several types of forgeries	Slow
Gorai et al. [18] (2016)	Bank Cheques, altered records	Texture Features (Gabor Filters and Local Binary Patterns)	"Unsupervised, no prior knowledge, and consumed less time"	"Thresholding sometimes fails to extract the edges of used ink."

Fig. 2. Examples of facial manipulation according to [21]

3 Video-Processing-Based Forgery Detection Techniques

With the advent of sophisticated and easy-to-use media editing applications, manipulating a video has become available to the public. Video forgery is mostly performed on the frames of the video in many different ways (see Fig. 3). Video forgery detection has become a critical requirement to ensure the integrity of video data, especially, for videos that are related to public security or legal evidence. That is, the major challenge, in this case, is to determine whether a video is original when it is used as critical evidence for judgment [25, 26]. Image processing techniques are sometimes difficult to be used for video forgery detection due to the strong level of degradation after video compression for all the frames [27].

According to the literature [28, 29], video forgery can be *Spatial*, when the forgery is performed in pixel bits on the source of the video, *Temporal*, when the forgery is performed on a sequence of frames in the video, and *Spatio-Temporal* that is a combination of both aforementioned types of forgery (see Fig. 2). Based on the study of Shelke and Kasana [30], video forgery approaches can be either intra-frame (e.g., copy-move, splicing, or upscale crop) or inter-frame (e.g., deletion, insertion, shuffling, or duplication of frames). Afchar et al. [27] proposed an approach to automatically detect tampering of faces in videos. They focused on two hyper-realistic techniques used for video forgeries, namely, *Deepfake* and *Face2Face*. The authors used a low-computational cost deep learning approach with the mesoscopic properties of the frames in the detection of forgery in videos. The proposed approach has several limitations, for instance, the output frames show blurry due to the limited encoding space.

Fayyaz et al. [31] proposed a video forgery detection technique that was based on noise residue correlation with SPN and with noise residue from the previous frames in a video. Their approach was designed to be suitable with the videos that have attacked frames. However, their approach was complex and needs a lot of stages and calculations to perform the detection. Aloraini et al. [32] suggested a method to detect "Object-Based Video Forgery" and estimate the movement of removed objects based on spatial decomposition, temporal filtering, and sequential analysis. They focused on detecting removed moving objects from a video scene that is taken from a static camera. The first step was applying spatial decomposition to the video frames using the Laplacian Pyramid. Then, they applied a temporal high pass filter to detect edges spatially and highlight variations temporally. Subsequently, detecting pixel changes that often happen near the boundary of a removed object. Therefore, a sequential analysis was implemented temporally to detect changes in pixels. The video forgery was proved if there existed pixels that were changed from large spatial regions and last for a short duration. Finally, the removed object's movement was estimated by summing all the tested pixels' changes of the video frames. The experimental results showed that object-based video forgery detection performance with this approach outperforms other approaches such as the work of [34] concerning precision. Also, more robustness was obtained against compressed and lower resolution videos. This approach could effectively estimate the movement of various sizes of removed objects using spatial decomposition. The drawback of this approach was that the sequential analysis phase was computationally expensive, which needs more development to reduce the computational cost.

Mathai et al. [35] used "Statistical Moment Features and Normalized Cross-Correlation" factor for detecting forgery and localization in videos. They studied on the issues related to the duplication that can be performed on a video such replacing or duplicating a small region of a video with another region in the same video. The main goal of the Mathai's work was to distinguish duplicated content in a video sequence. For each frame-block (set of a certain number of continuous frames in the video), the features from the prediction-error array were extracted. The normalized "Cross-Correlation" of the features among duplicated frame-blocks is high compared to other non-duplicated ones. The duplication was confirmed using a calculated threshold, which is based on the MSE. In addition, the proposed method aimed to figure out the duplicated block location. The results showed that the method was useful in the detection rate of forged frames. Wang et al. [36] used DCT coefficient for predicting frames. Their approach was efficient in detecting any change in frames (deleted and inserted frames). However, DCT approach is considered to be sensitive when the tested video has noise. Another approach proposed by Nguyen et al. [37] used Capsule-forensics for Deepfake. The approach was efficient when a swap occurs in faces within the video frames. Although this approach produced a high level of detection, it has limitations when the video attacker adds some noise to the video. Other approaches in the literature used the statistical features of the videos when detecting the forgeries. The study of Aloraini et al. [31] used the statistical features (e.g., mean and variance) for detecting object removal from videos. This approach was efficient with static video background, but it struggled with the dynamic video background. This issue appeared even when using other statistical features of the video. Kharat et al. [38] used SIFT features for detecting the duplication of frames in a video. The accuracy of this method reaches 99% but still has the issue of dynamic backgrounds.

The use of statistical features of videos needs more investigations aiming at having solutions when dealing with moving video backgrounds. Also, this kind of method may have high computational overhead because of the complex calculations of the correlations as confirmed in [39, 40]. Table 2 summarizes the aforementioned approaches.

4 Spectroscopy-Based Forgery Techniques

Many studies in the literature have taken the spectroscopy of documents for forgery detection. As mentioned in the introduction, the spectroscopy of a document can be obtained from different kinds of approaches and devices [41]. One of the most common technologies used in extracting the spectroscopy of documents is Laser-Induced Breakdown Spectroscopy and termed LIBS. Figure 4 depicts the way of how LIBS extract the spectroscopy from documents or materials.

The work of Lennard et al. [42] focused on the applications of LIBS in the investigating questioned documents. The study used the most common types of materials available in markets such as office papers, writing inks, inkjet inks, and laser printer toners. The authors tested the results obtained from LIBS against other methods such as laser ablation inductively coupled plasma mass spectrometry (LA-ICP-MS). The findings showed that LIBS reflected significant differences (from 99.8 to 100% compared to LA-ICP-MS) between different batches of the same and different brands of materials in the used

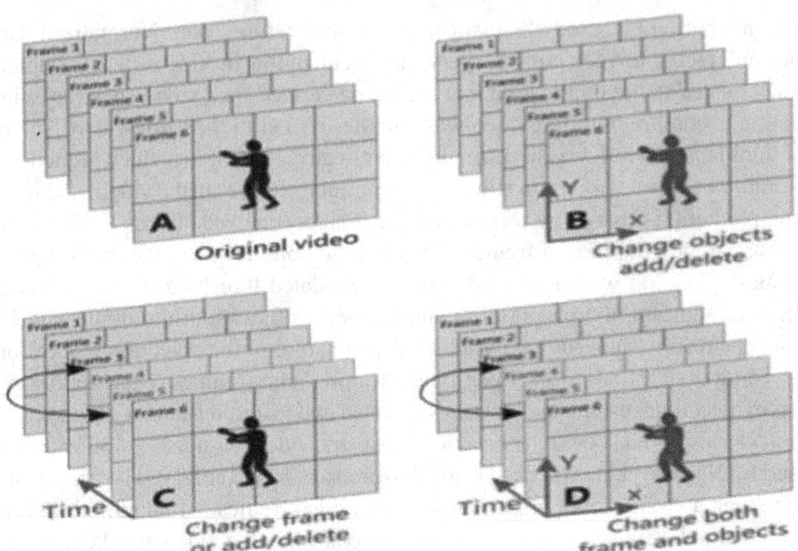

Fig. 3. Manipulating a video clip. A) is the original video, B) spatially forged video, C) temporally forged video, and D) spatiotemporal forged video [33].

samples. On the other hand, Elsherbiny and Nassef [43] investigated the wavelength dependence of LIBS for sample questioned documents. They examined thirty black gel-ink pens of ten brands aiming at identifying the variation of the chemical composition of the inks. Moreover, they aimed to distinguish among these types of inks with minimum mass removal and minimum damage to the document. The results showed that LIBS was able to distinguish the types of inks compared to IR LIBS at the same laser pulse energy. Furthermore, these results supported the ability of the LIBS using both the visible and IR lasers to be developed and benefited for the sake of forensics science. Gál et al. [44] studied the spectral features in "UV-VIS-NIR" and IR regions of laser and inkjet prints aiming at performing forensic analysis for documents. They assessed the abilities of "Non-Destructive" molecular spectroscopy approaches in distinguishing laser toners and inkjet inks. "The reflectance spectra of inkjet print in UV-VIS-NIR region areas were measured on fiber-optic reflectance spectroscopic system Ocean Optics. It includes HR 4000 spectrometer and the reflectance spectra of laser prints in the Infrared Region (IR) were measured on Excalibur FTS 3000MX (Digilab, USA) spectrometer with ATR adapter with diamond crystal. The authors found that the shapes of spectra of various black LaserJet prints and inkjet prints generally differ in the spectral regions UV-VIS-NIR and IR. They also found that the resolution of individual spectra was not reliable enough for analysis purposes. Moreover, the use of these spectrums in identifying individual printers should be enhanced by a computational chemometric method.

Table 2. Summarizing the video-processing-based forgery detection techniques.

Authors	Methodology	Advantages	Limitations
Fayyaz et al. [30] (2020)	Noise Residue Correlation with SPN	Accurate	Complex and needs a lot of stages and calculations
Kharat et al. [37] (2020)	Statistical Features (SIFT Features)	Efficient in frame duplication (accu = 99%)	Not efficient for moving background
Aloraini et al. [36] (2020)	Statistical Features (Mean and Variance)	Accu. = 96% for object removal	"Insufficient for moving background video."
Nguyen et al. [35] (2019)	"Capsule-Forensics for Deepfake"	Face Swapping accu. = 95%	"Not robust against an intentional attack."
Aloraini et al. [31] (2019)	Spatial decomposition, Temporal Filtering, and Seq. Analysis	Effective, accurate, and robust	The sequential analysis phase was computationally expensive
Afchar et al. [26] (2018)	Deepfake and Face2Face	Low-computational cost	The output frames show blurry due to limited encoding space
Mathai et al. [33] (2016)	"Using Statistical Moment Features and Normalized Cross-Correlation Factor"	Accurate	High computational cost
Wang et al. [34] (2016)	DCT Coefficient and Frame Prediction Error	Efficient in detecting deleted/inserted frames	Sensitive to noise

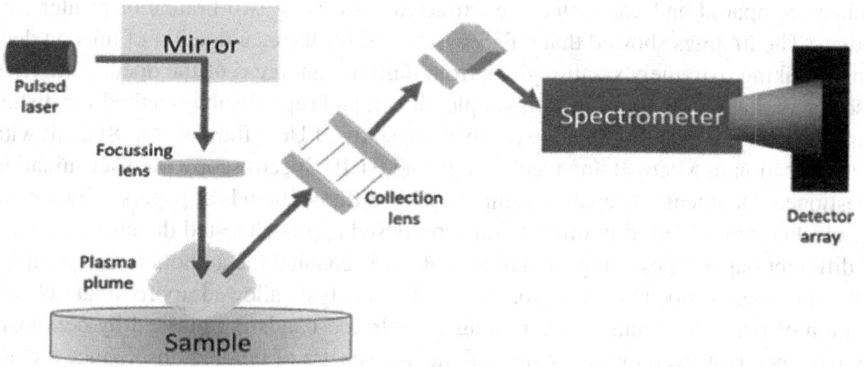

Fig. 4. LIBS method in extracting spectroscopy.

Another study by Hui et al. [45] analyzed printing ink by analyzing the elements of the print-ink-samples. In the analysis, they used the Principal Component Analysis (PCA) technique to distinguish the power of the LIBS technique for the samples. The samples used in the analysis were black printing inks from three types of printers; namely, viz. inkjet, laser-jet, and photocopier of different brands. They also used one control sample (blank/white A4 paper). The authors collected "200 LIBS" spectra from each sample. Each spectrum in the samples was accounted for a spot in the sample. Their proposed method comprising: (1) normalization was performed on the spectra between replicates, (2) the spectrum was divided into "*smaller relevant regions*" to perform spectra overlay, (3) Using NIST atomic spectra database, they identified the elements of interests with peak toleration of "0.12 nm" to "0.51 nm". The results showed that when using the LIBS method with the PCA technique enabled to provide discriminative evidence on elemental differences among all the different printing inks. They also showed that this approach is effective in terms of time and cost. Besides, their approach does not need sample pre-treatment steps and can be considered as a useful approach for the forensic questioned document.

Cicconi et al. [46] used LIBS for testing issues related to the commercial inks. The study performed a classification of "Pen Inks" on different paper types. Also, they analyzed a questioned document's signatures and toners. Then, they identified up to seven characteristic metals for the tested inks. This allowed to "Fully Discriminate" all black inks on one paper type. They authors found that when the inks were examined on ten different types of papers, for several reasons, the classification rates were reduced for some of them. "This was due to the presence of the same elements in both the ink and the paper ablated simultaneously with ink. The differential penetration of inks into paper is another reason. The experiments repeated at three crossing points, each involved a pair of blue or black inks were successful in five out of six cases. After they obtained the results, they said "LIBS was able to correctly identify the differences in three inks used for signatures on one of the three pages and the use of various printing inks on each page of the document", which approved their method".

Moreover, the literature shows different kinds of techniques when dealing with questioned documents. The work of Ameh and Ozovehe [47] used Fourier Transform Infrared Spectroscopy (FT-IS) to investigate the inks extracted from printed documents. The authors compared and contrasted the extracted inks using two brands of printer cartridges. The findings showed that FT-IS was useful for the examination of inks on documents taking extremely small regions from unimportant areas of the document. They also found that FT-IS was a useful, simple, direct, and reproducible method for distinguishing printing inks. In the same context, the study of Udristioiu et al. [48] dealt with the application of Micro-Raman technology and FT-IR Spectroscopy for discriminating questioned documents. They used samples of six different brands of papers, which were the most commonly used in offices. Their proposed approach tested the characteristics of different paper types using Raman and IR. This enabled the authors to discriminate different types of documents. Also, this kind of analysis allowed approximate classification of paper materials by examining the infrared bands not masked by cellulosic components. However, the study showed that the spectra of infrared absorbance are not definitive and Raman spectroscopy has the ability to provide complementary information that can lead to a fast and efficient analysis for questioned documents.

Raman technology has been widely used in forensic science for analysing questioned documents of different types of inks. Raza and Saha [49] analyzed stamp pad inks that were produced by different manufacturers. They studied the feasibility of "Raman Scattering" as an effective tool in forensics. They analyzed 9 different stamp inks using Raman spectroscopic and "HPTLC" methods. The findings reflected the efficiency of the proposed approach for inks classification. They proved that "Crystal Violet" was the main coloring agent that existed in the stamping ink. Zięba et al. [50] investigated degraded papers using Infrared and Raman spectroscopy. They investigated the age of documents and their types. They used three types of paper in the experiment and then selected different spots on each paper type. Their approach investigated the possibility of distinguishing the ages of samples. Their proposed approach involved "2D correlation" analysis on Noda's method using "ATR FT-IR" spectra as input data for producing the correlation maps. The results showed that the pattern of 2D maps gave insight into the samples degradation mechanism, which is of interest for many researchers in the field of forensics. Buzzini et al. [51] investigated the discrimination criteria of inkjet printer inks by Raman. Inkjet-printed documents produce "Microscopic Colored Dots (MCD)" that can be detected using a "Microscopical" approach coupled with Raman spectroscopy. The general aim of the studying was "to investigate whether the Raman data collected from the three cyan, magenta, and yellow microscopic colored dots constitute, coupled, a chemical signature of enough discriminating quality to provide trustworthy investigative leads in a time effective and non-destructive manner". The criteria were crucial to achieve discriminations between inks of the same and different brands and even the same models. Although Raman technology is efficient in characterization of colorants, the study showed that the contribution of minor peaks within Raman spectra improves the discriminating power of the technique. The joint consideration of the three colored components was also effective in distinguish inkjet printer ink samples, especially those from the same brand and in some cases from the same model. The results of this study showed that "spectral differences are observed where Raman spectra from different samples differ completely concerning the location, number, and relative intensity of Raman bands", the authors said. Differentiations were also commonly observed in cases where Raman patterns from different samples yielded similar Raman bands along with a variable number of different bands. In addition, spectral differences were also observed in cases where the general Raman patterns were indistinguishable except for a small number (1 to 3) of minor peaks.

Verma et al. [52] proposed a method for analysis of laser printer and photocopier toners by spectral properties and chemometrics. The research aimed to provide a non-destructive forensic documents discrimination methodology that could be considered as the routine analysis of the suspected documents in forensic science laboratories. Multivariate analysis (PCA-Principal Component Analysis) technique was used, which involved building up a set of orthogonal PCs, where each PC represents a set of data features that describe data variance as a whole. About 99.59% pair-wise discrimination power for laser printer toners and 99.84% pair-wise discriminating power for photocopier toners, were recorded based on comparing qualitative and quantitative analysis.

The methodology was efficient and reliable in the discrimination process without the need to destroy the samples. The technique requires the availability of special device like LIBS, that may not be available in a wide range. Borba et al. [53] proposed an approach to distinguish blue ballpoint pen inks using Raman spectroscopy and chemometrics. The research aimed to assess whether the combination of Raman spectroscopy and chemometric tools was good enough to be used in differentiating between blue ballpoint pen inks. The used methodology included 2 phases: 1) preprocessing phase that involved selecting the appropriate derivative that would prohibit baseline and fluorescence contributions, signal normalization to facilitate comparison among ink spectra, building up dataset table, and spectral channels autoscaling. 2) Data Analysis that included exploratory analysis using PCA (Principal Component Analysis) and HCA (Hierarchal Component Analysis). In addition, Ink classification analysis using PLS-DA (Partial Least Squares- Discriminant Analysis. PLS-DA derived models were able to achieve >97% classification rate. Baseline and fluorescence contribution can affect the spectra quality and spectral band shape; therefore, a preprocessing step was necessary to prohibit these effects.

Zieba-Palus and Kunicki [53] proposed a method to integrate the micro-FTIR, XFR, and Raman methods for examining the inks of documents. The research aimed to study the ability to achieve a high distinguishing rate between ink samples by mixing destructive and nondestructive spectrometric methods. The perform this integration as follows: a) IR spectra were extracted from samples and compared to those extracted from standard dyes from Polish ink producers. The comparison showed qualitative similarity. b) Raman spectra were performed on the samples. Ten measurements were performed for several (5–7) points on a line formed by the ink. c) Three X-Ray fluorescence measurements were carried out for each sample of the examined ink to obtain elemental composition information for each sample. The results showed that approximately 95% of blue and black inks were distinguished based on IR and Raman Spectra, whereas 90% of discrimination was achieved for the gel inks samples examined with IR & Raman methods only. The discrimination power can be increased if elemental composition information were considered. The proposed methodology combined the best of both worlds, the chemometric and spectrometric methods. In case the examined sample was unrecognizable by spectrometric methods, it will diffidently be recognized by its elemental composition information. The proposed methodology can lead to the destruction of the examined document. Table 3 summarizes the described works along with their advantages and limitations.

According to the aforementioned approaches, most of the approaches used LIBS and Raman technology for extracting the spectrums of documents. Then, these spectrums are almost analyzed using some mathematical and statistical approaches.

Table 3. Summarizing the spectroscopy-based forgery detections techniques.

Authors	Document used	Methodology	Advantages	Limitations
Cicconi et al. [45] (2020)	Documents with Signatures	LIBS spectroscopy	Ability to differentiate between different kinds of inks	Difficulties in examining same inks on different types of papers
Hui et al. [44] (2019)	Black Printing Inks	LIBS spectroscopy with Principal Component Analysis (PCA)	Consumed short time, low cost, and does not need sample pre-treatment steps	NA
Ameh and Ozovehe [46] (2018)	Printed Documents	FT-IS	Simple, useful, reproducible, and direct method	Complex
Buzzini et al. [50] (2018)	Inkjet Printer Inks	Micro-Raman spectroscopy	Efficient	High computational cost
Verma et al. [51] (2018)	Inks of Laser Printer and Photocopier Toners	Spectral Properties and Chemometrics LIBS with PCA	Efficient and reliable	NA
Zięba et al. [49] (2017)	Degraded Papers	Infrared and Raman spectroscopy	Efficient	Complex
Zieba-Palus and Kunicki [53] (2016)	Several Types of Inks	Micro-FTIR, Raman spectroscopy, and XRF	Efficient	The detection power is increased if elemental composition info. were considered, which lead to the destruction of the examined document

5 Conclusions

This review presented the state-of-the-art in the field of forgery detection in forensics science. The review investigated three aspects in forgery detection, namely, *Image Processing Techniques*, *Video Processing Techniques*, and *Spectroscopy-Based Techniques*. This work can be used as a reliable guide for the researchers who recently start their journey in the field of forgery detection since it provided the main and the most effective approaches in the three main aspects of the field. Moreover, the selection of the technique used in performing the forgery detection was based on many factors such as the type of the questioned documents (e.g., currencies, official certificates, images, or even video files), and the available tools (e.g., software and devices). Besides, the experience, qualifications, and background of researchers can also play a significant role in selecting the appropriate method.

This review showed a lot of approaches that can be adopted and each of which has advantages and limitations. In general, there is a trade-off between the accuracy of the adopted approach and the complexity. This means, complex approaches usually obtain a more accurate detection rate. Therefore, it is crucial to comprehend the approach and its main limitations before adopting it aiming to have an approach that meets the goal. Also, researchers should be aware of the cost of the tools, devices, and software that will be used when they try to design forgery detection approaches. In this context, researchers try to integrate the characteristics of more than one approach to develop an efficient approach in terms of cost and accuracy. Finally, in the future, this review will support researchers and developers of digital forensics in having a wider view of the approaches used in the literature.

Acknowledgment. We would like to thank the Computer Science Dept. at the University of Mosul/Iraq for all the support provided to achieve this research. We also would like to thank the Iraqi Ministry of Interior for all the support in our project.

References

1. Roux, C., Crispino, F., Ribaux, O.: From forensics to forensic science. Curr. Issues Crim. Just. **24**(1), 7–24 (2012)
2. Garfinkel, S., Farrell, P., Roussev, V., Dinolt, G.: Bringing science to digital forensics with standardized forensic corpora. Digit. Invest. **6**, S2–S11 (2009)
3. Henderson, S.: How do people manage their documents?: an empirical investigation into personal document management practices among knowledge workers, Doctoral dissertation, ResearchSpace@ Auckland (2009)
4. Deshmukh, A., Wankhade, S.B.: Deepfake detection approaches using deep learning: a systematic review. Intell. Comput. Netw. 293–302 (2021)
5. Morelato, M., et al.: Forensic intelligence framework—Part I: induction of a transversal model by comparing illicit drugs and false identity documents monitoring. Forensic Sci. Int. **236**, 181–190 (2014)
6. Pollitt, M.: A history of digital forensics. In: Chow, K.-P., Shenoi, S. (eds.) Advances in Digital Forensics VI, pp. 3–15. Springer, Heidelberg (2010). https://doi.org/10.1007/978-3-642-15506-2_1
7. Bicknell, D.E., Laporte, G.M.: Forged and counterfeit documents. In: Wiley Encyclopedia of Forensic Science (2009)
8. Casey, E.: Digital Evidence And Computer Crime: Forensic Science, Computers, and the Internet. Academic Press, London (2011)
9. Chambers, J., Yan, W., Garhwal, A., Kankanhalli, M.: Currency security and forensics: a survey. Multimed. Tools Appl. **74**(11), 4013–4043 (2014). https://doi.org/10.1007/s11042-013-1809-x
10. Pavia, D.L., Lampman, G.M., Kriz, G.S., Vyvyan, J.A.: Introduction to spectroscopy. Nelson Education (2014)

11. Shipp, D.W., Sinjab, F., Notingher, I.: Raman spectroscopy: techniques and applications in the life sciences. Adv. Opt. Photonics **9**(2), 315–428 (2017)
12. Markiewicz-Keszycka, M., et al.: Laser-induced breakdown spectroscopy (LIBS) for food analysis: a review. Trends Food Sci. Technol. **65**, 80–93 (2017)
13. Chalmers, J.M., Edwards, H.G., Hargreaves, M.D. (eds.): Infrared and Raman Spectroscopy in Forensic Science. Wiley, Hoboken (2012)
14. Muthukrishnan, R., Radha, M.: Edge detection techniques for image segmentation. Int. J. Comput. Sci. Inf. Technol. **3**(6), 259 (2011)
15. Dixit, R., Naskar, R.: Review, analysis and parameterisation of techniques for copy–move forgery detection in digital images. IET Image Proc. **11**(9), 746–759 (2017)
16. Barad, Z.J., Goswami, M.M.: Image forgery detection using deep learning: a survey. In: 2020 6th International Conference on Advanced Computing and Communication Systems (ICACCS), Buenos Aires, Argentina, pp. 571–576. IEEE (2020)
17. Zou, M., Yao, H., Qin, C., Zhang, X.: Statistical analysis of signal-dependent noise: application in blind localization of image splicing forgery. arXiv preprint arXiv:2010.16211 (2020)
18. Gorai, A., Pal, R., Gupta, P.: Document fraud detection by ink analysis using texture features and histogram matching. In: 2016 International Joint Conference on Neural Networks (IJCNN), pp. 4512–4517. IEEE (2016)
19. Cruz, F., Sidere, N., Coustaty, M., D'Andecy, V.P., Ogier, J.M.: Local binary patterns for document forgery detection. : 2017 14th IAPR International Conference on Document Analysis and Recognition (ICDAR), vol. 1, pp. 1223–1228. IEEE (2017)
20. Tolosana, R., Vera-Rodriguez, R., Fierrez, J., Morales, A., Ortega-Garcia, J.: Deepfakes and beyond: a survey of face manipulation and fake detection. Inf. Fus. **64**, 131–148 (2020)
21. Yu, N., Davis, L., Fritz, M.: Attributing fake images to gans: analyzing fingerprints in generated images. arXiv preprint arXiv:1811.08180 (2018)
22. Rossler, A., Cozzolino, D., Verdoliva, L., Riess, C., Thies, J., Nießner, M.: Faceforensics++: learning to detect manipulated facial images. In: Proceedings of the IEEE/CVF International Conference on Computer Vision, pp. 1–11 (2019)
23. Marra, F., Saltori, C., Boato, G., & Verdoliva, L.: Incremental learning for the detection and classification of gan-generated images. In: 2019 IEEE International Workshop on Information Forensics and Security (WIFS), pp. 1–6. IEEE (2019)
24. Wang, Y., Dantcheva, A.: A video is worth more than 1000 lies. Comparing 3DCNN approaches for detecting deepfakes. In: FG'20, 15th IEEE International Conference on Automatic Face and Gesture Recognition, May 18–22, 2020, Buenos Aires, Argentina (2020)
25. Stamm, M.C., Wu, M., Liu, K.R.: Information forensics: an overview of the first decade. IEEE Access **1**, 167–200 (2013)
26. Afchar, D., Nozick, V., Yamagishi, J., Echizen, I.: MesoNet: a compact facial video forgery detection network. In: 2018 IEEE International Workshop on Information Forensics and Security (WIFS), pp. 1–7. IEEE (2018)
27. Christian, A., Sheth, R.: Digital video forgery detection and authentication technique-a review. Int. J. Sci. Res. Sci. Technol. (IJSRST) **2**(6), 138–143 (2016)
28. Upadhyay, S., Singh, S.K.: Video authentication: issues and challenges. Int. J. Comput. Sci. Issues (IJCSI) **9**(1), 409 (2012)
29. Shelke, N.A., Kasana, S.S.: A comprehensive survey on passive techniques for digital video forgery detection. Multimed. Tools Appl. **80**(4), 6247–6310 (2020). https://doi.org/10.1007/s11042-020-09974-4
30. Fayyaz, M.A., Anjum, A., Ziauddin, S., Khan, A., Sarfaraz, A.: An improved surveillance video forgery detection technique using sensor pattern noise and correlation of noise residues. Multimed. Tools Appl. **79**(9–10), 5767–5788 (2019). https://doi.org/10.1007/s11042-019-08236-2

31. Aloraini, M., Sharifzadeh, M., Agarwal, C., Schonfeld, D.: Statistical sequential analysis for object-based video forgery detection. Electron. Imaging **2019**(5), 543–551 (2019)
32. Richao, C., Gaobo, Y., Ningbo, Z.: Detection of object-based manipulation by the statistical features of object con-tour. Forensic Sci. Int. **236**, 164–169 (2014)
33. Mathai, M., Rajan, D., Emmanuel, S.: Video forgery detection and localization using normalized cross-correlation of moment features. In: 2016 IEEE southwest symposium on image analysis and interpretation (SSIAI), pp. 149–152. IEEE (2016)
34. Wang, W., Farid, H.: Exposing digital forgeries in video by detecting double MPEG compression. In: Proceedings of the 8th Workshop on Multimedia and Security, pp. 37–47 (2006)
35. Nguyen, H.H., Yamagishi, J., Echizen, I.: Capsule-forensics: using capsule networks to detect forged images and videos. In: ICASSP 2019–2019 IEEE International Conference on Acoustics, Speech and Signal Processing (ICASSP), pp. 2307–2311. IEEE (2019)
36. Aloraini, M., Sharifzadeh, M., Schonfeld, D.: Sequential and patch analyses for object removal video forgery detection and localization. IEEE Trans. Circuits Syst. Video Technol. (2020)
37. Kharat, J., Chougule, S.: A passive blind forgery detection technique to identify frame duplication attack. Multimed. Tools Appl. **79**, 1–17 (2020). https://doi.org/10.1007/s11042-019-08272-y
38. Kuznetsov, A.: Digital video forgery detection based on statistical features calculation. In: Twelfth International Conference on Machine Vision (ICMV 2019), vol. 11433, p. 114332O. International Society for Optics and Photonics (2020)
39. Al-Sanjary, O.I., Sulong, G.: Detection of video forgery: a review of literature. J. Theoret. Appl. Inf. Technol. **74**(2) (2015)
40. Kucharska-Ambrożej, K., Karpinska, J.: The application of spectroscopic techniques in combination with chemometrics for detection adulteration of some herbs and spices. Microchem. J. **153**, 104278 (2020)
41. Lennard, C., El-Deftar, M.M., Robertson, J.: Forensic application of laser-induced breakdown spectroscopy for the discrimination of questioned documents. Forensic Sci. Int. **254**, 68–79 (2015)
42. Elsherbiny, N., Nassef, O.A.: Wavelength dependence of laser induced breakdown spectroscopy (LIBS) on questioned document investigation. Sci. Just. **55**(4), 254–263 (2015)
43. Gál, L., Belovičová, M., Oravec, M., Palková, M., Čeppan, M.: Analysis of laser and inkjet prints using spectroscopic methods for forensic identification of questioned documents (2013)
44. Hui, Y.W., Mahat, N.A., Ismail, D., Ibrahim, R.K.R.: Laser-induced breakdown spectroscopy (LIBS) for printing ink analysis coupled with principle component analysis (PCA). In: AIP Conference Proceedings, vol. 2155, no. 1, p. 020010. AIP Publishing LLC (2019)
45. Cicconi, F., Lazic, V., Palucci, A., Almeida Assis, A.C., Saverio Romolo, F.: Forensic analysis of commercial inks by laser-induced breakdown spectroscopy (LIBS). Sensors **20**(13), 3744 (2020)
46. Ameh, P.O., Ozovehe, M.S.: Forensic examination of inks extracted from printed documents using Fourier transform infrared spectroscopy. Edelweiss. Appl. Sci. Tech. **2**, 10–17 (2018)
47. Udristioiu, F.M., Bunaciu, A.A., Aboul-Enein, H.Y., Tanase, I.G.: Application of micro-Raman and FT- IR spectroscopy in forensic analysis of questioned documents. G U Fen Bilimleri Dergisi (G. U. J. Sci.), **25**(2), 371–375 (2012)
48. Raza, A., Saha, B.: Application of Raman spectroscopy in forensic investigation of questioned documents involving stamp inks. Sci. Justice **53**(3), 332–338 (2013)
49. Zięba-Palus, J., Wesełucha-Birczyńska, A., Trzcińska, B., Kowalski, R., Moskal, P.: Analysis of degraded papers by infrared and Raman spectroscopy for forensic purposes. J. Mol. Struct. **1140**, 154–162 (2017)
50. Buzzini, P., Polston, C., Schackmuth, M.: On the criteria for the discrimination of inkjet printer inks using micro-Raman spectroscopy. J. Raman Spectrosc. **49**(11), 1791–1801 (2018)

51. Verma, N., Kumar, R., Sharma, V.: Analysis of laser printer and photocopier toners by spectral properties and chemometrics. Spectrochim. Acta Part A Mol. Biomol. Spectrosc. **196**, 40–48 (2018)
52. Borba, F.D.S.L., Honorato, R.S., de Juan, A.: Use of Raman spectroscopy and chemometrics to distinguish blue ballpoint pen inks. Forensic Sci. Int. **249**, 73–82 (2015)
53. Zięba-Palus, J., Kunicki, M.: Application of the micro-FTIR spectroscopy, Raman spectroscopy and XRF method examination of inks. Forensic Sci. Int. **158**(2–3), 164–172 (2006)

A New Secret Sharing Scheme Based on Hermite Interpolation and Folded Magic Cube Rules

Rafid Abdulaziz[1], Ali Sagheer[2], and Omar Dawood[3](✉)

[1] College of Education for Pure Sciences, University of Anbar, Anbar, Iraq
rafid.alhashimy@uoanbar.edu.iq

[2] Al-Qalam University College, Dean of Al-Qalam University College, Kirkuk, Iraq
dean@alqalam.edu.iq

[3] College of Computer Science & IT, University of Anbar, Ramadi 31001, Iraq
omar-abdulrahman@uoanbar.edu.iq

Abstract. In this paper, a modern secret sharing scheme has been proposed that deal with set of variables points along specific polynomial. The main idea is to establish the dimension of magic cube into a secret point at a Lagrange polynomial equation. The secret value can be reconstructed from set of cooperated dealers or participants according to predefined threshold. The core idea is how to reconstruct a full magic cube of six dimensions across single key solution. The proposed method adopted Hermite mathematical comprehension that allows minimum number of participants with k-points under definition of a polynomial with degree $k - 1$ to reconstruct the secret properly. The proposed scheme supposed each dealer has his own share and any group of shareholders at the decided threshold together they can recover the secret. The proposed idea gave a good implementation and fast secret recovery with new mathematical orientation.

Keywords: Shamir's secret sharing · Magic square · Magic cube · Hermite interpolation · Lagrange

1 Introduction

Secrets sharing is an important cryptographic principle to people ever since humans started to interact with each other. There are a lot of information which we do not want other people to know, while there is other information which we could not risk landing in the wrong hands. One example perhaps would be our ATM passwords [1]. In modern cryptography, the security of data is fully dependent on the security of the keys used. As most of the ciphers are public knowledge, one can easily encrypt and decrypt any message if they know the key involved. For some highly confidential data, it's not always good to have a single person in control of the key and to secure the data. This has led to the need for Secret Sharing Schemes, which allow keys to be distributed among a group of people, with a pre-specified number of them needing to input their share in order, to access the key [2].

In 1979 Shamir [3] and Blakley [4] introduced the concept of secret sharing through threshold schemes. Their models were based on polynomials and finite geometries.

P. Liatsis et al. (Eds.): TIOTC 2021, CCIS 1548, pp. 352–364, 2022.
https://doi.org/10.1007/978-3-030-97255-4_26

Since 1979 many researchers have taken the basic concept of a threshold scheme and used other mathematical structures to adapt threshold schemes to meet the needs of many practical situations [5]. Secret sharing plays an important role in protecting important information from getting lost, destroyed, or into wrong hands. A secret can be shared among *n* participants. At least *t* or more participants can reconstruct the secret, but (*t* -1) or fewer participants can obtain nothing about the secret. To share another secret, the secret dealer must redistribute every participant *s* secret shadow [6, 7]. Secret sharing is an important topic in modern cryptography whose goal is to break one (or more) secret(*s*) into pieces called shares and distribute them among persons called participants in a way that whenever a predetermined subset of these participants pool their shares, the secret(*s*) can be recovered. One of the famous members of this family is (*t, n*) threshold secret sharing. In this method, *t* or more participants who pool their shares can reconstruct the secret(*s*) [8].

2 Related Works

Muthukumar, K. A., & Nandhini, M in [9], have introduced the performance of two algorithms viz., secret sharing algorithm and information dispersal algorithm that are compared and modified secret sharing algorithm and which is proposed for medical data sharing. Phenomenon of secure medical data sharing in cloud environment is discussed with two algorithms Secret sharing algorithm and information dispersal algorithm and their concerns are analyzed with different complexities. This modified secret sharing algorithm is proposed to overcome the issues faced by the existing algorithms. Through this algorithm, medical data can be shared in secured way according to the data requested by the client. The existing drawbacks are overcome in this proposed one and it can be used for dynamic database without affecting the users. It is very well suited for sharing high sensitive data in multi cloud environment. Also Further work is recommended to improve the system performance and increase the flexibility of system.

Lan, Y., Wu, C., & Zhang, Y. in [10], have proposed a secret sharing-based key management (SSKM). SSKM utilizes the advantages of hierarchical architecture and adopt two-level key mechanism, which can efficiently enhance and protect the all over network security and survivability. Different from previous works, the SSKM distributes keys based on secret sharing mechanism by the clustered architecture, which not only localizes the key things but also keeps scalability. The SSKM provides various session keys, the network key for base station (BS) and cluster heads (CHs); the cluster key between the cluster head and member nodes. The SSKM dynamically generates different keys based on different polynomials from BS in different periods which can protect the network from the compromised nodes and reduce the high probability of the common keys. The SSKM can prevent several attacks effectively and reduce the energy consumption. The Salient advantage of this work is addressed challenging security issues by localizing key things based on secret sharing theory. This paper presents the network key and cluster key and generate new keys from various polynomials by Lagrange interpolation formula. Meanwhile, SSKM has an authentication mechanism to ensure the scalability, which can not only authenticate the new sensor but also can isolate the compromised node.

Diaconu, A. V., & Loukhaoukha, K. in [11], have proposed a newly designed image cryptosystem that uses the Rubik's cube principle in conjunction with a digital chaotic cipher. Thus, the original image is shuffled on Rubik's cube principle (due to its proven confusion properties), and then XOR operator is applied to rows and columns of the scrambled image using a chaos-based cipher (due to its proven diffusion properties). This work develops novel permutation—substitution image encryption architecture, based on Rubik's cube principle and digital chaotic cipher. The proposed encryption system includes two major parts, chaotic pixels substitution (in order to achieve desired diffusion factor) and Rubik's cube, principle based, pixels permutation (in order to achieve desired confusion factor). Different keys were used for shuffling and ciphering procedures, and while a tent map was used to generate image's ciphering matrices, each row's and column's intrinsic properties were used to compute the number of their circular shifts. Comprehensive experimental tests have been carried out, and numerical analyses have shown robustness of the proposed algorithm against several cryptanalytic attacks. Likewise, the performance assessment tests attest that the proposed image encryption scheme is fast and highly secure. Although a much smaller key space is used, but still large enough to face against exhaustive attack, with a smaller key size, the proposed encryption scheme presents better results, compared to those of previously proposed ones.

Feng, X., Tian, X., & Xia, S. in [12], have introduced a novel image encryption algorithm based on the discrete fractional Fourier transform and an improved magic cube rotation scrambling algorithm. Through fractional Fourier transform and position scrambling, the proposed algorithm can achieve double image encryption in the time-frequency domain. Compared the encrypted images and decrypted images, the proposed image encryption algorithm has better performance than only using fractional Fourier transform.

3 Hermite Interpolation Method

Hermite interpolation is an extension of Lagrange's interpolation. When using divided differences to calculate the Hermite polynomial of a function f [13, 14].

To suppose that a function f(x) is defined on a closed interval [a, b]. given n + 1 data points $x_0, x_1, x_2, \ldots, x_n$, $(a \le x\_i \le b, x\_i \ne x\_j \, for \; i \ne j)$, and values.

$$F_k = f(x_k), f_k' = f'(x_k), k = 0, 1, 2, \ldots, n$$

Suppose we want to find a 2n + 1 dimensional polynomial P(x) such that P(x) satisfies.

$$P(x_k) = f_k, p'(x_k) = f'k, k = 0, 1, 2, \ldots, n$$

The problem here is to find such a polynomial *P(x)* that is called Hermite interpolation.

Here, it is known that we can get an unique 2n + 1 dimensional polynomial P(x) by the following equation.

$$\text{P(x)} = \sum\nolimits_i^n f_i \, h_i(x) + \sum\nolimits_i^n f_i' \, g_i(x)$$

Where two 2n + 1 dimensional polynomial $h_i(x)$, $g_i(x)$ satisfy.

$$h_i(x_j) = \begin{cases} 1 \; i = j \\ 0 \; i \neq j \end{cases}$$

$$g_i(x_j) = 0 \text{ for any } \; \text{I, j}$$

And

$$h_i'(x_j) = 0 \text{ for any } \; \text{I, j}$$

$$g_i'(x_j) = \begin{cases} 1 \; i = j \\ 0 \; i \neq j \end{cases}$$

This is called Hermite interpolation.

4 Magic Square and Magic Cube Rules

Magic squares have been studied for at least three thousand years, the earliest recorded appearance dating to about 2200 B.C., in china. In the 19th century, Arab astrologers used them in calculating horoscopes, and by 1300 A.D. magic square had spread to the west. An engraving by the German artist embedded the date, 1514, in the form of two consecutive numbers in the bottom row, because the concept of a magic square is so easily understood, magic squares have been particularly attractive to puzzles and an amateur mathematicians [15].

An n × n magic square is a permutation of n2 distinct numbers, 1, 2, 3,···, n^2 (each number is used once), in a square matrix, where the sums of the numbers in each row, each column, and the forward and backward main diagonals are equal. This sum is normally called the magic constant. According to whether size n is an even or odd number, a magic square can be called an even order or odd order one. Further, the even order magic squares can be classified into doubly even order and singly even order ones depending on whether or not n can be divided by 4 [16].

The magic constant (MC), magic vector or magic number, these terms are synonyms that can be calculated by the derivative formula (1).

$$\text{MC} = \frac{n^2(n^2 + 1)}{2} \tag{1}$$

Thus, 3 * 3 normal magic square must have its rows, columns and diagonals adding to MC = 15, MC = $3(3^2 + 1)/2$ = 15, 4 * 4 to MC = 34, 5 * 5 to MC = 65 and 8 * 8 to MC = 260, and so on. The Magic Sum (MS) is another significant term that includes the summation to all the numbers by (rows, columns and diagonals) in a magic square uses the following formula (2).

$$\text{MS} = \frac{n^2(n^2 + 1)}{2} \tag{2}$$

The MS for 3 * 3 = 45, MS for 4 * 4 = 136, MS for 5 * 5 = 325, MS for 8 * 8 = 2080 and so on, other method for calculating MS is by multiplying the MC by dimension of the magic square [17].

The following Fig. 1 below is a simple example of a magic square of order 3 with 9 values arranged consecutively in the magical order. So, suppose MC is the number that each row, column and diagonal must be add up to a vector numbers, and (P) is a pivot element for the numbers through which the magic square is determined and constructed. The pivot element in the magic square represents the center element in the middle square as it explained and mentioned with shaded central number, and through which can be determined some properties of the magic square.

8	1	6
3	5	7
4	9	2

Fig. 1. Magic square of order 3

The pivot element at any magic square of odd order with sequential numbers can be calculated with the following formula:

$$P = \frac{(n^2 + 1)}{2}$$

For example: the following two examples include pivot computing in magic square of order three and order five.

$$P = \frac{(n^2 + 1)}{2} = \frac{(3^2 + 1)}{2} = 5$$

$$P = \frac{(n^2 + 1)}{2} = \frac{(5^2 + 1)}{2} = 13$$

And so on Here, is another formula to determine the pivot element in non-sequential odd order numbers that might begin with indeterminate integer number, or have a period, in another word that have difference between the numbers greater than one. As stated below in Eq. (3). Where N = square order, A = starting number and D = difference number that represents the difference between the successive and the previous numbers. The Fig. 2 below states three of different examples a, b and c respectively that explains the whole notation [18].

$$P = \frac{(2 * A + D(n^2 - 1))}{2} \tag{3}$$

$$P = \frac{(2 * 54 + 3(3^2 - 1))}{2} = 66$$

$$P = \frac{(2 * 17 + 5(3^2 - 1))}{2} = 37$$

$$P = \frac{(2 * 3 + 2(3^2 - 1))}{2} = 11$$

75	54	69
60	66	72
63	78	57

(a) N=3, A=54, D=3

52	17	42
27	37	47
32	57	22

(b) N=3, A=17, D=5

17	3	13
7	11	15
9	19	5

(c) N=3, A=3, D=2

Fig. 2. Three magic square of order three with constant difference

A magic cube of order n is a 3-dimensional n * n * n matrix (cubical table)

$$Q_n = [q(i,j,k);\ 1 \leq i,j,k \leq n]$$

Containing the natural numbers 1, 2, 3,…, n3 in some order, and such that.

$$\sum\nolimits_{x=1}^{n} q(x,j,k) = \sum\nolimits_{x=1}^{n} q(i,x,k) = \sum\nolimits_{x=1}^{n} q(i,j,x) = \frac{n(n^3+1)}{2} \text{ For all } i,j,k = 1,$$

(Note that in a magic cube we make no requirement about the sums of elements on any diagonal). The triple of numbers (i; j; k) called the coordinates of the element q(i; j; k) (Fig. 3).

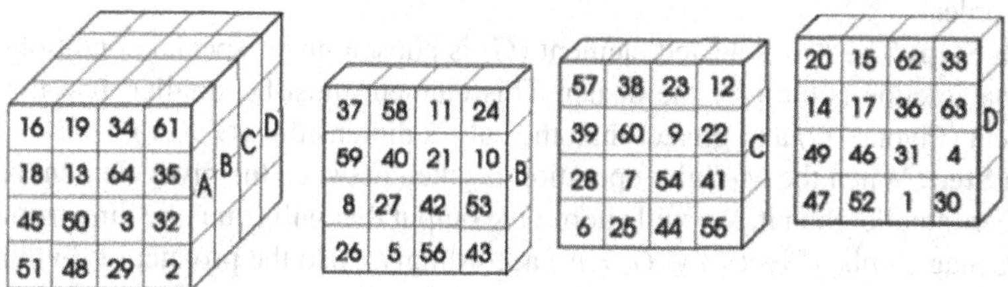

Fig. 3. Magic cube

A magic square of order 1 is a magic cube of order 1. Just as a magic square of order 2 does not exist a magic cube of order 2 does not exist either [19]. The basic feature of magic cube is that the sum of all numbers in each layers, each column, each row and main space diagonal is equal to single number, this number is called as magic constant of a cube, denoted by M3(n).

$$M_3(n) = \frac{n(n^2+1)}{2}$$

According to the theorem stated by M. Trenkler, magic cube can be constructed from the combination of magic square and two orthogonal Latin squares [20].

5 The Proposed Secret Sharing Method

The main objective behind the adopted magic cube idea is to transfer the magic cube properties from the dealer to a group of trusted subscribers. The pivot element of one of the six magic squares is selected from the magic cube and sent within a polynomial (secret) to the participants. In addition to sending another selected element (The element of G) to the subscribers through which will be obtained the characteristics of the magic cube and then reconstructed the original magic cube again. The following steps describe the main notations for the mixing of magic cube with secret sharing using Hermite interpolation.

- **First Step:** Build a magic cube of odd order from six magical squares, and the magic cube numbers start from a dedicated number with a specific difference value between the numbers.
- **Second Step:** The pivot element is selected from the first magic square of the Magic Cube to use it as a secret value in the polynomial to compute the main points (x_i, y_i) and its derivatives $(y\prime_i)$ and send them to the participants.

$$F(x) = (pivot) + a_1 x + a_2 x^2 + \ldots + a_{k-1} x^{k-1} \text{ mod } prime \tag{4}$$

$$F(x) = a_1 + 2 \cdot a_2 \text{x} + \ldots + \text{k} \cdot a_k \cdot x^{k-1} \text{ mod } prime \tag{5}$$

- **Third Step:** Magic cube properties are sent to subscribers to be rebuilt again according to the some parameters likewise (Start value, Difference value, Pivot element and the cube order).
- **Forth Step:** The new selected element (G) is chosen under special conditions after the magic cube is built by the dealer. This element must be smaller than the pivot element (Pivot > G) and greater than the cube's dimensions ($G > N$).
- **Fifth Step:** When the Modular operation is taken between the pivot element and the numbers smaller than it. We will choose the output that will equal the dimensions (N) of the magic cube (Pivot Mod $G = N$) accordingly. Also the product of dividing the (G) element on the dimensions of the magic cube will represent the difference (D) value according to (G Divide N = Difference).
- **Sixth Step:** After sending the points and (G) number to the participants. The Hermite interpolation is used to reconstruct the secret again to obtain the pivot element (secret).

$$H_{2n+1}(x) = \sum\nolimits_{j=0}^{n} f(x_j) H_{n,j}(x) + \sum\nolimits_{j=0}^{n} f'(x_j) \hat{H}_{n,j}(x) \tag{6}$$

Where

$$H_{n,j}(x) = \left[1 - 2(x - x_j)\hat{L}_{n,j}(x_j)\right] L_{n,j}^2(x) \tag{7}$$

And

$$\hat{H}_{n,j}(x) = (x - x_j) L_{n,j}^2(x). \tag{8}$$

- **Seventh Step:** After obtaining the pivot element, it will calculate the (Pivot Mod G) to get the Dimensions (N) of the Magic cube, and (G Divide N) to obtain the difference (D) between the Magic cube numbers.

- **Eighth Step:** After obtaining (Pivot, Dimensions and Difference) of the magic cube, it is easy to obtain the starting number (A) of the Magic cube by the equation regarding the Eq. (10) below:

$$\text{Pivot} = \frac{(2*A) + D*\left(N^2 - 1\right)}{2} \tag{9}$$

$$\text{Start Number} = \frac{(\text{ Pivot } *2) - D*\left(N^2 - 1\right)}{2} \tag{10}$$

Example:
Assume that a folded magic cube of odd order (5 * 5) consisting of six magic squares, starting by the number 5 and with a constant difference between the sequential numbers is 3 as shown in Fig. 4.

53	74	5	26	47
71	17	23	44	50
14	20	41	62	68
32	38	59	65	11
35	56	77	8	29

1st Square

128	149	80	101	122
146	92	98	119	125
89	95	116	137	143
107	113	134	140	86
110	131	152	83	104

2nd Square

203	224	155	176	197
221	167	173	194	200
164	170	191	212	218
182	188	209	215	161
185	206	227	158	179

3rd Square

278	299	230	251	272
296	242	248	269	275
239	245	266	287	293
257	263	284	290	236
260	281	302	233	254

4th Square

353	374	305	326	347
371	317	323	344	350
314	320	341	362	368
332	338	359	365	311
335	356	377	308	329

5th Square

428	449	380	401	422
446	392	398	419	425
389	395	416	437	443
407	413	434	440	386
410	431	452	383	404

6th Square

Dimension = 5, Difference = 3, Start = 5

Fig. 4. The magic cube

The Pivot element (41) of the first magic square is selected in the magic cube to be the secret within a polynomial. After that select the other coefficients randomly within the polynomial to produce (y_i) as stated in Eq. (11), additionally, compute the derivative of polynomial to deduce the ($y\prime_i$) as stated in Eq. (12). The magic cube properties are represented in the Hermite interpolation with the following important parameters:

Where n = participants, k = threshold, D = difference.

$$n = 6, k = 3, p = 53, p > s \text{ and } p > n$$

$$F(x) = (pivot) + a_1x + a_2x^2 + \ldots + a_kx^k \quad mod\ prime$$

$$F(x) = 41 + 9x + 11x^2 \quad mod\ 53 \tag{11}$$

And

$$f'(x) = a_1 + 2 \cdot a_2x + \ldots.. + K \cdot a_kx^{k-1} \quad mod\ prime$$

$$f'(x) = 9 + 22x \quad mod \quad 53 \tag{12}$$

As a result; six points (x_i, y_i) and (y'_i) of the polynomial are calculated and sent to six trusted subscribers (n) by the dealer as explained in Table 1.

Table 1. $(X, f(x))$ and the derivative $(f'(x))$

(x)	$f(x)$	$f'(x)$	Points $(x, f(x))$, $(f'(x))$
1	8	31	(1, 8), (31)
2	50	0	(2, 50), (0)
3	8	22	(3, 8), (22)
4	41	44	(4, 41), (44)
5	43	13	(5, 43), (13)
6	14	35	(6, 14), (35)

Compute a suitable (G) number that fits to the pivot element and the dimensions (D) of the cube to be $(G = 18)$. Pivot $> G$, $G >$ Dimension (N).

$$41 > 18 > 5$$

Distribute the generated six points to six subscribers accompanied by the element (G). The selection of any three points $(k = 3)$ to reconstruct the secret (Pivot) will be verified:

For Example: $D_0 = (1, 8, 31)$, $D_1 = (2, 50, 0)$, $D_2 = (3, 8, 22)$.
Compute the Hermite interpolation:
First compute the Lagrange polynomials and their derivatives:

$$L_{2,0}(x) = \frac{x - x_1}{x_0 - x_1} * \frac{x - x_2}{x_0 - x_2} = \frac{1}{2}x^2 - \frac{5}{2}x + 3, \quad L'_{2,0}(x) = x - \frac{5}{2} = -1.5$$

And

$$L_{2,1}(x) = \frac{x - x_0}{x_1 - x_0} * \frac{x - x_2}{x_1 - x_2} = -x^2 + 4x - 3, \quad L'_{2,1}(x) = -2x + 4 = 0$$

$$L_{2,2}(x) = \frac{x - x_0}{x_2 - x_0} * \frac{x - x_1}{x_2 - x_1} = \frac{1}{2}x^2 - \frac{3}{2}x + 1, \quad L'_{2,2}(x) = x - \frac{3}{2} = 1.5$$

The polynomials $H_{2,j}$ and $\widehat{H}_{2,j}$ are then:

$$H_{n,j}(x) = [1 - 2(x - x_j)\hat{L}_{n,j}(x_j)]L^2_{n,j}(x)$$

$$H_{2,0}(x) = [1 - 2(x - 1)(-1.5)]\left(\frac{1}{2}x^2 - \frac{5}{2}x + 3\right)^2 = -18$$

$$H_{2,1}(x) = [1 - 2(x-2)(0)]\left(-x^2 + 4x - 3\right)^2 = 9$$

And

$$H_{2,2}(x) = [1 - 2(x-3)(1.5)]\left(\frac{1}{2}x^2 - \frac{3}{2}x + 1\right)^2 = 10$$

$$\hat{H}_{n,j}(x) = (x - x_j)L^2_{n,j}(x)$$

$$\widehat{H}_{2,0}(x) = (x-1)\left(\frac{1}{2}x^2 - \frac{5}{2}x + 3\right)^2 = -9$$

$$\widehat{H}_{2,1}(x) = (x-2)\left(-x^2 + 4x - 3\right)^2 = -18$$

And

$$\widehat{H}_{2,2}(x) = (x-3)\left(\frac{1}{2}x^2 - \frac{3}{2}x + 1\right)^2 = -3$$

Finally,

$$H_5(x) = (-18 * 8) + (9 * 50) + (10 * 8) + (-9 * 31) + (-18 * 0) + (-3 * 22) = 41$$

Therefore,

$$H_{2n+1}(x) = \sum\nolimits_{j=0}^{n} f(x_j)H_{n,j}(x) + \sum\nolimits_{j=0}^{n} f'(x_j)\hat{H}_{n,j}(x)$$

$$\mathrm{F(x)} = 41 + 9x + 11x^2$$

After obtaining the Pivot element and (G) elements, it is possible to deduce the dimensions (D) of the original Magic Cube:

$$\begin{aligned} \text{Pivot Mod G } &= \mathrm{N} \\ 41 \,\%\, 18 &= 5. \end{aligned} \tag{13}$$

By the same steps deduce the difference (D) between the numbers of the original Magic Cube according to the Eq. (14):

$$\begin{aligned} G/N &= D \\ 18/5 &= 3 \end{aligned} \tag{14}$$

After gotten the following parameters (Pivot, Difference and Dimension), the starting number (A) can be obtained by:

$$\text{Start Number } = \frac{(\text{ Pivot } * 2) - D * \left(N^2 - 1\right)}{2}$$

$$\text{Start Number } = \frac{(41 * 2) - 3 * \left(5^2 - 1\right)}{2} = 5$$

Finally, the six participants will have the ability to rebuild the original magic cube again as shown in Fig. 5 below (Table 2):

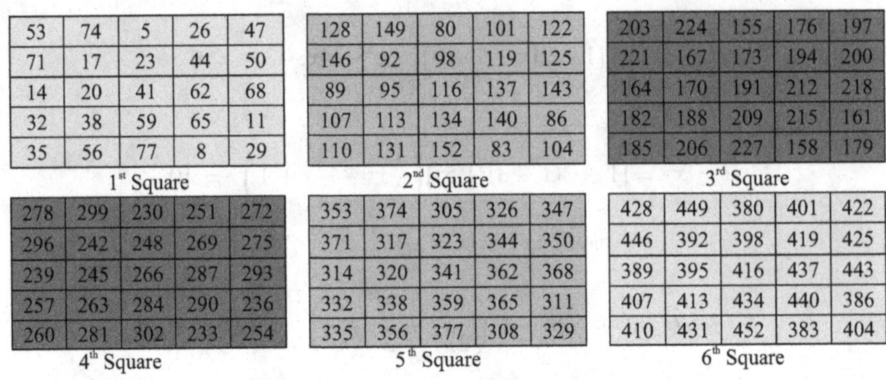

53	74	5	26	47
71	17	23	44	50
14	20	41	62	68
32	38	59	65	11
35	56	77	8	29

1st Square

128	149	80	101	122
146	92	98	119	125
89	95	116	137	143
107	113	134	140	86
110	131	152	83	104

2nd Square

203	224	155	176	197
221	167	173	194	200
164	170	191	212	218
182	188	209	215	161
185	206	227	158	179

3rd Square

278	299	230	251	272
296	242	248	269	275
239	245	266	287	293
257	263	284	290	236
260	281	302	233	254

4th Square

353	374	305	326	347
371	317	323	344	350
314	320	341	362	368
332	338	359	365	311
335	356	377	308	329

5th Square

428	449	380	401	422
446	392	398	419	425
389	395	416	437	443
407	413	434	440	386
410	431	452	383	404

6th Square

Fig. 5. The reconstructed original magic cube

Table 2. The proposed algorithm

1) Initialization of Algorithm
a- Choose a magic cube with six magic squares of odd order
2) Constructing Magic Cube (odd order)
a- The magic cube starts with a Start Number (*A*)
b- Choose the dimensions of the cube (*N*) and the amount of the difference between the cube numbers (*D*)
3) Encryption Process
a- Choose the Pivot element of the first magic square in the magic cube to be (secret) within the polynomial $f(x) = \text{pivot} + a_1x + a_2x^2 \; mod \; prime$, compute the polynomial derivative $f'(x) = a_1 + 2.a_2x \; mod \; prime$
b- Conclusion Six points of (x_i, y_i) and $\left(y_i'\right)$
c- Send points and its derivatives to six trusted subscribers
d- Determine the Threshold value
4) Generating (G) element
a- Chose the element (*G*) with conditions (Pivot > *G* > *N*)
b- The selected *G* number should satisfy the condition of (Pivot Mod *G* = *N*) and (*G* Divide *N* = *D*)
c- Send the (*G*) number to subscribers publicly
5) Decryption Process
a- Reconstruct the secret again by a specified number of subscribers (Threshold) to get the Pivot element via Hermite Interpolation
b- Pivot Mod *G* = *N*

(continued)

Table 2. (*continued*)

c- $D = G$ Divide N where the resultant integer is taken and the remainder value is ignored
d- After acquiring the properties of the magic cube (Pivot, D and N), the starting number (A) of the magic cube can be obtained through:
Start Number $(A) = \frac{(\text{Pivot} * 2) - D * (N^2 - 1)}{2}$
6) Reconstructing Magic Cube
a- Reconstructed the original magic cube through the characteristics obtained by the participants

6 Conclusion

A secret sharing scheme has been addressed where no single share can reveal any information without cooperation with other shareholders. In case one or more participant was fake then the secret cannot be reconstructed. The present method depended basically on folded magic cube with Hermite mathematical formula. The main reason for the folded magic cube is to exploit the magic cube characteristics in embedding the secret value. The dimension cube acts the main value that distributed among the shareholders across the Hermite interpolation. Hermite polynomial represents a new direction method toward the new variant of Lagrange equations that distribute the secret efficiently. The proposed method produced a good implementation and an efficient secret reconstruction for the secret value.

References

1. Tieng, D.G., Nocon, E.: Some attacks on Shami's secret sharing scheme by inside adversaries (2016)
2. Narani, S.: Social secret sharing for resource management in cloud. arXiv preprint arXiv: 1302.1185 (2013)
3. Shamir, A.: How to share a secret. Commun. ACM **22**(11), 612–613 (1979)
4. Blakley, G.R.: Safeguarding cryptographic keys. In: Proceedings of the National Computer Conference, vol. 48, no. 313 (1979)
5. Dawson, E., Donovan, D.: The breadth of Shamir's secret-sharing scheme. Comput. Secur. **13**(1), 69–78 (1994)
6. Pang, L.J., Wang, Y.M.: A new (t, n) multi-secret sharing scheme based on Shamir's secret sharing. Appl. Math. Comput. **167**(2), 840–848 (2005)
7. Peng, K.: Investigation and survey of secret sharing in verifiable distributed systems. In: 2011 12th International Conference on Parallel and Distributed Computing, Applications and Technologies, pp. 342–347. IEEE (2011)
8. Tadayon, M.H., Khanmohammadi, H., Haghighi, M.S.: Dynamic and verifiable multi-secret sharing scheme based on Hermite interpolation and bilinear maps. IET Inf. Secur. **9**(4), 234–239 (2014)
9. Muthukumar, K.A., Nandhini, M.: Modified secret sharing algorithm for secured medical data sharing in cloud environment. In: 2016 2nd International Conference on Science Technology Engineering and Management, ICONSTEM 2016, pp. 67–71 (2016)

10. Lan, Y., Wu, C., Zhang, Y.: A secret-sharing-based key management in wireless sensor network. In: Proceedings of the IEEE International Conference on Software Engineering and Service Sciences, ICSESS, pp. 676–679 (2013)
11. Diaconu, A.V., Loukhaoukha, K.: An improved secure image encryption algorithm based on Rubik's cube principle and digital chaotic cipher. Math. Prob. Eng. (2013)
12. Feng, X., Tian, X., Xia, S.: A novel image encryption algorithm based on fractional Fourier transform and magic cube rotation (5), 1008–1011 (2011)
13. Tomoko Adachi. (2015). Multi secret sharing scheme based on Hermitian interpolation (New contact points of algebraic systems, logics, languages, and computer sciences).
14. Adachi, T., Okazaki, C.: A multi-secret sharing scheme with many keys based on Hermite interpolation. J. Appl. Math. Phys. **2**(13), 1196 (2014)
15. Al-Najjar, S.A., Nuha, A.R., AAl-Heety, F.: Computation of odd magic square using a new approach with some properties. Eng. Technol. J. **30**(7), 1203–1210 (2012)
16. Duan, Z., Liu, J., Li, J., Tian, C.: Improved even order magic square construction algorithms and their applications in multi-user shared electronic accounts. Theoret. Comput. Sci. **607**, 391–410 (2015)
17. Heinz, H.D., Hendricks, J.R.: Magic squares lexicon: illustrated, published by HDH as demand indicates. 15450 92A Avenue, Surrey, BC, V3R 9B1, Canada, hdheinz@ istar. ca [ISBN 0-9687985-0-0]. John R. Hendricks, 308, p. 151 (2000)
18. Dawood, O.A., Rahma, A.M.S., Hossen, A.M.J.A.: Generalized method for constructing magic cube by folded magic squares. Int. J. Intell. Syst. Appl. **8**(1), 1 (2016)
19. Trenkler, M.: Magic cubes. Math. Gaz. **82**(493), 56–61 (1998)
20. Rajavel, D., Shantharajah, S.P.: Cubical key generation and encryption algorithm based on hybrid cube's rotation. In: International Conference on Pattern Recognition, Informatics and Medical Engineering (2012)

Investigation on the Impact of Video Games on People Who Use New Technology

Hoshang Kolivand[1], Shiva Asadianfam[2](✉), and Daniel Wrotkowski[1]

[1] Department of Computer Science, Liverpool John Moores University, Liverpool L3 3AF, UK
h.kolivand@ljmu.ac.uk

[2] Department of Computer Engineering, Qom Branch, Islamic Azad University, Qom, Iran

Abstract. Nowadays, every fourth person in the world is a player, which means that there are two billion players in the world, the gaming industry is enormous and the average person, several times during everyday life, encounters something related to games. The impact that games have on the modern world is massive. In particular popular games that have different types of influence on players and those messages from this game are not necessarily good things. The main task of this project is to reduce the impact of games that have negative aspects of our society in particular violence. This project objective is to create a program that will help a person examine if this person can play games that contain violence. The secondary objective is to post materials that show how long a person can use various gaming devices and encourage young people to spend more time without games. This project's program aims to inform a person can play games that contain violence, to inform what the negative aspects of prolong use different gaming devices are and to inform of better ways to spend time without any electronic devices.

Keywords: Video games · Game and people · New technology · Player

1 Introduction

Games that are full of violence can make people who play these games more likely to use violence than people who play games without violence. Especially young people who have contact with such games more than once a day. A similar situation is also in the case of drugs. When tested with one negative effect associated with the use of violent video games, she is exposed to violence. This exposure can lead to anti-social or aggressive behaviour, aggressive thoughts, or physiological stimulation [1]. Young people should know more about what they play and what the game contains. More importantly, their parents are aimed at the welfare of their children and loved ones who buy these games. Depending on the person and the circumstances, these negative aspects may affect their development and future. At first, it may have negligible effects, and over time it can turn into a big problem. Parents should be aware of what their children play and think about it from a socialist point of view. First of all, the values that such game brings, the learning from game brings and the possibilities to change a child's behaviour by this game [2]. Games are beautiful and attract many people. In particular, children who learn about the

P. Liatsis et al. (Eds.): TIOTC 2021, CCIS 1548, pp. 365–379, 2022.
https://doi.org/10.1007/978-3-030-97255-4_27

world. Children are absorbed in the openness of the open-world or the exciting plot of the game. Such a person or child spends more and more time, and sometimes such a person does not knowingly hurt themselves because extended or incorrect use of games may have an adverse health effect.

Studies have shown that kids or teens who play games may be more likely to have ADHD symptoms when compared to children who do not play games [3]. Games can have a negative effect not only on the mind but also on the body. Most often, this is manifested in the form of video-induced seizures or obesity. There may also be other symptoms such as skeletal, postural, and muscular disorders, in particular, carpal tunnel syndrome, tendonitis, and nerve compression [4]. There are more and more players in the world; a large part of this community is children. Children spend much time in the virtual world, but it has excellent benefits such as the development of imagination. However, it will be underestimated by many other factors that are important for the development of young people, such as exploring the world, creating new friends or spending time together with the family. The child should spend much less time playing games and more time outside or just with other people such as family and friends. This study aims to create software which guides people if they are allowed to play a specific type of game and inform them about how long they can play and inform them about adverse effects. Creating several simulations that together will create a small game. The simulation will be carried out by using a set of VR goggles. In this project is to check how a person reacts in a given simulation. The second goal is to check whether the use of virtual reality may affect a person and bring more attention to the game's impact on a person. This project aim is to create a program in which is 3D based and can be fully operational by a set of VR goggles in the program Unit which is using a C# programming language. The objectives of this study are: to investigate about (a) Popular games, especially what they are contains, (b) danger to mental and physical health by prolonged use of games, (c) young people and their parent to spend more time without games, to design a framework for this project simulation, to create simulations to show how long the use of games affect persona and a better way to spend time for children and their parents, to implement a test that will check whether a person can play games that contains violence or not, to evaluate and confirm the results of a human test with this project framework.

The organization of this paper is as follows: In Sect. 2, a review of previous studies related to games and people is investigated. In Sect. 3, the methodology of research is presented in detail. In Sect. 4, the experimental results are described. Finally, in Sect. 5, a general conclusion is drawn.

2 Literature Review

There are many methods to reduce violence, immature language, or the use of drugs. Such as identifying both perpetrators and victims, and potential victims of violence, and developing corrective actions to solve the problem, such as launching remedial programs and organizing support for both victims and perpetrators, launching individual counselling, instructional programs, support groups, or therapy. Sometimes a conversation with a person who has experience with this type of rows can have a good effect on such a person will help to show the right way and give much good advice. Individual counselling is proper because it helps give personal support and help cope with the problem. The support group is a method that aims to gather people who have similar experiences and share it with the rest of the group, e.g., personal experience, feelings, and treatments. This type of action can fill the gap in need of emotional support and give mutual understanding because friends and family may not necessarily know what a person is going through. It is an excellent method to help a group of people overcome a given problem, and it is better than individual counselling [5].

Therapy is a suitable method for people who has a massive problem with games, and they need help. Because it helps to change a person's thinking into a positive one, in this case, change a person's behaviour no longer relied on violence, a bad language, and drugs. The negative thing is that this type can last for years, depending on the therapist, patient, and how complex the problem can be [6]. The method includes in this project is designed to act before violence or drugs occur at all. Aims to check if a person is susceptible to such things and direct that person not to use games that contain such negative things. If the use of games affects a person, and this game contains violence, there is a risk that this person will be more susceptible to violence and may get a harmful situation. Similar action is also in the case of drugs because if it is popular in games, it can also affect a person to start using them, which is also bad for that person. If a person who is susceptible to this type of thing will not be in contact with this type of thing and will know that such things hurt their development will make them less susceptible to using drugs or using any of these bad things. These methods are designed to inform people what a given game contains or what are the harmful effects of using various types of gaming devices, e.g., prolonged use of VR sets. These devices may cause people to know what games to buy or use and will know how long they can use them.

3 Research Methodology

The task of this project is to check the impact of games on the person. An application will be designed and created to meet the requirements of this project. First, the data will be collected and studied. Then checking the available technology and simulation engine to create the application and all simulations that meet the requirements of this project. Then the design of the application and the implementation of all things that were designed to meet planned objectives. When the application is ready to carry out tests and after few corrections of bugs. The application will be used to carry out tests with people and collect data. When enough data is collected, the phase of the test will be complete, and the project summary will be created. The primary purpose of this application will be to perform simulations in which the test person will check the impact of the games in which the person played and check if the person had minimal contact with the games how they will behave. The simulation will contain three-level which each one will be carried out in different environments. After completing the test, the result will be given. If the result is positive or negative, the information will be displayed and instructions on what to do next. Figure 1 show the research methodology of this study.

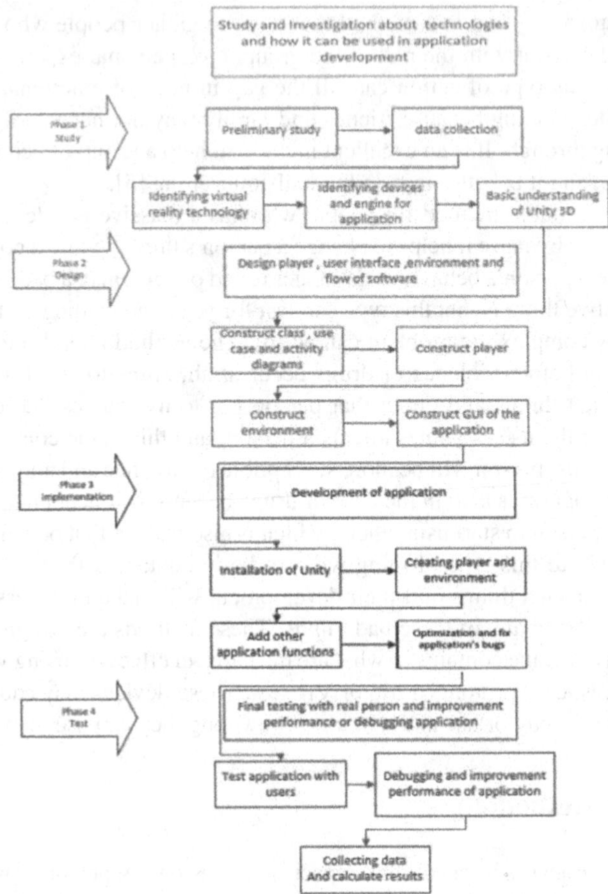

Fig. 1. Research methodology

3.1 Phase 1- Study

3.1.1 Preliminary Study

In Preliminary research, data will be collected by browsing the information needed to understand what games are in the modern world. First of all, how they work with people, how they affect people and what encourages them to continue using them, and in particular how they affect children. What is violence in games and why is it important to learn about it. What are the harmful effects of continued use of games, and what are they caused in the human body? An indication of how big games are in modern times as well as the fact that games operate on a global scale and are part of a large part of people on earth. Paying attention to what games for children contain and what effects it may have. Checking this based on many articles and the work of many people will allow to gathering knowledge and understanding of all the above questions. Reading many works and drawing conclusions that are needed for this project.

3.1.2 Data Collection

The data that is collected in this project is an essential part of this project. Data collected in this section will be used to determine how games affect people's minds. Following this information will allow us to continue to prepare the basics for level design. Each level that will be aimed at checking a person how this person will behave in a given situation and whether a person who has had contact with games will behave as in the game or behave rationally. It will then be necessary to note why it is essential to pay attention to how important it is to take care of good mental health and to show how VR technologies work with the human mind.

The second thing that is needed in this part of the project is to collect data for alternative solutions to spend time without the use of electrical devices. The goal will be to help parents and young people to spend more time without games and to draw parents' attention to checking the games they are buying for their children because they may harm the young mind.

3.1.3 Identifying Virtual Technology

This project will be based on the program, which will be carried out using VR technology. Therefore, it will also be essential to study this invention, because it is part of the technology that is also developing at high speed and is commonly used in games. Because google VR is a great way to feel being in the middle of a simulation fully. This is an excellent way to realistically run the test and collect better test results, because this technology has already been used many times in various tests and, for example, in the treatment of various phobias. It will also be essential to check how this technology affects people's mind.

3.1.4 Identifying Devices and Engine for Application

The program will be written in the Unity program. Unity is often used as a game development engine. The programming language that will be used is C #. When all functions and items inside will be fully interactive with the help of goggles and pads from the HTC VIVE device. The person who will be taking the test will be in the same zone as in Fig. 2. This person will have goggles on his head that will show the image from the simulation and pads that will allow interaction in the simulation. In addition, two scanners will check the position of the goggles and the pads and transfer them to the computer, which will allow them to operate in the simulation in real-time.

3.2 Phase 2 – Design

3.2.1 Construct Class, Use Case and Activity Diagrams

The class diagram shows how the system works together to model parts of the system and how they work together. With the use of diagram case, it will be possible to show how to meet one or more requirements for users when using the application and to show a fragment of functions provided by the system and determine the functional requirements of the system. The activity diagram will be used to model activities and scope to show what the user will have to do at each level.

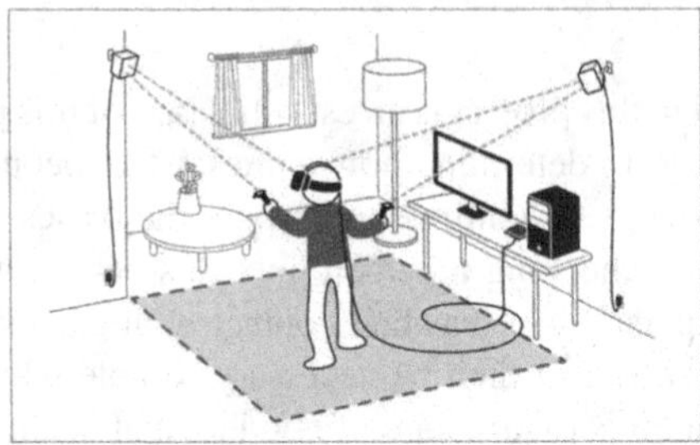

Fig. 2. This how HTC Vive works in the selected area [7]

3.2.2 Construct Player

After choosing the VR goggles, the user will see the menu in which he will be able to choose one of several options this application will offer. During the application, the user will be able to use the functions such as completing the test, posting the harmful effects of prolonged computer use, and how to better spend time without electronic devices, and for parents the importance of how games affect their children's minds. At the beginning of the test, the app will ask how many hours per week the user plays games. The test will consist of checking the user's decision. Namely, the user will have to behave rationally in places where the simulation will force the user to do something that a normally mentally healthy person would not do. When the user does not do what the game will cause him to subtract a point, but in the test, he will get points. The reverse happens when the user does what the simulation commands the user and gets the point in the game but loses one point in the test if a person, animal or object becomes damaged. When the user completes the levels, the application shows the results and the information is displayed, which gives him some tips on what games he should play and whether to limit the time that devices should spend in games.

3.2.3 Construct GUI of the Application

A graphical user interface will allow the user to freely use the simulation and temporarily change between the three main functions. The GUI will display the main menu, which will have three essential functions and options for exiting the application. While using the educational functions, information about the given object will be displayed. For example, when the user selects options to see one of the ways to spend time outside of games, the app will display information and an example. The GUI's main task will be to allow the user to interact with functions and objects.

3.3 Phase 3 – Implementation

3.3.1 Installation Unity

Installing unity involves preparing all that will be used when implementing this project. Installing VR set up and connecting all components. When all components are working in simulation and from real-time input that means green light to start working on implementing all function in application and creating all levels and graphical interfaces.

3.3.2 Crating Player and Environment

Creation of a camera that will function as a real-time player's field of view and will forget the HTC sensors will track the user's head movement. Creating an environment allows the user to move around in this project; the user teleports around the board. Create all objects and maps so that the user can interact with it. Creating a GUI so that the user can change between levels and functions.

3.3.3 Add Other Application Functions

Creating two levels in which the user can read and interact with objects for educational purposes. Signing all tables and objects. Each table will contain specific information for the displayed object which will stand above the table.

3.3.4 Optimization and Fix application's Bugs

After creating all levels, objects and functions. It will be necessary to check the individual simulation elements in order to check whether the functions assigned to them. In the during the test, there will few tests to check whether the information is collecting. Also, whether the correct result is shown after the test and the correct information is shown. At educational levels, all boards show what they present. Checking if the menu works as a tool or allowing the use of each function of the application. When all functions are functional. Everything will be ready to start collecting information from real people.

3.4 Phase 4 – Test

3.4.1 Test Application with User

The test consists of passing three levels; each test gives a point for good behavior and subtracts a point for bad behavior. A positive result must be obtained to pass the test. If the test is positive, information about the network is used, and games can be played. In case of a negative result, it shows information about what games not to play and the need to limit the use of games. Additional two educational levels provide information for educational purposes.

3.4.2 Debugging and Improve Performance of the Application

In case of any errors during the simulation. All faults and bugs will be removed immediately for the best operation of the application during the simulation. All this to achieve a goal which is to collect as much as possible the test data.

3.4.3 Collecting Data and Calculate a Result

After completing the testing phase, the data will be collected. All activities of this project can be collected and confidently say video games have a significant impact on people who use modern technologies or that have a low impact on modern people.

3.5 Diagrams

The task of this project is to create a simple simulation of coats that will be fully compatible with devices from HTC VIVE. The calibration of HTC VIVE set with Unity is required. When all plugins have will be added, and the VR set will be fully functional with Unity. This calibration will allow starting creating levels with the help of the objects that are available for free—the first creation of levels. Then menu and transitions between levels. After adding all models, Project can be able to proceed to the function generation phase. For example, the functions of firing a bullet from a gun. The first possibility should be to lift this gun utilizing a function that allows the pad to interact with objects in the simulation. In the steppe, then trigger function will be added, while the user presses the button on the pad the gun will fire the projectile. Then this bullet will hit the target and add points to the result, after adding all the functions at each test level and educational level. To educational levels, music has been added so that the user can relax while reading the information that this level contains. When all levels are functional, it is time to check the account for abnormalities—in the end, checking if each level is functional and ready for the human test phase.

Figure 3 represents the class structure of this application. It is divided between class such as System class which start and close application and lunch simulation. Simulation class allow the user to choose between education levels and test level. Simulation class will use information from the User class, and Test level class will lunch test. Test level class will collect data from test class, and Education level contains full use information that user can access that are being stored in an item class.

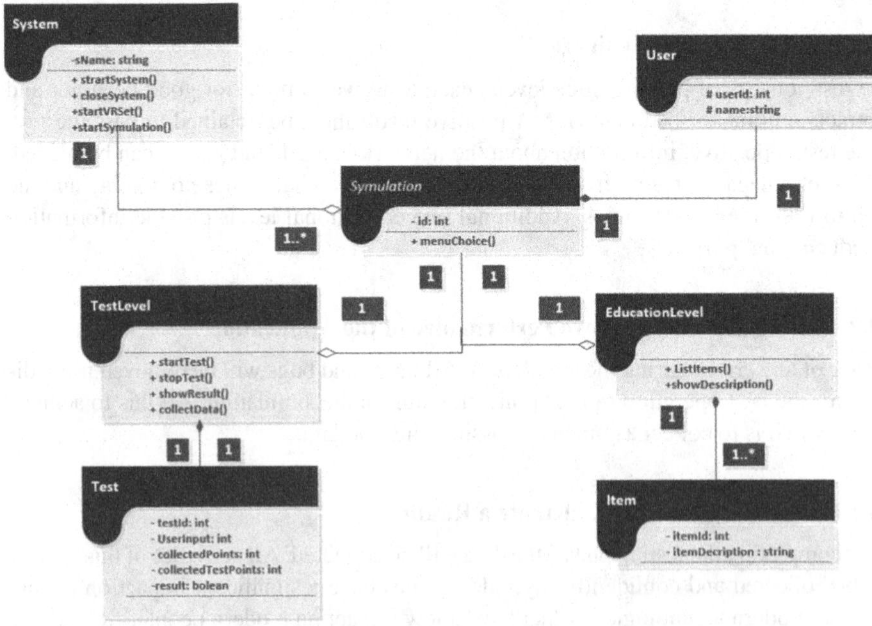

Fig. 3. Class diagram of this project application

At each level, the user must obtain the minimum amount to move to the next level. However, the real goal is to pass each level without harming people, other people's property or animals. When users advance each level, the game adds points. The user only gets one point for passing the game without damage. Points are deducted if the user intentionally begins to cause damage to everyone and everything that happens around him. User can enter and exit the educational level whenever the user wants.

4 Experimental Result

This part of the project is to conduct a test on ten people of different ages. The goal is to examine the impact of games on the behavior of a person in each situation. The first level checks the behavior of a person at a given level with the rules. The second level in the application is to check the behavior of people without the rules shown but commonly known rules of behavior in the real world. The third level is to check the player's behavior without any rules. Each user has 3 points, loses one point if the user injures a person, animal or other people's property. The test is successful if the user has one or zero points. The test is successful when the user has 2 or 3 points.

4.1 Tests Results

There are the results after conducting ten tests with people different in age. Two results with one point, six results with two points and two results with 3 points shown in Fig. 4. Most of the results are with 2 points. Result of 5 people who are players one result with 1 point, three results with two points and one result with 3 points (Fig. 5). Most of the result is with two points.

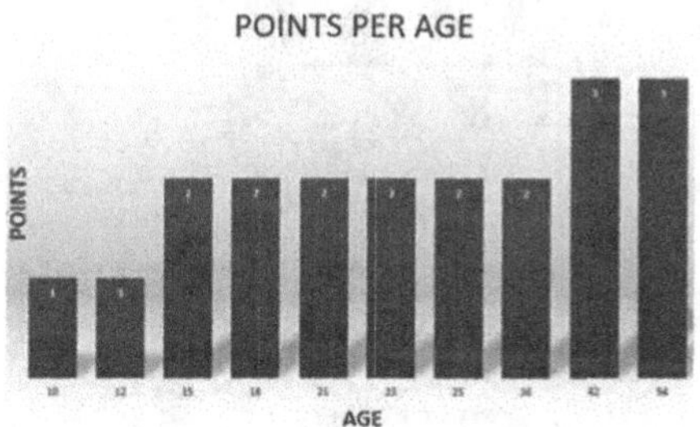

Fig. 4. Point per age

Result base on five people who are not players. One result with 1 point, three results with two points and one result with 3 points (Fig. 6). Most of the result is with two points.

Result of all test based on points. There are two results with one point, six results with two points and two results with 3 points shown in Fig. 7. Result of each test. Only two tests are with negative results, and there are eight positive results. Most people pass this test based on Fig. 8.

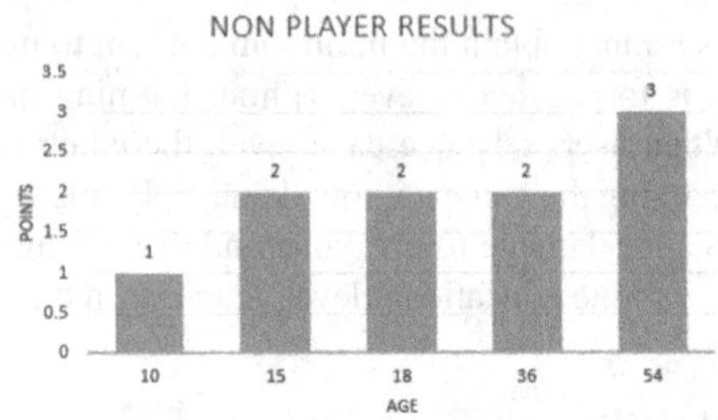

Fig. 5. Non-player results

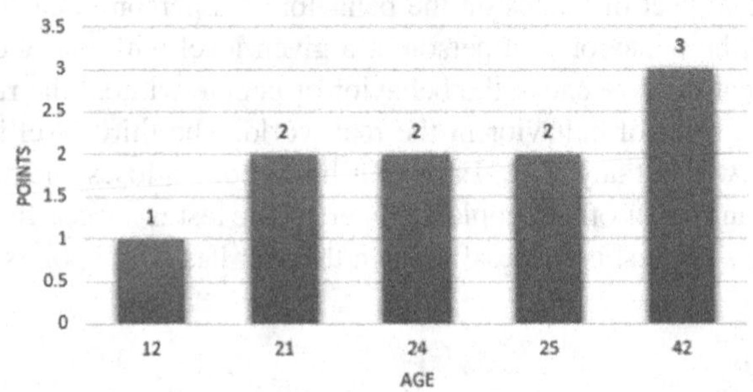

Fig. 6. Player results

ALL 10 TESTS REUSLTS

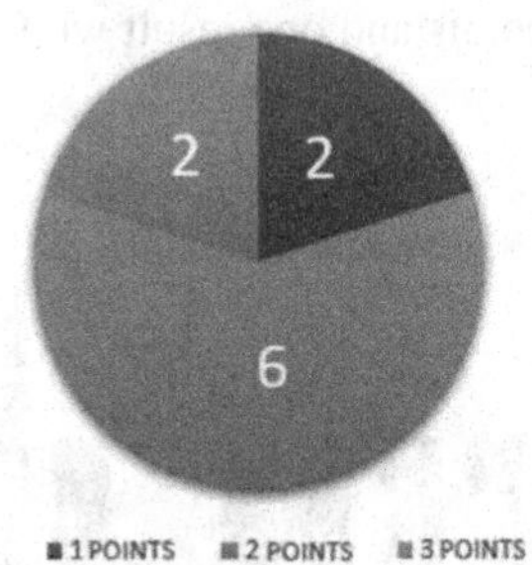

Fig. 7. All 10 test results

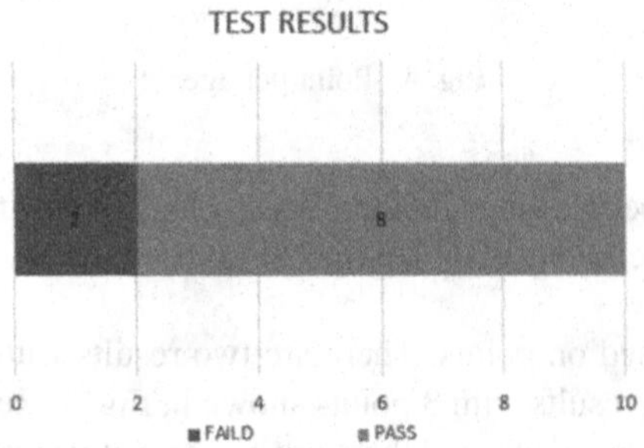

TEST RESULTS

2 8

0 2 4 6 8 10

FAILD PASS

Fig. 8. Test results

Based on grope age from Fig. 9 which was a divide on three parts young people from age 1–18, young adults from age 19–25 and adults from age 26–60 three was mostly young people with number 4, then their young adults with number 3 same as adults with number 3.

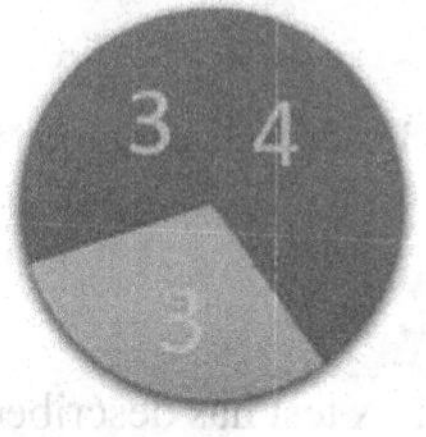

Fig. 9. Age groups of people who participated in the test

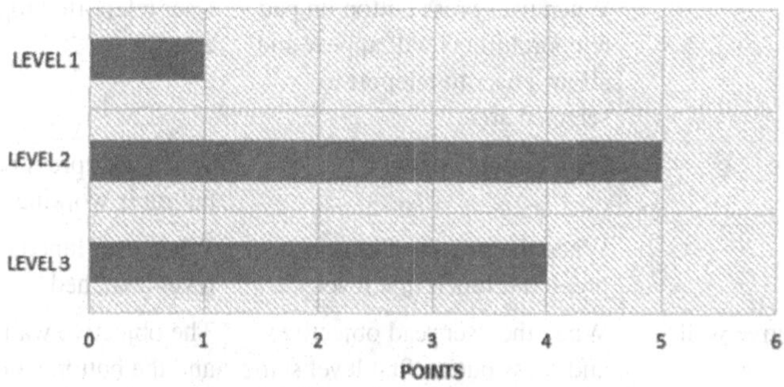

Fig. 10. Lost points per level

Base on lost points in Fig. 10, most people lost marks in level 2 simple by hitting an animal on the road, and second was level 3 where people just cut through a person that appears on stage. There was only one person that shoots a person on level 1, and that was ten years old child. Base on the group age from Fig. 11. Most people who lost a point where young people. The second was young adults and just one lost point by an adult.

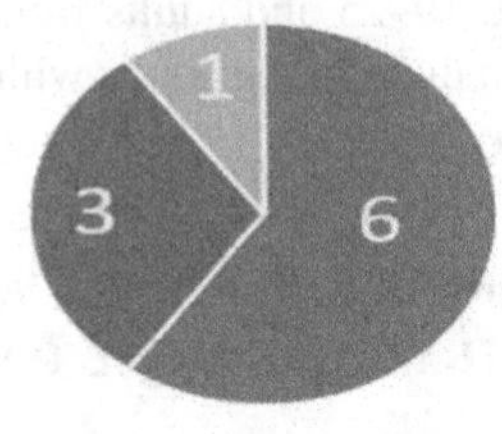

Fig. 11. Lost points per grope age

4.2 White Box Test

Table 1 show white box test. White box test has described the expected result and actual result for each test.

Table 1. White box test

Test	Expected result	Actual result
Teleportation	When user press button on pad teleportation is will appear and allow a user to teleport to selected area	User teleported to selected area
Menu Buttons	Each button works	When user press button, the button is working
Start test	When the press test button is pressed it lunch first level	When user lunch test, first-level launched
Level 1 - objective wall	When the user read objectives and press button first level starts	The objective wall appeared, and the button worked
Level 1 - Gun	User can take, move and shoot a gun	Gun is working as it should. User can take, move and shoot a gun
Level 1 - Target and points	When the bullet hit red, yellow or gravy target it will add points to the user score	a bullet hit the target and points were added to the player's score
Level 1 - Human appears	The person appears on shooting range when a player reaches 50 points	Persona appeared when the score is 50 points

(*continued*)

Table 1. (*continued*)

Test	Expected result	Actual result
Level 1 - Shooting person	When user shoot person user's score increases 10 points and decrease 1 point in the main score	Bullet hit a person. Person disappeared from level. Points 10 point were added to the user's score, and one point remove from the main score
Level 1 - Next level	When the user reaches 100 points in level 1. First test end and move user to the next level	The user reached 100 points and has been moved to the next level
Level 2 - objective wall	The objective wall appears with the second wall. When the user read objectives and press button first level starts	The objective wall appeared, the second wall with how to move in the car also append Start button worked
Level 2 - Human	Human should walk across the street when the user is close. If the user hit human, it will disappear from level, and one point will be removed from the main score	Human start to walk when the user is close. User hit human, and human disappeared from level, and one point has been removed from score
Level 3 - human	When the user reaches enough point, the human will appear on the level and start moving forward to the user. User cut human, and the point will be removed from the main score	Human appeared on the level, and user cut human, and one point has been removed from the main score
Test End and test result	When a user reaches 100 points on the third level, the test ends. The application will calculate and shows the result	The test has ended, and results from the test have appeared
Launch educational level 1	When the user selects the education level 1 button, it will move the user to the education level, and the user can move around the level	User has been moved to the educational level and can move around in the selected area
Launch educational level 2	When the user selects the education level 2 button, it will move the user to the education level, and the user can move around the level	User has been moved to the educational level and can move around in the selected area
Exit application	When the user presses the exit button, the application will close	The application has closed

4.3 Black Box Test

The purpose of this test was to check the impact of games on a person and to see if a person can play games. The test is divided into three different parts to check whether a person can pack people or animals, or even someone else's property. Thanks to this, anyone can check if a person who is playing games, taking into account that the game is in which violence is found, will quickly hit other objects or living beings. This test will efficiently and quickly come to light because for a person absorbed in violence will not see the difference from playing with violence with another simulation. Only nobody mentioned that this test is a game. Even though everything here looks like the game is a test that some who did this test did not pass. Therefore, the next section contains the pros and cons of this application. Table 2 show black box test. Black box test has described the expected result and actual result for each test.

Table 2. Black box test

Test	Expected result	Actual result
Menu level	User select what user wants to do in this application by pressing one button from Menu	User first move around level then selects one option from the menu
Test level 1	User should read objectives, then press button to start the first level. Next, the user should grab the pistol shoot target and reach 100 points. User should not shoot a person that will appear on the first level	User read objectives, read shooting range rules that are on behind the wall. Then the user grabs a gun and starts shooting. Some user shoots a person that appears on the level. Some users do not shoot a person that appears on the level
Test level 2	User should read objectives and second wall with how to move the car on the level Then the user should lunch test and move forward by car. User should not hit human, car or animal. User should stop on a red light	User read all objectives and read how to move by car. User start test by pressing a button on the wall. Most of the user stop when a human appears on-road and when the light turns reds. Most user hits animal that appears on the road
Test level 3	User should read objectives. Then the user should press a button to start the third level. User should cut all boxes with two sabres and reach 100 points. During cutting all box person will appear, and the user should not cut this person	User read objectives and start the test by pressing a button. User cut all boxes and reach 100 points. Some user cut through a person that appears on the level

(continued)

Table 2. *(continued)*

Test	Expected result	Actual result
Educational level 1	User should enter read each board with information and leave whenever the user wants	Most of the user read all information. Some users read- only information that is interesting for them
Educational level 2	User should enter read each bord with information and leave whenever the user wants	Most of the user read all information. Some users read- only information that is interesting for them

5 Conclusion

Based on the results collected during the test, it can be stated that the application is successful. The application collects data as it should and in places where it should be collected. The collected data is divided into three age categories. The youngest from 1 to 18 years of age, young adults 19–25, and adults 26–60. Taking into account the age of the most errors young people have made, which can be a little frightening, because young people are most exposed to negative aspects of games. The worst part is that the younger the person, the more likely he is to be able to harm based on test results. Another important thing is the fact that there are just two young people and they are the only ones who on the first level, where there are instructions not to shoot or aim at people, shot the man who entered the shooting range. Children need to know that they cannot hurt other people even if this happens a game. Parents must explain to their children that they do not harm other living creatures. Based on the test results, the least indicated games are for children because they most often made mistakes and did not pass the test. It is essential to restrict children's access to games and to give kidnapped education to parents so that they know what is best for their children.

References

1. Vegel, A.: Critical perspective on language learning: TBLT and digital games. In: Proceedings of the TBLT in Asia 2018 Conference (2018)
2. Anderson, C.A.: An update on the effects of playing violent video games. J. Adolesc. **27**(1), 113–122 (2004)
3. Chan, P.A., Rabinowitz, T.: A cross-sectional analysis of video games and attention deficit hyperactivity disorder symptoms in adolescents. Ann. Gen. Psychiatry **5**(1), 1–10 (2006). https://doi.org/10.1186/1744-859X-5-16
4. Tumbokon, C.: The positive and negative effects of video games. Raise Smart Kid (2019)
5. Oskarsson, B., Gendron, T.F., Staff, N.P.: Amyotrophic lateral sclerosis: an update for 2018. In: Mayo Clinic Proceedings. Elsevier (2018)
6. Swift, J.K., et al.: The impact of accommodating client preference in psychotherapy: a meta-analysis. J. Clin. Psychol. **74**(11), 1924–1937 (2018)
7. Crider, M.: Oculus Rift vs. HTC Vive: which VR headset is right for you. The Vive Has Better Tracking Technology (2017)

Author Index

Aal-Nouman, Mohammed I. 223
Abdali, Taj-Aldeen Naser 3, 266
Abdulaziz, Rafid 352
Abdullah, Hikmat N. 282
Agustianto, Khafidurrohman 195
Akbar, Shahzad 182
Al-Hemiary, Emad H. 31
Ali, Yossra Hussain 108
Ali, Zaydon L. 46
Al-Joboury, Istabraq M. 31
Almukhtar, Khalid A. K. 335
AlOmar, Mohamed Khalid 310
Al-Qassab, Rahaf A. 223
Aman, Azana Hafizah Mohd 266
Amjed, Alaa 335
Asadianfam, Shiva 365
Attarbashi, Zainab S. 3
Azamuddin, Wan Muhd Hazwan 266

Basori, Ahmad Hoirul 195

Dawood, Omar 352

Elshaboury, Nehal 324
Ettiyagounder, Punarselvam 299

Falcarin, Paolo 61
Falih, Muntasser S. 282

Gull, Sahar 182

Hameed, Mohammed Majeed 310
Hashim, Aisha Hassan Abdalla 3
Hassan, Rosilah 3, 266
Hassan, Syed Ale 182
Hassan, Wid Ali 108
Hussain, Mays Dheya 150
Hussein, Adil Yousef 61
Hussein, Mohammed K. 209

Ibrahim, Nuha Jameel 108
Ibrahim, Sarmad K. 253

Jalaludin, M. R. 237

Karrupusamy, Rajakumari 299
Khalaf, Osamah Ibrahim 299
Khaleel, Deiaaldeen 310
Khaleel, Faidhalrahman 310
Khamiss, Nasser N. 209, 253
Khan, Mudassir Hasan 150
Kolivand, Hoshang 365

Ladeheng, Hasnisha 122
Loganathan, Ganesh Babu 16

Mahdi, Muthana S. 46
Mahdi, Qaysar Salih 16
Mahmood, Basim 79, 335
Mahmood, Yasir 79
Mansur, Andi Besse Firdausiah 195
Mohammed, Duraid Yahya 135, 150
Mohd Aman, Azana Hafizah 3

Nazmi Asna, N. A. N. 237
Nor Shahrudin, N. S. 237
Nur, Al Mohi 3

Othman, Mohammad Mustafa 16
Ouda, Ghazwan K. 93

Rehman, Amjad 182
Riskiawan, Hendra Yufit 195

Sadad, Tariq 182
Sadiq, Ahmed T. 61
Sagheer, Ali 352

Saihood, Qusay 167
Saleh, Idris Hadi 16
Sarfraz, Mohammad 150
Sengan, Sudhakar 299
Setyohadi, Dwi Putro Sarwo 195
Sharma, Dilip Kumar 299
Sidek, Khairul Azami 122, 237
Sonuç, Emrullah 167

Thary, Hayder Hussein 135

Wiryawan, I. Gede 195
Wrotkowski, Daniel 365

Yas, Qahtan M. 93

Zidan, Khamis A. 135, 150

Printed in the United States
by Baker & Taylor Publisher Services